The Kennedys

Books by John H. Davis

The Guggenheims
Venice
The Bouviers

The Kennedys

Dynasty and Disaster
1848-1984

John H. Davis

McGraw-Hill Book Company

New York   St. Louis   San Francisco
Hamburg   Mexico   Toronto
London   Sydney

For Nancy

See permissions on page 864

2 3 4 5 6 7 8 9 A R G A R G 8 7 6 5

First paperback edition, 1985.

ISBN 0-07-015860-6 {H.C.}
ISBN 0-07-015862-2 {PBK.}

Library of Congress Cataloging in Publication Data

Davis, John H.
The Kennedys, 1848-1984.
Bibliography: p. 798
Includes index.
1. Kennedy family: 2. Kennedy, John Fitzgerald,
1917–1963—Family.   I. Title.
E843.D37 1984   973.9'092'2 [B]   83-19566
ISBN 0-07-015860-6 (h.c.)
ISBN 0-07-015862-2 (pbk.)

Book design by Roberta Rezk

Author's Note

THE FIRST TIME I became interested in the Kennedys was in mid-November 1952, not long after John F. Kennedy defeated Henry Cabot Lodge, Jr., for the Senate. On November 10 I had lunch with Jacqueline Bouvier, one of my cousins on my mother's side, at the Mayflower in Washington, and one of the things we discussed was her budding relationship with the new senator from Massachusetts. Although Jacqueline was not to become engaged to Kennedy until six months later, I sensed at the time that my mother's family might well have a Kennedy in-law one day. From that time on I took a more than casual interest in the Kennedys.

After the wedding in Newport in September 1953, many Bouviers, myself among them, became convinced that it was only a matter of time before the John F. Kennedys would go all the way to the White House. In fact, when we all met there on January 20, 1961, the day of President Kennedy's inauguration, the first thing we all said to one another was "Didn't I tell you it would happen?"

Although individual members of the Bouvier family visited the Kennedys in the White House from time to time, it was not until November 25, 1963, that the entire family met again in Washington. This time it was for the funeral and burial of John F. Kennedy. It seemed only yesterday that we had been celebrating his inauguration.

Meanwhile, I had been thinking about a book on the Bouvier family for some time. Since my branch of the family was in possession of all the most important Bouvier family papers, stretching back to 1817, and since I had a wide acquaintance with the living generations, I was in an excellent position to write the book. By the mid-sixties I was deep in researching both the Kennedys and the Bouviers. The result was *The Bouviers: Portrait of an American Family*, published by Farrar, Straus & Giroux in 1969.

After *The Bouviers* came out, I began contemplating a book on the Kennedys. I had gathered a good deal of information on them and had been with the family during some of their moments of greatest joy and deepest sorrow; I felt I had the knowledge and experience to write the book.

However, so many things were happening to the Kennedys at the time—the Robert Kennedy assassination, the Kennedy-Onassis remarriage, Chappaquiddick—it became clear to me that a Kennedy family history would inevitably seem incomplete. Something momentous could quite likely happen during the printing, or immediately after publication of the book that would quickly date it.

After the accident at Chappaquiddick (the summer of 1969) and Ambassador Kennedy's death shortly thereafter, the curtain did seem to come down on the Kennedy era, and one could conceive of a Kennedy history that would begin in the mid-nineteenth century and end in 1969. Still, a lot was stewing beneath the surface. Books coming out on the JFK assassination indicated that more had occurred between 1960 and 1963 than had met our eyes and ears at the time. Then in 1975 the Senate began its investigation of the intelligence agencies, and several of the darkest secrets of the Kennedy White House years began finally to see the light of day.

What else boiled beneath the surface? One mysterious individual, discovered by the Senate Intelligence Committee to have been a friend of President Kennedy, announced she was going to write a book about the relationship. In 1976, largely as a result of key discoveries made by the Senate Intelligence Committee, the House decided to reopen the investigation of the assassination of John F. Kennedy. Certainly no book on the Kennedys should be published without benefiting from the hearings of the assassinations committee, and, quite possibly, from the revelations of the late President's mysterious friend.

John F. Kennedy's friend published her book in 1977, and the House Committee on Assassinations issued its final report on March 29, 1979. After I digested these (without access, however, to the final report's twelve supporting volumes, which were issued several months later), I began constructing an outline for a book on the Kennedys that would span the years 1848–1979.

By the fall of 1979 I had my outline written and was ready to go to the publishers with a proposal. Then, in November, Edward M. Kennedy declared his candidacy for the presidency, and a whole new chapter in the Kennedy drama suddenly opened up, one that could conceivably generate an entire book of its own. The question now was whether to proceed with my previous plan. I was attending a reception for Rose Kennedy in Palm Beach in late November when I made up my mind to proceed. A brief chat with Mrs. Kennedy about her son's recently announced candidacy triggered my decision. If Ted Kennedy won the nomination, and then the presidency, that would be one ending to the book. If he lost, it would be another. One thing was clear: I could not postpone writing this book forever. Upon my return to New York from Palm Beach, my agent began submitting my proposal to the publishers.

During the spring and summer of 1980 I followed closely Edward Kennedy's campaign for the Democratic nomination, attending many campaign events; then, in the fall, I went to Ireland to investigate and experience the Kennedys' roots in Dunganstown, county Wexford, where I spent several days with the Kennedys' Irish cousins at their farm. From Ireland I went directly to East Boston— just as Patrick, the first Kennedy immigrant, had done in 1848—to investigate the family's American roots. The writing was completed in July 1983, and the editing and rewriting in January 1984. An epilogue, covering the events of 1984, was added to this edition in November, 1984.

I wish to emphasize that, although I have been privileged to have been with the Kennedy family during certain momentous occasions, this book is not, by any means, an authorized family history. All conversations with members of the Kennedy family reported herein were held informally during the years 1953 to 1983.

Furthermore, although I am related to the Bouvier family, the interpretation of Kennedy family history this book expresses is entirely my own and does not reflect the attitudes, opinions, or ideas of anyone in the Bouvier family but myself.

John H. Davis
New York
November 1, 1984

Contents

"*For the greatest enemy of the truth is very often not the lie—deliberate, contrived, and dishonest—but the myth—persistent, persuasive, and unrealistic.*"

> John Fitzgerald Kennedy
> Yale University
> June 11, 1962

"*Here the ways of men part: if you wish to strive for peace of soul and pleasure, then believe; if you wish to be a devotee of truth, then inquire.*"

> Nietzsche to his sister,
> June 11, 1865

Part 1

ORIGINS, 1848–1888

Yankee completely. On the road to this great collapse
_____ they had stopped at nothing including stuffing _____
ballot box and buying votes. "Don't get mad, get even _____

1. The Kennedys of Dunganstown

THE BOREEN from Dunganstown to New Ross is lined on both sides with giant, interlacing oaks and beeches, giving the narrow, shadowed roadway the feeling of a dark-green tunnel. Beyond the rows of tall trees stretch, unseen from the road, sunny open fields of hay and barley and sugar beets separated by old, mossy stone walls and hedgerows, and beyond these roll broad green pastures dotted with sheep and cattle.

Here and there the boreen occasionally breaks out into the open countryside to reveal an old, ruined abbey or a vine-clad Norman tower surrounded by clouds of crows. Roughly midway between Dunganstown and New Ross the road suddenly opens up to the great stone walls and barns and weathervanes of the Stokestown estate, the largest in the area, which has been in the same family since 1650. Then, after revealing this surprise, it returns once more to dark-green shade.

The traffic down the boreen is slow and infrequent: shepherds and their flocks, horse carts on the way to market, beggars, destitute emigrants bound for the ships of New Ross. In the year 1848, one of the regular travelers down the boreen was a young farmhand from Dunganstown by the name of Patrick Kennedy. Although little is known, or can be known, about the Kennedys of Dunganstown in the middle of the nineteenth century, enough basic information has come down to us that we can reconstruct, with reasonable accuracy, the daily life of young Patrick, destined to emigrate to Boston and found what would become one of the most powerful families in twentieth-century America.

Two or three times a week Patrick hauled a load of his father's barley down the boreen from Dunganstown to the brewery in New Ross while his father and two older brothers remained at work on the farm. After a forty-minute ride, Patrick's loaded horse cart rattled into the bustling little seaport of New Ross on the river Barrow, a town of 15,000 souls in 1848. Soon he was alongside the river, passing wharves jammed with fishmongers and sailors and lined with sailing vessels. From this port, and others like it, ships would occasionally sail for America, principally to the city of Boston. After delivering his load of barley, Patrick frequently lent a hand at barrelmaking in the brewery's nearby cooperage. An enterprising young man, he had gradually picked up the trade of the cooper, a skill that would be valuable to him in years to come.

Dunganstown was a farming community of some 200, about six miles downriver from New Ross in county Wexford, southeast Ireland. The Kennedys lived there in a one-story cottage, near a crossroads toward the end of the boreen. The whitewashed cottage was built of stone, clay, and sod and had a yellow-gray roof of thatched straw and grass. Like most Irish peasant cottages, the house blended into the landscape of rolling meadows as if it were a tree or a rock: there was a near-perfect harmony between the works of man and the elements of nature.

There were four rooms in the Kennedy cottage, each with its own door to the outside. One room was the kitchen/dining room/living room/storeroom, and its center was the great open hearth. Here, around an ever-burning fire, the family huddled on cold winter evenings, discussing the most important family problems, taking their hot potato soup before going to bed. In the other rooms were the beds and wardrobes. Sixty-four-year-old Patrick Kennedy, Sr., and his wife, Mary Johanna, slept in the same room with the young, unmarried children, Patrick Junior and

Mary. In the remaining two rooms slept the other sons and their families: John Kennedy, the eldest at 39, his wife, Mary, and their 5-year-old boy, Patrick; and the middle son, James Kennedy, 33, his wife, Catherine, and their little boy, who was also named Patrick. There were several outbuildings on the property—small barns, sheds, and other living quarters—one of which still survives. The entire farm comprised some twenty-five acres—a substantial property in 1848—and on this land the Kennedys raised cattle and sheep and planted sugar beets, potatoes, and malting barley, with each member of the family down to the most recent child having his or her assigned chore. They also kept a few pigs and chickens and had a small orchard and vegetable garden which provided the family table with fresh apples, pears, currants, peas, cabbage, parsnips, and turnips. Daisies and dandelions, purple foxglove, and wild arum lilies dotted the fields.

Although they had to pay the absentee landlord an extortionate rent, the Kennedys of Dunganstown were by no means poor. In 1848 they were among the best-off farmers in the community, and, although they would suffer their share of reversals during the terrible time of the evictions, they would prosper more and more in the years to come.

The community of Dunganstown had not changed substantially since Cromwellian times, when there had been a large-scale redistribution of the land. Besides the farmers, there were the fishers, who took salmon, trout, eels, bream, and pike out of the river Barrow, and the smith, the weaver, the miller, and the butcher, trades responsible for some of the most common English surnames today. From time to time a family of tinkers would camp by the crossroads, trade with the farmers, and scare the mothers to death, for the tinkers had a reputation for childsnatching. The crossroads were also the sites of dances, held so that the marriageable young men and women of the hamlet could meet one another. There was a Catholic church at nearby Ballykelly, which was the Kennedys' parish and to which they would one day contribute the main altar, and a Protestant church at Whitechurch, near the river. Kennedys were buried in the graveyards of both churches, the oldest recognizable Kennedy grave inscriptions going back to 1738.

By 1848 Gaelic and Norman Ireland had entirely disappeared, and Dunganstown and all of Ireland were under the merciless heel of the British. Dunganstown was ultimately ruled by a representative of the Crown, and most of the land was owned by rapacious absentee landlords, many of whom lived in Britain and rarely visited their Irish holdings.

The Kennedys of Dunganstown were Roman Catholics, and as such they and all the other Catholics in Ireland paid an enormous price for their religious allegiance. The Protestant British had imposed the infamous penal laws on the Roman Catholics of Ireland, which, in effect, completely prevented the Catholics from bettering themselves socially or economically. Here was a brutal tyranny imposed not over a dissident minority, but over the majority of a population. As a contemporary put it, the penal laws "were aimed at depriving the majority of the Irish people of all wealth and ambition, to make them poor and keep them poor." If you were a Roman Catholic in Ireland you could not sit in Parliament or join the armed forces, nor could you be employed in any kind of government service or enter the legal profession. Furthermore, you could not teach or maintain schools, and it was against the law to send your children abroad to be educated. In addition, Catholics could not keep firearms to protect themselves against outlaws and could not own a horse worth more than five pounds. To make matters worse, no Catholic was permitted to purchase land, and he or she could not lease land for more than thirty-one years.

From time to time the Irish rose up in rebellion against this repugnant, hypocritical repression that had been initiated in the name of Protestant Christianity. In the year of the Great Rebellion of 1798, the father of Patrick Kennedy, Sr., had probably fought in the Battle of Vinegar Hill in county Wexford. But always the insurrections were put down by the British garrisons at great cost of Irish lives. Between 1798 and 1848 some improvement was made in the Irish condition; then, just as prospects for relief from British tyranny seemed near, the great famine swept Ireland, reducing the population to helplessness.

The famine was caused by a fungus that made potatoes suddenly rot in the ground, turn black overnight, and give off a horrible smell. Since the potato was the staple of the Irish family's diet, being almost the *entire* diet for some of the poorer regions, a failure of the potato crop simply meant there was no food. The potato blight reached Ireland from England in 1845, and the Irish potato crop failed in 1846, 1847, and 1848. Thousands died of starvation, malnutrition, scurvy, typhus, or dysentery. By 1851 the population of Ireland had been reduced by 2 million, a million from death and another million from emigration to escape death.

The great famine, as widespread and destructive as it was, did not, however, seriously affect the Kennedys of Dunganstown. Though their own potato crop no doubt failed, they had other crops to fall back on. But they did suffer one very adverse consequence. The absentee landlords, unable to collect rents from famine-devastated areas, greatly increased rents in the more prosperous areas, and the county of which Dunganstown is a part was one of the most prosperous agricultural areas of Ireland, as it still is today. After the famine-induced rent gouging set in, farmers like Patrick Kennedy, Sr., found themselves pouring out all their hard-earned income in rent and interest on loans. And Kennedy had eight other mouths to feed off his twenty-five acres.

For Patrick Kennedy, Jr., the consequences of the famine were not dire, but they were certainly foreboding. As he envisioned the future, he saw only more drudgery ahead—farm laborers like himself worked a six-day seventy-hour week—with little monetary reward. Furthermore, since he was the youngest son, he could never hope to call the farm his own. As soon as his father died, it would pass automatically to his oldest brother, John. And even if, by chance, the farm ever did fall to him, he could still easily be evicted by an absentee landlord.

There was only one way out: America. The very word

America to the likes of Patrick Kennedy in 1848 was synonymous with hope, opportunity, promise. On his trips to New Ross he had seen the crowds of emigrants along the wharves, waiting to board the ships for America. In 1848 some 13,000 of his compatriots emigrated to Boston alone. And he had heard all the stories of friends with relatives in America who had sent back enthusiastic letters and envelopes fat with dollars.

So, one day in October 1848, as Ireland was reeling from the potato blight and ports like New Ross and Cork and Limerick were filling up with poor, sick, and starving wretches from all over the country, Patrick Kennedy of Dunganstown, age 25, set out for America. If he was typical of most of the young male emigrants of his day, he first took the short walk with his mother, Mary, to the church at Ballykelly and received the priest's blessing. Then returning to the homestead, he said goodbye to his father and mother, his brothers, John and James, their wives and little boys, and his sister, Mary. There was much crying and embracing and lots of last-minute advice and well-wishing. Then Patrick Kennedy shouldered his satchel, which contained all his material possessions, accepted some food from his mother, waved a last goodbye to everyone, and made his way down the dark, tree-lined boreen to New Ross.

At the quay at New Ross, a new world suddenly opened up for him. Strange faces from all over county Wexford were there—men and women, young and old, sick and healthy—with their satchels and bags, waiting to board the three-masted bark with its huge folds of sail and shrouds of rigging. Interspersed among them were piles of cargo, casks of ale and water, and old worn chests, waiting to be lifted aboard. The quay was also crowded with agents, peddlers, and sailors. Soon the roll call sounded, Patrick shouted, "Here, sir!" when his name was called and walked up the gangplank to his destiny.

2. Coffin Ship from New Ross

WHAT TRANSPIRED during the forty days it took Patrick to cross the Atlantic can only be surmised. But by piecing together written accounts of similar voyages and what little information has come down to us about Patrick's crossing, we can reconstruct Patrick Kennedy's probable shipboard experiences.

Once aboard, he and his fellow steerage passengers were led down through a hatch in the deck into the hold of the ship. There each was assigned his or her quarters for the voyage, a dark, boxlike space about ten feet wide, five feet long, and three feet high. In this communal bunk Patrick was to live with six to ten other male passengers for the next forty days.

On most transatlantic sailing vessels of the day, the entire steerage space, which usually accommodated some 800 men, women, and children, was about seventy-five feet long, twenty-five feet wide, and five and one-half feet high. An aisle, or passageway, five feet in width, ran down the center of the space, separating the partitioned pens, or bunks, on either side of the ship. Cooking stoves were set up in the passageway. At the fore and aft ends there were rude semienclosed toilets, or water closets, for the women.

There were no portholes of any kind except the overhead hatches. Since the hatches, the only sources of ventilation, were usually battened down, the air below was close and foul. Only rarely, in the very best of weather, would the master permit the passengers to venture out on deck. Otherwise they had to spend most of the forty-day crossing in their penlike bunks or in the always-crowded passageway.

It was, of course, impossible to stand up in the three-feet-high bunks, and a person over five and one-half feet tall could not stand up in the aisle without stooping. Thus, when the weather ran foul, a person would not be able to stand erect for days on end.

The steerage passengers were required to bring their own stores, but these were never sufficient for the voyage. After a week or so, a passenger's water inevitably ran out, and he or she would have to drink the strictly rationed water provided by the ship. So foul did this water become by midvoyage that it had to be "sweetened," or disinfected, with vinegar. The captain always laid in a large personal store of hardtack, salt pork, oatmeal, rice, beans, and potatoes, but he would not release these until a passenger's stores ran out. Then he would extort the last penny, or possession, from the passenger in return for enough rations to last for the remainder of the voyage.

Sometimes, especially during heavy weather, when the hatches were shut and the ship pitched and rolled, the scene in steerage was indescribable. Every day brought its share of human calamity and human violence. Under the swinging lanterns and to the relentless sound of creaking timbers and pounding waves, babies screamed and children cried. The sick vomited and moaned, women shrieked in childbirth, and men fought over a few inches of bunk or over an insult to a county of origin. A passenger caught stealing another's rations was pummeled by his fellow passengers. Rape was a common occurrence, as crew members took advantage of the chaos below decks during storms to molest female passengers.

The stench from the crude water closets was often unbearable. And always the sea seeped through cracks in the hatches, and bilge water oozed through the floorboards into the passageway and the bunks. There were constant battles with rats, which infested every corner of the steerage. Cholera, dysentery, yellow fever, smallpox, and measles ravaged both young and old.

As the voyage proceeded, the death rate increased each week. The sailors walked down the passageway every morning and called out for the dead bodies and the garbage, hauled both up through the hatches, and threw the combined refuse overboard to the sharks that constantly trailed the ship. "Coffin ships," these were called, and indeed the only coffins the dead had were the ships they died in. Only one in three passengers was to arrive at the ship's destination alive. The others were buried at sea without ceremony and without benefit of last rites, for there were usually no priests on board.

Amid these sporadic scenes of violence and death, the steerage passengers got to know one another. They walked up and down the passageway; they visited each other's pens; they cooked and ate with one another in the crowded aisle. On especially fair days, the survivors would gather above decks, turn their faces toward the sun, breathe in the fresh salt air, count their blessings, and remind each other that the promised land was only sixteen, or ten, or six days away.

One passenger Patrick probably met early in the voyage was a 27-year-old colleen from county Wexford named Bridget Murphy. The only evidence we have of the meeting is an assertion by Loretta Connelly, granddaughter of Patrick and Bridget and sister of Joseph P. Kennedy, that Patrick and Bridget met and became engaged aboard ship on their way to America. Bridget was making the voyage with her father and mother, who were also fleeing British tyranny, rapacious landlords, and the ravages of the potato blight. After their first meeting in the steerage passageway, Bridget and Patrick no doubt took advantage of every possible opportunity to see each other again, and by the time the gray headlands of Boston Harbor appeared through the fog, the two young survivors had drawn close. Patrick Kennedy had told Bridget Murphy that as soon as he had saved up enough money in Boston they would get married, and Bridget had given him her consent.

3. Haven on Noddle's Island

PATRICK KENNEDY'S activities during his first months in Boston can only be conjectured from scant family records and recollections and accounts of the cooperage industry in the mid-nineteenth century. But from those and from what is known about the experiences of Irish immigrants in Boston at the time, we can draw a fairly accurate picture of his early days in America, beginning with the moment the harbor pilot came on board the immigrant ship.

When the pilot came on board that cold, gray November day in 1848, all the passengers could see of Boston were several flat, uninviting islands emerging from the morning mist. The largest of these was Noddle's Island, and it was to this island that the pilot directed the ship.

As the ship glided slowly past the other islands, Governor's, Bird, Hog, there were feverish preparations both above and below decks. Accounts had to be settled. Bags and chests had to be packed. Children and belongings had to be gathered up.

A pause at quarantine, a shuffling of papers between the inspectors and the master and first mate, and then, with the dazed survivors now on deck, some too sick to walk, others so fatigued they could hardly stand, a few still active and healthy, the great vessel was towed to a wharf on Noddle's Island.

As the ship neared the wharf, Patrick Kennedy took note of the maze of wooden barriers and pens and the large crowd awaiting him and the other passengers, and wondered what was in store for him. Hurriedly, he bade farewell to Bridget and her family, promising to meet them on Sunday in the church nearest to the wharf, and was soon in the wooden maze, where inspectors and officials looked at his documents and his money, peered down his throat, thumped his chest, affixed tags to him, took the tags off, and finally delivered him to the crowd of hustlers waiting impatiently beyond the barrier.

As soon as Patrick cleared the maze, a man leapt forward, introduced himself, and asked Patrick where he was from. When the startled Patrick told him county Wexford, the hustler offered him a slug of whiskey and told him he would take him to a place where there would be plenty of lads from county Wexford.

Soon the greenhorn was led to one of the many boardinghouses along Border Street, which faced the wharves, where, for one dollar a week, paid in advance, he rented a small room already occupied by several other men. He was told where the sink and the privy were—a sink and a privy shared by all forty men in the boardinghouse.

Noddle's Island was the largest of the five islands in Boston Harbor, all destined one day to be joined by landfill to create East Boston. When Patrick Kennedy landed there, it was a busy port and shipbuilding center. The British Cunard lines had their Boston terminus on Noddle's Island, and Donald McKay, the famous shipbuilder, had his shipyard on Border Street. To Patrick the place appeared not too different from New Ross. It was filled with sailing vessels and teeming with his fellow Irish, and, as he soon found out, there was a cooperage on Sumner Street, not far from Border. But it still was an island. Its only communication with the mainland, with Boston proper, was by ferry. More than likely Patrick would have preferred to be on the mainland, but like most immigrants, he didn't have the money to go in search of lodgings and work there.

He had to go to work right away. He had no time to explore.

He was also in stiff competition with all the other Irish immigrants who were pouring into Boston at the time. Records show that between 1846 and 1851, 63,831 Irish arrived in Boston (as compared with 11,608 British and 186 Italians). Those who remained in Boston had to find jobs. Feeling this pressure, Patrick probably wasted no time in going straight to Daniel Francis's cooperage and brass foundry on Sumner Street, the principal cooperage on Noddle's Island at the time. Mr. Francis made beer and water barrels and ship castings, and when he saw Patrick's ability with the adze and the croze, he gave the young man a job. The work was twelve hours a day, seven days a week.

Although he soon became aware that he would be working much harder on Noddle's Island than in New Ross and Dunganstown, Patrick must also have realized that he was a very fortunate man. He had a job, and it was a skilled job. Most of the immigrants had come over as unskilled labor. All they knew was farm work, and all they had to offer America was the cheapest labor of all, the strength of their backs. If Patrick hadn't brought a trade, he might have been totally lost in the new world. He might never have been able to make enough money to marry and raise a family. In 1850 there were only 289 coopers in Boston, 79 of whom had been born in Ireland. But there were 7007 common laborers, 4650 of whom were Irish. Patrick Kennedy, among the Irish workingmen of Boston, was a notch above most. The overwhelming majority of the Irish who came to Boston at the time of the famine died early, were reduced to lifelong indigence, or returned to Ireland.

Patrick Kennedy plunged into his work at the cooperage with all the energy he could muster. For he had a clear, immediate goal: marriage to Bridget Murphy. Making casks for holding liquids is a job requiring great skill. The trick is to produce a cask that is absolutely watertight, has exactly the requisite capacity, and is strong enough to withstand a pressure of forty pounds per square inch. To accomplish this the cooper must have strong arms and hands, good eyes, steady nerves, the ability to work with sophisticated tools, and the patience of a craftsman. The barrels Patrick Kennedy made held beer brewed on Noddle's Island, the beer he drank with his fellow exiles after work. By starting off making beer barrels, Patrick unwittingly began a Kennedy family tradition that would last for almost a century—that of being connected with the beer and liquor business.

For Patrick, life on Noddle's Island was not an enormous improvement over life in Dunganstown. His living conditions were more squalid. This was a brutal day-to-day existence. It did not take long for young Patrick to realize that loyalty to family, respect for one's neighbor, and dutifulness to tradition, qualities valued in Ireland, were of little use to him in the new world. Harsh, pushy, competitive qualities were needed in this land, the qualities of the upstart and the go-getter, qualities that had been despised by his mother and father and the other staid, conservative farmers of Dunganstown.

Patrick also learned that in America there was no freedom without money. On Noddle's Island you could barely move without spending money. The ferry from Border Street to downtown Boston cost two cents each way, and it was the only way to get to the mainland.

As for the city of Boston, it was, to the likes of Patrick Kennedy, an utterly impenetrable world. It was perhaps the worst kind of American city for an immigrant to come to—settled, smug, and elitist. The white Anglo-Saxon Protestant was everywhere in full control of banking, commerce, manufacturing, education, and government. The Irish, and there were 35,287 of them in Boston in 1850, were utterly despised. The want ads in the Boston newspapers read "None need apply but Americans" and "Positively no Irish need apply." What few blacks there were in the city at the time stood a better chance on the job market than did the Irish. If the English overlords of Ireland had been oppressive and unfair, the New Englanders were even more so, and far more hypocritical. They saw only one use for the Irish: cheap labor, the cheapest labor possible. They took the Irish girls into their homes as domestic servants and gave the Irish boys picks and shovels and put them to work in gangs laying the railroads and highways. The Boston Brahmins paid an Irish colleen $2 a week and gave her an airless back room. Colleens were called "potwallopers," "biddies," and "kitchen canaries." The men, who were not paid much more, were called "greenhorns," "clodhoppers," "micks," and "paddies." Those who shoveled muck for a living were called "muckers."

Without family or friends or a boss concerned with his needs, an exile in a hostile society that despised his kind, to whom could Pat Kennedy of Noddle's Island turn for comfort, companionship, affection, and moral support? To the lovely Bridget Murphy and her family. And to the Catholic church.

The first Sunday after his arrival on Noddle's Island Patrick went to Holy Redeemer Church, not far from the docks, met the Murphys there, and attended mass. Holy Redeemer, a homely little building faced with a forbidding gray stone, was the first Catholic church built in East Boston, and it became the haven for all the Irish exiles of Noddle's Island.

Meeting Bridget and her mother and father at Holy Redeemer on Sundays and holy days of obligation became a fixed habit in Patrick's new life. Although he had to go to work at the cooperage right after mass, he could at least be sure of meeting the Murphys there and of making an appointment to visit Bridget in the shanty in which she and her parents lived. On holidays, and rare days off, Patrick and Bridget would probably spend four pennies apiece and take the ferry over to Boston to gaze at all the finery there. Other days, when they didn't have the money for the fare, they would go out on one of the docks off Border Street and just peer at Boston across the harbor. Finally, after nine months of steady courtship and unremitting labor in the cooperage, Pat had saved up enough money to be able to marry Bridget. The logical choice for the wedding ceremony was Holy Redeemer, but it appears that Patrick and Bridget already had their sights set higher, for records show they chose the much grander Cathedral of the Holy Cross on mainland Boston. They were married there on September 28, 1849, then went to live in a tenement not far from the wharves of Noddle's Island, where they began to raise a family of their own.

4. Patrick and Bridget

ISOLATED ON NODDLE'S ISLAND from both Boston proper and the rest of the nation, the newlywed Patrick and Bridget Kennedy probably knew very little, and cared very little, about what was going on elsewhere in the great, brawling young nation beyond Boston Harbor in 1849. Their own America was little more than an Irish enclave, a transplant from the "auld sod."

The major ferment in the country at the time was in the west and southwest, certainly very remote from Noddle's Island. General Zachary Taylor, one of the heroes of the recent war with Mexico, was President, having just succeeded the powerful James K. Polk. Most of the recently enlarged nation that Taylor had been elected to govern was still undeveloped and unsettled. This was preindustrial America, a land of small, intimate cities and vast, empty, largely unexplored open spaces full of virgin forests and unmined mountains. The United States, victor in a two-year trumped-up war with Mexico, had just acquired still largely unsettled California, Nevada, Colorado, Arizona, parts of Utah, and almost all of New Mexico. During the two years prior to the Mexican War the United States had annexed Texas, which had also once belonged to Mexico. In 1849 the California gold rush was just beginning. The Indians had not yet been entirely subdued, and many tribes still roamed the western plains at will. Women did not have the vote, and the overwhelming majority of the blacks were still enslaved.

In the world at large 1848–1849 was a time of social unrest and revolution. In 1848 Karl Marx published his *Communist Manifesto,* and socialist revolutions broke out in Paris, Vienna, Budapest, Berlin, and Frankfurt. This ferment did not significantly touch America, where the pursuit of wealth and privilege was still in its infancy.

At the time of the marriage of Patrick Kennedy and Bridget Murphy very few American families had attained anything approaching the enormous wealth some of Patrick and Bridget's descendants would attain in the next century. The ancestors of Henry Ford had arrived from Ireland only fifteen years before and were still dirt farmers in Dearborn, Michigan. John D. Rockefeller, son of a modest upstate New York trader and traveling salesman, was only 9 years old. Andrew Carnegie was only 13. The Mellons, the Morgans, and the Guggenheims had not yet made their vast fortunes. The first Guggenheim had, in fact, arrived in America the same year as Patrick Kennedy. Only the Astors, du Ponts, and Vanderbilts were on their way to attaining great wealth.

That some of their descendants would one day attain great wealth was, of course, a thought that most likely never occurred to Patrick and Bridget, for the young couple was compelled to begin married life at almost the very bottom of the economic ladder and to lead, throughout their entire marriage, an existence very close to the bone. The Liverpool Street tenement in which Patrick and Bridget Kennedy settled down to married life was a short block from Border Street and the wharves, about a block and a half from the cooperage in Sumner Street where Patrick worked, and two blocks from Holy Redeemer Church. The tenement itself was a plain, three-story wooden house with an open stairway in back. It was one of a long row of buildings that shared a common backyard filled with trash and reeking with open drains.

There were many families—almost all Irish—to each tenement, and there were always many persons to a room. Those rooms were very small, but small rooms were easier to heat, and winters in Boston Harbor were damp and terribly cold. Since the houses were cheaply constructed, the roofs often leaked. The windows were small and were generally kept closed against the stench of the yard in summer and the bitterness of the cold in winter. There were no closets—clothes were hung on pegs on the walls—and little furniture, only a bed, a table, and a couple of chairs. There were no kitchens in the tiny apartments. Tenants set up their stoves in the rooms in which they lived. A single sink with a narrow drain and one privy served the entire house. Frequently the privy was out of repair, the drain was blocked, and the backyard was turned into a cesspool. In such an environment disease spread rapidly, and there were frequent epidemics. So unhealthy were conditions in these tenements that the average Irish immigrant managed to live for only fourteen years after arriving in the United States, making the mortality rate of the poor in Boston higher than that of the poor in any city in Europe.

Conditions in the tenement in which the Kennedys lived were almost comfortable compared with conditions in which other Irish immigrants lived. Some families had to live in attics that were only three feet high or cellars that were frequently flooded with seawater. One cold, damp cellar was reported by the police "to be occupied nightly as a sleeping apartment for thirty-nine people."

When Patrick and Bridget were married, he was 26 and she was 28. Patrick continued working as hard as ever in the cooperage, and Bridget managed to pick up occasional part-time work as a hairdresser and a salesclerk in a notions shop.

Soon the children began coming along. On August 9, 1851, a daughter, Mary, named after both her grandmothers, was born. Then, a little over a year later, on December 4, 1852, another daughter, Johanna, named after Patrick's mother, was born. A son, John, named for Patrick's oldest brother in Ireland, arrived on January 4, 1854, and then another daughter, Margaret, was born on July 18, 1855.

In 1855 tragedy struck the crowded household on

Liverpool Street. Little John Kennedy died on September 24. Patrick and Bridget had lost their only son. The blow was a financial as well as an emotional one, for a family of nothing but daughters held the potential for economic disaster. But fortunately Bridget gave birth to another boy three years later, whom they named Patrick Joseph. Patrick Joseph, born January 14, 1858, was a healthy little boy. Nine years after their arrival in America, with Patrick 35 and Bridget 37, the Kennedy family was complete—three daughters and a son and heir.

Proudly Pat Kennedy reported news of the birth of his son and father's namesake back to Dunganstown. How long it took for the Kennedys of Dunganstown to receive the good news is anybody's guess. A round-trip correspondence in those days took at least three months. In the early 1850s the Kennedys of Noddle's Island had received terrible news from home. John and James Kennedy had become caught up in land agitation, joining a widespread revolt against the British absentee landlords. Abruptly their rents had been raised; they had refused to pay, and, since leases were short and expired leases went to the highest bidder, they had been evicted. The entire family had then squatted by the roadside near the Dunganstown crossroads while the two brothers hired themselves out to those neighboring farmers who had managed to keep their lands. The Kennedy property was not restored to the family until 1866, when the first of the great Irish land-reform acts was passed.

In 1858 times were bad for the Boston Kennedys as well. A severe financial panic had caused widespread unemployment in nearly every sector of business. Patrick Kennedy, father of four, was probably laid off during the crisis—laid off and forced to spend much of his day either fruitlessly looking for work or sitting around his tiny apartment with Bridget and their children, wondering if the terrible financial depression that now gripped all of America would ever end. And then the feared enemy of the poor struck.

Cholera had first come to Boston shortly after the Irish immigration began in earnest. After 1850, this disease and other epidemic diseases began to spread, decimating Irish working-class neighborhoods on the mainland—Half Moon Place and Fort Hill. Then, in the late fifties, it crept across the harbor to East Boston, and to the Liverpool Street area near the docks. In the year of the panic, when the tenements were crowded day and night with unemployed workers and their families, the dread disease struck all around the Kennedys. Every day, they watched corpses being carried down the back stairs of the tenements in their row. Then, in the fall, it came into the Kennedy household.

One day Patrick came down with a raging fever and nausea; his skin turned a yellowish-green. No medical assistance could be found. Bridget and the three girls, Mary, Margaret, and Johanna, sat helplessly by with the infant, Patrick Joseph, as cholera consumed the head of the little family. Patrick, Sr., had doubtless not worked in weeks and so there was little money to buy food, much less medicine.

When the priest from Holy Redeemer finally arrived, Patrick Kennedy had already turned a dark grayish-green. He died—penniless, it is supposed—at age 35 on November 22, 1858, ten years after arriving in America, and one hundred and five years, to the very day, before his great-grandson, the President of the United States, would die from an assassin's bullet in Dallas, Texas.

5. The Widow of Border Street

IT WAS LEFT to the widow Bridget to carry on. Not long after Patrick's untimely death she moved to 25 Border Street, near the docks, and somehow scraped up enough money to open a small store. The store, a notions shop, was downstairs and the living quarters upstairs, so she was within earshot of the children while she worked. She sold a bit of everything—groceries, toiletries, household articles—and her customers were probably mostly housewives, the spouses of Irish immigrants. Other customers were transients from the ships that docked near her shop—sailors, passengers, agents—and as activity in the port increased, so did her business. As soon as her daughters, Johanna, Margaret, and Mary, were able, they no doubt helped their mother in the store, waiting on customers, keeping accounts, and making deliveries. When Patrick Joseph came of age, he too helped out in the little store on Border Street.

Fortunately the economic depression that had struck Boston so catastrophically in 1858 did not last long, and by 1860 the economy of Noddle's Island had begun to revive. In that year alone thirty-two ships and one bark put in to the docks along Border Street from the East Indies, and one ship and one bark arrived from Russia, fifteen ships and seventeen barks arrived full of cotton from southern ports, thirteen brigs and one hundred and nine-

23

teen schooners came from other Atlantic coastal ports, and
ninety-two other assorted vessels put in not far from Bridget
Kennedy's notions shop.

From the little that has come down to us about Bridget,
we can conclude that she was a strong, cheerful woman,
and the people of Noddle's Island liked and respected her.
To her most trusted customers she probably extended credit
and this, of course, assured her a steady, loyal clientele.
This clientele formed the financial base from which she
derived her modest income; it would one day form the
political base from which her son, Patrick Joseph, would
launch his career in public life.

But the store was not Bridget's only money-making
activity. When Mary and Johanna were old enough to mind
the shop, she took the ferry over to Boston several times
a week to work as a hairdresser at Jordan Marsh, the big
department store. Here she had a chance to come into
contact with the beautiful and wealthy "Yankee" women,
women of Protestant British stock. With their fine dress
and elegant manners and conversation, they must have
seemed very remote and foreign to the young widow from
county Wexford.

Sometime in 1866 the Kennedys of Noddle's Island
received word from home that through the Land Act of
that year their land had been restored to the Kennedys of
Dunganstown. In fact, not only had their land been restored, but the Kennedys had been granted the twenty-
five acres they had once rented. Gradually, John Kennedy
and his brother James would build their holdings up to
fifty acres, and their descendants would more than double
that. As Bridget and her children entered the 1870s, it
could be said that the Kennedys of Noddle's Island had
not substantially improved their lot over that of their Irish
aunts and uncles and cousins during the twenty years they
had been in America. Of the three Kennedy brothers,
clearly Patrick, the immigrant, had been the least fortunate.

Soon, however, the Kennedys of Noddle's Island began
asserting themselves in various ways. While Bridget continued to run her notions shop and work as a hairdresser,

Patrick Joseph, anxious to make some money, dropped out of school and went to work on the East Boston docks as a stevedore and roustabout. On September 22, 1872, Johanna Kennedy, 20 years old, married a laborer by the name of Humphrey Mahoney, who later became a janitor at the Cushman and Paul Revere schools; the young couple moved into an apartment not far from Bridget's at 79 Border Street.

By 1881 Patrick J., now 23, had saved up enough money as a dockworker to begin a lager beer retail business, and by 1884 he had opened a saloon on East Boston's Haymarket Square and had his own wholesale and retail liquor businesses at 2 Elbow Street and at 81 Border Street. He had not drunk away the money he had earned on the docks like so many of the other dockworkers. The temperate Kennedys were to profit from drinkers in this way for the next seventy-five years.

In 1882, Margaret Kennedy, 27, married a clerk by the name of John T. Caulfield and settled in Revere; the following year Mary Kennedy, 32, married one Laurence Kane, a teamster, and moved into a house at 23 Border Street, right next to her mother. What a relief it was for the breadwinning Bridget to have all her daughters find good solid husbands with jobs! Although a laborer, a clerk, and a teamster were not a lawyer, a doctor, and a banker, Bridget had probably not hoped for more. She was just grateful that her daughters had found men who could put a roof over their heads and buy them something to eat.

And what an incredible success young Patrick Joseph was becoming! His liquor businesses were booming, and at only 25 years of age he was running one of the most popular saloons in East Boston. "P. J.," the customers called him. Many of these customers were no doubt the sons of Bridget's customers. A handsome, well-built young man with fair skin and light-brown hair flecked with red, sporting the handlebar moustache which was fashionable at the time, P. J., dressed in a big white apron and sleeve garters, held court from behind the bar of his saloon, made friends with everybody, heard everybody's problems, gave out free drinks to people he thought could be useful to him, and gradually built up a constituency of his own. Between his customers and Bridget's, the Kennedys of Noddle's Island acquired a following—so large a following that in 1885, when P. J. was only 27, the young saloon-keeper ran as a representative from East Boston to the Massachusetts state legislature and won. It was the first of what were to be five terms in the state legislature for P. J. Kennedy. The long political career of the Kennedys in America had begun.

In 1887, two years after his election, P. J. delighted his mother again by marrying Mary Augusta Hickey of Brockton, the daughter of another well-off saloonkeeper and sister of the mayor of Brockton. The Hickeys were, from a financial standpoint, a cut above most of the other Irish families in the Boston area. They lived in a large house in Brockton and even kept a young Irish girl to wait on table and do the heavy housework.

After the wedding in the Church of the Holy Redeemer, P. J. and Mary Kennedy moved into a modest apartment at 151 Meridian Street, one of the main thoroughfares of East Boston, not far from Bridget's notions shop and P. J.'s liquor businesses and saloon. Here they raised their children and received an endless stream of petitioners desiring favors from the new state representative.

By now Bridget, at age 67, was failing. The hard-working shopkeeper of Border Street had arteriosclerosis and heart trouble and some days was unable to run the shop. Confined to her quarters above the store, she was comforted in her last days by visits from her four children, three of whom lived close by, and from her loyal following of customers.

On December 17, 1888, she suffered a cerebral hemorrhage, and she died three days later, leaving a modest estate to her children; her legacy to them included $825 worth of stock in her notions store, $375 worth of household furniture, and a $1000 mortgage on the property at 25 Border Street. Considering what she had started out with, it was a sizable property. Her grave can be seen today in the cemetery of the Cathedral of the Holy Cross. The grave of her husband, Patrick, has never been found; his body had most likely been shoveled into a pauper's common grave along with those of hundreds of other cholera victims.

About two and a half months before her death, Bridget's life had been brightened by the birth of a son to P. J. and Mary. At last Bridget had a grandson who could carry the Kennedy name into the future. This infant, named Joseph Patrick Kennedy, would someday make a mighty fortune and become ambassador to the Court of St. James's and the father of a President of the United States.

Part 2

THE LONG CLIMB
1888-1960

6. The Kennedys of East Boston

BY THE TIME P. J. Kennedy celebrated New Year's Day 1889 from behind the bar of his Haymarket Square saloon, the Kennedy family had been in the United States for forty years, and both its founders were dead. It was no longer an Irish immigrant family; it was an American family now, and at its head was a 31-year-old saloonkeeper and state representative with a wife and son and three married sisters.

Although his sisters' husbands were still in the laboring class—one was a school janitor, another a clerk, and the other a wagon driver—P. J. had clearly moved up into the middle class. As he climbed to ever greater financial, social, and political heights, the families of his sisters—the Mahoneys, the Caulfields, and the Kanes—would remain far behind and, with the exception of Mary Kane's son Joe, would eventually fade out of sight, becoming either unknown to, or ignored by, the later Kennedys.

Extraordinary as P. J.'s early success was, however, his bailiwick was still East Boston, a social, economic, and political backwater in the Boston of the 1890s. A series of islands floating about the entrance to Boston harbor, it was even *physically* out of the mainstream of Boston life. This insularity inevitably bred in the East Bostonian the mentality of the outsider.

31

There is something homely and forlorn about East Boston. Its three-decker wooden houses look shabby and a little sad. Its three-story brick tenements with their narrow, unadorned entranceways and windows have little of the style or exuberance of their counterparts in Boston proper. Its few public buildings of consequence have no distinction whatsoever. Its miles of shoreline are unredeemed by parks and promenades: they are just miles of docks and yards and vacant lots. And then there is always the gray fog rolling in from the Atlantic and the heavy, damp cold.

The engineers of the East Boston Company had laid out the town on a geometrical grid, with Meridian Street, the street on which the Kennedys lived, running along the western edge, paralleling Border Street and the docks. Great workhorses pulled trolleys up and down the tracks that ran Meridian's length. The houses along Meridian, though more comfortable and attractive than the shanties along Border Street, were narrow and spare. The small three-decker house in which the P. J. Kennedys had their apartment was only about sixteen feet wide, having a very narrow, unadorned entrance and three narrow slits for windows across each floor. It was a place that was, to use one of H. L. Mencken's expressions, "as homely as an old woman with a black eye." Meridian Street led at one end into East Boston's principal square, Maverick Square, which contained Noddle's Island's finest hostelry, Maverick House, a red brick building of railroad station architecture in which P. J. was to open still another saloon. The stores along Border and Meridian in which the Kennedys shopped had gas lamps, coal stoves, papered walls, sawdust floors, and a meager selection of goods compared with the stores of downtown Boston. In the 1890s gas lamps lit the damp, dingy streets, and coal stoves were used to heat most of the houses. In fall and winter the soot poured out the chimneys and settled over everything, turning all buildings gray. Horse-drawn wagons and pushcart peddlers rumbled up and down the narrow cobblestone streets. As always, great mounds of rubble and garbage collected in the backyards and empty lots. Surrounding all were the shipyards and graving docks for the construction and repair of wooden clipper ships, the passenger and cargo terminals for the vessels that arrived from and departed for all parts of the world, and the saloons and whorehouses for the ships' crews. It was a damp, foggy, salty, beery, brawling, isolated, and forlorn Irish world, East Boston, and it was Kennedy territory for eighty years.

But, unpromising and removed as was this curious backwater, the Kennedys were to turn the place to immense personal advantage. First they would make East Boston their own private fiefdom. Then they would use it as a base to make the entire state of Massachusetts their own principality. And finally, out of this was to come the short-lived kingdom of the Kennedys.

As the undisputed boss of Ward 2, P. J. Kennedy became the chief dispenser of political patronage on Noddle's Island. Since saloons were the political caucus rooms, campaign headquarters, and poor men's clubs of the day, Kennedy the saloonkeeper ran the places where most political business was conducted. He also loaned money, put up bail, and provided the beer, wine, and spirits for weddings and wakes. In addition, he ran an informal court of justice in which he mediated disputes, much as the Mafia dons did when they began to appear on the scene a generation later. Because he was fair and honest and strong in his dealings, he became immensely popular. After his success as a state representative, he was elected a state senator for three one-year terms. Successively he was appointed Boston election commissioner (one of four), a post he held for five years at a salary of $5000 a year, wire commissioner, and acting fire commissioner. In each instance, his appointment was unanimously confirmed.

He was also, at different times, chairman of the Democratic Ward Committee, member of the Democratic State Central Committee, and delegate to the Democratic National Conventions in 1892, 1896, and 1900, the conventions that nominated Cleveland, then Bryan, then Bryan again. In 1898, when an internecine war broke out between Irish party bosses, P. J. had the audacity to take on the boss of bosses, Martin "the Mahatma" Lomasney, and defeated him by moving the Democratic state nominating convention away from Lomasney's ward to P. J.'s own East Boston Maverick House. In 1899, in recognition of his ability to "deliver" East Boston in an election, he was accorded the immense honor of being invited to join the Democratic board of strategy, an unofficial body (there were four members) known as "the mayor makers," and as such he became one of the four most powerful backroom politicians in Boston.

Back-room politician. The description must be emphasized. For P. J. Kennedy was, above all, a politician behind the scenes. He was not good at posturing and disliked making speeches. He was good at making deals, working out compromises, mediating disputes, and controlling patronage, deciding who got what.

In his heyday, when he became chairman of the board of strategy, P. J. would meet secretly with the other three mayor makers—Joe Corbett of Charlestown, "Smiling Jim" Donovan of the South End, and John F. "Honey Fitz" Fitzgerald, the pride of the North End—in Room 8 at Quincy House on the edge of the North End, near Scollay Square, a place that came to be known as "the hub of the Hub." The secret political meetings in Room 8 would always begin at noon over a sumptuous lunch provided by the hotel. By the end of the meal Boston might have a new mayor, or tax collector, or police commissioner.

By this time, around 1900, Boston politics was almost wholly dominated by the Irish. Ever since Hugh O'Brien's startling election as Boston's first Irish Catholic mayor in 1884, the Irish had steadily acquired more and more political power at the expense of the Yankees. By the turn of the century, a little over fifty years after the great famine had brought the Irish to Boston, they had vanquished the Yankee completely. On the road to this great collective success, they had stopped at nothing, including stuffing the ballot box and buying votes. "Don't get mad, get even,"

"Do to others or they will do to you," "Win at all cost," were their mottoes.

Win at all cost. This was the code P. J. Kennedy, East Boston ward boss, and his fellow Irish pols lived by, and this was the code P. J. was going to pass on to his children and to his children's children. No, there would be no coming in second for the Kennedys.

7. Young Joe

AS EXTRAORDINARY as P. J. Kennedy's rise from the docks to political power was, it was still a parochial career, confined for the most part to Noddle's Island, East Boston, and gave little promise of ever lifting the Kennedy family across the harbor and into the mainstream of American life. It is, in fact, reasonable to assert that if it were not for one all-important family decision, taken sometime around 1900, the Kennedys would have remained an East Boston clan forever, as did P. J.'s sisters' families, some of whose descendants still live on Noddle's Island.

That all-important family decision was to pull young Joseph Patrick Kennedy, then 13 years old, from the East Boston Catholic Xavierian School and ship him across the bay to the famed Boston Latin School, a Protestant institution frequented by the sons of old-line Yankees from the West Side, Beacon Hill, and Back Bay, which boasted among its many distinguished alumni Cotton Mather, Benjamin Franklin, John Hancock, John Quincy Adams, Ralph Waldo Emerson, Henry Adams, Charles Francis Adams, and George Santayana.

It was a daring decision for P. J. and Mary Kennedy to make. Their kind did not ordinarily go to Boston Latin, a Protestant stronghold and one of the best preparatory schools in the country, but rather remained in the neighborhood Catholic schools among people with whom they were born and raised. By sending young Joe over to Boston Latin, P. J. and Mary were gambling on a much more ample future for their son than the docks and saloons and political clubs of Noddle's Island could provide.

Before the abrupt move to Boston Latin, young Joe Kennedy had lived the life of any Irish kid in East Boston: taking his lessons from the nuns, getting into fistfights in the alleys, picking up a few coins selling newspapers, working in a haberdasher's, lighting gaslights in the homes of Orthodox Jews on the holy days, and doing odd jobs for his father's sundry businesses, which came to include a small East Boston bank, the Columbia Trust. Joe was a pugnacious little boy with reddish-blond hair, a freckled face, protruding teeth, a solid, muscular, well-coordinated body, and a quick temper.

Most of the boys Joe played with were tough, poor East Boston Irish kids who were never to leave Noddle's Island. They always needed money, and, because P. J. did not believe in handouts, Joe was no exception. He and his friends were forever dreaming up ways to make a dollar. One of Joe's earliest ventures was to take a few homing pigeons of his own to Boston Commons in order to lure Commons pigeons back to Noddle's Island where he would sell the birds for roasting. He also organized a Noddle's Island baseball team, which he called the Assumptions after a school he had attended, rented a ball park, sold tickets for the games, and ended up making a modest profit for the season. Thus, from his earliest years, the future financial titan showed an eager inclination to turn a dollar, often in very imaginative ways.

Before sending little Joe off to Boston Latin, P. J. and Mary Kennedy made another important decision: to leave their modest quarters on Meridian Street and move to a much larger house on Webster Street near Jeffries Point. Now Joe could, in theory at least, bring his new friends back to his father's house and not be ashamed.

By this time, the Kennedy family of East Boston had grown to include two more children, both girls: Loretta, born in 1892, and Margaret, born in 1898. As they grew older, the two sisters doted on their older brother, Joe.

On Sundays there would be big family gatherings at the new house on Webster Street. Mary Kennedy's brothers would come over: James Hickey, a police captain in East Boston, Charles Hickey, funeral director and mayor of Brockton, and Dr. John Hickey, a graduate of Harvard Medical School. (Whether P. J.'s sisters and their husbands were invited too is debatable; they were a whole social class beneath the Hickeys, and now beneath their own brother.) Young Joe used to marvel at the blaze of ribbons and medals that decorated the chest of his uncle, Police Captain Jim Hickey. He also marveled at the political activity that revolved around the family home. His earliest indoctrination into the ways of the wardheeler came on the day two of P. J.'s political retainers burst into the house with the news that they had each cast 128 votes that day. The young boy learned his political cynicism early and never forgot it.

What young Joe learned at Boston Latin is less sure. His grades were poor to average, and he had to repeat an entire year. But he compensated for his lack of scholarship in various ways that hinted at the kind of career he would have. He became a colonel in Boston Latin's cadet regiment and won the city drill competition for his school. He was on the school's first-string baseball team for four years and was captain for two. In his senior year, with an average of .667, he won the Mayor's Cup as the batting champion of the city high school league. Presenting him the cup was the Honorable John F. Fitzgerald, a friend and political associate of his father's, and a man destined to play quite a role in Joe's life.

But young Joe Kennedy was at Boston Latin not only to study and play sports. He was also there to meet and mingle with the sons of proper Bostonians, and here the record is mute. One can only imagine that, as the only East Boston Irish kid in the school, Joe Kennedy had to prove himself to the others. He did it mostly on the baseball diamond, with that extraordinary batting average, which was the envy of all the boys at Boston Latin. In his senior year, Joe Kennedy was elected president of his class.

P. J. and Mary Kennedy set their sights high again

when it came time for Joe to go to college. Ordinarily Irish Catholic boys from East Boston didn't go to college, but if one did, he would go to one of the two Catholic colleges in the Boston area, Boston College or Holy Cross. The Catholic hierarchy at the time frowned on young Catholics' going to Protestant Harvard, and the Cardinal of Boston frequently exhorted the faithful not to send their sons to such a heathen place. But Mary Hickey Kennedy's brother John had gone to Harvard, and it was to Harvard that she wanted to send her son. Fortunately, young Joe was accepted.

If Joe Kennedy had encountered social snobbery among his Brahmin classmates at Boston Latin, we can imagine the rejection he encountered at America's most aristocratic institution of higher learning, the preserve of the Adamses, Saltonstalls, Lawrences, Lowells, Cabots, and Lodges.

Again, he did not do very well at his studies, but that was not his main interest. Joe's primary focus was on advancing himself socially. Unfortunately for him, Harvard was, from a sports standpoint, many leagues above Boston Latin, and so he could not rely on his baseball prowess to elevate his prestige on campus. Although he made the freshman baseball team, he did not make the varsity his sophomore or junior year, and he won his letter in his senior year only by virtue of some political pressure, as we shall see.

The greatest disappointment Joe Kennedy suffered was not being elected to Porcellian, or A.D., or Fly, Harvard's most prestigious clubs; he was elected to D.U., a distinctly minor club, and he was not elected in his junior year, as was normally the procedure, but during his senior year, which was considered very late.

A similar snub had been inflicted on a near contemporary of Kennedy's, Franklin Delano Roosevelt, who did not make "Porc" either. Both men were to react to the exclusion in different, but powerful, ways. Roosevelt, as President, was to come down hard on the rich and well-born and be labeled a "traitor to his class." Kennedy was to rake the rich Yankees over the business coals, to best them in the race for wealth. But the snubs he had received gave him a complex he never overcame. So painful were they, that for the rest of his life, right down to the inauguration of his son as President of the United States, he was never comfortable in the company of people outside his own class.

Perhaps an incident that occurred on the baseball diamond at Harvard indicates why Joe Kennedy was not a favorite of those classmates he had hoped would elect him to one of the top clubs. It is related by Richard Whalen in his biography of the ambassador.

It seems that Joe was terribly anxious to win his letter in baseball his senior year, but he had not been permitted to play in a single game, having been beaten out at first base by one Charles "Chick" McLaughlin. However, during the ninth inning of the final game of the season, against Yale, with Harvard leading four to one, Chick McLaughlin, who was now pitcher and captain of the team, suddenly took his coach by surprise by asking him to put Kennedy in for the final play, thus assuring him of winning his varsity letter. The coach gave in, time was called, and the tall redhead got up from the Harvard bench and relieved the first baseman. When play was resumed the Yalie at bat hit an easy grounder to first and was put out by Kennedy. By all rights McLaughlin, as captain, deserved to keep the winning ball, especially since it was he who had allowed Kennedy to win his much-desired "H." But when McLaughlin asked for the ball, Kennedy shook his head and said, "I made the putout, didn't I?"

After the game, when McLaughlin was asked why on earth he ever put Kennedy in the game, he confessed that a few days before the game some of P. J. Kennedy's wardheelers had spoken privately to him. It seems they were aware that Chick wanted to apply for a city license to operate a movie theater after he graduated from Harvard. "Either you put Joe in the game, or no license," was their message. And it came straight from the mayor maker, P. J. Kennedy, boss of East Boston.

8. Enter the Fitzgeralds

ALTHOUGH JOE KENNEDY did not make a top club at Harvard, just being a Harvard graduate put him in an exclusive club—opportunities opened up to Harvard men that did not open up to anyone else. One such opportunity was the chance to marry the beautiful and charming Rose Fitzgerald, the daughter of the mayor of Boston.

Joe had first met Rose at a combined Kennedy-Fitzgerald family picnic in 1895 at Old Orchard Beach in Maine. Joe was 7: Rose was 5. They met again and again over the course of eight summers at the same resort. By the time Joe graduated from Boston Latin, the relationship was serious, but Rose's father opposed it. When Joe asked Rose to a dance at Boston Latin, Fitzgerald would not let her go. Joe and Rose contrived to meet, however, at parties, libraries, lectures, even streetcorners. Once at Harvard, Joe intensified his courtship. He invited Rose to the junior prom. But once again, the Honorable Mayor refused to let her go and took her off to Palm Beach instead. Rose later confessed in her memoirs that she never dreamed of disobeying her father.

Upon graduating from Harvard, Joe relied on his father's political influence to land a job as a state bank examiner at $1500 a year. Graduating from Harvard and winning the position impressed Mayor Fitzgerald a good deal, and his opposition to Joe began to abate somewhat.

For a year and a half Joe traveled throughout the eastern part of the state, going over bank ledgers and financial statements and, of course, being away from his beloved Rose much more than he would have liked. The work taught him a lot about banking, a field young Kennedy wanted to get into, but when he actually confronted the world of banking in Boston he soon realized that it was strictly a Yankee preserve and that he, as an East Boston Irishman, stood little chance of penetrating it.

A year and a half later, a crisis at the Columbia Trust, the little Noddle's Island bank P. J. Kennedy had a considerable interest in, gave Joe's career a sudden new turn. It was a time of bank mergers in Massachusetts, and First Ward National wanted to take over Columbia Trust. At a loss, P. J. Kennedy turned the fight over to his now-experienced son, who promptly went into action, gathering proxies and borrowing money to buy additional stock. During this struggle some of Joe's Harvard buddies came in handy, rallying to his cause. After a bitter, suspenseful battle, Joe succeeded in raising enough support and money to save the bank. He personally went into the hole to the tune of $45,000, possessing no assets but his abilities—his first of many big gambles. Having saved the bank, he then informed the directors, of whom his father was one, that he wanted to be president of the bank, and they promptly elected him to that position. Kennedy, at 26, now advertised himself as the youngest bank president in the country; newspapers picked up the story and gave it a big splash, even though the assertion was spurious. Out in the sparsely settled western states there were bank presidents of even younger age. When the Honorable Mayor heard the news he took a wholly different attitude toward Joe—a bank president would not be such a bad match for his favorite daughter.

Much has been made in books and articles of the fact that Joe Kennedy was "the youngest bank president in America." Rose Kennedy, in her memoirs, even asserted he was the "youngest bank president in the world." The truth is that the position was not nearly as important as it sounded, and Kennedy never would have got the job

had he not been the son of one of the principal owners of
the bank. The Columbia Trust was a tiny bank in East
Boston, with a capital of only $200,000 and a surplus of
only $37,000 when Joe took it over. The claim to be
"youngest bank president in America" was pure Kennedy
hype.

Nevertheless, the hype hit its mark, and Mayor Fitz-
gerald was finally persuaded to give his blessing to Joe and
Rose. The two childhood sweethearts, who had known
each other for some nineteen years, were married in
Cardinal O'Connell's private chapel on October 7, 1914.
After the reception the couple left for a two-week honey-
moon at the Greenbrier in White Sulphur Springs, West
Virginia.

The Fitzgeralds had now joined the Kennedys, and
it was to be a very fruitful relationship for both sides. The
Fitzgeralds were what was known in Boston as "high Irish,"
a cut above the Kennedys. The Fitzgerald clan of Ireland
had enjoyed a long and distinguished history. The family
had originated in Italy, where their name was Gherardini.
For their help in his invasion of England, William the
Conqueror had awarded the family a castle and a title. By
the time the family settled in Ireland, the name had been
transformed into Fitzgerald—Fitz deriving from the French
word *fils*, meaning son. *Fils* of the Gherardinis became
Fitzgerald. The family remained in Ireland for eight centuries before members migrated to the United States.

By the time of that migration the once powerful and
mighty clan had descended into poverty. Rose's grandparents, Thomas Fitzgerald and Rosana Cox, came from
the same part of Ireland as the Kennedys, county Wexford,
where they had been farmers. Emigrating to America at
the time of the potato famine, they first settled in South
Acton, Massachusetts, where Thomas found work as a
farmhand while his wife began producing a family of eleven
children, eight of whom survived, seven boys and a girl.
One of these was John Francis Fitzgerald, the future mayor
of Boston.

After some years Thomas Fitzgerald moved his family to the North End of Boston, where he opened a grocery

and liquor business. His wife died six years later, and in 1885 he himself died, leaving an estate of $18,000 to his sons.

Son John F. Fitzgerald had in the meantime entered Harvard Medical School, with the hope of becoming a doctor, but upon the death of his father he dropped out to raise and support his six surviving brothers. Though he was not the oldest, he became mother and father to all six. He washed dishes, made beds, scrubbed floors, sifted ashes, and brought up scuttles of coal and firewood, climbing three flights of creaky stairs. He washed and dressed his brothers, fed them, and sent them off to school, then went out and earned money to keep the family together.

John F. Fitzgerald, a dapper, ebullient little man who came to be known as "Johnny Fitz," "Fitzie," and "Honey Fitz," prospered in everything he undertook. He began to accumulate a sizable amount of property, married a most elegant lady, Mary Josephine Hannon, and eventually embarked on a political career that saw him rise from the state senate, where he sat with P. J. Kennedy, to the Boston Democratic board of strategy, where he also sat with P. J. Kennedy, to the U.S. House of Representatives (the first Catholic ever to be elected to that body), and finally to the mayoralty of Boston.

With Mary Hannon, Honey Fitz had five children: Rose, Eunice, Agnes, John F., Jr., and Thomas. Rose, the oldest, was born in 1890 in the second-floor kitchen of a small three-story tenement at 4 Garden Court in the heart of Boston's historic North End, one of the oldest residential areas of the city. Rose's father had a deep and abiding interest in early American history, and he used to take his favorite daughter out on long walks through the North End. From this experience Rose herself developed a lasting interest in history, which she later transmitted to her own children.

From her earliest years Rose demonstrated an above-average intelligence. She graduated from Dorchester High School near the top of her class at the early age of 15. She was exceptionally pretty, too, and was chosen by her senior class as the most beautiful girl in the school. Her sister Agnes also possessed great beauty; once when her father took her and Rose to the White House to meet William McKinley, the President remarked that Agnes was the prettiest girl who had ever set foot in the White House, an observation that wounded Rose's vanity not a little bit.

After graduating from high school, Rose was sent to a strict finishing school in Prussia, the Blumenthal School, where she mingled with the daughters of European nobility and followed a curriculum built around the German concept of *Kinder, Kirche,* and *Küche.* The indoctrination must have stuck, because the three K's were precisely what Rose was to concern herself with for the rest of her long life.

When she returned to Boston, speaking French and German and enriched by her exposure to European culture, Rose founded the Ace of Clubs, which rapidly became the top Irish women's club of Boston. This idea was something of a retaliation against Boston Brahmin women whose clubs excluded all Irish, including the "high Irish." In her autobiography Rose characterized the Cabots and Lodges of Back Bay as "a self-perpetuating aristocracy, a closed society." She expressed no rancor in her book, but she couldn't have helped feeling some resentment in her youth over being excluded from their society. She was beautiful and intelligent and educated, the daughter of the mayor of Boston, yet she was never invited to a Back Bay house or party, nor could she ever join a Back Bay club.

Rose's mother was a shy, retiring woman, and so Honey Fitz frequently enlisted his lively, outgoing eldest daughter as hostess at political events. It was invaluable training for the future ambassador's wife, yet, because of the deep mutual antagonism between the Yankee Protestants and the Catholic Irish in Boston, Rose never really felt very comfortable unless she was hostessing an affair for her own kind of people. The hostessing and politicking for her energetic father occupied most of Rose's time until her marriage to Joe Kennedy.

After returning from their honeymoon in White Sul-

phur Springs, Joe and Rose settled down to married life
in a seven-room wooden-frame house with clapboard sid-
ing on a small lot with trees and bushes in the Boston
suburb of Brookline. The house, at 83 Beals Street, is now
a museum. In it were born three of their first four children:
John, Rosemary, and Kathleen. Joseph, Jr., their first child,
was born in a rented summer house in Hull, near Nantasket, a resort town on the Atlantic coast.

9. Fitzie, King of the Dearos

HE WAS five feet two inches tall, had a compact muscular body, and a square, big-jawed face that was to someday reappear in his grandson Teddy. He was dapper, flamboyant, energetic, and talkative in the extreme; he would give a speech on any subject at the drop of a hat. As one contemporary described him, "He could talk to you for ten or fifteen minutes at the rate of 200 words a minute, without letting you cut in more than two or three times, then pat you on the back and tell you how much he enjoyed the conversation." "Fitzblarney," it was called. Another contemporary observed, "If John F. Fitzgerald were wakened from slumber in the dead of night and asked to speak on any subject under the sun, or elsewhere, he will readily, not to say willingly, arise from his couch, slip his frock coat on over his pajamas and speak eloquently for two hours and seventeen minutes on that subject."

He was called, among many nicknames, "The Little General," "The Little Napoleon," "Boston Johnny," and "King of the Dearos." This last appellation derived from Fitzgerald's constant affectionate reference to his birthplace as the "dear old North End." After a while all North Enders, most of whom were Irish, came to be known as "dearos," and, later still, all supporters of Honey Fitz came to be known by that name.

During the 1910 mayoral campaign he adopted the

song "Sweet Adeline" as his own, made it his campaign
song, and sang it to political audiences over and over again.
When President Franklin D. Roosevelt sent him on a goodwill mission to Latin America, he sang "El Dulce Adelina"
from Colombia to Argentina.

His personal slogan was "Work harder than anyone
else," and his political slogan was "A bigger, better, busier
Boston." He was possessed of inexhaustible energy and
was typically on the go eighteen hours a day, needing only
four or five hours of sleep. His mental and physical energy
was so prodigious he could outcampaign any politician who
ran against him. Three times he ran for the U.S. Congress
and won, becoming the only Democratic congressman from
New England and the only Catholic in the House of Representatives. Twice he was elected mayor of Boston, serving six years in that office. His charm was legendary.
Someone said his smile "looked like it had been built from
the bottom up."

His political savvy and relentless campaigning were
marvels to his contemporaries. A fastidious dresser, he
would go about slapping backs in a high, stiff collar, a
morning coat, pepper-and-salt trousers, sporting a bou-
tonniere and wearing a black derby. He had a "wake squad,"
which attended, in his behalf, every wake in the city of
Boston. He had his minions consult the obituaries every
day, and he sent every new widow a personal letter of
condolence. He organized the "John F. Fitzgerald Marching and Singing Club" and had them perform at political
rallies and march in parades. He helped the homeless,
orphans, and widows, who called him "Mr. Fixit." He was
famous for making everyone feel like his next-door neighbor. He held huge picnics for people who ordinarily got
no recreation. And he took good care of his "dearos,"
too, inventing dozens of offices for them. For example,
when he became mayor he created the superfluous post of
city dermatologist and gave it to a "dearo" at a salary of
$4000 a year. He was very conscious of the uses of pub-
licity—a trait which would reappear in his grandsons—
and a master at using it. At Thanksgiving and Christmas
he personally distributed food baskets and presents and

made sure he was in the range of a newsman's camera
when he gave a basket of fruit to a crippled child, or a box
of candies to a bent old lady, or a bottle of champagne to
a blind man.

Fitzie's tireless politicking became legendary in Boston. In his first two years in office as mayor he gave an
average of six speeches a day and attended two dinners
and three dances a night, for a combined total of 1200
dinners, 1500 dances, 200 picnics, and 1000 meetings.

For years Fitzie waged a relentless, all-out war against
the Brahmins of Back Bay, whom he accused of being
narrow, selfish, and bigoted. By the early twentieth century
there were more Irish in Boston than in Dublin, over 60
percent of the total registered voters in Boston were Irish,
and still the Brahmins would not take them into their clubs,
businesses, and financial institutions. In his celebrated
Mortmain speech of 1911 Honey Fitz roared: "If Boston
could disinherit about twenty-five men from Back Bay who
have their hands clutched about the throat of commercial
and industrial Boston, this city would attain a growth in
the next ten years almost unbelievable."

So popular did Honey Fitz become in Boston that
even Presidents courted him in the belief that Fitzie could
"deliver" the city in a national election. He knew Mc-
Kinley, Taft, and Franklin D. Roosevelt and visited the
White House many times. When his grandson, John Fitzgerald Kennedy, won a seat in Congress in 1946, representing the same district Fitzie had once represented, he
predicted that the young man would go all the way to the
White House.

During the last four decades of his long, octogenarian
life, Fitzie was as active, if not as successful, as ever. In
1912 he was chairman of the Massachusetts delegation to
the Democratic National Convention and hence was briefly
in the national spotlight again. In 1914 he withdrew from
the mayoral race and his great rival, James Michael Curley,
became mayor of Boston. In 1916 he ran for the U.S.
Senate against the powerful and detested (by Fitzie) Henry
Cabot Lodge, Sr., and lost by only 33,000 votes. (It was
left to his grandson to take revenge: JFK beat Henry Cabot

Lodge, Jr., for the Senate in 1952.) In 1918 Fitzie ran for the U.S. House of Representatives again, this time against "Weeping Peter" Tague. The election was disputed. Fitzgerald was seated, then later removed when instances of illegal registration and voting fraud were uncovered. In 1922 he ran for governor of Massachusetts and lost by over 60,000 votes. In 1925 he entered the race for Congress again, bringing his little grandson, John F. Kennedy, with him while he campaigned in the wards, but he eventually withdrew. Years later JFK recalled witnessing his grandfather perform "The Irish Switch" in masterful fashion, as Honey Fitz shook the hand of one supporter, talked animatedly with another, while smiling affectionately at a third. In 1930 he entered and withdrew from the primary for Governor, and in 1942, at age 79, the never-say-die Fitzie was defeated in the Democratic primary for the U.S. Senate. In 1934 he was appointed to the Boston Port Authority and served with that body until 1948. He died in 1950, at age 87, having lived to see his son-in-law become a multimillionaire and his grandson occupy his old seat in Congress. But he was denied the satisfaction of celebrating that grandson's victory over Lodge. Later Boston named the John F. Fitzgerald Expressway, cutting through the dear old North End, after him, and John F. Kennedy named one of the presidential yachts the *Honey Fitz*.

10. The Capitalist

WHEN JOE KENNEDY was asked to list his profession for the twenty-year report of his Harvard class, he replied, somewhat facetiously, "Capitalist."

The description, however, was apt. It would have been misleading if he had described himself as a businessman. For Kennedy was emphatically not a businessman in the commonly accepted usage of the term. Although he eventually came to hold a few corporate positions, he was chiefly a lone operator who bought and sold, taking his losses and his profits. Mostly his profits. By 1957, forty-five years after his graduation from Harvard, *Fortune* magazine listed him as the twelfth richest man in the United States.

The origin of the Kennedy fortune remains somewhat a mystery. The Kennedy wealth seems to have grown in bits and pieces from speculation in a variety of businesses; it is still uncertain how Kennedy made his initial stake. We know that the Rockefeller fortune was made from oil, the Ford fortune from automobiles, the du Pont fortune from chemicals, and the Guggenheim fortune from metals. But the Kennedy fortune was not made from any one business activity. Rather it was made helter-skelter from gambling on any number of dissimilar businesses, some legal, some not.

Joe Kennedy's career as a money-maker began while

he was still at Harvard. During his senior year, Joe, in partnership with another son of Irish immigrants, Joe Donovan, bought a bus for $600 and went into the tourist business, taking sightseers to historic places in Boston, Concord, and Lexington. With Donovan driving the bus and Kennedy at the microphone, they cleared $5000 during the summer, a princely sum in those days.

Victor Lasky, in his book that debunks John F. Kennedy, presents another dimension of this episode, which he attributes to the bookkeeper of the Colonial Auto-Sightseeing Company. To discourage competition from this rival company, according to the bookkeeper, Joe's future father-in-law, the mayor of Boston, under pressure from Joe's father, the boss of East Boston, upped the license fee of the Colonial Auto-Sightseeing Company from $2000 to $3000 a year. Once a month a young Harvard student would show up at the company offices to collect the augmented fee. The student was Joseph P. Kennedy.

While he was a state bank examiner, Joe took a vacation in Europe, his first trip abroad. Before leaving, he invested $1000 in a one-third interest in a nascent real estate outfit, Old Colony Realty. It was a company that capitalized on the misfortunes of others, particularly poor people. It took over defaulted mortgages on modest two- and three-family three-decker tenements, repaired and painted the houses, then quickly resold them. By the time Kennedy returned from his European travels he had made enough money from Old Colony to pay for his entire trip. By the time of America's entry into World War I Kennedy's initial $1000 investment was worth $25,000.

While he was president of Columbia Trust, young Kennedy acquired a reputation for being quick to call a loan and foreclose a mortgage. How many poor Irish and Italian families he destroyed is not known. The important thing was that at 26 years of age he was already in a position to cast into the street people who were in the same position his grandfather Patrick had once been in.

Kennedy himself was heavily in debt at the time; the debt could only have spurred his ambitions, especially with a growing family to support. It will be recalled that he had

had to borrow $45,000 to rescue Columbia Trust; in addition, he borrowed another $2000 as a down payment on his $6500 Brookline house. With $47,000 to pay off, and no assets other than his ambition and talent, young Joe had to be alert for every opportunity that might come his way.

While at Columbia Trust he tried very hard for a seat on the board of directors of the Massachusetts Electric Company and finally won one. When asked by a friend why he was so anxious for the seat, he replied: "Do you know of a better way to meet people like the Saltonstalls?"

One person "like the Saltonstalls" Kennedy met was a rich and influential Yankee lawyer by the name of Guy Currier. Currier, a lobbyist for Bethlehem Steel, needed an assistant manager for Bethlehem's booming Fore River shipyard, which was building warships for World War I, and offered the job to Kennedy. Kennedy accepted the position and turned over the presidency of Columbia Trust to his father. P. J. then ran the bank for the remainder of his life. (His death certificate described him as a "banker," not a saloonkeeper.)

With the United States involved in World War I, Kennedy came to supervise a labor force of 22,000 shipyard workers, who, at the height of production, built and launched thirty-six destroyers in only twenty-seven months. Kennedy worked hard, too hard, and developed neuritis and an ulcer, ailments that plagued him for the rest of his life. Ever ready to seize opportunities to make money, Joe took note of the inadequate commissary facilities at Fore River and opened the Victory Lunchroom, which eventually fed thousands of shipyard workers a day. With $20,000 a year in salary, plus bonuses, plus profits from his lunchroom, the young capitalist was not doing badly.

As an unexpected bonus, Kennedy met the young assistant secretary of the Navy, Franklin D. Roosevelt, who paid Fore River a visit to inspect production and who impressed Kennedy greatly at their meeting. Years later, when Roosevelt made his bid for the presidency, Kennedy was flattered that Roosevelt remembered him and threw his financial support behind the Hyde Park aristocrat, with highly favorable consequences for himself and his family.

Of course, Kennedy's Harvard classmates sneered at Joe's not going off with the rest of his class to fight "the war to end all wars." But Kennedy justified his dodging of military service by maintaining that he did more for the war effort at Fore River than he ever could have as a combatant, which was probably true.

After the war, Fore River, now without the military contracts, had to cut back drastically, and Kennedy realized he'd better look for another job. He found one as manager of the stock department in the Boston branch of the brokerage house of Hayden, Stone.

How he landed this plum has become a legend in the brokerage business. In 1919 he requested a meeting with Galen Stone, senior partner of the firm bearing his name and chairman of the Atlantic, Gulf and West Indies Steamship Line. Kennedy was granted a brief interview. He showed up for the meeting on time and was told Stone had had to cancel and was, in fact, on his way to the rail station to catch a train to New York. Undeterred, Kennedy immediately took a cab to South Station, boarded the train, found Stone, and cornered him for four hours on the way to New York. Stone was so impressed by Kennedy's aggressive salesmanship that two weeks later, after checking out his references, he gave him the job as stock department manager at $10,000 a year.

Joe Kennedy was now, at 31 years of age, entering the first really big money-making period of his life. He was in an excellent position to learn something about the stock market and to profit from that knowledge. Like any novice in the market, Kennedy experienced his ups and downs, mostly downs, and was soon able to formulate one of his immortal Wall Street dicta: "With enough inside information and unlimited credit, you are sure to go broke."

The dictum was somewhat facetious because Joe Kennedy knew the importance of inside information to the stock market plunger, and he profited enormously from obtaining it. Not long after he joined Hayden, Stone, Galen Stone, the principal stockholder of the Pond Creek Coal Company, told Kennedy he had quietly sold his interest in Pond Creek to Henry Ford, who intended to fit the company into his growing industrial empire. Kennedy, never afraid to go out on a limb, borrowed all the money he could and bought 15,000 shares of Pond Creek at $16 a share. When news of Henry Ford's plans to take over Pond Creek hit the papers, there was a wild stampede to buy Pond Creek stock; Kennedy sold out at $45 a share, making a whopping $435,000 profit, which, after repayment of his $225,000 loan, netted him $210,000.

With that speculative feat having won him quite a measure of respect at Hayden, Stone, Kennedy took another plunge. Movies had recently begun to appear on the scene, and he quickly saw the vast money-making possibilities in them. Going into partnership with Guy Currier, he headed a group of investors that purchased control of thirty-one movie theaters throughout New England. After a while, the chain bought the regional franchise for Universal Pictures. In the years that followed, the chain was such a consistent money-maker that Kennedy, whose usual practice was to unload properties soon after he bought them and take his profits, held on to his interest for forty years.

Gaining confidence in his money-making abilities from each new successful venture, Joe Kennedy was quick to see that a lot of easy money could be made from stock pools. Stock pools were nothing but a massive, institutionalized deceit, and they were eventually banned. The idea was for a brokerage house to create a wild flurry of buying and selling of a particular stock, and in so doing attract a lot of unwary outsiders to buy the stock. When the stock hit the pool operators' aimed-for price, they would dump all their stock, take their profits, and leave all the suckers they had attracted high and dry.

The first pool Kennedy managed at Hayden, Stone was in the stock of Todd shipyards. Adroitly he and his associates bulled the stock up to an exaggerated value, then, at the moment of the most feverish buying on the part of the gullible public, Kennedy, with an exquisite sense of timing, ordered a dump. Kennedy and his fellow members of the pool made huge profits, and thousands of little investors lost their shirts. "It's easy to make money in this market," he declared to a friend. "We'd better get in before they pass a law against it."

Fortunately for Kennedy, but not for millions of unwary investors, there was no law passed against stock pools until Roosevelt appointed him the first chairman of the Securities and Exchange Commission. By that time, Kennedy had made a small fortune off stock pools, and he could afford to put an end to the practices by which he had made his money.

But Joe Kennedy in the early twenties had more than one string to his business bow. It is now generally conceded that even though the Eighteenth Amendment, prohibiting the importing, sale, or manufacture of intoxicating liquors, was passed in 1919, the Kennedys, father and son, still remained in the liquor business. If, as it is now widely assumed, the Kennedys were indeed bootleggers during the thirteen years of prohibition, it explains where Joe Kennedy earned at least some of the capital he needed to speculate in the stock market. Certainly he did not get it from his father, for P. J. was not a wealthy man and would leave an estate of only $57,000 when he died in 1929, most of which went to his two daughters.

Since Kennedy's business papers, now in the John F. Kennedy Library in Boston, are still kept secret, what evidence we have that Joseph P. Kennedy earned his capital through bootlegging is mostly circumstantial. For example, several of Joe Kennedy's Harvard classmates of 1912 told his biographer, Richard Whalen, that Kennedy supplied all the liquor for his class's tenth reunion in 1922. According to one of these, Raymond S. Wilkins of Boston, Kennedy was his class's "chief bootlegger" for all class get-togethers. For the tenth reunion, which was held on the beach in front of the Pilgrim Hotel at Plymouth, Massachusetts, Kennedy apparently had his agents bring the liquor in by boat. "It came ashore the way the Pilgrims did," Wilkins told Richard Whalen.

Years later, several major underworld figures testified that Joseph P. Kennedy was one of the most ruthless competitors in the bootlegging business throughout the twenties and early thirties. In 1973 Frank Costello, former boss of the Luciano crime family, told author Peter Maas that he had been in the bootlegging business with Joe Kennedy before the repeal of prohibition and that they had a bitter falling out. "I helped Joe Kennedy get rich," Costello told Maas. It seems he told the same story to Cosa Nostra leader Joseph Bonanno, for it turned up in Bonanno's 1983 autobiography, *A Man of Honor*.

Archcriminals Lucky Luciano and Meyer Lansky were also in the bootlegging business during the roaring twenties. One of their former lieutenants, "Doc" Stacher, interviewed in Israel in 1976 just before he died, told journalists that Kennedy had been involved in some vicious fights with Mafia bootleggers and that a lot of bad blood had developed between Kennedy and the mob at the time. Other major underworld figures, such as Sam Giancana, boss of the Chicago syndicate, have alluded to Joe Kennedy's bootlegging activities during prohibition. Giancana even went so far as to tell one friend, who was also a friend of John F. Kennedy's, that Kennedy Senior "was one of the biggest crooks who ever lived."

If all this is true, it clears up the mystery of the origin of the Kennedy fortune. For no matter how brilliant a stock market speculator Joe Kennedy turned out to be, he still had to have initial funds with which to speculate. True, it was possible to buy stocks on margin during the roaring twenties, but margin never reached 100 percent, and there were collateral requirements for heavy borrowing. What probably occurred, then, was that upon the commencement of prohibition the already existing Kennedy liquor businesses simply went underground. What lends credence to this supposition is that immediately after prohibition was repealed in 1933, lo and behold, there was Joe Kennedy right in the thick of the Scotch, rum, and gin business.

In 1923, Joe Kennedy, at 35, had apparently made enough money from bootlegging and stock market pools not only to be able to pay off his debts, but also to be able to go in for speculative ventures on a large scale. While still maintaining his affiliation with Hayden, Stone, he went into business by himself, establishing an office in Boston under the masthead "Joseph P. Kennedy, Banker." From this office he launched a bid to gain control of the Film Booking Office of America, a British-owned film distribution outfit with a booming business that had gotten into a credit squeeze. Using every tactic imaginable, including cornering the Prince of Wales in a Paris restaurant under false pretenses in order to secure a much-needed letter of introduction, Kennedy, after a long battle, won control of Film Booking and made himself president and chairman of the board.

At this time, in the mid-nineteen-twenties, Joe Kennedy did a remarkable thing. He had made a lot of money, but he had no intention of hoarding it. He knew that if his children were to be able to enjoy a high and secure social position someday, they had to have money of their own. Accordingly, he established the first of three trust funds for his children, with Rose as trustee. Each of his seven children (Jean and Teddy were not yet born) would begin receiving an income from his or her trust fund at age 21. At age 45, one-half of the principal of the trust fund would be divided equally among all his surviving children. As Kennedy's wealth grew, significant additions to the fund were made, and in 1936 and 1949 two more trust funds were established. These trust funds would eventually guarantee each of Kennedy's eight surviving children, and his wife, over $20 million apiece, all provided within Father Joe's lifetime.

Much has been made of these trust funds by journalists, biographers, and historians. It has been asserted that Joe Kennedy gave all his money away to his children "so they wouldn't be afraid to talk back to him." It has also been asserted that what Kennedy wanted was to ensure his children's future social status. Joe's son John, however, produced a different interpretation. Stating in 1959 that the oft-repeated "so they wouldn't be afraid to talk back to me" story was pure myth, Jack Kennedy told reporters that his father was speculating very heavily at the time and because of his neuritis and acute ulcers was in precarious health. Fearing he could possibly be hit with crushing losses or could be incapacitated by illness, he wanted to make at least some of his money safe for his family, and so he set up the funds in his children's names.

Whatever the motive, these trust funds did prove to be of enormous advantage to his children. With each child automatically receiving income from a million dollars or more in capital after his or her twenty-first birthday, and with the distribution of income and principal from the other trusts falling due at various ages, the Kennedy children were free to devote themselves to pursuits other than making money. They were liberated economically. But to countervail, in a sense, this wonderful freedom, Joe and Rose Kennedy planted such exalted political and social ambitions in their children that they really were not so free to pursue lives and careers of their own choosing after all. Even though their wealth enabled them to be anything they wanted, to develop any potential within themselves— they could have been painters, composers, writers, scientists, teachers, philosophers, any of the not very remunerative professions—none of them became anything but what their father and mother intended they become. Think for a moment what would have happened in the family if one of the Kennedy boys decided he wanted to become a watercolorist or a ballet dancer. Thus, even though Joe Kennedy gave all that money to his children, those children were compelled to realize his ambitions with the money, and, in a very real sense, they served *his* purposes with it, and his alone.

11. The Snub

WHILE JOE KENNEDY was out assembling one of the great fortunes of his time, Rose Kennedy was busy at home in Brookline raising what was to become the most famous family in mid-twentieth-century America.

As that family, and Joe's income, grew, Rose and Joe decided they needed a larger house, and so in 1921, not long after Kathleen was born, they sold the house on Beals Street and bought a twelve-room house at 131 Naples Road, in a more fashionable section of Brookline. The house had higher ceilings than the place on Beals Street, a larger living room, and a very spacious front porch, which Rose divided with folding gates so that each child could have his or her own play area. Soon after they moved in, Rose gave birth to Eunice, named after her sister, and later Patricia (named after the two Patricks) and Robert.

From all accounts Rose was a devoted, conscientious, loving mother. A contemporary observed: "She would leave any party to be home in time for a baby's feeding." She took genuine delight in each new child that came along, and each child added to her sense of fulfillment as a woman. She expressed her philosophy of motherhood, perhaps not a fashionable one in this feminist age, in her autobiography: "I looked on child rearing not only as a work of love and duty, but as a profession that was fully as interesting and challenging as any honorable profession in the world, and one that demanded the best I could bring to it."

Later on in her autobiography Rose emphasized her exalted concept of motherhood by asserting she would rather be the mother of a great son or daughter than the author of a great book, or the painter of a great masterpiece. "What greater aspiration and challenge are there for a mother than the hope of raising a great son or daughter?" she asked.

Whenever the weather was fair, Rose took her youngsters on walks along the tree-shaded streets of Brookline. She would wheel one in the baby carriage, accompanied by three or four toddling along beside or after her. While on these walks, she never failed to take the children with her to church for a visit. Rose, who apparently never questioned the tenets of her religion for an instant during her entire life, wrote in her autobiography: "I wanted God and religion to be part of their daily lives."

She also taught the children catechism, because she was compelled to send them to a Protestant school, the Dexter School, located conveniently close to the house on Naples Road.

Rose also became the principal disciplinarian in the household, largely by default. She later observed in her autobiography that while Joe was working at the Fore River shipyards he "came home only to sleep," and the only time she and their children saw him was on Sundays, when they would all go to P. J.'s or Honey Fitz's for a big family luncheon. As a disciplinarian, Rose did not hesitate to use physical punishment, "because when they're very young that's the only thing they understand."

Bringing up nine children is a strenuous job, demanding, among many virtues, extraordinary patience. The burden of answering all the childen's questions and giving all the endless explanations fell on Rose, and evidently she bore it stoically and cheerfully. Joe once observed of her: "I don't think I know anyone who has more courage than my wife. In all the years that we have been married, I have never heard her complain. Never. Not even once. That is a quality that children are quick to see."

It also fell to Rose to give the children their allowances, and so the Kennedy children's earliest memories of receiving money—and they would receive handouts all their lives—were of receiving it from Mother Rose. Each child from age 5 received ten cents a week, with raises coming on each birthday. Thus on payday each week she had to remember what each of her nine children's allowance was. She tried to teach frugality, but none of her children was ever frugal.

She also taught the children a certain emotional repression or detachment. Any excessive emotional display was discouraged. By her own example, and through frequent admonition, she taught her children to hide their true feelings, fearing that if they showed their feelings too openly it would make them vulnerable to taunts and attacks. Prudish in the extreme, she also discouraged sensuality in her children and developed an aversion to all sexual innuendo. In her daughters she was quick to note and condemn the slightest display of sensuality. Later, when she came to learn of her husband's extramarital escapades, she raged and despaired inside, but refused to show her feelings. Coolly she would introduce Joe's girlfriends to eligible bachelors and then watch them fade out of his life.

Rose (and also Joe) also discouraged "Irishness" in their children. They had both taken so many brutal snubs because of their Irish backgrounds that they were determined that their children would not have to suffer similar humiliations. Both Joe and Rose dropped all contact with their relatives in Ireland (while P. J. had kept up with the Kennedys of Dunganstown) and avoided those American relatives who still displayed markedly Irish characteristics, like brogues. Absolutely no Irish history or culture was instilled in the children. On the contrary, Rose went out of her way to take her children to the old North End, and to Lexington and Concord, to instill *American* history in them. Later some of them, notably President Kennedy, acutely felt the lack of contact with his Irish roots, and made a concerted effort to compensate for it. The great homecoming to Dunganstown in 1963 was part of that effort.

One thing Rose and Joe did promote in their children to an exaggerated degree was clannishness. Rose Kennedy once told a journalist: "Years ago, we decided that our children were going to be our best friends and that we never could see too much of them." In a very real sense Joe and Rose substituted their children for friends and saw far too much of them for their own good. Fearing always the social snub, they sought to create their own society, within the family, where no one would ever have to suffer the indignity of taking a snub from another. The result was an *excessively* friendly (to each other) and cohesive family, destructive of individuality. Why bother to make friends, adapt to other people, when all your best friends are right in the bosom of your immediate family? Don't develop any personal characteristics or attitudes that would clash with your best friends, the members of your immediate family. Getting along together was more important than cultivating any markedly individualistic traits. This clannishness was to be particularly annoying to future Kennedy in-laws, who always felt somewhat left out at family gatherings. After marrying Jack Kennedy and moving to the family compound in Hyannis Port, Jacqueline Bouvier was often dismayed by her husband's insistence on dining with his mother and father and sisters and brothers every night. "Can't we *ever* have an evening together, just the two of us, alone?" she would plead.

On the surface things appeared to be going well for the Kennedys of Brookline. But, in reality, all was not well. Try as they might, the Kennedys never really fitted into the predominantly Protestant Brookline community. For all his phenomenal accomplishments, the doors to Boston's social inner sanctum would always and forever be closed to Joe and his family, and he could never hope for his darling daughters to be invited to join one of the top debutante cotillions of Boston when they came of age.

And then came the snub at Cohasset. The Kennedys of Brookline, after spending several summers on the Cape in predominantly Catholic Nantasket, where the Fitzgeralds maintained a summer home, decided in 1925 to storm the Yankee bastion of more fashionable Cohasset. Joe, flush with financial success, applied for membership in the Cohasset Country Club and was promptly blackballed. He and Rose and the children spent the entire summer being snubbed by the community. Behind the clapboard walls of the old Cohasset Country Club the self-satisfied Yankee members snickered: "You know his father was a saloon-keeper in East Boston, and she's the daughter of that *dreadful* Irish mayor we once had, you remember 'Honey Fitz'?"

The experience in Cohasset was the last straw for the Kennedys. In 1926, declaring that "Boston is no place to bring up Catholic children," Joe Kennedy sold the house on Naples Road in Brookline, put his family into a private railroad car, and moved them to a house he had bought in Riverdale, on the northern edge of New York City.

In New York the Kennedys would find the social acceptance they felt they could never have attained in Boston.

12. "Only a Fool Holds Out for the Top Dollar"

AT THE TIME the Kennedy family moved from Brookline to New York, Joe Kennedy was spending most of his time away from his family and away from New York.

Shrewdly sensing that there was big money to be made in the burgeoning new movie industry, he had gone to Hollywood in January 1926, a few months before moving the family to New York, with hopes of becoming a film producer. After testing the waters there, he remained, living in a big Beverly Hills mansion with swimming pool and tennis court for three and a half years, only occasionally making a trip east to see Rose and the children. By the time he returned home in the summer of 1929 he had succeeded in producing no fewer than seventy-six films and making some $6 million.

Joe Kennedy's sojourn in Hollywood has become a legend in itself. For it was here that he met and fell in love with one of the most celebrated actresses of the day, Gloria Swanson, who became his business partner and wife-away-from-home during his entire Hollywood stay. Miss Swanson, who died in the spring of 1983, wrote an account of her relationship with Joe Kennedy in her autobiography *Swanson on Swanson*, published in 1980. In this book the petite star told of a Joe Kennedy in tears over the failure of their film *Queen Kelly*, emitting "little high-pitched sounds . . . like those of a wounded animal whimpering in a trap," of a Joe Kennedy in passion, making love to her like "a roped horse, rough and ardent, yearning to be free," and of a Joe Kennedy who nearly ruined her financially by making her take the $800,000 loss for the failure of *Queen Kelly*. Miss Swanson also intimated in her book that she had a son from Kennedy, whom she named Joseph, and that Kennedy wanted to leave Rose and the children and marry her. When I asked her about this at a dinner at "21" in the fall of 1981, expressing my skepticism, she said it was "absolutely true." Then, when I asked her for an interview for this book she looked at me coyly and said: "Yes, but I might as well warn you, it's going to cost you an awful lot of money." In the end I decided her assertion that Joe Kennedy intended to leave Rose to marry her was absolutely untrue. Joe Kennedy was much too devoted to his family to do something that foolish.

Joe Kennedy's assault on the film industry turned out to be a typical Kennedy get-in, get-out operation. Referring contemptuously to the reigning film producers of the time—Zukor, Mayer, Loew, and Goldwyn—as "a bunch of pants pressers" (most of them had been in the clothing business), he vowed "to take them to the cleaners." However, like the pants pressers, Kennedy felt little sense of artistic or social responsibility as far as films were concerned. He was in films to make money and that was the only reason he was in them. "The mediocre that appeals to most" was his formula for success.

Assisting Kennedy in his attack on the pants pressers were the Four Horsemen, his rough and tumble but incredibly efficient cadre of Irish right-hand men: Eddie Moore, his long-time assistant, after whom he would name his last-born son, Teddy; Charlie Sullivan, who with his beefy red face looked, in the words of Gloria Swanson, "like a typical Irish cop"; E. B. Derr, who performed intricate financial calculations instantly in his head as he walked pigeon-toed through the gardens of the big house on Rodeo Drive; and Ted O'Leary, who also took care of Kennedy's liquor businesses, which, since the advent of prohibition, had gone underground.

After producing scores of trashy horse operas and

fast-paced adventure stories, all geared to the lowest common denominator of public taste, Kennedy became aware that the movie industry was heading toward a period of mergers and consolidations, and he schemed and worked hard to position himself to take advantage of the trend.

First he hooked up with David Sarnoff of RCA, whom he allowed to buy an interest in Film Booking Offices (FBO), an American film producing company, for $500,000. Then he approached Edward F. Albee of Keith-Albee-Orpheum, or KAO as it was called, offering to buy 200,000 shares of KAO stock for $4,200,000. Albee at first demurred; then, because he became convinced the price was right for him, he decided to sell, and Kennedy took over as chairman of the board, bringing the Four Horsemen with him. Albee believed that Kennedy would keep him on as president, but after Joe took over as chairman, he ruthlessly removed him.

After securing for himself the chairmanship of KAO, while still retaining the chairmanship and presidency of FBO, Kennedy became associated with Pathé as a "special adviser." By the spring of 1928 he was earning $2000 a week at FBO, $2000 a week at KAO, and $2000 a week at Pathé, for a combined yearly income of $312,000—and this did not include all the stock options he had received. As if this were not enough, he also took on the management of Gloria Swanson's career and reorganized her Gloria Productions.

Eventually he also became chairman of the board of Pathé and a "special adviser" to First National at an annual salary of $150,000. He and his Four Horsemen had taken over Hollywood. They were running three major film companies, Gloria Swanson's career, and almost running a fourth.

In October 1928 Kennedy's best-laid plans all fell into place. In a masterstroke of business maneuvering he arranged the merger of FBO and KAO with RCA Photophone to create Radio-Keith-Orpheum, or RKO, as it came to be known, a company with assets of $80 million, and received $150,000 for arranging the merger. David Sarnoff then came in as chairman of RKO and Kennedy cashed in all his stock. He exchanged 75,000 shares of KAO stock for an option on 75,000 shares of new RKO "A" stock at $21 a share. Mike Meehan, the legendary Wall Street trader, and an acquaintance of Kennedy's, then put a pool together and bulled the stock up to $50 a share. Kennedy quickly exercised his options, making a profit of over $2 million. At about the same time, Kennedy and Guy Currier sold their remaining interest in FBO for $5 million.

Kennedy was now virtually out of the film business, although he was still somewhat involved with Pathé and Gloria Productions. He had made himself about $6 million richer in a little less than three years. He then moved to liquidate his remaining interests in Pathé and Gloria Productions. He was an in-and-outer by temperament and now he wanted out. For his Hollywood wheelings and dealings, however, Kennedy paid a considerable price. The tension left him thirty pounds underweight, suffering from neuritis and ulcers, and so exhausted that he had to be hospitalized for several weeks.

Joe Kennedy had gone to Hollywood in 1926 to make money and he had accomplished exactly that. Now, in the spring of 1929, at 41 years of age, he was, for the first time in his life, a genuinely wealthy man; he was a multimillionaire with perhaps a net worth of $6 to $8 million. Now, for the first time in his life, he felt reasonably certain that he could provide adequately for the future of his children, and his children's children, and that the name of Kennedy would endure.

By 1929 the big bull market, fueled by the most exuberant commercial optimism the world had ever known, was raging like a great, unchecked fire. People were buying stocks with no thought of their intrinsic values. Everyone was out to double, even triple their money.

Having made a lot of money, Joe Kennedy now worked to hold onto what he had made. For a speculator, he suddenly turned very conservative. To everyone's surprise he refused to be enticed into the market and did not reinvest the huge profits he had made selling his FBO and RKO stock, preferring to keep the proceeds in cash.

When people asked him why he had suddenly turned so bearish, he told them that when shoeshine boys were handing out tips and calling the turns in the market, as he had seen them doing, it was time to get out. Besides, as he was fond of saying, "only a fool holds out for the top dollar."

Accordingly, during the summer of 1929, while most of the big Wall Street operators were buying like mad, Joe Kennedy was quietly selling, deserting the market by degrees.

Kennedy was not alone in his refusal to be swept along in the speculative madness. William Crapo Durant, the big-time pool operator who had founded General Motors, had got out in May. John D. Rockefeller, Jr., had begun converting to cash in June. And Michel C. Bouvier, head of the Bouvier clan, which would one day give Joe Kennedy a daughter-in-law, had had the sense to maintain a cash reserve of $1 million during the summer buying madness and had unloaded most, but not all, of his common stocks before September, thereby salvaging at least $3,800,000 of his $7 million fortune. Furthermore, Bouvier, who at 82 was close to being the senior member of the exchange, had also had the sense to sell his rights to a second seat for the top dollar—$125,000—only nine days before the first panic in prices.

Joe Kennedy's future daughter-in-law, Jacqueline Bouvier, a grandniece of M. C. Bouvier, was born at the height of the bull market, on July 28, 1929, in Southampton, Long Island. Both her father, John V. Bouvier III, known in society as "Black Jack," and her grandfather, John V. Bouvier, Jr., held seats on the New York Stock Exchange at the time. On October 19, about two and a half months after Jacqueline's birth, came the first catastrophic decline in stock prices. Then, on October 24, a day known to history as "Black Thursday," came the greatest decline in stock prices in the history of the Exchange to that time. John V. Bouvier, Jr., kept a diary of the crash. On Tuesday, October 29, the worst day in the history of Wall Street, he recorded: "XXXX *Blackest Panic Day of All.* Record 16,410,000 shares traded. No bids at last prices. No bids—no bids."

On this day, which many who lived through it would remember above all other days in their lives, huge blocks of stock—25,000; 50,000; 100,000 shares—were dumped on the market for whatever they could bring. With no buying support at any price in some stocks, floor brokers found themselves at the close of trading with pockets full of unexecuted orders to sell. Specialists like John V. Bouvier III, whose function was to provide buying support when there was none, faced the possibility of financial ruin if they fulfilled that function to the letter of the law. As a result, at the closing gong, specialists' wastepaper baskets were as full of unexecuted sell orders as the commission brokers' pockets. After the huge drifts of paper were swept away from the floor by the night cleaners, analysts estimated that if all orders received that day had been executed, there would have been a 20-million-share liquidation that would have driven prices even lower than they actually fell. As it turned out, Auburn Motors sank another astounding 60 points, Allied Chemical was down 35, Electric Auto Life was down a whopping 45, and General Electric was down 28. From New York to San Francisco the financial hopes of millionaires and of retired seamstresses and schoolteachers had been shattered in a matter of hours, and within the financial community the mood had become one of near-total demoralization and exhaustion.

Although there were a few upturns during the next few days that confirmed bulls called rallies, the general trend continued dismally downward. On November 6, John V. Bouvier, Jr., recorded in his diary, "Market opened with severe decline. Steel went to a new low at 166. Exchange closed at 1:00 P.M. Jack's $100,000 profits [off short sales] swept away." And on November 13, the day on which the lowest prices of 1929 were reached, John V. Bouvier, Jr., recorded: "no bids in many stocks." By then the *New York Times* index had fallen 249 points from the September 3 pinnacle of the bull market, and over $30 billion worth of securities value had gone down the drain.

How did Joe Kennedy react to this financial catastrophe? Although he was filled with dread, he nevertheless remained calm and quietly sold the market short, making perhaps about a million dollars in so doing. Satisfied with his profits from short sales, he still remained very apprehensive. Later he wrote, "I am not ashamed to record that in those days I felt and said I would be willing to part with half of what I had if I could be sure of keeping, under law and order, the other half. Then it seemed that I should be able to hold nothing for the protection of my family."

For all Joe Kennedy's dread, however, he and his family not only did not suffer from the crash, they prospered from it, and, with the exception of the chief breadwinner, were even largely oblivious to it. Writing from Canterbury School in New Milford, Connecticut, in 1930, Joe's 13-year-old son, John Fitzgerald Kennedy, made a request: "Please send me the Litary (sic) Digest because I did not know about the market slump until a long time after. . . ."

As for the Bouviers, they managed to weather the storm, but not as successfully as Joe Kennedy. M. C. Bouvier emerged from the crash with almost $4 million in assets still intact. His nephew, and principal heir, John V. Bouvier, Jr., was much less serene. The $250,000 inheritance he had received from his parents nine months before the crash was at least halved in value by the great collapse. As for his son, John V. Bouvier III, he, like Joe Kennedy, had actually made money off the crash in short sales, only to have all those profits swept away in the debacle of November 6, known as "the crash after the crash."

The Kennedy and Bouvier families had entered the summer of 1929 with roughly the same net worth: Joe Kennedy with $8 to $10 million, M. C. and nephew and grandnephew with a combined $7,850,000. But owing to losses sustained by all three Bouviers and to the subsequent decimation of M. C.'s estate in 1935 by inheritance taxes, counterpoised, in turn, by Joe Kennedy's adroit manipulations, the fortunes of these two families diverged radically in the 1930s. The Kennedys went on to gain vast wealth and the Bouviers gradually lost ground. By my generation—and Jacqueline Bouvier's—there was almost nothing left.

Joe Kennedy had come through the crash not only unscathed, but richer. Still he felt very uneasy about the future. He had made a lot of money, and was ambitious to make more, but who, what, was going to protect that money? With millions of Americans now out of work, and more threatened with layoffs, with breadlines stretching around city blocks and former businessmen selling apples in the streets, there was a lot of resentment against the rich building up in the country. As the bleak thirties unfolded, Joe Kennedy began to turn his attention from business to politics. He and the country needed a savior, but where was a savior to be found?

13. Roosevelt, Scotch, and Gin

JOE KENNEDY had first seen Franklin D. Roosevelt in action at the Bethlehem shipyard at Fore River during the war when Kennedy was assistant manager and Roosevelt was assistant secretary of the Navy, and he had immediately conceived a vast admiration for Roosevelt's executive abilities. As Kennedy was to tell his friend William Randolph Hearst, Roosevelt was "the hardest trader" he'd ever run up against, a man of decisive action, a man who got things done, a man even tougher than he was.

Accordingly, when Roosevelt declared his candidacy for the presidency in 1932, Joe Kennedy temporarily abandoned his money-making activities to throw himself first into the drive to get Roosevelt nominated, then into the campaign to get him elected.

As it turned out, Kennedy was eminently successful in both campaigns. First he persuaded Hearst, who was in control of both the California and Texas delegations, to switch his allegiance from California Senator William G. McAdoo and Texas Governor John Nance Garner to Governor Roosevelt, thus assuring Roosevelt the nomination; then, as a member of Roosevelt's campaign executive committee, known as "the silent six," he worked himself to the bone to get his savior elected.

Upon Roosevelt's victory Kennedy let it be known to his friends that he would accept the position of secretary

73

of the Treasury. As such he could keep an eye on the country's money and, at the same time, his own.

After winning the election, President-elect Roosevelt retired to his lovely ancestral estate at Hyde Park, overlooking the Hudson, to put together a new government. Kennedy, spending the fall in New York and the winter in Palm Beach, waited. Nothing happened.

Meanwhile it was announced that Roosevelt's secretary of the Treasury would be William H. Woodin, an unspectacular businessman with no strong opinions who was an old friend of Roosevelt's. In time other important appointments were announced. To his utter consternation, Kennedy did not receive so much as a phone call from the President-elect.

Apparently Kennedy had incurred the distrust of one of Roosevelt's closest aides, the eccentric Louis Howe, who pointed out to his boss that since Roosevelt had vowed during his campaign to chase the money changers out of the temple, it would not be so wise to admit a money changer to the White House.

After FDR had taken office, an exasperated Kennedy finally made up his mind to pay a call on him to tell him face to face that he was waiting for his reward and that, as a son of an East Boston politician, he knew that favors and rewards were what politics was all about.

Roosevelt, the patrician whose ancestors had been squires of Dutchess County long before Patrick Kennedy left the cow pastures of Dunganstown, had always held the emotional edge over the Irish saloonkeeper's son, and at this meeting, talking as President of the United States, he held more of an edge than ever. Acting as if nothing had happened, Roosevelt greeted Kennedy with a "Hello, Joe, where have you been all these months? I thought you'd got lost."

"Lost? For Christ's sake I've been down at Palm Beach sitting by the goddamn telephone all day waiting for your call," Kennedy was tempted to say, but instead muttered something about keeping busy tidying up some of his affairs.

"Well, come in and see us anytime you want," grinned the superconfident, above-it-all-now Roosevelt, as the crushed Kennedy slunk out the door.

Foiled in his effort to gain high office in Roosevelt's administration, Kennedy turned once more to the activity that had never failed him, making money.

Liquor had always been good to the Kennedys, who didn't drink much themselves but profited enormously from those who did. For over a decade the Kennedy liquor business had had to operate outside the law in the vicious world of the bootleggers, but now Roosevelt was out to end prohibition. Many states had aleady ratified the constitutional amendment to repeal prohibition. "Repeal fever" was beginning to consume Wall Street and the business community. Who was going to cash in on the coming liquor boom?

Joe Kennedy was. And a Roosevelt was going to help him.

While campaigning for FDR in the summer of 1932 Kennedy had come to know Roosevelt's tall, lanky son James quite well. Why not use him now to line up some Scotch and gin franchises in England?

Accordingly, in September 1933, two months before the repeal of prohibition, Kennedy took James and his wife, Betsey, in tow and dragged them off to England with himself and Rose, intimating to the President's son that of course there would be something in this venture for him, too. By then enough states had voted to repeal prohibition to lead Kennedy to believe liquor would be flowing again in his late father's saloons by the end of the year.

With the President's handsome son lending luster to his presentations, Kennedy coolly wrapped up appointments as U.S. agent for Haig & Haig Scotch, Dewar's Scotch, and Gordon's gin. He then created the firm of Somerset Importers to import and store case upon case of Scotch under "medicinal" licenses obtained through high-placed connections in Washington. Kennedy's total initial investment in Somerset, including costs of franchises and licenses, was $100,000.

On December 5, 1933, prohibition was repealed and

Kennedy was sitting pretty, with his warehouses stacked to the rafters with cases of Haig & Haig and Dewar's and with plenty of space available for the coming shipments of Gordon's gin and Ron Rico rum, another lucrative franchise he was to obtain. But Kennedy was far from alone among former bootleggers anxious to cash in on the repeal of prohibition. Half the underworld had the same idea. Thus among travelers to Britain in search of liquor franchises in 1933 there was also the crime boss Frank Costello, who succeeded in becoming the exclusive U.S. agent for King's Ransom and House of Lords Scotch. Upon returning to the States with these trophies, Costello established Alliance Distributors, a company in direct competition with Kennedy's Somerset Importers. Soon other members of the mob began getting into the legitimate, "depression-proof" liquor business, including such major crime bosses as Charles "Lucky" Luciano and Meyer Lansky.

Thus while it appeared that Joseph P. Kennedy was serenely weathering the great depression by calmly raking in enormous profits from Americans' appetite for hard liquor, the appearance was only partially true. For the business of Kennedy's Somerset Importers was far from serene. In reality, Kennedy was once again embroiled in a vicious war with the mob. We can only imagine to what lengths mobsters like Frank Costello, Lucky Luciano, and Meyer Lansky went to make sure certain bars, restaurants, and night clubs bought only their Scotch and gin and not Joseph P. Kennedy's. And we can imagine how the equally tough Joe Kennedy retaliated. Years later, when two of Kennedy's sons, John and Robert, were going after the mob tooth and nail, people wondered whence came the Kennedys' extreme animosity toward organized crime. The public, of course, was unaware that Joseph P. Kennedy had been warring with the mob for years, first as a bootlegger, then as the owner of Somerset Importers.

For some twelve years Joseph Kennedy kept up this war, experiencing victories and defeats. Then, in 1946, when his son Jack was running for Congress and he feared that his liquor business might become a liability to Jack's candidacy, he sold Somerset for a cool $8 million, realizing a whopping profit of over eighty times his original investment.

But what happened to young Jimmy Roosevelt, in his bid for legitimate liquor profits? Apparently, because of subsequent parental pressure, he got nothing out of the junket. It would not have appeared seemly for the President's son to have profited so enormously from his father's position, especially in a depression. Kennedy had duped him entirely, had used him shamelessly, and, in a sense, had now finally received his campaign reward.

14. "The Judas of Wall Street"

BUT THE REWARD Joe Kennedy *really* wanted, an important post in Roosevelt's administration, did finally come. When the announcement was made that he was to be chairman of the new Securities and Exchange Commission nobody could believe it.

"A grotesque appointment," complained the *New Republic*.

"I say it isn't true. It is impossible. It could not happen," wrote columnist John T. Flynn.

On Wall Street the appointment was greeted with utter disbelief. Joe Kennedy the pool operator would now be in a position to ban pools. Joe Kennedy the short seller would now be in a position to ban short sales. It was traitorous. For thirty pieces of silver, which, in this case, was the prestige of a high appointment, Joe Kennedy was going to betray all his old friends on the Street.

But Roosevelt knew precisely what he was doing. "Set a thief to catch a thief" had been his thinking behind the appointment. And so far as Kennedy was concerned, he had no "friends" on the Street to betray. In his cynical opinion they were all a bunch of greedy sharks who would eat their grandmothers for breakfast if they could make some money out of it. He, Joe Kennedy, was not Wall Street. He had taken Wall Street.

*　　　*

Joe Kennedy performed well as chairman of the SEC. He possessed genuine executive ability, self-discipline, and phenomenal drive. This was the most powerful office he had ever held. Now he was in a position to put a brokerage firm out of business or close down a major exchange, if he saw fit. All of a sudden brokers, bond salesmen, and stock, bond, and commodity exchange officials were inundated with government forms to be filled out; they saw their offices invaded by scores of SEC men, bent on inspecting their files and procedures.

For many brokers it was a humiliating experience. It is particularly interesting to note how the SEC affected the business of the family of Joe Kennedy's future daughter-in-law. The Bouviers, it will be remembered, had three of its members on the New York Stock Exchange at the time of Kennedy's appointment.

M. C. Bouvier, the oldest member of the Exchange, who had been in business on Wall Street for over fifty years and who was certainly guilty of many practices Kennedy would now find objectionable, suddenly was inconvenienced daily by having to open his firm's voluminous files to SEC officials, who would then take up unconscionable amounts of the dean of Wall Street's valuable time asking him about certain of his business practices.

John V. Bouvier, Jr., who had spent more of his career as an attorney than as a stockbroker, and who had voted for Roosevelt, to his later regret, recorded in his diary throughout the year 1935 that he was spending as much time at M. C. Bouvier & Co. dealing with the SEC and its attorneys as he was selling securities, with consequent loss of income.

And his son, John V. "Black Jack" Bouvier III, a specialist on the floor of the Exchange, was suddenly being denied the exercise of certain practices that had earned him his living.

For example, Bouvier was frequently a short seller. To prevent the sometimes precipitous declines in stocks being sold short, where each sale would automatically induce another sale, Kennedy put through a ruling that a short sale could take place only if the given stock had risen first. It was an excellent rule, and it helped stabilize the market, but it cost people like Bouvier money.

Another measure that directly affected John V. Bouvier III and other specialists, was a ruling that they could not buy the stocks they specialized in "on the way up," only "on the way down." Previously a specialist could buy stock in an issue when he noticed unusual interest in the stock on the part of the investing public. Watching the stock go from $39\frac{1}{2}$ to 40 between 10:30 and 11:00, he could buy it at $40\frac{1}{4}$ at 11:15 A.M. and sell it for $41\frac{3}{4}$, or more, at 2:00 P.M. Furthermore, if he took a big enough position in the stock, he could attract more attention to the issue and thereby help it go higher than it would have had he not bought as much. The opportunities for quick, painless profits for the specialist, given this state of affairs, were almost limitless. Kennedy put an end to the racket, however, by requiring that a specialist be allowed to purchase a stock he specialized in only on the downswing, or at a lower price than that of the preceding sale. In 1934, the year that Kennedy assumed the chairmanship of the SEC, Jack Bouvier recorded a net trading loss of $43,000, leading one to believe that he bought too many stocks "on the way down" that stayed down.

To Wall Street brokers Kennedy may have become a Judas who strangled their business in return for prestige, but for the securities and exchange industry and the economy of the nation, he was ultimately a godsend. Kennedy put through countless rulings that acted to stabilize markets and protect the investing public from fraud and corruption, measures that are still in force today. Kennedy's strenuous efforts to make the SEC a success won him the gratitude and friendship of President Roosevelt, who saw Kennedy often during his tenure as chairman and came to value his counsel.

While Kennedy was ramming these new measures down the throats of brokers and exchange officials, he lived with his perpetual flunky Eddie Moore in a vast, wooded estate he rented in Maryland, called Marwood, far from Rose and the children, who remained in New York. The enormous house, which overlooked the Potomac, had twenty-five rooms and contained such luxurious appurtenances as gold-plated bathroom fixtures and a movie projection room that could seat a hundred people. Here he could entertain a few lieutenants and an occasional girlfriend in the evening without getting caught up in the Washington social whirl. According to Eddie Moore, Kennedy took very good care of himself at this time. He did not drink or smoke, paid close attention to his diet, never stayed up late, and exercised regularly. The young ladies who visited were always taken home early by the chauffeur.

Joe Kennedy was a great lover of classical music, though, true to his exaggerated "macho" philosophy, he never told anyone except his closest associates for fear it would make him seem "arty" or effeminate. In the lonely evenings at Marwood, for Rose and the children rarely visited from New York, he would turn on the Victrola and let the vast halls echo with the works of Beethoven, Brahms, and Wagner.

By the middle of 1935 Joe Kennedy was well on his way to becoming, for the first time in his life, a national figure. This was what he had wanted above all. This was a major step, even several steps at once, in the long climb out of the forlorn alleys of Noddle's Island, East Boston. Now he was not just another millionaire, a quick-buck artist; now he was a statesman, friend, and confidant of the President of the United States.

15. The Importance of Winning

> Daddy was always very competitive. The thing he
> always kept telling us was that coming in second
> was just no good. The importamt thing was to win—
> don't come in second or third—that doesn't count—
> but win, win, win.
>
> **Eunice Kennedy Shriver**

THIS SCENE of near-fratricidal mayhem could have taken place in any one of the Kennedy residences: An insulting remark, a dare, or a taunt sets off another violent row between Joe Kennedy, Jr., and his younger brother Jack. The two boys set upon each other, punching, kicking, shoving, scratching. Locked in combat, they wrestle to the floor, making a commotion that has their little brother Bobby cowering on the sidelines in terror. Finally, inevitably, the physically stronger Joe pins Jack beneath him, then lets him up to limp away, beaten, bruised, and humiliated, while Joe savors, once again, his preeminent position in the family, Daddy's favorite, the family star.

The scene shifts: Joe and Jack are racing their bikes on the street outside the house. Joe has won a few races; Jack has won a few. Now one dares the other to a race around the block in opposite directions to see who comes back to the starting point first. They take off, each tearing around the block in a different direction. Then, as they pedal furiously to the starting point, Joe purposely rams Jack's bike in a head-on collision. Joe gets off his bike unhurt. Jack, thrown to the pavement, requires twenty-eight stitches to sew up his wounds.

The scene shifts again: It is now many years later. John F. Kennedy has emerged from his service in the Pacific war as a military hero, while his older brother Joe, a naval aviator who has not yet seen combat and is itching to get overseas, has to satisfy his dreams of glory ferrying aircraft from San Diego to the east coast.

Attending a large birthday party for his father in Hyannis, while on leave from his base, Joe Junior is stunned to hear a guest at the party, a Massachusetts judge, propose a toast: "To Ambassador Joe Kennedy, father of our hero, our *own* hero, Lt. John F. Kennedy of the United States Navy." Speechless, his face flushed, a false smile on his lips, Joe Junior, sensing his dethronement, lifts his glass and drinks the terrible toast. Later his roommate at the base is shocked to see him return crushed and to hear him sob in bed after the lights are out.

Another scene, another time, another son: Joseph P. Kennedy, following his youngest son, Teddy, in a sailing race on Nantucket Sound, notices the boy commit several grave tactical errors and then slack off at a crucial moment in the race. Later, back at the house, he gives the boy a tongue-lashing on the porch, pointing out all his errors, scorning his slacking off, and telling him that if he can't win, he shouldn't enter the race.

While Joseph P. Kennedy was in Hollywood adding to his fortune and in Washington adding to his reputation as a public servant, his large family of nine was growing up principally under the care and influence of his wife, Rose. But after Kennedy resigned from the SEC in 1936 and was finally able to spend extended periods of time at home, he saw more and more of his children, while Rose saw less and less, and soon *he* was the principal influence in their lives.

In the mid-nineteen-thirties the Kennedys divided their time among three large homes: a large $250,000 red-brick Georgian house with a movie projection room in the basement, in a five-acre wooded park in Bronxville, just outside of New York City; a fifteen-room, nine-bath, $125,000 white-frame clapboard house, also with projection room and, in addition, a tennis court, on two and a half acres of lawn sloping to the water, in Hyannis Port, Cape Cod; and a six-bedroom $100,000 Spanish-style stucco house with a red-tiled roof, designed by Arthur Mizner, on two acres of lawn facing the ocean on North Ocean Boulevard in Palm Beach. Of these three residences it was the house in Hyannis Port that was the most beloved by the family, and it was principally here that the family ethos of winning at all cost was formed and nurtured.

The place in Hyannis was a spacious, comfortable, old-fashioned house that had been built around 1900 on a height overlooking Nantucket Sound. A large green lawn sloped gently from the house to a beach and a breakwater where the Kennedys and their neighbors kept their boats. The place was ideal for children. The lawn became a football field and a baseball diamond. The beach became the scene of swimming meets. And Nantucket Sound became the scene of the celebrated Kennedy sailing races.

At seven o'clock in the morning all the children had to report promptly on the lawn for calisthenics under the tutelage of their own physical education instructor. After breakfast there were swimming and sailing and tennis lessons, and later there were competitions in all three sports. Eunice Kennedy recalled these contests:

> Even when we were six and seven years old Daddy always entered us in public swimming races, in the different age categories, so we didn't have to compete against each other. And he did the same thing with us in the sailing races. And if we won, he got terribly enthusiastic.

There was, of course, one extremely sensitive exception in the Kennedy household. No one ever expected Rosemary to come in first; for Rosemary was mentally retarded, so retarded that she never learned to use a knife and fork and her meat had to be cut up before it was served to her.

In a family committed to an ethos of winning, winning, winning, having Rosemary around was always an anguishing problem. The sweet, shy, affectionate girl, who looked a bit like her mother, could not stand commotion or violence of any kind and was, from her earliest years, a spectator, rather than a participant, in sports.

For years Joe and Rose were so ashamed of having this hopelessly incompetent child in their midst that they never told anyone about her condition. The exponents of the win-at-all-cost philosophy could not bear the idea of having a perpetual loser in their midst.

Since Rose Kennedy took no fewer than seventeen pleasure trips to Europe in the mid-nineteen-thirties, Joe Kennedy often had all the children to himself at Hyannis. Aided by his oldest son, Joe Junior, he drilled his own fiercely competitive code of life into his children with relentless insistence. It was a code that would one day be in force in the highest office in the land, sometimes with disastrous results.

Joe Kennedy ran a tense, Spartan household at Hyannis Port. The children were expected at meals five minutes ahead of time, and if one was late, he or she got hell. When Father Joe spoke to a child at meals he expected to receive an intelligent answer back, no small talk or wisecracks. Activities and competitions were planned for each day, and all children were compelled to adhere to the schedule and to excel in the given competitions. Tensions among the perpetually driven children ran high, and fights among them were frequent and vicious. The Kennedy children were never allowed to relax and be themselves. They were never allowed to grow up at their own individual paces and in their own special ways. To rebel against a parent's wishes, to strike out independently on one's own, was unthinkable. No Kennedy child, especially a son, would ever dream of refusing to enter a competition his father cared about. The Kennedy children may have possessed a lot of courage, but there are many kinds of

courage, and they never had the courage to rebel against
their father.

The kind of rigid parental molding Joe Kennedy enforced in his family can breed men and women of action,
with strongly competitive instincts, but it can also breed
people who never fulfill their unique individuality as human
beings, and therefore go through life suffering from a be-
deviling incompleteness that can, in turn, cause destructive
behavior. It was no accident that all four Kennedy sons
went into politics. (Joe Junior became a delegate to the
Democratic National Convention in 1940 and openly aspired to the presidency.) That's what Joe Senior told them
to go into, even though they were not all, by any means,
fitted naturally to be politicians, least of all statesmen. Jack
Kennedy had a strong literary bent which he never had
the time to fully develop because he was too busy trying
to fulfill his father's political ambitions. Bobby was too
awkward and generally unprepossessing to function convincingly in the highest office, but he was a natural advocate and prosecutor, a talent he should have perfected
and never did. Teddy gave evidence of being a natural
politician, but even he did not always seem comfortable
in the role. Furthermore, none of the brothers was capable
of initiating imaginative new programs or of developing
creative new ideas, an essential quality in a President,
because they were never allowed to become truly independent. And yet each one of these Kennedy sons felt he
had to try for the highest office in the land. Because Daddy
told them that they had to try for it, that they had to be
number one, that coming in second was losing. It was this
kind of thinking that ultimately caused many men to lose
their lives in the Bay of Pigs and that started America
down the road to the massive tragedy of Vietnam.

What gave Joe Kennedy this nearly maniacal urge
to win and have his children win? I believe the urge stemmed
from a radical personal insecurity, with roots stretching all
the way back to Dunganstown, county Wexford. Joe Kennedy came from a despised and conquered people. Bru-
talized by the British, the Irish were, in turn, exploited
and snubbed by America's Protestant ruling class upon

their emigration to the United States. Joe Kennedy was painfully conscious of a social inferiority all his life. He was frequently embarrassed by his paternal aunts and uncles—the Mahoneys, the Caulfields, and the Kanes—who remained in the laboring class. He did not want to know about his cousins in Dunganstown, whom he ignored entirely. He had taken it on the chin at Harvard and at Cohasset and at many other places. And he was determined that his children were not going to get the same treatment. All his children were going to benefit from multimillion-dollar trust funds so they wouldn't have to work for a living, as he had had to do. And his sons were going to try for the highest political offices; they would be governors, senators, perhaps even Presidents. Then, and only then, would the Kennedys finally be beyond all snubs and discriminations.

And so at the big house in Hyannis Port the Kennedy ethos of winning was continually drilled into the children by the obsessed pater-familias. And the day was not far off before the entire world became a witness to the drama he set in motion.

16. Kennedy for Roosevelt

IN AUGUST 1936 a new book entitled *I'm for Roosevelt* hit the stands, and it immediately attracted widespread attention. Its author was Joseph P. Kennedy.

Kennedy had worked on the book, in collaboration with the journalist Arthur Krock, throughout the first six months of 1936. When he sent a draft to President Roosevelt in June, the President did not immediately react. Kennedy did not receive so much as an acknowledgment that the manuscript had arrived. Roosevelt was up for reelection that fall and was terribly busy. Angry and hurt, Kennedy urged the President's secretary, Missy LeHand, to try and get a written reaction from her boss. Finally, to Kennedy's immense relief, it came:

> Dear Joe,
> *I'm for Kennedy.* The book is grand. I
> am delighted with it.
> > Yours Sincerely
> > Franklin

Kennedy had the letter framed and hung in his house at Hyannis Port. Shortly thereafter, Roosevelt told Kennedy he wanted the book to come out in August, in time for the campaign. The publisher, Reynal and Hitchcock, rushed it into print.

Joe Kennedy was understandably anxious about the

book because he had pinned his future political hopes on it and on its subject, the indomitable patrician from Hyde Park. If this book helped Roosevelt's campaign significantly, Kennedy would be in for a reward—a big reward this time, one even bigger than the chairmanship of the SEC.

In a statement of purpose toward the beginning of the book Kennedy told an enormous lie.

"I have no political ambitions for myself or for my children," he wrote, "and I put down these few thoughts about our President, conscious only of my concern as a father, for the future of his family and my anxiety as a citizen that the facts about the President's philosophy be not lost in a fog of unworthy emotion."

The truth was he had enormous political ambitions for himself *and* his children, and this, along with getting Roosevelt elected, was his chief motivation for writing the book.

In *I'm for Roosevelt* Kennedy put forth the thesis that Roosevelt had saved capitalism, and he berated the many businessmen who had foolishly opposed the President. Instead of venting their hatred for Roosevelt, Kennedy said, they should be down on their knees thanking him for saving their fortunes. In the book Kennedy argued for a planned economy and increased regulation of business, telling his readers that such a plan would be good for business and the nation.

Kennedy, it must be remembered, held a deep contempt for businessmen, especially big businessmen. "Big businessmen are all overrated," he once told his son Jack. He knew what he was talking about. If anyone knew big businessmen, it was Joe Kennedy. Before writing *I'm for Roosevelt* Kennedy had spent another profitable interlude in the land of big business, and it had not increased his respect for the breed who reigned there one bit.

After resigning from the SEC in the fall of 1936, Kennedy suddenly came very much into demand as a business consultant. When RKO, which he helped found, ran into trouble, David Sarnoff asked Kennedy to draft a new management plan for the company. Kennedy accepted the challenge, completely reorganized the corporation, chopping down whole forests of deadwood, and charged Sarnoff $150,000, minus $30,000 in accountants' expenses, for the job.

Immediately after that operation, Paramount came to him seeking help. Paramount at the time was a huge, mismanaged company weighed down with a colossal debt. Kennedy was made a "special adviser" and given a free hand. Again the deadwood fell; again frightened executives heard Kennedy's tough refrain: "You're through; it's all over." After innumerable heads had rolled, Kennedy accepted a fee of $50,000.

The Hearst organization came next. With his vast empire falling apart, and creditors hounding him from all over the globe, William Randolph Hearst, Kennedy's old friend, turned to him in desperation. Hearst's income had once been about $1,500,000 a month, now he faced not only a drastic reduction of income, but catastrophic capital losses. Kennedy agreed to help reorganize the Hearst Corporation at a salary of $10,000 a week. Hearst's one request was that it not take long. Once again Kennedy took out his hatchet, this time chopping down whole newspapers, one of which, the *New York American,* was losing $1 million a year. In the end, after considerable bloodletting, the Hearst empire was saved.

Kennedy emerged from these consultant jobs with a renewed contempt for big businessmen, men who didn't know how to run a business. Well, he had showed them how.

When *I'm for Roosevelt* came out, Joe Kennedy was delighted that journalists and radio commentators from coast to coast frequently mentioned his book during the campaign. He was also delighted that it sold well. There was no doubt about it: the book had become a factor in the election.

During the campaign, Roosevelt, in one demagogic speech after another, lashed out at the "malefactors of great wealth," appealing over and over again to the resentments of the poor and oppressed. It turned out to be precisely the right strategy. Since, in this year of economic depression, the poor and oppressed greatly outnumbered the malefactors, Roosevelt won the election over Landon by the largest plurality in U.S. history.

After the great victory Joe Kennedy again sat by the telephone waiting for his reward, telling friends that for the $600,000 a year he was paying in income taxes the reward better be quite a plum. This time the call came quite soon, but it brought a raisin, not a plum.

Kennedy was invited to head the newly created Maritime Commission, an agency designed to revamp the nation's declining merchant marine. Roosevelt had thought Kennedy appropriate for the job because of his experience in shipbuilding at Fore River during World War I. Deeply insulted, Kennedy reluctantly accepted the appointment.

There were no bigger plums to be had. Kennedy had wanted the Treasury, but Secretary Morgenthau and his wife were such close friends of the Roosevelts that requesting Morgenthau's resignation was unthinkable. Kennedy took the agency appointment, but he extracted a promise from the President that if he did a good job he could then have something better—a cabinet post, perhaps, or an ambassadorship.

Then, suddenly, the picture changed entirely. Robert Worth Bingham, a prominent Louisville newspaper publisher who had been United States ambassador to Great Britain since 1933, became ill and was compelled to return to America and tender his resignation. Roosevelt now had to choose a successor. He knew Kennedy wanted the job, but he was understandably reluctant to appoint a Boston Irishman to the position, an act he told people would be "the biggest joke in the world."

Kennedy, however, did possess many qualifications for the job. He was a good friend of Roosevelt's, a loyal Democrat, a generous contributor to the party, and a skillful executive and negotiator. And he had enough personal means to afford the job, which paid a pitiful $17,500 a year plus $4800 in expenses.

When the President finally, through his son Jimmy, told Kennedy that he could have the ambassadorship to the Court of St. James's, Joe was overwhelmed. From now on, he would be called "Ambassador." The social stigma under which he had lived all his life would be lifted, and the high status he so ardently desired for his children and grandchildren would be virtually assured.

17. The Ambassador of Appeasement

IT WAS A damp, cloudy day in March when Joseph P. Kennedy arrived in Plymouth as U.S. ambassador to Great Britain. As his launch proceeded through the fog and drizzle, it was battered by high waves and gusty winds, and by the time it reached shore the new envoy was so shaken up he appeared "nervous" to his greeters on the landing.

Kennedy was accompanied only by his personal public relations man, Harold Hinton, a situation that presaged a new and eventually controversial approach to the ambassadorship, for American envoys, as a rule, never maintained their own public relations personnel. Rose and the children, and the ever-faithful Eddie Moore, were due to arrive later in the month.

The year was 1938 and the political air in Europe was charged with unusual tension. Hitler had remilitarized the Rhineland in violation of the Versailles Treaty, and was now menacing Austria. Eleven days after Kennedy's arrival in England, German troops would be marching through the streets of Vienna and Hitler would be setting his sights on Czechoslovakia.

Entering the monumental ambassadorial residence at 4 Grosvenor Gardens, Kennedy realized that his new surroundings were perfectly matched to the gloom of the weather and the world situation. However, he lost no time in publicizing himself and his family in every way he could. After all, that was one of the goals of his ambassadorship: to gain further fame and prestige for the house of Kennedy. With his personal PR man seeding the British papers with all manner of intriguing and flattering stories about him, something that was not generally done in the diplomatic world at the time but was certainly in the Kennedy tradition, Joe Kennedy soon gained a reputation for being a publicity seeker, and, as the president of the Bank of England put it, "a man permanently on the make."

Although he soon became popular with the rank and file, it wasn't long before Kennedy's style became offensive to many Englishmen of position and influence. Ambassador Joe Kennedy greeted callers to his embassy office with his feet up on the desk, chewed gum incessantly, swore profusely, frequently lost his temper in public, and once referred to the Queen as "a cute trick."

All this was not lost on the British aristocracy. David Koskoff, one of Joseph P. Kennedy's biographers, mentioned some of their reactions in his book. Lord Francis-Williams remarked that Kennedy was "a tycoon who seemed to me when I met him to combine all the disagreeable traits of all the very rich men I had ever met with hardly any of their virtues." Sir Henry Channon was briefer and blunter when he observed that Kennedy's "chief merit seems to be that he has nine children." And Harold Ickes, in his diary, referred to a remark made to him by Sir Josiah Wedgwood, of the Wedgwood china family, writing: "At a time when we should be sending the best that we have to Great Britain, we have not done so. We have sent a rich man, untrained in diplomacy, unlearned in history and politics, who is a great publicity seeker and who is apparently ambitious to be the first Catholic President of the United States."

But Kennedy's social climbing and publicity seeking were relatively harmless compared to his initial misreading of the European political situation. A few hours before Hitler's soldiers occupied Vienna, Joe Kennedy wired Roosevelt that he believed Hitler was bluffing. Then, when Hitler marched into Austria and announced its annexation to the Third Reich, barely eleven days after Kennedy arrived in England, Kennedy stated: "The march of events in Austria made my first few days here more exciting than they might otherwise have been, but I am still unable to see that the central European developments affect our country or my job." Later he added further to his total misreading of the situation by saying: "I am sure I am right that none of these various moves has any significance for the United States, outside of general interest." He capped his wishful thinking by predicting publicly that there would be no war in Europe.

On September 12, 1938, at a mass rally in Nuremberg, over which 1000 spotlighted swastikas waved, Adolf Hitler demanded immediate justice for the German-speaking peoples of Czechoslovakia's Sudetenland; he was greeted by a mighty roar of "Sieg Heil! Sieg Heil! Sieg Heil!" The Czech crisis, which had been brewing for some time, was now a political reality.

Scarcely a month before that rally, Joseph P. Kennedy had submitted a speech for clearance by the State Department. In the speech Kennedy had written: "I can't for the life of me understand why anyone would want to go to war to save the Czechs." Roosevelt had the remark stricken from the speech and told Henry Morgenthau, "The young man needs his wrists slapped."

On September 29, 1938, a grim-faced Chamberlain, dressed in black and carrying a rolled black umbrella, met Adolf Hitler in Munich's Nymphenberg Palace, with not one Czech present. After thirteen grueling hours of relentless discussions, the British Prime Minister capitulated to every one of Hitler's demands. Returning to England, the weary Chamberlain announced to a cheering multitude at Heston airport: "I believe it is peace in our time." Later, at 10 Downing Street he announced that he had brought "peace with honour." At this, London went wild and, according to David Koskoff, Joe Kennedy exclaimed to Jan Mazaryk, "Now I can get to Palm Beach after all."

But there was one Englishman who did not approve of the Munich pact. Winston S. Churchill stood up on the floor of the House of Commons the next day to cry, "We have sustained a total, unmitigated defeat!" Roosevelt allowed the eloquent Churchill to rail against the pact over U.S. radio on a nationwide hookup: "We are confronted now with racial persecution, religious intolerance, deprivation of free speech, the conception of the citizen as a mere soulless fraction of the state. To this has been added the cult of war," Churchill thundered. Then, after elaborating further on the Nazi menace, he asked:

> Is this a call to war? Does anyone pretend that preparation for resistance to aggression is unleashing war? . . . I declare it to be the sole guarantor of peace. We need the resolute and sober acceptance of their duty by the English-speaking peoples and by all the nations, great and small, who wish to walk with them. Their faithful and zealous comradeship would banish from all our lives the fear which already darkens the sunlight to hundreds of millions of men.

But such issues as racial persecution, religious intolerance, deprivation of free speech, and the conception of the citizen as "a mere soulless fraction of the state" evidently meant little to Ambassador Joseph P. Kennedy. Steadfastly he defended Chamberlain's capitulation, which he had consistently encouraged, on the grounds that neither Britain nor France was militarily prepared to fight Germany over Czechoslovakia.

Joe Kennedy was a curious phenomenon, a hard fighter for himself and his family, but not for anybody else. Even the infamous *Krystallnacht* failed to shock Kennedy out of his pacifism in regard to the Nazis. Not long before this event the German ambassador to Great Britain, Herbert von Dirksen, had written in a dispatch:

> Today, too, as during former conversations, Kennedy mentioned that very strong anti-Semitic tendencies existed in the United States and that a large portion of the population had

an understanding of the German attitude to-
ward the Jews. . . . from his whole personality
I believe he would get on well with the
Führer.

Whether von Dirksen's purported conversations with
Kennedy were accurate or not, we shall never know. What
is known is that Kennedy made only a halfhearted attempt
to help get the remaining Jews in Germany out of the
country and resettled elsewhere, and continued to support
Chamberlain and other appeasers and to advise Roosevelt
not to get involved in the European crisis.

Then, on March 31, 1939, Britain involved herself
directly in the European crisis by announcing that if Germany invaded Poland she would go to war. When, in the
early hours of September 1, 1939, Germany attacked Poland, the world held its breath. Would Britain honor its
pledge? The question was asked of Joseph Kennedy by
U.S. Secretary of State Cordell Hull. Kennedy replied,
"No."

Once again the U.S. ambassador to the Court of St.
James's had misread the situation. On September 3, Neville Chamberlain summoned Kennedy to 10 Downing Street
and showed him the declaration of war he would read at
Parliament the following morning at 11. Everything he had
worked for, he told Kennedy, had "crashed in ruins."

As soon as he got back to the embassy, Kennedy
phoned his boss to tell him the awful news. It was 4 A.M.
in the White House when Roosevelt picked up the receiver
to hear Joe Kennedy's frantic voice repeating over and
over, "It's the end of the world, the end of everything,
the end of everything."

On September 27, 1939, Poland fell to the Nazis and
the agony of Polish Jews began. Many would end up in
the ovens of Auschwitz.

According to David Koskoff, Kennedy had privately
told a friend, one Bill Hillman: "I'd sell a hundred Polands
down the river rather than risk the life of one British soldier." Now, he strongly advised Roosevelt to stay out of
the war, telling him, "the real fact is that England is fighting

for her possessions and her place in the sun," and the United States had no stake in this struggle. "This is not our fight," he told an audience in East Boston during a brief trip home.

By contrast, Churchill, now first lord of the Admiralty, had just stated in a speech to the House of Commons: "[This] is a war viewed in its inherent quality, to establish, on impregnable rocks, the rights of the individual, and it is a war to establish and revive the stature of man."

Meanwhile, Kennedy's defeatist statements began to irritate the English not a little. David Koskoff recorded some of their strongest reactions. Sir Robert Vansittart of the Foreign Office attributed Kennedy's attitude to "only the narrowest personal motives," and called him "a very foul specimen of double-crosser and defeatist. He thinks of nothing but his own pocket. I hope that the war will at last see the elimination of his type." And Sir John Balfour of the American desk at the Foreign Office called Kennedy "malevolent and pigeon-livered."

But Kennedy persisted in his anti-British, antiwar stance. He publicly stated that the war would bring about the "collapse of capitalism" and the "destruction of democracy," and "there was no justification for the U.S. to enter the war."

Then came May 1940. Germany invaded Holland and Belgium, the British army answered King Leopold's appeal for help by moving into Belgium, Neville Chamberlain resigned as prime minister, and the King invited Winston Churchill to form a new administration. In his maiden speech to the House of Commons as prime minister, delivered on May 13, 1940, Churchill offered his countrymen nothing "but blood, toil, tears and sweat," then went on to make one of the most moving declarations ever heard in the Commons:

> You ask, what is our policy? I will say: it
> is to wage war, by sea, land and air, with all
> our might and with all the strength that God
> can give us: to wage war against a monstrous
> tyranny, never surpassed in the dark, lament-

able catalogue of human crime. That is our policy. You ask, What is our aim? I can answer in one word: Victory—victory at all costs, victory in spite of all terror, victory however long and hard the road may be.

When in June the British and French armies were forced to retreat before the German blitzkrieg and finally had to evacuate Europe at Dunkirk, Kennedy went into a virtual panic, told Lord Camrose of the *Daily Telegraph* it was only a matter of "days before Paris is snatched," and advised the British government to transfer its gold reserves and royal family to Canada. He also began worrying that the Germans would capture the British fleet and use it to invade the United States.

Hitler, with Churchill, was well aware that he had to break Britain or lose the war. He therefore unleashed a furious air campaign, bombing English towns and cities in an effort to destroy the morale of the English people. Within the first three months of the air raids 14,000 English civilians lost their lives and 20,000 were seriously wounded.

Ambassador Kennedy's response to this onslaught was to announce that he would not remain at the ambassadorial residence in London more than thirty days after the bombing began. He then rented a seventy-room country mansion in Sunningdale, about thirty miles from the limits of the bombing, and moved himself and his family into it. He also wrote to Cordell Hull: "To enter this war, imagining for a minute that the English have anything to offer in the line of leadership or productive capacity in industry that could be of the slightest value to us, would be a complete misapprehension."

Moving out to Sunningdale subjected Kennedy to an outburst of criticism in the press. Not long before, Sir Robert Vansittart had remarked: "Whilst we do not regard Mr. Kennedy as anti-British, we consider that he is undoubtedly a coward."

As Kennedy persisted in his isolationist position, and began spending more and more of his days, and almost all of his nights, in Sunningdale, he drew more and more criticism from the British. Labour's Hugh Dalton was more outspoken than most, saying: "I always regarded him as a defeatist and a crook."

By now Roosevelt had made up his mind to circumvent his ambassador and toward that end sent World War I hero, Col. William J. "Wild Bill" Donovan, former commander of the Fighting 69th Regiment, to Britain for a firsthand view of what was going on.

Donovan reported that England's morale was high, and that, in his opinion, she could successfully resist a German attack. This was in direct contradiction to Kennedy's estimate of the situation. In addition to reporting on Britain's ability to stand up to the Germans, Colonel Donovan also took the trouble to transmit back to Washington many unflattering comments he had heard about Ambassador Kennedy. They did not go unnoticed at the White House.

Roosevelt now began carrying on a wholly secret diplomacy with Churchill, circumventing Kennedy entirely. Britain desperately needed ships, arms, and munitions and pleaded with Roosevelt to release them. It would not be long before Churchill delivered his dramatic radio appeal to the American people: "Give us the tools and we will finish the job!"

While Churchill pleaded, Kennedy continued to oppose aid to Great Britain on the grounds that it would be contributing to an already lost cause. In late November Kennedy returned to the States and conferred with Roosevelt. Harold Ickes recorded in his diary: "The President said that, as might be expected, Joe Kennedy was utterly pessimistic. He believes that Germany and Russia will win the war and that the end of the world is just down the road." Ickes then went on to observe: "I suspect that Joe has been worrying about his great fortune for a long time and the London atmosphere has not helped him any." Ickes then confirmed this observation by reporting a talk he had had with Kennedy: "He said Germany would win, that everything in France and England would go to hell, and that his one interest was saving his money for his children."

Meanwhile, a much-offended and vengeful Joe Kennedy began talking with various individuals, including Lord Beaverbrook, about abandoning Roosevelt in the upcoming presidential election and throwing his support to Wendell Willkie instead. Roosevelt was intent on seeking a precedent-shattering third term in the White House, and since his intention had aroused so much opposition, he needed all the help he could get. When he heard that Kennedy had spoken to Lord Beaverbrook about abandoning him and endorsing Willkie, and then learned that Henry Luce was willing to help write Kennedy's speech endorsing the Republican, he realized Kennedy had him where he wanted him. Reluctantly he called the ambassador home for "consultations." Perhaps he could talk old Joe into endorsing him for a third term while still circumventing him as ambassador.

When Kennedy announced he was returning to the States for an indefinite length of time, the blitz was on and the bombs were raining down on London every night. The British, and the Americans living in London at the time, were shocked to learn that Kennedy was leaving at such a critical moment in the battle of Britain. Kennedy's air attaché, Gen. Raymond Lee, went on record: "From a soldier's point of view, he is deserting his post at a critical time." Others commented that Kennedy should have been going about inspecting damage and giving help to the wounded and homeless, something he rarely seemed moved to do.

On October 23, 1940, two years and nine months after he assumed his duties in London, Joseph P. Kennedy returned home, bringing with him a British air-raid siren which he would eventually install at his house in Hyannis Port to be used to announce meals and other important family events. He was greeted by Rose and four of his children and dozens of reporters, and was handed messages from President Roosevelt and Senator James Byrnes. Roosevelt wanted to see him at once and requested Kennedy phone him immediately upon reaching New York.

On the way to New York from the airport Kennedy unburdened himself to his wife. How Roosevelt was ignoring him. How the British were shunning him. By God, he was going to get even. He was going to resign as ambassador and then deliver a ringing endorsement of Wendell Willkie for President. But the coolheaded Rose, after listening to the tirade, gently talked him out of his revenge. She reminded him of the political code on which they had both been brought up: Remain loyal and grateful to people who do you favors. Roosevelt had made him the first Catholic ambassador to the Court of St. James's, and for this he should be eternally grateful.

Nevertheless, Kennedy was furious and hurt over how he had been treated in London and couldn't wait to vent his rage on Roosevelt. When he got to New York he rang up the President immediately. Roosevelt was lunching in the Oval Office with Sam Rayburn and Lyndon Johnson when the call came through. Years later Johnson recalled the episode. "Ah, Joe, it is so good to hear your voice," said Roosevelt, winking at Rayburn and Johnson, "I want you to come to the White House tonight for a little family dinner. I'm dying to talk to you." As he said these last words Roosevelt put his index finger to his throat and pulled it across as if to slit it, smiling at Rayburn and Johnson as he did.

Roosevelt received the Kennedys in a most affable mood. He allowed Kennedy to vent all his pent-up anger and frustration. Then, when Kennedy was through, Roosevelt defused his mood entirely by agreeing with him on practically everything. The President deplored the people at the British desk in the State Department and promised Kennedy there would be a cleaning of the Augean stables after the election.

The subject of the election had finally been broached. Roosevelt told Kennedy he expected him to endorse him for a third term, the sooner the better. At this juncture the two men retired to a study for a private conversation, leaving Rose alone with Senator and Mrs. Byrnes.

What Roosevelt and Kennedy said to one another

in that room was never reported by either one of them, but it is clear that a deal was made. Years later John F. Kennedy said that Roosevelt had assured his father that he would have Roosevelt's endorsement as Democratic candidate for the presidency in 1944. In return for this Kennedy was to endorse Roosevelt's third term. But Clare Boothe Luce, whose husband had hoped Kennedy would endorse Willkie, stated to Michael R. Beschloss that when she had expressed her amazement at his endorsement of Roosevelt, Kennedy had said, "I simply made a deal with Roosevelt. We agreed that if I endorsed him for President in 1940, then he would support my son Joe for governor of Massachusetts in 1942."

And so during the closing week of the campaign, Joseph P. Kennedy swallowed his pride and, speaking to the nation over a coast-to-coast hookup, endorsed Franklin D. Roosevelt for a third term. Kennedy that night lied to his nationwide audience, telling them that no secret negotiations had been going on between Roosevelt and Churchill that might lead America into war. Therefore his, Kennedy's, children, and all America's children, would be spared. It was not until four years later, when World War II was practically over, that the secret negotiations between Churchill and Roosevelt were finally revealed.

After Roosevelt won the election, by a surprisingly small margin, Kennedy handed in his resignation as ambassador, telling Roosevelt in no uncertain terms that he wanted it accepted. Roosevelt was only too happy to agree— but asked him to remain in the position until he found a successor.

Joe Kennedy never fully realized the extent of the Nazi menace, especially in regard to the Jews. He admired the Germans' capacity for hard work and their efficiency, and he thought they were the logical leaders of Europe. He also thought the Jews were exaggerating their plight. He told people that Jews were not the only refugees in the world and that "the Jews who dominate our press" were threatening the peace of the world, and, by extension, the lives of his sons and the integrity of his fortune.

Kennedy also was never able to feel any great sympathy for the English and *their* plight. He could never overcome his East Boston Irish prejudice against the tormentors of his ancestors. It was something ingrained in his being, in his flesh and blood and bones. A certain Alec Tuck of the British Foreign Office was once traveling in the same plane with Franklin D. Roosevelt, Jr., and Joseph P. Kennedy. Following a minor altercation with Tuck Kennedy told Roosevelt, "I hate all those goddamned Englishmen from Churchill on down."

Meanwhile telegrams and letters from all over the United States poured into the White House complaining of Ambassador Kennedy. Among the many (which are now on file in the FDR Library in Hyde Park) was one from John Boettiger, the president's son-in-law, about a film Kennedy had advised the Hollywood producers not to make because it might offend Hitler and Mussolini. According to Boettiger, Kennedy's remarks had "terrified" the film magnates.

Roosevelt himself was terrified by Kennedy's remarks. He now believed Kennedy was going to organize an appeasement movement, which would be well-financed and very vocal, and which would, of course, be in direct opposition to the President's foreign policy. For years Roosevelt had wanted a showdown with Kennedy, but he had put it off until after Kennedy helped get him elected. Now the election was past, and Kennedy was defying his policies. The time for the showdown had come.

Roosevelt summoned his ambassador to his estate in Hyde Park the weekend before Thanksgiving of 1940. Precisely what the two men said to each other was never revealed, but Roosevelt reportedly said to his wife barely ten minutes after the meeting began, "I never want to see that son of a bitch as long as I live. Take his resignation and get him out of here!" Eleanor reminded him that Kennedy had been invited for the entire weekend, that guests were expected for lunch, and that the next train from Rhinecliff to New York did not leave until two.

"I don't give a goddamn," said Roosevelt, "you drive him around Hyde Park, give him a sandwich, and put him on that train."

Joseph P. Kennedy's political career came crashing down that day in the cool, fall weather of the Hudson River Valley, and he knew it. He was now officially in disgrace. The prize he had so desperately craved—America's highest diplomatic appointment—had backfired in his face. "The greatest joke in the world" had turned out to be not so very funny. Harold Ickes was prompted to write in his diary:

> He [Kennedy] was an outstanding example of what the president can do in the way of an appointment when he is at his worst. Despite the fact that Kennedy was nothing but a stock market gambler, with no political background and no social outlook, the President brought him here to make him chairman of the SEC. . . . Kennedy made a stiff fight to become secretary of the Treasury and Morgenthau blocked him there. . . . As a consolation prize, the President sent him to the Court of St. James's. . . . Now he is back here undertaking to sabotage the President's foreign policy.

On Sunday morning, December 7, 1941, in the middle of a peacetime weekend, the empire of Japan struck American bases on Hawaii, Guam, Midway, Wake, and the Philippines, incapacitating, in one stroke, the U.S. Pacific Fleet at Pearl Harbor and destroying most of the Pacific Air Force on the ground. During the surprise raid the battleships *Arizona* and *Oklahoma* were lost, along with many lesser vessels, and over 3000 American men and women were killed or wounded. Simultaneously, Japanese troops invaded Thailand, Malaya, the Philippines, and Shanghai and sank the British battleships *Repulse* and *Prince of Wales*.

At the time of the attack on Pearl Harbor and the other American and British bases, Joseph P. Kennedy was enjoying a leisurely weekend in Palm Beach with Rose and those children who were on hand. Joe Junior and Jack were conspicuously missing. Joe was in training to be a naval aviator and Jack was already an ensign in the U.S. Navy.

Kennedy reacted swiftly and positively to the Japanese attack. At 6:20 P.M. on "the day of infamy" he fired off a telegram to President Roosevelt:

> Dear Mr. President
> In this great crisis all Americans are
> with you. Name the battle post. I'm
> yours to command.
>
> Joe Kennedy

Kennedy then waited, as he had waited many times before. Finally a form letter from the President's secretary, Stephen Early, arrived. It merely acknowledged receipt of Kennedy's message.

Two months went by and there was no word from the White House except for a rumor that Roosevelt was wondering why Kennedy had not volunteered for some form of war service. Many former enemies of the New Deal, and opponents of Roosevelt, had volunteered for service in the war effort; Roosevelt had overlooked his differences with them and had given them important jobs. But Kennedy was a special case. The bald fact was that Kennedy's remarks and actions over the past two years had caused Roosevelt to distrust his judgment and his motives. It had not been so long ago that Kennedy had opposed his lend-lease scheme, the cornerstone of his policy toward Great Britain. Nor had it been very long ago that Stephen Early had showed him a letter about certain off-the-record remarks Kennedy had made to a graduating class at Notre Dame. Those remarks of Kennedy's had reduced to three points:

1. Hitler was the greatest genius of the century, and from a military standpoint, was capable of things that could not be coped with by Britain or anyone else.
2. Hitler's diplomatic ability was superior to

      anything the British could hope to muster.
      His economic buildup in Germany in the
      eight or nine years that he had been in power
      was unbelievable.
3. Britain was hopelessly licked, and there would
      be a negotiated peace within sixty days.

And then there was the persistent talk of Kennedy's
lucrative Scotch and gin interests. A German invasion could
ruin Kennedy's source of income. A negotiated peace with
Hitler would ensure that there would be no German take-
over of Great Britain and Kennedy's liquor franchises would
remain intact.

Thus when Roosevelt surveyed the ranks of those
men who could possibly be counted on to help the war
effort, he could overlook the strong differences he had
with Republicans like Henry Stimson and Colonel Knox
and isolationists like General Robert E. Wood and Richard
Stewart, all of whom were eventually given top-level jobs.
He experienced a much greater reluctance to overlook the
differences he had with his former ambassador to the Court
of St. James's.

And so Joe Kennedy was sidelined during the war.
In England he may as well have never existed, so thoroughly was he ignored. When Churchill had welcomed the
new ambassador, John G. Winant, in a speech before the
Pilgrim's Club, he had never even mentioned his predecessor's name.

With the war gathering momentum on all fronts, and
the United States performing production miracles at home
in preparation for the great offensives in the Pacific and
in Europe, Kennedy, who loved to be in the thick of things,
found himself consigned to oblivion. Nobody sought his
help or counsel. He had become an untouchable.

But Joe Kennedy was far from finished. "Don't get
mad, get even," had been one of his father's favorite mottoes. The time had come to get even.

Elections for the Senate were coming up and Roosevelt wanted to make sure he had a Democratic majority

in that body. Accordingly, he handpicked the popular Democratic congressman, Joseph Casey, to run in the primary for U.S. senator from Massachusetts.

Kennedy immediately decided he would contest Casey in the primary. He wouldn't mind beating Roosevelt's handpicked man himself and gaining a seat in the Senate. But since he was not officially a resident of Massachusetts he could not run. He went to his first cousin, Joe Kane, for advice on whom to back instead.

This first cousin of Joe Kennedy's was one of the most influential back-room politicians in Boston. Short and stout, he went about in a fedora hat with one side of the brim turned down, and talked rapidly out of the side of his mouth, like a Hollywood gangster. Among his many offices, he had been secretary to Congressman Peter Tague of Boston's eleventh district. Tague had beaten Honey Fitz for the seat when Fitzie had been disqualified for "voting irregularities." That made Kane an enemy of Honey Fitz. Nevertheless, when cousin Joe Kennedy came to him and asked him who he should back to run against Roosevelt's Casey in the primary, Kane observed that the 89-year-old Fitzie was not doing anything at the time. Joe persuaded his aged father-in-law to run on a platform of opposition to Roosevelt.

Two weeks before the primary FDR had the nerve to phone Kennedy in Boston, urging him to make a speech in behalf of Casey. Kennedy told him he did not think it was proper to make a speech against his father-in-law. "I know," said Roosevelt, "I've been in politics."

As it turned out, Casey beat Honey Fitz by 28,000 votes in the primary. But Joe Kennedy's goal was reached. The fight had split the Democrats and allowed the Republican incumbent, Henry Cabot Lodge, Jr., to beat Roosevelt's man in the general election.

In gaining this small revenge, Kennedy showed, once again, that principle meant nothing to him. His family traditions and beliefs were anti-Republican and anti-Brahmin, and here he had helped a Republican Brahmin win. He was a professed New Dealer and he had helped an anti–New Dealer win. Once more Kennedy had used politics solely for his own narrow ends, this time in a personal vendetta.

But Joe Kennedy obtained only a temporary satisfaction. Political treachery was something Roosevelt never forgot; after the Massachusetts senatorial election of 1942, Joe Kennedy was consigned to the lowest rung of the political hell, utter oblivion, and he was compelled to witness America's and England's "finest hour," their greatest military victory in all their history, from a position of personal defeat and disgrace.

18. The Grand Design

As THE WAR raged on, summers at Hyannis Port became lonelier and lonelier for Joe and Rose Kennedy. In June 1943 Kathleen left for England to work with the Red Cross. Jack was already in the South Pacific. Joe Junior was in Norfolk about to go overseas. And now Bobby was itching to get into the Navy too. Couldn't his father pull a few strings and get him into the V-12 program at Harvard? Joe Senior was not very enthusiastic about that idea. Having two sons destined for combat was worry enough.

During the lonely summers of the war years, Joe Kennedy took to brooding on the collapse of his political career, and worrying about the war and the fates of his oldest sons. All that he had dreaded most, all that he had worked so hard to avoid, had come to pass: the world was in flames, and his two oldest boys were in the raging center of the conflagration.

"I am so damn well fed up with everything," he wrote in March 1943, "and so disgusted at sitting on my fanny at Cape Cod and Palm Beach when I really believe I could do something in this war effort, that it is better that I don't see anybody."

Meanwhile, to Joe's further dismay, his sons were itching to get into action and were even pressing him to use his influence to help them. Ens. John F. Kennedy had been initially assigned a desk job in naval intelligence, helping to edit a news digest for the chief of Naval Operations in Washington. After the bombing of Pearl Harbor he tried to get sea duty and failed. Discouraged over not being able to realize his dreams of military glory, Kennedy reverted temporarily to his other self, his playboy self. There were a lot of beautiful young women in Washington at the time, and young Kennedy played the field. Eventually he became involved with a stunning Danish beauty, Inga Arvad, a former Miss Denmark who was ostensibly working as a reporter for the *Washington Times-Herald* but who the FBI came to believe was a Nazi sympathizer, perhaps even a Nazi spy. Inga, in fact, had attended Field Marshal Goering's wedding, at which Adolf Hitler was best man, and had interviewed *der Führer* after the wedding. Before long, Ens. John F. Kennedy and Inga Arvad, whom Kennedy called "Inga Binga," were sharing a Washington apartment, despite the fact that Inga was married at the time. Since Jack Kennedy was in naval intelligence and Inga Binga was suspected of being a Nazi spy, J. Edgar Hoover decided to tap their apartment and the hotel rooms in which they occasionally spent the night. To Hoover's delight he found that the couple had "engaged in sexual intercourse on a number of occasions" and that Kennedy had disclosed to Inga "in general terms his tentative official assignment plans" and some sensitive information about presidential assistant Harry Hopkins. When this news reached Kennedy's immediate superior, Capt. Howard Kingman, Kingman was all for throwing Kennedy out of the Navy. However, the director of the Office of Naval Intelligence, Capt. Samuel Hunter, intervened in Kennedy's behalf and had him reassigned to the 6th Naval District Headquarters in Charleston, South Carolina. As it turned out, the transfer did not keep Inga and Jack from seeing each other, and the FBI succeeded in secretly recording their encounters in Charleston also.

Meanwhile, Joe Kennedy had learned of the affair and the fact that Hoover had secretly recorded his son in compromising acts and conversations with the Danish beauty. He was determined to put an end to the relationship. According to Joan and Clay Blair, Jr., in their carefully researched book, *The Search for JFK,* Joe Kennedy got in touch with his good friend James Forrestal, who was then undersecretary of the Navy, and persuaded him to assign Jack to sea duty. Kennedy was then transferred to officer training school. After specialized PT-boat training at Portsmouth, Melville, and Newport, young Kennedy was dispatched to the war in the South Pacific.

The irony of it all was, of course, that had Kennedy not got involved with a suspected Nazi sympathizer, he might not have ever got sea duty and therefore would never have acquired that "war hero" status that was to launch him on his meteoric political career.

The credit for getting Jack out of the tentacles of Inga Arvad belonged, of course, to Joe Kennedy, ever on the alert for the inevitable pitfalls that lay in his sons' paths. But, as it turned out, much serious damage had already been done by Jack's association with Inga Binga. FBI Director J. Edgar Hoover held in his files those recordings of John Kennedy's amorous conversations with the reputed Nazi sympathizer, and who knew what use he might make of them in the future?

Meanwhile Joe Junior had chosen a branch of the service that sent shivers of anguish down his father's spine. "Wouldn't you know?" Joe Senior exclaimed, "*Naval aviation,* the most dangerous thing there is!"

Joe Kennedy personally presented his oldest and favorite son with his wings and commission in May 1942 with tears in his eyes. Young Joe was subsequently sent off to reasonably safe duty in Florida, then Puerto Rico, and later Norfolk, much to his father's relief. But Joe Junior let it be known to his father and his commanding officer that he wanted action, and the action he wanted most was against Hitler's Luftwaffe in Europe. This time, however, Joe Senior did nothing to further his son's desires. No, he was not going to send his favorite boy into the very mouth of hell.

Frustrated himself at not being part of the war effort, Kennedy, in virtual exile, began writing his diplomatic memoirs, in collaboration with James Landis, who was dean of Harvard Law School at the time, as a way of settling old scores. These memoirs, which were to reveal to the world how Roosevelt and Churchill secretly maneuvered America into the war, never saw the light of day. They are now in a file marked "closed" in the John F. Kennedy Library in Boston.

The summer of 1943 saw Joe Kennedy both disappointed over the way his political career had gone awry and frustrated over not being able to do anything about the war, which he feared could claim the lives of his sons. Nevertheless, he was far from beaten. *His* political career might be over, but that of his son Joe was just beginning. He could run Joe for the House in 1944, when the young man would be 29, or for either the House or the governorship in 1946, when he would be 31. After several terms in the House, or a term as governor, Joe would be ready to challenge Henry Cabot Lodge, Jr., for the Senate in 1952. Then, after a term or two in the Senate, full of brilliant accomplishments, Joe would be ready to run for the presidency in 1960, when he would be 45, or in 1964, when he would be 49.

Meanwhile Joe Senior would also be grooming Jack and Bobby for important responsibilities. If anything should happen to Joe, Jack would be duty bound to pursue the political career he had envisioned for Joe. And the same went for Bobby, if anything should happen to Jack. When his boys came back from the war he would show Roosevelt and Churchill and "all those goddamned Englishmen" who the Kennedys were.

19. The Making of a Hero

ON AUGUST 3, 1943, a messenger appeared at the Kennedy house in Hyannis Port and delivered a telegram to Ambassador Joseph P. Kennedy. It was from the United States Navy, and it announced that his son, Lt. J. G. John F. Kennedy, was missing in action.

Stunned by the news, which seemed to confirm his very worst fears about the war, Kennedy put the telegram in his pocket and said nothing about it to Rose and the children. He would wait for the next telegram, the one which would report Jack had been found, or was still missing, before saying anything. Until then he would keep the awful news to himself, hoping his family would not detect his unease.

As it turned out, Jack, through a combination of his own volition and his forced transfer out of naval intelligence because of the Inga Arvad affair, had got himself involved in the thick of the fighting in the Pacific War. In fact, he could not have picked a hotter corner of the fighting if he had cut his orders at the Bureau of Personnel himself.

Entire books have been written about Lieutenant Kennedy's military exploits in the Solomons, but for the purposes of this narrative, we shall concentrate principally on what was made out of those exploits rather than dwell on the exploits themselves.

Briefly, then, John F. Kennedy, commanding officer

of a PT boat on patrol in the Solomons, became involved in a naval action in Blackett Strait between two islands in the Solomon group. Through apparent negligence on his part and the part of his crew, his PT boat was cut in two by a Japanese destroyer, the only such mishap in the entire history of World War II. Subsequently, Kennedy displayed remarkable courage, compassion, and stamina by towing his wounded chief engineer, Patrick McMahon, to safety on an island, clenching a strap from the chief's life jacket between his teeth and swimming for four hours with McMahon on his back. Later Kennedy and his second in command, Lennie Thom, devised an ultimately successful rescue effort, enticing islanders to bear messages carved in coconut shells back to naval headquarters.

There were two journalists present at the final rescue—Leif Erickson of the Associated Press, and Frank Hewlitt of the United Press. They apparently were not going to cover the rescue at first, but when they heard that Lieutenant Kennedy, son of the former ambassador to the Court of St. James's, was CO of the destroyed 109, they decided to cover the story, such had become the drawing power of the family name.

When, on or about August 10, Joe Kennedy was informed by the Navy Department that his son Jack had been rescued, he immediately ran to tell Rose what had happened. Later, however, Joe and Rose feigned that they first heard about the rescue on August 20, when Leif Erickson's AP articles characterizing Jack Kennedy as a hero hit the front page of the *New York Times*. The reason for the subterfuge was to hide from the public the fact that they had inside sources in the Roosevelt administration who, in violation of official censorship regulations, had kept them informed of what was going on.

That the PT-109 episode hit the front page of the *New York Times* largely because his son was the principal figure in the episode was a fact not lost on Joseph P. Kennedy. As he rambled about the place in Hyannis in the wake of the event, feeling happy and relieved, he began thinking of other ways of exploiting his son's heroism in battle.

On the morning of June 12, 1944, a gaunt, sallow young man, who had recently celebrated his twenty-seventh birthday and who was about to undergo back surgery, stood before the commanding officer of the Chelsea Naval Hospital in Boston and received the Navy and Marine Corps medal for "extremely heroic conduct as Commanding Officer of Motor Torpedo Boat 109 following the collision and sinking of that vessel in the Pacific War area on August 1–2, 1943." John F. Kennedy was now a certified public war hero.

The medal had been "in the works" for some time, and it now appears some pressure might have been applied to help move it along its way. For reasons only the records of the Navy Awards Board, which are permanently closed to the public, could ever reveal, the awarding of the medal had been held up for nine months. The secretary of the Navy during this period had been Frank Knox, and Knox, for reasons of his own, had been sitting on the matter. Knox died in office of a heart attack in the spring of 1944, and Joseph P. Kennedy's good friend, James V. Forrestal, who, it will be recalled, as undersecretary of the Navy had helped Jack Kennedy finally get sea duty, was sworn in as secretary on May 19. On that same day Forrestal signed the citation for Kennedy's medal and made the award official.

Meanwhile, the Kennedy publicity machine had cranked up to hype Jack's heroism for all it was worth, and it would be worth more in the years to come than any of the Kennedys dared imagine at the time. Five days after Jack received his medal, John Hersey's long article on the PT-109 sinking appeared in the *New Yorker* under the title "Survival." The article, which was written with the cooperation of Kennedy and several of his shipmates, stressed the dramatic rescue and hardly mentioned the failed military action in Blackett Strait.

While it was certainly good publicity for the piece to appear in the *New Yorker*, it was not good enough for Joe Kennedy. What kind of a circulation did the *New Yorker* have? Damn little, so far as he was concerned. Accordingly Kennedy Senior buttonholed *Reader's Digest* editor Paul

Palmer, who had been introduced to him by the ever-faithful Arthur Krock, and persuaded him to condense the Hersey article for his magazine. The piece came out in the *Digest* in August to a vast audience, and if there had been little mention of the failed military action in the Hersey piece, there was no mention of it at all in the *Digest* condensation. This omission would not have been so significant if the article had not received further publication, but, as it turned out, the *Digest* condensation was destined to be reprinted over and over again, at the behest of the Kennedys, usually to coincide with Kennedy political campaigns. Thus a distorted version of the PT-109 episode was what the American people eventually received as gospel.

The failed military action, however, was very much on Jack Kennedy's mind at the time of the articles, and also on the minds of his shipmates. Kennedy himself referred to the 109 episode as a "disaster" in a letter he wrote to another PT captain, Al Cluster, and at the Miami PT shakedown unit where Kennedy ended his military service, one of Kennedy's fellow PT skippers, Nick Niklovic, stated: "There was a lot of criticism in the Navy about the loss of the 109. MacArthur is supposed to have said that Jack should have been court-martialed, but I think he denied it. Jack was actually in a lot of trouble over that, so we never said a word about it." And when Barney Ross, third in command on the 109 at the time of its sinking, was questioned about the Hersey article, he said:

> Our reaction to the 109 thing had always been that we were kind of ashamed at our performance. I guess you always like to see your name in print and that Hersey article made us think maybe we weren't so bad after all . . . so I suppose my reaction to the article was to be pleased with myself. I had always thought it was a disaster, but he made it sound pretty heroic, like Dunkirk.

The reality, of course, was that "the 109 thing" *was* a disaster, a very genuine disaster that resulted in the loss of two lives and one naval vessel. What is more, it was a disaster that could possibly have been averted if Kennedy's crew had been more alert and his boat in a better state of readiness. For it was later revealed that at the time of the collision the crew was not at general quarters and the engines were muffled and idling. The second in command, Lennie Thom, was lying on deck. Crewman Harris was asleep. Crewman Kirksey was lying down on the starboard side. Maguire, the radioman, instead of being in the charthouse monitoring the radio, was in the cockpit talking with Kennedy. There definitely seemed to be a lookout deficiency. No one on the PT-109 had spotted the Japanese destroyer's wake until it was too late, and wakes could be seen at a distance of 1800 yards in those phosphorescent waters. Furthermore, at the moment of the ramming, Kennedy apparently had only one engine in gear, which was against PT operating procedure when a boat was in a combat zone. With only one engine in gear, and the others idling, it meant that Kennedy could not, without extreme difficulty, have got out of the way of an oncoming ship determined to ram him.

But such was the Kennedy genius for turning misfortune, and even incompetence, to advantage, that the "PT-109 thing" became one of the most powerful weapons in the Kennedy publicity arsenal. In fact, it could be said without exaggeration that Jack Kennedy's political career was virtually launched from the deck of a sinking PT boat.

To be fair to Jack Kennedy, however, it was not *he* who hyped the episode out of all semblance to reality, but his father. By all accounts, Jack Kennedy remained modest about his naval exploits and often expressed embarrassment over being called a hero. Still, it was Kennedy's good fortune that the volume of favorable publicity generated by the PT-109 rescue episode was such that the episode completely distracted future journalists and historians from probing into what had been for him a distinctly checkered naval career.

The immense flood of publicity made Jack Kennedy into a national celebrity during the last months of that career. It was, for him, a welcome emollient in a period of acute physical and psychological distress. After receiving his medal, Kennedy underwent a very painful back operation, endured a long, tedious convalescence, and was finally discharged from naval service in December on a medical disability, which he never collected.

As might be expected, Jack's much publicized war heroics seriously exacerbated the already intense sibling rivalry between himself and Joe Junior. The two oldest Kennedy sons were very different from one another, and, although the Kennedys strove to promote a public image of family unity and love, the relationship between Joe and Jack was always tense and, as we have recounted, occasionally even violent.

Joe Kennedy was a handsome, vital, gregarious, tough, bright, quick, pugnacious young man who had proved himself to be a born leader of men ever since he was a child acting as sergeant major of the Kennedy household in substitution for his frequently absent father. At prep school (Choate), he won the Harvard Trophy, awarded to the sixth-former who best combined scholarship and sportsmanship. Later, at Harvard, he was one of the most popular men in his class, graduated cum laude, and won his letter in sailing. After graduating from Harvard, he ran for a seat as a delegate from Massachusetts to the Democratic National Convention of 1940 and won. At the convention he exhibited an almost perverse independence by voting for Farley instead of Roosevelt, in opposition to most of the other Massachusetts delegates. Charming, intelligent, and brimming with energy, Joe Kennedy, Jr., seemed destined for sure political success. Sometime during Joe Senior's term as ambassador to Great Britain, young Joe and his father conceived the exalted ambition of one day capturing the White House for the house of Kennedy.

Joe Kennedy, Sr., in fact, once confirmed this in an indirect way, writing: "Joe used to talk a lot about his being President some day and a lot of smart people thought he would make it. He was altogether different from Jack, more dynamic, more sociable and easy-going. Jack was often shy, withdrawn and quiet."

Although he possessed an attractive personality in

many respects, there was nevertheless a cold, hard arrogance to Joe's makeup which made him difficult to get along with. His brother Jack once described him as having "a hot temper," "an intolerance for the slower pace of lesser men," and "a way of looking that would cut and prod more sharply than words." He did not hesitate to confess in later years that Joe had been a severe problem to him in his boyhood.

For, egged on by his parents' relentless philosophy of winning, of not entering the game unless one could be the leader, Joe Junior was determined to maintain his position as captain of the Kennedy children. For this position his only serious rival was Jack. What resulted was a sibling rivalry that went far beyond the norm. Theirs was a contest with no compromises possible, from which there could emerge only a victor and a vanquished, and which could only be settled once and for all by the elimination of one of the contestants.

Whenever possible in this protracted struggle, Joe, who was heavier and physically stronger than Jack, used direct tactics. Dispensing with words, which Jack knew how to use just as well, if not better, Joe would go right into physical attack, usually a brutal one, and would almost always win. In sports he would be easy on others and tough on Jack. He would toss a football softly to a friend but always threw a bullet at Jack.

To get even with Joe, Jack always had to resort to indirect tactics, ones requiring more brains and charm and deviousness than brawn. He used humor, impishness, charm, and cleverness to get a temporary upper hand. Fortunately Jack possessed these traits and qualities in abundance.

As might be expected, given the intensity of the sibling rivalry in which he was trapped, Jack Kennedy would be utterly delighted whenever Joe fell on his face. In a letter Jack wrote to his father from Choate he did not disguise his glee over his older brother's occasional misfortunes:

> When Joe came home he was telling me how
> strong he was and how tough. The first thing

he did to show me how tough he was was to
get sick so that he could not have any Thanksgiving dinner. Manly youth. He was then going
to show me how to Indian wrestle. I then threw
him over on his neck. Did the sixth formers
lick him? Oh man he was all blisters, they almost paddled the life out of him. He was rough-
housing in the hall a sixth former caught him,
he led him in and all the sixth formers had a
swat or two. What I wouldn't have given to be
a sixth former. They have some pretty strong
fellows up there if blisters have anything to do
with it.

Joe was very much like his father, exhibiting many
of his father's more unpleasant traits such as his compulsion
to advertise his drive and masculinity. Joe, like his father,
had a biting, venomous sense of humor; Jack had a ban-
tering, friendly sense of humor. Joe, like his father, was
a "bastard"—he seemed to have inherited his father's killer
instincts—whereas Jack was considered a nice guy.

While at Harvard, Joe and some of his tougher buddies used to go over to East Boston looking for brawls in
working-class barrooms, the sort of places his grandfather
P. J. used to operate. If, by chance, during his rounds, or
on any occasion, for that matter, Joe ever heard someone
utter a slur on his family, he would attack him on the spot.

So far as women were concerned, Joe preferred strippers, showgirls, actresses, models, and married women to
unmarried "nice girls," and he was not so much interested
in a relationship as in a conquest. One of his favorite sports
was pirating Jack's girlfriends when they would go out
together. If Jack would excuse himself to go to the men's
room or to greet a friend at another table, Joe would move
in on his brother's date and, if he could, spirit her out of
the place before Jack came back. Later Jack would attempt
retaliation and get thrashed, as usual.

Unlike Jack, an avid reader who would spend a good
deal of time alone with his books, Joe was very much an
activist and a roamer, a young man at home in the bar-

room, the nightclub, the gambling casino, and the race-track. His idea of being adult was to dress up, stick a big cigar in his mouth, and take an actress or a model to the track for some heavy betting on the horses.

Perhaps Jack's greatest success in prep school was making friends, and indeed the capacity to make and hold friends was one of Jack's most positive qualities. When Jack traveled, he usually traveled with a friend. Joe, however, while superficially gregarious, rarely formed any deep or lasting friendships and preferred to travel alone.

Jack was frequently ill in both his childhood and adolescence, so ill at times as to lead one to believe his maladies were psychosomatic reactions to his older brother. Jack decided not to enroll at Harvard, but at Princeton instead, so he would not be in direct competition with Joe in college, although after dropping out of Princeton due to illness he did ultimately enter Harvard College. Later Jack chose to avoid direct competition with his brother again, entering Yale Law School instead of Harvard Law, as Joe had done.

Always painfully conscious of not being as physically capable and robust as Joe, Jack was frequently compelled to resort to extreme stratagems to gain respect for what limited physical prowess he had. Once, while sick with fever and flu, he escaped from the Harvard infirmary to train for the swimming trials to get on the squad that would face Yale, seriously undermining his fragile health in the process.

But gradually, in a quiet, unspectacular way, Jack was gaining an ascendancy over Joe in many areas. Jack graduated from Harvard magna cum laude, whereas Joe graduated only cum laude. With the help of the doggedly faithful Arthur Krock, Jack transformed his Harvard thesis into a book published under the title *Why England Slept*, which became a book club selection and sold enough copies to land on some best-seller lists. Joe did not publish anything. Jack was promoted to lieutenant junior grade in the Navy while Joe was still a lowly ensign. Then, to Joe's utter horror and dismay, Jack became a bemedaled war hero while Joe had yet to see significant action in the war.

With the *New Yorker* and the *Reader's Digest* trumpeting his younger brother's heroic exploits to the world, Joe was desperate. Jack was clearly the most famous and celebrated offspring of Ambassador Joseph P. Kennedy. He had to do something spectacular to regain his preeminence, and he had to do it *soon*. The war would not last forever.

20. Death in the Skies:
The First Derailment

IT WAS JUNE 1944. If Joe was going to outdo his younger brother's heroics he had to see action soon. With Italy defeated, and Germany and Japan now decidedly on the defensive, there was very little time to lose.

On June 12, while his younger brother Jack was receiving his medal, Joe Junior was in England, frustrated by the fact that he had yet to inflict serious injury on an enemy plane or ship.

Then, on the following day, the first German V-1 rocket bomb hit London, with devastating psychological effect. Soon dubbed "buzz bombs," these revolutionary new weapons were actually small, pilotless gyro-stabilized aircraft capable of traveling 350 miles an hour and delivering an explosive charge greater than any bomb devised thus far. They were, in effect, the atomic bombs of their day. During the next two days the Germans fired 300 V-1s from their elaborate launching machines on the Dutch and Belgian coasts. Seventy-three of them struck London, killing thousands of civilians and terrorizing millions more. The V-1 seemed to be the ultimate weapon, Hitler's last desperate attempt to turn the tables on the Allies. Clearly something drastic had to be done to combat the V-1s. Intelligence sources were claiming that Hitler was even planning to launch them on New York. Hastily, a plan was devised and volunteers were called to fly perhaps the most dangerous aerial mission of the entire war: to destroy the German V-1 rocket launchers on the Dutch, Belgian, and French coasts. Joe Kennedy was the second pilot called, and he volunteered without a second thought. This was the kind of assignment he had been waiting for. This would surely enable him to outdo Jack. He could almost read the newspaper headlines already: "Lt. Joseph P. Kennedy, Jr., knocks out German V-1 rocket launchers, saving London from destruction, and is awarded the Navy Cross."

As it turned out, the Allies were more prepared for the buzz bombs than anyone had thought. A British spy had found out about them long before; a certain Flight Officer Lady Constance Babington-Smith had identified their launching sites from high-altitude reconnaissance photos even before the first V-1 was launched. Plans to incapacitate the launchers were well underway by D day, and, in fact, some 100,000 tons of bombs had already been dropped on suspected launching sites.

But they had done little damage, as the massive barrage of V-1s of July 13–15 proved. What was needed was a more imaginative solution than simply dumping tons of bombs on suspected launchers. That was too hit or miss. What was needed was a way to hit the launchers directly, with no margin of error.

The solution eventually arrived at was to completely disembowel a B-17 Flying Fortress, load it with more explosives than had ever been gathered on one plane before (twelve times the load of a V-1 rocket), equip it with remote-control guidance and arming systems, and send it crashing directly on top of a V-1 launching site. The pilot and copilot would get the plane off the ground, remain in it until the remote-control guidance and arming systems were electronically activated from the mother ship, and then bail out and parachute to presumed safety before the aircraft reached the English Channel. The great danger to the pilots and copilots of the mission lay in the fact that they would have to bail out at high speeds and low altitudes, the worst conditions for parachuting.

The first planes equipped to fly these missions were the Army's B-17 bombers. But it soon appeared necessary also to equip the Navy's PB4Y's for the sacrificial missions. That was where Joe came in.

While the Navy was belatedly getting its PB4Y's ready, the Army went ahead with its own anti-V-1 missions. None of the first four of these missions proved successful. One pilot was killed, one lost an arm, and another suffered a badly sprained back and had four teeth knocked down his throat. In succeeding flights, over half the pilots suffered major injuries. All of the planes were lost. None, of course, reached their targets.

All of this was known to Joe Kennedy as he prepared to fly the terrible mission in a gutted Navy PB4Y at the top secret base of Fersfield, in Suffolk, northeast of London. While he was preparing for the mission, the *Reader's Digest* condensed article on Jack's heroic rescue efforts in Blackett Strait appeared to a worldwide audience. Joe certainly received a copy and it must have goaded him on even more.

Then, sometime between August 10 and 12, a certain Lt. Earl Olsen, an electronics officer assigned to the top-secret project, discovered that the remote-control arming device for the firing system on Joe's plane was faulty. Olsen warned Kennedy's commanding officer and was ignored. He then got Kennedy's roommate's ear and the roommate, Ens. Jimmy Simpson, warned Kennedy. Joe ignored the warning.

Olsen was terribly upset. He was convinced the arming device was faulty. If it was indeed faulty, then the 20,570 pounds of Torpex and 600 pounds of TNT Joe and his copilot would be carrying could explode in midair for any number of reasons: radio static, a jamming signal, excessive vibration, excessive turbulence, an enemy radio signal. Overwhelmed with misgivings, Earl Olsen approached Joe Kennedy on the day of the mission as Kennedy was coming out of the hangar and heading for his aircraft. Breathlessly he told Joe that the arming-firing system was faulty and that he was wholly within his rights to call off the mission if he so chose. "Just tell your skipper," Olsen said, "he'll understand." After a brief moment of reflection, Kennedy said, "No, I don't think I will. I think

I'm gonna fly it . . . but thanks anyway, Oley, I know you mean well. I appreciate it."

Around 6 P.M. the evening of August 12, 1944, Joe Kennedy's flying bomb took off from Fersfield with its deadly cargo and commenced flying a zigzag course designed to have the explosive-laden aircraft reach its destination—the V-1 launcher—at 7 A.M. the following morning. Soon after takeoff the mother plane took remote control of the aircraft, and all Joe had to do was sit back and wait for the mother plane to arm the payload. After this was accomplished he was free to bail out over whatever stretch of English countryside he thought looked most benign. Once safely on the ground he would make his way to the nearest phone, call the base, and have them send a car and driver. Then, back at the base, he would wait for news of the devastation of the target. At approximately 6:20 P.M., the mother plane sent out the radio signal to arm the payload; seconds later, the plane exploded in midair over England with two tremendous blasts. Joe and his copilot, Wilford Willy, were instantly blown to pieces. No trace of the bodies has ever been found. The huge blast flattened several houses, barns, and sheds below. Old-timers in the area still remember the titanic blast, "the greatest airborne explosion over Britain in World War II."

Later, during the investigation, it was determined that Lieutenant Olsen had indeed been right about the arming device: it *had been* faulty and Kennedy had been reckless, not only with his own life but also with the life of his copilot, in not heeding Olsen's advice. Later still it was determined that the whole mission had been futile, for when the Allies finally captured the V-1 launching sites in France, they were found empty, abandoned sometime before the inauguration of the desperate Army and Navy missions designed to destroy them.

How did the Kennedys in Hyannis take the terrible news? Only one witness has recorded the reaction: Rose Kennedy.

I remember that it was Sunday afternoon and we all had lunched outside, picnic style, on our big porch at Hyannis Port. It was about two in the afternoon, and Joe Sr. had gone upstairs for a nap. The younger children were in the living room chatting quietly so as not to disturb their father; I sat reading the Sunday paper. There was a knock at the front door. When I opened the door two priests introduced themselves and said they would like to speak with Mr. Kennedy.

This was not unusual: Priests and nuns fairly often came to call, wanting to talk with Joe about some charity or other matter of the church in which he might help. So I invited them to come into the living room and join us comfortably until Joe finished his nap. One of the priests said no, that the reason for calling was urgent. That there was a message both Joe and I must hear. Our son was missing in action and presumed lost.

I ran upstairs and awakened Joe. I stood for a few moments with my mind half-paralyzed. I tried to speak but stumbled over the words. Then I managed to blurt out that priests were here with that message. He leaped from the bed and hurried downstairs, I following him. We sat with the priests in a smaller room off the living room, and from what they told us we realized there could be no hope, and that our son was dead.

Joe went out on the porch and told the children. They were stunned. He said they must be brave: that's what their brother would want from them. He urged them to go ahead with their plans to race that day and most of them obediently did so. But Jack could not. Instead, for a long time he walked on the beach in front of our house.

There were no tears from Joe and me, not then. We sat awhile, holding each other close, and wept inwardly, silently.

Then Joe said:

"We've got to carry on. We must take care of the living. There is a lot of work to be done."

Later Joe retreated to his room and locked the door. For weeks he remained relatively alone, listening to classical music for hours on end. Friends of the family have since observed "he was never the same again." According to Arthur Krock young Joe's death "was one of the severest shocks to the father that I have ever seen registered on a human being." For the rest of his life Joe Kennedy was unable even to talk of his son Joe. When, in conversation with friends, or writers, Joe Jr.'s name came up, he would either change the subject, or leave the room.

Then, a little over two weeks after Joe Junior was killed, with his family still reeling from the shock, another message arrived at the rambling wood-frame house at Hyannis Port: daughter Kathleen's husband, William Cavendish, Lord Hartington, whom she had only recently married, was dead. He had been leading a column of Coldstream Guards up a country lane in Normandy when a German sniper's bullet felled him as he marched.

The 25-year-old Kathleen, her favorite brother and her husband now gone, immediately flew back to England to be with her husband's family in their sorrow. It had only been two weeks before that she had flown to Boston to be with *her* family in their sorrow over Joe.

Kathleen never returned to her mother country, except for a brief visit, just as she never returned to her mother church, two facts the Kennedys were at great pains to keep from the American public. A Kennedy abandoning America? A Kennedy abandoning the Catholic church? For years the Kennedys suppressed the awful truth. But Kick remained true to herself and to her husband's memory, becoming perhaps the only child of Joe and Rose Kennedy to emancipate herself from the family. Remaining in London, she became, in the words of one observer, "more a Cavendish than a Kennedy." Eventually she fell in love with another Englishman, Peter Milton, Earl of Fitzwilliam, a man in his midthirties and one of Britain's wealthiest peers. Defying her father, who steadfastly opposed Fitzwilliam—just as he steadfastly labored to see that word of the romance never reached the American press, and it never did—she persisted in seeing him, and eventually made up her mind to marry him.

On May 13, 1948, Lord Fitzwilliam chartered a small plane to take himself and Kathleen to Cannes for a brief holiday and a trip to Fitzwilliam's stable of racehorses near the Riviera resort. The weather that day was unfit for flying. Rain and fog drenched Europe from England to southern France, and there were powerful winds. Against all advice, Kathleen and Fitzwilliam decided to brave the storms which were raging over the continent and proceed to Cannes. A few hours after takeoff the small, light plane, tossed about by high winds, was blown into the Crevennes Mountains in the Ardeche near Privas. Kathleen and her lover were killed instantly.

Joseph P. Kennedy was vacationing on the Riviera at the time. Kathleen had hoped to introduce him to Fitzwilliam during their trip and get his blessing on their relationship. When he was notified of the crash, he rushed to Privas and waited in a driving rain at the foot of the mountain against which Fitzwilliam's plane had crashed for Kathleen's body to be brought down. Hours passed; then a simple wooden cart, drawn by peasants, appeared in the mountain path. When it reached Joe Kennedy, he saw that it contained the battered remains of his beloved daughter.

So ended the lives of Joe Kennedy's favorite son and daughter, both killed in the air before reaching their thirtieth birthday. One wonders whether the ambassador ever, for a second, pondered whether the values he had instilled in them were partly responsible for their premature deaths. Probably he didn't, for Joe Kennedy was not prone to self-examination. He was simply not an introspective, reflective person. His entire being was aimed toward the acquisition of power.

That Joe Kennedy, Jr., died in a vain and rash quest to outdo his younger brother's heroics and reconquer his position of preeminence in a family whose members were driven to insane recklessness by the competitive code he had instilled in them, probably never entered Joe Senior's head. What mattered most now for Joe Kennedy was that his grand design had been derailed. The great goals he had failed to achieve himself, and therefore wished his oldest son to achieve, not the least of which was the attainment of the presidency of the United States, had once again eluded his grasp. Who, what, could put his plan on track again?

21. Jack's Turn

NOT LONG AFTER the news of Joe's death reached Hyannis Port, the Kennedy family began planning memorials to their fallen son, and the United States Navy began planning ways to memorialize his heroism in war.

Jack, the literary one in the family, began putting together a book of impressions and memories of his brother which was eventually published under the title *Joe: As We Remember Him.* Each member of the family, and many friends, contributed to the volume. Among the tributes Jack paid his brother in the book was one that revealed what he himself felt he now had to live up to: "I seriously think that of all the people I have ever met Joe had truly the mark of greatness in him."

Rose's desire to commemorate her dead son took the predictable form of a religious memorial. She and her husband donated an altar in memory of Joe to the Church of St. Francis Xavier in Hyannis, the embellishment of which was supposed to symbolize young Joe's fateful mission. Against a light-blue sky the artist painted a pair of golden Navy wings flying from St. George of England toward St. Joan of Arc.

The following summer the Department of the Navy awarded the Navy Cross posthumously to Joseph P. Kennedy, Jr., and named a new destroyer after him. The Navy Cross was a higher decoration than the one Jack had received a year before, and so, in a certain perverse sense, Joe had finally gone one up on his younger brother, which had been his intention all along. The destroyer named after Joe was destined to play quite a role in the history of the Kennedy family and our country. It was christened in 1945 by Joe Junior's goddaughter, Jean Kennedy, with almost the entire Kennedy family present. In February 1946, Seaman Robert F. Kennedy reported for duty on the *USS Joseph P. Kennedy, Jr.* Years later, the *USS Joseph P. Kennedy, Jr.* became the first ship to stop a Russian freighter off Cuba during the blockade initiated by President John F. Kennedy at the height of the Cuban missile crisis.

In August 1946, in the midst of Jack Kennedy's first campaign for Congress, Joseph P. Kennedy presented Archbishop Richard Cushing of Boston with a check for $600,000 to be used to construct the Joseph P. Kennedy Jr. Convalescent Home for disadvantaged children. Instead of presenting the check himself, Kennedy Senior had his son Jack, the candidate, actually hand the check to the archbishop in front of the newspaper photographers at the founding ceremony. Later on during his son's campaign, Joe Kennedy announced the creation of the Joseph P. Kennedy Jr. Foundation to help retarded children, into which he was to pour several million dollars. It has since proved to be the most lasting memorial to his fallen son.

Undoubtedly the specific charity for which Kennedy's foundation was created had something to do with the fact that Kennedy had a retarded child. The ambassador had always felt that his daughter Rosemary's mental retardation was due to some defect within himself. This unreasonable though entirely human assumption loaded him with a sense of guilt that was intensified after what is widely assumed to have been a prefrontal lobotomy was performed on Rosemary in 1941.

The dangerous and controversial operation (a common treatment before the advent of tranquilizers and mood-altering drugs) was performed after Rosemary had become hyperactive and unmanageable. Rose Kennedy, in her autobiography, referred to the operation as "a certain form of neurosurgery," and went on to state that "the operation eliminated the violence and the convulsive seizures, but it also had the effect of leaving Rosemary permanently incapacitated." To have such a person around a house full of vital, active, intelligent people, including observant guests, was awkward to say the least. Accordingly, not long after the lobotomy, Joe and Rose made the decision to confine Rosemary for life to a home for the hopelessly retarded, intensifying Joe Kennedy's sense of shame.

Much has been written on the subject of Jack Kennedy's decision to enter politics. Kennedy cronies and camp followers, like Dave Powers and the late Kenny O'Donnell have steadfastly asserted that Jack Kennedy would have gone into politics anyway, whether his brother had lived or died, whether his father had pushed him or not. But there is more than ample evidence to indicate that Joe's death and the ambassador's ambitions were decisive in forcing Jack into a political career.

Unquestionably the most convincing witness to this process was Paul B. "Red" Fay, Jr., an intimate of Jack's from PT-109 days and undersecretary of the Navy in the Kennedy administration. In his highly entertaining and informative book, *The Pleasure of His Company*, Fay reported that in the months following Jack's discharge from the Navy he gave up his ambition to become a "newspaper columnist commenting chiefly on politics" in favor of going into active politics, largely because of pressure put on him by his father. According to Fay, Jack fully realized at the time that "his father now saw him as the heir to the political traditions of the family." "I can feel Pappy's eyes on the back of my neck," Jack told Fay during one of their weekends together at Palm Beach.

Then one day during this same period, after Jack had been discharged from the Navy (in March 1945), he said to Fay, "with no special enthusiasm":

When the war is over and you are out there in sunny California giving them a good solid five and a half inches for a six-inch pavement [Fay was destined for his father's construction busi-

ness], I'll be back here with Dad trying to par-
lay a lost PT boat and a bad back into a political
advantage. I tell you, Dad is ready right now
and can't understand why Johnny Boy isn't "all
engines ahead full."

Fay concluded at the same time that "Jack seemed indif-
ferent to the idea of a political career."

Years later, when Hugh Sidey was interviewing Jack
and Fay in California for a cover story about Kennedy for
Time magazine, Kennedy went to great pains to discourage
Fay from intimating that his father was behind his political
ambitions. Since then almost all the Kennedy apologists
have attempted to cover up Joe Senior's crucial influence
on his son.

But Joe Kennedy himself had given the matter away
to Eleanor Harris in an interview for an article in *McCall's*
magazine in August 1957. "I got Jack into politics," he
told Harris, "I was the one. I told him Joe was dead and
that it was therefore his responsibility to run for Congress.
He didn't want to. He felt he didn't have the ability and
he still feels that way. But I told him he had to."

Even before he had begun thinking seriously of the
presidency, Jack Kennedy himself had given the matter
away. In an interview for an article in *McCall's* conducted
by the same Eleanor Harris, he stated: "My brother Joe
was the logical one in the family to be in politics and if he
had lived I'd have kept on being a writer. . . . If I died,
my brother Bob would want to be senator and if anything
happened to him, my brother Teddy would run for us. . . ."

Many years later, Arthur Krock, who was very close
to the Kennedys for a good part of his life, declared in his
Memoirs: "Ambassador Kennedy began definitely to plan
for Jack the political career he had designed for Joe Junior.
Until then, I think, he shared a belief which was mine that
Jack was suited to a career in journalism, in literature, or
in teaching." Later still, Krock, who is now dead, told
journalist Clay Blair, Jr., that Jack's entering politics to
take Joe's place was "almost a physical event: now it's
your turn." And that Jack was "not too happy about it."

As it turned out, his older brother's death, resulting in his own sudden accession to the role of heir apparent, turned out to have grave psychological consequences for Jack Kennedy. On a subconscious level, it must have made him feel terribly guilty. How could he expiate his guilt? The solution probably never rose to the level of a conscious intent but rather remained below the surface, urging him constantly to tempt fate.

That Kennedy had an inclination to flirt with death is suggested by his favorite poem, "I Have a Rendezvous with Death," by Alan Seeger, which he recited to his bride on the eve of their marriage.

> *But I have a rendezvous with Death*
> *At midnight in some flaming town,*
> *When Spring trips north again this year,*
> *And I to my pledged word am true,*
> *I shall not fail that rendezvous.*

22. Young Jack:
The Unlikely Prospect

IT FELL TO young Jack Kennedy to realize his father's ambitions. Chronically underweight and sick about fifty percent of his life, not able to beat Joe at anything, and too weak to be a consistent victor among the kids in the neighborhood and at school, yet constantly urged on by his parents to win, win, win, young Jack Kennedy was often driven to recklessness and "overdoing it." As a result, his system frequently broke down. The procession of illnesses that assailed the "frail" and "sickly" (as his mother described him) Jack Kennedy as a child and young man was harrowing. "Almost all his life, it seemed," Rose Kennedy wrote in her autobiography, "he had to battle against misfortunes of health." Brother Bobby confirmed this observation when he wrote: "At least one half of the days that he spent on earth were days of intense physical pain. . . . He had almost every conceivable ailment. . . . When we were growing up together we used to laugh about the great risk a mosquito took in biting Jack Kennedy—with some of his blood the mosquito was sure to die."

The chronology of Jack Kennedy's health problems—many are only just beginning to come to light, and several still remain hidden because his family has refused to release his medical records—is both astonishing and sobering. Our admiration for the man is reinforced by the knowledge of what he had to overcome to attain the physical strength and stamina he needed to make his arduous assault on the presidency. In the end, the heroism Jack Kennedy displayed in rescuing his shipmates from the wreck of the PT-109 was insignificant compared to the courage and determination he displayed in overcoming his own infirmities.

What were those infirmities? First of all, he was born with an unstable spine, as testified to by Dr. Elmer C. Bartels, who treated him at the Lahey Clinic in Boston. An unstable spine is a chronic, lifetime disability. It is a congenital malformation of the spinal column. Sometimes it causes no discomfort. Then, suddenly, it goes awry and the victim suffers excruciating pain. The pain can be occasionally relieved by hot baths, back braces, and painkillers, but the basic condition can never be cured. Secondly, Kennedy was either born with, or early in his life was stricken with, insufficient functioning, or atrophy, of the adrenal glands, a condition known in its extreme form as Addison's disease. Thirdly, he suffered from a set of debilitating allergies; he was highly allergic to dogs, horses, and certain kinds of dust and suffered coughing and sneezing attacks, skin rashes, and swollen glands as a result of these allergies. He was also periodically asthmatic and had a weak stomach; in his later years, he could not tolerate anything but bland foods. In addition, he suffered from poor eyesight, having to wear reading glasses from an early age, and was slightly deaf in one ear. Chronically underweight through his first thirty-five years, a symptom, perhaps, of his adrenal insufficiency, he was fed in his youth a diet of milk, cream, butter, creamed soups, chowders, and sirloin steaks, baked potatoes with butter, ice cream, chocolate malteds, and hot chocolate made from milk and topped with whipped cream, all of which he ate in large quantities without ever putting on so much as an extra pound.

Among the many maladies he supposedly suffered from, in addition to the above, were scarlet fever, measles, appendicitis, tonsilitis, frequent colds and influenzas, rashes, jaundice, malaria, sudden high fevers, and many injuries and bruises suffered in sports because of his inadequate physique. As a young boy his mother remembered him as "bedridden and elfinlike . . . with his bed piled high with books," a boy whose "body could not keep pace with his dreams," and several school and college friends remembered him as frequently pale, with lines around deep, sunken eyes, and a speaking voice that was sharp and high-pitched. Years later, when he and his doctors had begun to conquer his health problems, especially his unstable back and what we might presume was Addison's disease, he still watched his diet very carefully, tried hard to avoid bruises and infections (because of his adrenal insufficiency), wore corrective shoes (for his back) that made him look taller, wore a tight, eight-inch-wide cloth corset (also for his back) around his middle, which made him look even thinner, used glasses when reading, always kept a rocking chair in his office, always slept with a bedboard under his mattress, no matter where he traveled, and was constantly under massive medication (cortisone) for his adrenal insufficiency.

But to counterpose this baleful list of infirmities, Jack Kennedy possessed phenomenal stamina, endurance, and vitality, and during those periods when he was well, managed to enjoy life to the hilt, especially in his later years. At maturity he was over six feet tall, weighed an average of 165 pounds, and, as he grew older, developed strong muscles in his arms, chest, and legs.

There is a mystery to Jack Kennedy's health problems which could probably be cleared up if the John Fitzgerald Kennedy Library in Boston would release his health records, which are currently classified "closed." The suspicion is that many of his early ailments were, in fact, manifestations of but one ailment, Addison's disease, an ailment the Kennedy family had refused to admit Jack ever had, even though it was diagnosed in London in 1947, and again in 1951. In the advanced stages of Addison's disease the slightest infection or instance of acute stress can bring on an "Addisonian crisis," resulting in severe debility, accompanied by confusion, nausea, fainting, and ending even in death.

In 1933, when Jack was 16, and a student at Choate,

Rose suddenly stopped entering illnesses on Jack's file cards. It was in that year that Jack suffered a severe illness, the true nature of which remains a mystery to this day. Headmaster George St. John made reference to it in a letter to Jack's father, and Jack's roommate at Choate, Lem Billings, has referred to it in various interviews, but its exact nature remains publicly unknown. Since St. John and Billings have stated that the illness (which was serious enough to land Jack in Boston's Lahey Clinic) left Kennedy so weak that he could no longer exert himself either in sports or in studies, one suspects that quite possibly the illness was the onset of Addison's disease, since one of the symptoms of that disease is a sudden loss of energy and vitality.

In the following year, his sixth-form year at Choate, Jack took a bad fall in football practice, hurt his knee, and aggravated his back condition. From that point on he moved with a slight limp, which usually went undetected, but was immediately noticeable when he climbed or walked down stairs.

Upon graduating from Choate, Jack followed in his older brother's footsteps by enrolling in the London School of Economics for the academic year 1935–1936 to study under the renowned socialist economist, Harold Laski. No sooner had he embarked on his studies in London than he became seriously ill with what his father later referred to, rather vaguely, in a letter to the Harvard Admissions Office, as a "recurrence of a blood condition." This "recurrence," possibly of his fifth-form illness at Choate, was so severe he was compelled to withdraw from the London School and return to the United States.

Once back at Hyannis Port the question arose: what to do with Jack now? Quickly Joe Kennedy went into action. It was very important that Jack not miss a year of college. Jack wanted to go, but the big question was which college? Harvard was the logical choice for a Kennedy, but Jack wanted to go to Princeton for two reasons: One, he didn't want to be in direct competition with his brother Joe at Harvard, who was doing very well; and two, his two best friends from Choate, Lem Billings and Rip Horton, were already enrolled in Princeton. Though Joe Senior was somewhat disappointed that Jack did not want to go to his alma mater, he nevertheless swiftly took measures to get his son into Princeton. He contacted his friend, an important Princeton alumnus, Herbert Bayard Swope, who was then editor-in-chief of the *New York World*, and got him to influence the Princeton dean of admissions to take Jack in, even though the school year had already begun. Such was the combined power of the Kennedy and Swope names that young Jack was admitted, in violation of official admissions policy.

And so Jack Kennedy entered Princeton in late October about six weeks after the fall term had begun. Throughout November he felt very weak and experienced great difficulty applying himself to his studies. His midterm grades were poor. He was not strong enough to take part in freshman athletics. Finally, in early December, he gave it all up and withdrew for reasons of ill health, claiming he had "jaundice."

There followed a two-month stay in Peter Bent Brigham Hospital in Boston, after which he joined his family in Palm Beach. After spending the holidays with the entire clan, Jack was dispatched to a ranch near Tucson, Arizona, to recover his health. He thus missed an entire academic year, a serious matter for a young man of such an ambitious family.

However, judging from Kennedy's later campaign biographies, and his self-submitted biography in *Who's Who,* one would never suspect the missing year. For Jack Kennedy and his family, and later his associates, always gave out that he spent the entire academic year 1935–1936 at the London School of Economics, studying under the liberal Harold Laski.

What went wrong with Jack Kennedy's health in London and Princeton? The Kennedy lips and the Kennedy health records are sealed. The only hint we have is the admission to his having had "jaundice." One of the symptoms of jaundice is discoloration of the skin, which is also a symptom of Addison's disease.

Whatever the case, Jack Kennedy was a sick young man throughout the academic year 1935–1936, and he must have felt himself to be a terrible disappointment to his father. Here was his hale and energetic older brother at Harvard performing well in both sports and studies and winning the full approval of both his peers and his parents, and here *he* was, unable to finish out his course in London, able to get into Princeton only because of pull, feeling guilty about being there, and not doing at all well in either his studies or in sports, and eventually having to drop out because of ill health. Such a record during one's first year at college certainly did not augur very well for the future.

It appears, however, that the winter and spring months in the dry, sunny air of Arizona did Jack Kennedy a lot of good. A fairly relaxed summer in Hyannis Port followed, during which Father Joe, pulling strings here and there, was able to get Jack into Harvard. Young Kennedy entered as a freshman in the fall of 1936, determined to make up for lost time.

Despite his chronic back trouble, history of illness, and lack of weight, Jack Kennedy went out for freshman football at Harvard and, as could have been predicted, was brutally mauled during a practice session in which his back was thrown completely out. Dragged from the field in terrible pain, the scrawny 145-pound end could hardly walk for days. Years later his back trouble was blamed by journalists and biographers on this Harvard football episode, when, in reality, what he sustained was simply an aggravation of his already unstable spinal condition.

While at Harvard, Jack Kennedy spent every summer in Europe. (It may be remarked, at this point, that the Kennedys were particularly attracted to Europe and became unquestionably the most cosmopolitan presidential family in modern American history.) In the summer of 1937 Jack took a trip through France, Italy, Germany, Holland, and England with his friend Lem Billings. During these months he visited Paris, the Loire Valley, Biarritz, Saint-Jean-de-Luz, Lourdes, the Riviera, Monte Carlo, Naples, Capri, Milan, Pisa, Florence, Venice, Rome, Munich, Nuremberg, Amsterdam, and London. It was Kennedy's first direct contact with European civilization, and, though he was not, and never would be, a linguist, he took to it with ease and delight. He and Billings visited every museum, castle, palace, and cathedral they could find and hiked endlessly over mountains, ruins, and ancient battlefields. They were wildly enthusiastic over the castles of the Loire; they climbed Vesuvius; they clambered over the ruins of the villa of Tiberius on Capri. One of the high points of the trip for Jack was a private audience with Eugenio Cardinal Pacelli, who knew his father, at the Vatican. At Lourdes both Jack and Billings got sick from bathing in the holy waters. According to Billings' account, they probably enjoyed themselves most on the Riviera and at Monte Carlo, where they apparently took some time out from visiting museums and cathedrals to indulge a bit in women and gambling.

But then the fun and adventuring came to an abrupt close toward the end of the trip in London where Jack fell suddenly, and unaccountably, ill. According to Billings, Kennedy's face "puffed up and he got a rash" and "terrible asthma." Billings diagnosed the malady as an allergic reaction to a dog they had bought in Amsterdam, but it may well have been something much more serious.

Returning to Harvard in the fall of 1937, Kennedy's health seemed to hold up. Then, in 1938, he became sick again. From February 23 to April 11 he was so sick he missed all his classes and spent several weeks in the infirmary. It was during this time that he did another reckless thing. Suffering from a high fever, he sneaked out of the infirmary to try out for the swimming team that would soon meet Yale. We have already noted that for someone with chronic adrenal insufficiency acute physical stress can be very dangerous. Kennedy did not make the swimming team, but he did get sicker. In late March he left Cambridge and went down to his parents' home in Palm Beach to recover his health in the warm Florida sun. It was not the first time he needed a warm climate to recuperate from a mysterious illness. It is worth noting, in passing, that untreated Addisonians have trouble coping with the cold.

From what we know, Kennedy got through the fall term of 1938 without suffering a serious illness, then withdrew from Harvard for the entire next semester (spring,

1939) to serve as a kind of secretary and emissary to his father, who was by then ambassador to the Court of St. James's. This turned out to be one of the great formative periods of John Kennedy's life, and it apparently unfolded without significant health problems. Jack served his father at the embassy in London at a time of great international crisis; attended the coronation of Eugenio Cardinal Pacelli as Pope Pius XII in Rome; met Giovanni Cardinal Montini, who was to become Pope Paul VI; was entertained in Paris by Ambassador William C. Bullitt, a friend of his father, traveled through Hitler's Germany and soon-to-be threatened Poland; went on to Leningrad, Moscow, and the Crimea; then traveled to Istanbul, Palestine, and Egypt; and on the way back to London visited beleaguered Prague and Vienna. Wherever young Kennedy went, his impeccable credentials, provided by his father, opened all the right doors. He got firsthand impressions of the Jewish-Arab standoff in Palestine and the mounting crisis in central Europe. It was an education worth six terms at Harvard, and it was to stand Kennedy in excellent stead when, twenty years later, as leader of the free world, he found himself dealing with great international crises.

On returning to Harvard after his long, stimulating trip abroad, Jack Kennedy the scholar suddenly caught fire. The formerly lackadaisical student became passionately interested in his studies; he wrote a thesis on Great Britain's unpreparedness to meet the Nazi threat that was so well received by his professors that it enabled him to graduate magna cum laude. During the writing he helped himself to the vast research facilities and materials available to his father, the ambassador.

The thesis was read by family friend Arthur Krock of the *New York Times*, who was so impressed that he encouraged Jack to publish it as a book. Jack consulted with his father, and they decided to go along with Krock's suggestion. Krock then helped the young Harvard graduate, who was in ailing health, write the book, which was eventually published under the title *Why England Slept*, with an introduction by none other than Henry R. Luce, head of Time-Life. Luce had, of course, been recruited to write the introduction by his friend, the ambassador to the Court of St. James's. Subsequent researchers found that young Kennedy had incorporated a good many of his father's letters in the book, passing them off as his own prose. The final result was "a work of many hands," as Kennedy biographer Clay Blair, Jr., put it; nevertheless, it sold well and received favorable reviews.

After Joe Kennedy himself read the final product, he wrote a revealing letter to his son in which he said, "You would be surprised how a book that really makes the grade with high-class people stands you in good stead for years to come." In other words, it was not the ideas, the style, the content of the book that impressed the ambassador, but its possible usefulness to advance the career of his son. The book, so far as Joe Kennedy was concerned, represented just one more step up in the long climb.

One person who was not terribly impressed by the book was Harold Laski. Writing the ambassador on July 20, 1940, he had this to say:

> Dear Joe:
>
> The easy thing for me to do would be to repeat the eulogies that Krock and Harry Luce have showered on your boy's work.
>
> In fact, I choose the more difficult way of regretting deeply that you let him publish it. For while it is the book of a lad with brains, it is very immature, it has no real structure, and it dwells almost wholly on the surface of things. In a good university, half a hundred seniors do books like this as part of their normal work in their final year. But they don't publish them for the good reason that their importance lies solely in what they get out of doing them and not in what they have to say. I don't honestly think any publisher would have looked at that book of Jack's if he had not been your son, and if you had not been Ambassador. And those are not the right grounds for publication.
>
> I care a lot about your boys. I don't want

them to be spoilt as rich men's sons are so easily
spoilt. Thinking is a hard business, and you
have to pay the price for admission to it. Do
believe that these hard sayings from me represent much more real friendship than the easy
praise of 'yes men' like Arthur Krock.

Yours very sincerely,

(signed) Harold J. Laski

It is unlikely that this letter was ever shown to Jack
Kennedy, and it is not mentioned by any of his chief apologists, all of whom tend to pass Jack's book off as a minor
masterpiece. The letter is on file at the Franklin D. Roosevelt Library in Hyde Park, but it is not at the John F.
Kennedy Library in Boston.

After graduating from Harvard, and while preparing
his book for publication, an ailing Jack Kennedy went to
the Mayo Clinic for some tests. There he was advised to
take a year off. The precise reasons for this advice are not
known since the Mayo Clinic will not give out information
on its patients. What is known is that Kennedy ignored
the advice and enrolled in the business school at Stanford
instead, even though he was not particularly enthusiastic
about becoming a businessman. Not long after the fall term
began, he fell terribly ill again and had to return east. Soon
he was back in the Lahey Clinic, and by January 1941 he
was in the New England Baptist Hospital in Boston with
a serious ailment, the exact nature of which has never been
disclosed.

Throughout his naval career Kennedy was frequently
ill, and during most of his final year in the Navy (1944) he
was in and out of several hospitals, some military, some
civilian. Among other treatments and medical procedures,
he underwent surgery of the back. One of his Navy buddies, Torbert Macdonald, visited him once during this period and found him "all strapped up," "suffering from a
recurrence of malaria," a weight loss of thirty-five pounds,
and "skin turned yellow"—all obvious symptoms of Addison's disease. After undergoing treatment for his back
and other as-yet-undisclosed ailments, Kennedy went to

his father's home in Palm Beach to recuperate and await his final retirement from the Navy, which occurred as we have seen on March 16, 1945, by reason of medical disability. Two months later Germany surrendered unconditionally to the Allies, and in August President Truman dropped the atomic bombs on Hiroshima and Nagasaki, forcing Japan's unconditional surrender. Not long after that momentous event, which put an end to the most devastating war of all time, Joseph P. Kennedy set up headquarters in Boston to begin masterminding his son's campaign for the Congress of the United States.

Joe Kennedy's opening gambit in this process was to accept a commission from Massachusetts Governor Maurice Tobin to make an "economic survey" of the state, which, for the ambassador, meant essentially a political survey for his son Jack. As it turned out, the appointment served many useful purposes for the Kennedys; it landed the Kennedy name in every newspaper in Massachusetts and enabled Joe to meet hundreds of influential people who could possibly be useful to Jack's eventual campaign. The ground was being prepared.

By the fall of 1945 Joe Kennedy had definitely decided to run Jack for Congress in 1946, and the idea had been seconded by everyone in the clan, with the possible exception of Jack. At a family reunion in Hyannis Port that September, after ex-naval officer Jack had returned from a period of rest on the west coast, the irrepressible Honey Fitz stood up at the luncheon table and adopting an uncustomarily serious expression and looking Jack straight in the eye, proposed a remarkable toast: "To the future President of the United States, my grandson, John Fitzgerald Kennedy." It was like a ceremony of knighthood. Jack was now anointed. Joe Kennedy's son, the unlikely prospect, the reluctant candidate, had been officially dispatched to his high, preordained, unwanted fate.

23. Selling Jack "Like Soap Flakes"

To FULFILL Honey Fitz's audacious prophecy young John Kennedy first had to get himself elected to some public office. But important public offices do not just grow on trees for the plucking. Then by sheer chance, just at the right time, an office suddenly did appear on the Massachusetts political tree—a seat in the House of Representatives representing Boston's eleventh district. It was a particularly ripe and potentially valuable plum, and the Kennedys were quick to pluck it.

The eleventh district seat opened up because James Michael Curley, Honey Fitz's former archrival, decided to give up his seat in the Congress and run for mayor of Boston again. The Kennedys and Fitzgeralds hated Curley, but they secretly helped him win the mayoral race so the much-coveted seat would open up. Curley ran in the November 1945 election and won. A special election to fill his seat in Congress was then scheduled for November 1946. For young John Kennedy, more or less at loose ends since his discharge from the Navy, this was his proverbial golden opportunity.

Boston's eleventh district was as ideal a political territory for Jack Kennedy to operate in as could be imagined. Both the Fitzgerald and Kennedy families had been closely associated with sections of it from 1848 to 1929. Joe Kennedy still owned East Boston's Columbia Trust on Maverick Square, and there were still a few people in the area who remembered old P. J. and his saloons and liquor businesses. Other areas included in the eleventh were not quite so congenial. Charlestown was a poor, working-class waterfront community composed mostly of Irish longshoremen and their families. Cambridge, seat of Harvard, was full of liberal intellectuals, and Somerville, seat of Tufts, was a predominantly working-class district with no Kennedy associations.

Despite his family's connections with the North End and East Boston, John Kennedy was, however, declared to be a carpetbagger as soon as he tossed his hat in the ring. And, in a very real sense, he was. He had never lived in the eleventh district himself and knew next to nothing of its constituents or problems.

However, John Kennedy was already quite well known throughout Boston. Before entering the race for Curley's seat he had received a strong dose of public exposure as a correspondent for the Hearst organization, which had assigned him to cover the first United Nations conference in San Francisco and the British elections. His father, who had been a long-time friend of William Randolph Hearst, had gotten him the job for the express purpose of getting his name in the papers. The Hearst organization gave him a flattering byline. Each article carried a small photograph of Kennedy with this short biographical sketch: "Lt. John F. Kennedy, recently retired PT-boat hero of the South Pacific and son of Ambassador Joseph P. Kennedy, is covering the San Francisco conference from a serviceman's point of view. Before the war he wrote the bestseller *Why England Slept.*" The articles went out to every paper in the Hearst chain.

It was while Kennedy was writing for Hearst that he is said to have decided that journalism was too "passive" an activity for him. He would have preferred to have been a participant at the UN conference rather than a reporter of its proceedings.

And so it was with a sense that he was doing the right thing for himself, as well as for his father, that John Kennedy plunged into the Democratic primary fight for the right to stand in the election for a seat in Congress representing Boston's eleventh. Shaking hands at receptions, giving political speeches, marching in parades, and charming people with his smiles were much more congenial activities for him than wrestling with his thoughts through long hours of solitude, even though he often confessed to friends that campaigning "embarrassed" him. In the end, I believe Kennedy genuinely *wanted* to be a writer but realized he lacked the temperament for it.

Actually there was very little in his experience, aside from family background, to equip him for the job he was seeking. He had never administered anything in his life. He had never run an office. He had never even held a full-time job, outside of the Navy.

But he always was, and always would be, a strong competitor. Those closest to him marveled at his stamina and zest for campaigning. His sister Eunice has been quoted as saying, "Jack hates to lose. . . . He hates to lose at anything. That's the only thing Jack gets really emotional about—when he loses."

Others have commented on what a sore loser Jack Kennedy was. He absolutely always had to win, win, win, to maintain his self-esteem. When he lost at something he would sulk, often get mean, and sometimes not even talk. As he grew older, and his responsibilities multiplied, he would even take exaggerated precautions *not* to lose. Once when he was President, he was playing golf with a friend in Palm Beach; when it appeared toward the end of the match that he might lose, he had a secret serviceman suddenly announce that a message had just come over the radio that the President had to quit the match immediately to attend to an urgent matter. And once, while playing dominoes with Red Fay, when he was President and Fay was his undersecretary of the Navy, he again broke up a game, this time by abruptly overturning the domino board just before Fay was about to win. This kind of behavior goes way beyond normal displeasure at losing a game. This neurotic need to win was not guaranteed to produce in Kennedy the highest human happiness, but it would make of him a mighty contender in a race for a seat in the U.S. Congress.

And so a campaign was organized, with Father Joe the chief organizer and paymaster general. "We're going to sell Jack like soap flakes," he announced to his associates, and he promptly hired a public relations firm to mount, in his words, "the most elaborate professional advertising effort ever seen in a Massachusetts congressional election."

He also hired an astute campaign manager, his cousin Joe Kane. No one knew more families in the eleventh than Kane. He had grown up in the alleys of East Boston. He had also managed James Tobin's campaign for mayor against James Michael Curley in 1937. In 1942 Joe Kennedy had hired him to manage Honey Fitz's primary fight against Joe Casey. He had studied politics at the feet of his uncle, P. J. Kennedy, and his cousin Joe's father-in-law, Honey Fitz. He was tough, rude, and salty, and he knew his way around the back rooms of Boston Irish politics. Joe Kennedy felt he was the best political tutor his son could have, but he was somewhat skeptical of how well his refined and educated son would get along with him. To his relief, Jack hit it off beautifully with his tough older cousin.

Joe Kane had very definite ideas about how to sell Jack Kennedy to the eleventh district. When other people tried to horn in on his planning, he reacted sharply. One day while Kane was giving Jack a lesson in local politics, old Honey Fitz suddenly walked into the room to offer his two cents.

"Get that sonofabitch out of here!" yelled Kane. And that was the end of Honey Fitz so far as the campaign was concerned, save for a few grandfather and grandson photos.

Early in the game Kane decided to sell Jack almost exclusively as a young war hero with a superb record in combat. It was the immediate postwar period, with hundreds of thousands of veterans returning from the wars, and no one could get anywhere in politics unless he had an impressive war record. Accordingly, Jack was made commander of the newly organized Joseph P. Kennedy Jr. Veterans of Foreign Wars Post, which was to be his political base, and Kane devised a campaign slogan to go with the position: "The New Generation Offers a Leader." Jack Kennedy was packaged. Now he had to be sold.

To sell him Joe Kennedy left nothing to chance. He was fully aware that his son's campaign for a seat in the Congress was a first step in a long-range bid for the presidency of the United States. Nothing must be allowed to go wrong. Nothing must be allowed to stand in Jack's way. To make sure nothing went wrong, he, Joe Kennedy, would take overall charge of the campaign. He would raise the campaign funds, largely from his own pocket; he would interview and hire most of the key campaign workers; he would make most of the hard, crucial decisions. Joe Kane would be there for the day-to-day operations, but, behind the scenes, it would be the ambassador pulling all the key strings. Later, when asked what role he took in his son's campaign for the Congress, Joe said, "I just called people. I got in touch with people I knew. I have a lot of contacts. I've been in politics since I was ten."

And so the campaign began. It was not an easy task. Here was a millionaire's son, who was himself a millionaire yet had never held a job in his life outside of military service, running in a district composed mostly of longshoremen, railroad workers, truck drivers, small shopkeepers, bartenders, and waitresses.

From the very beginning of the campaign Jack Kennedy's universal appeal to women was exploited. Kennedy liked to refer to "womanpower, the untapped resource." As a professional womanizer and charmer, he uttered the now-famous phrase "the older women will want to mother you, and the younger ones will want to make love to you." If you could harness this dual power, you were in. Women constituted over fifty percent of the registered voters.

And so teas for young ladies, and not-so-young ladies, were organized, including the famous "Boston tea party" in Cambridge's Commodore Hotel where 1500 young women were invited to come, "in their best gowns," to meet young John F. Kennedy, the handsome millionaire's son. "Every girl there was dreaming that lightning would strike," commented Kennedy aide Dave Powers, and another aide, Patsy Mulkern, said, "Every girl there was gonna be Mrs. Kennedy, for crissakes." It was quite a challenge for Jack. He had to make every girl in that ballroom feel he liked *her*. But this was his forte. Jack the attentive listener, Jack the man who seemed always so interested in *you*.

There were many other things on which to capitalize. There was the death of Joe Junior. There were Kennedy's exploits in the Solomons during World War II. When he gave his first speech at the Joseph P. Kennedy Jr. Veterans of Foreign Wars Post, the hero received so much attention in the press that one wag was wont to describe his appearance as "the second coming of Christ." We know now that the war hero image was greatly overblown; the action in the Solomons out of which Kennedy's "heroism" arose was, in reality, a minor naval disaster. We also know now that the ambassador lobbied incessantly for Jack's medal and that it was he who arranged for John Hersey's account of the PT-109 episode, "Survival," to appear conspicuously in the *Reader's Digest* and had them distributed to every single voter in the eleventh district.

Allied to his heroism in war, Kennedy was also able to capitalize on his infirmities, which, in the public's imagination, were associated with the wounds of battle. The women voters especially were deeply touched by the sight of the handsome young war hero on crutches.

Then, of course, Jack Kennedy was finally able to capitalize on perhaps his two biggest assets of all, his money and his family. Joe Kane, paraphrasing one of Napoleon's most famous remarks, stated early in the campaign that the three most-needed ingredients in a political campaign were money, money, and money. And Joe Kennedy had responded by letting everyone involved know that the sky was the limit. He would spend as much as was needed to get Jack elected.

As for the family, they all pitched in and helped as best they could: Bobby, just out of the Navy, Eunice, Pat, and Jean—and, of course, Rose. Rose Kennedy was especially helpful. According to Richard Whalen, biographer of Joseph P. Kennedy, she would display her card index file on her nine children to the family-minded Italian women of the North End, dressing very simply for her appearance before them. Then, later the same day, on her way to speak to the elegant ladies of Chestnut Hill, she would change her jewelry, put a mink stole around her shoulders, and speak to the good society ladies of the latest fashions she had recently seen in Paris. Who was the real Rose Kennedy, the North End housewife or the millionaire's wife able to buy at the Paris fashion shows? It didn't make any difference. Appearance was what counted. Appear to be all things to all people. The image projected *to any one particular group* was what counted.

In all fairness to Jack Kennedy, he worked very, very hard. His close political aide, Dave Powers, whom he had recruited out of a three-decker tenement in Charlestown, testifies that Kennedy was up at 6:30 every morning and remained in constant motion, often walking on crutches for the next fourteen to eighteen hours. One cold autumn morning he was down at the Charlestown wharves greeting the longshoremen at the gate to the port as they reported to work. Another morning he was at Maverick Square greeting passersby. He visited the three-decker tenements of Charlestown. He paraded with the veterans to the point of physical collapse. John Kennedy campaigned as if he were driven. His speeches were often bland and phony, but they were always delivered with a feeling of urgency and conviction. This phenomenal drive came from two related sources: the all-but-pathological fear of losing and his father. Old Joe was sitting there behind the scenes, spending all that money, pulling all those strings. He could not let his father down. It was unthinkable. Push on. Push on. Down to the docks at dawn to pump the longshoremen's hands. Out to East Boston to greet the children and grandchildren of those of the eleventh who had known his politician grandfather, P.J., had received favors from him, and had drunk in his saloons. Off to the ladies' teas, tittering with the women of the eleventh—old, middle-aged, and young—being son, brother, and potential lover, or husband, to all of them. Not leaving anything to chance, not leaving one stone unturned in this first crucial political debut which was to pave the way for the inevitable, prophesied assault on the White House.

As all the world knows, Jack Kennedy won the "wild, free-for-all" Democratic primary, then went on to bury his Republican opponent in the election. Soon the eleventh became a "safe seat" for the Kennedys. No one even challenged Jack Kennedy in the next election two years later. Kennedy then went on to a singularly undistinguished career in the House as an often absentee congressman. He confided to intimates that the House bored him, and it became apparent that a seat in Congress was, for him, little more than a stepping-stone in the long climb to the highest political office in the land.

24. Joe Senior: Making Money Again

WITH HIS SON JACK safely elected to Congress, and presumably on his way to a brilliant political career, Joe Kennedy turned his attention once more from politics to his original occupation: making money.

Joe Kennedy enjoyed making money. It was a kind of a game with him. Having become a master of the game he did not have to work quite as hard at it as he used to, and hence his enjoyment of it was greater than ever. As he told his friend and aide, James Landis: "You know, I used to work hard. Now I sit here by the pool and make more money than I ever did."

Actually, Joe Kennedy had turned his attention to making money again some time before his son's campaign for the Congress. It was just that after the campaign he was able to devote more time to it. During the early 1940s Kennedy had become aware that real estate values in New York City were very depressed. Many areas of the city had fallen victim to a seemingly chronic economic blight. Even midtown Manhattan was depressed. A lot of fine buildings were up for grabs.

It was at this time that Francis Cardinal Spellman introduced Kennedy to John J. Reynolds, a tough Irish real estate operator from the Bronx who had made a lot of money speculating in real estate for the Catholic church, and specifically for the archdiocese of New York. Kennedy

hit it off right away with Reynolds, and together they decided to plunge aggressively into the Manhattan real estate
jungle. Before long Joe Kennedy was on his way to making
an entirely new fortune.

Kennedy needed more money. The New Deal's
"confiscatory" income taxes were taking a tremendous bite
out of what was left of the family income after the children
received *their* incomes from the two substantial trust funds
Joe had established for them in 1929 and 1936. And now
that he planned to finance political campaigns for one or
more sons, he needed to bolster both his capital and his
income. Furthermore, his scale of living had become enormously expensive. Maintaining large houses full of servants
in Bronxville, Hyannis, and Palm Beach, taking care of
poor Rosemary, and sending eight children to expensive
prep schools and colleges was a colossal drain on his resources. As he confided to a friend in the early 1940s,
"Now my income does not meet my expenses and I have
one of the biggest incomes in the world."

And so, in the early 1940s, Joe Kennedy plunged
into real estate with the firm intention of making as much
money as he could while market conditions were so favorable. Who knew? If all went well, he might one day
have the opportunity of financing even a *presidential* campaign. That would take a hell of a lot of money. He went
from success to success, growing bolder throughout the
forties and fifties, and by 1960 Joe Kennedy had made a
whole new fortune, his fourth since he had made his initial
three in the stock market, movies, and liquor.

The Kennedy-Reynolds real estate investment strategy was relatively simple. Reynolds would scout potential
acquisitions and bring the most promising ones to Kennedy's attention. Kennedy would then consult with his
financial advisers and decide on a buy. A very small down
payment on the property would be made and a huge, low-
cost mortgage taken out. As soon as the building was under
Kennedy-Reynolds control, its tenants would be confronted with huge rent hikes. If they paid up, fine; otherwise new tenants would be found. The jacked-up rents
would pay the interest on the mortgage, the taxes, and the

upkeep, leaving Kennedy with a profit of from 15 to 20 percent on the investment. When the time was ripe, Kennedy-Reynolds would then sell the property for a lot more than what they had paid for it, often quintupling the original investment.

It would be tedious to enumerate even a small fraction of Joe Kennedy's real estate deals in the 1940s and 1950s as he and Reynolds raided Manhattan. But his operations were by no means confined to office properties on that island. He bought a large tract of land along the Pelham Parkway in the Bronx, office buildings in White Plains, Albany, Chicago, and São Paulo, shopping centers in several states, and lands and buildings in Miami and other parts of Florida. In addition, he purchased a substantial ($30 million) interest in the Hialeah racetrack, a twelve-mile strip of land along Florida's then undeveloped west coast, a 49.9 percent interest in 2740 acres of non-coastal Florida lands, and vast tracts of potential oil-bearing lands in Texas.

His biggest coup of all, however, was buying Chicago's gigantic Merchandise Mart, at that time the world's largest privately owned commercial building. Marshall Field had built the twenty-four-story structure, containing a whopping ninety-three acres of rentable space for $30 million in 1929–1930. Now, in 1945, Kennedy picked it up from a financially troubled Field for only $12,956,516, putting a mere $456,516 down and borrowing the remaining $12.5 million from the Equitable Life Assurance Society.

Immediately Kennedy-Reynolds launched a major advertising campaign for the Mart, made a few changes in the building to create more rentable space, and hiked the rents. Soon they were renting out more space than Field ever had and at much higher rentals. Within twenty years the value of the building would sextuple, and its annual rental income would increase to $13 million, or more than what Kennedy originally paid for the building. Today the Mart is worth well over $200 million and constitutes the Kennedy family's single largest investment.

John J. Reynolds estimated that Kennedy made well in excess of $100 million in real estate alone between 1942 and 1960. Evidently Kennedy relied almost wholly on Reynolds' judgment regarding a property, usually buying it sight unseen (as he did with the Merchandise Mart). And the remarkable thing was that Kennedy made most of his extraordinarily profitable deals just sitting by his pool with a sunhat on his head, a towel around his middle, and a telephone in his hand.

It was typical Kennedy business, buying and selling, getting in, getting out, always going right to the heart of every business opportunity, "cutting through the crap," as Joe used to say, never letting any consideration get in the way of making the biggest possible profit on the deal.

This philosophy, however, eventually got him into some trouble. In 1944 New York City officials began investigating complaints against rent gougers, and the name of Joseph P. Kennedy figured prominently in many of the worst complaints.

By the late 1950s the press began to take an interest in Joe Kennedy's growing wealth. *Fortune* magazine ran an article on the wealthiest Americans in 1957; the article estimated that Kennedy's personal fortune was somewhere between $200 and $400 million. The figure utterly astonished Rose Kennedy, who did not have the vaguest idea of her husband's net worth. (According to her autobiography she and Joe never discussed money or business affairs.) One day, after her son had become President and her husband had become paralyzed, Rose was found rummaging wildly in the attic at Hyannis by Joe's nurse, Rita Dallas. According to Mrs. Dallas, who reported the episode in a book, when she asked Mrs. Kennedy what she was doing, she replied that she was trying to find where her husband kept all his money.

Money meant a great deal to Joe Kennedy, and he estimated people in relation to how much money they had. Red Fay recalls an incident on the golf course in Palm Beach that vividly shows where Joe Kennedy's values lay.

We were held up on every one of the first four holes by the twosome in front of us. Mr. Kennedy was angered by the third delay, and by the fourth tie-up he was fuming. Finally, he shouted ahead, "Bill, if you want us to come through, just let us know."

Bill nodded, indicating that he would let us know.

"Before the depression that guy used to be worth 35 or 40 million dollars," Joe Kennedy said. 'Now he would be lucky if he could scrape together two or three millions, and he's still acting like he had it."

Was *Fortune* magazine's estimate of Joe Kennedy's wealth in 1957 accurate? Kennedy himself thought he was worth "around $200 million" in 1960, with the bulk of his wealth in real estate acquired since 1941. That meant that there were only around fifteen to twenty people in America richer than he was. It meant also that he was richer than either Nelson or David Rockefeller. It meant, according to one of his biographers, David E. Koskoff, that, aside from the major oilmen, he was "the richest self-made millionaire in America."

After 1960 Joe Kennedy stopped speculating in real estate and turned his attention to protecting his vast wealth through investments in tax-sheltered oil ventures and tax-exempt municipal bonds. His new overall investment strategy had become "make the most of the opportunities created by the tax laws."

Accordingly, he began getting out of real estate and into highly speculative, hit-or-miss oil ventures, as he joined syndicates that were backing wildcatters looking for oil in Texas and Oklahoma. Roughly half these ventures produced dry holes, the other half gushers. "Batting 500," he told a friend, "in a new ballgame, that's not a bad average."

Kennedy also began backing small Texas drilling companies, writing off 60 percent of the drilling costs and benefiting from the then-current 27.5 percent oil depletion allowance. Three of his most profitable oil partnerships were Mokeen Oil Company, with sales in the early sixties of $3 million; Kenoil, a Houston-based outfit holding oil leases with substantial royalty income; and the Sutton Producing Company of San Antonio, whose operations Kennedy kept tabs on via his poolside telephone in Palm Beach, never once bothering to visit the Lone Star State.

Having done spectacularly well in real estate during the 1940s, Joe Kennedy established still another set of trust funds for his seven surviving children (Joe Junior and Kathleen were now dead) in 1949. Actually what he did was to buy many real estate and oil properties in the name of "the children of Joseph P. Kennedy," then integrate these properties into the trusts he had already established. Apparently the ambassador was very concerned about his children's finances, because, as he once confided to an associate, "none of my children has the slightest interest in making money, not the slightest," and several of them, notably his daughters, he regarded as spendthrifts.

The precise allocation, or distribution, of income from the various Kennedy enterprises remains to this day a carefully guarded family secret. Kennedy established two corporate entities to administer his business, the Park Agency, Inc., and Ken Industries, both of which were headquartered, along with the Joseph P. Kennedy Jr. Foundation, in New York City—in the Pan Am Building until very recently, when they moved to lower Park Avenue. Stephen Smith, who married Jean Kennedy, continues to manage these privately held family businesses, and he releases no information on them except that required by law. Since the Kennedy Library in Boston will not permit *anyone* (not even Kennedy court historians) to consult the financial records of Joseph P. Kennedy, John F. Kennedy, and Robert F. Kennedy, all of which are classified "closed," any overall estimate of Joe Kennedy's wealth must be an educated guess based on certain disclosures made at various times, notably during political campaigns, as required by law.

From what has been pieced together, it can be stated, with reasonable accuracy, that by the end of 1961, the first year of John Kennedy's presidency and the year in which Joe Kennedy suffered a massive stroke, Joe Kennedy's aggregate fortune (including trust funds for children and the foundation) was in the neighborhood of $300 million, roughly subdivided as follows: children's trust funds established in 1926, 1936, and 1949, $75 million; the Joseph P. Kennedy Jr. Foundation, another $75 million; miscellaneous real estate, another $75 million; and oil interests, tax-exempt municipal bonds, stocks, and cash, another $75 million. This meant, among other things, that in 1961 his seven surviving children had about $10 million each, which, in turn, meant that each could dispose of pretax income of anywhere from $500,000 to $1 million a year, depending on the rate of return on his or her investments at the time. (During political campaigns individual income was sometimes drastically reduced because a "tithe" was levied on all to support the particular campaign in progress. Thus, during campaigns, those six children not campaigning for office would receive their substantially reduced monthly checks from the main office accompanied by a little note: "You have just made a political contribution.")

This was, of course, what Joe Kennedy had struggled so mightily for: his children's financial security and what it could obtain for them in power. Money-making had been, for him, wholly devoted to supporting his family and promoting his ambitions for them. He himself required few luxuries. He and Rose did not live in especially luxurious houses, did not collect expensive art or racehorses, and did not own fleets of Rolls Royces. The money Joe Kennedy had fought so hard for was made essentially for his family, and especially for his sons and their careers.

Joe Kennedy succeeded admirably in realizing his twin goals. By purchasing so many of his major properties in the name of "the children of Joseph P. Kennedy" (including the mammoth Merchandise Mart) he minimized the eventual tax on his estate. And in guaranteeing his son John a six-figure annual income, and earmarking enormous additional sums for his political campaigns, he gave him a huge boost in his quests for a seat in the Senate in 1952 and a desk in the Oval Office in 1960. Few men in American history succeeded in their ultimate financial goals as completely as Joseph P. Kennedy. In the end, he got everything he wanted.

25. Settling Old Scores:
Kennedy over Lodge

No SOONER did young Congressman-elect John F. Kennedy land in Washington to take his seat in the House of Representatives than he immediately established what would become a sort of branch office, or secondary headquarters, of the Kennedy family in the capital. Far from cutting the umbilical cord and striking out on his own, as most 29-year-old American men do, Jack Kennedy set up a household in a three-story rented house in Georgetown that became, in essence, simply an extension of his father's home.

In addition to the young congressman, the Georgetown household was composed also of sister Eunice, cook Margaret Ambrose, who was on indefinite loan from the Joseph Kennedy household, and valet George Thomas, a faithful retainer obtained by Father Joe through his friend Arthur Krock. Paying the rent, utilities, and salaries was Paul Murphy, Daddy's paymaster at the Park Agency in New York. It wasn't long before this menage became a full-fledged Kennedy enclave in Washington. Father Joe and Mother Rose were frequent overnight visitors. While they were in residence they would gather intelligence on their son's personal life from the cook and the valet and take appropriate remedial action, if warranted. Other members of the family, including various Fitzgeralds, were also frequent visitors. Freshman Congressman Jack Kennedy, we can be assured, did not enjoy very much privacy or independence. A throwback to an earlier era, when large, extended families sticking together were the norm, the Kennedys were an anachronism in mid-twentieth-century America. There was little "typically American" about them.

Here then was young Jack Kennedy, a millionaire in his own right at 29, benefiting from an unearned income in excess of $100,000 a year, in addition to his earned congressman's salary of $20,000, beginning life on his own, served by a full-time cook and a full-time valet, and mothered by a full-time sister.

Eunice Kennedy, it should be emphasized, not Jack, had been the real leader in the family after Joe Junior died. An extremely bright, energetic, high-strung young woman, she was the most natural leader in the family after Joe, a girl with an authoritative personality and tremendous drive who could be incredibly tough when she wanted to be, a true chip off the old block. It was she who had wanted her father to pick *her* to run for Congress. Jack had been a somewhat reluctant candidate, whereas she would have given anything to be a candidate. But, in the Kennedy scheme of things, daughters were not supposed to have *that* kind of ambition. They were supposed to get married and breed lots of healthy babies.

It was already something of an extraordinary assertion of independence that Eunice, at 24, was working hard in Washington as an executive secretary for the Justice Department's Juvenile Delinquency Committee. The model daughter of a rich and privileged family, she had always been interested in juvenile delinquency and in handicapped children, probably as a result of the long, drawn-out trauma of growing up with a severely retarded sister.

Eunice's function in the new Kennedy household in Washington was to be the new congressman's hostess and watchdog. Since she too was benefiting from an unearned income in excess of $100,000 a year, the two young Kennedys at 1528 31st Street could well afford to entertain their friends, family, and colleagues at home. Assisted, as few people their age ever are, by two full-time servants, they were to offer food and drink to an endless stream of visitors, including, of course, Jack's parade of girlfriends. One of these last was the controversial Inga Binga whom Joe Kennedy (and the FBI) had forbidden Jack to see. Evidently, Jack saw her for the last time while he was in residence at 1528 31st Street. Eunice's presence did not cramp her brother's style, for years later, according to author Clay Blair, Jr., Inga told her son, Ronald McCoy, born some nine months after her last encounter with Jack Kennedy, that his father was *not* her husband, the actor Tim McCoy, whom she had married six months before Ronald was born, but John F. Kennedy.

This last matter would have no significance whatsoever if it were not for the fact that J. Edgar Hoover had kept a running file on the relationship between John Kennedy and Inga Arvad ever since Kennedy ran afoul of the alleged Nazi-sympathizing Danish beauty while serving in naval intelligence during the war. Inga Binga became something Kennedy wanted very much to keep under wraps. Only two people knew very much about the affair: Inga herself and J. Edgar Hoover. Both were in a position to damage his political career. Realizing this, Kennedy would eventually take strong precautionary measures, especially in Hoover's regard, to make sure the affair never came to light.

No sooner did Representative John Kennedy arrive in Washington to take his seat in the Eightieth Congress, than he immediately, and somewhat self-consciously, asserted his independence from both his party's leadership in the House and from his father. Deliberately he arrived late to minority whip John McCormack's first Democratic party caucus just before the opening of Congress. McCormack was from South Boston, and he had been in the Congress twenty-six years. A freshman congressman was supposed to defer to a man like McCormack, but in the case at hand the hotshot rich man's son was not about to defer to an old Boston pol just because he had been around the House for twenty-six years.

And just because his ambitious father had recently paid for a very expensive political campaign, that did not mean that he, Jack Kennedy, was going to advocate Joe Kennedy's beliefs and policies in Congress. It was the beginning of the "cold war" and President Truman had just enunciated the Truman Doctrine of aid to beleaguered countries which could conceivably "go communist" if help were not forthcoming. The doctrine was the beginning of foreign aid and would eventually lead to the Marshall Plan and the reconstruction of Europe and Japan. The policy of "containment" was being formed. Old Joe Kennedy, ever the isolationist, was against it. His son Jack was for it, and voted for it in the Congress. Thus, at the beginning of his public life Jack Kennedy broke with his father ideologically and became an internationalist committed to "containing" the threat of communism by aiding countries supposedly vulnerable to the Russians and their satellites.

The ideological differences between father and son did not, however, prevent the father from continuing his relentless promotion of his son. Through incessant lobbying via a New York press agent by the name of Steve Hannagan, Joe Kennedy got his son Jack named one of the "Ten Outstanding Men of 1946" by the U.S. Junior Chamber of Commerce. Still another example of Kennedy hype and self-promotion, essentially meaningless because engineered by the Kennedys themselves, the nomination nevertheless gave a boost to Congressman Jack's prestige—at least among those who took such nominations seriously.

Descriptions of Kennedy by intimates during his first year in Congress reveal an impatient, often bored young man, always in a rush, always late to meetings and appointments, leaving a trail of clothes, papers, and bills behind him for his valet and his secretary to pick up. According to his secretary, Mary Davis, he struck one as being a "lackadaisical, provincial New Englander with ill-fitting suits hanging from an emaciated frame," who always seemed to be in a last-minute rush. A careless dresser, he often shocked his more fastidious colleagues in the House, like young Richard M. Nixon, by appearing late on the House floor wearing a sports jacket, khaki pants, and sneakers.

He was both careless with and oblivious to money.

He almost never carried any money on him and was apparently so uninterested in his own investments that his father once complained to an associate: "Jack has absolutely no understanding of his own finances." When his secretary or one of his friends paid a taxi fare or a restaurant check for him, he habitually "forgot" to pay it back. He often borrowed small amounts from friends without repaying them. His dates were frequently dumbfounded when, at the end of an evening in a restaurant or a night club, they were forced to pick up the tab because he had no money. His larger expenses were often paid by his or his father's subordinates, so he himself rarely had to write out a sizable check. Rent, telephone, and utilities were paid by his father's New York accountant, Paul Murphy. Office furniture came directly from the family-owned Merchandise Mart in Chicago free of charge. Actual money, it seems, rarely had to pass through Kennedy's hands. In disposing of an income of over $100,000 a year, he hardly ever touched cash.

Much nonsense has been written about John Kennedy's obliviousness to money and the fact that he rarely carried any cash on his person, as if this were a feather in his cap. "He had so much money but it didn't mean anything to him; he was completely unmaterialistic," goes the refrain. But I believe Kennedy's attitude toward money was distinctly neurotic. He had been given so much money at such an early age, and he felt unworthy of it, guilty about it. One way to overcome these feelings was to play at being poor. Wealthy people, especially very wealthy people who have inherited their money, always love to have others pay their way. It makes them feel less different, less guilty about having so much more than everybody else. Having a friend or secretary pick up his tab no doubt made Kennedy feel good. As to the wisdom of entrusting to a young man who had "absolutely no understanding of his own finances" a vote toward the spending of the American taxpayers' money, no one at the time seemed prompted to raise the issue.

Jack Kennedy had a curiously undistinguished career as a congressman. He was frequently annoyed by the House

seniority system. He was impatient with the poor constituents of the eleventh district and eventually left almost all
the day-to-day casework regarding them to his assistant,
Ted Reardon, who had been a close friend of Joe Junior's
(and one of the heirs to his estate). He was frequently
absent from sessions in the House. About the only issues
he took a really impassioned stand on were low-cost housing for veterans and the Taft-Hartley Labor Act, two matters dear to the hearts of the working-class district he
represented. Stating publicly that "the leadership of the
American Legion has not had a constructive thought for
the benefit of the country since 1918," he castigated the
organization for not energetically pressing for low-cost
housing for veterans. He also voted against the Taft-
Hartley labor bill and voted to sustain Truman's veto of
that bill. Beyond taking these stands, Kennedy did not
accomplish very much in the Congress. By the end of his
first two-year term he realized the House was not for him
and consciously used his next two terms to run for the
Senate, which he felt would be more in his league.

The late William O. Douglas characterized Congressman John F. Kennedy as "disinterested and bored in
Washington." "Time hung heavy on his hands," Douglas
observed, "he had nothing of consuming interest, he never
seemed to get into the mainstream of any tremendous
political thought, or political action, or any idea of promoting this, or reforming that, nothing." "He was sort of
drifting," Douglas went on, "and when he started drifting
he became more and more a playboy."

Much of what Douglas said was true. A study of
Kennedy's record as a congressman reveals there was really
no central core to his beliefs. On practically every issue it
appears that he simply weighed the votes he would receive
from his district if he voted for it, and the votes he would
receive if he voted against it. By and large, he voted the
interests of his predominantly poor, working-class constituency, going along with the liberals on those Truman
Fair Deal measures appealing to low-income voters and
then switching to join the conservatives in voting on foreign
policy matters. As one of Joseph Kennedy's biographers,

Richard Whalen, observed, young John Kennedy's politics were "as self-centered as his father's fortune building."

But there was, quite possibly, another reason for Kennedy's lackluster performance in Congress: his Addison's disease. The attack came during a trip to Europe around the middle of his first year of service. President Truman and his secretary of state, George Marshall, recommended to the Eightieth Congress the Marshall Plan for Europe; it was to become the most extensive program of economic aid in the history of the human race. During the summer of 1947 many congressmen headed for Europe to investigate economic conditions there for themselves. Kennedy decided to go with a couple of his fellow members of the House Subcommittee on Labor. His trip was to also include a spell in Russia studying "labor conditions" under communism.

Before business, however, there was pleasure—an extended visit with his sister Kathleen and some of her friends at Lismore Castle in southern Ireland's county Waterford.

Lismore Castle is an ancient, twelfth-century structure that had once belonged to Sir Walter Raleigh and now belonged to Kathleen's father-in-law, the Duke of Devonshire. It is not very far from the Kennedy's ancestral homestead in Dunganstown. Among the guests that were to gather there for the house party were Sir Hugh Fraser, Anthony Eden, and Pamela Churchill, the divorced wife of Winston Churchill's son, Randolph. For Jack Kennedy the stay at Lismore Castle represented both a vacation from his first stint as a congressman and a chance to spend some time with his sister Kathleen, of whom he was very fond.

It also represented an opportunity for Kennedy to make a nostalgic trip into the land of his ancestors. His Aunt Loretta (one of his father's sisters) had suggested he try to look up some of his third cousins at Dunganstown, a few hours' drive south of Lismore Castle. Kennedy made the trip with Pamela Churchill, who characterized the old farm with its thatched-roof cottage and muddy yard full of pigs and chickens as "Tobacco Road." "She had not understood the magic of that afternoon," Kennedy later observed. When they got back to Lismore Castle, Kathleen, who had already adopted the airs of a duchess, asked, somewhat patronizingly, whether her remote cousins "had a bathroom." She was told they did not.

Soon after the trip to Dunganstown, Kennedy suddenly fell ill and was compelled to telegraph to his administrative assistant, Ted Reardon, for special medicine. Confined to his room in the damp, drafty old castle, he grew steadily worse. On September 21 he was flown to London in the company of Pamela Churchill to pick up some medicine sent from the States and promptly collapsed. Admitted to a London clinic, a certain Dr. Davis told Pamela Churchill "that young American friend of yours, he hasn't got a year to live." Dr. Davis recognized Kennedy as a victim of advanced Addison's disease and diagnosed his collapse as a severe Addisonian crisis.

By this time endocrinologists had developed a synthetic substance that compensated for an adrenal gland's inability to secrete the hormone cortisone, and Kennedy received injections of this substance, called desoxycorticosterone, or DOCA. These injections probably saved his life.

On October 11 Kennedy sailed for Boston from Southampton on the *Queen Mary*, having been forced to give up his European tour. He spent the entire voyage in the ship's hospital. An ambulance met him in New York and took him to a chartered flight to Boston from LaGuardia. He was taken off the plane at Logan Airport on a stretcher. Reporters from the Boston papers were on hand to greet him; the Kennedy family gave out to them that the young congressman had suffered a recurrence of the "malaria" he had contracted in the South Pacific during the war. In reality Kennedy was so sick from Addison's disease that he was administered extreme unction. He was subsequently told that he would probably not live beyond his middle forties.

At Boston's Lahey Clinic Kennedy was given injections and implants of desoxycorticosterone, and he soon recovered. When he returned to Washington to resume his duties as a congressman, he did so under a cloud of pessimism about his health. He had an unstable back that would not improve, forcing him occasionally to use crutches, and he was now a fully diagnosed Addisonian who would probably not live beyond the age of 45. Was there really much point to beating his brains out in Washington? Because of his precarious health he could never hope to realize his father's ambitions. It now appears quite certain that Kennedy's lackluster first term in Congress was in direct relation to his discouragement about his health.

Then, in 1949, cortisone was discovered, and entirely new vistas were suddenly opened up for victims of Addison's disease. By 1951 cortisone could be taken orally, and Kennedy was ingesting 25 milligrams daily. He was also receiving periodic implants of 150 milligrams of DOCA pellets in his thighs.

Cortisone has a truly magical effect on Addisonians. Soon after he began taking the synthetic hormone, Kennedy's health and stamina began to improve dramatically, and he underwent something of an emotional transformation. His discouragement about his health left him and he suddenly "got ambition." It was then that he made a firm decision to run for the Senate in 1952.

Actually, as has already been pointed out, no sooner had Kennedy been reelected to the House in 1948 than he began, in a sense, running for the Senate, for from then on he spent as much time touring Massachusetts—giving speeches in Gloucester, Greenfield, Holyoke, all over— as he spent on the floor of the House. It was just that he did not formally declare his candidacy until 1951.

When he finally did declare, many observers felt that the Kennedys had finally bitten off more than they could chew. For young John Kennedy, age 34, had had the audacity to challenge none other than the redoubtable Henry Cabot Lodge, Jr. Lodge was the grandson of the distinguished U.S. senator Henry Cabot Lodge, Sr., who had won international fame by opposing President Woodrow Wilson's League of Nations. Lodge Senior had also given Kennedy's grandfather, Honey Fitz, his last serious defeat. The Lodges exemplified old Yankee society, the sort of people who had discriminated against the Irish Kennedys. Henry Cabot Lodge, Jr., was the very incarnation of the well-born, educated, cultured New Englander who could trace his ancestry back to the earliest days of the Massachusetts Bay Colony. Furthermore, as a politician he seemed invincible. He had decisively beaten three Irishmen for the Senate: James Curley, Joseph Casey, and David Walsh.

John F. Kennedy's candidacy for the Senate went beyond politics and into class warfare. It put the Kennedys squarely in opposition to Massachusetts' old Yankee establishment, the very class that had forced Joe Kennedy to leave Boston. For Joe Kennedy the Lodge battle placed his deepest pride on the line. It would be a fight with no quarter given, and he was confident of victory. Not long after Jack declared his candidacy, Joe Kennedy wrote his old friend Lord Beaverbrook: "You know me well enough to know that we wouldn't be in this if we weren't going to win."

Even though the odds against beating someone like Henry Cabot Lodge, Jr., appeared enormous, the Kennedys had three things in their favor. The first was money. The new Kennedy money was much more plentiful than the old Lodge money. The second was Jack Kennedy's incredible charm and tireless zest for campaigning. The third was the fact that the Irish and the Yankees were no longer so much at each other's throats. They had begun to coalesce and ally themselves against all the newcomers—the Italians, Jews, and blacks. This meant that Kennedy could count on a lot of Yankee supporters.

As the Kennedys conceived it, the greatest danger lay in Eisenhower's simultaneous candidacy for the presidency. It had been Henry Cabot Lodge, Jr., who had enticed Eisenhower from his post as commander of NATO forces in Europe and convinced him to run for the presidency. (Lodge, in fact, had personally led the fight against the candidacy of Taft.) Eisenhower was so popular he could conceivably sweep all the other Republicans into office with him. Jack Kennedy had to somehow make his personality prevail over Lodge's and Eisenhower's. As it turned out, the campaign became almost wholly one of personality. Kennedy and Lodge thought pretty much alike, and there were few issues dividing them. Promotion of personality was a Kennedy forte, and so the way the campaign evolved—into little more than a popularity contest—clearly favored Kennedy.

The Kennedys soon developed a strategy. It was, quite simply, to saturate the state of Massachusetts with Kennedy. While Congressman Kennedy was off on his many speaking tours of the state he had accumulated a large card-index file of promising young people he met along the way who might someday be counted on to work for him in a political campaign. This file was now activated, and messages from Kennedy went out to names in all the 39 cities and 312 towns Kennedy had visited.

The Kennedys also solicited an enormous number of nominating signatures—2500 are required by law and that was about all the incumbent Lodge bothered to collect. By contrast Kennedy collected 262,324 signatures from all over the state and had his aides mail thank-you letters to all of them, a hitherto unheard-of procedure in Massachusetts politics.

But the biggest effort was reserved to win the female voters. Kennedy had capitalized effectively on his appeal to the women of Boston's eleventh district in his congressional campaigns; now he attempted to capitalize on that appeal statewide.

Teas were organized and held in every city in the state. Women in various communities were asked not only to bring themselves, but also to bring their best lace and linen tablecloths and their silver services. They were apparently delighted to do so. There was a certain thrill in associating with the now-famous Kennedy family, in being able to do something for them. As the campaign progressed Kennedy began to sense that his sex appeal for young women was stronger than his "son appeal" for older women, and so more and more younger women were invited. Kennedy was often accompanied by one or more members of his family. A typical invitation would ask a woman to a "reception in honor of Mrs. Joseph P. Kennedy and her son, Congressman John F. Kennedy." At the party there would be a receiving line, and each female would get a chance to shake the handsome Jack Kennedy's hand and perhaps even receive a peck on the cheek from him. Dave Powers would stand near the receiving line with a clicker, counting the number of women who filed by. Thirty-three major tea parties were held, attended by some 70,000 young women. Kennedy's margin of victory over Lodge would be 70,737 votes, corresponding almost exactly to the number of women who attended the teas.

Successful as the tea parties were, however, they did not, by any means, characterize the overall tenor of the campaign, so far as Jack Kennedy was concerned. For the candidate it was largely a grueling ordeal, involving much pressure, pain, and discomfort. As Dave Powers recalls, it was racing a train to a railway crossing to get to a speaking engagement at the Knights of Columbus in South Hatfield on time; it was sleeping in "a crummy small-town hotel, with a single electric light bulb hanging from the ceiling over the bed and a questionable bathtub down at the far end of the hall"; it was Kennedy in his topcoat shaving at a sink in the men's room of a bowling alley at Danvers, with a dirty mirror above the basin and only cold water in the faucet; it was traveling in almost constant pain, hiding the crutches in the hotel room or in the car; it was leaving one of those teas full of bouncy hopeful women, where he had smiled and beamed for three hours, looking like the happiest, most relaxed young man in the world, and returning to the car, leaning back, letting his smile finally drop, closing his eyes in pain, then, arriving back at the hotel, going to his room on crutches, and collapsing into a tub of steaming hot water—the end of a day in which he had been in almost perpetual agony since he had got out of bed at 6 A.M. With an engine of ambition like that, no opponent of Jack Kennedy's stood a chance. As long as Jack didn't break he was invincible.

Yet Kennedy needed every last ounce of ambition in his struggle against Lodge. The campaign had actually got off to a shaky start under the direction of Joe Kennedy and his following of old Boston Irish pols. The candidate himself had sensed this and had tried to give more power to his young cohorts, people like Kenny O'Donnell, Larry O'Brien, Dave Powers, and Sarge Shriver.

But it was not until Bobby Kennedy was recruited as campaign manager that the campaign really began to take off. Bobby Kennedy was then a 26-year-old fledgling lawyer, just out of the University of Virginia Law School, a shy, awkward, reserved young man who knew next to nothing about Massachusetts politics. Not long after he went to bat for his older brother he metamorphosed into "a tough, cocky, ruthless, field general," as Kenny O'Donnell described him. As campaign manager he worked from 8 A.M. to midnight, and, according to O'Donnell, "saved the campaign and made it click."

Not only Bobby but all the other Kennedys pitched into the fray. Rose Kennedy, in her role as a Gold Star mother, went through her various metamorphoses yet again. And the girls—Eunice, Patricia, and Jean—also pitched in and answered the phones, mailed envelopes, and poured tea.

There was a crucial debate with Lodge in Waltham, organized by the League of Women Voters. Here a relaxed, youthful-looking Kennedy took on the older, more distinguished-looking patrician and soon proved to be quicker, smarter, and surer of himself than the Boston Brahmin. Dave Powers and Kenny O'Donnell stood backstage and relished watching the somewhat stiff Lodge reacting to Kennedy by "nervously squeezing and flexing his hands behind his back." The photographs in the Massachusetts papers the next day told the story: a grinning, bushy-haired, toothy Kennedy jabbing his fist at the reserved, overdignified Yankee aristocrat, who looked rather taken aback by the whole encounter. In a campaign in which personality weighed far more than any issue, the photos resulting from the debate became powerful weapons and the Kennedys made the most of them.

Publicity again was the key. The Kennedy campaign released 900,000 copies of an eight-page tabloid on Jack with the photos of Joe Junior and Jack on the cover under the headline: John Fulfills Dream of Brother Joe Who Met Death in the Sky over the English Channel. Inside this family-concocted publication were drawings of Jack Kennedy rescuing shipmates in the South Pacific and a reprint of John Hersey's article on the saga of the PT-109. The Kennedys spared no expense to get the publication into circulation. The tabloid was sent out to every registered voter in the state of Massachusetts.

But the Kennedys were rarely content to deploy just one or two big guns in a political assault. They hauled out yet another cannon, this time a financial one. It was a timely loan of $500,000 to Mr. John Fox, the financially troubled publisher of the *Boston Post*. The loan apparently saved the *Post* from folding and miraculously caused the paper to suddenly endorse the candidacy of John F. Kennedy. According to Richard Whalen, who reported the loan in his biography of the ambassador, both Joe Kennedy and John Fox denied the loan was made for political purposes, but people drew their own conclusions.

Right up until the closing weeks of the campaign Henry Cabot Lodge, Jr., had been so confident of victory that he had spent an inordinate amount of time stumping out of state for Eisenhower. Meanwhile the Kennedy campaign had been reaching a crescendo at home. When word of his defeat came, the twelve-year veteran of the Senate was utterly stunned. "It was all those teas," Lodge later told reporters, "it was the teas that beat us."

It was far more than the teas that elected young John F. Kennedy to the U.S. Senate. The Kennedys had mounted, as a biographer of Joe Kennedy put it, "one of the most methodical, most scientific, most thoroughly detailed, intricate, and disciplined and smoothly working campaigns in Massachusetts history." They had forged a political machine that was to prove virtually unstoppable.

The victory, of course, gave the Kennedys immense satisfaction. Jack Kennedy had overcome both serious physical infirmities and widespread prejudice against Irish Catholics to win his Senate post. Joe Kennedy, now 64, enjoyed through his son Jack a victory and an acceptance that had been denied him throughout his life. This victory did much to ease Joe Kennedy's deep-seated feelings of resentment and inferiority. It helped to make up for all the snubs and persecutions he had endured because he was just an East Boston mick.

As it turned out, Jack Kennedy began campaigning for the vice presidency the day he arrived in the Senate in January 1953. Part of that campaign involved a secondary campaign, that of winning a wife. For the bachelor image was no longer of great utility. It was appropriate for the handsome congressman seeking a seat in the Senate, but not for a U.S. senator with his sights on still-higher office. Before long he would have to disappoint every one of those 70,000 Massachusetts women who had apparently given him his margin of victory over Henry Cabot Lodge, Jr.

26. Toward a New Image:
The Senator and Jacqueline Bouvier

It WAS IN November 1952 on a gray, drizzly day in Washington, not long after Jack Kennedy's victory over Lodge, that I first had a chance to talk with cousin Jacqueline about her relationship with the newly elected senator from Massachusetts.

I was an ensign in the Navy at the time, stationed aboard a ship that had just returned from a five-month tour of duty with the Sixth Fleet in the Mediterranean and was now undergoing drydock repairs at Newport News, Virginia. I was sent to Washington to research and write a history of my ship.

Jacqueline was also in Washington at the time, working as an "inquiring photographer" for the now-defunct *Washington Times-Herald* at $42.50 a week. It was an ideal society girl's job, for it didn't require a great deal of time or effort and it gave her a good excuse to interview rising young politicians, like John F. Kennedy and Richard M. Nixon, and, in general, to meet a lot of people she would not have otherwise had an opportunity to meet. Since she continued living at the Auchincloss estate, Merrywood, with her mother and stepfather, she didn't have to live on her salary.

I had not seen much of Jackie since the summer of 1949 when I was a cadet at the Reserve Officers Candidate School in Newport, Rhode Island. I was granted one twenty-four-hour liberty each week. During that interval I would occasionally go out to Hammersmith Farm, or the Newport Country Club, or to Bailey's Beach as a guest of the Auchinclosses. Jackie's mother, Janet Lee Auchincloss, was my titular godmother; at least she had officiated at my christening, and she did her godmotherly duty, somewhat half-heartedly I sensed, by getting her serviceman godson guest privileges at both the Golf Club and at Bailey's Beach. I remember it was quite a relief from the hot parade grounds, the deafening gunnery practice, the cramped barracks, and the boring navigation and seamanship courses to get out on that breezy golf course.

I went up to Hammersmith Farm that summer perhaps three or four times. Relations between the Auchinclosses and the Bouviers were not particularly friendly at the time (Janet's divorce from Jack Bouvier had been an ugly one that had spawned many animosities), and I couldn't help sensing a sort of defensive chilliness on the part of Janet and her husband toward me.

Jackie and I had both turned 20 that summer; we had not been together since the summer of 1947 in Long Island, when, in the last years of our grandfather Bouvier's life, we had spent parts of July and August at his lovely East Hampton estate, Lasata. Somewhat to my surprise, I found the Newport Jackie to be unusually distant and reserved, and rather full of self-importance over being a member of the Auchincloss clan, which, I sensed, she felt was a good deal grander than the Bouvier clan in which we had all grown up. Up there, in the vast hilltop gloom of Hammersmith Farm, surrounded by her stiff, ultraformal mother, her tall, rigid, uncommunicative stepfather, and assorted Auchincloss steprelatives, she had seemed very tight, nervous, and somehow trapped.

There was something coldly formal and removed about Hammersmith Farm. I remember the large, drafty rooms filled with heavy, dark Victorian furniture. I have an image of Jacqueline perched on the arm of a dark-brown sofa talking with me stiffly, nervously, while her stern-faced mother sat nearby scrutinizing us and listening carefully to every word we said. So far as Janet was concerned, I belonged to the enemy camp, the Bouviers, and therefore bore watching.

Even down at Bailey's Beach, that exclusive preserve of Newport's landed gentry, Jackie seemed to affect a remoteness that set her apart. Invariably the young men around her would be the most "social" in the club, and I remember being quite disgusted with her for wasting her time with so many *unimpressive* socialite types, whom, I recall thinking to myself, I would love to have taken back to the base for a session or two on the drill field. Jackie seemed to gravitate toward boys who had important family names or European titles, no matter what they were like in terms of personality or intelligence. When she was in East Hampton I remember she spent an inordinate amount of time hanging around the White Russian emigré, Prince Serge Obolensky, who was old enough to be her father.

Jackie, it must be observed, was not terribly attractive at this somewhat awkward stage of her life (the beauties in the Bouvier family then were Jackie's younger sister, Lee, and her oldest cousin, Edith Bouvier Beale). Like Jack Kennedy she grew into her full attractiveness as she grew older.

At any rate, in that summer of 1949, while she was still enrolled at Vassar, a place she never liked, and still a prisoner of the Auchinclosses at Hammersmith Farm, Jacqueline struck me as being neither exceptionally attractive nor particularly vital or exciting, just another rather uptight, bored Newport society girl, like dozens of others lolling around Bailey's Beach, waiting for some young socialite to come over and invite them for a swim, or a sail, or a spin in a Piper Cub.

Now, however, three and a half years later in Washington, Jacqueline appeared much more at ease, and much more lighthearted, and much more beautiful. Although she was still living with her mother and stepfather at Merrywood, she did enjoy an added measure of freedom, at least during the day, as a journalist and photographer, and it showed in her high spirits. Not long after I arrived in Washington for the writing assignment, we met for lunch at the Mayflower. I noticed immediately that she was in a particularly good mood. During our lunch she was more her old, pre-Newport self, witty and charming and somewhat mischievous. Washington, I thought, was doing her a lot of good. Or was it that young Kennedy guy I heard she had been going out with who was putting her in such a good mood?

After chatting about this and that for a while, trying to catch up on each other's lives, I asked her if there was anything to the rumors I had heard that she and Kennedy were getting serious about each other.

"I've seen a few items in the gossip columns, and there's a lot of scuttlebutt around town about you two," I observed, whereupon she laughed and went into an amusing discussion about how vain he was.

"You know, he goes to a hairdresser almost every day to have his hair done," she said, in that low, breathless whisper of hers, "so it'll always look bushy and fluffy."

I nodded, without saying anything.

"And you know," she went on, "if, when we go out to some party, or reception, or something, nobody recognizes him, or no photographer takes his picture, he sulks afterwards for *hours*."

"Really?"

"Really. He's so vain you can't believe it."

"Maybe he's just ambitious," I said.

"Oh sure, he's ambitious, all right," she said, "he even told me he intends to be President some day," and she tossed her head back and laughed again.

We both laughed for a few seconds over that; then I said, "Listen, he's an old Navy man; I'd like to meet him."

"Sure," she said, "I can arrange it easily. When he comes back to D.C. you can just go right over to the Hill and attend a hearing or something. Then you can get together with him afterward, have lunch maybe, out of a paper bag."

I told her that would be great, then we switched to other topics, talking mostly about our Bouvier relatives, and particularly about our eccentric Aunt Edie and her forty cats, a favorite topic of conversation among the Bouviers.

"Wait 'til I introduce Jack Kennedy to Aunt Edie," she said, laughingly. "You know, I doubt if he'd survive it. The Kennedys are really terribly *bourgeois*."

"Well," I said, "if you ever feel like terminating the relationship, just bring him up to Gray Gardens some weekend."

She laughed. "The cat hairs alone would drive him crazy. You know he's allergic to animals, especially horses. Imagine me with someone allergic to horses!"

I could not imagine it. Next to herself, Jacqueline loved horses more than anything in the world. When not studying or working, her life was virtually horses, and horses would remain her chief recreation in the years to come.

After what turned out to be an immensely enjoyable lunch, Jackie "interviewed" me and took my picture for her column. The interview and photo appeared in the November 11, 1952, *Times-Herald*. Exactly one week before that Eisenhower had been elected to the presidency and John F. Kennedy to the Senate. Whom Jackie voted for is anybody's guess; most likely it was Eisenhower. Throughout her youth Jackie, like her father, mother, stepfather, and all grandparents, had been a staunch Republican, and had been an especially fervent admirer of Wendell Willkie, whose campaign buttons she had collected as a girl.

As it turned out, I was not to meet Jack Kennedy until over a year later. A Senate pass I still have in my possession, signed by Kennedy, indicates that I met him on January 28, 1954. I had just got out of the service and was in Washington seeing a second cousin, Thomas Gates, who was then Eisenhower's undersecretary for the Navy and who would later become his secretary of defense.

I was very curious about this young senator whose PT-109 exploits were somewhat of a legend in the Navy. I had had a rather incredible career so far in the Navy myself, having become at 22 one of the youngest navigation officers in the Sixth Fleet upon the sudden collapse of our ship's navigator as we were entering the Bay of Naples, and I was anxious to swap a few sea stories. At the same time, I was somewhat uneasy. Although I was proud of what I had accomplished in the Navy, my greatest exploit had been to navigate a ship around the peacetime Mediterranean, a fairly routine matter, while Kennedy was a decorated veteran of World War II, twelve years older, and a certified war hero.

My chance to meet Kennedy that January came after attending a hearing of a Senate subcommittee on labor, of which Kennedy was a member. Through Jackie's intervention I had been given a pass by Kennedy's office to attend the hearing.

When I first saw Kennedy sitting there with the other subcommittee members at a long table on a kind of stage, or platform, I was surprised by his appearance. He was extraordinarily thin, almost emaciated, with a shock of thick reddish-brown hair tousled and "fluffed up," as Jackie had described. He looked as young as I was, if not younger.

During the hearing, which was very monotonous, Kennedy remained slouched in his chair, never sitting up straight once. From a slouch he would occasionally slide into a sprawl. Tapping his pen on the table, and sometimes on his teeth, yawning from time to time, and frequently changing position (because of his bad back?), he looked utterly bored. When, at one point, he did ask a question, he spoke casually, giving the appearance of complete indifference. For me, so ready to admire the man, it was a disappointing performance, although I could sympathize with his attitude because the proceedings were so dull.

After the hearing, I went up to the dais and presented myself. He told me his office had informed him I was coming, and he invited me to the Senate cafeteria for a quick lunch. The hearings, if I remember correctly, were scheduled to resume in an hour.

During lunch, off a self-service tray (his brown-bag lunches he ate at his office), I kept marveling at Kennedy's youthfulness. He looked almost abnormally young for a 36-year-old-man. Years later, when I learned he was a victim of Addison's disease, I found out that an abnormally youthful appearance, together with imperviousness to gray hair, was one of the more fortunate manifestations of the disease.

Probably because I was Jackie's cousin, and he was barely five months into his marriage, Kennedy seemed to bend over backward to be nice to me, and I was quite flattered by the attention. I have since learned that this was one of Kennedy's most appreciated traits. He gave people his undivided attention in conversation and appeared genuinely interested in what others had to say. He was that rare being in these times, a good listener, and he had the ability to make the person he was with feel exceptionally important.

After talking a little about the hearing, which he admitted bored him "shitless," he asked me about my naval service. I told him about my last tour of duty with the Sixth Fleet in the Mediterranean, about our vast joint NATO maneuvers, about how magnificent the enormous fleet looked combined in formation with the fleets of Greece, Turkey, Italy, and Great Britain, and how great the liberty was in such ports as Naples, Nice, Athens, and Palermo.

"Pretty good duty, if you ask me," he observed. "I guess when you were in the Med you must have put into Italian ports *a lot*."

I told him we had, especially Naples, where the southern wing of NATO, AFSOUTH, was headquartered (and where Kennedy would one day receive the largest and most tumultuous welcome of his political career).

"Who knows if we'll ever be able to make NATO work," he mused, "there are so many weak links in the chain."

"Well, all I can say is that the Mediterranean is surely *mare nostrum*," I observed. "All the Russians have to harass us with is a couple of radar ships disguised as fishing smacks."

"And we're gonna *keep* it *mare nostrum*, don't worry," he said emphatically.

We talked about NATO and the Navy for a while, and I became aware he had a deep love and nostalgia for the service. Then he took me somewhat by surprise by asking me what I thought of Italian women.

I told him I thought they were the toughest women I had ever known, and he observed, with a smile, that the women you meet while you're in the Navy are not always the sweetest. I agreed and after telling him I would be returning to Italy shortly on a Fulbright grant, he told me he would probably be going to Italy himself the following year on some fact-finding mission and would find out how tough Italian women were firsthand. "If you have any good numbers leave them for me at the embassy in Rome," he said with a twinkle. I laughed and assured him I would.

Our lunch then progressed to a protracted discussion of Mediterranean women, extending now to the Greeks, the Turks, and the Arabs, with whom I also had acquired some experience, since our ship had spent quite a bit of time in Greek, Turkish, and various North African ports.

"You must have had a field day," he grinned, "although I wonder a little bit about the sanitary conditions."

I soon became aware that the subject of women really gripped Kennedy, sexual adventurer that he was, and when the time came to leave, he appeared genuinely reluctant to return to the hearing. "And what about the Turkish girls? . . . And tell me about the Sicilians. . . . And did you make it with any Egyptians?" he kept on. Only once or twice during the lunch, which went by very quickly, did he bring up Jackie, and when he did it was only a passing reference. I remember wondering about his relationship with Jackie. How strong was it? How were they getting along?

Given the somewhat blasé and condescending attitude Jacqueline had displayed toward Jack Kennedy during that luncheon at the Mayflower in November 1952, I had remained somewhat skeptical of their relationship and had been very surprised in the spring of 1953, when I was again in the Mediterranean with the Sixth Fleet, to learn in a letter from my mother that Jackie and Jack were about to become engaged. Jackie's father shared office space with my father in New York, and he had confided to my father the devastating news that Joe Kennedy's son had approached him for his daughter's hand. It was too ironic to believe, since Jack Bouvier had regarded Joe Kennedy as his nemesis, the man whose policies as chairman of the SEC had put him in the red. Later, toward the end of the month, I read the official announcement in a copy of the Paris *Herald Tribune* I had picked up from a newsstand in Naples. So it was true, after all. Judging from my impressions of Jacqueline's attitude toward the senator seven months before, it was hard to believe. It was also hard to believe that Jack Bouvier, the arch-Republican who detested Joe Kennedy, would have approved of the union, but that is another story.

The intervening months—December 1952 to June 1953—had witnessed the blossoming of Jacqueline and Jack's relationship; Jacqueline had turned on the charm and Kennedy had responded.

Before November 1952 Jack and Jacqueline apparently had not taken each other very seriously. True, they had been going out with each other sporadically since June 1951, when during Kennedy's second term in Congress, Charles Bartlett, Washington correspondent for the *Chattanooga Times*, first introduced them at a dinner party in his Georgetown house. But at first it seems they did not interest each other in the slightest. Kennedy did not bother to call up Jackie after this first meeting, and Jackie, oblivious to Kennedy, merrily took off on a long trip to Europe with her sister a few days later without saying goodbye.

Love at first sight, it was not. Nor love at second, or third, or fourth sight. After Jackie and Lee returned from their trip, which they subsequently memorialized in their delightful book, *One Special Summer*, it was a while before Jackie saw Kennedy again, and when they finally did begin seeing each other, it was usually the result of chance meetings. Kennedy had so many girls on the string and was enjoying his bachelorhood so much that he had little time for a steady relationship. As for Jackie, she was never one to chase men, or even to show she liked someone, except in the most unobtrusive ways. Gradually, however, as her interest in Kennedy began to grow, she became a little less unobtrusive; she ventured to Capitol Hill to interview Representative Kennedy for her column and sent gourmet French meals to his office to replace his customary brown-bag deli luncheons. But still there were many inpediments to their relationship. The ever-gregarious Jack often brought along some friend, or political crony, or relative when he went out on a date with Jackie, something that never failed to annoy her. As a further discouragement, 1952 was an election year, and Jack, consumed with getting himself elected to the Senate, was much too busy to spend time courting one woman. Going after a lot of different women, in a series of superficial flirtations and one-night stands, was feasible, but spending a lot of precious time and energy assiduously cultivating one woman in particular was temporarily beyond his aims and capabilities.

Everything changed, however, in January 1953, when Jack took his seat as a freshman in the Senate. That January he escorted Jackie to Eisenhower's inaugural ball and invited her to the opening session of the Eighty-third Congress. From then on they saw each other more or less continuously. Free from the strain of campaigning for the Senate, Kennedy now began campaigning for Jacqueline Bouvier's hand. For he was now acutely aware that, given the American public's deep emotional need to have family men in the highest offices of state, he had to get married and raise a family to advance his career. And Jacqueline seemed to have the qualifications he sought in a wife. She was attractive, poised, intelligent, Catholic, and she came from not one, but two, supposedly prominent eastern families, the Bouviers and the Auchinclosses.

Plying her trade as journalist and photographer, Jacqueline continually piqued Kennedy with her articles and tantalized him with her travels. Knowing that Kennedy was reading her inquiring photographer column every day, she asked people such questions as: "Is your marriage a fifty-fifty partnership, or do you feel you give more?"; "Can you give any reason why a contented bachelor should ever get married?"; and "The Irish author, Sean O'Faolain, claims the Irish are deficient in the art of love. Do you agree with the author's opinion?"

Throughout Kennedy's courtship Jackie never forgot her father's advice to not give too much of herself, to always hold something back, and always appear hard to get. For a man of Kennedy's vanity and insecurity, it was a potent strategy. He simply could not conceive of a woman not falling all over herself to be in his arms. When Jackie occasionally stood him up, or did not return his calls, or left town without telling him, it wounded his vanity, aggravated his insecurity, fueled his desire, and spurred him on to conquer her.

By early spring 1953, almost two years after they first met, Jacqueline had apparently fallen in love with Kennedy and was determined to win him over. It was at this time that Jackie's father wrote his nephew, Michel Bouvier, that he believed Jackie was "in love" with Kennedy, whom he described in the letter as "this young kid who needs a haircut." That Jackie did, in fact, actually fall in love with Kennedy is also attested to by Red Fay, who, in describing his first meeting with Jackie just before her marriage to Kennedy, wrote:

> With all her sophistication, she could not conceal her love for Jack. . . . While we ate and talked, Jacqueline would reach for Jack's arm or hand, and speak with great delight of their coming marriage. She laughed. She almost sang. She did all the things a young, beautiful girl does when she is in love and the man she loves is with her.

For Jacqueline, Kennedy represented a big change from the few other men she had been involved with. Kennedy was the first young man with strength and guts she had ever become seriously attached to.

But what of Kennedy? Was he "in love" with Jacqueline? Who knows? When asked this question by his first biographer, James MacGregor Burns, Kennedy is said to have replied, "I'm not the heavy lover type." My own belief is that he knew himself when he gave out that answer and never "fell in love" with Jackie, or with anybody, for that matter—but that in time he definitely did come to "love" Jacqueline as much as it was within his power to love one woman. If Jack Kennedy was never "in love" with Jacqueline, he was undoubtedly fascinated by her, however. The Bouvier style was something very new and different for him and it intrigued him.

Meanwhile, Jackie, determined now to "get" Jack, resorted to every wile and stratagem her lively imagination could devise to ensnare him. Knowing that the Kennedys were insecure about their social status, and always on the defensive about it, she dropped hints here and there about her own glorious background, alluding now and then to the Bouviers, who had been in the New York Social Register continuously since 1889, the early American Ewings (her paternal great-grandmother's family from Caroline County, Maryland), who had been officers under Washington in the Revolution, and the illustrious Auchinclosses.

Shrewdly she did everything possible to hide her Irish background, which, ironically, predominated in her genetic makeup, for her mother was of 100 percent Irish extraction, fully as Irish as the Kennedys. (Strictly speaking, since her father was one-fourth French and three-fourths English and her mother was totally Irish, Jackie herself was one-eighth French, three-eighths English, and one-half Irish.) No, Jack Kennedy did not want an Irish Catholic bride, he wanted a *French* Catholic bride; so Jackie never breathed a word about her Irish ancestry and studiously kept her mother's relatives from meeting him, lest they destroy the illusion she was trying to build up.

In addition, Jackie also fostered an illusion of personal wealth so Kennedy would not think she was after his money. While in Washington, she had Kennedy out to Merrywood, and he could see that Jackie and her mother lived in even grander style than the Kennedys did. He received a similar impression when he visited the imposing Hammersmith Farm. But the hidden truth was that Jackie, as a mere stepchild of Hugh D. Auchincloss, did not stand to inherit a cent from the Auchinclosses. Hugh D. had several children of his own to leave his money to. And there was little likelihood Jackie would ever inherit much money from her father, since it was well known in the Bouvier family that Jack Bouvier had already run through several small fortunes. Actually, at the time Kennedy was courting Jacqueline, she had exactly the same amount of money I had—$3000, left to her by our grandfather Bouvier in 1947. Her only other financial resources, beyond an occasional handout from her mother, were her weekly salary from the *Washington Times-Herald* and the regular $50 a month allowance her father sent her from New York. Yet, on these modest resources, and in her opulent Auchincloss settings, Jackie always managed to *look* rich, so that Kennedy never dreamed she was virtually penniless. Later, after the honeymoon, when the bills began coming in, it was something of a shock for Kennedy to find out that Jackie had no money of her own at all.

Perhaps the most shrewd and tantalizing ploy Jacqueline pulled on Kennedy during their courtship was to go off to London to cover the coronation of Queen Elizabeth II in the spring of 1953. Taking off with hardly any advance warning, and certainly not telling Kennedy she was going to miss him, she made it clear in the stories and letters she sent back to Washington that she was having a marvelous time in London, going to all the balls and parties and meeting lots of handsome and exciting men. Kennedy evidently fell for the ploy because not only did he meet her at the airport, but not long after she returned, full of stories about Perle Mesta, Prince Philip, the Queen, and all the wonderful men she had met, he finally asked her to marry him.

During this period Jacqueline freely engaged in journalistic practices she was later to condemn and abhor with every fiber of her being. She intercepted two nieces of Mamie Eisenhower's on their way to school and elicited indiscretions from them that enraged their mother, Mamie's sister. When she was in London she went around trying to get juicy tidbits about the royal family from people who knew them. Jackie also went out of her way to interview Elizabeth's ladies-in-waiting, something she would bitterly regret when, ten years later, she found herself in a position similar to the Queen's, and her secretaries were vulnerable to the same sort of questioning.

The questions inevitably arise: How suited were Jacqueline Bouvier and John F. Kennedy to one another, and why did they decide to get married? My belief is that Jacqueline was more suited to Jack and his purposes than he was to her and hers and that marrying into the Kennedy clan was, for Jackie, something of a mistake, a denial of her being.

Jacqueline Bouvier and John F. Kennedy came from two radically different backgrounds and traditions, and it was not easy for either one, especially Jackie, to reconcile the differences. Furthermore, they possessed radically different emotional and sexual temperaments. Jacqueline was no Inga Arvad. She was basically demure. She had been brought up to downplay and repress her sexuality. As a young woman, she had a reputation for being sexually remote. Kennedy, on the other hand, was a classic sexual adventurer, a libertine who thoroughly enjoyed the hunt, the chase, and the conquest, who took women where he found them and discarded them as quickly as he took them. Combining two such temperaments in marriage means that one is bound to get hurt, and, in the case of the John F. Kennedys, it was Jacqueline who was hurt the most. It is not a very happy thing for a young wife to be continually betrayed by her husband.

Much has been made of Jack Kennedy's sexual life. As each year passes, more and more women float to the surface out of his erotic past. His type was not the type most suited to the overprotected, restrained, very proper, straightlaced society girl. Jacqueline Bouvier was very aloof with men. As a young girl she was the classic virgin princess. I went to scores of the subscription dances she went to in New York, saw her at dozens of college weekends at Princeton and Yale, and scores more debutante parties in Greenwich, Rye, Watch Hill, Glen Cove, Locust Valley, Southampton, and other watering places of the northeastern seaboard. The boys always had the same complaint: "Gee, what's wrong with your cousin? She's a real cold fish, isn't she?" "God, you can't get *near* that cousin of yours, can you?" And so it would go. The complaint was delivered to me many times over when Jackie and I were in our late teens and early twenties. Jackie just didn't "give out."

What did Jack Kennedy, the womanizer who had always favored the company of models, starlets, actresses, and adventuresses and who had avoided marriage like the proverbial plague, see in *this* girl? He saw primarily someone of "class," as his father would say, who would advance his social status and his political fortunes. If he had not come from such a social-climbing family and did not have such powerful political ambitions, he would probably never have got married at all. He often frowned on the marriages of his friends, claiming that their wives spoiled their company forever, and he himself waited a long time before finally marrying.

This is not to say that Jack Kennedy did not have other good reasons for marrying Jacqueline Bouvier. Jackie is very good company; she is bright and witty and can often be fun to be with. Like Kennedy, she is a good conversationalist, with the same ability to listen with interest to others. Since 90 percent of marriage is spent in conversation, this was an important, positive aspect of their relationship.

The trouble was—for Jackie, at least—she and Jack were rarely alone together. Jack Kennedy was terribly fond of his male friends and his family. He had this damnable tendency to always have people around. If it wasn't Bobby, or one of the "rah-rah girls," as Jackie called Jack's sisters, or Ethel, or Sarge, it was some politician, or crony, or one of his school, college, or Navy buddies. If you were with Jack Kennedy you always had to share him with someone else. Time and again Jackie would be driven to distraction in Hyannis Port by Jack's desire to have every single meal with his parents, brothers, and sisters. And when he finally got into the White House, what did he do but have his old school friend Lem Billings down to visit every weekend! This, in addition to his later constant association with crony

Dave Powers, whom Washington gossipers were to dub "John's other wife."

But why did Jacqueline Bouvier need John F. Kennedy? She needed him to fulfill the overriding commandment of her social class at that moment in time: *marry well*. And marrying well meant, above all, marrying a rich man—not necessarily a man exceptionally suited to your personality, temperament, or to your particular ideals and aspirations, but a man with a lot of money. Jacqueline knew, as did all the Bouviers of her generation, myself included, that she would never inherit very much money from her own family, and, since she had no profession of her own, she *had* to marry well to survive economically in the manner in which she had been raised.

And so, in the summer of 1953, at the beginning of the Eisenhower era of the American presidency, Jack Kennedy promised to give up his precious and much-loved bachelorhood, and Jacqueline Bouvier promised to give herself up to the Kennedys. For her it was a great leap into the unknown, into a world that was basically alien to her temperament and interests, but which promised certain emotional and financial rewards. For Kennedy it was the attainment of a new image, an image destined to help him replace the Eisenhower era eight years later with a whole new style of life and statecraft, the regal, reckless, short-lived, incandescent Kennedy-Bouvier moment in American history.

27. The Bouviers (and the Lees): Of Style (and Steel)

> *The beauty of a race or family, the charm and benevolence of their whole demeanor, is earned by labor: like genius, it is the final result of the accumulatory labor of generations.*
>
> *One must have made great sacrifices to good taste, one must for its sake have done many things, left many things undone.*
>
> *. . . one must have preferred beauty to advantage, habit, opinion, indolence.*
>
> *Nietzsche*

I

IT WAS ONE of the promises of John F. Kennedy's engagement to Jacqueline Bouvier that the alliance would lift the Kennedys up one last, vital social notch in their long climb out of the East Boston slums. For by the time Jack and Jacqueline announced their engagement, the Bouviers had enjoyed significant wealth for over a century, had been in New York society since the 1880s, and had married into several eminent white Anglo-Saxon Protestant families, including one with roots deep in America's colonial past.

John F. Kennedy was fascinated by the institution of Society, with a capital S, and not a little insecure about his own status in relation to it. He often wondered about the so-called social leaders who seemed to have the power to determine and proclaim who was in, and who was out, of Society. Who, what, gave these arbiters—whether they were party hostesses, editors of the Social Register, gossip columnists, or chairmen of admissions committees—their special power? And what exactly were the criteria for admission into the Social Register, "the 400," and the most exclusive clubs? Once, after he had become President, Kennedy surprised Red Fay by remarking: "Do you know it is impossible for an Irish Catholic to get into the Somerset Club in Boston? If I moved back to Boston, even after being President, it would make no difference."

That Jacqueline Bouvier was in society thoroughly fascinated the socially insecure Kennedy. It meant, among other things, that she possessed a mysterious something that he did not have. There was, in fact, something missing in the Kennedy status. For all their money and political power they were still, by the lights of those mysterious social arbiters, incomplete.

It remained for the Bouviers, in the person of Jacqueline, to involuntarily supply those missing dimensions, to lend the Kennedy image a more highly polished tone, a measure of historical depth, and a special sense of aesthetic individualism that takes several generations to develop.

By the time Jacqueline and I reached the age of reason and became aware of the family in which we were being raised, the Bouvier style had been developing for well over a hundred years and had reached practically the status of a cult, a cult that included, in addition to aestheticism, ancestor worship and preoccupation with history.

The Bouvier cult developed as a result of an extraordinary family success in the nineteenth century, one so total and complete and spectacular that the family never got over it.

The Bouviers had been, in the eighteenth century, a modest "petite bourgeois" family of artisans living in the ancient Provençal village of Pont-Saint-Esprit on the river Rhone about seventy miles from the Mediterranean. André-

Eustache Bouvier, the father of the founder of the American Bouviers, was a *menuisier-ébéniste,* or cabinetmaker, who made furniture by hand in a small shop that is still standing, 300 years later, in Pont-Saint-Esprit. Like others of his class, he had been caught up in the revolutionary fervor of the times, and eventually became a follower of Napoleon Bonaparte, whose avowed aim was to topple all the reigning European monarchs from their thrones, install his puppets in their places, and attempt to spread the ideals of the French Revolution throughout Europe. André-Eustache's son, Michel Bouvier, who had been apprenticed to his father and had spent a good deal of his youth in the family shop in Pont-Saint-Esprit, enlisted in the service of the Bonapartists, fought in the Napoleonic wars, and finally went down to defeat with the emperor at Waterloo.

After Waterloo, those who had served Napoleon were declared criminals by the Royalists, subject to imprisonment or the guillotine, and Michel Bouvier was compelled to escape from France to save his life. He chose to escape to America, and arrived in New York, with very little money, on August 6, 1815, along with many other French refugees from the Napoleonic wars. After knocking about New York for at least a year, he settled permanently in Philadelphia.

Fifty-nine years later, in 1874, Bouvier died in his vast Italian renaissance mansion in Philadelphia, leaving an estate of approximately $1 million to his large family of three sons and seven daughters. Unlike the Kennedys, who took three generations to realize the classic American dream, Bouvier had realized it in one generation, his own. As the Philadelphia papers reported at the time, it was "an unqualified success story." Very few immigrants to America had accomplished what the poor French veteran of Waterloo had accomplished within the compass of his own lifetime.

To parallel Michel Bouvier's American adventure with that of the Kennedys during the same period (1815–1874), we find Michel establishing himself as a cabinetmaker in Philadelphia; marrying; raising a family of twelve children; befriending and working for another French emigré to Philadelphia, Napoleon's brother, Joseph Bonaparte; eventually giving up cabinetmaking to engage in the mass production of furniture; becoming an importer of marble and a manufacturer of veneers; and finally moving on to real estate speculation, including the acquisition of some 63,000 acres of coal lands in West Virginia—all before the first Kennedy had left the barley and potato fields of Dunganstown.

Subsequently, during the period in which poor Patrick Kennedy, the immigrant barrelmaker, wore himself out in the slums of East Boston (1848–1858), Michel went on to acquire a total of 153,000 acres of West Virginia coal lands, along with substantial parcels of choice real estate in Philadelphia, marry his sons and daughters into some of the finest old Main Line families—the Drexels, Pattersons, and Ewings—and build his vast renaissance palace on North Broad Street. Thus, by the time Patrick Kennedy succumbed to cholera in his cramped East Boston tenement, as poor as when he had left Ireland, Michel Bouvier was already a rich man who had made the ritual return in triumph to his birthplace in France and had married his children into distinguished old American families.

In the decades that followed, the gulf between the Bouviers of Philadelphia and the Kennedys of East Boston widened. During the period 1858–1874, in which Bridget Kennedy, the indomitable widow of Border Street, ran her little notions shop near the East Boston docks and raised her family of one son and three daughters, never fully emerging from the poverty she had lived in all her life, Michel Bouvier put the capstone on his phenomenal career by piling up a million-dollar fortune in real estate and stocks and bonds and buying seats for two of his sons on the New York Stock Exchange, over half a century before a Kennedy was to set foot on Wall Street.

Those sons, who were only slightly older than P. J. Kennedy, plunged into the business of making money on Wall Street with gusto. By the mid-1920s, the oldest son, John Vernou Bouvier, who had produced the family heir, John Vernou Bouvier, Jr., had amassed around $500,000, while the youngest son, Michel C. Bouvier, known as M. C., had piled up a fortune of around $10 million for himself and his three unmarried sisters.

A year after P. J.'s son, Joseph P. Kennedy, was born (1888), the Bouvier brothers turned up in the first edition of that American Almanac de Gotha, the New York Social Register. By the time P. J. Kennedy was elected to the Massachusetts State Senate, M. C. Bouvier was a multimillionaire doing business with the likes of J. P. Morgan, Jay Gould, and Cornelius Vanderbilt.

Doubtless, as one of the princes of Wall Street in a day when Wall Street was almost more powerful than the government and politics and politicians were looked down on socially, M. C. would have regarded the state senator from Massachusetts with some condescension.

As the Kennedys and Fitzgeralds then proceeded to grow in political power in Boston, the Bouviers continued to grow financially and socially in New York and its environs. They established sumptuous residences in the city, and in Narragansett and East Hampton, and cultivated an unusually high style of living, becoming collectors of fine antiques and paintings and entertaining on a lavish scale. During this period (1890–1920) the wealth of the Bouviers far outstripped that of the Kennedys. M. C. Bouvier was to leave an estate of close to $4 million, while his near Kennedy contemporary, P. J., would leave only $57,000.

It was not until the late 1920s that the Kennedy financial fortunes began to catch up with those of the Bouviers. By the time Joe Kennedy had made his initial stake from bootlegging and had milked the film industry of some $6 million, the two families stood about equal in terms of net worth. By the time the Kennedy fortune was six years old, the Bouvier fortune had been in existence for seventy-five years.

After the crash of 1929, the fortunes began to diverge slightly, as the shrewdly opportunistic Joseph P. Kennedy embraced Roosevelt's New Deal, and profited from it, while the conservative Bouviers vehemently opposed Roosevelt and the New Deal, and suffered from it.

Then, slowly but inexorably, the Kennedys, under

the dynamic leadership of Joseph P. Kennedy, began to move ahead of the Bouviers—and just about everyone else—on the financial front, leaving the Bouvier heir, John V. "Black Jack" Bouvier III, Jackie's father, far, far to the rear. By the time Jacqueline Bouvier and John F. Kennedy announced their engagement in the summer of 1953, Joseph P. Kennedy had piled up a fortune worth approximately $250 million, while his counterpart and near contemporary in the Bouvier family, "Black Jack" Bouvier, saw his net worth plummet to a mere $250,000. Thus, while her own family, in the person of her father, the Bouvier heir and hope, was beginning to sink financially, Jacqueline Bouvier reached out for the life ring proffered by the Kennedys, a family on the rise just as her own family had been decades ago.

The decline in the Bouviers' financial fortunes was not, however, accompanied by a corresponding decline in their style and manner of living. Rather it was during their decline that their style reached its full flower. The Bouvier devotion to aesthetic values had roots deep in the culture of Provence. The Bouviers had been Provençal artisans. For decades they made furniture which today bears the description Provençal. The first Bouvier who came to America was himself an artisan, and his finely wrought tables, chairs, and secretaires are considered valuable antiques today.

After he made his fortune, Michel Bouvier became a collector of antique furniture and objets d'art. In 1854 he moved his large family and all his possessions into a thirty-room Italianate town house in Philadelphia that became a veritable museum of French Empire and early American furnishings. The vast house contained, in addition to living quarters for twenty people plus servants, two large drawing rooms, a music room with a grand piano, a library, a gaming room, an enormous dining room, and a private chapel. In back there was a formal garden with an elaborate fountain made from creamy white Carrara marble Bouvier imported from Italy, and vineyards and greenhouses. In these sumptuous surroundings the Bouviers lived from 1854 to 1878, assisted by a cook, three chambermaids, a coachman, a footman, and a gardener. Here, in this setting, a taste and style were formed and consolidated which were to be refined in later generations and eventually absorbed by a mid-twentieth-century descendant, who then, for a brief moment, expressed it to the entire world.

It is worth noting, for the sake of perspective, that by the time Michel Bouvier had made his fortune and moved his family into his North Broad Street mansion, John D. Rockefeller was only a $25-a-month assistant bookkeeper in a Cleveland commission house, Patrick Kennedy was still a beer-barrelmaker in East Boston, and the future automotive Fords were still dirt farmers in Dearborn, Michigan.

After Michel Bouvier died and his house in Philadelphia was sold (to La Salle College), two of his sons and three of his daughters moved to New York and set up households in Manhattan brownstones into which they poured their parents' accumulated possessions and added new collections of their own.

The four-story brownstone home of M. C. Bouvier on 46th Street, just west of Fifth Avenue, soon became a showplace in New York and remained one for fifty-five years. Here M. C. and three of his unmarried sisters lived formal, ceremonious lives for over half a century, making those countless little "sacrifices to good taste," showing in dozens of ways that preference for beauty and style over "advantage, habit, opinion, indolence" that would eventually result in the marked Bouvier taste with which Michel's great-great-granddaughter transformed the White House in the early 1960s.

The decor in the Bouvier brownstone on West 46th Street was a melange of French Empire, Victorian, and early American, with red and gold the dominant colors. There were red velour portieres with golden tassels draping the doors. On red damask walls hung huge, floor-to-ceiling gilt-framed Louis XV mirrors. Statues on marble pedestals were everywhere: busts of Napoleon, Greek gods, neoclassic goddesses. Elaborately brocaded footstools abounded among the Empire fauteuils, and there were over two dozen

Empire clocks on the tables and mantels. A beautifully carved golden eagle, a gift from Joseph Bonaparte to Michel Bouvier, hung from one of the red damask walls, and there were tables and chairs made by Michel Bouvier scattered throughout the house. On a sideboard in the dining room I remember there was displayed a magnificent gold service in a red-velvet-lined case. Into this world Jacqueline Bouvier and I were first introduced as infants. Our last visit was made at the age of 5. For suddenly, with the death of M. C., it was all over, and the Bouvier brownstone on West 46th Street vanished like a dream.

After the inevitable auction, many of the old brownstone's contents, which either had not been sold or had not been put up for sale, found their way into Grandfather Bouvier's homes—his apartment at 765 Park Avenue and his lovely East Hampton estate, Lasata, on Further Lane. It was at the ivy-draped Lasata, with its charming sunken Italian garden and sweeping lawns, that the Bouvier cult of beauty reached its maximum intensity. No one who experienced Lasata during his or her formative years could ever again escape its influence. It established standards of taste against which all other places would be judged for the rest of one's life. For most of us, after Lasata was gone everything that came next was second-rate.

Grandfather Bouvier and his wife Maude bought Lasata in 1925, and the Bouvier family congregated there every summer until Grandfather Bouvier's death in 1947. In this era East Hampton was far from the trendy resort it is fast becoming today. It was, rather, a simple, somewhat quaint summer place of stately mansions belonging mostly to wealthy New York families, superimposed upon an old colonial village with families and houses going back to the seventeenth century. The pervasive atmosphere of the place was dignified, weathered, and uncommercial, a place of old elms, ancient windmills, village greens, town ponds, saltbox houses, and stately mansions separated by bright green lawns and dusty potato fields. Old post-and-rail fences, smothered in honeysuckle, ran along narrow country lanes.

The Bouviers' Lasata was spread out over fourteen

elaborately cultivated acres off Further Lane, the nearest
road running parallel to the ocean. A long bluestone driveway curved under an arbor of young maples, past magnificent, sweeping lawns, leading to the large, ivy-covered
stucco house, which resembled an English country manor
but with its own special eastern-Long-Island shingled and
gabled roof. Giant elms shaded the house from above, and
clumps of rhododendrons enveloped its base. With all the
ivy clinging to its walls, the house appeared entirely shrouded
in green, giving it a veiled, mysterious feeling.

Beyond one lawn there was a red-clay tennis court
surrounded by a blackthorn hedge and a high wire fence
entirely draped in trumpet vines. Everywhere there were
groves of beach plums and wild roses. Out back, toward
Middle Lane, which bounded the property on the landward
side, stretched a magnificent cornfield, and nearby was an
orchard of apple, pear, and peach trees, a large truck
garden, and an equally large cutting garden full of flowers
for the house.

From these gardens a long grape arbor led back to
the stables, paddock, and jumping ring, where there were
box stalls for eight horses and a small L-shaped pavilion
containing feed and tack rooms. It was here, in the jumping
ring, that the future First Lady spent hours and hours of
her youth putting her horses, Danseuse, Pas d'Or, and
Stepaside, through their paces, learning that cool self-
mastery that was to benefit her so much, when, for a second
of history, she occupied the center of the world stage.

Returning to the main house, one passed the tool
sheds and garage, with upstairs apartment for the chauffeur, and eventually arrived in Lasata's chef d'oeuvre, the
formal Italian garden, winner of scores of horticultural
prizes. Here, surrounded by high hawthorn hedges, was a
large sunken area divided into neat geometrical patterns
by mossy brick walks and immaculately clipped box hedges,
in the manner of a classic Italian garden of the Renaissance. Beds of delphiniums, marigolds, zinnias, and snap-
dragons sparkled between dark-green hedges and weathered
red pathways. A large, bird-spattered stone sundial stood
on a small patch of lawn between the hedgerows, and at

the far end of the garden stood two charming baroque statues of French shepherds. The centerpiece of the garden was an old, moss-hung fountain wreathed in a tangle of yellow roses and spilling into a dark pool of fish, the whole shaded by delicate lindens and willows.

At the height of the East Hampton season during the early 1940s, it was not uncommon to find seventeen Bouviers at lunch at Lasata on a Sunday afternoon. The formal dining room was painted a dull, mustard yellow and contained a huge, heavy, Jacobean oak refectory table, capable of seating twenty, plus a smaller table, in an alcove, for the children.

As was customary in the Bouvier family, carelessness in dress and manners was not tolerated. The family's devotion to beauty and style would not permit it. Even in the most uncomfortably hot and humid weather, the men and boys wore jackets, shirts, and ties, and the women and girls wore sleeved dresses and stockings. And in those days there was no air conditioning. From his throne at the head of the long oak table, Grandfather Bouvier, wearing a high, stiff collar and tie with jeweled stickpin, enforced an exacting code of behavior. If a grandchild did not sit up straight, keeping his elbows off the table, he would be sent, after one or two unheeded warnings, to his room. Slumping was a sin against good form. Correspondingly, if a grandchild, when asked a question, replied in sloppy English, he or she would be severely reprimanded. Once again, the cult of beauty demanded those repeated "sacrifices to good taste"—in manners, clothes, and speech—and that consistent preference for beauty over "habit, opinion, indolence" that Nietzsche over a century before, had regarded as so essential to the development of style.

For the Bouviers, the beauty and luxury of Lasata seemed the normal, everlasting order of things. But it was all destined to come to an abrupt and irredeemable end upon Grandfather's death and the sale of his house and possessions. One summer Jack Bouvier was living in the splendor of Lasata, pampered by a retinue of servants; the next summer he was lucky if he could rent one miserable room, with no room service, in the Sea Spray Inn. It was not until his daughter Jacqueline entered the White House that a member of the Bouvier family was to live in surroundings comparable to Lasata again.

If the Bouvier ethos was primarily concerned with beauty, style, individualism, and enjoyment, it was correspondingly unconcerned with the competitive values of the Kennedy ethos. But those values were not lacking in the future First Lady's background. For Jacqueline Lee Bouvier was also a Lee.

II

The Lees were Irish, in some ways more Irish than the Kennedys. Not much is known about them, but enough solid information has come down to enable us to piece together a reasonably accurate sketch of their history. Arriving in America from Ireland sometime during the time of the famine in the 1840s, the first Lee settled in New York City and fathered a son, James Lee, who eventually married a young colleen by the name of Mary Norton. In 1877 James and Mary produced a son of their own, whom they named James Thomas Lee.

James T. Lee, destined to become the grandfather of the future First Lady, was a remarkable man. Eleven years younger than Joseph P. Kennedy, he enjoyed a rags-to-riches career almost as spectacular as the ambassador's.

After growing up in a rough Irish neighborhood on New York's Lower East Side, where he attended public school, Lee went to the City College of New York, from which he took a B.S. degree; he then worked his way through Columbia where he earned both an M.A. and a law degree. For a while he practiced law in Manhattan. Successful speculation in real estate led to his first significant money. In 1903 he married Margaret A. Merritt, daughter of Irish immigrants, who bore him, in turn, three daughters—Marion, Winifred, and Janet—and from whom he became totally estranged even though he continued living with her all his life. In 1916, at the time the Joseph

P. Kennedys began producing their first children, Joseph Junior (1915) and John Fitzgerald (1917) in Brookline, Lee joined the legal department of the Chase National Bank and rapidly became a vice president. Later he was enticed away from Chase to the New York Central Savings Bank, now the New York Bank for Savings, where he swiftly rose to become president and chairman of the board. He remained in these positions until he was 80, piling up a large fortune, mostly in real estate, which, at the time of his death in 1972 at age 95, was conservatively estimated to be worth in the neighborhood of $12 million. Among the lucrative buildings he owned was 740 Park Avenue, destined to become one of the most prestigious addresses in the city.

James T. Lee was every bit as tough an Irishman as P. J. or Joe Kennedy. I remember him as a short, stocky man with a large nose, full lips, and a dark complexion, a man of gruff, no-nonsense manners, perpetually chewing on a wet, unlighted cigar. The last time I saw him was at the Maidstone Club in East Hampton in the summer of 1965. I hadn't seen him since 1947, when Jackie and I were teenagers, and we talked briefly. When I asked him, perhaps tactlessly, why he hadn't attended John F. Kennedy's inauguration, at which everyone had found him conspicuously missing, the archconservative Republican let out a volley of oaths that left no doubt how he felt about the Kennedys. Later I found out that not once during Kennedy's brief term as President did Lee ever visit his granddaughter in the White House.

James T. Lee began taking his family down to East Hampton for the summer in the 1920s. By then he had made his money and was anxious to establish his family in society. But because of his obscure origins, somewhat uncouth manners, and gruff way of speaking, the social doors did not automatically burst open. Since his origins were so obscure, Lee became known to East Hampton's old guard as "the mystery man," and since he was thought to "look somewhat Jewish" was snidely referred to by some as "Mr. Levy." People snickered at the curious habit he had of sitting on the beach in a gray business suit, shirt, tie, and straw hat, noting that since he had worked so hard all his life, he had never taken the time to learn how to dress and behave at play. They also whispered about Lee's wife, Margaret, with whom he never spoke—no, *never*—and his Irish mother-in-law, Mrs. Merritt, who was reputed to have greenhorn manners and "a brogue you could cut with a knife" and who was not allowed to come downstairs in the Lee house to greet guests for fear of hurting the family's social chances. Mrs. Merritt took care of all the knitting, sewing, and ironing in the household, functioning almost as a servant. Whenever there were guests in the house, the old Irishwoman would be forced to sit at the top of the stairs and content herself with just listening to what was going on below.

The Lees in the 1920s were a family very similar to the Kennedys, a nouveau riche, Irish-American family on the rise, financially and socially, tough as nails and ambitious to climb the ladder of social success.

The Lee toughness and ambition were transmitted from the father to his daughters, especially to his daughter Janet, who early in life had set her heart on a brilliant marriage and vast future riches. Janet Lee possessed extraordinary strength (and an extraordinary temper) as a young woman, and that strength was nowhere more exemplified than in the riding ring. A short, compact woman with narrow shoulders, a somewhat flat chest, and muscular legs, Janet was a natural athlete who easily obtained complete mastery of her mounts. For ten years she was one of the outstanding horsewomen of the east, regularly winning blue ribbons wherever she competed, from the East Hampton Horse Show to the National Horse Show in New York's Madison Square Garden. Members of the Bouvier family today remember her as a fierce and determined competitor in the ring, a woman who would not let anything stand in the way of winning, whether the contest was a horseshow, a bridge game, or a man.

That same sense of competitiveness she brought to the more serious business of social climbing. With all her heart and mind Janet Lee was determined to make it into society. She succeeded, temporarily, with her marriage to

John V. Bouvier III, and when that marriage fell apart she picked up the pieces and tried again, this time landing no less a catch than the wealthy, socially impeccable Hugh D. Auchincloss, member of a family that had more money than the Bouviers and an equally distinguished lineage. From that moment on, Janet Lee became that curious phenomenon in American society, an Irish WASP.

Just as the Bouviers transmitted their highly developed sense of style to Jacqueline, so the Lees transmitted their toughness and ambition to her. But later, in the presence of the Kennedys, and especially at the time of her engagement to JFK, this side of her character and background was kept securely under wraps. Jacqueline Bouvier was a *French* Catholic. She had *French* culture and charm and an aristocratic *French-English* background. This was the image of herself Jacqueline propagated. Little did the Kennedys realize that, in addition to the refined French aristocrat, they had at the same time admitted to their family a tough, ambitious Irish Catholic like themselves.

28. Young Jacqueline

AUGUST 1936: With Joseph P. Kennedy, chairman of the SEC, commuting between Washington and Hyannis Port, the Kennedys were enjoying another summer on the Cape. Not far away, only a hundred miles as the crow flies, their future in-laws, the Bouviers, were enjoying another radiant summer in East Hampton.

John Vernou Bouvier, Jr., the patriarch of the clan, had just come into a $1.5 million inheritance from his late uncle, M. C. Bouvier, and was living in renewed splendor with his wife, twin daughters, and their children at Lasata. His eldest daughter Edith, the family nonconformist, known as "Big Edie," was living with her beautiful daughter, "Little Edie," and sons Bouvier and Phelan, at their hedge-enclosed, ivy-hung Gray Gardens on Appaquogue Road, not far from Georgica Beach. Son Jack Bouvier was living with wife Janet, nephew Michel, and daughters Jacqueline and Lee, at Wildmoor, JVB Jr.'s other house, a charming old wooden-frame structure, clapboarded and shingled, with a widow's walk overlooking acres of potato fields, a cattail swamp, and the distant, roaring Atlantic.

Jack Bouvier was living in one of his father's houses to save money. His father may have just come into a substantial inheritance, but for stockbroker Jack Bouvier, times were rough. The new SEC chairman was cracking down on the stockbrokers, and particularly on specialist brokers like Jack Bouvier, the stock market was in the doldrums, and the country was in the depths of the worst depression in its history. In the preceding year Jack Bouvier had managed to make around $35,000 from commissions and trading, a goodly sum in those days, but his expenses had remained around $40,000. In 1936 his expenses continued to be about $40,000, while his income fell below $30,000, due, in part, to certain regulations Joe Kennedy had instituted. Already he had had to endure the humiliation of having to move himself and his family into a duplex apartment owned by his father-in-law, James T. Lee, at 740 Park Avenue, for which Mr. Lee asked no rent, only obedience. Now he was also having to spend the summer at his parents' mercy. And this is not to mention the loans his father and father-in-law had made to him over the past two years, with little chance he would be able to repay them in the foreseeable future.

However, to behold the family of John Vernou Bouvier III at Wildmoor, otherwise known as the Appaquogue House, in the summer of 1936, one would never have suspected times were difficult. The six-bedroom house, with its ten acres of lawns and potato fields and sweeping views in every direction, was more than ample. Jack's maroon Stutz town car and Lincoln Zephyr stood sparkling in the bluestone driveway, looking as if they had just come out of the showroom. Magnificent dogs cavorted around the bright green lawns: Sister, the peppy little white bull terrier, Caprice, the fluffy, shaggy Bouvier des Flandres, and the great King Phar, the splendid, bounding, booming Harlequin Great Dane. Boarding at the stables at Lasata were all the Bouvier horses: Gandhi, Stepaside, Pas d'Or, Clearanfast, Arnoldean, and Danseuse, with their grooms, Willie and Murphy. The JVB III's might not have been able to pay the rent in New York and East Hampton, but feeding and caring for three pedigreed dogs and six thoroughbred horses they could afford.

In a certain sense, the John V. Bouvier III's were trapped by the exalted social status Jack had inherited in New York and eastern Long Island. Jack was not just in the Social Register, he was also listed in "the 400," a compendium that was supposed to define the 400 most socially distinguished families in America. In the New York Sunday *News* on July 2, 1933, an article appeared about the opening of Belle's Hampton Country Club between East Hampton and Southampton; the article observed in part, "But the social respectability and acceptability of Belle's newest supper club was established once and for all with the arrival of Mr. and Mrs. John Vernou Bouvier, pillars of the East Hampton summer colony." The children were quite aware of this high status. I remember distinctly the Bouvier grandchildren gathered at Lasata one rainy day debating whether the Bouviers were in the upper upper, or the middle upper, or the lower upper class; the fatuous consensus was that we were in the upper upper class. (Thus, as most of us were to find out, there was plenty of room for downward mobility.) As Jack Bouvier used to tell his daughter Jacqueline: "Jackie, you never have to worry about keeping up with the Joneses, because we *are* the Joneses. Everyone has to keep up with *us*." But, on the other hand, the Joneses had to keep up with themselves. For the John V. Bouvier III's in East Hampton in 1936 this involved a certain amount of strain.

For little Jacqueline Bouvier, aged 7 in 1936, the problem of keeping up appearances on dwindling resources was, of course, nonexistent. True, she overheard her mother's occasional temper tantrums over money, her incessant quarrels with Jack over other women, other men, the horses, the dogs, the nurses, herself and her little sister, Lee, but, all in all, the summer of 1936 was, for Jacqueline, a lovely, secure time, a time when her mother and father and all the Bouviers, in all their branches, were together in one big, united, prosperous family, enjoying the beauty and bounty of East Hampton to the hilt. It is safe to assume that the little girl with the black hair and wide-apart eyes never dreamed for an instant that the strains beneath the glittering surface would soon snap the fabric of her little family's life and things would never be the same again.

In the summer of 1936, when breadlines were forming across the nation, Lasata was fairly bursting with glory, and Jacqueline made the most of it. While her other little cousins would be off at the Maidstone Club, aimlessly splashing in the surf, Jacqueline, dressed immaculately, as usual, in her custom-made riding habit—boots, leggings, jodhpurs, derby, ascot, long-sleeved shirt—and clutching her little whip, would be putting one of her horses through its paces with great purpose and determination. For hours and hours the sturdy little girl with the kinky black hair and broad cheekbones would trot and gallop around the ring on her magnificent chestnut hunter, Danseuse, taking the jumps like a champion, while her admiring mother, also in riding habit, and adoring father, in his familiar tan double-breasted gabardine suit and polo shirt, coached her from the post-and-rail fence, assisted by young Michel and the grooms.

From the age of 4 on, young Jacqueline Bouvier had succeeded in obtaining complete mastery over huge stallions; she won her first blue ribbons at horse shows at 5, which was something of a marvel to the Bouviers, none of whom, except Michel, were particularly enamored of horses or even enjoyed riding. Jackie may have betrayed a certain shyness and insecurity in one-to-one social situations, but before a crowd of onlookers in the riding ring, she always remained in perfect control and almost never faltered. My earliest vivid recollection of Jackie is of her at the age of 5 or 6 riding in a horse show before a large crowd of spectators. I have this distant but clear memory of the entire Bouvier family, from Grandfather in his Panama down to the tiniest tot, hanging over the rail at the East Hampton Riding Club watching little Jackie take the jumps cleanly and neatly, then gather in yet another blue ribbon at the annual summer horse show.

It was principally her achievements as an equestrienne that made Jackie special as a child. In other respects she was more or less an average youngster, her only other distinguishing characteristics being a tendency toward tomboyishness, for Jacqueline was a physically powerful little girl, and a distinct tendency toward aloofness. Jackie always was, and will ever be, a loner, and somewhat of an outsider to American life.

If my first memory of Jacqueline comes down from

the riding ring, my second stems from the stables at Lasata. As a little girl in East Hampton, Jackie rarely did what her other little cousins did. While they were chasing around on the lawns or climbing trees, she would be off in the solarium of the main house sketching (which she was very good at) or writing a poem, or, more likely, she would be out back in the stables with her beloved horses, helping the grooms with the feeding and the currying and the braiding. Jackie could do this for hours and hours, and later, as an adolescent, it often seemed she preferred horses to human beings, so frequently did she forsake the company of her peers for the company of her first and greatest love, her horses.

Although Jack and Janet Bouvier and their daughter made a stunning impression at the horse shows on eastern Long Island, things were far from serene in the John V. Bouvier III household in the summer of 1936. After his children were born, Jack Bouvier, the eternal Don Juan, had begun playing around again, and when Janet got wind of these affairs she flew into uncontrollable rages. Admittedly it was not a particularly free-from-temptation situation for an attractive young married couple (well, not *so* young: Jack was 45 and Janet 29). Janet was down in East Hampton all week with the children, leaving Jack alone weekdays in New York. After a rough day on Wall Street Jack was wont to distract himself in the evening. Inevitably, after a few drinks in the Polo Bar of the Westbury, he would fall into the arms of some woman, who would then be enormously impressed by the fabulous duplex he lived in at 740 Park Avenue, not being told, of course, that it belonged to Jack's father-in-law. My father, who frequently ran into Jack in restaurants, used to remark on how stunningly beautiful these women were. When Jack would return to East Hampton on the weekend, Janet, by comparison, looked something like an old shoe. Occasionally one of these ladies-met-in-New York would show up at some event in East Hampton at which Jack and Janet would be present. Janet would note the easy familiarity between her husband and the woman and would fly into a fury when they returned home.

Once a photographer took a picture of Jack flirting with another woman while in the presence of his wife at a Tuxedo Park horse show. Whether the picture was ever published before it appeared in this book is not known, but it is safe to assume that Janet found out what was happening behind her back and may even have seen the photo, in which Jack is standing at the rail, next to a beautiful young woman, Virginia Kernochan, who, along with Janet, is sitting on the rail. In the picture Jack is holding Miss Kernochan's hand while Janet looks the other way. He was quite obviously doing this in full view of everyone at the show. It was a humiliation Janet would never forget.

Underlying these timeless marital problems there was always the problem of money. The country was in a depression, and Wall Street would simply not pick up. Jack was earning a mere fraction of what he had been making before 1929, when his net worth had been around $750,000. After the repeal of prohibition he had made over $2 million in liquor stocks. But gambling, both in the market and outside of it, and high living had reduced his net worth to just a little over $100,000 in 1936. While his living expenses remained the same, for neither he nor Janet was able to cut down on any of their luxuries, his income had dropped precipitously.

As might be expected, relations between Jack and Janet Bouvier were no better at Old Man Lee's apartment at 740 Park Avenue. Jacqueline's nurse, Bertha Newey, testified at the eventual divorce proceedings that Janet "was always tired and upset so that when you [Jack] arrived home from the office she took it out on you." She further testified that the Lees constantly interfered in the Bouvier household:

BOUVIER: Do you recall that after returning to New York after a very stormy summer in East Hampton, one day Mrs. Lee tried to slap Jacqueline in the face?

NEWEY: Yes.

BOUVIER: What did Jacqueline do to deserve such treatment?

NEWEY: Positively nothing. Mrs. Lee, losing her temper, as she usually did, attempted to slap Jacqueline in the face, and I tried to shield her and received the blow myself, and then I very properly returned it to Mrs. Lee. A grandmother should never slap a child in the face and that's the reason I slapped her.

What effect did all this have on the young Jacqueline? Despite all the mush that has been written about Jacqueline's childhood, particularly by her "official" biographer, Mary Van Rensselaer Thayer, Jacqueline had a very unsettling childhood and, as a consequence, she developed into a very neurotic child. Jackie's immediate family situation, far from being a favorable influence on her growth as a human being, was something *she had to overcome*. We shall see how she eventually learned to turn it to her material advantage.

Further proof of the turbulence of Jacqueline's early family life comes from another employee of the Bouvier household, one Bertha Kimmerle, known as "Mademoiselle," who was employed by the Bouviers from August 1937 to December 1938. In the eventual divorce proceedings she described Jacqueline as "an unusually bright and alert, but high-strung child, a little difficult to manage." As to the Bouvier household, Miss Kimmerle further testified: "the air of the menage was not one of peace or of happiness."

Despite Jacqueline's unsettled, and frequently upsetting, home life, the young girl did fairly well in almost everything she undertook, proving that her own considerable mental and physical endowments were strong enough to overcome the family environment. She was very good at her winter ballet lessons and was a consistently better-than-average student at school, clearly superior to what her future husband was at a similar age. In fact, about the only hint that something was wrong in her young life was her extreme mischievousness and unmanageability at school. At Miss Chapin's in New York, the headmistress, Miss

Stringfellow, was compelled to scold and lecture the young Jacqueline more than any other girl in her class, so fractious and uncooperative was she when she first entered Chapin. Neglected at home by her mother, overindulged by her adoring father, and constantly upset by her parents' quarrels, the little girl had no settling influence at home. It remained for Miss Stringfellow to settle Jackie down. Years later Jacqueline was to confess to a biographer that Miss Stringfellow had been "the first great moral influence" in her life.

Still, the young Jacqueline had a great deal to cope with in her home life, and at the end of that summer of 1936 something happened that sent her little world crashing down around her: she was told that her mother and father were going to separate. The separation agreement, which went into effect on October 1, 1936, stipulated that "the parties mutually agree to continue to live separate and apart from each other for the period of six months from the date of this agreement." Provisions were then made for the termination or extension of the agreement after the six-month period. It was further stipulated that

> Mrs. Bouvier, during the life of this agreement, shall have the custody of the children of said marriage and shall, except as hereinafter provided, maintain, educate, clothe, and support said children until they shall have attained their majority out of payments hereinafter provided to be made by Mr. Bouvier. It is understood and agreed that Mr. Bouvier shall have the right to visit the children at all reasonable times and places and shall have the further right on Saturday afternoons and Sunday mornings to have them with him at his own home or elsewhere as he may wish.

Furthermore, the agreement provided that for the six-month period "Mr. Bouvier agrees to pay to Mrs. Bouvier on the first day of each month, commencing October 1, 1936, $1050 for her support and maintenance and for the support and maintenance of said children."

And so Janet remained with her daughters at the apartment her father owned, and Jack Bouvier moved to one room in the Westbury Hotel. The separation was a severe blow to Jack in many ways, and he never really recovered from it. First of all, he lost continuous association with his beloved daughters, and Jack Bouvier loved his daughters more than anything else in the world. Secondly, he was compelled to shell out half his after-tax income to Janet, leaving him only around $1000 a month to live on. But to further complicate his position, the estate of M. C. Bouvier, deceased, began pressing him for payment of the $25,000 loan M. C. had made him in 1930, and the federal government began pressing him for some $16,045.64 in back taxes—this, in addition to a $23,000 income-tax claim against him that was pending in the courts at the time. It was a bleak situation; the accountant who prepared the figures on which his separation agreement was based calculated that if all real and contingent liabilities were to be settled by the end of the year, John V. Bouvier III's net worth would sink to a mere $56,509.36.

Lee Bouvier at 3 was too young to feel consciously the effects of this catastrophe, but Jackie at 7 felt them intensely and was, as a result, driven more into herself than ever. At subsequent Bouvier family gatherings her aunts and uncles and cousins began to sense an embarrassed, sheepish air about her, as if she were ashamed of something.

It was an altogether perplexing time for the little girl. Now she went to Thanksgiving and Christmas and Easter at Grandfather Bouvier's apartment at 765 Park Avenue without Mummy. All the other cousins had their mothers there, but she didn't. Then, in an effort to counteract the Bouvier influence on her daughter, Janet redoubled her efforts to subject her to the influence of her own family, the Lees. But there was a strained atmosphere in the Lee household because Mr. Lee never spoke to his wife and Mrs. Lee's Irish mother was always hanging around in the wings. Jacqueline didn't like the Lee household—she liked to be with the Bouviers. But this predilection for her father's family enraged Mummy. Finally, after a long period

of utter perplexity, Jacqueline learned to play off one parent against the other. And as she succeeded admirably,
especially with her father, she learned the great lesson of
her life: With a little charm, and a little cunning, you could
get almost anything you wanted out of a man.

After the six-month trial separation was up, a period
marked by profound unhappiness for all concerned, Jack
and Janet decided to try and live together again. The East
Hampton season was about to roll around once more and
Jack was able to convince Janet that it would be "good
for the children" if they spent the summer together out in
their glorious playground on eastern Long Island.

Accordingly, Jack rented a cottage on the dunes for
the season, and as soon as Jacqueline got out of school
the reunited John V. Bouvier III's headed down to their
East Hampton paradise in Jack's maroon Stutz.

Fortunately for posterity we have a document that
tells more or less what went on in that dunes cottage in
the summer of 1937. It is a sworn statement by Jacqueline's
and Lee's governess that summer, Bertha Kimmerle, made
on June 9, 1939, "in the matter of the matrimonial affairs
of John V. Bouvier III and his wife, Janet Lee Bouvier."

Bertha Kimmerle began her long and detailed account, writing:

> I had been in the home of Mr. and Mrs.
> Bouvier for barely a week when I could not
> help but notice that the relations between the
> two were strained and irritable. . . . This at-
> mosphere in the household . . . consisted,
> among other things, in the lack of companion-
> ship on the part of Mr. and Mrs. Bouvier for
> each other. She was a lady that unmistakably
> had a will, and was generally engaged in doing
> what she wanted, when she wanted and where
> she wanted. It was thus a matter, if not daily
> at least of frequent occurrence, that Mrs. Bou-
> vier was not home, and the children, consis-
> tently without their mother, were always in my
> company.

On the other hand Mr. Bouvier was left in his own house quite alone, but his love for the children, and their very joyous love for him, I could easily see. Both were devoted to him, and both sought his company whenever it was possible. This was particularly so when Mrs. Bouvier, day after day, would leave him alone in the house. He seemed to get a real pleasure out of the children's companionship and it was equally clear that they got the same pleasure in romping, playing, and talking with and to him.

This was particularly so in the case of Jacqueline, who, as I have said, was an unusually bright child, with a passionate fondness for horses. Little Lee was a lovable little mouse, not as high-strung or as alert as her sister, but strong, sweet, and affectionate.

Whether it was lack of sympathy on the mother's part, or indifference, or because she was occupied with other thoughts, I do not pretend to say, but I did notice a certain reserve when the children were in the presence of their mother that they never showed when in the presence of their father. Moreover, Mrs. Bouvier was a lady of quick temper which she showed many times toward Mr. Bouvier and which many times she showed toward the children. Indeed I had not been in their home more than ten days when Mrs. Bouvier gave Jacqueline a very severe spanking because the little girl had been too noisy in her play. She would spank Jacqueline quite frequently and became often irritated with the child, but for no reason that I was able to see.

On Sunday, September twenty-sixth, Mrs. Bouvier called her father over to the house. I could gather that she was mad because Mr. Bouvier had not, while in town, gotten himself a lawyer for some purpose. I do know that when the three, that is, Mr. Bouvier, Mr. Lee, and Mrs. Bouvier, were together in a very noisy argument, little Jacqueline rushed up stairs to me and said: "Look what they are doing to my daddy!" and at the time Jacqueline was in tears.

So ended the summer of 1937. In October Janet, Jacqueline, Lee, and Bertha returned to the apartment at 740 Park Avenue, and Jack went to Lasata for some much-needed rest. Later Jack attempted to cohabit with Janet and the children once more at 740 Park, but the experiment did not last very long. Soon he was back in his one room in the Westbury Hotel, and instead of spending his evenings with his beloved daughters he was reduced to prowling the Westbury's Polo Bar. With some of the most beautiful girls in New York dropping in there every evening for cocktails the place was not without its consolations.

What then happened in the fall-winter of 1937–1938? Bertha chronicled it all in her sworn testimony.

Janet evidently plunged into an active social life as soon as she got back to 740 Park. She would stay out late almost every night and not get up until noon the next day, when she would quickly pull herself together for a luncheon date. The children were always left with Bertha, who was later to testify:

> Mrs. Bouvier left the apartment many weekends, leaving the children alone. This I would say occurred at least twice a month during the fall and winter of 1937 and 1938. I recall particularly that Mrs. Bouvier left them on New Year's Eve and was absent on New Year's Day, having gone to Tuxedo with some man. It was at this time that Mr. Bouvier had already left 740 Park Avenue and when the children expressed a great eagerness to see their father, Mrs. Bouvier struck me as being jealous of the children's affections for him. I recall distinctly how this jealousy worked. Little Lee was crying for her father and Mrs. Bouvier said to me: "If

Lee crys [sic] for her father spank her." The child still cried but I did no spanking.

I may truthfully say that Mrs. Bouvier had a very quick and at times violent temper, which she showed not only to Mr. Bouvier, but on many occasions when she was angry with me and with the children to whom she would frequently yell, and yell is the only correct word to use.

And so the winter and spring of 1938 unfolded at the Bouvier household at 740 Park Avenue. Janet was leading a hectic social life involving a continual round of luncheons, bridge parties, dinner parties, and late nights. Jacqueline and Lee were left largely in the care of Bertha Kimmerle. Occasionally Jack Bouvier would slip over to the apartment when Janet was out and have a rousing time playing with his girls. Then on Saturday afternoons, when, as per the separation agreement, he had Jacqueline and Lee all to himself, he would go overboard in indulging his daughters' every whim and fancy.

Saturday afternoons and Sunday mornings thus became very special occasions for Jacqueline and Lee. On Saturday afternoons Jack and his girls would make a round of the shops, picking up expensive toys at F.A.O. Schwarz and clothes at Bloomingdale's and Saks. Then he would take them to a pet shop and let them pick out a dog for a romp in Central Park, telling the pet owner they wanted to try the dog out, that they could not tell whether they really wanted to buy the dog until they had spent some time with the animal in the park. For an hour or two the happy threesome would tear around in the park with the new dog, then Jack would take the animal back to the pet shop and tell the owner they had decided not to take it. The next weekend they would go to a different pet shop and do the same thing with a different dog. This was repeated Saturday after Saturday, to the utter delight of Jacqueline and Lee.

Sunday mornings Jack would arrive at 740 Park Avenue in his black Mercury convertible and would announce his presence with a special honk of the horn. As soon as the girls heard it they would tear out of the apartment, down the elevator, and race through the lobby and out to the car shouting, "Daddy! Daddy! Daddy!"

Jack would then scoop them up in his arms and take them to the car, telling them he had a big secret. "What is it? What is it?" they would scream. "Well," he would say, "between you and me and the lamppost it may be . . ." "What? What?" they would cry. "It may be a, a sundae at Schrafft's . . . or a horseback ride in the park." Then, just as he was about to tell them which it was he would suddenly push them down below the dashboard, gun the accelerator, and cry, "Cheese it, the cops!" whereupon the girls would scream as Jack tore down the avenue in a mock escape from the police.

Oh, Daddy was so much fun to be with! After the horseback ride in the park it would be time for lunch. If it was just an average Sunday he would take them to the Polo Bar of the Westbury for club sandwiches on protein bread, enjoying the admiring stares of the other diners as he strode in, dressed elegantly in a dark-blue pinstripe suit, high, custom-tailored starched collar, homburg on his handsome head, with two of the prettiest little girls in New York.

If it was a special Sunday, a holiday, or a family milestone, he would proudly take his girls to Grandfather Bouvier's for a big family luncheon where Jackie and Lee would have a chance to hug and kiss their adored grandfather and play with all their Bouvier cousins. The lunch, prepared by a cook and served by two maids, would inevitably be a culinary delight, and after huge helpings of shrimp cocktail, stuffed turkey or roast beef, and vanilla ice cream with chocolate sauce and cake, Jack would take his happy girls back to their mother's. As they approached the Lee apartment building, which was only a block away from Grandfather Bouvier's, Jackie and Lee would begin to cry, and once they were back in the care of Bertha (for Janet would rarely be there to greet them), they would be weeping uncontrollably.

The situation was definitely unfair to Janet. She had

them on her hands during the difficult times. Jack had them for the fun times. The fact that they consistently preferred to be with their father drove her to distraction. Soon June rolled around, and this time Janet put her foot down about sharing a house in East Hampton again with Jack. No, this time she was going to rent her *own* place at Bellport, without telling Jack where it was, while Jack rented his usual cottage on the dunes in East Hampton.

What went on in the Bouvier households in Bellport and East Hampton in the summer of 1938? Much of the same. Janet spent most of her time out, and Jacqueline and Lee spent an unhappy summer waiting to join their father in East Hampton. Bernice Anderson, a maid in the Bouvier household, testified at the eventual divorce proceedings:

> The children, with the atmosphere the way it was and their mother highly nervous and irritable, were not happy at Bellport, and Jacqueline frequently spoke about running away and going to her father's house at East Hampton. Once, when her mother was away, Jacqueline asked me to help her find her father's number in the telephone book as she was so unhappy she wanted to talk to him without delay. In fact, I never saw two happier children than the day Mr. Bouvier called for them at Bellport.

That August of 1938 in East Hampton turned out to be one of the happiest times in Jacqueline's and Lee's young lives. For a month Jack and his girls, one 9, the other 5, did everything together. I was in East Hampton myself that summer, staying at Lasata, and I remember well the happy, boisterous times we all had together, the riotous birthday party at Lasata on August 4 for my mother and her twin sister, and the huge family reunion on August 12 to celebrate Grandfather Bouvier's seventy-third birthday. Jack brought his daughters along to both parties at which our irrepressible Aunt Edith, who had the build, and almost the voice, of an opera star, led the singing and many poems were read. In addition to these lively family gatherings, there were, of course, all the wonderful times with the dogs and horses, with King Phar and Danseuse. Jack let nothing, absolutely nothing, stand in the way of giving Jacqueline and Lee the most wonderful summer they ever had.

Jack Bouvier loved to show his beautiful young daughters off to his friends and to parade them before his family. One of his best friends that summer was a certain George de Mohrenschildt, a White Russian émigré who worked in New York and summered in Bellport. De Mohrenschildt was, among other things, a "beau" of Jack's sister, Michelle, who was staying with her father at Lasata. Jack wanted to show off his daughters to de Mohrenschildt, and as soon as he got them from Janet he introduced them to his friend. De Mohrenschildt took to them at once and soon Jack, Jacqueline, Lee, de Mohrenschildt, and Michelle were a happy fivesome, doing everything together. A tall, robust, handsome man, with a self-styled "provocative personality," de Mohrenschildt got to know the whole Bouvier family, including the beleaguered Janet, that summer and became particularly fond of young Jacqueline. After the breakup of Jack and Janet's marriage, and the breakup of his own romance with Michelle, George de Mohrenschildt wound up in Texas, where, by a strange twist of fate, he became the chief mentor and friend of a young man by the name of Lee Harvey Oswald, the husband of another Russian émigré.

According to Bertha Kimmerle, Jack Bouvier

. . . was during this holiday the most careful of fathers, particularly regarding the children's routine day as to their hours of play, a time for rest, a time for their meals, their going to bed, and their swimming exercises in the morning at the beach, and Jacqueline's riding in the afternoon . . . and it is a fact that they were very sorry weeping little girls when Mr. Bouvier's custody came to an end, and they were compelled to return to their mother who was staying with her father, Mr. Lee, in East Hampton.

Janet had, by this time, given up her cottage at Bellport and gone to live with her father. Bertha Kimmerle went along and described what it was like at Mr. Lee's:

> The experience with Mr. Lee, so far as food and routine was concerned, was exactly the opposite as that they had gone through at Mr. Bouvier's. There was really no established hours for meals, and the children would be served with canned foods, canned soup, and canned fruit, as in comparison with the fresh vegetables, fruits, and soups they received at their father's home [all from the garden at Lasata].

After the summer was over, Mr. Lee forced his daughter Janet to give up the duplex in his building at 740 Park Avenue, claiming it was too large for her, and Janet, Jacqueline, and Lee went to live in an apartment Janet rented at 1 Gracie Square. She took Bertha Kimmerle and Bernice Anderson with her. The latter testified to the unhappy life at 1 Gracie Square at the eventual divorce proceedings:

> I was at 1 Gracie Square with Mrs. Bouvier and the children from Oct. 1, 1938, until two or three days before Thanksgiving Day of the same year. Here things were about as they were at Bellport, if not worse. Mrs. Bouvier always stayed in bed until 12:00 o'clock, getting up only in time for lunch. Mrs. Bouvier was highly nervous all during this time that I was with her at this address, and drank even more than at Bellport and almost every night she used to take sleeping pills (Allonal) to put her to sleep. . . . Mr. Lee was a constant dinner guest, at least once a week; they would talk late into the night.

What Janet and Old Man Lee talked about was strategy to nail Jack Bouvier in a divorce action. Bernice Anderson's final testimony in regard to Janet was clearly slanted in Jack Bouvier's favor:

> Jacqueline used to say on many occasions that she hated her mother. Jacqueline and her mother frequently had yelling spells; she would yell at Jacqueline and Jacqueline would yell back at her mother. In fact they both were very highstrung and Mrs. Bouvier seemed to be by far the worse of the two. In closing I would say that the children were not happy with their mother at Bellport or at Gracie Square. They always seemed very happy when they were allowed by their mother to go see their father, in fact it was almost pathetic.

For Jack Bouvier, his 9-year-old daughter, Jacqueline, was everything, his reason for living. And for Jacqueline, her father was what she loved more than anything else in the world. And yet they could not be together. They had to be content with these occasional "visitation periods"—a stolen evening here, a stolen evening there, a Saturday afternoon, a Sunday morning.

To make matters worse Janet and her father were quietly hatching a plot to do away with Jack altogether, to get him totally out of her life. If Janet could divorce Jack Bouvier, and marry again, then she could get the children removed from their father once and for all. Jack, of course, was unwilling to grant Janet a divorce, for the very reason that upon a possible remarriage Janet could make it very difficult for him to see his children.

The only grounds for "absolute divorce" in New York State at the time was adultery. If you could prove adultery you did not have to have the consent of the other partner. Accordingly, Janet and her father devised a plan to trap Jack in an adulterous situation. A detective was hired to shadow Jack Bouvier night and day, and a certain "Scandinavian blonde" was persuaded to entice him. Before long Janet and Old Man Lee had their "evidence."

And so in January 1940, Janet brought a suit for divorce on the grounds of adultery against Jack Bouvier, giving her charges out to the press. On one Friday in early January pictures of Janet, Jacqueline, and Lee appeared in four New York papers in connection with the ugly suit. Soon, because of syndication, the picture and notice of the suit were in almost every city in the country. The text of the article in the January 26, 1940, issue of the New York *Daily Mirror* was as follows:

> SOCIETY BROKER SUED FOR DIVORCE
> A line in the Social Register will be cracked right in two if Mrs. Janet Lee Bouvier of 1 Gracie Square has her way. Mrs. Bouvier asks alimony and custody of two children, Jacqueline and Caroline. Mrs. Bouvier claims the society broker who lives at 765 Park [Jack was then temporarily living with his father] was over friendly with another socialite, Marjorie Berrien, as well as with unnamed women in his summer home in East Hampton.

Janet's reckless publishing of charges of adultery against her husband did have an aftermath, the serious damaging of Jack Bouvier's reputation in New York, and the effect on his two daughters was devastating. At Chapin, Jacqueline had to put up with the snickers of her schoolmates. At Sunday and holiday luncheons at Grandfather Bouvier's, she had to put up with the snickers of her aunts and uncles and cousins. All of a sudden she was the daughter of a black sheep, a man in disrepute, an adulterer! It was all over the papers, all over the country. The little girl was mortally ashamed. From this point on young Jacqueline was to crave one thing above all others: respectability. Somehow she would find a way of overcoming the embarrassment of her parents' divorce.

As it turned out, Janet and her father were unable to make their sensational charges stick, and the suit for divorce on the grounds of adultery in New York State was eventually dropped. Nevertheless, the damage was done. Janet's charges had been published nationwide, but the dropping of them saw not a line of print. Jack was so embittered he agreed to a quickie Nevada divorce, and Janet packed up and went off to Reno with the children.

The period from 1940 to 1942 was a confusing and trying time for Jacqueline and Lee. With their parents divorced and Janet not yet remarried, they were in sort of a disreputable limbo. But, in fact, the entire period of marital squabbles, 1934 to 1942, was a trying and confusing time for Jackie and Lee. When they were with their mother, all they heard were bad things against their father and the Bouviers. When they were with their father, all they heard were bad things about their mother and the Lees.

Eventually, at a certain indeterminate point, Jackie and Lee ceased crying and began playing off one parent against the other. It was a tactic that would stand them in excellent stead when they eventually entered the marital wars themselves against the Radziwills, the Kennedys, and Onassis, far bigger game than their beleaguered parents ever contended with.

29. Up to the Auchinclosses

JANET BOUVIER returned to New York from Reno with her daughters and her divorce decree at the end of July 1940; by August 1 Jack and his girls were reunited in East Hampton. This time Jack had shrewdly rented a house right next to the Riding Club. No sooner did Jacqueline unpack her bags than she raced over to the club to see Danseuse. When she finally was in the stall with her arms around the animal's neck, the tears were streaming down her face. Jack Bouvier was very happy. His house near the Riding Club and Donnie would keep his beloved girls away from Janet, at least for a while.

Janet Bouvier was spending this summer at her new apartment at 1 Gracie Square, going out to East Hampton to visit her father and mother on weekends. But even though she had finally got her divorce, her problems were far from over. She was a 34-year-old divorcée with no marketable skills, other than her attractiveness as a female, living part-time with two daughters on $1050 a month from her ex-husband, wholly dependent on his living up to his divorce agreement. A job was out of the question, because first of all, she couldn't do anything but ride horses, and, secondly, she believed that women of her station should not work. Consequently, her only avenue toward a better life was to find a new husband. Desperately she searched. Her life became an endless round of luncheons, cocktail parties, dinner parties, and late nights in search of the right man.

Her search was, of course, complicated by the fact that the man had to be rich, the richest possible. She had grown up in a large, spacious house with servants, and nothing less than the circumstances in which she had been brought up would suit her. Besides, she had to raise and educate two young daughters with already expensive tastes.

And so the great search wore on. Jack's sisters used to joke about it endlessly. Since the first "heavy beau" Janet acquired after the divorce was a man named Zinsser and she had gone through the alphabet to reach him, they used to laugh about Janet going "from A to Z" in her search. In the end, nothing came of the romance and she was back searching again. Then, one weekend, friends by the name of Meyers invited her down to Washington where they introduced her to a certain Hugh D. Auchincloss, a stockbroker—and a far wealthier one than Jack Bouvier. When that seemed to catch on, Jack's sisters laughed that after going from A to Z, she then went from Z back to A again.

Meanwhile, as Janet was continuing her search for her marital salvation, Jack was having the time of his life with his girls in East Hampton. He took them over to Lasata on August 4 for his twin sisters' birthday; he brought the horses over, too, and he and the girls began giving them daily workouts in the ring in back of the house. Soon Jackie and Lee were back in competition in the local horse shows, and Jack was able to boast to his father that Jackie had "cleaned up," as he used to say, at the East Hampton show, winning everything that she had gone into, including jumping for girls and boys under 20 years of age.

After the summer was over, Jackie and Lee returned to their mother at 1 Gracie Square, and Janet immediately began making it more difficult than ever for her daughters to see their father. Jack was quick to react to this new turn of events. He chided Jacqueline for not phoning him, pointing out to her that since they were now separated the phone was the only thing left that could keep them together. He also pointed out that he was boarding her beloved Danseuse at a stable on West 66th Street, but, if she was not considerate of him, he could easily remove the animal to the country where she would never get a chance to see it.

Meanwhile Janet remained in ill temper over her family situation, marked, as it was, by such an intense rivalry with her ex-husband for the time and affection of her daughters. Admittedly, her position was most awkward. As it turned out, it was left to Mr. Auchincloss of Washington to provide Janet with a new life.

After a courtship of some months, during which time Janet tried hard not to seem too available, Auchincloss proposed and Janet accepted. The two divorcés married in June 1942, at about the time Ambassador Kennedy was opposing lend-lease and John F. Kennedy was seeing action in the Solomons. After a brief honeymoon, the 54-year-old Hugh D. Auchincloss installed his new wife and her daughters in his huge seventy-five-acre Hammersmith Farm, which overlooked Narragansett Bay. They would spend the first summer of their marriage there before Mr. Auchincloss brought his bride back to Merrywood, his vast McClean, Virginia, estate that overlooked the Potomac.

So all of a sudden, Janet was married to a man far wealthier than Jack Bouvier and had two vast estates to command. Friends and former in-laws could not help smiling as they beheld her now in some of her old haunts, like the Colony Club in New York, appearing very much above it all. And later they were to collapse with laughter when they read in the papers and magazines that Janet's own family, the Lees, who were as Irish as blarney and shamrocks, were suddenly promoted to the southern aristocracy, as possible descendants of Robert E. Lee. This piece of genealogical hype is still being propagated by the tour guides of Hammersmith Farm (now a museum, described as a "summer White House 1961–1963").

The Auchinclosses, a most distinguished old family, were clearly a giant step up in the world for the socially ambitious Janet Lee Bouvier. The first Auchincloss, a Scotsman from Paisley, had emigrated to America in 1803, twelve years before the Bouviers and forty-five years before the Kennedys, had entered the dry-goods business, and had done well, though not spectacularly well. One of his sons, John, then married into a family connected to two of the oldest colonial families of New England, the Winthrops and the Saltonstalls. From then on the Auchinclosses made a succession of brilliant marriages, allying themselves to such distinguished American families as the Van Rensselaers, the du Ponts, the Tiffanys, the Vanderbilts, the Jenningses, and the Rockefellers. It was through the Jennings connection that Hugh D. Auchincloss acquired his fortune. His father, Hugh Dudley Auchincloss, Sr., had married Emma Brewster Jennings, daughter of Oliver B. Jennings, one of the founders, along with John D. Rockefeller, of Standard Oil. A large share of the vast Jennings oil fortune was passed down to Emma Auchincloss, who, in turn, passed it on down to her son.

Hugh D. Auchincloss, Jr., known to family and friends as "Hughdie" or "Uncle Hughie," eventually invested a sizable portion of his inheritance in the Washington-based brokerage firm of Auchincloss, Parker, and Redpath, in which he became a general partner. Before marrying Janet Bouvier in 1942 Auchincloss had been wed to Maya Charapovitsky, daughter of a Russian naval officer, from whom he had had a son, Hugh D. III, known as "Yusha." Then in 1935, after divorcing Maya, he had married Nina Gore Vidal, daughter of the blind senator from Oklahoma, T. B. Gore, and mother, by her first marriage, of the eminent author, Gore Vidal. With Nina Gore Vidal, Auchincloss had had two more children, a daughter, Nina Gore, and another son, Thomas Gore, called Tommy.

Thus, when the newlywed Janet Auchincloss brought her daughters Jacqueline, aged 13, and Lee, aged 10, up to Hammersmith Farm, the two Bouvier girls were compelled to adjust to the presence of three other children in the house: Yusha, Nina, and Tommy. Gore Vidal had left the menage upon his mother's divorce from Mr. Auchincloss. Now it would not be long before Janet would cement herself to the Auchinclosses for good by producing from Hughdie two more children: Janet Jr., born in 1945, when Hughdie was 57 and Janet 39, and James, known as Jamie, born in 1947 when his father was 59 and his mother 41.

And so a whole new life suddenly opened up for Jacqueline and Lee Bouvier. They were Auchinclosses now, as well as Bouviers and Lees. Or so it should have been. But while Janet was busy linking herself and her children to the Auchinclosses, Jack Bouvier was not idle. Though he began circulating a slogan around the Stock Exchange after the marriage—"Take a loss with Auchincloss"—in reality, he was not about to take a loss with Auchincloss.

He redoubled his efforts to weld his beloved daughters to his own family, and in so doing he started a battle for the loyalty and affections of Jacqueline and Lee that was to drag on for the next fourteen years and in the course of those years profoundly influence the character of the future First Lady.

The first thing he did was to insist that Jackie and Lee spend the summer of 1942 with him in East Hampton. Thus, no sooner had they been brought to Hammersmith Farm after their mother's June wedding to Hughdie than they were shipped down to Long Island to join their father. To lure them down, Jack kept their horses at the East Hampton Riding Club, not permitting them to be sent to Newport under any circumstances.

For Jack Bouvier, the summer of 1942 was one of the best he ever enjoyed. Not only did he have his girls for an entire month, he also fell in love. The lady in question was a young, attractive English woman who was married to an officer in the British army, temporarily attached to the Pentagon. While the Britisher labored away in Washington, his wife spent the summer frolicking in East Hampton. It wasn't long before she met the handsome, dashing Jack Bouvier, and it wasn't long after that that she was spending nights in Jack Bouvier's rented house on the dunes. I first became aware of her existence in early August, when, upon entering the men's section of the Bouvier cabana at the Maidstone Club one day, I beheld Uncle Jack entwined with this lovely lady on the floor of the shower room. Soon she became virtually a member of the family.

Uncle Jack's British ladyfriend made a very big

impression on me that summer, and I was only Jack Bouvier's 13-year-old nephew. The romance had every tongue in the Bouvier family wagging. Since, in those days, couples in East Hampton, especially at the Maidstone Club, were not particularly demonstrative of their affections, it was exciting to see Jack Bouvier and his British lady together. They walked arm in arm, they held hands, they hugged and kissed unabashedly, they made love wherever they found themselves: in the Bouvier cabana, at Jack's house, behind the dunes. Jack, no doubt, knew that Jackie and Lee would carry back tales of the beautiful young woman to Newport for Janet's entertainment.

In any case, Jack had a marvelous time that summer with his three women. They rode together. They swam together. They went to parties together. Jack even brought his love to Bouvier family gatherings at Lasata, where she was practically treated as his wife. In time the liaison would have fateful consequences and would be a source of tremendous concern to Jacqueline when she became First Lady, but that is another story.

Although Jack Bouvier had had a surprisingly enjoyable summer in 1942, when fall rolled around it was another matter. Now his two darlings were no longer a few blocks away from his New York apartment, they were way down in McClean at Merrywood. Now he had to be content with an occasional letter or phone call from his daughters.

To further distress him, business on Wall Street was not what it used to be. With the new regulations Joe Kennedy had instituted, it was getting harder and harder for an in-and-out trader like Jack Bouvier to make any decent money.

As it turned out, Jackie and Lee did not come up to New York for Thanksgiving because Janet wanted to have them spend the first Thanksgiving of her new marriage with their stepfather. Jack was desolate, and he confided a new doubt to my mother and father—he was beginning to wonder whether his daughters really loved him. There never had been any question before about the bond between him and Jacqueline. But now Jacqueline had a new man in her life. It would not be long before Jack entered into a bitter and protracted rivalry with Auchincloss, and it would not be long either before Jackie learned to play the rivalry for all it was worth. To get something out of Daddy, all she had to do was mention Uncle Hughdie. And to get something out of Mummy and Uncle Hughdie all she had to do was mention Daddy. Thus her sharply divided family life became a valuable schooling in personal relations, making her a far shrewder person than she would have been had her parents remained united. Jacqueline Bouvier's link to the Auchinclosses was to have far-reaching consequences in her life. If her mother had not married Mr. Auchincloss, it is doubtful whether Jacqueline would have ever met and married John F. Kennedy.

30. The Battle for Jacqueline

THE FOURTEEN-YEAR BATTLE between Jack Bouvier and the Auchinclosses for the time, affections, and loyalty of Jacqueline and Lee Bouvier was waged largely between East Hampton and Newport in the summer and New York and Washington the rest of the year. Although it was merely a protracted family quarrel, its outcome would have a fleeting influence on the history of the United States.

Each side in the struggle had its specific advantages and handicaps. Jack Bouvier was a much more charming man than Hughdie Auchincloss and much more fun to be with, but Auchincloss had much more money than Bouvier had, and he possessed a decided temperamental advantage: He was calm and cool in a crisis and Jack was not.

Jack Bouvier was not, strictly speaking, an alcoholic, but he had a tendency to drink excessively in a crisis. He got terribly drunk at his mother's funeral in 1940. On low-volume days on Wall Street he would return home from the office and drown his sorrows. When he didn't hear from Jacqueline and Lee for weeks he would drink away his pain. Hugh Auchincloss was just the opposite. Nothing ever seemed to phase him, or fluster him. It was this characteristic that was to be decisive in the battle for Jacqueline.

Nevertheless, the early returns seemed to be in Jack's favor, and 1943, to Jack's surprise, became a very good year. Jackie and Lee had difficulty adjusting to the Auchincloss menage in Virginia and missed their Daddy very much. Uncle Hughdie wasn't nearly as much fun to be with as Daddy. And the Auchincloss children could not help but regard Jackie and Lee as intruders. Jack was easily able to lure his girls up to New York for Easter and to East Hampton for August.

Actually, the most important loss Jack took that summer was his wartime love, who returned to England with her husband. Some months after her return, she surprised Jack by informing him she had given birth to twins, a boy and a girl, reminding him that she hadn't been living with her husband nine months before their birth, but with him. She hastened to add, though, that she and her husband were going to bring the twins up as their own children. Jack swallowed this momentous news and did not tell his daughters, but Jackie was to find out on her own one day, and the realization was to worry her to death when the Kennedys began trying to build up her image.

Even though he was not nearly as wealthy as Hugh Auchincloss, Jack Bouvier soon found that the most effective way of manipulating his daughters was through money. Both Janet and Hughdie were very tight with their money, and Janet wanted Jack to pay for everything for Jacqueline and Lee, from their toothbrushes to their tuition. Consequently Jackie and Lee became wholly dependent on their father financially. Jack took advantage of that dependence by paying their way when they did his bidding and withholding all largesse when they did not. After a while he began accusing them of taking advantage of him, of getting in touch with him only when they were up against it financially. "You come visit me in New York only when you are absolutely broke," he told Jacqueline, "then as soon as you collect your check you disappear and spend it like water." Money was too hard to make, he continually advised her, for her to throw it away so recklessly.

On January 17, 1948, his father, Major Bouvier, died, and Jack, as one of the executors of the will was involved in the settling of the estate. Among other matters, there were legacies of $3000 to each grandchild of John V. Bouvier, Jr., including, of course, Jacqueline, Lee, and me. It was the first significant money any of us had ever received up to that time.

Because Janet was worried that Jack would try and gamble with her daughters' $6000 inheritance, she and Jacqueline and Lee began badgering him about what he was going to do with the money. Considerably annoyed by this, he assured them that he had no intention of putting the money into stocks, because he felt that stock was not a suitable investment for young women. In the end he put the money into U.S. Treasury bills, which at the time paid next to nothing.

Jacqueline, meanwhile, had entered Vassar in the fall of 1947, much to Jack's delight, and he wholeheartedly undertook to pay her entire tuition there, plus books and living expenses, happily aware that it was much farther from Poughkeepsie to Merrywood than it was from Poughkeepsie to New York.

But Jack's adversaries were not inactive. One way or another Janet Auchincloss would lure her daughter away from her father's grasp. One way was to schedule dental appointments for Jacqueline in Washington rather than in New York. This, however, only succeeded in enraging Jack to the extent that he refused to pay his daughters' dental bills unless they went to a New York dentist.

Besides keeping a wary eye out for Janet and the Auchinclosses, Jack also kept a vigilant eye out for the boys in his daughter's life. He took a very protective attitude, becoming particularly annoyed at Jacqueline once when she went to New Haven to see a boy who purposely kept her until after the last bus had gone back to Poughkeepsie, forcing Jackie to return to Vassar as best she could. Calling him a cad and a bastard, he told Jackie that she should always make herself hard to get and not jump at any short-notice invitation from a boy. Never let a boy think you are easy, he advised her.

As the year 1948 wore on, and summer approached, Jack began to get nervous over whether his daughters would want to spend some time with him in East Hampton or would forsake him for Newport. Unfortunately for his prospects, Lasata had been willed not to him but to his twin sisters, Maude and Michelle, so he no longer had that as a lure. In fact, to use the stables and the riding ring he would now have to ask permission of his sisters.

As his anxiety over the summer began to mount, and he heard nothing of his daughters' plans, he grew extremely upset with them. When they wrote asking for money, he told them that he was fed up with never hearing from them unless they needed their allowances. Finally Jacqueline broke the awful news to him: She was going to spend the summer in Europe. Reacting sharply, he reminded her that he was only told of the trip after all her plans had been made and that he imagined Janet was behind the whole junket because it was to take place precisely during the time when Jackie was supposed to be visiting him. However, in the end, he confessed that the trip would probably have educational value, and he approved it on condition that upon her return, she spend at least one week with him before going back to school. If she did not agree to this he would cut off her allowance for good and not give her any spending money for her European trip. He proposed that they discuss these matters over dinner at 7:30 P.M., May 16.

Jacqueline kept her appointment with her father and evidently poured on all her charm, for by the end of her visit Jack had not only agreed to help pay for her trip to Europe, but had also given in to her plan to redecorate his apartment, something she had been wanting to do for a long time.

The pattern of transgression and chastisement, followed by forgiveness after an effusion of charm, was one that would be repeated over and over again in Jackie's life. At first she dimly perceived how potent her charm could be. Then, as it got her out of more and more scrapes and won her more and more unexpected rewards, she finally realized she held a weapon that could charm favors out of even the most powerful men in the world.

As it turned out, the redecoration project irked Jack Bouvier not a little. His apartment at 125 East 74th Street was rather drab and staid; still, Jack was not convinced of any need to refurbish it. Telling Lee that he believed Jackie came to his apartment not to see him but only to redecorate the place, he canceled the $201.58 worth of draperies Jackie had ordered from Bloomingdale's and called off all future redecorating plans. Future victims of Jackie's redecorating mania would not be so successful at dismantling her plans.

After the redecorating project fell through, Jacqueline took off for her first trip to Europe. She went with fellow Vassarites Julia Bissell of Wilmington and Helen and Judy Bowdin, stepdaughters of Edward F. Foley, Jr., undersecretary of the Treasury at the time. The four girls were chaperoned by a Vassar teacher, Miss Helen Shearman.

Through Secretary Foley an invitation was wangled for Jacqueline and her friends to attend a royal garden party at Buckingham Palace, where they met King George VI and Queen Elizabeth and had a chance to shake hands with Winston Churchill. It was the 19-year-old Jacqueline's first glimpse of royalty, and it thrilled her to the bone.

In the fall of 1948 Jackie returned to Vassar, Lee returned to Miss Porter's, Jack returned to his apartment at 125 East 74th Street, and the same family pattern as in previous years unfolded with depressing predictability.

Eventually the two girls became embroiled in a rivalry over what their father did for them. Lee complained that Jackie got a lot more out of Jack than she did, and Jackie complained that her father did more for Lee than for her. Jack complained that both girls continually exploited him.

Jackie and Lee also criticized their father for his girlfriends, several of whom were not much older than they were. To their relentless taunts he would reply that he would much rather go out with the girl in question (who was almost never someone from his own class or milieu) than what he would refer to as "those old bags in Newport," such as Mrs. Fahnestock, Mrs. Douglas, or Miss Holmsen, who were supposed to represent society.

Relations between Jack Bouvier and his daughters continued in this stormy way throughout the fall of 1948;

then, upon the advent of the new year, Jack suddenly took his older daughter to task. He accused her of being out-rageously extravagant, of charging countless items of cloth-ing to him without his permission. He chided her for blowing her entire monthly allowance on just one dress. He accused her of being selfish, telling her that the trait was going to get her into a great deal of trouble. As evidence of her selfish attitude, he cited a recent discussion they had had about his will and some of its bequests; during that dis-cussion she had argued against one legatee's getting any-thing at all. Jack observed that Janet had never been generous in her whole life, and he advised Jackie not to become like her mother but to be more generous toward others.

Despite these occasional outbursts, life went on and Jack's relationship with his girls continued as before. If he was not inveighing against them over preferring the Au-chincloss world to his, he was forever giving them advice on how to behave with men. He told Lee that he was delighted that she had come to the conclusion that most men were "rats." Jacqueline, he observed, was a pretty good example of a girl who played the field, and he advised Lee to follow her lead.

But he reserved his most fervent advice on men for Jacqueline. Over and over again he would tell her never to forget that all men are disreputable, that she should always make the boys come to her, that she should never go after them or show them that she liked them, for that was absolutely fatal.

It was in the spring of 1949 that Jacqueline was ac-cepted into the Smith Group Junior Year Abroad program, which, for her, meant an academic year at the Sorbonne in Paris, commencing the fall of 1949. Jack was delighted she was admitted and told her so in several letters he wrote her throughout the spring of that year. It was undoubtedly an honor, and so far as Jack's purposes were concerned, it promised to keep Jackie out of the Auchinclosses' clutches for at least a year.

At about this time Jackie and her father began to devote some thought to what Jackie would do the year after she returned from the Sorbonne. Jackie was fed up with Vassar. She had not taken to college campus life and spent every weekend in New York or Washington or at some men's college. Furthermore, the Vassar girls had not particularly taken to her, for they had refused to admit her to the Daisy Chain, an honor analogous to being tapped for an important sorority. This rejection fell as a hard blow upon young Jacqueline's pride, and she became determined not to have anything to do with Vassar anymore.

For a while she toyed with the idea of dropping out of college altogether and becoming a photographer's model in New York. This idea, however, did not appeal to her father. Although he was fully aware that Jackie was unhappy at Vassar, and was willing to countenance the idea that she spend her senior year in New York studying designing and drawing, Jack Bouvier was against having his elder daughter work as a fashion model. And that was that.

Jack proposed that after her year in Europe Jackie should come live with him in New York and take a part-time job in his office at fifty dollars a week. Telling her that she would probably be a good influence on him, helping him to keep out of trouble, he reminded her that by living in his apartment she would save rent and utilities and so could spend her salary on clothes and cosmetics. Since she would be working only part-time, he added, she would have all the time in the world to pursue her interest in drawing and designing.

Not long after Jack spun out his dream for Jackie's future, she disappointed him once again by choosing Merrywood over him. Jack had hoped she would visit him over Easter vacation (1949); however, not only did she not visit him, she didn't even have the courtesy to phone him Easter Sunday! Angrily he told her that if that was what she wanted she could stay at Merrywood for good, adding that if she did he would cut off her allowance and her charge accounts at Bloomingdale's and Saks. He also told her in this outburst that she hadn't made the Daisy Chain at Vassar because the other girls realized she had no school spirit, what with her spending every college weekend off the campus and not participating in any extracurricular activities.

Meanwhile Jack made arrangements to have Jacqueline stay with him at a rented cottage in East Hampton from July 14 to 31. From there she would go to Hammersmith Farm in Newport. And on August 24 she would sail with the Smith Group for her year of study in Europe. Jack Bouvier was apparently somewhat reluctant to go to East Hampton this particular summer because of the presence of the hated Lees. He could not abide his former father-in-law, James T. Lee, and Mr. Lee could not abide him. But since they both belonged to the same club, they could not very easily avoid one another. In fact, to get from the Bouvier cabana to the beach one had to pass directly in front of the Lee cabana. Thus Jack would be compelled to walk past the glowering Old Man Lee every day on his way to take his morning swim. Telling Jackie how much this pained him, Jack confessed that he only put up with the ordeal because of the love he still had left for his favorite daughter.

Jackie did join her father in East Hampton, and for two weeks they swam and sunned at the Maidstone, rode horses at the Riding Club, and went to dinners and parties at the Devon Yacht Club. On August 5, after a wonderful reunion, Jackie took off for Auchincloss country. Jack fully expected to receive some word of thanks from his daughter after she left, but none came. Angrily he reminded her that during the two weeks following her stay with him she had never phoned him once. And she had spent twenty days with him in East Hampton, charging all her expenses at the Maidstone Club to him and buying half a dozen dresses and two steamer trunks for her forthcoming trip to Europe! It was especially galling to him because while she was with him she had made at least two long-distance calls an evening to her mother, at his expense, and it was he, of course, who was paying for her Smith Group year at the Sorbonne.

It must have been something of a relief for Jack Bouvier when his elusive Jacqueline sailed for Europe on August 24. Now he didn't have to worry anymore about her preferring Hammersmith Farm or Merrywood to 125 East 74th Street. And he could safely nurture those dreams about Jackie living with him upon her return and working in his firm on Wall Street.

To Jack Bouvier's surprise and delight, his relations with his older daughter actually improved while she was in Europe for her year of study in France. The only thing that really worried him about Jackie's spending a year in Europe was the possibility that she might get emotionally involved with some no-good Frenchman or Italian, two breeds of men Jack Bouvier had a low opinion of, despite his own French ancestry. He therefore kept a steady stream of advice flowing across the Atlantic, writing her at least once a week. When Jacqueline, attending an intensive French language program at the University of Grenoble, expressed a desire to go to Corsica, Jack strongly advised her not to go, informing her that Corsica was a very tough place and indulging in a long harangue about how she was a striking-looking girl who would easily attract the unwanted attention of men wherever she went.

After completing her language course at Grenoble and taking a trip to Italy, Jacqueline settled down to life in Paris, staying with the Countess de Renty, at 78 Avenue Mozart, in the 12th arrondissement. The Countess was a widow whose husband had died in a German concentration camp. With her daughter, Claude, who was exactly Jackie's age, she lived off a small independent income and took in boarders. She did all the cooking for the seven boarders in her household. There wasn't much heat in the apartment, and Jackie was forced to do most of her studying in bed under a heavy quilt. It was a somewhat dreary life, as the courses at the Sorbonne, all in French, were quite demanding, and the winter weather was generally bad. For occasional relief from her routine, Jackie would go horseback riding in the Bois de Boulogne.

Jacqueline took advantage of the Christmas break at the Sorbonne to do some more traveling in Europe. Among the places she went was England, and among the people she looked up there was her father's former wartime sweetheart, with whom she had become very friendly. It had been about eight years since the woman had left the States with her husband. Jackie knew the lady had had twins shortly after her return, but she never had been told whose children they were. Now, on her vacation jaunt to England, Jackie came face to face with the twins, and to her utter consternation saw that they were almost exact replicas of herself! The same broad faces, the same wide-apart eyes, the same prominent chins, the same dark hair, the same complexion. They were Bouviers, all right; they were *her* brother and sister. We do not know whether she said anything about it to her hosts at the time, but, as soon as she got a chance, she wrote her father about it. Jack replied in January that Jacqueline was dead right about the twins.

The confirmation must have hit the impressionable 20-year-old Jacqueline like a thunderbolt. Her father had concealed his paternity of the twins for all these years! And she and Lee had had this real, live, blood brother and this real, live, blood sister over there in England for all this time! This was indeed a terrible secret that no one should ever know. Zealously Jacqueline guarded it, and when her first husband, John F. Kennedy, began to rise in American political life, she lived in constant fear that somehow, sometime, the secret would leak out. As it turned out, her fears proved unfounded, for the secret never spread beyond her family and that of her British half-brother and half-sister, both of whom eventually died tragic deaths while only in their twenties.

Not long after Jacqueline returned to Paris from her Christmas vacation travels, something came up that bothered Jack very much. Jackie informed him that the Auchinclosses were coming over to travel with her in Europe during February. This was ominous news indeed. Anxiously he expressed the hope that her mother and her husband would not interfere with Jackie's work.

As it turned out, Jacqueline traveled extensively with her mother and stepfather, even visiting Hitler's retreat in Berchtesgaden and the former Nazi concentration camp at Dachau, outside Munich. Jack himself would have loved to have been the one accompanying her, but it was not to be. Nor was it to be in the future either. He had been hoping against hope that he would be able to visit Jackie in Europe himself, possibly at Easter, but while he was dreaming, she had made other plans. All of a sudden, in response to his overtures about coming over for Easter, she told him she was going to Spain "with a friend." Severely piqued by this, he retaliated by telling her that Lee was now the apple of his eye, his right eye, and that she perhaps was now the apple of his left.

What irked Jack no end was the fact that he was footing the bill for her entire stay abroad and he was not able to visit her, yet the Auchinclosses, who were not contributing a cent to her studies or her upkeep, were able to visit her and enjoy her company. What would she do, he asked, if he couldn't find time to send her her allowance on the fifteenth of the month?

But Jacqueline knew what she was doing. She knew that all she had to do was write her father a couple of charming, loving letters, and he would continue sending her allowance and paying for her year in France. Meanwhile, she could cry poor to her mother and Uncle Hughdie and wangle a little money out of them too.

Then one day Jacqueline scared Jack to death by writing him that she now had a glamorous beau who was on the staff of Premier Bidault. This was bad news for Jack indeed. Anxiously he told her not to get involved with this man, observing that a man who is an attaché always is more polished than other men. He urged her not to fall for that glamorous attaché, to take her time. She had plenty of that ahead of her. He begged her to wait until she was 23. Then she could do as she pleased, provided, of course, he liked the guy. As it worked out, Jacqueline was to heed her father's advice not to get deeply involved with anybody until she was 23. It was in her twenty-third year that she became engaged to John F. Kennedy.

Meanwhile, Jack Bouvier continued to dream of Jackie's future. She still did not want to return to "that damn Vassar" after her year at the Sorbonne and was toying with the idea of staying with her father in New York. It was an idea that gave Jack Bouvier immense happiness as he sat in his drab little apartment at 125 East 74th Street with his housekeeper, Esther, and discussed the furnishings for Jackie's room and the organization of the menage upon Jackie's return.

But Jack, in indulging these dreams, was underestimating Janet Auchincloss. For Janet, as usual, was not inactive. When, during her trip with Hughdie to see Jackie in Europe in the winter of 1950, Janet heard of some of these tentative New York plans, she became determined to thwart, at all cost, Jack Bouvier's plans to have his daughter live with him in New York.

Janet realized she had to exploit both Jackie's intense dislike of Vassar and her great love of Merrywood, with its wonderful riding country and serene views of the Potomac. What better way than to find a college for her in the Washington, D.C., area that would accept all her Vassar and Sorbonne credits and enable her to graduate on schedule? Or perhaps there were other possibilities. *Anything* would be preferable than to have Jackie go live with her father in New York.

Among the several possibilities Janet came up with was *Vogue* magazine's Prix de Paris contest. The winner was to receive the opportunity of spending six months in *Vogue*'s Paris office as a salaried editor. Janet sent Jackie the entry blanks; Jackie filled them in, wrote the obligatory essay on "People I Wish I Had Known," and won the contest. It was a great honor and a great opportunity: six salaried months in Paris on the staff of a great international fashion magazine.

So that was one possibility. Another was to get Jackie admitted to a university in Washington. When Janet and Hughdie returned to Merrywood after seeing Jackie in Europe, they went at this with a vengeance, finally paving the way for Jackie to enter George Washington University in the fall of 1950 as a senior.

In the end, the Auchinclosses dictated and Jacqueline obeyed. Jacqueline was not to go to New York and live with her father and work in his office. Furthermore, Jacqueline was to renounce the *Vogue* Prix de Paris. One year in Paris was quite enough in the eyes of the Auchinclosses. After a summer in Europe Jacqueline was to return and enter George Washington University in Washington, D.C.

When Jacqueline finally got around to telling her father about George Washington University, he was predictably angry and disappointed. He finally gave up all hope of ever having his beloved daughter live with him in New York. From this point on, Bouvier family members felt that Jack went into something of a decline. Imitating his eccentric sister Edith, he began leading an increasingly reclusive existence. He was almost 60 now, and the only life prospect that ever gave him any real hope and expectancy and joy was that of having Jackie live with him in New York and work in his firm. With that hope dashed by Janet, what was there left to live for?

In May 1950 Jack Bouvier underwent a serious cataract operation that left him weak and dispirited and away from Wall Street for two months. He rented a cottage in East Hampton for July and August, hoping his daughters would join him in his convalescence, but neither one of them had the compassion or thoughtfulness to come. Jackie continued her European travels, and Lee trotted off to a summer at Larry Larom's dude ranch in Valley, Wyoming, while Jack lashed out at his "ungrateful" daughters.

All was not bleak, however. On the same day that Jack fired off his salvos at Jackie and Lee, Jackie sent him a telegram from the *S.S. Liberté* announcing that she would be home shortly. Her ship would dock at 4 P.M. the following day at Pier 88, West 48th Street. Overjoyed, Jack sent her a most revealing telegram:

> CAN'T WAIT   HURRY HURRY   YOU CAN LEAVE
> EVERYTHING AT MY APARTMENT INCLUDING
> YOURSELF   LOVE   DAD

The intensity of feeling expressed in the telegram was evidence of the special relationship Jack Bouvier had with his older daughter. She was not only his favorite daughter, she was his "best girl," the great love of his life. To see Jack Bouvier walking arm in arm with Jacqueline down Park Avenue in the early fifties was to see a most distinguished-looking gentleman with a most beautiful young lady who seemed, from their affectionate attitude toward one another and animated conversation, involved in a very special relationship. Whatever it cost Jack Bouvier, emotionally and financially, to maintain Jacqueline, it was worth it in the end. For, as things had been going in his life, Jackie was virtually his whole reason for being.

1950 had been a trying year for the aging Jack Bouvier. In addition to his long and painful illness, he had had to witness the sale of Lasata by his twin sisters (which they accomplished primarily to pay him a cash bequest from his father's estate) and the subsequent dismantling of the house and stables, an event that effectively put an end to the grand era of the Bouvier family. Reacting somewhat petulantly to the whole situation, he went over to the great house just before it was to be consigned to the new owner's agent and indiscriminately tagged dozens of Bouvier family papers and heirlooms for destruction. When my mother and I arrived in a station wagon in April 1950 to cart away the last contents of the house, I was startled to see that Uncle Jack had tagged many historically important items for the pyre. I was a history major at Princeton at the time and to me this was sacrilege. Quickly I gathered up all the old Bouvier family photographs, the Civil War letters of Louise Vernou Bouvier to her son, and all the private papers of Michel Bouvier the first, M. C. Bouvier, and Lasata's former owner, John Vernou Bouvier, Jr.—all these in addition to several old Bouvier ancestral oil portraits and other valuable family memorabilia. Many of these letters and documents were to appear in my book *The Bouviers*, and some of them appear for the first time in this book. The irony of the situation was that it was Jack Bouvier's daughter, Jacqueline, whose career was to make the Bouvier papers historically significant, and yet if Jack had had his way not one scrap of Bouvier family history would have escaped the incinerator.

At any rate, the sale of what had been the focal point of the Bouvier family for so many years was a blow to Jack and all the family. (The estate was sold for $40,000; today it is worth around $10 million.) Now, whenever we went to East Hampton we no longer had the radiant, spacious Lasata to stay in; we were reduced to staying in small inns and motels. Now, Jack, Jacqueline, and Lee no longer had a place to board their horses and a ring of their own to ride in. Could Jack ever hope to coax Jacqueline and Lee down to East Hampton again with Lasata no longer in the family? It was doubtful, when they had the vast Hammersmith Farm in Newport at their disposal.

Jack Bouvier was in a despairing mood in the winter of 1951 when something happened that suddenly changed everything: Jackie fell in love with a young Wall Street stockbroker by the name of John G. W. Husted, Jr., son of a prominent New York banker. Husted, like Jack Bouvier, had graduated from Yale, and his parents, who lived in Bedford Village, in Westchester County, shared many acquaintances of Jack Bouvier's. The Bouviers and the Husteds were of the same world, and this meant that if Jackie married John chances were Jackie would be removed from Auchincloss country forever.

Thanks to Jackie's infatuation with the young Husted she visited New York much more often than she would have had she not been involved with him. This was a great consolation to Jack, because when she was in the city she stayed, of course, in his apartment. For some four months or so the relationship prospered; Jackie went to Bedford to meet Husted's parents, and Husted presented Jackie with a diamond and sapphire engagement ring that had belonged to his mother. Then, after an engagement party given by the Auchinlosses at Merrywood, Janet began thinking very seriously about the whole thing. And the more she thought about it, the more she disliked it.

The big question was money. Upon querying Husted, Janet learned he was making $17,000 a year. That was not a bad income in 1951 for a young man just starting out on Wall Street, but it wasn't enough for Janet. Jack Bouvier was making around $45,000 a year in 1951 and Janet's husband, Hughdie, was making in excess of $100,000. $17,000 a year looked terribly paltry to her. Furthermore, after making discreet inquiries, she learned that the Husted family fortune was not very substantial; it was unlikely that young John might someday come into a significant inheritance.

Money meant everything to Janet, and so she told Jackie bluntly that she could not afford to marry John Husted. Janet had her eyes set on far bigger game for Jackie than a $17,000-a-year stockbroker, no matter how nice he was. Janet wasn't sure who that big game would be, but, judging from her own marital luck, something promising was bound to turn up. After all, hadn't she once been on the beach with nothing but Jack Bouvier's $1050 a month to keep her body and soul together, when, lo and behold, none other than Hugh D. Auchincloss had suddenly appeared? Monday she had been living with her back up against the wall, and Tuesday she was the mistress of two vast estates. Who knew? Something like that could turn up for Jackie, too.

But, of course, Janet's plans for her daughters were always at variance with Jack's, and as the two girls came of marriageable age the distances, emotional and geographical, between Jack and Jacqueline and Lee widened.

By January 1, 1951, those daughters were back at their old tricks. All day, New Year's Day, Jack Bouvier waited in his apartment at 125 East 74th Street for the calls from Jacqueline and Lee. But the calls never came. The girls' thoughtlessness was crushing. Jack Bouvier entered 1951, his sixtieth year, feeling abandoned and alone.

Nevertheless, he still held out hope for Jackie and Lee to visit him in East Hampton that summer. Then the two girls dashed those hopes by announcing they were going to take a long trip through Europe, a trip to be financed by Janet and Uncle Hugh. They embarked on June 7, 1951, only a week after Jacqueline first met Representative John F. Kennedy, and remained abroad until September 15, 1951.

Jacqueline and Lee subsequently memorialized the trip in a whimsical and often charming book they wrote in 1951, just after the trip was over, entitled *One Special Summer*. The book remains one of the few revealing statements Jackie and Lee ever made about themselves and was written and illustrated with exceptional wit and charm.

It reveals, first and foremost, the Bouvier sisters' sense of humor. From reading their account, it appears they simply laughed their way through Europe. They saw the ridiculous in everything and were constantly making fun of everyone they met—of everyone, that is, but Bernard Berenson, the American art dealer and scholar of the Italian Renaissance, whom they looked up in Florence.

For a day the Bouvier sisters visited Berenson at Vallambrosa. The first thing they talked about was love, and the first thing Berenson wanted to know was "Why did Mummy divorce Daddy?" The question went unanswered in *One Special Summer*, but the girls did record that Berenson advised, "Never follow your senses—marry someone who will constantly stimulate you—and you him."

"The only way to exist happily is to love your work," he told these two young beauties, who would never work until circumstances more or less compelled them to when they were both widows in their forties. "Anything you want, you must make enemies and suffer for," he went on. "Don't waste your life with diminishing people who aren't stimulating, be with life-enhancing people." After the Berenson episode, the Bouvier sisters' narrative turned hilarious again as they ridiculed nearly every human being they met on their subsequent travels to Spain, Rome, Naples, and Venice. Their most devastating satire was reserved for a group of United States senators they met in Madrid.

Nowhere in the entire narrative is the U.S. representative from Massachusetts mentioned—nor is Jack Bouvier, although Janet and Uncle Hugh are given a few lines.

One of the last pages in *One Special Summer* carries a montage entitled *Dreams of Glory*. It depicts Lee in a long gown with a most aristocratic expression on her face; it is captioned, "Carolina, Duquesa de Bronxville." Jackie, in a regal costume and a crown, is described as "Jacqueline, Fille Naturelle de Charlemagne."

These two youthful dreams of glory are most revealing. The Bouvier sisters did not dream of themselves as someday representing something on their own, like Lee

Bouvier, interior decorator, or Jacqueline Bouvier, editor, as young girls today would dream. They saw themselves as aristocrats in relation to some man—Lee as the wife of a duke and Jacqueline as the daughter of an emperor. Curiously enough, both were to achieve these dreams. Lee went on to marry a prince, and Jackie became the wife of two modern-day "monarchs," both much older than herself. Jacqueline at 21, then, did not envision herself as a wife, but as a daughter of some immensely powerful man, as a fairy-tale princess. It was an attitude she never quite relinquished.

After the one special summer in Europe, Jacqueline's third extended stay on the Continent, she returned to Merrywood and through the auspices of Uncle Hugh landed the inquiring camera girl job with the *Washington Times-Herald,* which, in turn, propelled her into seeing John F. Kennedy again. Thus it was that taking the job Hugh Auchincloss had found for her, rather than the job her father had offered her, was crucial in determining her fate.

By the spring of 1953, the battle for Jacqueline included a third contender, the freshman senator from Massachusetts. As the relationship developed, Jacqueline began to worry about the problem of introducing him to her father. Knowing only too well her father's anti–New Deal, anti–SEC, and anti–Joe Kennedy feelings, she was justified in experiencing some trepidation.

The fateful meeting finally took place in a New York restaurant one spring evening, and to Jackie's immense relief the two men hit it off beautifully. It was almost impossible not to like Jack Kennedy. His charm was simply too overwhelming. No one could resist it. As the evening wore on, Jacqueline was the one who found herself somewhat left out, so animatedly did Jack Kennedy and Jack Bouvier talk to one another. Soon Jack Bouvier was taking his prospective son-in-law to the New York Stock Exchange luncheon club and was showing him around the trading floor of the Exchange.

When Jack Bouvier finally did bestow his blessing

on their engagement, he did it with the sure feeling he had made a friend in Jack Kennedy and would not therefore lose his daughter entirely.

Meanwhile, Lee had announced her engagement to Michael Canfield, son of the publisher Cass Canfield and member of the staff of Winthrop Aldrich, American ambassador to Great Britain. The wedding was set for April 18 in Washington, and Jack Bouvier was to give the bride away.

Although he was very proud of Lee, Jack Bouvier did not relish the thought of attending the reception at Merrywood under the eyes of Janet, Uncle Hugh, and Old Man Lee. Steeling himself for the ordeal, he took the train from New York to Washington under the watchful eye of my mother and her twin sister, who did not allow him as much as one drink on the way down. It turned out to be most beneficial for Jack to have his sisters with him, for during the train ride he was able to vent his spleen against Janet, the Lees, and the Auchinclosses at will. By the time they arrived in Washington he was all talked out. Carefully steering him away from anything resembling a bar, my mother and aunt got him to the wedding in good shape, where, under the eyes of his enemies, he gave his daughter away to young Canfield in style. Later, at the reception at Merrywood, he found himself in the heart of Auchincloss country for the first time in his life, and it was not hard for him to realize why Jackie and Lee liked it so much. It was a gray, drizzly day, but the great Virginia estate, with its lovely Georgian house and distant view of the Potomac, looked beautiful beyond words. He and the twins took a quick tour of the estate, admiring the rolling green meadows and the thick woodlands, the country in which Jackie loved so much to ride, and he reluctantly conceded it was every bit as beautiful as Lasata had been at the height of its glory. Later, as the reception drew to a close, Jack had to summon all his strength to keep from breaking down. Finally he had seen what Hughdie Auchincloss had been able to give his beloved daughters over the past ten years.

When Jack Bouvier returned to New York he soon

realized that the Bouvier-Canfield wedding had been but a dress rehearsal for a much grander event, the wedding of his daughter Jacqueline and Senator John F. Kennedy. It was set for September 12, 1953, at Newport, and the reception was to be held at Hammersmith Farm. Already it was being billed by the press as "The Wedding of the Year."

31. The Wedding

PREPARATIONS for the marriage of John F. Kennedy to Jacqueline Bouvier began in June and required three and a half months to complete.

By June blessings on the marriage had been obtained from all families concerned except the Lees. Old Man Lee's dislike of Joe Kennedy was just too intense to allow him to countenance the marriage of one of his granddaughters to a Kennedy. Janet, however, approved of the union, with some reservations. The Kennedys were precisely that big game she had been after for Jackie. But, the Kennedy fortune notwithstanding, she felt the Kennedy family was socially beneath her daughter, so that, in a sense, Jackie, in marrying John Kennedy, would be "marrying down." Her ideal would have been for Jackie to marry into a family like the du Ponts, or the Vanderbilts, or the Mellons, a family combining big money *and* distinguished lineage. And so, Janet, while bestowing her blessing on the marriage, nevertheless maintained a slightly superior attitude toward Jack Kennedy and the other Kennedys. Red Fay commented on this in his book, *The Pleasure of His Company,* when he referred to a request of Jack's for him to pay special attention to Janet during the prenuptial festivities because Janet had, in Jack's words, "a tendency to think I am not good enough for her daughter."

If the Auchinclosses had some slight misgivings about

the marriage, the Bouviers and the Kennedys had none. Jack Bouvier liked Jack Kennedy so much at first sight, and considered the young senator such a bright prospect for the future, that all his reservations about the Kennedys faded away. The same can be said about the other members of the Bouvier family, all of whom were captivated by John F. Kennedy. As for the Kennedys, they accepted Jacqueline with enthusiasm. When Jack Kennedy first introduced Jackie to his family, Father Joe was impressed by Jackie's wit and spunk and class, and the other members of the clan had to admit she was a young woman of unusual beauty and grace.

As it turned out, the marriage offered benefits to all concerned. For John F. Kennedy it promised to give a big boost to his political career. Soon he would be a married man with, he hoped, children, just what they wanted out there in the heartland. For the Kennedy family it promised to enhance their general social image. For Jack Bouvier it promised to get Jackie out of the Auchinclosses' clutches once and for all, and, since the Kennedys were so wealthy, it further promised to relieve him forever of the burden of giving Jackie an allowance and paying all her bills. What a relief it was going to be to have the Kennedys pay all those unauthorized charges in department stores! For Janet Auchincloss the Kennedy money and ambition promised prestige and honors yet to come. For Jacqueline Bouvier it was the fulfillment of every young woman's dream. For, in the relatively old-fashioned, nonfeminist era of the early fifties, when women were not supposed to have careers of their own, a young woman was supposed to marry the richest and most handsome man she could find. In John F. Kennedy Jacqueline found the near-impossible combination: a man who was young, handsome, *and* rich— and rich in his own right, not just a candidate for an inheritance.

On June 25 Mr. and Mrs. Hugh D. Auchincloss gave an official engagement party for Senator John F. Kennedy and Jacqueline Bouvier at Hammersmith Farm, and an official announcement of the engagement was made in the papers. To this event John Vernou Bouvier III was pointedly not invited. As the father of the bride, he was deeply offended. But he would eventually have his day. They certainly could not prevent him from taking Jackie down the aisle during the wedding ceremony.

After June 25 the wedding preparations picked up steam. The following Monday Jack Kennedy began feeding his secretary, Evelyn Lincoln, names for invitations. At first they were to be only "close friends." Before long the list was to swell to include practically the entire Senate and almost every Democratic politician in Massachusetts. For over a month the question of invitations consumed the young senator, but, as soon as Congress adjourned in August, he promptly took off with his old Harvard roommate, Torbert Macdonald, on a trip to Europe, leaving Jacqueline to manage the wedding plans. Chartering a yacht, Kennedy and Macdonald, who would later be elected to Congress from Massachusetts, spent several weeks sailing off the coast of France, ending the trip with a fling in Stockholm and London.

The trip, of course, astonished Jacqueline. Here they were only a few weeks from the big day and her betrothed takes off for an extended trip to Europe with an old buddy. It was a portent of things to come. Kennedy could never cut down on seeing his old buddies or members of his immediate family, and Jacqueline was to feel continually left out, or ignored, while he temporarily dropped her to devote all his attention to a Red Fay, or a Torbert Macdonald, or a Lemoyne Billings, or a Bobby Kennedy.

They were really two very different people, the Boston Irish senator from Massachusetts and the society girl from New York, East Hampton, and Newport, and their relationship in marriage was bound to be stormy.

When Jack returned from his last fling to Europe, his wedding day was not far off. Soon the elaborate prenuptial festivities would begin. These included two bachelor dinners, innumerable luncheons and teas, and a big bridal dinner in Newport.

While Kennedy was cavorting in Europe and Jacqueline was frantically preparing at Hammersmith Farm, Jack Bouvier was getting ready in New York and East

Hampton. Planning carefully, he ordered his cutaway considerably in advance, so the tailor would be able to make all the necessary alterations in time. A fastidious dresser, Jack Bouvier was very careful about such details as the width of lapels, the cut of pockets, the length of sleeves and trousers. Since he liked to show plenty of linen, he liked to keep his jacket lapels low on his neck and his sleeves a little on the short side. Jack Bouvier assembled his wardrobe meticulously that summer of 1953. Striped trousers just the right width and breaking ever so slightly over his shoes. Gray vest just the right length so it would not come down too far beneath the lapels of the cutaway. Immaculate linen. His late father's pearl stickpin. A new pair of gray suede gloves.

Then, to complement the wardrobe, he went down to East Hampton to get some exercise and work on his tan. At the big wedding in Newport he was going to show everyone—the Auchinclosses, the Kennedys, Uncle Hughdie, Joe Kennedy—who Jackie's *real* father was.

Meanwhile, in Newport and Hyannis, plans for all the prenuptial events were proceeding apace, and invitations were being sent out. Among the events scheduled were a big bachelor dinner in Boston ten days before the wedding, a house party at the Kennedy compound at Hyannis Port for the ten bridesmaids and fourteen ushers, a smaller bachelor dinner at Newport's Clambake Club, and a big bridal dinner the night before the wedding, also at the Clambake Club, to be given by Mr. and Mrs. Joseph P. Kennedy.

Jack Bouvier waited for the invitations to at least some of these events to arrive at his apartment at 125 East 74th Street, but they never came. He had not expected to be asked to the big bachelor dinner in Boston, to which mostly Massachusetts politicians had been invited, but he had expected to be invited to the intimate bachelor dinner at Newport and the big bridal dinner the night before the wedding. After all, he *was* the father of the bride, and he had every right to be accorded a place of honor at those festivities.

But, once again, he had underestimated Janet Auchincloss. For Janet had determined to exclude her ex-husband from all the prenuptial celebrations. Assuming control of all the arrangements for the wedding not already appropriated by Joe Kennedy, she took charge of the bride's half of the invitation lists and of all the seating at the various parties, pointedly excluding her ex-husband from everything.

Meanwhile, the prenuptial events began to unfold. On September 2, 350 people, including Kennedy's campaign chairmen from every section of Massachusetts and many of the senator's old buddies, assembled at the Parker House in Boston for a bachelor dinner in honor of John Kennedy. Bob Kennedy was one of the principal speakers, and Red Fay observed that when he got up to make his speech he was "ashen white. His hands quivered and his voice quaked. When he finished," Fay observed, "you could almost feel the audience's relief." It would be a while before the shy, awkward Robert Kennedy would succeed in acquiring some poise on his feet.

The second bachelor dinner was held at Newport's exclusive Clambake Club a few days before the wedding. It was a much smaller affair, an intimate black-tie dinner for close friends and male relatives of the bride and groom, and was hosted by Hugh D. Auchincloss. Red Fay acted as master of ceremonies. He advised Jack Kennedy to offer the first toast to the bride and after the glasses were drained to have everybody throw them into the fireplace. This was done and the fine crystal glasses with which Auchincloss had had the table set were all duly shattered against the hearth. Immediately, according to Fay, "a shaken host, Hugh D. Auchincloss . . . called the waiter to replace the glasses." Soon the new crystal was on the table and Jack Kennedy rose again. "Maybe this isn't the accepted custom," he said, "but I want to again express my love for this girl I'm going to marry. A toast to the bride." At that, everyone raised his glass again, toasted the bride, and hurled his glass into the fireplace a second time. By now Hugh Auchincloss's Scotch instincts had been stirred. Disappearing momentarily into the pantry, he returned to the table looking a bit more relieved. Soon the waiter brought out a set of glasses that, in Red Fay's words, "could have fitted very nicely into the rack at Healy's ten-cent restaurant."

Came the day of the dinner given by Mr. and Mrs. Joseph P. Kennedy for the bridal party. By now Jack Bouvier was ensconced in Newport's Viking Hotel and was confidently awaiting an invitation to the bridal dinner. After all, since he was to give the bride away at the wedding ceremony the next day, he certainly was a bona fide member of the "bridal party."

What went on via telephone between Jack Bouvier and Hammersmith Farm that day is known only to the survivors. What is known is that Jack Bouvier was not invited to the bridal dinner, and it crushed him. In fact, he was not even given a chance to see his beloved Jacqueline the day before her wedding. Jack Bouvier had taken his share of insults from the Auchinclosses and his share of neglect from his daughters, but this was the most devastating snub of all. Granted, he was not a big millionaire like Joe Kennedy or Hughdie Auchincloss, but he did come from a distinguished old family and he *was* the father of the bride. Furthermore, despite the Auchinclosses' money, it was he who had singlehandedly supported Jacqueline her entire life. Wasn't he, by all rights, entitled to a place of special honor at the bridal dinner? Jack Bouvier went to bed at the Viking Hotel that night a deeply wounded man.

Meanwhile, the celebrants at the bridal dinner had a merry time. Kennedy's buddies gave riotous toasts, and Kennedy and Jacqueline gibed at one another. The 36-year-old groom, in his speech, announced he was giving up his bachelorhood to remove Jacqueline from the fourth estate where she could conceivably threaten his political future. And the 24-year-old bride told everyone what a failure Kennedy had been as a suitor. Apparently during his entire courtship he had not sent her one single love letter, only one measly postcard from Bermuda. Jackie held it up for all to see. Its message was

Wish you were here.

Jack

If Janet Auchincloss had played a preponderant role in the prenuptial events, it was Joe Kennedy who took charge of the actual marriage ceremony. His aim was simple: to produce an extravaganza that would gain his son national attention. First of all, he saw to it that in addition to the society friends of the Auchinclosses and Bouviers, who were really not worth very much to his purposes, there would be plenty of distinguished members of the press, especially political commentators and national magazine reporters, in attendance. In addition, he saw to it that invitations were sent to notable society columnists, syndicated columnists, film celebrities, congressmen, and important political figures, such as the Speaker of the House. Then he engaged the archbishop of Boston, Richard Cushing, to celebrate the high nuptial mass, assisted by Msgr. Francis Rossiter and no fewer than three other distinguished Catholic clergymen—Bishop Weldon of Springfield, the Very Rev. John Cavanagh, former president of Notre Dame, and the Rev. James Keller of New York, leader of the Christopher movement. To top it off he engaged a celebrated tenor, Luigi Vena, to sing the "Ave Maria" and saw to it that the bride and groom received the apostolic blessing of Pope Pius XII.

September 12, 1953, was a magnificent day. Though it was a bit on the windy side, the sky was clear and it was warm enough to allow the ladies to wear their summer dresses with reasonable comfort.

Busily the bride and groom began pulling themselves together for the wedding, Jacqueline at Hammersmith Farm, Kennedy at the guest house provided by the Auchinclosses. At Hammersmith Farm the mood was one of nervous excitement. In addition to the normal excitement associated with such an event, there was the problem of John Vernou Bouvier III. The bride wanted very much to be given away by her real father. But the bride's mother did not want that. She wanted her daughter to be given away by her stepfather, Hugh D. Auchincloss.

While Jack Bouvier was preparing for the wedding at the Viking Hotel the other members of the Bouvier family, my mother and father and my mother's twin sister and her husband, Harrington Putnam, were getting ready at the Hotel Munchener King. It had been decided that my father and Mr. Putnam would pick Jack up at the Viking, take him back to the Munchener King to get the twins, and then all five would then head for St. Mary's.

If Jacqueline felt under great tension as she dressed for her wedding, Jack Bouvier was practically on the verge of a fit. Having taken two devastating snubs from the Auchinclosses on preceding evenings, he was in a confused, but fighting mood. He adored his beloved Jacqueline and wanted so badly to make her proud of him on her big day, but at the same time the wedding ceremony and the reception to follow had been organized by his hated rivals, the Auchinclosses, and by that scoundrel who had ruined his business, Joseph P. Kennedy. Thus he was confronted with a situation so explosive that to think about it even for an instant was sufficient to raise his blood pressure ten points. But, as he looked at himself in the dresser mirror in his hotel room, he had to admit he looked pretty good. Tanned and fit, he could not help but make a splendid impression on everyone present.

When my father and Mr. Putnam arrived, they found Jack Bouvier half dressed and in a state of extreme agitation. He had his dress shirt and striped trousers and his gray, double-vested vest on but was still without his tie or cutaway or shoes. Looking about the room, my father quickly ascertained that room service had been busy that morning with the demands of the Viking's most honored guest. In addition to the breakfast tray, with its remains of scrambled eggs, bacon, toast, and coffee, there was also an ice bucket full of ice and a bottle of whiskey. And, standing on the dresser, along with brush and comb and whisk broom, was a half empty highball with droplets of condensed water dripping down its sides.

"How are you coming along, Jack?" my father and Mr. Putnam asked almost simultaneously.

"Great. Never felt better in my life," came the reply.

As my father and Harrington Putnam walked around the room, gauging the scene, my mother and her twin sister, back in the Munchener King, were putting the finishing touches on their makeup and their outfits, when suddenly the calls began coming through from Hammersmith Farm:

"Is Jack all right?"

"Do you think Daddy is up to it?"

"How's everything with Jack Bouvier?"

To which the twins replied, "We don't know. John and Put have gone over to the Viking to find out."

By now anxieties at Hammersmith Farm were reaching the level of hysteria. Would Jack Bouvier be able to make it? A call to the Viking earlier had found Jack somewhat thick-tongued. Perhaps Uncle Hugh should maintain himself at the ready. For the first time in what was to be a long succession of times, Jacqueline found herself trapped in the web of Kennedy publicity. She desperately wanted her father to give her away, but with all those reporters, columnists, and photographers Joe Kennedy had invited to the wedding, could she risk a Jack Bouvier unsteady on his feet? Wouldn't it be safer, from a publicity standpoint, to have Uncle Hugh escort her down the aisle? As she was dressing for the most important day in her life, these must have been the thoughts running through the young bride's mind.

Meanwhile, back at the Viking Hotel, my father and Harrington Putnam were trying to assess the situation. They saw Jack Bouvier drain his highball as he began working his tie into his high stiff collar. He had trouble with the tie, and Putnam had to help him. Then he couldn't find his pearl stickpin. Before long he was going over to the tray and ice bucket to pour himself another drink.

In contrast to the tense preparations at Hammersmith Farm and at the Viking and the Munchener King, John F. Kennedy was dressing calmly and collectedly. Kennedy usually functioned best in a crisis, and he was looking forward to the spotlight. It was conceivable that if the pictures turned out well, the wedding could land him on a few front pages. So all was serene in the Kennedy camp. Father Joe and Mother Rose were in fine shape, and Bobby and Teddy and the girls were also coming along fine.

Back in the Bouvier-Auchincloss camps, however,

the tension was mounting. A chain of communications had been established: Hammersmith Farm to the twins at the Munchener King, the twins to their husbands and brother at the Viking then back to Hammersmith Farm. Desperately my father and Harrington Putnam were trying to determine whether Jack Bouvier was fit to perform. He was by no means drunk, but he had had a few drinks, and the big question was whether he could walk a straight line and hold himself steady throughout the ceremony. What was to be avoided, at all cost, was to have the father of the bride stumble or fall flat on his face in front of 600 people, who included members of the nation's press. Finally, to thwart that possibility, Harrington Putnam took the whiskey bottle, when Jack wasn't looking, and hid it in the closet.

While my father and Mr. Putnam were discharging the heavy responsibility of trying to determine whether Jack Bouvier was fit to walk down the center aisle of St. Mary's, the twins at the Munchener King were being deluged by frantic calls from Hammersmith Farm. Finally Janet got on the phone and demanded to know if Jack Bouvier had been drinking. My mother took the call, and hedged, trying to protect her brother. But Janet would not let up. Finally Mother had to admit that her brother had had "one or two" drinks.

"Then we don't want him at the wedding!" Janet snapped. "We don't want him even if he has taken only one or two *sips*."

"But John and Put think he can perform," my mother pleaded.

"I don't care. Don't bring him. If you do, Jackie and I will never speak to you again."

"I'll check with the Viking one more time," my mother said, and hung up.

Now things were down to the wire, and the responsibility hung heavy on all concerned. Back at the Viking, Jack had begun to rail at the Auchinclosses and how they had excluded him from all the prenuptial events, an ominous sign. However, my father and Mr. Putnam took this in stride—my father had spent half his life listening to Jack

Bouvier rail against the Auchinclosses—and ultimately came to the decision that Jack could function adequately. By now he was fully dressed and looked splendid in his immaculate, beautifully fitted cutaway and deep East Hampton tan. True, his tongue was a little thick, and there was a slight unsteadiness to his gait, but he was coherent and physically fit. There was no doubt about it in my father's or in Harrington Putnam's minds: Jack Bouvier could take Jacqueline down the aisle at St. Mary's and do himself and her proud.

This was communicated to the twins at the Munchener King, who, in turn, communicated it to Hammersmith Farm. But the twins were wasting their breath. Janet Auchincloss would not hear of it. Hugh was now ready to give Jackie away. Time was running out. Soon they would all have to leave for St. Mary's. If the twins brought Jack Bouvier with them, Janet would not let him in the door, and there would be an ugly scene. "Keep him there," Janet urged, "don't let him out of his room . . . even for *one second.*"

Janet was so emphatic with her threats that the twins had no choice but to accede. A call was made to the Viking, and, after a heated discussion, it was decided that the twins would go on to the wedding and my father and Harrington Putnam would remain behind at the Viking to look after Jack. This is exactly what happened, and so my father and Mr. Putnam missed both the wedding ceremony and the reception at Hammersmith Farm.

Now Janet had the wedding the way *she* had wanted it, with her husband, Hugh D. Auchincloss, taking Jackie down the center aisle. For Jackie it was a deep disappointment, but she could do nothing about it. By now Jackie was no longer her own master. She was already a prisoner and tool of the Kennedy political machine. From now on she had to do what was good for the Kennedy image. If it was good for the Kennedy image to go along with her mother's wishes and have her father excluded from her wedding, she had to accept it.

So be it. Jacqueline's task now was to overcome her disappointment, summon her reserves of strength, and rise to the occasion, which she did magnificently. Triumphing over the high tensions of the morning and her disappointment over her father, she made a radiant, confident bride to the 600 notables cramming St. Mary's and the thousands who lined the avenue leading to the church.

Walking down the aisle on the arm of the tall, solid, stately Hugh D. Auchincloss, who performed his office with calm dignity, Jackie radiated a serene beauty to the multitude assembled. Only a few people, mostly members of the Bouvier family and their friends, noted that she was not on the arm of her father. As she walked down the aisle, her twin aunts burst into tears, remembering the drama of the past two hours and envisioning her brother in his magnificent cutaway and tan being held prisoner in the Viking by their husbands.

Although oceans of publicity on the wedding poured out of Newport, few people had the vaguest idea of what Jacqueline had gone through. In her first few minutes as a Kennedy she had not only risen to the occasion, knowing she was being married before the eyes of the nation, but she had risen to it under most distressing circumstances. The smiles she gave out from the arm of Hugh D. Auchincloss came from deep reserves of strength. From now on her life would be an unbroken succession of rising to great occasions, a series of rehearsals, as it turned out, for that one great occasion, when, before the eyes of the entire world, she performed her last wifely duty to John F. Kennedy.

By the time the ceremony was over and the guests had begun to drift over to the Hammersmith Farm for the reception, Jack Bouvier had calmed down somewhat and was eating club sandwiches for lunch in his room at the Viking with his two captors, my father and Harrington Putnam. There had been a couple of brief struggles when Jack had lunged for the door in an effort to escape his overseers, only to be restrained and hauled back into the room. But by 3 P.M. he was completely sober and could have easily joined the revelers at Hammersmith Farm. Still, the orders from Janet had been not to let him out of sight for a second. Thus he sat in his room with his two in-laws during the entire reception, drinking coffee and talking about how terribly everyone had behaved toward him during the past three days. The battle for Jacqueline was over.

The John F. Kennedys spent their wedding night at the Waldorf-Astoria in New York. The next day, a Sunday, they flew to Mexico City on their way to Acapulco. Because Kennedy's secretary, Evelyn Lincoln, had forgotten to furnish them with their birth certificates, the Mexican authorities at the Mexico City airport refused to let them officially into the country. For three hours Kennedy tried to track down the appropriate officials at the American Embassy, who were all off duty, while Jacqueline sat by making pointed remarks, in her inimitable way, about the mighty United Sates senator who was unable to enter a friendly country. Finally, after much annoyance and embarrassment, they were admitted to Mexico and were able to proceed on to their honeymoon in Acapulco. Jackie had fallen in love with the villa she and Jack had stayed in on a previous visit to Acapulco with her mother and stepfather. It was all pink, and its various levels climbed a terracotta-colored cliff overlooking the Pacific. Once ensconced in the retreat, Kennedy immediately phoned his secretary in Washington to complain about the lack of birth certificates, and Jackie wrote her father a long letter of "forgiveness," which one of Jack Bouvier's partners, John Carrere, who saw the letter, told me was "one of the most touching, compassionate letters" he had ever read, one that "only a rare and noble spirit could have written." The wording and tone of the letter seemed to indicate, however, that Jacqueline did not know of her mother's role in preventing her father from attending the wedding. That role she was to learn about when she next visited her father in New York.

Jack Kennedy loved the sea and as soon as he got a chance in Acapulco he was off deep-sea fishing in the Pacific. His nearly unbroken string of luck held: On one outing he landed a tremendous nine-foot sailfish, which Jackie insisted on having stuffed and mounted as a me-

mento of their honeymoon. During his remaining senatorial years the gigantic fish hung in Kennedy's Senate
office. Later it was moved to the White House and was
hung in the room directly opposite the President's office.
It now hangs in the John F. Kennedy Library in Boston,
a sole trophy of the events of September 1953.

32. Setbacks and Recoveries

SOMETIME during the fall of 1953, after Jacqueline returned from her honeymoon, she visited her father in New York and received a scolding from him over what had happened in Newport. According to his version, it was all the fault of Janet and the Auchinclosses that he had been prevented from giving her away to John F. Kennedy. He had been treated shamefully, having been excluded from all the prenuptial events and then forcibly restrained, at the behest of Janet, from giving his own daughter away at her wedding. Jacqueline took these remonstrances in stride, as she always did. The important thing was that she had got through the ceremony with no outward mishaps or embarrassments.

As it turned out, Jack Bouvier's rivalry with Hugh Auchincloss was not over yet. The next clash came over the annual get-together of the Association of Stock Exchange Firms on Febraury 15 at the Shoreham in Washington. Jack Kennedy, Jack Bouvier, and Hugh Auchincloss had all been invited. Jack Bouvier thought his son-in-law should sit on the dais, but Auchincloss insisted that Kennedy sit at the Auchincloss, Redpath, and Parker table.

When Jack Bouvier learned that there was a possibility Kennedy might sit at the Auchincloss table he flew into a rage. He had just discussed the whole outrageous wedding episode at Newport with Jackie and now here was her husband about to sit down at Hugh D. Auchincloss's table at the Stock Exchange banquet as if nothing had happened; it was more than he could bear. Angrily he called both Kennedy and Jackie, urging Kennedy to sit on the dais where he belonged. It must have taxed all of Kennedy's resources as a politician to handle this situation. Where the senator finally sat is not known. We can only assume that Jack Bouvier did everything possible to prevent Kennedy from sitting at the Auchincloss table.

The Bouvier-Auchincloss rivalry continued to drag on after the Stock Exchange dinner and did not really end until Jack Bouvier's death in 1957. Years later some of his nephews were to express regret that Jack never lived to see the firm of Auchincloss, Redpath and Parker go bankrupt and Hammersmith Farm sold to raise cash for his rival's depleted estate.

Jackie's relations with her father during the early years of her marriage remained more or less the way they had always been: sequences of neglect, recrimination, and reconciliation. Jack Bouvier tried to understand his daughter's attitude toward him, attributing her neglect to her manifold duties as a senator's wife, but as time passed and he grew older and lonelier, it became increasingly hard for him to excuse it.

Early in 1955, Jack Bouvier sold his seat on the New York Stock Exchange for a mere $90,000 (seats in 1929 had brought as much as $625,000, and in 1968 they would bring $515,000) and retired from business on a capital of approximately $200,000, which, at ten percent, could have yielded him a retirement income of $20,000 a year. It was a far cry from his uncle's, or his father's, retirement incomes, which had been $500,000 and $150,000 a year, respectively.

Without anything to do and suffering from a variety of ailments—slipped disc, chronic sinusitis, irisitis, and a diseased liver—Jack Bouvier treasured more than ever a call, or a visit, from his favorite daughter. But the calls and visits were few and far between.

Jack Bouvier, however, had one last card to play to

enforce a measure of loyalty from his daughter: his last will and testament. For strange as it may seem, Jacqueline Kennedy still had no money of her own, other than the $3000 left her by her Grandfather Bouvier in 1948, which had been so conservatively invested it never grew beyond $8000. In 1955 she was therefore wholly dependent on the Kennedys from a financial standpoint, not a terribly comfortable position to be in.

Assuming Jack Bouvier did not gamble his $200,000 away, Jackie stood to inherit anywhere from $80,000 to $90,000 from her father some day. This would give her a little leverage in the face of the Kennedys' incessant demands. No, Jackie could not afford to be disinherited by her father, even though that possibility was very remote. She would have to divorce Kennedy and marry an Auchincloss for such a drastic thing to happen. Still, it was not worth taking chances on; Jack Bouvier did hold a strong card, beyond father-daughter love, to bind Jacqueline to him as he entered his last years.

Meanwhile, John F. Kennedy's congenital back trouble had grown steadily worse, so that by late 1954 he was forced to go around on crutches and was finally compelled to undergo a very dangerous back operation, a double fusion of spinal discs. Kennedy's doctors, cognizant that the senator's inadequate adrenal system would make him highly vulnerable to infection and might prevent his bodily defenses from functioning adequately, had recommended that the operation be done in two separate stages, but the reckless Kennedy demanded that it all be done in one operation, thus vastly increasing the risk he might not survive.

The story of the surgery is well known. After surviving the long operation, during which his spinal column was laid bare, Kennedy hovered between life and death. There were times when his doctors gave up all hope, then, suddenly, he would rally. At one point he fell so low that his family and a priest were summoned, and he was given the last rites of the church. At his son's bedside Joe Kennedy broke down and cried. The press covered the crisis as if Jack were already President. But the Kennedy family withheld the real reason why the operation had been so dangerous.

During Kennedy's stay in New York Hospital, Jack Bouvier, who lived not far away, was a constant visitor, and Jacqueline hardly ever left her husband's side. All concerned agreed that Jackie was extraordinary in the way she buoyed her ailing husband's spirits.

Finally, in December, Kennedy was judged well enough to go to his parents' home in Palm Beach to convalesce. It was during his convalescence in Palm Beach that he, one of his political aides, Theodore Sorensen, and several university professors collaborated to write *Profiles in Courage*, a book he dedicated to Jacqueline and which won him what is now considered a controversial Pulitzer Prize.

Profiles in Courage was concerned with, in Kennedy's own words, "problems of political courage in the face of constituent pressures." It was a fine book and deserved much acclaim. However, it now appears reasonably certain John F. Kennedy did not write it. Kennedy evolved the idea, assembled much of the material, took copious notes, dictated many ideas and facts to secretaries, and played a preponderant role in organizing the work, but there is no evidence he ever wrote a draft of the book, not a first draft, a second draft, or a final draft; these were done, in typical Kennedy style, by his paid minions.

Kennedy was either too unwell, or too busy, to have had the time for such a demanding undertaking in late 1954 and the first ten months of 1955, the year in which the book came out. During this period he endured two major spinal operations, one of which almost took his life, and spent significant periods of time in the hospital on three other occasions. Furthermore, when he was well, he was often away on trips throughout the country, and between August and October 1955 he was touring Europe. There was simply no way he could have written an entire book under these conditions, and the notes, tapes, and miscellaneous manuscript material pertaining to the book at the Kennedy Library in Boston prove it. There are many notes in Kennedy's almost illegible scrawl on yellow sheets of paper; there are many tapes of Kennedy's voice dictating rapidly and almost indecipherably to secretaries; but there are no Kennedy drafts of the book itself on file. Instead of being written by Kennedy, it is now generally conceded that the drafts of *Profiles in Courage* were written, in part, by Prof. Jules Davids of Georgetown University, a teacher of Jackie's, and Theodore Sorensen, with major contributions from professors Arthur Schlesinger, Jr., James MacGregor Burns, Allan Nevins, and Arthur Holcombe. Sorensen then wrote the final, unified version, which, of course, Kennedy went over very carefully, making his corrections, deletions, insertions, and additions. At least this is the opinion of Herbert Parmet, the Kennedy biographer who has done the most research on the subject. Nevertheless, despite the fact that all he did was organize, oversee, and edit the book, Kennedy was not above accepting a Pulitzer Prize for *Profiles:* Receiving the award was good for his political career and that was all that really counted in the end.

The success of *Profiles* brightened an otherwise dreary period for the John F. Kennedys. Kennedy's illness and convalescence during the fall of 1954 and winter of 1955 placed great strains on his marriage; then, in 1955, Jackie suffered a miscarriage, and in 1956 she gave birth to a stillborn child in Newport shortly after her husband lost the vice presidential nomination in Chicago. Kennedy was not with Jackie at the time of this last traumatic event, for he had flown to the Riviera to confer with his father about his political fortunes and to get in a bit of yachting around Capri and Elba with friends, knowing full well his wife was expecting a child momentarily. We may imagine Jackie's anguish, giving birth to a premature, stillborn child with her husband 5000 miles away and completely out of touch. But, in Jack Kennedy's world, politics and the Kennedys always came first. Jacqueline was all too frequently made to realize that, at certain times, she occupied a distinct second place.

Despite this disconcerting aspect of her marriage, however, Jacqueline strove to be a good wife to John F.

Kennedy. There was a persistent rumor that Jackie, fed up with always having to play second fiddle to her husband's political ambitions and his family, and troubled by gossip about his reputed liaisons with beautiful women, threatened to divorce Kennedy and thereby compromise his political career, whereupon Joe Kennedy gave her a million-dollar bribe to remain with Jack. The rumor has never been proved true, and there is strong evidence that it is false, for Jack Bouvier's personal secretary, John Ficke, told me that after Bouvier died and his estate was being settled, Jacqueline was terribly anxious to receive her legacy of $79,700 and kept bothering him for it. The settlement of Bouvier's estate occurred in late 1957, some time after the 1956 birth of her stillborn child. It is not likely that Jacqueline would have pressed her father's estate for a mere $79,700 if she had $1 million from Joe Kennedy in the bank.

Jack Bouvier's sudden death from cancer in August 1957 at Lenox Hill Hospital in New York was a shock to Jacqueline, for she had had no idea her father had been so ill. Upon learning the news, she flew to New York from Newport and was joined there by her husband from Washington. She and the senator stayed at Joe Kennedy's New York apartment and were assisted in making the funeral arrangements by my mother and father and by a cousin, Michel Bouvier.

My mother remembers that Jack Kennedy was still having trouble with his back, despite all the operations and hospitalizations, and often seemed to be in considerable pain. Despite this he made a special effort to assure Jack Bouvier a prominent obituary by personally delivering the text and a photo (obtained by Jackie from one of her father's girlfriends) to the managing editor of the *New York Times*. At the time my father, who had accompanied him, was struck by the brashness of the young senator, who let no secretaries, receptionists, clerks, or assistant editors prevent him from going right into the managing editor's office with the obituary and photo.

Jacqueline was no less forceful. She astonished my mother and father by quickly taking charge of the funeral arrangements and decisively organizing everything from obtaining the photo of her father to selecting his casket.

For the last rites in the Bouvier chapel in St. Patrick's she rejected the conventional flower arrangements usually produced for funerals in favor of displaying sprays of summer flowers in white wicker baskets. "I want everything to look like a summer garden," she told her twin aunts, "like Lasata in August." Later, at the burial in St. Philomena's cemetery in East Hampton, she had the gravesite heaped with the most appropriate flower she could think of—bachelor's buttons.

After the burial, the Bouviers and their friends expected to have lunch with Jacqueline and the senator, or at least have tea or a drink together. Jacqueline was in favor of the idea, but Kennedy was in too much of a hurry to get back to Hyannis Port. Quickly saying goodbye to everyone in his typically rushed manner, he whisked Jackie off to a private plane which soon had them over Long Island Sound on the way to the Cape. Everyone was disappointed they did not have a chance to reminisce about Jack Bouvier with Jackie, but there was little time for such superfluities for the John F. Kennedys now. Jack Kennedy was about to run for reelection to the Senate, a race he had to win overwhelmingly if he was to be a contender for the big prize in 1960. The funeral and burial of his wife's father was a distraction from that pursuit. Even today, twenty-five years later, East Hamptoners, "the locals," who loved Jack Bouvier, talk disparagingly of Kennedy's precipitous exodus from the burial that hot August afternoon.

When Jack Bouvier's estate was inventoried, the net taxable estate was found to be worth only $171,994, indicating he had spent a good deal of his principal since retiring. Among the curiosities of the inventory was a debt of $4773 owed to Jack's housekeeper, Esther Lindstrom, to whom he had left no legacy, for "noncompensated services over a period of two years." Taxes and various individual bequests amounted to $12,578, so the "rest and residue" of the estate, which was to be divided equally between Jacqueline and Lee, amounted to $159,416.

Her father's legacy was the first respectable sum of money Jacqueline ever received, and she received it in her twenty-eighth year. It was not, by her new Kennedy standards, very much money; still it was better than nothing. True to her extravagant ways, one of Jacqueline's first major expenditures from her inheritance was a flashy white Jaguar for her husband for Christmas 1957, only a month or two after her father's estate was settled. According to Theodore Sorensen, Kennedy, sensitive to the political implications of driving around in such an ostentatious car, returned it to the dealer with regrets.

Jackie's extravagance was, at the time, a great source of friction between her and her husband. Years later, Mary Gallagher, a personal secretary to Jacqueline, reported in a book that Kennedy would pore over his wife's enormous expenditures with unbelieving dismay. Now he was getting the treatment Jack Bouvier had received for so many years.

Jackie must have felt in a good mood to buy her husband a white Jaguar for Christmas in 1957. The time of troubles was clearly over. The operations, hospitalizations, miscarriages, and quarrels were at last behind them.

Of course one great source of new happiness to the John F. Kennedys in late 1957 was the birth, by caesarian section, of Caroline Kennedy. The two had wanted a child so badly, and Jackie had had such terrible difficulties with her two previous pregnancies that the successful birth of a healthy daughter was like a godsend, almost too good to be true.

Caroline Bouvier Kennedy was christened on December 13 in St. Patrick's near the Bouvier altar, erected in memory of her great-great-great grandparents, Michel and Louise Bouvier. Many members of the Bouvier and Kennedy families were present. Bobby Kennedy and Jackie's sister, Lee, were the godparents. My mother attended to many of the religious arrangements and recalls the extreme annoyance of the cathedral's authorities at all the television cameramen, photographers, and reporters present. But Jack Kennedy had that senatorial election coming up the following year, and possibly a national election coming up two years later, and he needed all the exposure he could get. He therefore wanted to make his daughter's christening into an important media event. While my mother had been attending to the religious aspects of the ceremony, Kennedy had been attending to the publicity aspects. The two clashed head on, as a much irritated cathedral clergy and an overzealous fourth estate met under a blinding glare of klieg lights and flashbulbs while the little baby was baptized. Although the feelings of the priests were bruised, Kennedy's purposes in the end were realized. The christening of Caroline Bouvier Kennedy was widely covered both on television and in the press. With his major troubles behind him and a baby daughter now to bolster his image, Kennedy, as the crucial year 1958 drew near, was once again on the road to his high destiny.

33. Going All the Way: The Buildup

IN the John F. Kennedy Library in Boston, a film about the life of Kennedy plays continuously in the small theater. At a certain moment in the film, somewhere during the two years between Kennedy's unsuccessful bid for the vice presidency in 1956 and his triumphant reelection to the Senate in 1958, the film's narrator intones, in a voice full of distant drama and accompanied by the sounds of cheering crowds, that it suddenly occurred to Kennedy that he could "go all the way." This flash of intuition then led Kennedy to prepare for the 1960 presidential campaign a full three years before that campaign was to begin. It was not that at a certain point during the course of his political career he was seized with a special vision concerning the future of his country and his role in that future. It was simply that at a certain moment, sensing the upsurge in his popularity, John F. Kennedy became reasonably sure he could win a presidential election. To win, for a Kennedy, was the important thing. The vision, if any, would come later.

Accordingly, with no particular program for the country in mind, certainly with nothing approaching the vision of a Franklin D. Roosevelt in 1932 or a Ronald Reagan in 1980, but with a clear certainty he could "go all the way," John F. Kennedy began his campaign for the presidency of the United States. It made little difference what Eisenhower-Nixon had accomplished, or even what he, Kennedy, had accomplished during the past eight years. He knew that what he had accomplished, primarily, was building constituencies and winning elections. No, in the age of television what mattered most was tone, feeling, spirit, image—if you could convey a better *feeling* and a more sparkling *image* than your opponent, you could win.

1957 was a good year. No fewer than 2500 speaking invitations poured into Kennedy's Senate office in 1957. *Time* magazine did a cover story on him (Henry Luce was, as we know, a friend of his father). He won a seat on the Senate's prestigious Foreign Relations Committee, thanks to the Democratic party's leader in the Senate at the time, Lyndon Johnson. He was even elected to Harvard's Board of Overseers, an appointment that gladdened the heart of old Joe Kennedy no end.

Still, for all the honors and preferments he received, there nevertheless remained some big hurdles to leap if he were to make it all the way to the White House in 1961; the biggest hurdle was the Senate race of 1958. Not that Kennedy feared he would not get reelected. There was no question about that. What concerned him was what his margin of victory would be. He simply had to get a tremendous vote that would break all records if he was going to convince the Democratic leaders he could win a presidential election.

To roll up a tremendous vote, the Kennedys went to work with a vengeance. Bobby Kennedy, who had been serving with Jack on the McClellan committee investigating labor racketeering and organized crime, took on the job of campaign manager. Ted Kennedy and Steve Smith were also brought in to receive their political baptism of fire. And, of course, the ambassador was always there in the background, pulling strings, feeding stories to journalists, and writing checks.

It was a hectic campaign, and Kennedy worked like a horse. The pace was killing. Larry O'Brien, one of Jack's handlers, later told the press: "We ran the senator in one day through fifteen speaking appearances in fifteen cities and towns, from Chelsea to Gloucester, and had him back in bed by 11:00 P.M."

Kennedy also spoke in many other states. He had shrewdly decided to use his Senate reelection campaign as a means to become better known nationwide. Now his famous card-index file of useful names would grow to include possible supporters in every state in the union.

Of course, there were also the teas for "women in their best gowns." However, with Jack Kennedy now married, these were not quite so successful as in the past. What was the point of a young woman going to a Kennedy tea if there was no chance of a romance with Jack Kennedy?

As it turned out, Senator Kennedy received his record-breaking vote, getting 1,362,926 votes to his opponent Vincent Celeste's 488,316 or 73.6 percent of the total. It was a tremendous victory, and it accomplished exactly what it was supposed to accomplish: It convinced the Democratic party leaders that Jack was a phenomenal vote-getter and definitely a possible presidential candidate.

For Kennedy himself, the end of the Senate reelection campaign was the beginning of his presidential campaign. As aides Ken O'Donnell and Dave Powers put it, no sooner was the Senate fight over than they "were already thinking of the next ballgame."

The problem was how to get Jack better known nationwide. To accomplish this, Joseph P. Kennedy chose the written word. He had cultivated some of the most influential gentlemen of the press—William Randolph Hearst, Henry Luce, and Arthur Krock, to name a few—now he would get them to go to bat for Jack. They and countless other journalists. Among his many publicizing efforts, Joe managed to get the *Saturday Evening Post* to do an article on the entire family, eventually entitled "The Amazing Kennedys," in which Jack Kennedy was portrayed as a clean-cut, smiling young man who was "trustworthy, loyal, brave, clean, and reverent." It was the first of a stream of flattering articles on the family. The great buildup had begun.

Throughout 1959 the American people were given an enormous dose of Kennedy, almost all of it originating from the Kennedys themselves. Major features on Jack and Jackie and the other Kennedys began to appear in

Life, Redbook, The Ladies' Home Journal, Look, Coronet, the *Washington Post,* and the *Reader's Digest.*

And then there were the books, both by and about John Kennedy. Prof. James MacGregor Burns wrote an official, "authorized" biography of Jack that portrayed him as a combination hero and saint. According to Kennedy scholar Herbert Parmet, Ted Sorensen put together a book to please the liberals called *A Nation of Immigrants,* which went out under Jack Kennedy's name. Articles by John F. Kennedy, also written largely by Sorensen, began appearing in such prestigious publications as the *New York Times Magazine,* the *Reporter,* and *Foreign Affairs.* And, of course, the Pulitzer Prize–winning *Profiles in Courage* was constantly pushed as John F. Kennedy's masterpiece.

It was therefore not a very great surprise to anyone when, on Saturday, January 2, 1960, Jack Kennedy made his formal declaration of candidacy in the caucus room of the Senate. Political observers duly noted the adroitness of the timing—catching the public's attention right after the first of the year and choosing a Saturday for the formal announcement. The Kennedys, as master manipulators of public opinion, were quite aware that more people read the Sunday papers than the dailies.

34. Going All the Way: The Blitz

"A BAREHEADED, coatless man, lithe as an athlete, his face still unlined, his eyes unpuffed with fatigue, wandering solitary as a stick through the empty streets and villages of Wisconsin's far-northern Tenth Congressional District."

So was John F. Kennedy described by Theodore H. White, who trailed the young candidate for the Democratic nomination as he made his dogged way through the primaries. It was not easy going. In Wisconsin Kennedy traveled through all the state's electoral districts, no matter how remote and underpopulated some of them were. He traveled 185 miles through the bleak, empty tenth, making his way through cold, desolate country, to be seen by only 1600 people, 1200 of whom were too young to vote. But no corner of the state was too far out of the way for the determined John F. Kennedy. With his system pumped full of cortisone, and popping an occasional amphetamine, he made his indefatigable rounds. Of the other candidates for the nomination—Hubert Humphrey, Adlai Stevenson, Stuart Symington, and Lyndon Johnson—only Humphrey was out there trudging through Wisconsin's winter desolation, and Humphrey was not covering nearly as much territory as Kennedy. But the others didn't want the nomination as badly as Kennedy did. Not even Lyndon Johnson wanted it as badly as Kennedy did, though he certainly wanted it very badly. Humphrey wanted it if he did not have to work too hard and spend too much money to get it. Adlai Stevenson wanted it if it was handed to him on a gold platter. Stuart Symington wanted it if it was handed to him on a silver platter. Lyndon Johnson wanted it if he could get it by making deals in the cloakrooms of the Senate. But John F. Kennedy wanted it with the same killer instinct with which his father had wanted to build a fortune.

But it was not just John F. Kennedy who wanted it. It was the entire Kennedy family. The drive for the 1960 Democratic nomination, and then for the presidency, was a concerted family effort. Every member of the Kennedy family was as active as he or she could possibly be in the campaign.

Managing the campaign on an eighteen-hour-a-day basis was Robert F. Kennedy the relentlessly driving, 34-year-old brother of the candidate. A classic puritan, moralistic and wholly committed to the work ethic, Bobby Kennedy believed in getting up very early in the morning, then working uninterruptedly until he virtually dropped from exhaustion at the end of the day. Whatever he went into, he went into to win. He expected the same attitude from his subordinates, whom he drove with equal zeal.

Then came the other young males in the family, the candidate's youngest brother, Edward, and his brothers-in-law Stephen Smith and Sargent Shriver. Teddy and Sarge were "area commanders," in charge of certain geographical zones of the campaign, and Stephen Smith was made overall administrative director, in charge, among other things, of collecting and disbursing funds. Shriver also functioned as Kennedy's aide in charge of issues, such as agricultural policy, urban affairs, and civil rights.

And then there were all the Kennedy women: Rose, and Jean, and Eunice, and Patricia, and Ethel, and Joan, and Jacqueline, each with her own area of responsibility.

And on top of these were all the "honorary Kennedys," all those loyal friends of Jack's and of the others, who had become members of a sort of permanent Kennedy gang: people like Lem Billings, and Red Fay, and Ben

Smith, and Bill Walton, and Whizzer White, and countless others. They too were given their areas of responsibility.

Behind the scenes, well in the background, was the unquenchably ambitious father of the candidate. Joe Kennedy made unlimited amounts of money available and prevailed upon his media friends to publish flattering portraits and on his political network to line up delegates.

One of the first, and most important, contributions Joe Kennedy made to his son's campaign was to form the Ken-Air Corporation, purchase for the corporation a $385,000 Convair prop airplane, and then lease it to the candidate at $1.75 a mile. The plane, which JFK named the *Caroline*, became a tremendous advantage. While Hubert Humphrey either wasted time waiting around airports for commercial flights or lumbered about in his campaign bus, Jack Kennedy tore here and there in the *Caroline*, covering more territory in less time and at less expense.

Ever mindful of the vulnerability of his son's reputation, Joe Kennedy also took care of cultivating the one man in America who could seriously threaten his son's career: FBI Director J. Edgar Hoover. Well aware that Hoover kept in his files tapes of Jack Kennedy's encounters with Nazi-sympathizer Inga Arvad, the ambassador did everything in his power to soothe and satisfy the director.

Unlike most of the other candidates, John F. Kennedy had decided not to wait until the convention in Los Angeles in August to nail down the nomination, but "to blitz the primaries" and, in so doing, nail down the nomination long before the convention opened.

As it turned out, the two most important were in Wisconsin and West Virginia. If Kennedy, the northeastern Catholic, could whip Humphrey, the midwestern Protestant, in a state neighboring Humphrey's own Minnesota, he could probably beat anyone anywhere.

Deciding on a saturation campaign, the entire Kennedy family invaded Wisconsin in March, determined not to leave a square mile unvisited by a Kennedy. Fanning his sisters throughout the state, Robert Kennedy made Pat,

Jean, and Eunice attend a minimum of nine gatherings a day each, an endless round of breakfasts, luncheons, teas, and dinners.

So overwhelming was the Kennedy presence in Wisconsin during the primary that Hubert Humphrey, complaining that the Kennedys "were all over the state," compared himself to "a corner grocer running against a chain store." Even though Wisconsin was his neck of the woods, the disconsolate Humphrey felt like an outsider in the state when confronted with the omnipresent Kennedys. He would pull into a community in his "over the Hump with Humphrey" bus, thinking he had the whole place to himself, and dammit, if Eunice, or Jean, or some other Kennedy wasn't already there holding a tea party for women voters.

As for the candidate himself, he was up every day at 6 A.M., sometimes even at 5, to go first to a meat factory, or a rail yard, or a dairy farm, to greet workers reporting for duty in the cold predawn, pausing for his customary breakfast of two four-minute boiled eggs, four strips of broiled bacon, coffee, milk, and orange juice and then launching into a day of speeches and handshaking that would not see him back in his hotel, soaking his aching spine in a hot tub, until 1 A.M. Sometimes, after a particularly lengthy handshaking session, Kennedy's hands would be scratched and bleeding. Even the unpolitical Jacqueline, who normally detested campaigning, was out shaking hands in Wisconsin. She turned out to be a valuable asset. When she accompanied Jack on his rounds Kennedy was frequently moved to remark to aide Dave Powers, not without a trace of jealousy in his voice, that "as usual, Jackie's drawing more people than we are."

So far as the crucial religious issue was concerned, the Kennedys played it with great cunning. While Jack Kennedy was denouncing religious prejudice and arousing sympathy by posing as a victim of anti-Catholic bigotry, his aides would be secretly flooding the state with inflammatory anti-Catholic leaflets, which Kennedy would then make reference to as an example of bigotry he had to combat. At least this was the view of journalist Marquis Childs and Humphrey's campaign manager, Gerald Heaney, who protested the practice at the time.

When the votes were tallied, Kennedy had won, but not by the margin he had anticipated; Humphrey, being somewhat consoled by the results, was moved to enter the West Virginia primary that followed. The Kennedy forces welcomed his entry. If Jack Kennedy, the northeastern Catholic, could beat the Protestant Humphrey in a Bible Belt state that was only 5 percent Catholic, then he had the nomination.

Campaigning with Franklin D. Roosevelt, Jr., whose father was beloved among the miners, Kennedy was delighted to hear Roosevelt say over and over again, "My daddy and Jack's daddy were just like that," as he, FDR Junior, held up two entwined fingers.

Of course, Joseph P. Kennedy and Franklin D. Roosevelt had not been "just like that," but it made no difference. The object was to win. One means was money. It was widely reported that during the West Virginia primary large amounts of Kennedy money wound up in the pockets of potential Kennedy voters. Charles D. Hylton, Jr., editor of the *Logan Banner,* reported that, in Logan County, payoffs "ranged anywhere from $2 and a drink of whiskey to $6 and two pints of whiskey for a single vote." Later, in December 1961, FBI listening devices picked up evidence of large Mafia donations to the West Virginia campaign that had apparently been disbursed through Frank Sinatra. It was this under-the-table money, used to make payoffs to key election officials, that was to be perhaps the deciding factor in the contest.

When the West Virginia votes were counted and showed Kennedy winning by a 60 to 40 margin, the Kennedy forces knew they had the nomination sewn up. Apart from his mob support, Kennedy had won under the most unfavorable circumstances imaginable. If he could win West Virginia, think what he could do in the big, populous, heavily Catholic industrial states of the midwest and northeast. As it turned out, from the West Virginia primary on,

Kennedy would go from victory to victory all the way to the convention in Los Angeles.

Meanwhile, as the primaries unfolded, Kennedy had initiated a relationship which was destined to have fateful consequences for himself and his coming administration. On February 7, during a campaign stopover in Las Vegas, his friend Frank Sinatra introduced him to a beautiful young woman by the name of Judith Campbell. According to Miss Campbell's account, which was accepted as true by a Senate investigating committee in 1975, the meeting took place in the lounge of the Sands Hotel, with brother Teddy present, and later moved on to dinner in the Garden Room and later to the Copa Room for the late show. Kennedy fell for the sensual, dark-haired Judith who bore a strong resemblance to Jacqueline; they had lunch the following day, they exchanged telephone numbers, and Jack told her he wanted to see her again soon.

For Jack Kennedy there was nothing out of the ordinary in this behavior. The Kennedys, father and sons, had their wives and their girlfriends. This was the way they lived. A little fling with Judith Campbell, an occasional, tension-relieving encounter with a beautiful young woman, would certainly lighten the burdens of the campaign. Anticipating an exciting and refreshingly distracting affair, Kennedy sent the lovely Judith a dozen roses on February 12, after phoning from California, and then proceeded to phone her nearly every day.

According to Judith's memoirs, on March 7 they met at the Plaza Hotel in New York. Apparently, their first sexual encounter was that night, and it was disappointing to Miss Campbell. She got the impression that she was there to just "service" the candidate. He did not appear to want to give very much, just take. Whatever happened, Kennedy became eager for more encounters. For he subsequently called her regularly from the campaign trail, from Wisconsin, West Virginia, Indiana, Washington.

As it turned out, this young lady was not just another pretty face; she was very well connected in the worlds of show business and organized crime, where she was regularly "passed around" among a certain set of not-too-reputable characters. It was in April, Judy claimed, that Frank Sinatra introduced her to one Sam Giancana, one of the most notorious underworld figures in America.

Did Judith Campbell know who Sam Giancana really was when Sinatra first introduced her to him? More than likely she had a vague idea but did not know of the full extent of his criminal activities. In fact, all she was ever to receive were vague hints of his power. Known by many aliases, Sam Giancana's real name was Salvatore Giangana, and by the time Sinatra introduced him to Judith Campbell he had been arrested more than seventy times. Among the crimes for which he had been arrested were contributing to delinquency, burglary, assault and battery, larceny, assault with intent to kill, possession of burglar tools and concealed weapons, bombing, gambling, and murder. His first murder indictment had occurred when he was 18. At that time he was released on bail; subsequently the sole prosecution witness was murdered. At the age of 48 he became the boss of all bosses of the Chicago syndicate, known as The Outfit. In this capacity he ruled over an executive staff of some 1000 criminals, who, in turn, gave orders to some 50,000 burglars, hijackers, counterfeiters, extortionists, narcotics peddlers, loan sharks, and murderers. It was estimated by the Chicago newspapers that the annual "take" from this vast criminal enterprise was somewhere in the neighborhood of $2 billion. According to his biographer, William Brashler, Giancana's word in the early 1960s became "law in Chicago, Cook County, Gary, most of the Midwest," and "his interests reached into Miami Beach, St. Louis, Arizona, California, Las Vegas, Mexico, Central and South America." This made Giancana one of the two or three most powerful criminals in the world.

Known as the "sour-faced Don" because of his perpetual scowl, Giancana reigned over his underworld empire through sheer terror. Anyone who stood in his way was coolly eliminated by one of his team of "enforcers." FBI bugs picked up conversations about one of Giancana's victims who had apparently been hung on a meat hook for two days while Giancana's executioners, Fifi Buccieri and Willie Daddano, tortured him to death "with an electric cattle prod, ice picks, a baseball bat, and a blow torch." By 1960 the Chicago police estimated that Giancana had ordered some 200 murders.

Judith Campbell probably did not know all this when she presumably first met Sam Giancana—introduced to her by Sinatra as Sam Flood—in the French Room of the Hotel Fontainebleau in Miami. The first time she sensed who he might be was at dinner with him at the Eden Roc Hotel. In her own words,

> From the way people behaved around him, Sam was obviously a man of "position." I was used to seeing the help jump whenever Frank walked into a restaurant, but with Sam they fell all over each other trying to please him. And he, on the other hand, acted like royalty, completely ignoring their existence, which seemed to spur them to even greater effort.

When Giancana found out that the beautiful Judith was also seeing the candidate for the Democratic nomination for President of the United States, he began pursuing her with a vengeance, although he was admittedly in love with a singer, Phyllis McGuire, at the time. Certain conversations between Giancana and his associates overheard by the FBI during its program of electronic surveillance of organized crime indicate that his shrewd gangster mind knew that if Kennedy succeeded in "going all the way," he, Giancana, might have a conduit to the White House, and possibly a means to avoid future prosecution by the government. Giancana had already taken out some insurance with the future Kennedy administration. Those December 1961 FBI listening devices were to record that one of the major mob contributors to Kennedy's West Virginia primary campaign had been none other than Sam Giancana.

But what of Jacqueline?

Did she know about her husband's budding affair

with Judith Campbell, and how did she react to it? I believe she knew, if for no other reason than that she had already had so much experience with this sort of behavior in her own father that she would certainly be on the alert for it in a husband. And she being such a sensitive, intelligent young woman, it would be very difficult to deceive her. How did she react? By turning away, as Rose had turned away. And by absenting herself from her husband's side for long periods of time. During 1960 Jacqueline actually saw very little of her husband. She wasn't in Los Angeles when he won the nomination, but Judy Campbell apparently was. And during the campaign against Nixon she remained most of the time at the Cape, ostensibly because she was pregnant with JFK Junior, leaving Kennedy free to see Judy at various stopovers during the campaign.

As it turned out, the sexual favors of Judith Campbell were not the only favors Kennedy accepted from the mob prior to the Democratic convention. According to godfather Joseph Bonanno, Kennedy attended a reception given by an Arizona rancher in the winter of 1959–1960, where he was introduced to Bonanno and other potential campaign contributors. And according to FBI reports obtained in 1979, through a Freedom of Information Act petition, by Sam Giancana's daughter, Antoinette, FBI listening devices recorded evidence of other Mafia donations to the Kennedy campaign made through the auspices of Joseph P. Kennedy and Frank Sinatra. Kennedy would accept additional favors from organized crime before his campaign was over, for, once the mob came to the conclusion that it would have a possible conduit to the President in Sinatra, a conduit who could take away "the heat," it gave Kennedy its full support. Because of Sinatra's role in mobilizing the mob's support, the mob was eventually to credit the singer with winning the presidency for Kennedy. Years later, Skinny D'Amato, a gambler close to Sinatra and Giancana, told author Ovid Demaris: "Frank won Kennedy the election. All the guys knew it."

Los Angeles, July 11, 1960: the Democratic National Convention. The entire Kennedy family, except Jackie, was on hand for John Kennedy's day of days. Kennedy was reasonably confident he had enough delegates committed to his candidacy to win; still he remained very touchy in regard to the possible injurious effects of adverse publicity. He was particularly touchy about any insinuations that he was merely a puppet of his father, and therefore not really his own man. While visiting Red Fay in Monterey before the convention opened, he gave a number of interviews to Hugh Sidey of *Time* magazine. Fay also participated in the interviews.

Turning to Fay, at a certain point, Sidey asked, "Red, how much influence do you feel that the senator's father has had on his career? Do you feel that he is the motivating force behind the amazing drive and ambition of the entire family?"

At this question Kennedy gave Fay a look of grave concern.

Fay replied, "Hugh, I think that Mr. Kennedy has been the most vital force in the careers of the Kennedy men and women, particularly after they left grade school and entered high school and college."

At this remark, Jack Kennedy, who was not in Hugh Sidey's line of sight while he was addressing Fay, grimaced and drew his finger across this throat, which immediately shut Fay up.

Later, after Sidey had left, Jack jumped on his friend:

> God, if I hadn't cut you off, Sidey could have headed his article "A vote for Jack is a vote for Father Joe." That's just the material *Time* magazine would like to have—that I'm a pawn in Dad's hands. That it's really not Jack Kennedy who is seeking the presidency, but his father. That Joe Kennedy now has the vehicle to capture the only segment of power that has eluded him. That once in the White House it will be Dad directing the policy with Nice Jack agreeing, "Right again, Dad."

As it turned out, *Time's* cover story on Kennedy, which came out just before the convention opened, was not the "kiss of death" Kennedy told Fay he feared it might be and probably gave his candidacy a boost. But the hypersensitivity to insinuations about the degree of his father's influence on him remained. Former President Truman annoyed him not a little by stating to the press, in regard to the Kennedy candidacy, which he opposed: "I'm not against the Pope, I'm against the Pop." And Eleanor Roosevelt irritated him considerably with her comments about his father and her much-publicized remark about JFK as epitomizing "the new managerial elite that has neither principles nor character."

Despite this opposition from a former Democratic President and the widow of the most powerful Democratic President of them all, Kennedy and his forces were optimistic as the convention opened on July 11. From the Kennedy command post on the eighth floor of Los Angeles' Biltmore Hotel, the superbly organized Kennedy forces kept track of each delegate to the convention, wooing some, cajoling others, catering to their every whim and fancy. The Kennedys saw to it that their "hospitality suite," where the delegates could come at any time of the day or night and meet real, live Kennedys, had the best food and drink and by far the prettiest girls. By comparison, the Stevenson, Symington, and Johnson suites were dull.

As things came down to the wire, Joe Kennedy, who was staying with Rose at the house of a close friend, the actress Marion Davies, was on the phone from morning to night making deals with the heads of certain delegations. He had masterminded the capture of all his son's New York City delegates, had brought in all the North Jersey delegates, and had been instrumental in bringing Richard Daley's Illinois delegates into the Kennedy camp. Now he kept tabs on all of them to make sure they did not stray from the fold.

On the day of the balloting Dave Powers greeted Kennedy with "Well, this is the day you've been waiting for. This is the day you will pick up all the marbles."

And "pick up the marbles" Kennedy did. On the first ballot it was 806 for Kennedy to 409 for Johnson, the other candidates' campaigns having in the meantime collapsed.

Immediately after the victory Kennedy phoned Jackie at the Cape and his parents at Marion Davies's. Then he was confronted with the problem of selecting a running mate. So engrossed had he been in his own campaign for the nomination, he had never been able to give the problem of selecting a vice president much thought. Realizing he needed the southern vote to be elected President, he asked his aides for a breakdown of that bloc. They immediately told him that out of a total of 409 delegates, 307 had gone for Johnson, only 13 for Kennedy, and the rest for other candidates. Without hesitation Kennedy made up his mind. He could not win without the southern vote, and Johnson would be the man to "deliver" that vote, including his big home state of Texas. He did not much care for Johnson as a person and did not much relish being in close association with him for the next four years, but he was pragmatic enough to realize he needed him, more than anyone else, to get elected. Thus, considerations of whether Johnson would make a good President, if anything happened to him, Kennedy, were secondary. As usual with the Kennedys, the important thing was to get elected, to win.

And so on to the fight with Nixon, with former adversary Johnson at his side. After an August hiatus, during which the candidates were compelled to attend a special session of Congress, the real campaign began. Kennedy was chomping at the bit. In the words of Theodore White, Kennedy took off from Baltimore's Friendship Airport on September 2 "as if to swallow the whole country in one gulp."

The official kickoff of Kennedy's campaign was a Labor Day speech by the candidate in Detroit. At this point in Kennedy's career his manner of speaking was still a bit awkward. He was often taut, tense, and rushed. And with his Harvard accent and habit of jabbing the air with his fist, he appeared unnatural to many. At his kickoff speech in Detroit many thought his fast-paced delivery sailed right over most people's heads. Later he learned to relax and his speaking became both more forceful and more graceful.

And so now began two months of the most grueling campaigning imaginable for John F. Kennedy—two months of getting up at six in the morning, after only four or five hours of sleep, and plunging into a ceaseless round of breakfasts, lunches, dinners, TV speeches, radio speeches, huge gatherings, with not a second available for privacy or reflection. Considering his health problems, his energy and stamina were extraordinary. "He doesn't eat, he doesn't sleep, he doesn't do anything to keep fit," said Jacqueline later, "but he thrives on it."

It wasn't long before it became apparent to most intelligent observers that the campaign was essentially a drive to reach emotions, with the issues a wholly secondary consideration.

Kennedy's greatest challenge was overcoming the anti-Catholic prejudice of the overwhelming Protestant majority. Since Catholics constituted only 26 percent of the population, this was an enormous challenge. He would have to somehow charm the Protestants into submission. There was no other way, since it was impossible to talk religion on the stump.

With Robert Kennedy, the human dynamo, the man who could work an uninterrupted eighteen-hour day on four or five hours' sleep, commanding the campaign, it was decided to concentrate the most time and energy on nine states whose combined electoral votes amounted to 237 of the 269 needed to win. These were New York, Pennsylvania, California, Michigan, Texas, Illinois, Ohio, New Jersey, and Massachusetts. Launching first a massive registration drive, Kennedy would then blitz these states.

An essential ingredient to the blitz was the cadre of the now-legendary advance men. It was one of their many tasks to produce "demonstrations" at airports and along motorcade routes, or wherever the candidate was supposed to appear and needed a crowd of well-wishers for the photographers and TV cameramen.

Kennedy's advance men soon proved particularly adept at whipping up the hysterical enthusiasm of large crowds. The trick was to find some segment of the electorate who would really go wild before the cameras. Kennedy's advance men soon realized this segment was young women. Harness the Kennedy sex appeal and you could orchestrate huge, wildly cheering crowds almost anywhere.

Before long, several new phenomena appeared in American politics. They were young women in their teens and twenties who somehow soon fell into three categories: the "jumpers," the "runners," and the "clutchers." The jumpers just stayed in one place and jumped up and down, screaming their heads off. The runners would break out of the police lines and run screaming toward the candidate as he arrived at an airport or rolled down a boulevard in a motorcade. The clutchers remained rooted in one spot, hugging and clutching themselves and screaming "He saw me! He saw me!" If an advance man could arrange for enough jumpers, runners, and clutchers to meet a plane or attend a motorcade, he was assured of a wild "demonstration" for the candidate.

Meanwhile, John F. Kennedy, in his campaign speeches, produced a hurricane of high-blown rhetoric.

We stand today on the edge of a New Frontier; the frontier of the 1960s, a frontier of unknown opportunities and paths, a frontier of unfilled hopes and threats. . . .

The New Frontier of which I speak is not a set of promises: it is a set of challenges. It sums up not what I intend to *offer* the American people, but what I intend to *ask* of them. It appeals to their pride, not to their pocketbook. It holds out the promise of more sacrifice instead of more security. . . .

The New Frontier of which I speak is the opportunity for all of us to be of service to this great republic in difficult and dangerous times.

I run for the Presidency in 1960 in the conviction that the people of this country are

willing to sacrifice—to give—to spare no effort . . . . for Americans life will be more difficult and more challenging in the 1960s than
it has ever been in the past.

It was heady stuff, and he reinforced it with the written word. In *Life* magazine on August 22 he had written,

Our national purpose consists of the combined purposefulness of each of us when we
are at our moral best: striving, risking, choosing, making decisions, engaging in a pursuit of
happiness that is strenuous, heroic, exciting and
exalted.

Kennedy also extended his rhetoric about the New
Frontier to the nation's intellectual and artistic life. He
called for "the pursuit of excellence in all phases of our
national life":

The problems now are so sophisticated and
technical that unless you have a partnership or
an interrelationship between the intellectual
world and the political world, you will not possibly be able to solve these problems which now
face us.

And the New Frontier for which I campaign in public life can also be a New Frontier
for American art . . . for we stand, I believe,
on the verge of a period of sustained cultural
brilliance.

Much of this, of course, came from the imagination
of Theodore Sorensen, but it also rose out of that rarefied,
idealistic streak that was very much a part of John F.
Kennedy's being. Kennedy, in a way, was a split personality—part tough, devilish sailor and part soaring poet.
His life was, in a sense, a struggle to reconcile the two.

As the campaign unfolded, it was very hard to determine where Kennedy stood on the issues. Sure there
was all the magnificent rhetoric, but behind it there was
almost no specific point of view or discernible social or

political philosophy. In reality, Kennedy had no ideology of his own beyond flexible pragmatism. He had been so busy all his political life running for office that he had never had the time to sort out his ideas and determine where he stood, emotionally and intellectually, on any of the great issues of the day. In the last analysis Kennedy was running for the presidency because he thought he could win.

The sheer courage and daring of John Kennedy's drive were little short of superhuman. Time and time again in the campaign against Nixon he had to fly right into the face of possible disaster. The two most notable examples of this were his appearance before the Protestant ministers in Houston and his debates with Vice President Nixon.

Since his Catholicism had become such an important factor in the campaign, Kennedy decided to confront the matter head on by accepting an invitation from the Greater Houston Ministerial Association to discuss his religion on September 12 in Houston.

A few days before the meeting, Theodore Sorensen had confided to a friend, "We can win or lose the election right there in Houston on Monday night." One is hard pressed to imagine anything more nerve-wracking for Kennedy than for him, the urbane, Harvard-educated, northeastern Irish Catholic, to confront an assemblage of Bible Belt Protestant preachers in Texas. He had listened to their interminable ranting many times over the radio while campaigning in Texas. He knew how stubbornly committed they were to their own faiths and doctrines.

Standing before 300 ministers, and an equal number of other onlookers, in the ballroom of Houston's Rice Hotel, he told them,

> I believe in an America where the separation of Church and State is absolute—where no Catholic prelate would tell the President (should he be Catholic) how to act, and no Protestant minister would tell his parishioners for whom to vote. . . .
>
> I believe in a President whose views on religion are his own private affairs, neither im-

posed upon him by the nation or imposed upon him as a condition to holding that office.

After his speech the ministers questioned him mercilessly. They all seemed to suspect that a Catholic President would perforce take his orders from the Pope, or at least a cardinal. Kennedy had to reassure them he would take orders from nobody: "May I just say that I do not accept the right of any ecclesiastical official to tell me what I shall do in the sphere of my public responsibility."

When it was all over, Kennedy appeared to have won the day. The applause he received seemed genuine, and, of course, the grace and charm of his personality could not possibly have left the preachers unmoved.

Then there were the great debates. Nixon foolishly went into them when he had everything to lose and Kennedy had little to lose and everything to win.

By 1960 there were some 40 million television sets in American homes. The instrument had a greater power to shape minds than any church, school, newspaper, or literature. Now, for the first time in history, two presidential candidates were to hold a debate before the cameras of this instrument. Estimates varied as to how many people actually watched the performances. Some said 70 million. Others thought that perhaps 120 million watched them.

There were four debates, and Kennedy was primed for them. From the first debate on it was clear to most people who was the more engaging and articulate candidate. Kennedy appeared calm, relaxed, and graceful as he adroitly fielded questions and remarks from the moderator, Howard K. Smith, and from the Vice President, always taking care to look at the camera—the people—rather than at the Vice President. Nixon appeared tense, frightened, haggard, and sweating as he addressed his not-too-convincing remarks to Kennedy, not to the people.

During the four debates, there was no real discussion of issues. What they accomplished was to allow the American people a chance to assess two personalities. Since the people had become accustomed to viewing glamourous actors and actresses on TV, it turned out to be no contest. Kennedy had glamour, style, charisma. Nixon was tense and awkward. After the last debate all the polls came to the conclusion that Kennedy had "won," and, as if to ratify that estimate, crowds began to turn out in greater numbers for him at his next campaign appearances. Some observers, in pondering the influence of television on the campaign, commented that had there been television in George Washington's time, he might never have become President, for he had an expressionless face and a wooden manner. Others observed that the half-paralyzed, confined-to-a-wheelchair Roosevelt probably wouldn't have been elected either had there been television in his time.

Be that as it may, it was the consensus of most observers that the debates finally turned the tide toward Kennedy. A political miracle—the election of the first Catholic President of the United States—now seemed at least a possibility. The Kennedys' long struggle against religious prejudice and social discrimination was nearing its resolution in a triumph of heroic proportions. With an Irish Catholic in the White House, not only would the Kennedys as a family be vindicated, but the pall of prejudice and discrimination toward *all* Americans not of white Anglo-Saxon Protestant origins would be removed.

35. Going All the Way: The Delivery

ON ELECTION NIGHT, November 8, 1960, the entire Kennedy family gathered at the family compound in Hyannis Port to await the election returns. The compound was a triangle of houses separated by contiguous lawns. At one corner of the triangle was the ambassador's sprawling seventeen-room house overlooking Nantucket Sound. Jack Kennedy's much smaller house, referred to by the family as a "cottage," was across the lawn about 100 yards away. Bobby Kennedy's larger house was nearer the ambassador's, facing Jack's back lawn.

For election night Bobby Kennedy's house had been converted into a communications and vote-analysis center. Machines and wires were everywhere. A switchboard, manned by fourteen telephone operators, had been installed in one room. A huge vote-tabulating machine had been set up in the dining room. Upstairs, Lou Harris, the pollster, went about his chores surrounded by an incredible tangle of telephones, computers, and assistants. The press headquarters had been established in Hyannis's National Guard Armory.

Anxiously, the Kennedys, assembled in Bobby's house amid the constant ringing of telephones, clacking of typewriters, and outpourings of radios and televisions, awaited the first convincing returns.

On election day the national vote is usually Republican until about five or six in the evening. The factory and office workers tend to vote in the evening, and they usually vote Democratic. If the Democrats are going to win they usually must have a very substantial majority built up before midnight on the east coast; later the traditionally Republican western farm state vote begins to come in, and it can annihilate an early Democratic majority if it is not substantial enough.

By 8 P.M the IBM main computer had predicted Kennedy would win the election by 56 percent of the vote. Soon after this encouraging news, the Pennsylvania returns came in, revealing a comfortable majority for Kennedy. The Kennedys were jubilant. A mood of euphoria prevailed at Bobby's house. The candidate's sisters were jumping up and down in Bobby's living room, clapping their hands, and Morton Downey, the ambassador's singer-friend, was passing out drinks and sandwiches and crooning "Did Your Mother Come from Ireland?"

At 10:30, with the entire Kennedy family peering at television screens at Bobby's house, the industrial states began to surge in, and it looked solidly Kennedy.

"Oh Bunny, you're President now!" cried Jackie.

"No . . . no . . . it's too early yet," replied the candidate, who knew more about national election returns than his wife.

Then word came that Ohio was going for Nixon, an acute disappointment for Kennedy, who had campaigned exceptionally hard in that state.

By 11 the mood in the Kennedy camp began to change. For it was then that ominous returns began to drift in not only from Ohio, but from Wisconsin, Kentucky, Tennessee, and the entire farm belt west of the Mississippi; all of these states were veering toward Nixon. Furthermore, Kennedy was not doing at all well in Illinois and Michigan, two states he felt he had to win to gain the election.

Then, as the Kennedys and their friends and supporters began to fall into dejection, there were two important, and, as it turned out, fateful telephone calls, one incoming, the other outgoing.

The incoming call was from Lyndon Johnson in Texas.

Calling from his ranch, where all during the campaign he had been furiously making deals, pulling strings, and twisting arms, Johnson told Kennedy that Texas "was close, but safe."

This was something of a relief. But what about that other pivotal state, Illinois? Such was Kennedy's anxiety about Illinois that he was moved to call Mayor Daley himself to see what the situation there was. Daley was not only the mayor of Chicago and leader of the Democratic party in Illinois, he was also the nominal boss of the Cook County political machine, infamous for its history of political corruption—*nominal* boss, because gangsters like Sam Giancana controlled many of Cook County's most populous wards. Ever since the 1920s politics and crime had gone hand in hand in Cook County, and by 1960 the situation had not changed.

Jack Kennedy's friend Ben Bradlee of the *Washington Post* was present when Kennedy made his call to Mayor Daley. As reported in his book *Conversations with Kennedy,* Daley reassured Kennedy: "Mr. President, with a little bit of luck, and the help of a few close friends, you're going to carry Illinois." As it turned out, it was a fateful statement. Who were the "few close friends" and how were they going to rescue what appeared to be a desperate situation?

While the chilly November air began to creep into Bobby's brightly lit house, with its hum and ring and clamor of phones, TV sets, typewriters, and computers, the night stubbornly refused to grant the election to the Kennedys. By about 3:30 A.M. John Kennedy had around 261 electoral votes, 8 short of victory. At this point the Kennedys watched a haggard Nixon appear on television, refusing to concede. After this, John Kennedy, munching on a sandwich, stood up and announced he was going to bed. The election, alas, was still up in the air. The final outcome would not be known for another four hours. According to Dave Powers, John Kennedy had remained the most calm, self-possessed person at Bobby's throughout the ordeal of the returns.

Cornelius Ryan, who was also present, confirmed this to me and added another dimension. He told me that Jack Kennedy was also the toughest person at Bobby's that night. When bad news flashed on the screen, Bobby would groan and his sisters would wail, but Jack would never flinch or look dejected; he would just mutter "shit" or "fuck it," without blinking an eye.

After Jack Kennedy left, Bobby Kennedy, the unquenchable campaign manager, stayed up throughout the remainder of the night, making frantic calls to California, Texas, Chicago, and Minnesota, continually checking the latest returns. As dawn approached, Kenny O'Donnell thought Bobby looked very perturbed and asked him why.

"I'm worried about Teddy," Bobby replied, "we've lost every state that he worked in out west. Jack will kid him, and that may hurt Teddy's feelings."

While Jack Kennedy was sleeping soundly in his cottage, word came to Bobby's command post that Jack had lost California but had squeaked by in Illinois and Texas, and had finally won in Michigan, Minnesota, and New Mexico, giving him a total of 303 electoral votes, to Nixon's 219. Apparently Jack had won.

As it turned out, the election was so close that a very small change in the vote in Texas and Illinois would have given the election to Nixon. Kennedy had won by 118,550 in the national popular vote, 49.7 percent to Nixon's 49.6 percent, or a margin of only one-tenth of 1 percent.

At 7 A.M. the U.S. Secret Service established a detail around Jack Kennedy's house. At 7:30 John F. Kennedy awoke to be informed he was the President-elect of the United States. After receiving this word, he had breakfast with Jacqueline and Caroline, then took a walk on the beach. To his surprise there were already Secret Service agents patrolling the stretch of sand where he had always gone for solitude and reflection.

When the vote was analyzed it immediately became apparent that Texas and Illinois had been the crucial states. Kennedy's margin of victory in Texas was a tiny 28,000 votes. His margin in Illinois was an infinitesimal 8858 votes.

Kennedy could not have won the election without Johnson delivering the vote in Texas and Mayor Daley and "friends" delivering the vote in Illinois.

On the basis of this analysis it became readily, but grudgingly, apparent that the selection of Lyndon Johnson as vice-presidential running mate had been the single most important decision of the campaign. Because Johnson had been on the ticket, Kennedy took not only Texas, but also such important southern states as Alabama, Georgia, Missouri, and South Carolina.

As the vote was further analyzed, it became more and more apparent that possibly the second most important decision of the campaign was made by Kennedy when, after Martin Luther King, Jr., was arrested in October and sentenced by a Georgia judge to four months of hard labor for driving with an out-of-state license, Kennedy, at the suggestion of his civil rights coordinator, Harris Wofford, called Coretta King and offered her and her husband his support. It was a risky decision that could have alienated the southern whites, but it probably brought Kennedy the black vote. Thanks to the assiduous publicizing efforts of the Kennedys, every black in the country knew that Kennedy had phoned Mrs. King—and that Nixon had not.

When the black vote was fully analyzed it was revealed that two-thirds of all blacks who had voted had voted for Kennedy. In Illinois alone some 250,000 blacks voted for him. There was little doubt that the blacks had helped win Illinois, New Jersey, Michigan, South Carolina, and Delaware. After the election was over, the novelist James Michener, who had taken part in the campaign, wrote, "The single event which came closest to being the one vital accident of the campaign was the call to Mrs. King."

But going out of the way to cultivate Mayor Richard Daley of Chicago had also been a crucial, and less accidental, decision of the campaign.

After the smoke of the election lifted, it was alleged by many close observers that the Illinois vote had been stolen. Mayor Daley had told Kennedy on the phone on election night, "With a little help from our friends, you will take Illinois." "Friends," in this case, was a euphemism for anyone in Cook County who could "deliver" the vote. The most powerful of these was Sam Giancana.

In Chicago there is a large, sprawling electoral district known as the West Side river wards, or the West Side bloc, and since the days of Al Capone it has been dominated by organized crime. The bosses who control these wards are so vicious, and their hold on the local machinery is so powerful, that the people are afraid to vote against the bosses' choices. In this pocket of corruption, registering to vote more than once, stuffing ballot boxes, forging vote tabulations, and intimidating voters are routine events. Anyone who doesn't go along with these practices might find his car mysteriously smashed, or his store burned down, or his wife strangled.

Estes Kefauver, in his book *Crime in America,* the fruit of his intensive investigation of organized crime, wrote, "There was no doubt in the minds of any of us, after the sort of testimony we heard in Chicago, that organized crime and political corruption go hand in hand." It was common knowledge that Richard Daley's election as mayor of Chicago came mostly as a result of votes from the West Side bloc.

Ovid Demaris, the journalist who helped edit and write Judith Campbell's memoirs, investigated the Illinois presidential election of 1960 and came to some unsettling conclusions. He found that Nixon had carried 93 of the state's 102 counties, yet he lost Illinois to Kennedy by 8858 votes. How was that possible? It was possible because of the extralarge vote for Kennedy from Cook County. Demaris calculated that a switch of 4500 votes in Cook County's 5199 precincts would have given Nixon the state's twenty-seven electoral votes, and, quite possibly, the national election.

After the election, Illinois Republicans initiated an unofficial recheck of 699 paper-ballot precincts in Cook County and turned up a net gain of 4539 votes for Nixon, enough to win the state. Later an official recount of the votes was blocked by the Daley political machine.

Giancana was later to boast to Judith Campbell that

he had "elected" Kennedy. Giancana was now sitting pretty. He was regularly seeing the girlfriend of the President-elect and, probably unknown to Kennedy, was under contract with the CIA to assassinate Fidel Castro. If ever there was a gangster presumably immune to prosecution it had to be Sam Giancana. He firmly believed that he had just too much on too many highly placed people to ever be prosecuted by the government again.

Hints of the extent to which Giancana was able to control voting in Cook County's West Side bloc were discovered through the FBI's program of electronic surveillance of organized crime. The relevant tapes came to light in 1979 when the House Select Committee on Assassinations published its twelve volumes of *Hearings and Exhibits* in support of its final report.

On October 23, 1962, an FBI listening device overheard Congressman Roland Libonati, whose administrative assistant, Anthony Tisci, was married to one of Giancana's daughters, tell Giancana political associates Pat Marcy, a ward committeeman, and John D'Arco, a city alderman, that he didn't even know who was running against him in the upcoming congressional elections because "any opposition is laughable." Libonati then went on to tell Marcy and D'Arco: "Last time you guys built me up to 98,000 votes and the other guy got 23,000."

And on February 28, 1963, Sam Giancana was overheard by an FBI bug referring to how Robert Kennedy would react to the outcome of a recent local election: "That will teach that little fucker who runs Chicago."

William Brashler, in researching his biography of Sam Giancana, *The Don,* made a study of how Giancana's forces rigged elections in Chicago's "river wards." Giancana's henchmen, he wrote, "controlled political slates and, in the best forms of buying, slugging, and bribery, they controlled the votes, in some years down to each individual vote." According to Brashler, scores of Giancana's "vote floaters" and "vote sluggers" would fan out on election day to coerce the voters. Brashler wrote, "The 1960 Kennedy-Nixon election played into Giancana's hands" as "the master vote counters of the city's river wards worked feverishly to deliver their man."

G. Robert Blakey, a Justice Department attorney under Robert Kennedy, who would become chief counsel for the House Select Committee on Assassinations, echoed Brashler's account. As chief counsel, Blakey had access to FBI files and tapes on political corruption in Chicago and took testimony from Ralph Salerno, a recognized authority on the subject and former police official who spent years as an intelligence analyst on organized crime for the New York Police Department. Based on the evidence that was presented to him, Blakey concluded that "thanks to massive vote stealing in Illinois and Texas . . . the Kennedy-Johnson ticket eked out its razor-thin margin of victory."

It must be emphasized at this point, however, that it is not my contention that Sam Giancana "delivered" the election to Kennedy, but that there is little doubt that he *helped* deliver it, unknown to Kennedy probably, and, what is more important, that *he thought* he had won the election for Kennedy.

The trails to the truth of this sorry matter are, by now, quite cold. However, a few of Kennedy's closest supporters have admitted, off the record, that the Illinois vote was probably stolen. One of these is that long-time Kennedy friend, adviser, and backer, Patrick Lannan of Palm Beach and New York, who worked hard throughout the campaign to get out the vote. Lannan once informed my agent that Kennedy was losing crucial Cook County until Mayor Daley "and friends" went to work stuffing ballot boxes and resurrecting the voters from the dead.

As for Mayor Daley, he was also convinced he had won the election for Kennedy. It was no mere coincidence that he became the second official visitor (after Truman) to the new President's office the day after the inauguration. Sam Giancana, of course, did not pay a call, but three and a half months after Kennedy was installed as President, his girlfriend, Judy Campbell, apparently did, the first of the many visits to the White House she was to describe in a book fifteen years later.

In view of what occurred in Illinois, the question immediately arises, did Lyndon Johnson steal the election in Texas? The answer to this question is best stated as another question: Would the egomaniacal Lyndon Johnson ever risk the embarrassment of losing his home state? Johnson had said it all when he told Kennedy over the phone that Texas was "close, but safe." According to Robert Blakey, of the some 100,000 Texas big-city votes "disqualified" by the state voting commission, the overwhelming majority of them had been for Nixon.

Richard Nixon in his memoirs wrote that he was urged by Republican leaders, including Eisenhower, to contest the election and especially the Illinois vote, but decided against it. Eisenhower even said he would personally raise the money for a general recount of the votes, and Nixon still refused to contest. In his book Nixon wrote that he did not contest because it would have been too divisive for the nation, but perhaps he too had some electoral shenanigans to hide.

Whatever the reason, the election had been so close as to be considered virtually a draw. If the combined fifty-one electoral votes of those two "delivered" states, Texas and Illinois, had gone to Nixon, Nixon would have become President of the United States with a majority of two in the electoral college.

Still it was something of a political miracle that a Catholic could win, if even by an infinitesimal margin, in such a predominantly Protestant country as the United States. However, it was a miracle bought at great price—the price not only of Joseph P. Kennedy's millions, but also of a large indebtedness to Lyndon B. Johnson and, though it was not acknowledged at the time, to the Chicago underworld. Betraying either of these last two vital helpers could possibly have terrifying consequences.

All this was, of course, far from the Kennedys' minds the day after the election. For them it was a great victory, as it most certainly was. They had once again proved they were consummate masters at winning elections. They had once again proved that they were supreme masters at building up and projecting idealized images of themselves through massive publicity blitzes and saturation advertising. Their victory, for it was very much a family victory, was the culmination of a long, sustained drive for power that had been in motion for decades, and they were fully justified in being immensely proud of their accomplishment.

Part 3

THE MORTAL CROWN,
January 20, 1961 –
November 25, 1963

36. Inauguration

THE THREE large buses bearing the sign KENNEDY FAM-
ILY above their windshields stood empty at the East Wing
of the Capitol. It was a cold, clear January noon in Washington, and John Fitzgerald Kennedy had just been sworn
in as thirty-fifth President of the United States.

Slowly the freezing guests who had attended the inaugural ceremonies drifted away from the Capitol through
the slush and snow toward the waiting limousines, cars,
and buses. A group of Kennedys and Fitzgeralds who had
not been assigned limousines were standing near the Kennedy buses along with a sizable number of the new First
Lady's family, who had not been assigned limousines either:
various Bouviers, Lees, and Auchinclosses. As one of the
First Lady's numerous cousins present, I was among this
latter group. Although we were all very elated, we were
also quite perplexed because no one seemed to know how
we were all supposed to get to Ambassador Joseph P.
Kennedy's luncheon for the President's and First Lady's
families at the Mayflower Hotel. We had been taken to
the Capitol in White House cars and told that buses would
take us to the Mayflower, but the only buses in evidence
were obviously reserved for the Kennedys.

"God, there must be a hell of a lot of Kennedys
around to fill all those buses," someone observed.

"Either that or they're stuffing the ballot box again," someone quipped.

But after nearly all of the Kennedy and Fitzgerald relatives had piled into the first bus, it was clear they would take up no more than three-quarters of one bus. What about the other two buses? Before long the answer came from a White House military aide equipped with a two-way radio. The First Lady's family members were to go to Ambassador Kennedy's luncheon in the Kennedy family buses. Immediately, we all made for the buses. Once inside, we were surprised to find that red carpets had been laid down the aisles.

And so, for a brief time—the time it took to go from the Capitol to the Mayflower—we all enjoyed the glory of being Kennedys on that momentous day in the history of the Kennedy family. It was a heady experience, and it gave me an invaluable insight into what it was like to be a Kennedy, what it *meant* to be a Kennedy.

Pennsylvania Avenue had been completely cleared of all traffic and parked cars. As the three large buses got under way, preceded by a police escort, I looked out the window ahead at the vast crowd in the intense cold. The passionate rhetoric of the new President was still ringing in my head:

"Let the word go forth, from this time and place. . . ."

"Of those to whom much has been given, much will be required. . . ."

"We will pay any price, bear any burden, meet any hardship, support any friend, oppose any foe, to assure the survival and success of liberty. . . ."

At a certain point the crowd began to wake up to the huge KENNEDY FAMILY signs on the buses and began cheering lightly. Soon all of Pennsylvania Avenue had erupted in a wild outburst of cheering and applause. Simultaneously the police escort's sirens began to screech and wail. By the time the three buses arrived at the Mayflower, the roar of the crowd was deafening.

A magnificent buffet was laid out over a vast table in the center of the Mayflower's rose and blue East Room, with round tables seating six to eight scattered about the room on either side. Soon a gathering of perhaps sixty or more Kennedys, Fitzgeralds, Bouviers, Lees, and Auchinclosses was milling around the food while Rose Kennedy and the other mother of the moment, Janet Auchincloss, attempted to do the honors.

It was an awkward situation. Most of the President's relatives had not met the First Lady's relatives, or had met them perhaps only once or twice before, either at the wedding in Newport in 1953 or at Jack Bouvier's funeral in 1957. It was well known to the Kennedys that the First Lady's three families were all ardent Republicans, who had probably not voted for Jack Kennedy. Furthermore, several members of the First Lady's families, my father and Jackie's stepfather, both stockbrokers, among others, held resentments against Ambassador Kennedy going back to Kennedy's days as the chairman of the SEC. And there were others among Jackie's relatives who detested Joe Kennedy. There was Jackie's maternal grandfather, James T. Lee, for example. Old Man Lee had refused to attend the inauguration.

Somewhat hesitantly, Rose Kennedy attempted to make the introductions. Noticing she was having a little trouble, Janet Auchinchoss stepped in, in her usual brisk way, to help out, and before long, the five families had more or less "met." Throughout the introductions, Ambassador Kennedy seemed oddly reserved and detached for someone whose son had just been inaugurated President of the United States. When my father shook his hand and congratulated him on his son's accession to the presidency, he simply nodded without uttering a word. I noticed he was equally blasé with the other congratulators and especially with the First Lady's towering stepfather, Hugh D. Auchincloss, to whom I believe Kennedy said hardly a word. Was this the dynamic Joe Kennedy who had made one of the great fortunes of modern times and fathered the most powerful political family since the Roosevelts? One would have never sensed it from his demeanor that momentous afternoon. He made absolutely no effort to ingratiate himself with his guests and displayed very little outward enthusiasm. Once he had shaken everyone's hand, he withdrew to his own fold—to his daughters and nieces and nephews—and stayed close to them, more or less ignoring his wife. Rose, too, appeared somewhat shy and withdrawn. She did not seem to be much at ease unless she was talking with a member of her own family. Granted, she had already spent an exhausting morning—rising early, after a late night, climaxed by an eight-inch snowfall and an immense traffic jam, going to mass in Georgetown at 8 A.M., walking home from mass in the snow because nobody would give her a lift, getting ready for the inaugural ceremonies at the Capitol—still she seemed oddly subdued and unsure of herself. As for the Kennedy sisters—Eunice, Jean, and Patricia—they hardly left each other's company, walking around in a tight little covey of their own. The Kennedy brothers were not present. Bobby Kennedy was attending the official luncheon in the old Supreme Court Chamber of the Capitol, and no one was sure where Teddy was.

Of course, the buffet was splendid and did tempt the guests from one another. Spread out over the vast center table were hot and cold hors d'oeuvres, hot soups, lobster Newburg, Alaskan king crab, blue points on the half shell, shrimp cocktail, roast turkey, duck a l'orange, roast beef, ham, pheasant, whole baked salmon, and varieties of salad, fruits, nuts, and sweets.

After helping themselves to the buffet, the guests faced the problem of where to go. There were no place cards on the tables, and no one seemed to be in charge of seating people. The Kennedys, however, already knew in advance where *they* were going and that was someplace *together*. Before long Rose and Joe and Pat and Jean and Eunice and a clutch of Fitzgeralds were all together at a group of tables on one side of the room, and the others—the Bouviers, Lees, and Auchinclosses—were left to fend for themselves. It wasn't long before the East Room of the Mayflower became a clearly divided arena. There were those of us who had been thinking about making a toast to Jack Kennedy, or a toast to Jackie, or a toast to the next four years, but we were soon discouraged from trying by the withdrawn, disassociated attitude of the Kennedys.

"Don't you understand?" one of my cousins said. "We're the enemy . . . that's all there is to it."

The enemy. I wondered. If we were the enemy it was all in the Kennedys' imaginings. Granted, the Auchinclosses were quintessential white Anglo-Saxon Protestants, the sort of people the Kennedys, as Irish Catholics, had been blackballed by in Boston, but the Bouviers were French Catholics and the Lees were Irish Catholics.

"Listen," someone said, "they think we are Henry Cabot Lodge . . . in other words, anathema."

The luncheon ended with fewer goodbyes and thank-yous than there had been introductions. Then the whole troupe, minus Ambassador and Mrs. Kennedy and the Kennedy sisters, who had limousines waiting, filed once again past the klieg lights, the photographers, the TV cameramen, the gawkers, the police, and Secret Service and into the KENNEDY FAMILY buses to head for the inaugural parade.

While Ambassador Kennedy's luncheon at the May-flower was unfolding in its stiff way, the official luncheon in the old Supreme Court Chamber of the Capitol was proceeding with due pomp and circumstance, and, as Arthur Schlesinger, Jr., has pointed out, with a tremendous "air of expectancy," toward its immediate sequel, the inaugural parade, and its ultimate one, the New Frontier. The official luncheon was being given by the joint congressional inaugural committee and included not only the new President and First Lady and new Vice President and his lady, but the new cabinet as well. New England boiled stuffed lobster was served as a gesture to John Kennedy, while prime Texas ribs of beef were offered in gesture to Lyndon Johnson. The dessert of pâtisserie bâteau blanche was, in Rose Kennedy's view, a gesture to Jackie's French ancestry. The luncheon was a resounding success, with the new President enjoying himself immensely.

Meanwhile, the three KENNEDY FAMILY buses were off again with their cargo of Fitzgeralds, Bouviers, Lees, Auchinclosses, and minor Kennedys, this time bound for the White House and the inaugural parade. Again the avenue had been totally cleared, and again there were the great mounds of ploughed snow and the vast crowds behind the mounds. At the sight of the Kennedy buses the expectant crowds broke into another roar; by the time all of us had taken our seats in the White House reviewing stand for the parade, the cheering was as deafening as it had been upon arriving at the Mayflower. It had also got much colder. The afternoon sun was now well into the western sky, and Washington had become bleak and forbidding. Once the parade began, it was impossible to keep still. Most of us were continually getting up and down as each new contingent of marchers appeared and passed, or we were running off to the coffee bar under the presidential stand. From where I was sitting I could see Jack Kennedy and Jacqueline in that stand quite clearly. Kennedy looked astonishingly fresh for a man who had had little sleep the night before and had already put in a very demanding day. Hatless, and occasionally coatless, in that freezing wind (he kept putting on and taking off his coat), he cheered each contingent as it marched by with apparently genuine enthusiasm, never letting up for a moment during the three and a half hours the parade took to pass the stand. Always curious, and eager to learn from any experience, Kennedy even put the parade to some practical use. Dave Powers, his White House man Friday, reports that when Kennedy noticed that there was not one black among the cadets of the Coast Guard Academy marchers, he was so outraged that he made it one of the first offical acts of his administration to see that blacks would be included in the academy band in the future.

As for the First Lady, she was not faring nearly as well as her husband. Everybody had noticed how detached she had looked during the inaugural ceremonies and how she and Jack seemed never to have exchanged a glance during the speeches and recitations. Now she looked even more withdrawn. She had given birth to her son, JFK Junior by caesarian section only two months before and was still not feeling entirely up to scratch. At least that was many people's interpretation of her demeanor. Grimly she hung in there, with her fur-trimmed pillbox hat pulled down over her ears and her hands in her fur muff, trying to look enthusiastic in the penetrating cold.

At about 3:30 or 4:00, some three hours before the parade would finally end, I noticed Jackie rise, shake hands with Vice President and Mrs. Johnson, pat Jack Kennedy on the shoulder, and leave the reviewing stand, accompanied by an Air Force aide. She had a lot ahead of her that afternoon and evening, a reception in the White House for her and the President's families, and five inaugural balls, and she had every reason to get some rest and have plenty of time to get dressed. She and the aide soon disappeared into the White House.

After she left, I got up and went down under the stands for a coffee. There was only one other customer at the bar, Bobby Kennedy. He was shivering uncontrollably, and he looked absolutely frozen. I wanted to shake his hand and congratulate him, but when I held out my hand, a secret serviceman quickly took me by the arm and asked for my identification. I produced it, was okayed, and then shook hands with the 35-year-old attorney general who was soon to mount the Kennedy war against organized crime. He appeared shy and uncomfortable and very, very young to be the chief law enforcement officer in the country. After a few perfunctory remarks about the freezing weather, he downed his coffee and strode back to the stands.

After a while the cold became unbearable to everyone but the President, and a general consensus was reached to go into the White House where the "Reception for Members of President and Mrs. Kennedy's Families," as it was billed on the invitations, was scheduled to be held following the parade. It was the first party to be held in the Kennedy White House, and it inaugurated a succession of perhaps the most stylish presidential parties ever held in the nation's history.

The reception was held in the State Dining Room on the ground floor of the White House. Though the guests who had abandoned the inaugural parade were an hour early, everything was already set up for the party. At the center of the State Dining Room was a huge mahogany table laden with everything the guests could desire: great silver urns of hot tea and coffee, great silver trays of cocktails and tall bourbons and water, coolers with bottles of vintage champagne, trays of canapes, sandwiches, cakes, petits fours, and cookies. On a smaller, separate table, a few feet away from the main table, rested an immense silver punch bowl filled with Russian caviar, an inaugural gift, we were told, from Chairman Khrushchev, the caviar surrounded by plates of crackers, toast squares, slices of lemon, and mounds of chopped egg. This great black mountain of caviar in its gleaming silver bowl soon became the focal point of the party.

Once again it fell to Rose Kennedy and Janet Auchincloss to do the honors, because, we were told, the First Lady was upstairs resting and wouldn't be down until later. And once again it was Janet Auchincloss who really took charge of the party. Rose Kennedy seemed slightly dazed and a bit unsure of herself. For one who had been hostess for her father, Honey Fitz, at Boston mayoral functions and hostess at countless embassy functions when her husband was ambassador to the Court of St. James's, she seemed strangely shy in the White House.

But Janet, fortunately, was fully up to the occasion. There were lots of newcomers, who hadn't been to the Mayflower luncheon, to introduce, and pretty soon the President and First Lady were due to show up, so she had her hands full. Janet's sisters' children, the Ryans and the d'Oliers, appeared, the Ryans fresh in from South America. Peter Lawford and Ted Kennedy finally showed up. My wife, Nancy, just off a flight from Rome, arrived. A Bouvier cousin who was thought lost, "Little Edie" Beale, strode in flamboyantly, giving notice she would become the life of the party. Lyndon Johnson's two daughters showed up. Jackie's sister, Lee, who had by then divorced Michael Canfield and married the Polish exile, Prince Stanislaus Radziwill, could not attend because of illness.

After picking up a bourbon and water and sampling some of the caviar, I went over to Ambassador Kennedy to thank him for the luncheon and congratulate him again on his son's winning the presidency. He was standing all by himself, several feet from the buffet. As we shook hands, I was struck by how slight he looked. I am a little over six feet and I had read he was the same height and strongly built. But, at 72 years of age, he seemed several inches shorter than I and much slighter, and this was before his first stroke. He shook my hand gently and very quietly accepted my congratulations.

"I guess you must be extremely proud of your son today," I said, for want of something more original to say.

"Oh yes, I guess it's quite an honor," he said very quietly.

Lord, I thought, Joe Kennedy's dream has been fulfilled. The long climb out of nowhere has climaxed with a Kennedy in the White House, the first American President to arrive at the office largely as a result of family ambition, and here he is acting so blasé about it all.

Then I asked him point-blank if he personally had some great vision for America that his son could help realize, and he laughed at me as if I were naive. Joe Kennedy's vision for America, I eventually realized, was simply to have his son President, to have the Kennedys at the summit of American political life. What vision he had was for a family, not a people.

I was about to say something else, as banal as my first remark, something about looking forward to seeing the President at the party, when my cousin Little Edie Beale came up and gave the ambassador a kiss. Little Edie Beale had known the Kennedys long ago in Palm Beach, long before Jackie had known them. Putting her hand on the ambassador's arm, she reminded him, rather tactlessly but jokingly, that she once had been semiengaged to his oldest son, Joe Junior and that if he hadn't been killed in the war he would be President instead of Jack and she would be First Lady, not Jackie. Joe Kennedy said nothing and took a sip of his drink.

It was at this point that a Bouvier cousin, Michelle Crouse, overheard Joe Kennedy mutter to someone: "Jesus Christ, I didn't know Jackie had so many goddamned relatives."

By now it was getting close to six and still the President and the First Lady had not appeared. It was clear why the President had not appeared—the band music of the inaugural parade was still audible. He would not be in until the parade was over. But what was the story on Jackie? "They say she's upstairs resting" was the word. Then Janet confirmed it by telling everyone her daughter was "up in the Queen's bedroom trying to relax." The disappointment was acute. Some of her relatives had flown thousands of miles to see her at this climatic moment of her life.

Despite the absence of the two principals, the party was, by now, booming. About 150 to 200 relatives and friends of the new President and First Lady, and also of Vice President and Mrs. Johnson, were milling around, albeit in separate enclaves, enjoying themselves.

Peter Lawford, easily the most gregarious of all the Kennedys, was going about shaking hands with everyone as if he had just been elected President. Hugh D. Auchincloss, tall and ruddy, was already pretty much in his cups. He had hardly said a word all day, and several Bouviers had observed he was not very steady on his feet. Being in the same room again with Joe Kennedy had apparently been too much for the ultra-Republican WASP stockbroker.

Meanwhile Janet Auchincloss was very hard-pressed to explain where Jackie was and why she wasn't coming down. It was her old ploy, I thought at the time; she always knew that playing hard-to-get made you more wanted, more missed. Despite her absence, however, the guests, after about an hour of warming up, were having a rousing time. Even the standoffish Kennedys appeared finally to be enjoying themselves. Ted Kennedy had stopped running around and was actually smiling at people. The Kennedy sisters were still together, but their glances over the room were not as furtive and suspicious as before. Joe and Rose appeared to be responding more enthusiastically to the relentless congratulations they were receiving, although they still seemed too unassuming and remote for the occasion, and there still seemed to be almost no rapport between them.

Then, suddenly, everyone became aware that the

band music had stopped. It was almost seven; the parade was two hours late in ending. Someone who had just checked the stands said everyone had left the reviewing box but JFK and his secret servicemen. Now, with no more cymbals, drums, and tubas sounding in the distance, an eerie silence fell over the White House. The guests in the State Dining Room, sensing that the President would soon appear, drifted toward the main entrance to the room.

There was a sudden commotion. Several secret servicemen burst into the room, forming a sort of horseshoe. And then, in the middle of the horseshoe, there was the new President, tall and erect in his cutaway, with a wonderful glow on his face, entering the White House for the first time as President.

The horseshoe widened and the President's relatives poured in. Mother, father, brothers, sisters, aunts, uncles, cousins, all flung their arms around his neck. Janet Auchincloss, next to whom I had been standing, ran up and kissed him on the cheek, crying, in an unusual burst of emotion for her, that he must be "so cold." My wife, Nancy, shook his hand and was bowled over by his energy. When it came my turn to shake his hand, I asked him how he felt and he said, "Great!"

He looked great, especially considering that in the last twenty-four hours he had attended Frank Sinatra's and Peter Lawford's preinaugural gala at the Armory and another party of his father's at Paul Young's restaurant in downtown Washington; had got up at 7 A.M. after about only three hours' sleep and gone to 8 A.M. mass in Georgetown; had then paid a call on a Georgetown neighbor; had gone with Sam Rayburn and John Sparkman to pick up the outgoing President and First Lady; and had stayed for coffee in the White House with the Eisenhowers for half an hour; was then sworn in at the Capitol, gave his inaugural address, attended the official luncheon in the Capitol, and reviewed the parade for almost four hours in intense cold. Yet here he was looking fresh and vigorous. He exuded energy and confidence. This was the JFK genius: a combination of energy, stamina, and charm, a magnetic radiance. "Magic," Jackie used to call it. His grandfather

Honey Fitz had had it, too. It ran in the Fitzgerald family. It was a great gift. When it was turned on, it was irresistible.

In contrast to his mother and father and sisters, John Kennedy gave of himself unstintingly. Even though he had been through such a demanding day, he greeted everyone at the reception warmly, no matter what his or her family, or party, was, and went out of his way to say a good word to each person who came up to him.

After he had been thoroughly greeted by everyone, he took a drink and asked where Jackie was.

"Oh, she's upstairs, resting," Janet Auchincloss said.

The President's face suddenly took on a quizzical expression, and, after a moment's pause, he said, "Well, I guess I better get on up there too."

Several minutes later he disappeared with his secret servicemen.

It was about this time that a little man in a black suit, a White House usher, came up to one of Jackie's older cousins, the six-foot-two, 210-pound Michel Bouvier, and told him that the First Lady wanted to see him upstairs. After Michel went away with the usher, everyone began speculating wildly about what Jackie was doing upstairs, why she didn't come down, and what she wanted to tell Michel. When he finally came down everyone surged toward him and inquired about Jackie. But he had nothing concrete to report.

"She's just resting, goddammit," he said, rather impatiently. "You know she's got to go to five goddamn balls this evening, don't you?"

"But can't she come down even for a *minute?*" someone asked.

"Not even for a *second,*" Michel replied firmly.

After this news the party began to break up. Joe and Rose Kennedy left without saying goodbye to anyone. The Kennedy sisters took off, too, with no adieus. Janet began to push Hughdie toward the door. The Bouviers and Auchinclosses gulped their last drinks and followed the exiting crowd. They too had to get ready for the inaugural balls.

Years later, Michel Bouvier revealed to me what had gone on in the Queen's bedroom of the White House that evening and why Jackie had not come down to greet the Kennedys and her family. He said, he had found the new First Lady sitting on her bed in a state of abject dismay, her eyes wide with fright and her nerves in pieces. People were coming and going: hairdressers, cosmeticians, wardrobe assistants, maids, secretaries.

"Oh, Miche," she said, in distressed tones. "I don't know what to do. Is everybody there?"

"Just about everybody."

"Also Uncle Hughdie?" Her voice was breathless.

"Yes."

She seemed to consider this. "I hope he's okay."

"Don't worry about him," Michel reassured her. "He's had a few, but he's holding up very well."

"And what about Big Edie?" Her large eyes widened.

"She stayed in East Hampton."

Jackie seemed relieved.

"And Little Edie?"

"She's here," Michel said.

"Oh, my God!"

"Don't worry, she's behaving herself."

"And what about Shella and Scotty?"

"Oh, they're down there, too, and just about all your other cousins."

"And Grampa Joe . . . and Rose?"

"They're *here*. They're all *here*."

She fell silent. Then she said:

"Oh, Miche, really. I can't go down, I can't go down, I really can't. I've got all these balls to go to and I've got to look good for them."

"But they're all waiting for *you*," Michel said. "All the Kennedys, all the Auchinclosses, all the Bouviers, the whole family, *everybody*."

"Did Jack say hello to everybody?"

"Yes, but they want to see *you too*."

"I don't care, I don't care. I can't make it. I can't make it. *I just can't. I can't.*" And, appearing very agitated, she got up to go to her dressing table.

Shortly thereafter, the President came into the room

in a T-shirt with a towel around his neck. "Hey, let's get on the stick, Jackie," he said. "Why weren't you downstairs at the reception?"

Jackie's nonappearance at the party for her and the President's families offended quite a few Bouviers, Lees, and Auchinclosses, and perhaps some Kennedys, and seriously dampened a few of her relatives' feelings of loyalty to her. However, others, myself included, knew the real reason for her not showing up was fear and shyness, not snobbery. She had always been very sensitive, very secretive, even timid, with her relatives. Ultimately I believe this attitude had its roots in the embarrassment she continued to feel over her father. Her relatives knew what had gone on behind the scenes at her wedding, and she probably imagined them still snickering about it. Many of those relatives had not seen her since then. And we now know about the fourteen-year battle between the Bouviers and the Auchinclosses for her time and attention, and the strained relations between the Bouviers and the Lees. Now the Kennedys were part of the mix. No, *anything* would have been easier for Jackie than to have faced her families in the White House that afternoon. All this, of course, was something the public never suspected, since Jacqueline seemed so at ease before vast gatherings.

But Jacqueline made the inaugural balls later on, at least a few of them, and to the millions of Americans who saw them on TV, she and Jack looked marvelous beyond belief. The inaugural balls were not, however, the only social events of the evening. There were several other parties going on, and John F. Kennedy, the indefatigable party goer, managed to attend no fewer than three of them that crowded evening. Anxious to impress some of his girlfriends whom he had invited to the inauguration, Kennedy, a man who struggled heroically throughout his marriage to lead simultaneously a married and a bachelor life, briefly attended a dinner party, without Jacqueline, before the first of the inaugural balls, given by friends and campaign workers, Jane and George Wheeler, at which one of his brightest flames, the actress Angie Dickinson, was present, escorted at his specific request by his old Navy buddy and ever-ready cover Red Fay. Then, during the second ball at the Statler-Hilton, Kennedy managed to slip away from the presidential box, leaving Jackie alone with the Johnsons, and went upstairs by himself to a party Frank Sinatra was giving for the stars who had performed at the inaugural gala the evening before. This gave him yet another chance to flirt with Angie Dickinson and mingle with people like Kim Novak, Gene Kelly, Tony Curtis, and Janet Leigh.

As it turned out, only one of Kennedy's "steady" girlfriends was not present in Washington that momentous evening—his favorite, Judy Campbell, the friend of the CIA-Mafia plotters. Although she had been invited to all the inaugural events, Miss Campbell chose not to attend because, as she later stated in her memoirs, "Too many people already knew about our relationship without my flaunting it before his wife on this most important day of their life."

The President stayed just long enough at the Sinatra party to thank all the stars who had performed at the gala, then rejoined his wife in the ballroom below. After the ball at the Statler-Hilton, the President and First Lady went on to the biggest ball of the evening, at the Armory, attended by over a thousand people.

For most of us, the ball at the Armory was a congested, inelegant, noisy, chaotic affair, and not in the least bit enjoyable. The noise level was so high one could not hear the music, and the waiters, taking short-cuts, were constantly getting in the dancers' way. Also, great herds of people were just standing there on the floor gazing up, transfixed, at the President and Jackie.

The silk-draped presidential box was located on the balcony overlooking the Armory floor, and my wife and I and other members of the Bouvier family were seated not far away. Given the way the Kennedys had behaved most of the day, when the TV cameras were not on them, their performance now was extraordinary, a thing of wonder to behold.

Powerful searchlights were trained on the presidential box, so that JFK and Jackie were always looking into a blinding glare. There was Jackie in her long white Oleg Cassini chiffon dress and high Kenneth chignon hairdo, smiling like the sun, with the equally radiant President on one side and a somewhat less-than-radiant Lyndon Johnson on the other. Behind Jackie sat her mother, looking quite uncomfortable, even cross, throughout the proceedings. She was accompanied by her stepson Yusha Auchincloss. Uncle Hughdie was not present, leaving a gap between Janet and Joan Kennedy, who was seated next to a very boyish-looking Teddy. Did Mr. Auchincloss refuse to come, or was he unable to attend? Nobody seemed to know. To the President's right sat Rose and Joe Kennedy, looking utterly transformed from the reception four hours before. Rose was wearing the same glittering Molyneux gown she had worn twenty years before when she had been presented to the King and Queen at the Court of St. James's, and Joe was wearing the same tie and tails he had worn then as ambassador. Both were beaming. Gone the unassuming indifference. Now, with the TV cameras zeroing in, they were greeting friends and relatives warmly, waving and shouting to other friends, slapping backs, hugging and kissing and grinning with joy.

Much later, on the way back to Italy, I reflected on the performance: Jackie looking so stunning at the ball, able to face enormous crowds—where, of course, the human contact is wholly superficial—but unable to face her relatives one to one, where the contact would be direct and personal; the new President and First Lady making a stunning impression before the cameras, giving the appearance of being reasonably united, but behind the scenes going their own separate ways; Joe and Rose Kennedy suddenly coming alive at the ball when, during most of the day, they had barely said a word to one another. What the public saw that evening on TV was, in the end, an illusion. That day the White House was not the mythical kingdom it would one day seem to be. It would be a long time before I could voice my impressions without arousing hostility and disbelief. For the Kennedys were the greatest masters of myth and illusion American politics had ever known, and one pricked their balloons at some personal risk.

In the midst of the ball at the Armory, as the Kennedys were preparing to leave to attend yet another ball, Jacqueline, in her own words, "just crumpled," and went back to the White House, leaving the President to attend the last two balls and a late night party without the First Lady. Jacqueline therefore spent her first night in the White House alone, staying in the Queen's Room, a guest bedroom traditionally reserved for royals and not ordinarily occupied by First Ladies.

The President still found the energy to attend a final postinaugural party at the Georgetown home of columnist Joseph Alsop, where he was feted by still more female admirers, drank a nightcap, and dined on hastily warmed-over terrapin. It was not until 3:22 A.M. that he left the party and returned to the White House, where he spent his first night as President alone in the Lincoln bedroom.

The next day was a Saturday, not always a workday in the White House, but Kennedy had ordered his entire staff to be at their desks by 9 A.M. He himself was at his desk in the Oval Office at 8:50, testing the buzzers and buttons, so eager was he to venture out into the New Frontier.

Two days before, on January 19, he had had his final business meeting with Eisenhower, at which he and the outgoing President had discussed, among other things, the recent (January 17) CIA-abetted assassination of Patrice Lumumba of the Congo, the deteriorating situation in Laos and South Vietnam, and the necessity of doing something about the growing menace of Cuba. It is not known whether they discussed the CIA's plan to assassinate Fidel Castro, which was well under way, but it is known that Eisenhower urged the incoming President to encourage the training of certain Cuban exile forces the CIA was financing, equipping, and drilling in Guatemala for a possible invasion of Cuba.

Vietnam and Cuba. Two days before these had been Eisenhower's concerns. Now, as John F. Kennedy tested the buzzers and buttons on his desk, they were suddenly his. He had already tasted the delights of the presidency. Soon he would know also its horrors.

37. Youth in Power

JOHN F. KENNEDY at 43 was the youngest elected President in the nation's history, and his wife, Jacqueline, was at 31 among the youngest First Ladies. The President's brother, Robert F. Kennedy, was at 35 the second youngest attorney general in American history. The administration John F. Kennedy assembled after his election turned out to be one of the most youthful in the history of the United States, and its methods and strategies perfectly expressed that youthfulness.

Among the President's key men, Robert McNamara, the new secretary of defense, was at 44 only a year older than John Kennedy, and McGeorge Bundy, the new special assistant for national security affairs, was at 41 two years younger than Kennedy. Younger still were two of the President's closest White House staff assistants, the men who wrote his speeches, Theodore Sorensen and Richard Goodwin, both only in their early thirties. In addition, several of the CIA officials whose reckless schemes would have considerable influence on the administration, men like Richard Bissell, author of the Bay of Pigs invasion, were also in the President's age group, as was the new assistant attorney general, later deputy attorney general, Nicholas Katzenbach, who was 39.

As it turned out, the youthfulness of the Kennedy brothers and their closest collaborators made for a special brand of government, one that soon revealed itself to be impulsive and battle-prone, a government that strove to circumvent bureaucracy, public opinion, and conventional channels, in favor of the shortcut, frequently the wholly secret shortcut, to the goal of the moment. Close observers came to call this brand of administration "guerrilla government." Its style was James Bond: intrigue, glamour, high risk, and action, often action for its own sake. Its method was not the tedious, time-consuming legislative process, but the master stroke, the coup.

Special assistant to the President Harris Wofford alluded to this aspect of the Kennedy modus operandi when he wrote, in his account of the administration, that the President once asked the CIA to bring him a "007" type who could give him some ideas about clandestine operations, and the CIA complied by sending a "pistol-carrying," "martini-drinking" soldier of fortune over to the White House. At this time the President kept a Special Forces green beret on his desk, and his brother was inviting Green Berets to his house for weekend demonstrations of counterinsurgency techniques.

When President-elect John F. Kennedy began to think seriously about whom he wanted in the top appointive positions of his government, he realized, to his chagrin, that he knew very few people beyond the politicians and party leaders he had been assiduously cultivating over the past fourteen years. Being very young, his and Jacqueline's own friends and acquaintances, men and women for the most part in their thirties and early forties, tended to be too young and inexperienced to rate consideration for jobs of enormous responsibility. Furthermore, since Kennedy's father had been his major financial backer, he was not compelled to pay off campaign debts by appointing a lot of heavy campaign contributors to high office.

Fully realizing his lack of acquaintances, Kennedy asked his brother-in-law Sargent Shriver to initiate a talent search for, in Kennedy's words, "the brightest and the best" in the land. Years later, David Halberstam would invert the phrase and use it as a title for a book about those very people Shriver had been asked to recruit.

But before Shriver's search bore fruit, Kennedy himself made two very important reappointments that would have enormous, perhaps even decisive, consequences for his administration. These were the reappointment of Allen W. Dulles as head of the CIA and J. Edgar Hoover as head of the FBI.

Ben Bradlee, Kennedy's close friend and then editor of *Newsweek,* told how flippantly these two fateful appointments were made. Immediately after the election, Kennedy invited Bradlee and his wife Toni over to his house in Hyannis Port to have dinner with him and Jacqueline and their artist-friend Bill Walton. After a happy dinner, Kennedy turned to Bradlee and Walton and said, "Okay, I'll give each one of you guys an appointment, one job to fill. What will it be?"

Walton spoke up first and said that Kennedy should replace J. Edgar Hoover, who had been director of the FBI for the past thirty-six years. Then Bradlee suggested he replace Allen Dulles, who had been in command of the CIA since 1953. After this recitation Kennedy laughed and said he would see what he could do.

The next day Bradlee was in Robert Kennedy's house, to interview the President-elect's brother when he overheard Jack Kennedy make two telephone calls from an adjoining room, one to J. Edgar Hoover, during which he told the FBI director how very much he wanted him in his administration, and the other to Allen Dulles, telling him how very much he wanted *him* in his administration. According to Bradlee's account, when Kennedy was speaking to Hoover, he "really laid it on thick."

The reappointment of Dulles as head of the CIA was to have disastrous consequences and clearly pointed up Kennedy's immaturity. Kennedy should have demanded to know precisely what Dulles was up to at CIA before reappointing him, but he apparently never even asked.

As it turned out, Dulles was up to things that would probably have shocked Kennedy greatly. Unknown to Kennedy, or to any of his closest aides, Dulles was preparing an invasion of Cuba by CIA-trained Cuban exiles and planning the assassinations of Patrice Lumumba of the

Congo, Rafael Trujillo of the Dominican Republic, and Fidel Castro of Cuba. Furthermore, in order to assassinate Castro, his agents had entered into an unholy alliance with organized crime. Kennedy, during the campaign, had vowed to fight organized crime with every weapon at his command. One of the mobsters he and his brother had gone after during their days on the Senate rackets committee was the same one the CIA had engaged to kill Castro, Sam Giancana.

Why did Kennedy reappoint Allen Dulles without checking into what he was doing? I believe it was because Dulles, as one of the sacred cows of the U.S. government, was too much of a father figure for Kennedy, "the son," to challenge. Kennedy, the classic father's son, was habitually too respectful of older men. It was part of his psychological makeup. To fire a man like Dulles was, for him, tantamount to firing his own father.

As for J. Edgar Hoover, reappointing him was to have possibly more fateful consequences than reappointing Dulles. Kennedy was, of course, well aware that civil rights for blacks would be a major domestic priority of his administration. The blacks had played a crucial role in helping elect him. And yet he also knew that the FBI director was antiblack, anti–civil rights, and anti–Martin Luther King. Furthermore, Kennedy knew that the war on organized crime would be another major domestic priority, and it was well known that J. Edgar Hoover had stubbornly refused to believe that such a thing as organized crime even existed.

Why then did Kennedy reappoint him? The conventional opinion on the subject is that since Hoover was such an American sacred ikon, firing him would be an unpopular act, and, after all, Kennedy did not have sufficient mandate from the American people, having polled less than 50 percent of the popular vote, to indulge in unpopular acts. But I believe the reason why Kennedy reappointed Hoover went deeper. Hoover had in his files those tapes of Kennedy's encounters with Nazi-sympathizer Inga Arvad; he had the goods on Kennedy. Hoover, who had lived with his mother all his life, was known to be an archpuritan, one bordering on all but pathological prudery. Crossing him in any way could have conceivably grave consequences for a sexual adventurer like Kennedy. By retaining Hoover, he at least had him under his control. Unfortunately, however, in retaining him he was to compromise severely both his civil rights and anticrime programs. To put it another way: In wanting to keep a lid on his past, Kennedy was willing to betray one of his key constituencies—the blacks—a group who helped put him in the White House, and to hamper his brother's forthcoming campaign against organized crime.

Closely allied to Kennedy's reappointment of Hoover was his most controversial appointment of all, that of his brother, Robert F. Kennedy, to the post of attorney general of the United States. His aide, Harris Wofford, and Sargent Shriver had dutifully prepared a list of candidates for this vital position, but when they presented the list to the President-elect, Kennedy said, "Why give me these? Bobby will be attorney general." Both Shriver and Wofford were much taken aback by this, even though the name of Robert Kennedy had already been bandied about as a possible candidate for the attorney general job. They had simply never taken the idea seriously. To appoint Bobby attorney general was out-and-out nepotism.

But John Kennedy insisted on making his brother attorney general for several reasons. For one, his father had urged him to do it, and, it has been shown, John Kennedy rarely, if ever, went against his father's wishes. For another, Jack Kennedy felt he had to repay Bobby for having been such a tireless and effective campaign manager. Bobby was a lawyer who had served competently on the McClellan antiracketeering committee. He was personally dedicated to fighting organized crime. What better way to use his talents than to have him serve as the chief law enforcement officer of the land? Then there was a last reason that must have weighed heavily on Kennedy's decision. The attorney general was the boss of the director of the FBI. By having Bobby in a position of direct authority over J. Edgar Hoover, it was unlikely that Hoover would ever open up those Kennedy-Inga Arvad files or any files he might have had on the ambassador. It is now known that Hoover did keep a file on the elder Kennedy's liquor enterprises. No matter what information Hoover ever got on the President, he would be less in a position to exploit it with the President's brother breathing down his neck.

And so John F. Kennedy appointed his brother attorney general of the United States, thereby making the chief executive and the chief law enforcement officer one. The power implicit in this union was mind-boggling. On the positive side, it meant that the Kennedy administration could go after organized crime as no other administration had. On the negative side, it meant that the President had virtually made himself immune to any prosecution for wrongdoing. It meant that he could get away with almost anything. (Later, when the Kennedy brothers were engaged in a concerted effort to sabotage Castro's Cuba, one Kennedy aide inquired of another whether the operation was legal. The response was "If Jack and Bobby say it's legal, it's legal.")

After the appointment was announced, the Kennedys were typically arrogant about it. Eunice Kennedy Shriver stated, "Bobby we'll make attorney general so he can throw all the people Dad doesn't like in jail. That means we'll have to build more jails." And John F. Kennedy said he was naming Bobby attorney general "to give him a little experience before he goes out to practice law."

Then there were all the other appointments, most of which were much less controversial. These were "the brightest and the best" who were going to sail America into the New Frontier.

First, there was Kennedy's personal White House staff, composed of his so-called Irish Mafia and his brain trust.

The Irish Mafia: Kenneth O'Donnell, a young, tough, dour, unpleasant man, who had played football with Bobby Kennedy at Harvard (and who once told me in Boston to "cool it, or else" if I ever thought of writing a book on the Kennedys); Lawrence O'Brien, jovial, energetic, master politico; Dave Powers, the ebullient storyteller from Charlestown, who had been with Kennedy from the beginning and who was now Chief Companion to the President, The Man Who Could Always Make The President Laugh.

The brain trust: Theodore Sorensen, young, midwestern, intelligent, sensitive, loyal, idealistic, eloquent, a man with an exceptional talent for writing the spoken word; Richard Goodwin, a young, ambitious, hard-driving lawyer who had graduated first in his class at Harvard Law and had served as a law clerk to Justice Frankfurter—an extremely talented political strategist and speechwriter; Pierre Salinger, colorful, likable, effective press secretary; John Kenneth Galbraith, the lanky Harvard economist who would go to India as ambassador in April; Walt Whitman Rostow, brilliant son of Russian Jewish immigrants, a Yale man, a Rhodes scholar and MIT professor; Arthur M. Schlesinger, Jr., the distinguished Harvard historian who would one day write a 1031-page history of the Kennedy administration.

Then there were the brilliant, high-powered executive types. Robert McNamara, secretary of defense, he of the round, rimless glasses and slicked-down hair, who Jacqueline thought was "the sexiest man in the cabinet." A true Kennedyite, if there ever was one. Young, energetic, efficient, a man who got things done. A workhorse, who routinely put in sixteen-hour days. A tough, no-nonsense man with a machinelike brain. Phi Beta Kappa at the University of California at Berkeley. Top student at Harvard Business School. A living computer. An austere man, "a rational puritan," someone you could count on to push himself and his subordinates to the limits of his and their capabilities. Kennedy was happy and proud to lure him away from the presidency of the Ford Motor Company.

Dean Rusk, secretary of state. Kennedy, as he himself admitted, wanted to be his own secretary of state, and so he was happy to find the quiet, mild-mannered, former Rhodes scholar from Cherokee County, Georgia, for the job. Rusk had risen from a poor white southern background to the highest echelons of the State Department and had then become president of the Rockefeller Foundation at only 43 years of age. Kennedy liked those credentials and the fact that he was not a flamboyant scene-stealer who would upstage him in the world theater. Rusk was a controlled, patient, modest man who would never clash with the President. He would be an obedient servant.

Then, in a class all by himself, there was that archetypal new frontiersman, the brilliant, controversial McGeorge Bundy, special assistant for national security affairs, and later coordinator of security affairs within the White House, a man destined to play a large role in the history of the sixties, especially in Vietnam. Bundy, the urbane aristocrat, descended, on his mother's side, from the ultra-Brahmin Lowells of Massachusetts. Bundy, of the cool, logical, mathematical mind, the intellectual machine who never displayed any emotion, let alone passion. Bundy, the consummate student, who excelled at Groton, entered Harvard with perfect scores on all his entrance exams, made Phi Beta Kappa, and went on to become dean of Harvard College at only 34 years of age. Bundy had everything John Kennedy wanted: youth, breeding, intellect, urbanity, and energy. Of all the new frontiersmen, Bundy came the closest to exemplifying the Kennedy ideal of the "brightest and the best."

Others qualifying for that description were Byron "Whizzer" White, former Rhodes scholar and all-American football player—another ideal Kennedy type—appointed deputy attorney general; Burke Marshall, a brilliant lawyer, appointed assistant attorney general for civil rights; and the wise and perceptive George F. Ball, appointed undersecretary of state after the forced resignation of Chester Bowles.

The Kennedys' attitude toward many of the older members of the administration was often contemptuous, or at best patronizing. John Kennedy did not much care for Adlai Stevenson, his ambassador to the UN, whom he considered a possible political threat, and he found Chester Bowles, one of his undersecretaries of state, "boring."

He also found his Vice President, Lyndon B. Johnson, boring, though he never would express his true feelings about him face to face. Kennedy could not help admiring Johnson's political ability, but he was never able to warm to him personally, finding the Texan boorish and overbearing. According to Ben Bradlee, Kennedy's contemptuous nickname for the Texan was "Landslide," a reference to the time when Johnson was first nominated to run for the Senate by a majority of only eighty-seven votes in the primary. Kennedy was hardly the man to use such a nickname.

Johnson would remain a great, lonely shark in the Kennedy administration, swimming around in circles, frequently rebuffed and left out, on perpetual lookout for the least crumbs of responsibility, respect, and praise that fell to him from the Kennedy table. Eric F. Goldman, the Princeton historian who became a special assistant to Johnson shortly after Kennedy's assassination, told me that the only person in the Kennedy circle who treated Johnson decently was the President. He may have called him "Landslide" behind his back, but to his face he was usually courteous and respectful. The other new frontiersmen, however, with the exception of Bundy, often treated him with open contempt. Since Johnson knew how important his role had been in getting Kennedy elected, the Texan did not take that contempt lightly.

As baleful as people like Johnson, Dulles, and Hoover were, it is unlikely that the Kennedy brothers dwelled on them for very long during the first months of their reign. The Kennedys were so heady with power, and so filled with high hopes, and, no doubt, so overjoyed at all the human brilliance and talent they had coaxed on board—more Rhodes scholars than any administration in history!—that they could easily overlook the sharks that swam beneath the shimmering surface of their influence.

For the Kennedys and their youthful crew of the brightest and the best, there were no doubts, suspicions, or hesitations. It was full speed ahead. The seas were all charted, and the best navigators in the country were on board.

38. Into the Bay of Pigs

EVER SINCE President Franklin D. Roosevelt's spectacular first hundred days in office, during which the new President rammed bill after bill through Congress, changing the very fabric of the nation's economic and political life, successive American Presidents have felt compelled to do something equally spectacular during *their* first hundred days.

President John F. Kennedy was by no means immune to this aspiration. In view of the extreme narrowness of his victory over Nixon, he regarded it as an absolute necessity that he do something spectacular during *his* first hundred days. As it turned out, Kennedy did do something spectacular. But, unfortunately for him and his administration, it was light-years away from what Eric F. Goldman called, in referring to Roosevelt's first 100 days, "the most controlled, directed, overpowered period in all the history of Congress." It was, instead, a spectacular fiasco, what Theodore Draper characterized as "a perfect failure" and Harris Wofford termed "a case study in how not to govern and how not to deal with world affairs."

The debacle of the Bay of Pigs, coming as it did on the ninetieth day of Kennedy's presidency, was all the more tragic for having occurred during a period of exceptionally high hopes.

"The Kennedy presidency," Arthur M. Schlesinger,

Jr., wrote, "began with incomparable dash." Although I had found the new President's family, especially the ambassador, exceedingly clannish and cold, President Kennedy himself projected an extraordinary feeling of power, hope, and optimism, and the prospect of a Kennedy administration generated an air of expectancy and excitement not felt in Washington since the FDR inaugural. I was forcibly struck by the enormous hope and trust the aides and officials I talked to expressed in their young leader. Say what you will about John F. Kennedy, he inspired tremendous love, trust, and devotion among his followers.

In his farewell address to the Massachusetts state legislature on January 9, 1961, Kennedy quoted the early governor of the Massachusetts Bay Colony, John Winthrop, in characterizing what he hoped would be the conscious example of his presidency: "We must always consider that we shall be as a city upon a hill—the eyes of all people are upon us."

From the beginning of his first 100 days in office, President John F. Kennedy set out to create an appearance of drive and hope and a personal image of attractiveness and mastery. The vehicles for projecting this appearance and image were the press and television. Never before in the history of the American presidency did a new President receive as much press during his first 100 days as did John F. Kennedy. Kennedy was the first President to hold live televised press conferences. His first one was held on January 25, 1961, and was witnessed by 60 million people. It was an unqualified personal success. Through his term, sixty-two more live press conferences would follow, to the delight of ever-vaster audiences.

A mighty river of magazine and newspaper articles flowed forth from the nation's presses during those 100 days that virtually inundated the American consciousness. Never before in the history of the presidency was a "first family" photographed as relentlessly as John F. Kennedy, his wife, Jacqueline, daughter, Caroline, and baby son, John F. Kennedy, Jr. It wasn't long before these attractive young people became the darlings of America, the most idolized American family perhaps of all time.

This was all relatively harmless, save for the fact that so much of the Kennedy image-building was contrived. When the American people beheld little Caroline "spontaneously" skipping around the Oval Office, they were all the more delighted because they did not know that the photograph was deliberately set up by the President and his image makers. Kennedy exploited his family for publicity with merciless calculation.

Then too the President and his aides fed the ravenous journalists gallons of hogwash, which only occasionally bore some resemblance to the truth. John F. Kennedy was consistently presented in the most flattering terms: he was brave war hero, devoted son, faithful husband, adoring father, wise statesman, inspired leader, ad nauseam. And his wife, Jacqueline, was the most beautiful, the most charming, the most brilliant, the most aristocratic, the most adoring wife and mother who ever lived.

Even serious biographers were caught up in the hero-worshipping. In William Manchester's *John F. Kennedy: Portrait of a President* we find this: "In a single address he has quoted Wilson, Goethe, Faulkner, Artemus Ward, Finley Peter Dunne, Swift, Emerson, Lord Asquith, Tennyson, and Queen Victoria. . . . If he weren't the leader of the west he would doubtless be leader of the west's literary elite." Of course, it is now known who wrote most of Kennedy's books, articles, and speeches.

And I remember so well having huge laughs with my wife, Nancy, over some of the American magazine articles about Jacqueline that reached us. What they poured forth about her and the Bouviers was so off base and so sentimental as to be downright embarrassing. Probably only a relative could know how off base such journalistic outpourings were. "How could Jackie permit this mush to be published?" I used to ask. Later I learned she had little or no say in the matter. The Kennedy people released what they wanted to be released, and that was all there was to it.

And so, accompanied by winds of all this favorable publicity, the Kennedy ship of state sailed forth, with flags waving and pennants streaming, toward that hoped-for spectacular coup which the skipper so ardently desired to fall within his first 100 days.

The establishment of the Peace Corps in March 1961 could hardly qualify as a spectacular coup, but it did, at least, represent something new, a clear example of the "invention, innovation, imagination" Kennedy had promised during his campaign. Eisenhower had termed the idea "a juvenile experiment," and others had ridiculed it as "Kennedy's Kiddie Korps," but Kennedy stood fast and signed an executive order creating the Peace Corps of national voluntary service on March 1, naming his brother-in-law Sargent Shriver as its first director. Twelve days later he took another auspicious step toward peace, this time in Latin America.

Latin America had long attracted the young President's interest as a possible arena for personal glory, and by the evening of March 13, on the fifty-second day of his presidency, Kennedy had made in that arena a promising start. Addressing the entire Latin American diplomatic corps in the East Room of the White House, Kennedy told the South Americans assembled that the revolution that started in Philadelphia in 1776 and in Caracas in 1811 was still unfinished; he went on to say:

> I have called on all people of the hemisphere to join in a new Alliance for Progress—Alianza Para Progreso—a vast cooperative effort, unparalleled in magnitude and nobility of purpose, to satisfy the basic needs of the American people for homes, work, and land, health and schools—techo, trabajo y tierra, salud y escuela.
>
> Let us once again transform the American continent into a vast crucible of revolutionary ideas and efforts—a tribute to the power of the creative energies of free men and women—an example to all the world that liberty and progress walk hand in hand.

Arthur M. Schlesinger, Jr., who was there, later observed that the meeting was an "extraordinary occasion."

The Venezuelan ambassador took Schlesinger's arm and said "we have not heard such words since Franklin Roosevelt." "The future of the hemisphere," observed Schlesinger, "did seem bright with hope."

But these were mere words. What Kennedy was actually doing in Latin America was something far, far different. For by the time he uttered those thrilling words to the Latin American ambassadors, he had already decided on approving a CIA-sponsored invasion of a Latin American nation that threatened to destroy all the goodwill and prestige he had built up since taking office barely two months before.

Consider the process of decision step by step. The CIA's plan to have Cuban exiles invade Cuba and overthrow Castro's government had been in existence before John F. Kennedy's election to the presidency, and had the blessing, in principle, of both President Eisenhower and Vice President Nixon. The operation had been conceived by CIA director Allen W. Dulles and his brilliant deputy director of plans (a euphemism for director of covert operations), Richard M. Bissell, as "a quick surgical elimination of a whole regime" in four stages: one, assassination of the leader; two, brief propaganda war directed at the Cuban people, three, invasion of Cuba by a brigade of CIA-trained and -equipped Cuban exiles; and four, fomentation of a local uprising.

John F. Kennedy probably did not hear about the plan until November 27, 1960, eighteen days after he had reappointed Allen Dulles director of Central Intelligence. (Dulles had briefed Senator Kennedy on Cuba on July 23 but had not mentioned the secret plan.) Kennedy was resting from the campaign at his father's house in Palm Beach when Dulles and Bissell came to brief him on the venture. Evidently they outlined only the bare bones of the top-secret operation. There would be an air strike against Castro's air force and an amphibious landing of CIA-trained Cuban exiles on the southern coast of Cuba, preceded and accompanied by a propaganda campaign inviting the Cubans to rebel against Castro. After securing a beachhead, the exiles would then "fade into the hills" and proceed to foment a popular uprising against Castro that would eventually result in the Cuban dictator's overthrow.

Kennedy did not approve, or disapprove, of the plan when it was first outlined to him at this meeting. He simply took it under advisement. Allen Dulles and Richard Bissell enjoyed large reputations in Washington; their ideas and projects were entitled to respect. As it turned out, Kennedy was not to discuss the plan seriously again until January 19, the day before his inauguration. As we know, it was then that he met with Eisenhower in the Oval Office and Eisenhower recommended that he approve the CIA's plan.

What did Kennedy think about the plan at the time? Since he kept many of his closest aides in the dark about it until mid-March 1961, and even later, it is difficult to say. One thing is certain, however, Kennedy wanted to do something spectacular during his first hundred days to offset the nagging narrowness of his victory over Nixon. What more spectacular thing could he do than overthrow Fidel Castro and return Cuba to democracy and freedom? It was just the kind of glorious exploit he was looking for.

There are several mysteries surrounding the November 27 meeting. One of them concerns the most important element in the CIA's plan: the plot to assassinate Fidel Castro. We do not know with certainty whether Kennedy was informed of the plot at this time. The idea was to dispose of Castro before the Cuban exiles invaded the island. Only by removing the Cuban dictator would the Cuban army be thrown into sufficient disarray as to be unable to repel the invaders. To accomplish this, Richard Bissell, as director of covert operations, had invited opinions from other CIA officers as to how the job might be done. One of these, Col. Sheffield Edwards, director of the CIA's office of security, suggested that members of organized crime, many of whom had been expelled from their Havana gambling casinos by Castro, recruit Cubans in Cuba to accomplish the killing. The idea appealed to Bissell because the American gangsters would be personally motivated and would constitute a perfect cover for the CIA's operation. Bissell, never flinching one minute from the immorality of the unholy alliance, ordered Edwards to proceed. Edwards and another CIA officer, James O'Connell, then recruited a man to recruit the gangsters. He was Robert A. Maheu, a former FBI man and head of Robert Maheu and Associates, a firm of private investigators based in Washington, one of whose most important clients was the eccentric industrialist Howard Hughes. Edwards and O'Connell asked Maheu to recruit the Las Vegas gangster Johnny Roselli to "finger" a Cuban assassin to eliminate Castro.

Roselli, who had started his professional life under Al Capone in Chicago, had run the crime syndicate's Sans Souci casino in Havana and was eventually chosen by Sam Giancana and the high commission of the Mafia to help run the mob's rackets in Las Vegas and southern California. In helping the CIA, Roselli imagined he would receive immunity from federal prosecution, and so he agreed to Maheu's proposal and, in turn, asked his friend and superior in the Mafia hierarchy, Sam Giancana, to help him with the job. Roselli needed Giancana to contact Santo Trafficante, Jr., boss of the Florida underworld and member of the national Mafia *commissione*, who had the vital contacts in Cuba.

Roselli, known to the mob as "Don Giovanni," was a slim, dapper, native-born Italian with sharp features, silvery hair, and cold blue eyes. He had a reputation for settling serious disputes without raising his voice. Edwards and Bissell were happy to recruit him.

We might point out here just how far removed an initiator of a conspiracy to murder can be from the actual commission of the crime. In this case the initiator was Allen W. Dulles, director of the CIA, and the chain of conspiracy ran from him to Richard Bissell to Sheffield Edwards to James O'Connell to Robert Maheu to John Roselli to Sam Giancana, and eventually to Santo Trafficante, Jr., and to the Cuban national who would actually perform the execution. To "prove" such a conspiracy would require witnesses, or confessions, or hard evidence, or reliable testimony, regarding the complicity of nine people, even though only one actually committed the murder.

Fortunately for Castro, the CIA-sponsored attempts against his life had already degenerated into a grotesque comedy of blunders some time before Roselli's recruitment. The devices proposed by the CIA plotters, before they hired Roselli and Giancana, came straight out of James Bond and bordered at times on science fiction. Some of them did not involve assassination, but merely attempts to destroy the Cuban dictator's image. The technical services division of the CIA produced a box of Castro's favorite cigars impregnated with a chemical supposed to induce disorientation. The idea was to get Castro to smoke one of these cigars just before delivering a speech. A somewhat similar plan involved spraying Castro's broadcasting studio with an LSD-like powder that would make him seem like a madman when he spoke. There was also a plan to dust Castro's shoes with an extremely powerful depilatory that would cause his beard to fall out. Soon, however, these benign plans were abandoned in favor of genuinely murderous ones. Now the CIA and its hired gangsters devised a vast range of exotic weaponry, from poison capsules to fatal bacterial powders to poison pens, along with such commonplace ordnance as high-powered rifles with supertelescopic sights. Somehow the CIA managed to sink the U.S. government into a medieval dungeon, with a moral profile worthy of the Borgias.

Abandoning the chemical disorientation ploys, the plotters turned to impregnating Castro's favorite cigars with a botulinum toxin "so potent that a person would die after putting one in his mouth." The cigars were duly consigned to a Cuban national who then apparently failed to get Castro to smoke one. The CIA never heard from the Cuban again.

Clearly it was time for the CIA to get some really professional assistance. To murder Castro, the CIA, in September 1960, offered Johnny Roselli $150,000, a very considerable sum for a single "hit." After the deal was made, Roselli and Maheu went on October 11 to Miami, where Roselli introduced Maheu to his "back-up man," Sam Giancana, who was really the boss from whom he had to obtain authorization to perform the hit, and to Santo Trafficante, Jr., the former boss of all mob rackets in Havana, who was to go to Cuba and make all the necessary arrangements there for killing the Cuban dictator. While these four were plotting, they were joined by the CIA support chief in Miami. By now the FBI had also become privy to the conspiracy and was busily engaged in "monitoring" it.

There followed a succession of attempts by Roselli-Giancana-Trafficante to poison Fidel Castro, all unsuccessful. But the CIA never gave up and continued to plot against Castro's life throughout 1961.

To what extent was John F. Kennedy made aware of these plots while he was President-elect and during his first months as President? The matter is still shrouded in mystery. The CIA had instituted the doctrine of "plausible denial" to protect presidents from blame over assassination attempts against foreign leaders. Nothing about the plots was ever written down, and they were always discussed in "circumlocutious" terms. Since the plot to assassinate Fidel Castro was the very linchpin of the plan to invade Cuba and overthrow the Castro regime, it seems inconceivable that Dulles would not have briefed President-elect Kennedy on the plot at their November 27 meeting. When Dulles's deputy director of plans, Richard Bissell, who had been present at the meeting, was questioned about this by the Senate Committee on Intelligence in 1975, he testified, under oath, that he believed Dulles had briefed the President-elect "obliquely of this auxiliary operation, the assassination attempt" at the meeting, adding that his belief was a "pure personal opinion."

On September 23, 1983, I interviewed the man who eventually took Bissell's place and later became director of the CIA, Richard Helms, on this point; Helms stated that he believed Bissell was correct, that, knowing him, he would not commit perjury before a Senate committee. Robert Maheu was of the same opinion. Testifying before the Senate Committee on Intelligence in 1975, Maheu stated, "The government felt it was important to dispose of Mr.

Castro as part of the overall invasion plan." "The government," he was led to believe, implied the authority of the President. John Roselli was of a similar opinion.

In the interim report of the Senate Committee on Intelligence, Senator Howard H. Baker, Jr., stated that it was his personal view "that on balance the likelihood that presidents knew of the assassination plots is greater than the likelihood they did not." And in the same report Senator Barry Goldwater stated, "The Select Committee has received circumstantial evidence that Attorney General Robert Kennedy was aware of the attempts on Fidel Castro's life before, during, and after they occurred. There can be no doubt of the unusual circumstances where the President has his brother as attorney general, and there can be no doubt of the close relationship existing between these two." Finally, committee member Senator Robert Morgan stated in the interim report: "During the course of these hearings, I have been impressed by the belief held by the principals that those alleged and immoral acts engaged in by our intelligence agencies were sanctioned by higher authority and even by 'the highest authority.' " Thus it seems likely that Kennedy learned about the plots "obliquely" from Dulles, without necessarily either approving or disapproving of them, at the November 27 meeting.

In addition, there is also the distinct possibility that Kennedy knew about the plots from another source, Judith Campbell. Although Roselli eventually testified before the Senate that he did not discuss the plots with Miss Campbell, he was in fear for his life when he so testified and was, in fact, murdered shortly thereafter. Judith Campbell also testified in 1975, not long after Roselli's murder, that she did not know about the plots, but then she also was in fear for her life. Giancana never lived to testify to Judith's knowledge of the plots, as he was murdered shortly before he was scheduled to appear before the Senate committee. There remains, then, only the faint suspicion that Kennedy could have known about the plots through his girlfriend, and may even have used her as a conduit to the plotters. Certainly the fact that, of all the women in America Kennedy could have been seeing, he chose the woman who was simultaneously seeing the two criminals his government had hired to kill Castro was an astounding coincidence. By the time of his November 27 briefing by Dulles, Kennedy had been seeing Miss Campbell for eight months, and her close friend Sam Giancana had already been recruited to assassinate the Cuban dictator.

Thus, when in February 1961 President John F. Kennedy began seriously reviewing the plan to invade Cuba, he probably was fully aware of the key element in the overall scheme: the plot to kill the president of Cuba. (Kennedy administration aides and cabinet members have subsequently denied that Kennedy had such knowledge, but it was Kennedy's modus operandi to operate secretly. When, in February 1982 it was revealed that Kennedy had secretly taped 325 Oval Office conversations, not one of his closest former aides claimed to know anything about them. All expressed utter astonishment, and, in some cases, dismay.) Today the general consensus, based principally on the 1975 Senate investigation, is that Kennedy knew about the plot against Castro, but that, since he probably did not know the CIA had hired Roselli and Giancana to carry it out, he was not using Miss Campbell as a conduit to the plotters.

Throughout February Kennedy ruminated on the CIA invasion plan; then, on March 11, only ten days after he established the Peace Corps, he held what turned out to be the decisive conference on the matter. Present at the meeting were Secretary of State Rusk, Secretary of Defense McNamara, Director of the CIA Dulles, Director of Covert Operations Bissell, the joint chiefs, and Kennedy's top Latin American advisers in the State Department. Also present was presidential adviser Arthur M. Schlesinger, Jr., who, in his own words, was so intimidated by all the high brass that he "shrank into a chair at the end of the table and listened in silence."

Schlesinger had opposed the plan from the moment he first heard about it and sent the following memorandum to Kennedy expressing his opposition: "This would be your first dramatic foreign policy initiative. At one stroke you would dissipate all the extraordinary goodwill you have generated so far."

Confused thoughts must have raced through the young Commander in Chief's mind during that momentous meeting. Kennedy had never run anything more than a PT boat, and now here he was the superior to Gen. Lyman Lemnitzer of the Army, chairman of the joint chiefs of staff, Marine Comd. David Shoup, and Adm. Arleigh R. "30-Knot" Burke, chief of naval operations, all of whom argued persuasively for the invasion during the meeting. As Kennedy, the 43-year-old neophyte, sat there before all those gold stripes and stars and rows of medals, he must have felt nearly as intimidated as Arthur Schlesinger, Jr. did. Add to the mixture the "living legend," Allen W. Dulles, and the "human computer," Robert McNamara, not to mention the brilliantly persuasive Richard Bissell, all plugging for the venture, and one can sense what an array of talent, power, and experience young Jack Kennedy was up against. After interminable discussions, Kennedy agreed to go along with the plan, provided no direct U.S. intervention would be required. It was a fateful decision, possibly the most fateful of his entire administration.

Looking back on the Bay of Pigs invasion, one is struck by the sheer madness and folly of it all. There was only one way that 1400 Cuban exiles, armed, trained, and guided by the CIA, could be expected to secure a beachhead against Castro's 200,000-man army, and that was with the unconditional support of the U.S. armed forces. Without that support, the mission was bound to fail.

Why then did Kennedy go along with the plan? To answer that question we must once again refer to the Kennedy family ethos of competition, confrontation, and winning. All his life John Kennedy was constantly in competition with someone. His first major adversary had been his older brother. After he took Joe Junior's place as the golden boy of the Kennedy family, he entered the big leagues of competition, running for political office, and was so good at it he was able to go all the way to the White House. But reaching the White House did not put an end to his competitiveness. His whole personality was geared to confrontation with an adversary. Now his adversaries were leaders of hostile states, people like Fidel Castro of Cuba and Chairman Khrushchev of the Soviet Union; and John F. Kennedy was not going to shrink from confrontation with a hostile foreign leader, not even the leader of the Soviet Union. What had he himself said in his inaugural address?

> We shall pay any price, bear any burden, meet any hardship, support any friend, oppose any foe, to assure the success and survival of liberty.

This was the primary justification for the invasion of Cuba. John F. Kennedy yearned for historical greatness. After Castro was finally overthrown, he would be able to go before the American people and tell them how he had made good his ringing inaugural promise.

Another reason why John F. Kennedy approved the invasion of Cuba may have been his inability to challenge the opinion and ideas of the older "father" figures behind the plan: Eisenhower, Dulles, General Lemnitzer, and Admiral Burke. Even though he had promised a radical departure from Eisenhower's policies during the campaign, he ended up following the same old Eisenhower-Dulles line.

Finally, it appears reasonably certain that there was yet another reason why Kennedy went along with the invasion plans. Allen Dulles had assured him that Castro would be "eliminated" before the invasion force hit the beaches. With its commander-in-chief dead, the Cuban army would fall apart and all the dissidents on the island would be encouraged to rise up against the regime. At least this was the theory.

The next big meeting about the invasion was held in late March. It was a convening of the National Security Council and included a new participant, Undersecretary of State Chester Bowles, who at the time was acting secretary of state in the absence from the country of Dean Rusk. After

Dulles and Bissell went over the plan, Bowles was utterly appalled. It was the first time he had heard about the operation, and he immediately voiced his opposition to it. His first thought was that Dulles should immediately be thrown out of office. In a memorandum to Rusk, he wrote, "We would be deliberately violating the fundamental obligations we assumed in the Act of Bogotá, establishing the OAS . . . the rumored invasion is illegal, immoral, and impractical."

Soon others joined Bowles in vigorously opposing the venture. Senator William Fulbright, chairman of the Senate Foreign Relations Committee, denounced it, saying "the Castro regime is a thorn in the flesh, but not a dagger in the heart."

After Fidel Castro captured over 1000 men of the exiles' brigade, Kennedy loyalists unjustly accused Bowles of informing the press that he had opposed the Cuban venture from the beginning. In his book *Of Kennedys and Kings*, Harris Wofford, the President's special assistant for civil rights, wrote that one day Pierre Salinger came up to him in a White House hallway and told him, "That yellow-bellied friend of yours Chester Bowles is leaking all over town that he was against it. . . . We are going to get him."

But the invasion plan had already leaked all over the place before the landing occurred. It had found its way into the *New York Times,* and, of course, Castro himself had become well aware of it.

Came April 4 and a final meeting of the National Security Council in the White House from which there would be no turning back. At this meeting Bissell told Kennedy that the invasion's chances for success were two out of three and that U.S. air support was needed to guarantee success. The joint chiefs then seconded Bissell, stressing the absolute need for air superiority. Kennedy, however, refused to give Bissell the go-ahead for a U.S. air strike against Cuban air bases and expressed strong reservations about providing U.S. air support for the invasion. So, as things stood at the end of the meeting, the invasion was on, but the extent of the air support was still indefinite. This would prove to be a fatal combination.

Meanwhile the plot to murder Fidel Castro was activated. Sometime in late February or early March the CIA's technical services division produced a batch of poison pills containing botulinum toxin, which in a test conducted on monkeys did, in the CIA's words, "the job expected of them." The pills were to be put in Castro's food by a Cuban contact, or "asset," of Florida mob boss Santo Trafficante, Jr. They would cause Castro to get sick and die within a couple of days, and no trace of the poison would be discovered in the autopsy. In early March the CIA gave the pills to Johnny Roselli, who, on March 12, met with Sam Giancana, Robert Maheu, Santo Trafficante, Jr., and a Cuban at the Hotel Fontainebleau in Miami for the purpose of passing the pills to the Cuban, who would then take them to the "asset" in Cuba, who would, in turn, actually perform the poisoning of Castro's food.

By mid-April, a week or so before the invasion of the Bay of Pigs, Roselli and Giancana met again at the Fontainebleau and were joined there by the President's girlfriend, Judy Campbell. Whether Miss Campbell's presence in Miami with the CIA-Mafia plotters at precisely the moment when the plan to kill Castro was nearing its final resolution was by coincidence or design is a matter of conjecture. Certainly, that the President's girlfriend should be there with those particular men at that particular time was an extraordinary coincidence.

By this time the mobsters' Cuban "asset" was in Havana on the verge of poisoning Fidel Castro. The poisoning was to take place in one of Castro's favorite restaurants, one in which he dined at least twice a week. The invasion was not far off. Anxiously all those concerned with the plot to murder the Cuban dictator—the CIA, Giancana, Roselli, Trafficante—were holding their breaths, waiting for news of Castro's "illness" and death.

It seems likely that President Kennedy was holding his breath too. For Dulles had probably assured him, in terms sufficiently circumlocutious to allow the President to "plausibly deny" knowledge of it, that Castro would be taken care of shortly before the invasion, and Kennedy, who was no fool, must have known that the elimination of Castro was the key to the operation.

But, as it turned out, Castro suddenly stopped frequenting the restaurant in which Trafficante's Cuban "asset" was employed, and the poisoning scheme came to naught. Time was now running out. The planned invasion was only a few days away.

Kennedy had kept some of his closest aides, and even some of his top appointees, in the dark about his Cuban adventure, and so when they were at last informed during the final countdown to the invasion, they were all the more disturbed. When Theodore Sorensen first learned of the plan, he burst into Kennedy's office in a state of obvious dismay. Kennedy knew at once what Sorensen was upset about, and when Sorensen began his complaint, Kennedy immediately cut him short, saying, "I know everybody is grabbing their nuts on this"; but Kennedy was not going to turn chicken.

Kennedys never turned chicken. On April 14 he flashed the green light to Bissell to proceed with the initial action, which was to bomb the Cuban air bases in an attempt to wipe out Castro's air force. Bissell had originally requested sixteen B-26s to accomplish the job. That was the minimum needed to attain the objective. But as the hour of decision approached, Kennedy backed down and authorized only six B-26s. They took off from a base in Nicaragua on April 14, manned by both CIA and American-trained Cuban pilots and bearing Cuban air force markings on their wings and fuselages.

When Bissell received the news that only six B-26s had taken off, he was utterly horrified. Hadn't the joint chiefs stressed the need for absolute air superiority? He couldn't believe Kennedy would weaken at the last minute and risk compromising the entire mission.

The following morning the news reverberated around the world that six B-26s with Cuban markings, but not belonging to the Cuban air force, had bombed Cuban air bases. Promptly the Cuban ambassador to the UN, Dr. Raúl Roa, accused the United States of initiating the attack.

It was up to Adlai Stevenson, the American ambassador to the UN, to reply to Roa in the afternoon. But Kennedy had never informed Stevenson of the invasion plan. When Stevenson called the State Department to find out what had actually happened, he was told that Cuban defectors in Cuban planes had bombed the airfields, and that that was what he was supposed to reply to the Cuban ambassador's charges. Stevenson did what he was told, only to soon find out that it was all a lie. Later, when he found out about the landing from the newspapers, he felt completely betrayed. When he eventually had to explain the whole mess to the UN General Assembly, he felt the experience was the most humiliating of his public career.

As it turned out, the six B-26s failed to wipe out Castro's air force, and a second strike became absolutely necessary. The Cuban exile pilots in Nicaragua were getting briefed on the strike when word suddenly came that it had been canceled. President Kennedy had been terribly upset by the adverse reaction to the invasion at the UN and had given the order to cancel the second strike. By now demoralization among the American military advisers and Cuban exiles had begun to spread. When Clayton Lynch, an American guerrilla trainer, heard about Kennedy canceling the second strike, he said, "It was like learning that Superman was a fairy."

But the worst was yet to come. The invasion force, led by five U.S. Navy destroyers with their hull numbers painted out, and including five merchant ships and two landing craft, was moving with wholly inadequate air cover, toward the Bay of Pigs on Cuba's southwestern coast. Everyone concerned with the operation was getting panicky. The original watered-down air strike had not destroyed Castro's air force by any means, and Castro's planes would certainly attack the approaching invasion force with everything they had.

At 4 A.M. on Sunday, April 16, President Kennedy was awakened with an urgent request to approve U.S. jet intervention from the carrier *Essex*, which was cruising in waters close to the Bay of Pigs. If the *Essex* would supply air cover to the invasion force, the invasion could succeed.

Kennedy, determined now to avoid further U.S. intervention, denied the request and ordered the *Essex* and its escort of seven destroyers further out to sea so that the warships would be at least thirty miles from the Cuban shore.

For the CIA planners, the American military advisers, and the Cuban exiles, this move by Kennedy was the last straw. It was letting the whole operation go down the drain. Soon Bissell's ships were crashing into the coral reefs of the Bay of Pigs and receiving merciless gunfire and bombardment from Castro's planes. When Lemnitzer heard about Kennedy's "pulling the plug," he characterized the President's move as "unbelievable, absolutely reprehensible, almost criminal."

During the next three days—April 17, 18, and 19—the Cuban exiles landed on the beaches of the Bay of Pigs, fought bravely against overwhelming odds, and were defeated by the army and air force of Fidel Castro. With inadequate air cover they were all sitting ducks. Castro's planes sunk two of their ships and drove a third onto the coral reefs that lined the western approach to the bay. When it was all over, on April 20, the ninetieth day of Kennedy's presidency, 114 men of the Cuban Brigade lay dead on the beaches, and 1189 others were captives of Castro's forces. Other casualties included four American pilots and nine Cuban exiles who later died in a sealed truck on the way to Havana.

As disaster followed disaster, the American planners and Cuban exiles were overwhelmed by a sense of betrayal. The CIA had promised the exile troops full air cover by CIA B-26s and, if that proved inadequate, "an American air umbrella." When President Kennedy reduced the first air strike by ten planes, canceled the second air strike, and prevented the Navy jets on the *Essex* from accompanying the invasion force, he virtually assured the failure of the operation. After the smoke cleared, the CIA, the U.S. military advisers, and the Cuban exiles were left numb with dismay. Soon their dismay turned to rage, rage against President Kennedy.

At the CIA command post, Walt Whitman Rostow

found a completely demoralized Richard Bissell. "It was inconceivable," Bissell told Rostow, "that the President would let the operation fail when he had all this American power."

On April 20 a badly shaken President Kennedy invited his old adversary, Richard Nixon, to his office and told him that the last three days had been the worst experience of his life. Nixon later told friends that he felt Kennedy had "turned chicken" when he let the operation fail.

In addition to Nixon, Kennedy also met on April 20 with the Cuban national involved in the unsuccessful underworld assassination plot, a meeting that was not discovered until the Senate Committee on Intelligence found out about it in 1975. That Kennedy could have met with this individual, whose name has never been revealed, without knowing what his mission had been, seems inconceivable. Given all the evidence reported in the committee's *Interim Report on Alleged Assassination Reports Involving Foreign Leaders,* it seems reasonably clear that Kennedy was quite aware of what the Cuban who had been recruited by Trafficante had failed to do. Indeed it now appears that Kennedy probably withheld the vital air support after he learned the attempt on Castro's life had been unsuccessful. When he learned that, he knew the invasion would fail anyway.

Kennedy later took full blame for the disaster, admitting to his associates that the Bay of Pigs affair was the worst defeat of his career. He believed, to his horror, that he had handed his critics a stick with which to beat him forever. In addition, Kennedy felt the failed Cuban operation had seriously affected his reputation as President and the reputation of the United States throughout the world. In postmortems with his aides, Kennedy agonized over all the mistakes and wrong decisions he had made. "Here the greatest military man in America, the former President of the United States, got this thing going and gave it to the CIA," he observed, "why should I, a young President, challenge their assumptions?" In the end he admitted that he had "probably made a mistake in keeping

Allen Dulles" and had certainly made a mistake in believing everything the CIA had told him about the plan's chances of success.

But Kennedy was by no means wholly to blame for the failure. Almost the entire government was to blame. They may have been the brightest of their generation, but that they were also the best was another matter. For the bald fact remains that the CIA-sponsored invasion was *wrong;* it was immoral. The United States had absolutely no legal or other right to attempt to overthrow another government. In the last analysis, Kennedy was not so much in error to have approved the project as he was *morally* at fault to have gone along with it.

A final question arises. How could two such experienced and intelligent men as Allen Dulles and Richard Bissell have ever concocted such a wild, unrealistic scheme?

I believe a combination of overconfidence, desire for fame and glory, and Anglo-Saxon misunderstanding of the Latin mentality were to blame. Both Dulles and Bissell had enjoyed spectacular successes in the past. They were convinced they could not fail. They were also both terribly ambitious. Dulles had always felt subordinate to his more famous brother, John Foster Dulles, Eisenhower's secretary of state. He desperately wanted to accomplish something that would put his reputation on a par with his brother's. As for Bissell, he was afflicted with the dream of the glory that would be his if he succeeded in overthrowing Fidel Castro. Finally the two men suffered from a faulty frame of reference, a set of assumptions that made them incapable of understanding the Cuban people and how they would react to a Yanqui invasion of their shores. To white Anglo-Saxon Protestants like Dulles, the Cubans, like the Vietnamese later, were inferior human beings who would most certainly buckle before the brains and power of the mighty CIA and its puppets. Allied to this attitude was a total misreading of the Cuban soul. The Cuban people worshipped Fidel Castro as only Latins can worship a great leader. To think that upon the arrival of a CIA-backed invasion of their country, the *campesinos* would spontaneously join the invaders and rise up against their beloved

Fidel amounted to nothing less than massive self-deception. The "brightest and best" undoubtedly possessed quick, efficient, mechanically agile minds, but the Bay of Pigs showed that many of them possessed minds lacking in intuition, feeling, imagination, sensitivity, and vision.

The Bay of Pigs fiasco was a major watershed for John Kennedy and his administration. Kennedy's dream of engineering a spectacular success within the first 100 days of his presidency was over. On the ninetieth day he had gone down in bitter defeat. Theodore Sorensen observed that for President Kennedy, after the failure "the exhilaration of the job was gone, he was no longer the young conquering hero. Suddenly it became one hell of a job."

The Bay of Pigs affair also revealed three things about Kennedy that were unsettling: one, that he was basically an interventionist, a fact that did not bode well in an age in which a nuclear holocaust could easily develop out of even a limited military intervention; two, that in foreign affairs he offered basically nothing new in going along with an Eisenhower-Nixon-Dulles plan, he was simply perpetuating the Eisenhower-Nixon-Dulles past; three, that he was still very young and immature. He had imprudently approved a mad, wild plan, and then, out of fear and inexperience, he had withheld the very support for the plan that might possibly have guaranteed its success.

But the Bay of Pigs affair did not permanently discourage Kennedy. According to both Sorensen and Schlesinger, Kennedy soon recovered his aplomb and began acting as confidently as he had before. Vowing he would "break the CIA into one thousand pieces," he eventually fired Dulles, Bissell, and CIA Deputy Director General Charles P. Cabell, though not until a decent interval had passed. He got rid of Chester Bowles, who had been a principal opponent of the CIA plan, replacing him as undersecretary of state with George W. Ball. After the bloodbath General Cabell publicly branded Kennedy a "traitor."

But firing Dulles, Bissell, Cabell, and Bowles did not rid him of the consequences of the Bay of Pigs disaster. There is little doubt now that it led directly to the Cuban missile crisis a year and a half later, since it encouraged Chairman Khrushchev to think Kennedy was weak enough for him to get away with installing missiles on Cuba.

This was a grave consequence, but, for Kennedy personally, perhaps the gravest consequence of all was the enemies he made as a result of the fiasco. With Castro, Dulles, Cabell, and the leaders of the Cuban exiles at the top of the roster, it was indeed a formidable list.

In addition to enemies, there was also a host of new doubters. I was told on good authority, by a former high-ranking official of the Department of Defense, that in the weeks following the Bay of Pigs disaster there were serious informal discussions at high levels of the government on the question of John F. Kennedy's competency to serve as Commander-in-Chief of the armed forces of the United States.

It has often been asserted by Kennedy court historians and memorialists that there was one positive aspect to the Bay of Pigs disaster, and that was its educative effect on the President. Kennedy *learned* a great deal from the episode and became a wiser man from the experience.

The record of Kennedy's post-Bay of Pigs administration, however, does not bear this out. Kennedy, in fact, proved unregenerate. Not long after the smoke cleared away from the Bay of Pigs, the President and his brother, the attorney general, initiated a concerted program to destroy Castro and his regime. This second effort at covert action and counterinsurgency in Cuba was named "Operation Mongoose," and it went into high gear in January 1962.

But that was not all. Along with Mongoose came a renewed commitment to covert operations, counterinsurgency, and military aid in another part of the world: South Vietnam. "We're in this one all the way," declared the President, and the attorney general, during a trip to Saigon in February 1962, seconded his brother by stating, "We are going to win in Vietnam. We will remain here until we do win."

When Kennedy took office in 1961 there were about 500 U.S. military personnel in South Vietnam. By the end of 1961 there were 3164, and by the end of 1963 there were 16,263, including combat support units, air combat and helicopter teams, and 600 Green Beret Special Forces, trained in guerrilla warfare. In the end, the Bay of Pigs adventure was not a book that had instructed an inexperienced young President and that was now closed. It was instead the prelude and stimulus to a disaster of incomparably greater proportions, one that would eventually destroy a President, divide a nation, and claim the lives of 57,939 Americans.

39. "The Enemy Within": Part I

> *If we do not on a national scale*
> *attack organized criminals . . . they will*
> *destroy us.*
>
> **Robert F. Kennedy**
> *The Enemy Within*

ONCE, during a hearing of the Senate rackets committee, committee member John F. Kennedy declared, "We have only one rule around here. If they're crooks, we don't wound 'em, we kill 'em." The remark set the tone for the Kennedy war on organized crime, the most massive and concerted in the nation's history.

In approaching the Kennedy war on organized crime it is necessary to go back to an extraordinary event that occurred three years before John F. Kennedy's election to the presidency, an event which, more than any other, alerted John and Robert Kennedy, and many others, to the existence of a national criminal network.

November 14, 1957, was a cold, wet, overcast day in the small upstate New York community of Apalachin. The bright autumn colors had, for the most part, turned to dreary browns and grays. A light mist hung over the lowlands, traveling silently through the trees.

Atop a wooded hill off McFall Road, not far from route 17, spread the 150-acre estate of Joseph Barbara, a wealthy "businessman." Not much was known about Mr. Barbara's businesses, other than the fact that he was supposed to own a Canada Dry distributorship, but the New York State Police did know that Mr. Barbara had a criminal record. Among other things, they knew he had been involved in bootlegging and gambling—and had been the chief suspect in two gangland murders.

For some time Sgt. Edgar D. Croswell of the State Police had been keeping Joseph Barbara's estate under close surveillance, monitoring the comings and goings of Mr. Barbara and his family and guests. For months, nothing out of the ordinary had happened around the Barbara estate. Then on November 13, Sergeant Croswell noticed an unusual number of expensive-looking cars bearing out-of-state license plates parked at a motel in nearby Vestal. Some of them were big black limousines manned by chauffeurs. From what Croswell was able to determine, they were driving back and forth between the motel and the home of Joseph Barbara.

The next day Sergeant Croswell, accompanied by his regular partner and two hastily recruited agents of the alcohol and tobacco tax division of the Treasury Department, paid a call on Mr. Barbara's estate. Arriving around 12:40 P.M., they were astonished to find ten cars in the parking area in front of the main house and over twenty-five parked near a barn. As Sergeant Croswell and his men cruised about taking down license numbers, they came across a cluster of around ten men talking near the garage, all dressed in expensive-looking dark suits, cuff-linked shirts, and flashy ties. As the officers pulled away, they heard a female voice, which they took to be that of Mrs. Barbara, yell from inside the house: "Hey, there's the state troopers!"

Sergeant Croswell sensed he had stumbled onto something very important. Upon leaving the Barbara estate, he immediately established a roadblock and checkpoint on route 17, near the intersection of McFall Road, and calmly proceeded to question every car that came down from the Barbara estate.

Meanwhile pandemonium had broken out in the Joseph Barbara house. Some of the guests took to the woods in their sleek, expensive suits and jeweled cuff links. One of these was Sam Giancana. Others raced to their cars to make as fast a getaway as possible. These soon encountered Sergeant Croswell on route 17.

The first car Croswell stopped contained Russell Bufalino, a well-known racketeer from Pittston, Pennsylvania, and Vito Genovese, one of the most notorious gangsters in America, a cold-blooded murderer who had amassed a $30-million fortune from gambling, narcotics, and other rackets. Croswell took their names, noted their license numbers, and, waving them on, waited for the next cars.

For the better part of the afternoon, Croswell and his men interviewed guests of Joseph Barbara on route 17. By the time they were through, they had a list of most of the top figures in organized crime in America. Among the most notorious crime bosses present at Apalachin that day were Tommy Lucchese, Joseph Magliocco, Carlo Gambino, Carmine Lombardozzi, Joseph Profaci, and John Bonventre, all leaders of major crime families in New York; Gerardo Catena, Joseph Ida, and Frank Majuri, a trio of leaders from New Jersey; Frank de Simone from California; Joseph Civello from Texas; James Colletti from Colorado; John Montana from Buffalo; and the notorious Santo Trafficante, Jr., from Tampa and Havana. In addition to these known professional criminals, there were well over a dozen individuals from the ranks of organized labor, men like James La Duca, secretary-treasurer of Local 66 of the Hotel and Restaurant Workers Union in Buffalo, and John Scalish of Cleveland, an associate of Teamsters official Louis "Babe" Triscaro, who was also at the meeting, and four representatives of the New York hod carriers union. The only major crime boss not present was Carlos Marcello of New Orleans, who preferred to send an underboss, his brother Joseph, to the gathering instead.

Of the fifty-eight men stopped and questioned by Sergeant Croswell that cold, wet November afternoon in Apalachin, it turned out that fifty had arrest records and thirty-five had convictions for serious crimes. Eighteen of them had been arrested, or questioned, in connection with murders, fifteen in connection with narcotics, and twenty-three with illegal use of firearms. A strong link to organized labor among the conferees was evident: twenty-two of the fifty-eight were involved with labor unions.

Later, upon further investigation, it was determined that the gathering at Apalachin had been a well-organized affair. Telephone records revealed that the conferees had been in close touch with each other for weeks. Reservations in local hotels and motels had been made considerably in advance—as had arrangements for provisions: nine days before the gathering, Joseph Barbara had placed an order with Armour & Co., of nearby Binghamton, for 207 pounds of steak, 20 pounds of veal cutlets, and 15 pounds of luncheon meat. It was thought at the time that the purpose of the conclave was to organize the narcotics, gambling, prostitution, and labor rackets of the United States on a nationwide scale, that territories, responsibilities, and chains of command were to be decided upon.

Later, however, Cosa Nostra soldier Joseph Valachi and boss Joseph Bonanno wrote, in their respective books, that the main purpose of the meeting was to "explain" Albert Anastasia's recent murder and introduce and "bless" Carlo Gambino as his successor and new "lord high executioner of Murder, Inc." Meetings of the *commissione*, Bonanno went on to explain, were mainly "political" and "social," and were not designed to actually organize criminal activity throughout the United States.

The Apalachin crime conclave occurred during the time of the hearings of the Senate Select Committee on Improper Activities in the Labor and Management Field, chaired by Senator John L. McClellan of Arkansas, better known as the McClellan committee. Chief counsel of the committee at the time was 31-year-old Robert F. Kennedy.

The McClellan committee hearings, the first major congressional investigation of organized crime, began on January 30, 1957, six years after its predecessor, the smaller, less extensive Kefauver committee of the early fifties. Senator McClellan had stunned the country, at the outset of his committee's investigations, by announcing, "There exists in America today what appears to be a close-knit, clandestine, criminal syndicate." Few Americans were willing to admit this in 1957. Now the Apalachin conclave proved it was true. What the American public subsequently learned about the Apalachin meeting it learned from the findings of the McClellan committee, which immediately conducted a full inquiry into the conclave. The findings turned out to be an eye-opener. For the first time the government possessed full, unequivocal evidence that a national crime "board of directors" actually existed.

During the course of the McClellan committee hearings, it also became shockingly apparent that much of organized labor in America was deeply involved with organized crime. In its first major investigation, the committee found Dave Beck, president of the Teamsters Union, had received $32,000 in illegal kickbacks and had helped himself to some $370,000 in union funds. As a result of these findings, Beck was eventually imprisoned for larceny and tax evasion. Following the Beck investigation, the McClellan committee turned its attention to the new Teamsters president, James Riddle Hoffa, who, it was soon discovered, was associated with two notorious gangsters, John Dioguardia (Johnny Dio) and Anthony ("Tony Ducks") Corallo. Among the many nefarious acts Johnny Dio was suspected of committing was hiring someone to throw acid in the eyes of journalist Victor Riesel, blinding him for life.

Robert F. Kennedy became so outraged by the arrogant manner and blatantly illegal activities of Jimmy Hoffa that he made it a personal crusade to put the Teamsters boss behind bars. In August 1958, his merciless grilling of Hoffa before a national television audience him that reputation of implacable prosecutor he was never able to shake.

During his term as chief counsel, Robert F. Kennedy directed a sizable organization with great skill and drive. He supervised a staff of fifty-five which eventually compiled 11 million words of testimony at a cost of $1,500,000. Throughout the proceedings Kennedy displayed extraordinary energy, determination, aggressiveness, imagination, and a phenomenal capacity for sheer hard work. At the end of his stint he wrote a book with John Seigenthaler about the experience, entitled *The Enemy Within*, in which he described the work of the committee and alerted the country to what he called "a conspiracy of evil" that he believed seriously threatened to destroy the American system. He eventually left the committee to devote himself to managing his brother's campaign for the presidency.

The battle against organized crime was a natural arena for the Kennedys. It involved confrontation with real enemies of the people and therefore appealed to their competitive, combative, and moralistic instincts. And it was one of the surest ways to attract favorable publicity. Ever since crime-buster Estes Kefauver had snatched the vice presidential nomination away from John F. Kennedy in August 1956, the Kennedys had appreciated the political value of being known as crime fighters.

Thus in January 1961 when John F. Kennedy took office as President and his brother took office as attorney general, it was only natural that the Kennedy brothers would address themselves to the threat of organized crime. They had been working in the field for the past three years and had become passionately dedicated to confronting the problem.

In his first interview as attorney general, Robert Kennedy told Peter Maas, the eventual author of *The Valachi Papers*, that fighting organized crime would be his "number one concern" as attorney general.

This was all very commendable, but, unfortunately, it was not the number one concern of his major law enforcement officer in the Justice Department, Federal Bureau of Investigation Director J. Edgar Hoover.

Hoover had long maintained that there was no such thing as a national crime syndicate in America, and he still clung to that view, despite the Apalachin revelations, at the time Robert Kennedy took office as attorney general. Even as late as January 1962, J. Edgar Hoover was on record as saying "no single individual, or coalition of racketeers, dominates organized crime across the nation." When, as a result of the shock of the Apalachin conclave, the FBI, in the persons of Deputy Director William Sullivan and assistant Charles Peck, drew up a special report on organized crime and distributed twenty-five numbered copies of it to the top twenty-five law enforcement officers in the government, Hoover flew into a rage. After reading a copy the day after it was circulated, he ordered each copy recalled and destroyed, saying the report was "baloney." The report was never heard of again.

It was as if the FBI director had buried his head in the sand. For by then there was no doubt about it: a coalition of gangsters, mostly of Sicilian descent, did indeed dominate organized crime on a nationwide scale, and had dominated it for some time, at least since 1931, the year the first meeting of the *commissione* was held.

Even I was aware of this as early as 1955. In that year I was living and studying in Naples on a Fulbright scholarship and had a chance to talk several times with Palermo-born Charles "Lucky" Luciano, who had recently been deported to Naples by the U.S. government. It was Luciano who had been responsible more than any other racketeer for modernizing or "Americanizing" the traditional Sicilian Mafia. The former boss of New York's Masseria family and founder of the national *commissione* of Mafia leaders, Luciano had been let out of prison in 1946, long before his sentence was up, because he had helped organize the Mafia-dominated New York waterfront behind the U.S. war effort and had also helped persuade the Sicilian Mafia to cooperate with the Allies during World War II. In what was perhaps the first instance of collusion between the U.S. government and organized crime, Luciano, whose word in the Mafia was absolute law, had given the word out, from prison, that the Mafia, in both the United States and Italy, should cooperate with the U.S. armed forces and not with those of Benito Mussolini or Adolf Hitler. Evidently, to have had the Mafia on the side of the Allies during the invasions of Sicily and southern Italy turned out to be immensely advantageous for the Allied cause.

I used to meet Luciano in his favorite Neapolitan restaurant, the California, on Via Santa Lucia, in which he was reputed to own an interest. Luciano, in Naples, was perpetually homesick for the States and used to hang out in the California because it was the only place in town where he could get a decent hot dog, or a hamburger. Also the place was heavily frequented by officers and enlisted men of the U.S. Sixth Fleet, who used to flatter him by asking for his autograph, which he would write on the California's menu.

In Naples in the mid-fifties, Lucky Luciano was a well-known figure who, though erroneously thought to have headed Murder, Inc., enjoyed something of the reputation of a Robin Hood. It was known he was receiving large sums of money from the mob in the States and was giving much of it to certain of the poor of Naples, especially to young unwed mothers, some of whom had supposedly been his mistresses.

In my first conversation with Lucky Luciano I found him sullen and depressed, but surprisingly frank and open, if a bit laconic. A short, slight man with a repulsive face, he did not possess the slightest aura of the romanticism Mario Puzo gave the Mafioso in his novel *The Godfather*, and Luciano had been the godfather of godfathers.

We talked over his favorite meal and I asked him how he was getting along. He said, "There's nothin' like the States." Then, in an obvious reference to the Italian criminal justice system, which is based on the Napoleonic code, he said, "Ya know, here they put ya in first, and ask questions later."

When I asked him if he ever had any pangs of conscience over his dealings with Murder, Inc., he said, "What the hell, it was just a business like any other. They performed a service an' got paid for it. That's all there was to it."

At a certain point in our discussion I asked him if it was true, as I had heard, that he was once the *capo di tutti i capi*, the boss of all bosses, and he said, "Yeah, I organized the syndicate in New York and L.A.; before me it was just a bunch a guys each goin' his own way."

"You must be a very good organizer," I observed.

"You gotta be a pretty tough guy," he replied.

If he had wanted to, J. Edgar Hoover could have sent one of his FBI agents to Naples to interview Lucky

Luciano about organized crime in America, and, I am quite sure, Luciano, who was very grateful to the government for having let him out of prison in 1946, would have been quite cooperative and enlightening, within the bounds of *omertá*. He would probably have told a lot about structure, although he would not have named many names. In any case, as the man who Americanized the old Sicilian Mafia, he certainly would have been a priceless mine of information.

But the truth of the matter was that J. Edgar Hoover did not *want* to know that such a thing as organized crime existed on a nationwide scale. He did not want to know, because if it did exist, it meant that he and the FBI had failed to prevent its growth and development over the thirty-six years of his administration.

Hoover's attitude was part of a national blindness, a collective self-deception, for by the time John F. Kennedy was inaugurated President, American freedom and liberty had been tragically abused on an enormous scale by large crime "families," often acting in concert. The Honored Society, or the Syndicate, or the Mafia, or La Cosa Nostra, or the Tradition, or the Outfit, whatever one chose to call it, was, by 1961, just as much an American institution as General Motors or the U.S. Senate.

But by 1961 the lords of organized crime were no longer underground, as they had been in the days of prohibition. Now the enemy within freely mingled with the luminaries of café society, Hollywood, and America's monied class wherever they were found. By 1961 there was scarcely an area of American life that was not corrupted in some way by organized crime.

It was a tribute to John and Robert Kennedy that, unlike the director of the FBI, and, for that matter, most of the government's other law enforcement agencies, they alone seemed to fully appreciate the size and influence of organized crime in 1961 and the enormous threat it posed to American institutions. Here was a huge criminal network that was routinely making a mockery of the Constitution, the Bill of Rights, and all branches of government—federal, state, and local. It was no exaggeration of Robert

Kennedy's to have identified it as the nation's prime enemy within.

When Lyndon Johnson was informed that John Kennedy was going to appoint his brother Robert attorney general he told a friend: "Dick Russell [the Senator] is absolutely shittin' a squealin' worm. He thinks it's a disgrace for a kid who's never practiced law to be appointed. . . . I agree with him. But I don't think Jack Kennedy's gonna let a little fart like Bobby lead him around by the nose."

Lyndon Johnson was not the only one who had been appalled over John Kennedy's appointment of his brother as attorney general. It had been a most unpopular appointment all the way around. But, as it turned out, it was perhaps John Kennedy's best cabinet appointment, if not his wisest. For Robert Kennedy, who turned 35 two months before he was sworn in, had had an education second to none in combating organized crime by virtue of his service as chief counsel of Senator McClellan's antirackets committee. While working for that committee he had helped uncover corruption in fifteen unions and fifty corporations. He had helped put corrupt labor leaders like Dave Beck, Jr., James G. Cross, and William E. Maloney behind bars. He had alerted the nation to "the conspiracy of evil" that was organized crime. And he had acquired a thorough knowledge himself of the structure, extent, and methods of organized crime, far more knowledge than J. Edgar Hoover had acquired in his thirty-six years as director of the FBI.

But being attorney general was much more than chasing crooks; it was also administering an immense $400-million-a-year governmental bureaucracy containing 32,000 employees, seven major divisions, three major offices, and three major bureaus, not the least of which was the Federal Bureau of Investigation. As his brother's campaign manager in both his senatorial and presidential campaigns, Robert Kennedy had gained considerable administrative experience by successfully managing large staffs and large amounts of money. He was probably a more capable administrator than most attorneys general within memory.

With so much administrative expertise and firsthand experience in fighting organized crime behind him, Robert Kennedy should have got off to a tremendous start as attorney general after his brother took office as President of the United States, but, unfortunately for him, and for the people of the United States, he had in his FBI director a most difficult man to contend with, a sly egotist whom his own deputy director, William Sullivan, once described as "one of the greatest con men who ever lived" and "a master blackmailer," a man who routinely broke the law, violated the Bill of Rights, and took orders only from himself.

In his book *Kennedy Justice*, Victor Navasky characterized the clash between Robert Kennedy and J. Edgar Hoover as that between "The Maximum Attorney General, the President's brother," and "The Ultimate Bureaucrat." It was to be a clash of monumental dimensions, and vast, possibly sinister, repercussions.

For Hoover, the very existence of an attorney general who was the brother of the President and who therefore had behind him the immense power of the presidency, was, in the words of one observer, an unprecedented threat. To have Robert Kennedy as his boss meant that Hoover could not enjoy that cherished special relationship with the President he had always enjoyed with previous chief executives. Now the attorney general, not the FBI director, had the special relationship.

Correspondingly, for Robert Kennedy, and especially John Kennedy, Hoover represented an unprecedented threat. As official keeper of the secrets, Hoover had enough material in his files to blackmail thousands, if not millions, of Americans, including the President of the United States. All he had to do was leak the John Kennedy-Inga Arvad relationship, or the $500,000 allegedly paid to one of Kennedy's former girlfriends (who had sued him for breach of promise during the recent campaign), and he could seriously tarnish the President's image.

Compounding the mutual threat was a conflict of ages. Robert Kennedy was only 35. J. Edgar Hoover was 65. Add the almost totally different mentalities represented by the generations to which each belonged and the conflict was intensified. After Robert Kennedy took office he happened to see a copy of the FBI tour guide one day. To his acute annoyance he found it contained this sentence: "Mr. Hoover became the Director of the Bureau in 1924, the year before the attorney general was born." Immediately the attorney general ordered the sentence stricken from the guide.

The conflicts multiplied. The attorney general and the FBI director had very different conceptions of the role and status of the FBI within the Justice Department. Hoover had gradually withdrawn the FBI from the control of the Justice Department, and previous attorneys general had let him get away with it. Kennedy, on the other hand, was determined to draw the FBI into his web of control. If Hoover didn't like it, he could lump it. Hoover perceived this attitude as hostile, the first hostile stance he had encountered from an administration in thirty-six years. With extreme reluctance he went along with it. Until 1961 no attorney general had ever succeeded in imposing his will on Hoover. Robert Kennedy was the first to get away with it. Lamented FBI man, and Hoover's closest friend, Clyde Tolson, "I guess we'll be stuck with the Kennedy clan until the year 2000." Years later Nixon recalled Hoover referring to Robert Kennedy as "a sneaky little son of a bitch."

There was also a sharp conflict of personality and style between the two men. Both John and Robert Kennedy did not like Hoover personally and experienced great difficulty calling him "Edgar." Hoover, a formal man, did not like the gregarious, informal, free-wheeling Kennedy brothers. It has been said that the two people J. Edgar Hoover hated most in the world were Martin Luther King, Jr., and Robert F. Kennedy. As for John Kennedy, Hoover made him acutely uncomfortable. The director was in the habit of sending the President reports on the sex lives and drinking habits of senators, congressmen, and high government officials. President Kennedy did not enjoy receiving these reports. Knowing that Hoover had compromising information on *him* in his files, he must have wondered whether Hoover, in sending him reports, was not indulging in a subtle blackmailing of the President.

Intellectually the Kennedy brothers were also far apart from the FBI director. As Navasky pointed out, Hoover was not ideologically motivated, he was bureaucratically motivated, whereas the Kennedy brothers, despite their pragmatism, held certain firm beliefs. Hoover and the FBI had become one and indistinguishable. Hoover's first thought when an important issue came up was not how it affected the pursuit of justice, or the fortunes of the American people, but how it affected the FBI. Robert Kennedy's position was exactly the reverse.

Hoover disapproved of Robert Kennedy's style. He disapproved of Kennedy letting his huge dog, Brumus, have the run of the fifth floor of the Justice Department, thereby violating the rules and regulations of public buildings. And he positively loathed the new attorney general's informal dress: the rolled-up shirtsleeves, open shirt, tie askew, disheveled hair, unpressed pants, a style which soon spread to other employees of the Justice Department.

Once when Hoover and Clyde Tolson arrived in the attorney general's office, they were horrified to find Kennedy in shirtsleeves, as usual, tossing darts at a board hung on a wall. What was even worse, during their conversation Kennedy *kept* tossing darts at the board. Hoover, who was used to receiving the undivided attention of the attorney general, was enraged. Later Tolson commented that it was "the most deplorably undignified conduct they had ever witnessed in a cabinet member."

As might be expected, when it came to the attorney general's program to fight organized crime, Hoover's ideas on the subject were very different. First of all, Hoover's obsession was communism, whereas Kennedy's main concern was organized crime. To obtain Hoover's full cooperation in his fight against what Kennedy told him was "a private government of organized crime resting on a basis of human suffering and moral corrosion," Kennedy had to overcome both Hoover's obsession with communism and his dogged insistence that organized crime did not even exist.

Soon after taking office as attorney general, Robert

Kennedy asked his FBI director for dossiers on the 1957 Apalachin conferees and was astonished to learn that Hoover didn't have any. He had dossiers on the sex lives of senators, but he did not have any on the most notorious criminals in America. Later Kennedy found out that Hoover had suppressed his bureau's report on the Apalachin conclave. What was the explanation of all this? Sheer human vanity and stubbornness. Hoover contended that if the FBI, with his all-wise self at the helm, and with all its sophisticated detection apparatus did not know about organized crime, how could it exist?

To add to Robert Kennedy's dismay he also found that there were in the federal government no fewer than twenty-seven independent, non-cooperating investigation and intelligence agencies, each going its own way, and none of them seemed particularly interested in fighting organized crime.

There was only one solution. Establish a National Crime Commission, uniting the functions of the FBI and the other twenty-seven agencies. But to this Hoover was adamantly opposed. He would not permit one shred of the FBI's authority to be taken away and united to some other bureaucratic entity.

And so, in the face of so much blindness, stubbornness, and lack of cooperation, Kennedy had to turn to his own department's Organized Crime Section to coordinate the government's anticrime program. He quadrupled the staff and funding of the Organized Crime Section, thus infuriating Hoover and lessening the FBI chief's authority in the field.

Finally, after weeks of reappraisals and reorganizations, Robert F. Kennedy was ready. There followed the most comprehensive and intensive campaign against organized crime in the history of the United States. As one observer put it, "Before Kennedy, attorneys general had merely *declared* war on organized crime. Robert Kennedy was the first to fight one." Commented another observer: "Robert F. Kennedy's zeal to break up the syndicate was reminiscent of a sixteenth century Jesuit hunting for heresy."

Robert Kennedy's program to attack organized crime was to be conducted in four separate campaigns: one, mobilizing the people and the Congress through speeches, books, articles, testimony, legislation, films, and publicity stunts alerting the nation to the danger; two, giving new, enhanced status, manpower, and money to the Justice Department's own Organized Crime Section; three, winning cooperation of all the other governmental agencies involved in fighting crime through visits, phone calls, meetings, and lunches, in which the sharing of information would be stressed; and four, sending out prosecutors to investigate, indict, and try cases involving organized crime.

The program needed able leaders, and so Kennedy hired Edwyn Silberling, a brilliant prosecutor who had worked with District Attorney Frank Hogan in New York, to be the new head of the Organized Crime and Racketeering Section of the Justice Department and Walter Sheridan, a former FBI man who had worked with Kennedy on the McClellan committee, to head up the new labor and racketeering unit of the Organized Crime Section.

Since Sheridan's unit was the one assigned to go after Jimmy Hoffa, it eventually became known as the "get Hoffa squad." Silberling's outfit, in turn, became known as the "whizz kids" because there were so many bright young men on its roster. With each new anticrime section and unit established in the Justice Department, Hoover saw his own power diminish. It would not be long before Kennedy would all but entirely ignore him in matters pertaining to organized crime.

One of Silberling's first efforts was to compile a list of top racketeers who had escaped the law. These were to be the priority targets, the first kingpins of organized crime the Kennedy administration would go after. As it turned out, the list started with 40 names and was to number 2300 by the time Kennedy left the Justice Department.

On the original list were such powerful "godfathers" as Mickey Cohen and Johnny Roselli from the west coast; Sam Giancana and Anthony Accardo from the midwest; Santo Trafficante, Jr., and Carlos Marcello from the south; and Frank Carbo, Joe Sica, Tony "Ducks" Corallo, Carmine Lombardozzi, and "Trigger" Mike Coppola from the east. Kennedy circulated the list among the government's twenty-seven investigative agencies, to the continuing fury of the FBI director, who, two years before, had termed such a list, compiled by his own deputies, "baloney."

But compiling lists was one thing. How to get the goods on these hoodlums, indict them, prosecute them, and send them to jail? Robert Kennedy would let no scruples stand in the way of his bringing these men to justice. Reversing the usual procedure of starting with a crime, then going after the criminals, Kennedy started first with the criminal, hoping he would catch him in a crime.

Accordingly, he put pressure on the IRS to single out people like Carlos Marcello, Santo Trafficante, Jr., and Carmine Lombardozzi for tax audits and tacitly allowed Hoover to conduct arguably illegal electronic surveillance of known criminals. He also sought to incriminate gangsters on the flimsiest pretexts. He indicted Louis Gallo and his father for giving false information on a Veterans Administration loan application. He nabbed Chicago racketeer Moses Joseph for giving false information on a request for a Federal Communications Commission license to operate a radio station. Joseph was then successfully prosecuted for perjury. And he got Joe Aiuppa for violating the Migrating Bird Act. (He was found to have over 563 mourning doves in his freezer, 539 over the legal limit.) The conviction was eventually overturned on the grounds of illegal search and seizure.

Before long Robert Kennedy was able to amass some impressive statistics. In 1960 there had been only 19 indictments of organized criminals. By the end of 1961, 121 criminals had been indicted. From only a handful of convictions in 1960, the Justice Department went on to convict 96 in 1961 and 101 in 1962. Among the most powerful racketeers Kennedy indicted were Anthony Accardo of Chicago, for tax evasion; Anthony "Tony Pro" Provenzano of New Jersey, for extortion; Carlos Marcello of New Orleans, for conspiracy to defraud; and Carmine Lombardozzi of New York, for tax evasion.

The case of Carlos Marcello particularly interested

Robert Kennedy. Marcello had been born in Tunisia of Sicilian parents who emigrated to the United States before Carlos was a year old. Carlos had never become a U.S. citizen and carried a Guatemalan passport, which he had allegedly obtained by paying a $100,000 bribe to the law partner of one of Guatemala's prime ministers. From childhood Marcello had been active in various rackets in New Orleans, especially gambling, prostitution, narcotics, and burglaries. By 1961 he had become one of the richest men in Louisiana, living on a 6500-acre, $22-million estate, Churchill Farms, and enjoying a personal fortune estimated to be in excess of $40 million.

Furthermore, the criminal organization Marcello headed, the oldest and most deeply entrenched Mafia family in the United States, had become by far Louisiana's largest single industry. Called the "Wall Street of the Cosa Nostra" because of its fiscal expertise, it had an annual income authoritatively estimated to be well in excess of $1 billion.

According to the House Select Committee on Assassinations staff report on organized crime, Carlos Marcello had become the undisputed boss of the Louisiana Cosa Nostra "with the corrupt collusion of public officials at every critical level, including police, sheriffs, judges, prosecutors, mayors, governors, licensing authorities, state legislators, and at least one member of Congress," all of whom the Mafia boss "substantially enriched."

By the time Robert Kennedy assumed the office of attorney general and mounted his war on organized crime, Marcello, who was still an illegal alien, had become the most powerful man in his state and one of the most powerful men in neighboring Texas as well. In Louisiana there was scarcely an area of life the Marcello organization had not penetrated, including even the Catholic church. I was told by a prominent New Orleans attorney that the Marcello organization was also the principal contributor to political campaigns in the state, often via private Catholic charities organizations, and "had probably even helped John F. Kennedy's 1960 presidential campaign indirectly in the hope of purchasing immunity." It is now known, through FBI reports, that Marcello also hoped to obtain immunity from government prosecution through Frank Sinatra's friendship with Joseph P. Kennedy.

Robert Kennedy was determined to deport Carlos Marcello to Guatemala, the country of his passport, and took steps in early March 1961 to have him thrown out. Accordingly, on April 4, 1961, when Marcello went to his local office of the Immigration and Naturalization Service for his required quarterly check-in, he was summarily arrested, handcuffed, and taken to the airport, where a U.S. Border Patrol plane was waiting to fly him to Guatemala.

Marcello was flown to Guatemala City and left there, without luggage and with almost no money. Before long Marcello's brothers remedied his condition by flying down from New Orleans, bringing him clothes and cash. But soon the president of Guatemala ordered him expelled and had him flown to a small village in the jungles of El Salvador. After a terrible ordeal trekking through the Salvadoran jungles, Marcello eventually reached a town on the coast, somehow arranged for a flight on a Dominican air force plane, and flew to Miami where he illegally reentered the United States.

Meanwhile, the Internal Revenue Service had slapped a $835,396 tax lien against Marcello and his wife. Then, on June 8, 1961, a federal grand jury indicted him for illegal entry. Some months later Robert Kennedy announced that the federal grand jury in New Orleans had indicted Marcello for conspiracy to defraud the United States in regard to his false Guatemalan birth certificate.

Robert Kennedy now had Carlos Marcello cornered, as he would have many other top criminal bosses cornered—men such as Jimmy Hoffa, Anthony Accardo, and Anthony Provenzano. The Kennedy anticrime program was underway, and it was working.

Marcello did not take Robert Kennedy's attack passively. In September 1962, Edward Becker, a Las Vegas gambler and promoter, visited Carlos Marcello at his enormous Churchill Farms estate. When, during the course of a conversation, Becker mentioned the name Robert Kennedy, Marcello immediately flew into a rage.

"Don't worry about that little Bobby son-of-a-bitch," Marcello exclaimed, "he's going to be taken care of. *Livarsi 'na petra di la scarpa.*" (The Sicilian expression means "Get the stone out of my shoe.")

And how was Marcello going to get the stone out of his shoe? According to Becker, he was going to find a "nut" to do the job, the way they do in Sicily, so that no one in his own organization would be blamed. But the "nut" was not going to hit Bobby, he was going to hit his brother. Marcello then used a Sicilian metaphor to explain his strategy. To prevent a dog from biting you don't cut off its tail, but its head. The President was the dog and the attorney general was its tail. If you cut off the tail, Marcello explained, the dog will continue biting; but if you chop off the head, the dog will die, tail and all. (Becker's story did not reach the FBI until 1967, and the FBI attempted to discredit it.)

Marcello, of course, denied making these statements to Becker when he was questioned about them by the House Select Committee on Assassinations on January 11, 1978, and so, in the end, all we have is Edward Becker's word that Marcello uttered them. The House committee concluded, after a thorough investigation, that there was a high probability that Becker had attended the Churchill Farms meeting and had heard Marcello utter his threatening remarks.

But even if Marcello did not utter them, they were symptomatic of the way American crime bosses were reacting to the Kennedy war on organized crime. It would not be long before FBI electronic surveillance of Cosa Nostra bosses would register actual, undeniable death threats from leading crime bosses against Attorney General Kennedy and his brother, the President of the United States.

The Bay of Pigs fiasco had earned President Kennedy the lasting enmity of Castro, Dulles, Cabell, the CIA, and the anti-Castro Cuban exiles. Now, thanks to his brother's anticrime program, two more groups joined the President's growing list of enemies: the FBI and organized crime. As disparate as these groups were, it was not inconceivable that one day some of them might come together and conspire to eliminate the source of their distress. Already two of them, the CIA and organized crime, had joined forces to attempt the murder of the president of Cuba.

40. The Imbroglio

WHILE Attorney General Robert F. Kennedy was mounting his war against organized crime, his brother the President was continuing his relationship with a woman closely involved with the very criminals he, Robert Kennedy, was pursuing.

White House telephone logs reveal that during the first months of the Kennedy presidency there was frequent telephone contact between Judith Campbell and the White House, but according to Miss Campbell's memoirs, she and the President did not meet until late April, a week or so after the Bay of Pigs.

Meanwhile, Judy was seeing a great deal of Sam Giancana. In the Mafia a man's rank is determined by how much fear he can generate. Judith Campbell was aware that, in Chicago, "one word from Sam and a restaurant would be closed, a union would strike, trash wouldn't be collected, a fire might break out." But, if we are to believe her memoirs, she evidently had no idea of the lengths to which Sam would go to generate such "respect." She apparently did not know that Sam Giancana had risen to supreme power in Chicago by terrorizing all opposition, that his enforcers, "Fifi" Buccieri, Rocco Pranno, and "Milwaukee Phil" Alderisio, reportedly had sealed Giancana victims alive in cement and tortured others to death on meathooks.

Also, unless she was consciously working for the mob, which seems improbable, it is unlikely that Judith knew that Sam Giancana had clashed with Robert Kennedy many times when Robert was chief counsel of the McClellan antirackets committee or that Giancana was now at the top of the attorney general's list of the ten most powerful criminals in the United States. At least this is the opinion of two experts on organized crime, Ovid Demaris and G. Robert Blakey, both of whom told me that they believed Miss Campbell was "just a girlfriend" of Giancana's and was not informed of the extent of his activities. In this heyday of organized crime, the crime bosses circulated so freely in society that it was often difficult for friends not directly involved to imagine the brutalities that went on beneath the surface of drinks in the Polo Lounge, or dinners at "21." Furthermore, it was contrary to the Mafia code to discuss mob business with girlfriends and wives.

In late March, Judy and Sam attended the wedding reception of Linda Lee, the daughter of fellow Chicago crime boss Tony Accardo, and one Michael Palermo. It turned out to be a lavish affair held at a big Italian restaurant, the Villa Venice, attended by the elite of organized crime in Chicago, and elsewhere, and observed by a horde of onlookers, whom Giancana called "the ants"— Feds, reporters, and photographers anxious to record who was present at the festivities. By now social evolution in the United States had progressed to the point where mob weddings received more attention in the press than so-called society weddings.

It was not long after the Accardo-Palermo wedding that Judy was reintroduced to Johnny Roselli, a Cosa Nostra delegate in Las Vegas and southern California, whom she had first met in the early fifties. Judith soon added Roselli to the roster of friends she would see on a regular basis.

Meanwhile, on the heels of the Bay of Pigs fiasco CIA Director of Covert Operations Richard Bissell temporarily shelved his plans to continue using Sam Giancana and Johnny Roselli in his attempts to murder Castro. But it was by no means the end of covert operations against the Cuban dictator. Bissell had established, with apparent White House approval, an "executive action capability," or standby facility to plan and carry out the assassination of foreign leaders, and just before he left the CIA he turned one of the programs, the operation against Castro, over to the CIA's William K. Harvey, a hard-drinking, gun-toting professional who promptly rehired Roselli to murder the Cuban premier.

Two weeks after the Bay of Pigs fiasco, on May 5, Judy Campbell claims she was in Washington, at the invitation of the President, and was staying at the Mayflower Hotel. It was a Friday and she had her first visit with Kennedy at the White House at 4:30 P.M. According to Judy's account, when Kennedy beheld her looking lovely in a magenta Dior suit, he exclaimed "what a way to end a day!" For a while they chatted, getting reacquainted, then Kennedy, who still had some business ahead of him, invited her back for lunch the following day, Saturday, at 1:30.

On weekends it was Jacqueline Kennedy's custom to go out to Glen Ora, the estate Kennedy had rented in Virginia riding country. Of course, the President also had another country retreat available at the time, one that would have cost him nothing—Camp David in the Maryland mountains—but since the place was so closely associated with Eisenhower, the Kennedys wouldn't even go and look it over. Besides, horses were half of Jacqueline's life, and the riding out at Glen Ora was among the best there was anywhere. And so, for Kennedy's and Judith's purposes, with Jackie and the children out at Glen Ora, the coast was clear.

According to Judith, she was taken to her assignation with the President on Saturday in a White House car and was met by Dave Powers, who escorted her to Kennedy. The President, who customarily took a swim in the nude before lunch, asked her if she wanted to take a swim with him, and she declined on the very feminine grounds that she didn't want to muss her hair.

After Kennedy's swim, Judith and the President had a lunch of cold soup and hamburgers (Kennedy had been put on a bland diet and could not eat Jacqueline's haute cuisine) upstairs in the family quarters.

How much did Kennedy know about the other associates of Judith Campbell? Since of the four protagonists of this drama, only one—Judith Campbell—has escaped murder, and since she is not talking for fear of her life, we shall probably never know the full truth. Recently, however, I learned something which, if true, sheds new light on the question. In her memoirs, coauthored by Ovid Demaris, Miss Campbell had declared she never told John Kennedy she was also seeing Sam Giancana. Yet Demaris told me in October 1983 that Judy had later confessed to him that she had lied about an important point in her book: she *had* told the President about her relationship with Giancana and Kennedy was *jealous* of it. Demaris assured me he believed Judy was telling the truth. But did Judy ever tell the President about Giancana's involvement in the CIA-Mafia plots against Castro? Demaris, who worked side by side with Judy for months on her book, thinks not, because he came to believe that Judy herself was unaware of the plots at the time.

What else do we know that sheds significant light on the problem? We now know several established facts. Assuming that Kennedy knew the CIA had plotted to eliminate Castro before the Bay of Pigs invasion, as Richard Bissell has testified, but that he did not know the CIA had hired gangsters to do the job, it is quite possible that he could have found out something about the nature of the CIA plot in late May 1961. For it was on May 22, 1961, that FBI Director Hoover sent a memorandum to Attorney General Robert Kennedy that told of the CIA's use of Sam Giancana in connection with "several clandestine efforts against the Castro government" that involved, in the memo's words, "dirty business." Although this memorandum did not mention assassination, an earlier memorandum in the FBI's files, dated October 18, 1960, revealed that Giancana had talked about his involvement in an assassination attempt against Castro, without indicating that the CIA was behind it. Hoover was aware of this earlier memorandum, and he could have easily assembled the entire picture of the CIA-Mafia plot against Castro's life from the two memoranda and revealed it to the attorney general.

Since the Kennedy brothers were such close confidants, it is reasonable to assume that Robert told the President about the Hoover memorandum and that, at the very least, President Kennedy came to know in late May that the CIA had used Sam Giancana in "dirty business" against the Castro government, and quite possibly knew the "dirty business" involved assassination.

Furthermore, since it now appears reasonably certain that Kennedy knew who else Judith Campbell was seeing, it also appears reasonably certain that he also realized her friend was involved in the CIA's "dirty business" and, in fact, may even have been monitoring it through Judy, even though Judy may not have been aware of it at the time.

Whether Kennedy already knew something about the CIA-Mafia plot against Castro, or was just finding out about it, or was not yet informed of it at this time, is, however, still unclear. Whatever the case, he continued his relationship with Giancana's girlfriend. For during the summer of 1961, White House telephone logs reveal that he, or his secretary, and Judith spoke over the phone an average of twice a week, and Judith, in her memoirs, claims Kennedy met with her a full five times. With Jacqueline conveniently up in Hyannis Port with the children for most of the summer, Kennedy apparently had carte blanche to entertain Judith at will.

That Kennedy continued seeing Judith knowing she was also seeing Sam Giancana, and possibly knowing that Giancana had been hired to kill Castro, was, of course, reckless in the extreme, especially since his brother had targeted Giancana as a top-priority candidate for investigation in his war against organized crime. But as we know, John Kennedy thrived on danger, risk, and intrigue.

Of her many alleged visits to the White House that summer of 1961, Judith, in her memoirs, wrote that the one she made on August 8 stood out as her most memorable.

Wearing an apple-green Chanel silk suit, she was,

by her account, met by presidential secretary Evelyn Lincoln, who escorted her to where the President was waiting in the family quarters. Again there were more questions about the private life of Frank Sinatra. (Ben Bradlee, in his *Conversations with Kennedy,* wrote that Kennedy had an insatiable appetite for this kind of gossip, especially for gossip about Sinatra.) Then, at a certain point in their conversation, Kennedy suddenly surprised Judy by asking, "Has Teddy phoned you?"

"No, why?"

"Boy, if Teddy only knew, he'd eat his heart out!"

According to Miss Campbell, it was during this meeting that Kennedy accused her, in front of Dave Powers, of spreading a rumor that he had once asked her to go to bed with him and another woman. She, of course, denied it, but the fact that Kennedy had brought it up, especially in front of Powers, soured her for the afternoon's fun. Nevertheless, they made a date to see each other again on August 24.

Upon returning to the Mayflower, after this abortive encounter, Judith was surprised to receive a visit from none other than Sam Giancana, who was in Washington "on business." Giancana was accompanied by his son-in-law, Anthony Tisci, then an administrative aide to Illinois congressman Roland Libonati, a known friend of organized crime who would soon be targeted by Robert Kennedy. Giancana at the time no doubt believed he was invulnerable to attack by the U.S. government. Though he was on Attorney General Robert Kennedy's top-priority list, he had recently been under contract with the government to assassinate a foreign leader, his pal Frank Sinatra was a good friend of the President, his girlfriend was a girlfriend of the President, and his son-in-law worked for a U.S. congressman.

There is some evidence that President Kennedy occasionally accommodated Congressman Libonati—possibly because of Judith's friendship with Giancana—and hence was undercutting Robert's war against organized crime. On October 23, 1962, an FBI listening device picked up a conversation between Libonati and Chicago politician John

D'Arco (that subsequently became part of the official record of the House Assassinations Committee) during which
Libonati characterized John Kennedy as a "sweetheart"
and his brother Robert as "cruel." Libonati went on to
describe how he had opposed an anticrime bill that had
been proposed by Robert Kennedy and had received a call
from Mayor Daley reprimanding him, whereupon Libonati
had phoned President Kennedy and asked him to stop his
brother Bobby from phoning Daley about such matters;
the President had apparently said he would oblige. Later,
when Robert Kennedy stated on television that his brother
wanted him to stay out of party politics because he was
the attorney general, Libonati took credit for the President's action.

   Judith Campbell's next alleged date with the President, on August 24, was a special one and occurred in the
evening—special because, after frozen daiquiris in the upstairs family quarters, Judy claimed Kennedy presented
her with a large diamond-and-ruby brooch. Reflecting on
this visit, in her memoirs, Judith wrote of Kennedy: "I
think he had a natural desire to be an elegant bum, to be
on the sea, under the sun, to play games and make love.
But that this was in conflict with his drive for power." It
was a perceptive observation. Theodore Sorensen said more
or less the same thing when he once observed that the
great, underlying conflict in John Kennedy's life was between "the lure of luxury and statesmanship." And something of the same intuition was expressed by Jacqueline
Kennedy when she wrote of her new husband in 1953:

   Men would call him thoughtful, sincere,
   They would not see through to the Last Cavalier.

   There followed more meetings. According to her account, Judy Campbell met with the President at New York's
Plaza Hotel again, at her apartment in Los Angeles, and
in Palm Beach. In addition, throughout the fall of 1961
she continued visiting Kennedy in the White House, now
often in the evening. Since Jacqueline came to spend more
and more time with her horses at Glen Ora, often as many
as four days a week, it would have been relatively easy for

Kennedy to schedule a visit from Judy when his wife was not around.

It was during her visits to the President in the fall of 1961 that Judy began to sense that JFK was apparently seriously contemplating a Kennedy family dynasty in the White House. Although he often complained to her of Teddy's immaturity, he felt that his brother Bobby would make an excellent President. "And don't forget the Grandkids," he once told her; they would be ready for the presidency in the 1990s.

Some corroboration of this plan for a Kennedy presidential dynasty also comes from Ben Bradlee, who reported a conversation with Kennedy in the White House over who would succeed him after his expected eight years were up. JFK said first they would run Franklin D. Roosevelt, Jr.; then, after his term was up, they would run Bobby. After Bobby's eight years, another suitable interval without a Kennedy in the White House would have to pass; then they would run Teddy and, after that, one of the grandchildren in the nineties. So grandiose were JFK's political plans, they literally encompassed the globe. In her memoirs, Judith Campbell quoted Kennedy as saying, in response to a remark of hers about Kennedys running the country for decades, "Yeah, maybe even the whole world."

Did Judith visit Kennedy in the White House as many times as she said she did? There is no way of telling for certain because the Secret Service's White House appointment slips during the Kennedy years, now in the JFK Library in Boston, remain closed to the public, as do the White House social files that might disclose her name among the invitees to the inauguration or to other social events.

The only concrete evidence we have, then, of the relationship is White House telephone logs indicating there were some seventy phone contacts between Judith and the White House between January 22, 1961, and March 22, 1962; certain FBI memoranda about the relationship that surfaced during the Senate intelligence investigations of 1975 and 1976, one of which was obtained by William Safire of the *New York Times* in 1978 under the Freedom of Information Act; and Judith's secret testimony, given under oath before the same Senate Committee on Intelligence, that convinced the members of the committee that there had indeed been a relationship between Miss Campbell and the President and also between her and Giancana and Roselli. This testimony, which will not be made public until 2025, was read in transcripts by counsel and some members of the House Select Committee on Assassinations in 1978. Chief Counsel G. Robert Blakey told me that the testimony convinced him an extensive relationship existed.

Thus that the relationship existed is beyond doubt. What remains open to question is its extent. In all likelihood it is reasonable to assume Miss Campbell exaggerated the extent of her relationship with both Kennedy and Giancana in her memoirs. At least this is the opinion of several former Kennedy White House aides and of Sam Giancana's biographer, William Brashler. (It is *not* the opinion of Miss Campbell's coauthor, Ovid Demaris.)

However, assuming that only a portion of what Judy Campbell asserted in her memoirs is true, the implications of her relationships with Kennedy and Giancana and Roselli are no less devastating. In pursuing Miss Campbell, Kennedy was making himself more and more vulnerable to blackmail from the underworld, not just from Sam Giancana and Johnny Roselli, but from all those other members of Cosa Nostra to whom Giancana and Roselli revealed the Kennedy-Campbell affair, and there were many. Professional Mafia assassin Jimmy "the Weasel" Fratianno told Ovid Demaris that the mob used to laugh their heads off over the relationship. I was told by a New York Teamsters official, with connections to organized crime, that it was well known in the underworld in the early sixties that one of Giancana's girls was seeing the President. Not since the days of Inga Arvad had Jack Kennedy been in such trouble over a woman.

On another level, JFK, in pursuing Judith Campbell, was dealing a blow to the very institution of the presidency. The President of the United States holds a unique office. Unlike the prime ministers of the parliamentary democracies, he is both head of state and head of government. As head of state he is a symbol, like the Queen of England, who must set an example of personal behavior for the entire nation. The President of the United States, as head of state, must be beyond reproach from the standpoint of moral conduct. As head of government he may indulge in the Machiavellian machinations of politics, but, as head of state, he, and his family, must set an example of personal conduct for an entire people.

Kennedy himself was well aware of this, and, by and large, his conduct as head of state was exemplary in almost every way. He consciously tried to behave as if he were "a city upon a hill" with "the eyes of all people" upon him.

And yet he risked having the eyes of all people discover his affair with Judith Campbell, an affair he carried on behind the back of someone who was rapidly becoming a national idol, Jacqueline. Why did President Kennedy violate his high ideals of conduct, on both an institutional and personal level, with his affair with Judith Campbell?

There are two ways of looking at it. Either he was conducting the affair for strictly "business" purposes, that is, using Judith as a conduit to the CIA-Mafia plotters, or simply as a spy on the mob, or he simply thought he could get away with a fling with one of the many girls Frank Sinatra had introduced him to. The Kennedys were not only rich, beautiful, and lucky, they were also closely protected by loyal minions who would never squeal. To this day Dave Powers and Evelyn Lincoln have denied Judith Campbell's visits to the White House, though Mrs. Lincoln, upon being presented with unassailable evidence of White House phone calls to and from Miss Campbell on White House logs, was forced to admit, in a 1975 Senate investigation, that such calls had indeed been made.

Yes, Kennedys were very well protected. John Kennedy, the political and sexual adventurer, who thrived on risks and crises, was no doubt sure he could get away with his fling with Judy Campbell. If he was using her as a conduit to the CIA-Mafia plotters, which is highly doubtful, his affair could be justified as business—dirty business, but still business. If, on the other hand, he was ignorant of her gangster friend's role in the plot to kill Castro, he could rely on his subordinates to keep the fling quiet, so that he could still appear to the public as "a city upon a hill." Whatever the case, the matter was destined to come to a head a year later when none other than J. Edgar Hoover confronted him with it over lunch at the White House.

41. Operation Mongoose

THE BAY OF PIGS fiasco was the most ignominious and humiliating defeat of the Kennedy brothers' political careers. A less competitive family might have conceded defeat and moved on to something else. But Kennedys did not concede anything; they fought back harder than before.

In the summer of 1961 they decided to strike back at Fidel Castro in a coordinated secret attack involving intelligence collection, propaganda, sabotage, guerrilla strikes, and assassination. Kennedy aide Richard Goodwin gave the program its name: Operation Mongoose. The Cobra, Cuba, had won the first test of will and strength. Now the Mongoose would strike back.

No doubt the Kennedys derived some measure of optimism over Mongoose's chances of success from the recently successful operation against the dictator of the Dominican Republic, Rafael Trujillo, who was assassinated by dissidents armed by the CIA on May 30, 1961.

That the Kennedy brothers apparently saw nothing wrong in the assassination of Trujillo was revealed by the Senate Committee on Intelligence in 1975, which noted in its *Interim Report:*

> There is no indication or suggestion contained in the record of those post-assassination

meetings, or in Robert Kennedy's notes, of concern as to the propriety of the known United States involvement in the assassination. Nor is there any record that anyone took steps following Trujillo's assassination to reprimand or censure any of the American officials involved either on the scene or in Washington, or to otherwise make known any objections or displeasure as to the degree of United States involvement in the events which had transpired. . . . Later the Agency described the project as a "success."

If the Kennedy government could eliminnate the leader of the Dominican Republic and establish its own puppet on the island, it could do so in Cuba as well, so the reasoning apparently went.

After the Bay of Pigs fiasco, President Kennedy's Cuba Study Group came to the conclusion that "there can be no long-term living with Castro as a neighbor," and the President accepted this conclusion. Almost everyone in the Kennedy administration agreed. President Kennedy declared he wanted to initiate "massive Mongoose activity." Robert Kennedy asserted he wanted to invoke "the terrors of the earth" against Castro. Robert McNamara stated, "We were hysterical about Castro at the time of the Bay of Pigs, and thereafter." Even the habitually dovish Arthur M. Schlesinger, Jr., who, it will be recalled, had argued against the Bay of Pigs adventure, wanted to do something forceful about the Cuban menace.

The Kennedy brothers were particularly hard on the CIA in regard to Cuba. In a 1975 Senate hearing, a high-ranking CIA official declared that sometime in the fall of 1961 Richard Bissell was "chewed out in the Cabinet Room in the White House by both the President and the attorney general for, as he put it, sitting on his ass and not doing anything about getting rid of Castro and the Castro regime." Bissell himself recalled the episode, stating, "During that entire period, the administration was extremely sensitive about the defeat that had been inflicted, as they felt, on the U.S. at the Bay of Pigs, and were pursuing every possible means of getting rid of Castro."

The first major meeting to establish Operation Mongoose was held in the White House on November 4, 1961. At this secret meeting Robert Kennedy stated, "My idea is to stir things up on the island with espionage, sabotage, general disorder, in an operation run essentially by the Cubans themselves." Later on that November, top-secret Operation Mongoose was born with the presidential directive to "use our available assets to overthrow Castro." It goes without saying that neither the Congress nor the American people were informed. In fact, it was not until 1975 that the operation surfaced.

Soon Operation Mongoose had its own specific organizational structure. The attorney general would be its unofficial supreme commander. Gen. Edward G. Lansdale, the legendary CIA operative who had helped Ramón Magsaysay defeat rebellion in the Philippines, had aided Ngo Dinh Diem in Vietnam, and was used as the model for the principal character in the national best-seller *The Ugly American,* was deputy commander. Beneath Kennedy and Lansdale there was to function the Special Group, consisting of Gen. Maxwell Taylor, McGeorge Bundy, Alexis Johnson, Roswell Gilpatric, Gen. Lyman Lemnitzer, and CIA chief John McCone. Within the CIA itself the special unit for Mongoose was called Task Force W.

Edward Lansdale, it seems, was possessed of a lot of wild ideas as to what Mongoose's activities would be. Among his many proposals he suggested deployment of nonlethal chemicals to temporarily incapacitate Cuban sugarcane cutters; employment of gangsters to attack Cuban police officers; covert operations to force defections of Castro's top echelon of communist officials; and a propaganda campaign to depict Castro as "the anti-Christ." All of this was supposed to result in "open revolt and overthrow of the communist regime."

On January 19, 1962, a top-secret meeting on Mongoose was held in the attorney general's office, during which Robert Kennedy urged that "no time, money, effort, or manpower, be spared" toward "the overthrow of Castro's regime." By now Robert Kennedy was as fired up about hounding Castro as he was about hounding the mob.

Then, on August 23, McGeorge Bundy issued National Security Council memorandum 181, a presidential decree calling for the immediate implementation of Mongoose "Phase B," a massive covert operation involving the initiation of a propaganda war, selected sabotage projects, and provocation of incidents designed to create tension between the Cuban and Soviet military.

Soon the CIA's special Mongoose unit, Task Force W, under the direction of William K. Harvey, established a huge nerve center on the campus of the University of Miami, code-named JM/WAVE, which had some 400 men working for it in Washington and Miami; maintained over fifty business fronts in Florida, a small navy of high-speed vessels, and an air force; and employed over 2000 Cuban agents, the whole at a cost of $100 million a year. The JM/WAVE station soon became one of Florida's largest employers and the second largest CIA installation in the world, after CIA headquarters in Langley, Virginia. A plausible argument could have been made that the American taxpayer was paying this annual sum for a Kennedy vendetta, and a secret vendetta at that. While all this secret bellicose activity was going on, Kennedy was publicly talking peace and promoting his celebrated Peace Corps.

It might be mentioned, at this point, that the Kennedys and the CIA were not the only ones out to get Castro in 1962. Castro's closing of the casinos, nightclubs, and bordellos in Havana and curtailing of most of the drug trade were costing the American mob, which had controlled all these recreations, over $100 million a year. In response to this catastrophe, Meyer Lansky, the "Jewish Mafia" boss, who, with Santo Trafficante, Jr., had the most to lose from Castro's crackdown, had reportedly offered a reward of $1 million for Castro's head.

Then, in addition to Operation Mongoose and the mob, there was that other ultrasecret anti-Castro operation, the CIA's new "executive action capability," a euphemism for what Lyndon Johnson was to someday call "a damn Murder, Inc., in the Caribbean." It will be recalled that Allen Dulles and Richard Bissell were fired from the CIA in the fall of 1961. Dulles was succeeded by John A. McCone and Bissell by Richard Helms, while William K. Harvey, who had been in on the original CIA-Mafia Castro murder plots, stayed on, now in charge of both the "executive action capability" and Task Force W.

It was in April 1962 that Richard Helms, responding to Kennedy pressure to do something about getting rid of the Castro regime, ordered Harvey to reactivate the plan to murder Fidel Castro. Believing there were too many hands involved, Helms and Harvey decided to eliminate Maheu and Giancana from the chain of conspiracy, leaving only Roselli and Trafficante, and their Cuban connections, to effect the disposal of the Cuban dictator.

And so in April there was yet another poison-pill attempt to eliminate Castro, initiated by Harvey and Roselli, that, like its predecessors, failed. It was to have been a triple assassination: along with Fidel, his brother Raúl and the professional revolutionary, Che Guevara, were supposed to have been eliminated. Then in June a three-man assassination team was sent by Roselli to ambush the Cuban premier, and it also failed.

To what extent were the Kennedy brothers involved in these murder attempts? John Kennedy is on record as publicly denouncing assassination of foreign leaders as an instrument of national policy, but we have seen that Kennedy's public pronouncements were often at odds with his intended actions.

Richard Helms testified at a Senate Intelligence Committee hearing in 1975 that the Kennedys had told him flatly "to get rid of Castro," and he assumed that meant by any means, including assassination. In an interview with me on September 23, 1983, Helms maintained the position, stating that he had no doubts whatsoever on the matter.

It was apparently at the August 10, 1962, meeting of the Special Group that the administration's plans to assassinate Castro came the nearest to being explicit. On May 30, 1975, at the height of the Senate Intelligence Committee's hearings, David Martin of the Associated Press interviewed General Lansdale about the August 10, 1962, meeting, and Lansdale told him that "acting on orders from President John F. Kennedy, delivered through an intermediary, he developed plans for removing Cuban Premier Fidel Castro by any means, including assassination."

At about the same time Jeremiah O'Leary of the *Washington Star-News* interviewed Lansdale and reported, "Retired Major General Edward G. Lansdale has named Robert F. Kennedy as the administration official who ordered him in 1962 to launch a CIA project to work out all feasible plans for getting rid of Cuban Prime Minister Fidel Castro."

On June 6, 1975, John McCone testified before the Senate Intelligence Committee that at the August 10, 1962, meeting of the Special Group Augmented, attended by Robert Kennedy, "liquidation of Castro" was discussed, adding that it was Defense Secretary McNamara who originally made the suggestion. Richard Goodwin corroborated this in his testimony before the committee by stating, "McNamara got up to leave during a discussion of how to get rid of Castro and said: 'The only way to get rid of Castro is to kill him . . . and I really mean it.' To this remark Robert Kennedy offered no objection." Goodwin added that the meeting was "etched in [his] memory." Thirteen years later, however, on July 11, 1975, McNamara testified to the Senate Intelligence Committee that he did not even recall the August 10 meeting and had no recollection of raising the assassination suggestion at that time.

William K. Harvey, the CIA officer who was directly in charge of certain plots to assassinate Castro, had absolutely no doubts about their ultimate authorization. On June 25, 1975, Harvey testified under oath before the Senate Committee on Intelligence that "the project" (the assassination plots) was authorized by the "highest authority," which to him meant the President of the United States. He further testified, as had Richard Bissell, that it would have been Allen Dulles, and only Allen Dulles, who obtained the presidential authorization and that he would have obtained it in such a way as to allow the President to plausibly deny giving the authorization should the occasion ever arise.

Thus, while neither John nor Robert Kennedy probably ever gave a direct order to the CIA to murder Castro, they gave orders comprehensive enough to include that possibility. Furthermore, whenever the CIA-Mafia plots were brought to their attention, they consistently looked the other way. In 1975 a Senate committee was presented with documents that clearly indicated that in May 1961 Robert Kennedy and J. Edgar Hoover "received information that the CIA was engaged in clandestine efforts against Castro which included the use of Sam Giancana and other underworld figures," and that they did nothing about it. Later, when the CIA told the attorney general flat out about the CIA-Mafia murder plots, Kennedy expressed disapproval only of the CIA using criminals, not of the plots themselves. Clearly the Kennedy brothers were playing a very dangerous game.

In a sea of operations that was always murky and often unfathomable, one thing was clear: The Kennedy ship of state was sailing on to an inevitable confrontation with Castro, or with his protector, Chairman Khrushchev of the Soviet Union.

42. The Imbroglio, Continued

ON FEBRUARY 27, 1962, not long after Operation Mongoose was launched, FBI Director J. Edgar Hoover sent a memorandum to Robert F. Kennedy that must have profoundly troubled the young attorney general. The memorandum stated that, during the course of the investigation of Johnny Roselli, the FBI had checked the gangster's telephone records and found he had made six calls to a woman by the name of Judith Campbell. This led to a check of Judith Campbell's own telephone records, which, in turn, revealed that Miss Campbell had phoned the White House twice in November 1961, on the 7th and the 15th. Hoover noted in his memorandum that Miss Campbell was friendly with Sam Giancana, whom he described as "a prominent underworld figure," and with Roselli, whom he called "one of the second group of forty hoodlums receiving concentrated attention." He ended the memo by observing that "the relationship between Campbell and Mrs. Lincoln [the President's secretary], or the purpose of these calls, is not known."

Hoover was probably lying in feigning ignorance of the nature of "the relationship between Campbell and Mrs. Lincoln" and the purpose of the calls. The FBI had been trailing Judith Campbell since November 27 as part of its surveillance of Giancana and more than likely knew she was also seeing the President. Those calls she made through

Mrs. Lincoln's office had probably been made to set up appointments with the President, for the dates of the calls corresponded to visits Miss Campbell subsequently claimed she made to the White House during the period in question, visits which she described in detail in her memoirs.

The FBI director was understandably reluctant to divulge all he knew about the Kennedy-Campbell relationship to the attorney general, and so he merely hinted at it in his memorandum to his boss. No doubt Hoover delighted in giving the attorney general this news. If, as Hoover believed, the President and the attorney general were bent on eventually replacing him, he now appeared to have enough information on the President to make that impossible, or, at least, very difficult.

What did Robert Kennedy do on February 27? Did he already know who Judith Campbell was? Since Jack Kennedy had met Campbell and had seen her often during the campaign and he, Robert Kennedy, had managed that campaign, it is reasonable to assume he knew who Judith was. Teddy Kennedy also knew Judith and, in fact, according to Judith, had become infatuated with her in Las Vegas at the same time Jack Kennedy had fallen for her. Is it possible, given the closeness of the three brothers, that the name of Judith Campbell never came up in their conversations? In any case, we shall probably never know whether or not Robert Kennedy knew, at this time, who Judith Campbell was. Nor shall we ever probably know how Robert Kennedy reacted to Hoover's memorandum, or what he did about it. All that is known for certain is that White House telephone logs show that calls continued to be made at about the rate of two a week between the White House and Judith Campbell until March 22, the day on which J. Edgar Hoover had a luncheon meeting with the President in the White House. Whatever Robert Kennedy did or didn't tell his brother about the Hoover memorandum, it evidently didn't stop the President from continuing telephone contact with Miss Campbell.

Hoover's visit to the President on March 22 was another matter. After that meeting, White House telephone logs record only one more call made between the President, or his secretary, and Judith Campbell and that occurred shortly after Mr. Hoover left the White House.

It is now generally assumed (and, according to the Senate Committee on Intelligence *Interim Report,* FBI briefing materials prepared for Mr. Hoover's meeting with Kennedy bear out the assumption) that the purpose of Hoover's visit to the President that day was to tell him what he knew about the President's meetings with Judith Campbell and perhaps to inform the President of the other men Judith Campbell was seeing.

John F. Kennedy must have been astounded by this intelligence. He must have been aware for some time that, through Judy, the mob had set him up. But he had not been aware that his FBI director knew about it. What a mess he had gotten himself, and his administration, into! It was also on March 22 that Hoover apparently disclosed all he knew about the Kennedy-Campbell-Giancana affair to the attorney general.

Judith Campbell, in her memoirs, wrote that she and the President continued to be in touch with each other into June. If this is true, Kennedy managed to phone her from an outside location, or from a direct White House line not connected to the switchboard, and warn her against phoning him at the White House..

As John Kennedy's relationship with Judy Campbell was drawing to a close, he and his brother had to absorb another shock regarding Giancana and Roselli.

Sam Giancana had another girlfriend, Phyllis McGuire. Giancana had become suspicious that Phyllis was cheating on him in Las Vegas with comedian Dan Rowan. Giancana asked Robert Maheu, the ex-FBI agent and current intermediary between the CIA and the Mafia, to run a wiretap on Rowan's phone, using the CIA to accomplish it, and Maheu and the CIA complied. The wiretap was then discovered by a maid, who brought it to the attention of Rowan, who in turn brought it to the attention of the federal government. Eventually the Justice Department instituted proceedings against Maheu for illegal wiretapping.

Early in May 1962, the CIA urged the Justice Department not to press charges against Maheu for fear Giancana's role in the wiretap would be revealed. The CIA obviously wanted to protect Giancana because of his role in the murder plots against Castro. The CIA told Robert Kennedy that Giancana had had a role in certain "clandestine efforts against Castro's government," something the attorney general already knew, but Kennedy remained unmoved, still adamant about pressing charges.

Then, on May 7, Laurance Houston, the CIA's general counsel, paid a call on the attorney general and told him the whole and awful truth. Houston told Kennedy that the CIA had contracted with Giancana and Roselli to murder Fidel Castro. Robert Kennedy was utterly appalled. Before then Kennedy had received only hints of the nature of this conspiracy. According to Houston, Kennedy's eyes got steely, and his voice became "low and precise." "I trust," he said to Houston, "that if you ever try to do business with organized crime again—with gangsters—you will let the attorney general know." Later he discussed the murder plots with J. Edgar Hoover, and Hoover recorded that Kennedy seemed very disturbed. Not so disturbed, however, about the plots themselves, as about who had been hired to carry them out. As Houston later observed: "He was mad as hell. But what he objected to was the possibility it would impede prosecution against Giancana and Roselli. He was not angry about the assassination plot, but about our involvement with the Mafia."

During the late spring and early summer of 1962 Harris Wofford, Kennedy's special assistant for civil rights, used to observe the President and the attorney general "huddled in the Oval Office, or walking together in the Rose Garden," as he described them in his book. What were they talking about? he wondered. Now he believes that one of the subjects they were pondering that spring was Judith Campbell and Sam Giancana and Johnny Roselli and Castro and the disastrous situation the President had gotten himself into.

More than likely, the crucial decision to continue the investigation of Giancana was made during a series of meetings. What is known is that the Justice Department's investigation of Giancana and Roselli continued, but the wiretap suit against Maheu was dropped.

Not long after Kennedy's break with Judy Campbell, Kennedy also terminated relations with the man who had brought him and Judy together and who had also introduced Judy to Sam Giancana: Frank Sinatra. Justice Department attorneys had told Robert Kennedy that their war on organized crime was being compromised by the President's friendship with Frank Sinatra, who, though not involved in organized crime himself, was on friendly terms with many mob bosses, including, of course, Giancana and Roselli. In the summer of 1962 President Kennedy was due to visit Sinatra's home in Palm Springs. Sinatra had even built a new wing on his house and had installed a helicopter pad on his property for the President's visit. But by then the President had become more prudent about his friendships. Telling his brother-in-law Peter Lawford, "I can't stay there [at Sinatra's] . . . while Bobby's handling the [Giancana] investigation," he stayed at Bing Crosby's home at Palm Desert instead, something that must have galled Sinatra, who often boasted of his friendship with the President. It also galled Sam Giancana, for he had pinned his hopes for immunity from government prosecution on his friendship wth Sinatra and Sinatra's friendship with the President. Sinatra was supposed to have been able to arrange the immunity, what is known in the underworld as "putting in the fix." When it turned out that he couldn't, Giancana, in the words of his biographer, William Brashler, became "furious" and "cursed the sight of the attorney general and fumed at the very mention of the Kennedy name." Before long, according to Brashler, Giancana and his lieutenants decided to do something about it.

Sam Giancana now held potentially ruinous information on the President of the United States and, knowing what he knew, was also in a position to blackmail the FBI and CIA agents who knew about the Castro murder plot. In view of this, he had every reason to believe he would be left alone.

But Robert Kennedy had other ideas. William Hundley, who became head of the Justice Department's Organized Crime Section, stated, "Bobby pushed to get Giancana at any cost." And from what we now know, it was true. The attorney general's pursuit of Giancana was second in vehemence only to his pursuit of Jimmy Hoffa.

It is possible, but not certain, that Robert Kennedy's determination to get Sam Giancana had been strengthened by what an FBI agent told him about a face-to-face encounter with Giancana at the time a team of FBI agents was trailing him and Phyllis McGuire and trying to question Miss McGuire.

"Whataya wanna know?" Giancana had yelled at one of the agents. "I'll tell ya, I'll tell ya anything ya wanna know."

"Okay," one agent piped up. "Tell us what you do for a living."

"Easy," laughed Giancana, "I own Chicago. I own Miami. I own Las Vegas."

Meanwhile Phyllis McGuire was being questioned by another agent, who had taken her from Giancana's side. When, after some time had passed, Phyllis had not returned, Giancana exploded at another agent. "Fuck you," he screamed. "Fuck your boss, too. Fuck your boss's boss. I'll get you for this. You lit a fire tonight that will never go out. You'll rue the day. I'll get you."

It wasn't long after the President's break with Judith Campbell that FBI agents intensified their hounding of Sam Giancana. As might be expected, Giancana lashed back. On June 30, 1962, a member of Giancana's crime family, Charles "Chuckie" English, accosted an FBI agent who was keeping Giancana under surveillance and told him that if Robert Kennedy wanted to talk with Giancana he should organize a meeting through Frank Sinatra. The implication was clear. Was this going to be the first step in Giancana's blackmail of the Kennedys?

As the FBI intensified its surveillance of Giancana, it also pursued Judy Campbell. After Robert Kennedy learned the mob had probably arranged to introduce her to his brother, had "planted" her on him as the underworld saying goes, he had set his FBI agents out to dog her in every way they could. In her memoirs Miss Campbell wrote, "I was followed, hounded, harassed, accosted, spied upon, intimidated, burglarized, embarrassed, humiliated, denigrated, and . . . finally driven to the brink of death."

It was, in her opinion, no way to treat a woman who had been intimate with the President for a year and a half. Joining forces definitively with Giancana, she told him, "Okay, Sam, I'm with you. If you have to fight them, I'll fight them, too."

In June 1963 Giancana became so exasperated by the FBI's lockstep surveillance that he did something unprecedented in the annals of organized crime. He sought a court injunction against the FBI for harassment on the grounds that the Bureau was depriving him of his constitutional rights to privacy. In order to obtain this injunction Giancana would have to swear in court that he was a lawabiding citizen, a representation that would open him up to cross-examination by government attorneys. The heads of crime families usually spend lifetimes trying to avoid such a situation. In going to court, Giancana had to feel fairly secure that the government would not want to question him.

When, toward the end of the court proceedings, Giancana was finally asked by the U.S. attorneys whether he was guilty of breaking any local, state, or federal laws that would warrant such FBI surveillance, Giancana unhesitatingly said, "No." It was a tense moment in the courtroom. Now the U.S. attorneys were free to question Giancana about every criminal act they suspected him of, and they possessed volumes of information on these. They could ask him about all the bribes, extortions, and gambling and narcotics operations he had been involved in. They could ask him about all the hit contracts he had given out. And he would be compelled to answer all the questions asked of him or face binding contempt charges.

As the hushed courtroom waited for the crossexamination to begin, the U.S. attorney, James P. O'Brien, stood up and startled everyone by waiving the right to cross-examination, saying that the government had no questions. It was an opportunity the Justice Department had been waiting for ever since the days of the McClellan committee hearings. But the order not to cross-examine had come down from none other than the attorney general of the United States, Robert F. Kennedy. The attorney general claimed that the Giancana petition was improper, and that the U.S. District Court in Chicago lacked jurisdiction in the matter. To have taken advantage of cross-examination rights would have lent sanction to an essentially improper petition.

The presiding judge then ruled against the FBI, ordering a reduction of their surveillance of Giancana. Now the FBI had to park at least a block from his house and remain one hole behind him on the golf course.

What was the reason Robert Kennedy decided, at the last minute, to forgo cross-examination of Giancana on a legal technicality? The reason probably was that by now Robert Kennedy knew too much about Sam Giancana. He knew that his government had hired him to assassinate Castro. He knew that Giancana had contributed to his brother's presidential campaign. And he knew his brother had been involved with Giancana's girlfriend. In cross-examining Giancana it was conceivable these facts would come out, and these were facts Kennedy hoped would never see the light of day. For the sake of his brother's and his government's reputations, he gave up the opportunity to cross-examine one of the most powerful criminals in the world. Thus Robert Kennedy and the U.S. government became hostages to the CIA's unholy alliance with the Mafia and the President's indiscretions with a Mafia woman. Giancana's schemes to "get something on" the Kennedys and the government had paid off.

Later on in the summer a court of appeals overturned the decision against FBI surveillance, and the intense surveillance of Giancana resumed. The government had finally got what it wanted without having to risk the cross-examination of the Chicago boss. When Giancana learned of the decision, he exclaimed to his lawyer, "They can't do this to me, I'm working for the government!"

Among the measures the FBI took to spy on Giancana was a program of electronic surveillance that resulted in a revealing collection of tapes. Transcripts of the tapes were made public during the House Select Committee on Assassinations inquiry, 1976–1979.

On December 12, 1961, at the time Giancana was losing hope that Sinatra could arrange immunity with the President, the FBI had managed to record the following conversation between Giancana and Johnny Roselli (one of Giancana's nicknames was Moe):

> ROSELLI: He's got big ideas, Frank does, about being ambassador or something. You fuck them, you pay them, and then they're through. You got the right idea, Moe, so fuck everybody. . . . We'll use them every fucking way we can. They only know one way. Now let them see the other side of you.
>
> I had a chance to quiz Sinatra in Las Vegas. . . . I said, Frankie, can I ask one question? . . . He says, Johnny, I took Sam's name, and wrote it down, and told Bobby Kennedy, this is my buddy. This is my buddy, this is what I want you to know, Bob. And he says Johnny, he. . . .
>
> GIANCANA, laughing: You could have answered it yourself.

On January 31, 1962, the FBI recorded a conversation between Giancana and John D'Arco, a Chicago city alderman, about the candidacy of Roswell Spencer, a former FBI man, in the coming election for Cook County sheriff. The exchange indicated that now Giancana no longer believed Sinatra had any influence with the President.

> GIANCANA: Spencer is like Kennedy. He'll get what he wants out of you, but you won't get anything out of him.
>
> D'ARCO: That fucker Kennedy! Is Sinatra gonna work on . . . ?
>
> GIANCANA: No.
>
> D'ARCO: I heard that the President, when he

        is in California, is with Sinatra all the time.

GIANCANA: He can't get change of a quarter.

D'ARCO: Sinatra can't?

GIANCANA: That's right. Well, they got the whip and they're in office and that's it. . . . So they're going to knock us guys out of the box and make us defenseless.

Later, after Giancana's disillusionment with Sinatra was complete, the FBI recorded a brief conversation between Giancana and another henchman, Johnny Formosa, during which Formosa suggested that because Frank Sinatra had not done what had been expected of him, he should be hit. The two gangsters' further remarks indicated how murderous their intentions had become:

FORMOSA: I could knock out a couple of those guys—Lawford and that Martin prick—and I could take the nigger and put his other eye out.

GIANCANA: No, I got other plans.

Robert Kennedy continued his investigation of Sam Giancana until the afternoon of November 22, 1963. On that afternoon the attorney general was scheduled to have a meeting with his Organized Crime Section about Giancana immediately after lunch, but events in Dallas forced him to cancel it. The meeting was never rescheduled, and subsequently the Justice Department's investigation of the boss of the Chicago underworld was temporarily dropped. Giancana would not come under fire again until the spring of 1965.

43. The Challenge of Civil Rights

As IF the secret war against Cuba and the open war against organized crime were not enough to absorb the Kennedy brothers' thoughts and energies, they also had to contend with the growing dissatisfaction of the blacks.

Neither John nor Robert Kennedy had evidenced much interest in the cause of black people until they were forced to. Theodore Sorensen, the most ardent Kennedy partisan, underscored this lack of concern in his book *Kennedy*: "Jack Kennedy had been privately scornful of what he called the 'real liberals,' and he knew comparatively little and cared little about the problems of civil rights and civil liberties." Jack Kennedy's experience with blacks had been pretty much limited to his relationship with his black manservant, George Thomas, who had been his personal valet ever since he was a 29-year-old congressman. This faithful retainer had played a not insignificant role in Kennedy's life, yet Kennedy rarely permitted himself to be photographed with him, for obvious political reasons. Robert Kennedy's experience with blacks was equally limited. Like his brother, he had gone to exclusive private schools where blacks were in such a minority as to be virtually invisible. "I won't say I stayed awake nights worrying about civil rights before I became attorney general," Robert admitted not long after he took office.

And yet, what little interest in civil rights the Kennedys displayed during the presidential campaign was enough to create vastly inflated expectations among the nation's black population.

During his campaign, John F. Kennedy had criticized President Eisenhower for not doing more in the area of civil rights, even though two civil rights bills had been passed during Eisenhower's administration, the first such bills since Reconstruction; then, after Kennedy was elected President, he failed to include a civil rights bill in his own legislative program until he was forced, by black activism, to include one. He did, however, promise, during the campaign, to end discrimination in publicly assisted housing "by one stroke of the presidential pen," as soon as he entered office. And he did come forth with a generalized, high-blown rhetoric on human rights in speech after speech, which led multitudes of black people to expect great things.

For example, although the following passage from Kennedy's inaugural address did not specifically refer to civil rights for blacks, it prompted a young black air force veteran, James Meredith, to apply for admission into the strictly segregated University of Mississippi the day after Kennedy delivered his speech:

> Let the word go forth from this time and place, to friend and foe alike, that the torch has been passed to a new generation of Americans . . . one unwilling to witness or permit the slow undoing of those human rights to which this nation has always been committed and to which we are committed today at home and around the world.

Despite the rhetoric, and despite its confrontational stance on a number of issues, the Kennedy administration was somewhat reluctant to deal with the nation's number-one domestic problem, racial discrimination. Harris Wofford, the President's civil rights assistant, attributed this to Kennedy's fear that pushing civil rights too hard might provoke a Senate filibuster which would jeopardize his entire domestic program.

Kennedy had promised to end discrimination in federal housing. Yet, once in office, he astounded Harris Wofford by doing absolutely nothing about desegregating federal housing and only took action when, twenty months after his inauguration, racial trouble was breaking out everywhere and blacks from all over the country were mailing him hundreds of pens and inkwells (which Kennedy ordered put on Wofford's desk).

In May 1961, not long before Kennedy's first trip to Europe and meeting with Chairman Khrushchev, the Freedom Riders took off in their buses to challenge racial segregation wherever they found it—in washrooms, restaurants, waiting rooms. Kennedy's first reaction was to have it stopped for fear it would cause him embarrassment in Europe.

"Stop them! Get your friends off those buses!" he exclaimed to Harris Wofford, as Martin Luther King, Jr., James Farmer, the Rev. William Sloane Coffin, and their friends headed for their confrontation with the rednecks and Klansmen of Georgia, Alabama, and Mississippi.

To his plea to black leaders that the Freedom Riders would cause him "embarrassment" in Europe, those leaders retorted, "But we have been embarrassed all our lives."

The truth was that, although President Kennedy saw the need to right the terrible injustices that had been forced on the American black, and had every intention of furthering the drive for full civil rights, he did not have, as Martin Luther King, Jr., once observed, a "deep passionate moral commitment" to the problem. It was for this reason that almost every major initiative in the blacks' quest for civil rights was begun by the blacks themselves.

As Harris Wofford, who was closer to the situation than anyone else, later explained it, "Each major decision [of Kennedy's] was made hurriedly, at the last minute, in response to black pressures, with no overall strategy."

It was an old story for Kennedy. He simply did not have a firm set of beliefs, or ideas, on the subject, just as he did not have a firm set of beliefs, or ideas, on many other subjects—space, the economy, foreign affairs—unless he was compelled to formulate one by external forces, because he himself had never taken time out from politicking to reflect, to establish a solid core of belief from which policies could one day flow. Kennedy's forte was winning elections. George W. Ball, Kennedy's undersecretary of state, expressed the Kennedy style succinctly in his memoirs: "Kennedy was the pragmatist 'par excellence': although he sometimes alluded to conceptual ideas in his speeches, his main concern was action and day-to-day results."

In the area of civil rights, Jacqueline was not a positive influence either. For Jacqueline Kennedy, with her strong bent toward aesthetic pursuits—her preoccupation with clothes, furniture, entertainments, interior decoration, and the fine arts—had little interest in social problems, least of all the problem of civil rights for blacks.

Strangely enough, though, her father's family had had a long history of concern for the blacks, one she could have taken great political advantage of had she so chosen. For it was one of Jacqueline's cousins, Louise Bouvier Morrell, who, together with her stepsister, Katharine Drexel, founded in 1891 America's first major organization to promote the welfare of blacks, The Congregation of the Sisters of the Blessed Sacrament for Indians and Colored People. This organization, established within the embrace of the Catholic church (for Katharine Drexel was a nun), and at first financed by Bouvier and Drexel money and later by the church and other private donors, founded some sixty-one schools and colleges for blacks throughout the nation, including Epiphany College in Baltimore and Xavier College in New Orleans, and eventually poured some $40 million into charities for blacks and Indians. In time this enterprise became the principal charitable concern of the Bouvier family. The wealthiest of Jacqueline Bouvier's forebears, Michel C. Bouvier, donated $25,000 a year to the Congregation.

In 1967 I interviewed the Mother Superior of the Sisters of the Blessed Sacrament at her convent in Cornwell Heights, Pennsylvania, and she told me that when Jacqueline entered the White House she wrote her a letter reminding her of her family's role in establishing the original Congregation for Indians and Colored People and suggesting she publicize it and perhaps make a contribution to it. To her immense surprise and disappointment, she received a five-line note of acknowledgment and a contribution of only twenty-five dollars. Jacqueline never mentioned to the press, at that time or subsequently, her family's connection to what was the first major concerted effort to ameliorate the condition of the blacks and Indians since Reconstruction.

Harris Wofford related an encounter between Martin Luther King, Jr., and Jacqueline which clearly showed what Jacqueline was *really* interested in. At a moment of great crisis on the civil rights front, Wofford was escorting King to a meeting with the President, for which he, as special assistant on civil rights, had already briefed Kennedy. Kennedy had asked them to come up to the family quarters to discuss what was on their minds. When Wofford and King entered the small elevator near the White House main entrance, the elevator, instead of going up to the family quarters, promptly plunged down to the basement, where Jacqueline Kennedy got on. She was dressed in blue jeans and had dust all over her face. When Wofford introduced her to Dr. King, she said, in that low, whispery voice of hers, "Oh, Dr. King, you would be so thrilled if you could just have been with me in the basement this morning. I found a chair right out of the Andrew Jackson period—a beautiful chair."

"Yes—yes—is that so?" replied King in a slow, deep voice.

Then, when they arrived up in the family quarters, Jacqueline said, "I've just got to tell Jack about that chair. . . . But you have other things to talk to him about, don't you?"

King, who had matters of life and death to talk about, commented to Wofford after Jacqueline had gone: "Well, well—wasn't *that* something?"

No doubt Jack Kennedy would have been much more delighted to learn about Jacqueline's chair than to meet with the civil rights crusader whose intensely moralistic attitude inevitably made him feel uncomfortable. But it was not just Dr. King who made Kennedy feel uncomfortable, it was the whole civil rights movement.

On May 4 James Farmer, leader of the Congress of Racial Equality (CORE), an organization based on Gandhian principles of nonviolent action to effect social change, led a party of blacks and whites on a bus journey into the south to test the blacks' right to use the same facilities as the whites in southern bus terminals.

It wasn't until the Freedom Riders arrived in Anniston, Alabama, that serious trouble erupted. There a hysterical white gang set fire to one bus and broke into another, beating up the riders. Later, when the one battered remaining bus arrived in Birmingham, it was met by the Ku Klux Klan, which promptly attacked the riders with lead pipes, bicycle chains, and baseball bats. The Birmingham police were strangely absent from the scene. Later it was found out they had been purposely excused from duty that day by Police Commissioner "Bull" Connor. The FBI, however, was on the spot, taking down notes on the clubbings and forwarding them to Director J. Edgar Hoover, who, however, did not bother to report them to his boss, the attorney general.

The Freedom Riders went next to Montgomery, where they were viciously attacked by a mob of rednecks armed with axe handles, chains, and clubs. It was during this bloody episode that a white Freedom Rider was brutally clubbed and one of Robert Kennedy's top aides, John Seigenthaler, who had been sent down to help the riders, was knocked unconscious. Again, the FBI stood by taking notes without attempting to aid any of the beleaguered riders.

Things went from bad to worse, and finally, on May 21, Robert Kennedy acted, with the reluctant approval of his brother the President. He sent down 500 federal marshals, under the command of new frontiersman Byron "Whizzer" White. When Martin Luther King, Jr., flew down to get in on the action, the governor of Alabama told Kennedy he could not guarantee Dr. King's safety.

Kennedy then ordered fifty federal marshals to meet Dr. King at the airport and escort him into Montgomery.

Robert Kennedy then called for a "cooling off period," and James Farmer replied, "We have been cooling off for 100 years. If we got any cooler we'd be in deep freeze." That was that. The Freedom Riders drove on to Mississippi, determined to invade the capital, Jackson. Once in Jackson, they were all promptly arrested and thrown in jail. When Robert Kennedy attempted to get them out of jail, they refused to budge.

Martin Luther King, Jr., had asked President Kennedy to do something about segregated facilities in bus terminals long before the Freedom Rides began, suggesting that the Interstate Commerce Commission (ICC) issue an order banning all bus segregation, and Kennedy had been indecisive. Now, in the face of what was going on in Montgomery and Jackson, he finally took action. Five months later, as a direct result of the Freedom Rides, the ICC, acting on Kennedy's request, banned interstate bus segregation.

But desegregation of buses and bus terminals wasn't nearly enough. Black leaders were calling for the barriers to voting in the south to be erased. They wanted school desegregation. They wanted equality of opportunity in employment. They wanted integrated housing.

Meanwhile, the Kennedys in Washington had to confront various embarrassing situations. Washington, D.C., is a predominantly black city. However, not only were blacks barred from membership in the city's most prestigious club, the Metropolitan, but a white member could not even take a black guest to lunch there. After failing to get the club to change its rules, Robert Kennedy, with the blessing of his brother, resigned, and Angier Biddle Duke, George Cabot Lodge, Charles Bartlett, and others followed suit.

That was a positive step. But then, in reaction to another embarrassing situation vis-à-vis the blacks, John F. Kennedy displayed less vigor. Many black diplomats in Washington had been refused service in restaurants along route 40 in Maryland and Delaware. When the ambassador of the Republic of Chad presented his credentials to the President, he told him, "I was thrown on my rear end as a result of entering the Bonnie Brae restaurant on route 40." The President then said he would do something about it, but what he did was to call his chief of protocol, Angier Biddle Duke, and tell him: "Can't you tell these African ambassadors not to drive on route 40? It's a hell of a road— I used to drive it years ago, but why would anyone want to drive it today when you can fly? Tell those ambassadors I wouldn't think of driving from New York to Washington. Tell them to fly."

By the spring of 1962 the black leaders had succeeded in pressing their demands on the Kennedys to such an extent that Attorney General Robert Kennedy was compelled to admit that as his war on crime was finally getting into high gear, civil rights was now also "a major priority" of his administration.

That Robert Kennedy had decided that civil rights was now one of his top priorities led him, once again, into confrontation with his FBI director, J. Edgar Hoover. Again, Hoover proved to be a stumbling block. Hoover had no interest in furthering the cause of civil rights for blacks. Quite the opposite, in the black-white struggle he took the side of the bigot and racist against the blacks.

When Hoover took over the FBI in 1924, at the age of 29, Washington was still a relatively provincial southern town where the blacks were still in their "proper places" as waiters in restaurants and private clubs, servants in homes, janitors in government buildings, and ushers in the White House. This, for Hoover, was the eternal order of things. When this order began to change, he could not accept it. Instead of adapting, he filled up with rage. The black who before was a subject of, at best, tolerance to him, now became a subject of hate.

He was indeed a strange man, J. Edgar Hoover, a man very close to being mentally ill. A monomaniac and a pathological prude who had carved out a secret kingdom for himself within the U.S. government, accountable to no one but himself, he kept, in the words of contemporary columnist Westbrook Pegler, "the greatest deposit of personal dirt ever amassed." This made his relationship to each passing administration little more than that of blackmailer to blackmailee. As a result, no senator or congressman dared challenge him, and no President dared fire him. And so he became utterly corrupted by his power. In time, he managed to make the FBI into an organization worthy of a totalitarian state. By the time Robert Kennedy became his immediate boss, Hoover had made the FBI into a virtual gestapo which regularly violated the Constitution and made a mockery of the Bill of Rights.

Robert Kennedy once asked Hoover how many blacks were FBI agents. For a while Hoover, in a rage, refused to give his boss an answer. Then he told him there were none. Finally, after noting the attorney general's acute displeasure, he claimed there were five (out of 5000). Actually there were none, and Hoover had seen to it there were none. The five the director had come up with were Hoover's chauffeurs, whom he had made special agents during the war so they would not be drafted.

As much as J. Edgar Hoover hated Robert Kennedy, it seems safe to say his hatred for Martin Luther King, Jr., was even greater. As Dr. King came into prominence in the fifties, with his founding of the Southern Christian Leadership Conference (SCLC) and his subsequent encouragement of and participation in such activities as the Freedom Rides, Hoover's hostility toward him hardened into an implacable hatred and a determination to destroy the civil rights leader.

Accordingly, Hoover formed, within the FBI, a secret, concerted, counterintelligence program named COINTELPRO, one of whose purposes was "to expose, disrupt, misdirect, or otherwise neutralize" Martin Luther King, Jr., and his Southern Christian Leadership Conference. Knowledge of the existence of this secret organization within a secret organization was to be kept from both the President and the attorney general.

William Sullivan, Hoover's number three man at the Bureau, later wrote that COINTELPRO was "a rough, tough, dirty, business . . . with no holds barred." And former FBI agent James Murtagh stated, in 1979, when during the House Assassinations Committee investigations, the existence of COINTELPRO had finally come to public light, "we were operating an intensive vendetta against Dr. King in an effort to destroy him."

Hoover also used COINTELPRO to gather information on the Kennedys. William Sullivan, in his memoirs, states,

> Hoover was desperately trying to catch Bobby redhanded at anything . . . and was always gathering damaging material on Jack Kennedy, which the President, with his active social life, seemed more than willing to provide. . . . I was sure he was saving everything he had on Kennedy, and on Martin Luther King, Jr., too, until he could unload it all and destroy them both. He kept this kind of explosive material in his personal files, which filled four rooms on the fifth floor of headquarters.

Sullivan went on, "Kennedy was aware that Hoover was an enemy, of course, and kept his distance. He never asked Hoover for any gossip or any favors. If he heard that Hoover was leaking any anti-Kennedy stories, JFK would call the director right away and ask him to put the statement on the record."

One of the reasons why Hoover was so anxious to get as much on the Kennedys as possible was his abject fear of being fired by them. On January 1, 1965, Hoover was to turn 70. The Kennedy brothers, sure of JFK's re-election to the presidency in 1964, were determined to get rid of him then. They already had a successor picked out: Courtney Evans, a section chief from the criminal division who was one of the few FBI men who had been befriended by the Kennedys. Word of this evidently got back to Hoover, and it filled him with fear and rage.

By then the Kennedy brothers had become more mistrustful of Hoover than ever. In 1964 Anthony Lewis of the *New York Times* asked Robert Kennedy whether he thought Hoover was just a nasty person or truly dangerous, and Kennedy replied: "No, I think he's dangerous." And to another interviewer, John Bartlow Martin, he said about Hoover: "He's rather a psycho. . . . I think it [the FBI] is a very dangerous organization. . . . He's senile and frightening."

With the Kennedy brothers becoming more and more identified with Martin Luther King, Jr., and the civil rights movement, and the FBI director secretly intent on destroying all three of them, and the movement, the stage was set for a drama every bit as deadly as the Kennedy-Campbell-Giancana-Roselli duel that was unfolding at the same time.

By the fall of 1962 the seed of hope that John Kennedy had planted in James Meredith's head with the high rhetoric of his inaugural address had sprouted into the next great civil rights disturbance of his administration.

On September 10, 1962, Justice Hugo Black of the United States Supreme Court handed down the decision and command that there be no further interference with the judicial order that had already been handed down that summer to enroll James Meredith in the University of Mississippi forthwith. Accordingly, Robert Kennedy, who by now had embraced Meredith's cause with all his heart, ordered federal marshals to accompany Meredith to the University of Mississippi to register on September 20. When Governor Ross Barnett issued a proclamation refusing Meredith's application for enrollment, it was immediately challenged by John and Robert Kennedy.

There followed several sharp verbal exchanges between the governor and the Kennedys, which resulted in the Kennedys naively accepting a distinctly dishonest deal: In return for the governor's police protection of Meredith, the Kennedys agreed to secretly enroll him not at Oxford, but at the state offices in Jackson. Then, no sooner had the deal been made than the governor went back on his word and canceled it.

Meanwhile reports were coming into Washington of angry, racist mobs attacking the federal marshals who were guarding Meredith on the university campus, and President Kennedy was compelled to go on the air to plead with them to desist. As it turned out, the broadcast did no good whatsoever, and the situation on campus deteriorated.

Clearly it was time to order the U.S. Army into Oxford, but Kennedy, as he had done during the Bay of Pigs crisis, delayed. Finally, a little after midnight, with wild mobs raging around the Mississippi campus, Deputy Attorney General Nicholas Katzenbach, who was in command of the federal marshals guarding Meredith, appealed again to Kennedy to send in the Army. Again Kennedy delayed.

When Kennedy finally made up his mind to send the troops in, it took over three hours for them to arrive from Memphis. By then there were two people dead and scores of marshals, students, and others wounded. It was amidst this carnage that James Meredith, protected by the U.S. Army, was finally enrolled in the University of Mississippi.

The bloodshed at Oxford profoundly shocked the south, and, for that matter, all of America and a good part of the world. It also deeply shocked the Kennedy brothers. It was obvious to many that they lacked a sense of southern history and had no idea how deep-rooted the racial problem there was. It was not, as they had imagined, a small bush that could easily be spaded up, but a giant oak with a hundred massive roots reaching deep down into centuries-old soil.

John F. Kennedy was finally shocked into fulfilling some of those campaign promises and rhetorical flights that had led people like Meredith to act the way they did. Finally, after twenty months of delays, and the receipt of hundreds of pens and bottles of ink, he fulfilled his campaign promise that with "one stroke of the presidential pen," he would desegregate all federally assisted housing.

This notwithstanding, for Martin Luther King, Jr., the President's action was "too little, too late." "It does no good," he stated, "to apply vaseline to a cancer."

Meanwhile the Kennedys managed to further outrage the black leadership with some of their judicial appointments. To Dr. King's utter dismay, John F. Kennedy saw fit to appoint the best friend and former college roommate of archconservative, anti–civil rights Mississippi Senator James Eastland to the federal bench. His name was William Harold Cox, and one of his first acts as a federal judge was to try and block the Justice Department's voter registration drive in Mississippi.

As Victor Navasky pointed out in his *Kennedy Justice,* "the Kennedys named no fewer than 25 percent non-law-of-the-land followers to lifetime judgeships in the Fifth Circuit, the district that encompasses . . . the heart of the deep south." Five of them, Navasky pointed out, "were singled out by students of judicial decision-making in the south as anti–civil rights, racist, segregationist, and/or obstructionist." This was in direct violation of the Kennedy rhetoric of May 20, 1961, when he called for judges of "incorruptible character, firm judicial temperament, and the rare inner quality to temper justice with mercy."

John Kennedy was now in a virtually no-win situation. If he did something significant for the blacks, he earned the hatred of the southern whites, his own FBI director, and, in many instances, gave certain black leaders an opportunity to tell him he was doing "too little, too late." If, on the other hand, he threw a sop to the south by appointing someone like William Cox to the bench, the entire black leadership would come down on his head. One wonders if he ever came to rue the day he allowed his rhetoric to arouse such high expectations among the black people of America.

In January 1963 the President's youngest brother, the 30-year-old Edward M. Kennedy, took office as the junior senator from Massachusetts, and George Wallace was inaugurated governor of Alabama. Teddy Kennedy's inauguration marked the first time in American history that three brothers held high office in the U.S. government at the same time. George Wallace's inauguration was less auspicious. During his campaign, Wallace had said he would place himself in the doorway of any schoolhouse in Alabama under court order to admit blacks. Later he was to shriek to his followers: "From this cradle of the Confederacy, this very heart of the great Anglo-Saxon Southland . . . I draw the line in the dust and toss the gauntlet before the feet of tyranny. And I say, Segregation now! Segregation tomorrow! Segregation forever!" Kennedy's confrontation with Wallace was now all but inevitable.

That confrontation finally came in the spring of 1963. On April 3, 1963, Martin Luther King, Jr., led thousands of black men, women, and children into one of the most racist cities of the south, Birmingham, Alabama, where, as they marched through the streets, demanding with placards and shouts an end to racial discrimination, they were set upon by police with dogs and high-pressure water hoses, and mobs of rednecks carrying clubs and chains. As the nation watched black women marchers torn from their children, clubbed, and dragged off to jail and heard Governor Wallace's strident denunciation of the march, people wondered why President Kennedy just sat in his rocking chair and watched the bloodshed on television.

Finally, the rednecks forced his hand. On May 11 they bombed the home of Martin Luther King, Jr.'s, brother and then the hotel at which Dr. King had been staying. Now President Kennedy had had enough. He federalized the Alabama national guard and sent a contingent of federal troops to the state, to the outrage of Governor Wallace. By May 14 a small army of some 3000 troops had been deployed in and around Birmingham.

The presence of the federal troops calmed things down a bit; then, when Governor Wallace attempted to prevent two blacks from enrolling in the University of Alabama, things began heating up again.

"I am the embodiment of the sovereignty of this state," Wallace shouted, "and I will be present to bar the entrance of any negro who attempts to enroll."

Wallace backed up his words by personally attempting to block the entry of the black students at the administration building, standing in that building's main entrance with outstretched arms. This time Kennedy took quick action and ordered the national guard to the campus. When the guardsmen appeared, armed to the teeth, Wallace backed down and the black students were duly enrolled.

That evening President Kennedy went on the air with

a ringing address to the nation, telling the American people that civil rights was "a moral issue as old as the scriptures . . . and as clear as the Constitution. . . . A great change is at hand," he cried, "and our task, our obligation, is to make that revolution, that change, peaceful and constructive for all." The following week, he concluded, he was going to send a civil rights bill up to Congress that was going to make the commitment "that race has no place in American life or law."

So finally Kennedy sent up his bill on civil rights. The date was June 19, 1963, almost two and a half years after his inauguration. What had he been waiting for? It now appears he had been waiting to be forced into making the move—either that, or waiting for the propitious moment when he felt his bill might stand a chance of getting passed. It was probably a combination of both.

The civil rights bill that Kennedy sent up to Congress (and that did not pass during his administration) turned out to be a cautious document. Clauses having to do with the desegregation of public facilities were limited to organizations having a substantial effect on interstate commerce. Federal aid was to be cut off to businesses which discriminated against blacks, but on an optional, not a mandatory, basis. There was no clause banning segregation in the schools, and there were no new voting rights clauses. John Lewis, chairman of the Student Nonviolent Coordinating Committee (SNCC), later denounced the bill, stating, "In good conscience, we cannot support the Administration's civil rights bill, for it is too little too late."

Not long after the bill was sent up, Medgar Evers, the Mississippi NAACP director who had encouraged James Meredith to fight his rejection by the University of Mississippi, was shot dead in front of his house. As a war veteran, he was buried in Arlington.

There followed, on August 28, 1963, the great Freedom March on Washington at the end of which some 250,000 people gathered near the Lincoln Memorial to hear Martin Luther King, Jr., utter his now famous words: "Free at last! Free at last! Thank God Almighty, we are free at last!"

As might be expected, J. Edgar Hoover was outraged by the march on Washington. The event filled him with such fury that after the crowds dispersed he became determined to destroy Martin Luther King, his movement, and its supporters, which included, of course, John and Robert Kennedy.

Both John F. Kennedy and Martin Luther King were fully aware of the mutual enemy they had in the FBI director. The President had had a meeting at the White House with the civil rights leader on June 22, two months before the Freedom March. King was surprised that no sooner did he arrive in the Oval Office than Kennedy led him right out into the adjacent Rose Garden for a stroll. There he told King that Senator Eastland and J. Edgar Hoover were furious over the coming march and that he, King, better be very careful about his utterances, for the FBI was keeping him under close surveillance. The President seemed so concerned and secretive that King later told his friend Andrew Young: "The President is afraid of Hoover himself. . . . I guess Hoover must be buggin' him too."

J. Edgar Hoover was not "buggin' " either the President, or Martin Luther King . . . yet. He *was* bugging a certain Stanley Levison, a New York lawyer who was a friend of King's and a supporter of his Southern Christian Leadership Conference. Hoover believed Levison was a communist and had obtained authorization to tap his phone for "reasons of national security."

Hoover's contention was without apparent foundation at the time, but that did not stop him from trying to use it as a pretext for tapping Martin Luther King, Jr.'s, telephone. On the grounds that it was imperative to find out whether the SCLC was infiltrated by communists, he asked his detested attorney general for permission to tap Dr. King's phone on July 23 and was refused. Then he told RFK that he had just discovered that Levison had begun phoning King again after a lapse of many months. Finally Kennedy gave in, and on October 21, 1963, authorized the director of the FBI to install a thirty-day wiretap on Martin Luther King. As it turned out, the authorization opened a Pandora's box of wiretapping and bugging of the civil rights leader. The fanatical Hoover, out to get King at any cost, tapped his telephones both in his SCLC offices and his home. In addition, Hoover's FBI agents would manage to conceal recording bugs in King's hotel and motel rooms at least twenty-one times when he was on the road.

How could Robert Kennedy, in good conscience, have allowed Hoover to tap Martin Luther King's phones? To determine whether Levison was a communist, it was sufficient to tap only Levison's phone. Why then was a two-way conversation necessary? In all probability he allowed the tap because, by now, the Kennedys were virtual hostages of the FBI director. Not only did Hoover have the Inga Arvad files and the report of an alleged $500,000 payoff to one of JFK's former girlfriends during the 1960 campaign, he now had the Judith Campbell files. Furthermore, as Harris Wofford has suggested, Hoover could conceivably damage the Kennedys' image by announcing or leaking the accusation that the attorney general refused to authorize wiretaps on a suspected communist.

What were the ultimate consequences of Kennedy's vacillating civil rights policies? On the positive side, Kennedy's sympathy helped give Martin Luther King, Jr., and other civil rights activists the courage to risk their lives to further their cause. Kennedy also helped to arouse the conscience of the nation in his televised speeches and press conferences. Finally, he proposed legislation that was to result in the Civil Rights Act of 1964, the first major step toward equal rights for blacks. Unfortunately, it was only a first step, and it didn't come soon enough. Kennedy's rhetoric may, in fact, have raised the expectations of the black people too high since the American people were not prepared to accept legislation that would provide for a complete end to discrimination. The terrible racial outbursts of the mid-sixties—in Selma, Watts, and Chicago's Southside—could have been related to exaggerated expectations that were never fulfilled.

Theodore H. White claimed that one of the great achievements of the Kennedy administration was "opening the gates" of American society to blacks and other minorities. This may have been due more to speechwriters Sorensen's and Wofford's rhetoric than to conscious intention on the part of the Kennedys. Although JFK had a real concern for involving blacks in government, Kennedy himself used to confess to intimates that he considered his role vis-à-vis black resentment as "a finger in the dike."

And what were the personal consequences for Kennedy?

As in the Cuban mess, he made enemies on both sides, among both blacks *and* southern whites. But the most potentially dangerous enemy to emerge from Kennedy's civil rights policy was the FBI and its director.

While the Kennedy brothers were consorting with the detested Martin Luther King, Jr., and belatedly sending their civil rights bill up to the Congress, Hoover was routinely receiving illegally taped threats against the President's and the attorney general's lives from those top figures in organized crime he had been tapping and bugging, without the attorney general's authorization, ever since the Kennedys' war on organized crime began. Quietly he had been placing these threatening tapes in his secret files, never revealing their existence, much less their contents, to either the President or the attorney general.

If President Kennedy's wavering Cuban policy had won him the enmity of the CIA, which he had vowed to "break into a thousand pieces," his equally wavering civil rights policy had won him the enmity of the FBI, whose director he was secretly planning to replace.

In alienating his two major investigative agencies, what was Kennedy doing, albeit unwittingly? He was denying himself the loyalty of the two agencies of his government that were fully capable of destroying him and his administration. And not only did the CIA and the FBI have the means and the expertise to destroy him, but they, as the two chief investigative agencies of the government, also had the means and expertise to impede and misdirect any investigation of that destruction.

44. Their Finest Hour

ONCE OPERATION MONGOOSE was launched, a clash with Fidel Castro and his ally, the Soviet Union, was inevitable. The CIA's Kennedy-backed secret war against Cuba, with its plans to sabotage Cuban mines and mills, cripple its sugar industry, foment rebellion within Castro's inner circle, conduct guerrilla strikes on the island, and murder the Cuban dictator, was an invitation to violent reprisal.

It is somewhat surprising, therefore, that the Kennedy brothers were apparently so shocked and surprised when, on October 16, 1962, they learned that the Soviet Union was secretly arming its Caribbean ally with intermediate-range nuclear missiles. In a very real sense, the presence of Soviet missiles on Cuba represented the chickens coming back to roost.

All the Kennedy court historians, without exception, register the same surprise in their various accounts of John F. Kennedy's administration, leading one to conclude they knew little or nothing themselves about the Kennedys' secret war. For a reading of Arthur M. Schlesinger, Jr.'s, *A Thousand Days*, Theodore C. Sorenson's *Kennedy*, Pierre Salinger's *With Kennedy*, and Kenneth P. O'Donnell and David F. Powers' *Johnny We Hardly Knew Ye* leaves one in total ignorance of Operation Mongoose. There is not one single line in any of these "official," "inside" histories of the Kennedy regime that even *hints* at the secret war against Cuba. Nor is it mentioned in Robert F. Kennedy's own memoir of the Cuban missile crisis, *Thirteen Days*, and Robert F. Kennedy, as we know, was the supreme commander of Operation Mongoose.

The truth of the matter is that Operation Mongoose was the great dark secret of the Kennedy administration, unknown even to many of President Kennedy's closest advisers and family members. Were it not for the Senate Select Committee to Study Governmental Operations with Respect to Intelligence Activities, specifically its investigation of alleged assassination plots involving foreign leaders (the Church committee) of 1975, we probably would still be ignorant of Operation Mongoose.

No wonder the American people were so shocked to learn that Chairman Khrushchev was arming Fidel Castro with ballistic missiles bearing nuclear warheads. If Sorensen and Schlesinger were kept in ignorance of the secret war, then the American people, whose taxes were financing Mongoose to the tune of $100 million a year, were left in complete darkness about it. Had the American people known that their own government was plotting the overthrow of Castro's regime and the murder of Castro himself, they would not have been so amazed that Cuba wished to defend itself.

In the last analysis, the Cuban missile crisis was not the result of an arbitrary, isolated act of hostility; the Russian missiles on Cuba constituted a justifiable defensive measure. In sending ballistic missiles to Cuba, Khrushchev was not only establishing a Soviet offensive capability near the American mainland, he was trying to protect Cuba from the belligerencies of the Kennedy government. In effect then, the Cuban missile crisis was actually brought on by the Kennedys themselves.

Before considering the Kennedys' response to the Soviet missiles in Cuba, it is necessary to backtrack to the other milestones of the cold war during John F. Kennedy's administration, for the missile crisis was but the culmination of a series of crises with the Soviet Union, going back to Kennedy's first spring in the White House. The first crisis, one that involved only indirect confrontation with the Soviet Union, had occurred five days before the ill-fated invasion of the Bay of Pigs. On April 12, 1961, Maj. Yuri Gagarin of the Soviet Union was rocketed into orbit aboard the spaceship *Vostok I* and made a complete trip around the earth in ninety minutes.

The Soviet space exploit profoundly shocked the young American President. It was now abundantly clear that the Soviets were way ahead of the Americans in the conquest of space. John F. Kennedy did not have a space program, and had very little interest in, or knowledge of, rocketry and astronomy; nevertheless, during a subsequent week-end he made a snap decision to put an American on the moon by 1970. This was to become Project Apollo and was to cost over $30 billion.

Nothing typified Kennedy's modus operandi more than this decision. Just as he had had no real passion for civil rights before becoming President, he had had no real passion for the space effort either. In both areas, his policies, as President, were generated mostly by external challenges. For Kennedy, Project Apollo was not so much an opportunity to enlarge human knowledge of the universe as it was an opportunity to get the best of the Russians, to "beat" them in the game of space. If the Russians had not launched a man into space, it is doubtful whether Project Apollo would have ever got off the ground.

Kennedy also wanted to "beat" the Russians in the arms race. Accordingly, he took steps to close the so-called missile gap in a concerted drive to attain nuclear arms superiority for the United States. His goal was to possess both an overwhelmingly powerful strategic nuclear deterrent and strong conventional forces for a "flexible response" to external aggression. By the end of 1962 he wanted 600 intercontinental ballistic missiles (ICBMs) and got them. By the end of 1963 he wanted 1000 and a military budget of $50 billion, the highest in history. He expressed his defense philosophy with his usual deftness: "We dare not tempt them with weakness. For only when our arms are sufficient beyond doubt can we be certain beyond doubt that they will never be employed."

The first major test of Kennedy's defense posture came in August 1961 over Berlin, a test that has come to be known in the Kennedy literature as the Berlin crisis. The Soviet Union had been anxious to sign a separate peace treaty with East Germany for some time, a treaty which would literally turn all of Berlin over to East Germany. The Allies, each of whom had jurisdiction over a specific sector of West Berlin, would then have to come to terms with East Germany over access to their individual sectors. What signing a separate treaty with East Germany really meant was squeezing the Allies out of West Berlin.

The thriving capitalistic economy of West Berlin had become a constant source of embarrassment to the Russians ever since the partition of Berlin after World War II. Communist East Berlin was chronically depressed. As a result, some 200,000 East Germans were flooding into West Germany through West Berlin each year.

Nikita Khrushchev, chairman of the Presidium of the Supreme Soviet, was anxious to stanch this embarrassing flow, and so when President Kennedy met with him in Vienna, in June 1961, he announced to a startled Kennedy that he was going to sign a separate peace treaty with East Germany within six months. If the United States insisted on defending its rights in West Berlin after this treaty was signed, he would, subject to further negotiations, make war. In the meantime, if the United States wanted to negotiate, he would listen.

In a talk with Kennedy at the Soviet Embassy in Vienna, Khrushchev shouted at him that his decision to sign the treaty allowing East Germany to seize West Berlin in December was firm and irrevocable, and "you can tell that to Macmillan, de Gaulle, and Adenauer. If that means war, the Soviet Union will accept the challenge."

To this barrage JFK replied, "It's going to be a cold winter."

The Berlin crisis was on. Charles de Gaulle had warned Kennedy in Paris that Khrushchev would try and bluff him on the issue, but still John F. Kennedy was shaken. "West Berlin," he declared to the world, "will be the great testing place of western courage and will. Our commitment, going back to 1945, and Soviet ambitions, meet in basic confrontation."

John Kennedy had been used to confronting a powerful rival since early childhood. Because of this early conditioning, Kennedy had a tendency to overreact to any challenge. Now, faced with a threat of war from Chairman Khrushchev, Kennedy reacted with measures that startled the world. He immediately called for $3.25 billion more in defense appropriations. He doubled, then tripled, the draft. He called up 150,000 reservists and initiated a program of civil defense from nuclear attack.

Kennedy's civil defense program was alarming, and indicated the degree to which he overreacted to the crisis. He requested financing from Congress to

> identify and mark space in existing structures . . . that could be used for fallout shelters in case of attack, to stock these shelters with food, water, first-aid kits and other minimum essentials for survival; to improve air-raid warning and detection systems . . . and to take other measures that will be effective at an early date to save millions of lives, if needed. In the event of an attack, the lives of those families which are not hit in a nuclear blast and fire can still be saved—if they can be warned to take shelter and if that shelter is available.

This was nothing less than preparation for nuclear war.

On August 13, Khrushchev acted. Suddenly he had East German troops throw up barricades at all the entry points into West Berlin; then the East Germans began building the Berlin Wall. Soon it would be virtually impossible for an East German to enter West Berlin without risking his life.

Kennedy's reaction to this initiative was to send 1500 troops of the first battle group, Eighth Infantry, down the autobahn from West Germany into East Germany and on into West Berlin. It was a dangerous and unnecessary action, for if the U.S. soldiers had been challenged by East German forces, World War III could easily have been ignited. But they were not challenged, and, once inside West Berlin, they did nothing. They allowed the East Germans to go ahead building their wall. Subsequently Kennedy called on the Soviet Union to agree to negotiations over the status of West Berlin, negotiations were held, and Khrushchev agreed not to sign a separate peace treaty with East Germany. Khrushchev had found a relatively peaceful solution to the problem of the East Germans escaping into West Berlin—the Wall—and stopped at that. The crisis was over. Although the U.S. and her western allies bitterly criticized it, it was really the Wall that saved them from war.

At the height of the crisis Kennedy had decided not to go to Hyannis Port for the weekend because, as he told an aide, it would be an "inappropriate place from which to start World War III." If the world had come close to nuclear war during the Berlin crisis of 1961, observers are generally agreed that during the Cuban crisis the world came the closest to nuclear holocaust since the so-called nuclear age began.

Time and events have certainly proved that John F. Kennedy's Cuban policy was totally misguided. Kennedy should have made an accommodation with Castro a cardinal point of his administration. Kennedy might well have been able to convince Castro to come over to his side and thus prevent Cuba from becoming a satellite of the Soviet Union.

One can easily imagine what the impact of a state visit by Jack and Jacqueline Kennedy to Havana could have meant to Cuban-American relations at the time. With the charming, Spanish-speaking Jacqueline at his side, it is possible the charismatic Kennedy could have established a rapport with the Cuban dictator that could have conceivably overcome Castro's antipathy for America. Instead he chose the path of confrontation.

Furthermore, since John Kennedy had backed down at the last minute in the Bay of Pigs, denying the invasion forces the full support that would have assured their success, Khrushchev believed Kennedy was weak, and he was encouraged to gamble on a confrontation in Cuba.

In the meantime (early 1962), the CIA and the Kennedys had launched Operation Mongoose. By the time of the missile crisis there were some 600 CIA case officers in and around Miami directing some 3000 Cuban agents out of some fifty business fronts with fleets of warplanes and ships at their disposal. President Kennedy had called for "massive Mongoose activity" against Castro, and when quick results were not forthcoming, he and his brother roundly criticized the two big chiefs of the operation, Edward Lansdale and Richard Helms, goading them to step up their efforts. In response to this goading, Richard Helms, as the CIA's deputy director of covert operations, was compelled to revive the CIA's plan to murder Castro through its alliance with organized crime.

When President Kennedy first learned of the missiles he cried out in anger: "He can't do this to *me!*" And Robert Kennedy, in his book *Thirteen Days,* wrote, "The dominant feeling was one of shocked incredulity. We had been deceived by Khrushchev, but we had also fooled ourselves."

The Kennedys had indeed fooled themselves, but not in the way Robert had meant.

On July 2, 1962, Fidel Castro's brother Raúl, minister of the armed forces, went to Moscow with intelligence reports of how the Kennedy administration, through its secret Operation Mongoose, was plotting to overthrow his brother's regime by force. Meeting with Khrushchev, he requested military aid, and Khrushchev agreed to begin installing intermediate-range ballistic missiles on Cuba in the fall.

The first reports of the installation of Russian missiles on Cuba were made by Cuban refugees and informants to Senator Kenneth Keating of New York on August 31, 1962. Keating advised the Kennedy administration, and, disbelieving the reports, the Kennedy administration did nothing. Further reports of strange military constructions on Cuba reached Washington throughout September, and the administration still didn't believe them. As late as October 14, Kennedy's National Security Adviser McGeorge Bundy was denying reports of missiles on Cuba on ABC's

"Issues and Answers" program. Later on that same day, aerial photographs of the missile installations, taken by a U-2 reconnaissance plane, arrived in Washington; the missile crisis was on.

President Kennedy examined the photographs and summoned his National Security Council. At the meeting it was decided that Khrushchev had to remove the missiles or the United States would be compelled to invade Cuba and destroy all the missile installations.

On October 22 President Kennedy announced to the Soviet Union and the world that he was aware of the installation of the Soviet missiles on Cuba and demanded their immediate withdrawal. He then announced a "quarantine" of ships carrying weapons to Cuba, and further announced he had put U.S. strategic forces on full alert, warning the Soviet Union that "any missile launched from Cuba would be regarded as a Soviet missile" and would be met with "a full retaliatory response."

The Soviet response came two days later, on October 24, and it was equally strong. Khrushchev ordered the Soviet Union's forces on full alert and threatened to sink any U.S. ship that stopped a Russian ship on the way to Cuba.

The stage was now set for a thermonuclear war. In such a war, Defense Secretary Robert McNamara was to estimate, during the first hour 100 million Americans and 100 million Russians would die.

Meanwhile the U.S. Navy had deployed 180 ships in the Caribbean, entirely surrounding the island of Cuba and effectively blockading the country. President Kennedy's orders to the Navy were to stop any vessel seeking to enter a Cuban port to ascertain whether or not it was carrying weapons. If it was carrying weapons it would not be allowed to proceed. If it then continued to proceed it would be fired upon.

In addition, Kennedy ordered the Army's First Armored Division out of Texas and into Georgia and put five more divisions on full alert. He also ordered the entire B-52 bomber force, carrying nuclear weapons, into the air.

Preparations were also begun for a full-scale invasion

of Cuba. This would involve deployment of an army invasion force of 250,000 men and a force of 90,000 Marines and airborne units, and would mean at least 500 air sorties against missile installations and air fields on Cuba. Robert McNamara estimated that U.S. casualties in an invasion would amount to roughly 25,000. Soon there would be an initial force of 150,000 men in Florida ready to invade Cuba. The battle lines were now drawn.

There followed the extraordinarily tense last four days of the now-famous "thirteen days" of the Cuban missile crisis. During this crisis John F. Kennedy proved to be considerably more poised and mature than he had been during the Bay of Pigs invasion. This time he would not listen to the gospel according to the CIA. This time he listened to his own counsel, and to that of his brother Robert. And this time, for the first time, he showed he was made of truly presidential timber.

A committee had been formed to help the President and his brother deal with the crisis. It was named the "Ex Comm" (Executive Committee of the National Security Council) and counted among its members such prominent new frontiersmen as Robert McNamara, Dean Rusk, McGeorge Bundy, Theodore Sorensen, and Roswell Gilpatric. The group also included Gen. Maxwell Taylor, chairman of the joint chiefs, and, from time to time, Lyndon B. Johnson and Adlai Stevenson.

And so John and Robert Kennedy and the members of the Ex Comm waited to see what was going to happen when the first ships encountered the U.S. naval blockade of Cuba. The President had confided to Robert that he believed there was a one in three chance that the crisis would result in nuclear war.

It must be pointed out here that midterm elections in the United States were only two weeks away. John Kennedy had never had much of a hold on Congress, and he certainly did not want to lose any Democratic seats, and thus lose what little hold he had, in the coming elections. To allow the Russians to leave the missiles in Cuba he believed would be disastrous for the elections.

Although President Kennedy remained remarkably

calm throughout the crisis, the waiting to see what the Russian ships would do when they reached the U.S. quarantine line took its toll on his emotions. Just before word came about the Russian ships arriving at the line, "his hand," in the words of Robert Kennedy, "went up to his face and covered his mouth. He opened and closed his fist. His face seemed drawn, his eyes pained and gray." The moment of truth was at hand. If the Russian ships tried to run the blockade, the Navy would fire on them and World War III might conceivably begin.

It was more or less at this time that Bertrand Russell worsened Kennedy's mood by sending him the following telegram:

> YOUR ACTION DESPERATE . . . NO CONCEIVABLE
> JUSTIFICATION. WE WILL NOT HAVE MASS
> MURDER . . . END THIS MADNESS.

As the Kennedy brothers and their advisers waited to see what would happen at the blockade, the U.S. military continued to urge an immediate invasion of Cuba. Gen. Curtis Le May wanted to bomb all the missile sites and airfields at once and send an invasion force of 250,000 men to wrest the island from Castro once and for all. "But what would the Russians do if we did this?" asked President Kennedy. "Nothing," replied General Le May. Both John and Robert Kennedy rejected the idea.

The most dramatic moment in the entire crisis came on October 25 when several Soviet ships stopped dead in the water before the U.S. naval blockade. A Russian submarine was among them; it too did not attempt to run the blockade. Relieved, President Kennedy awaited a response from Chairman Khrushchev to his demand that the Soviet missiles be removed from Cuba.

Khrushchev's response was soon in coming. On October 26, the day after the Russian ships stopped before the American blockade, Khrushchev sent Kennedy a long, rambling, emotional letter offering to withdraw the missiles in return for a pledge from the U.S. government not to invade Cuba. This was followed the next day by a tougher letter in which Khrushchev offered to withdraw the missiles from Cuba if the United States agreed to withdraw its missiles from Turkey.

The U.S. missiles in Turkey (and Italy) were considered obsolete, and Kennedy had already given orders that they be eventually replaced, but he did not respond sympathetically to the idea of a trade. He called a meeting of the Ex Comm to consider the two letters. Several of those in attendance were to remark later that in these meetings President Kennedy was always the calmest person in the room.

Six members of the committee wanted to dismiss Khrushchev's proposals and to bomb and invade Cuba immediately. The majority was more conciliatory. Adlai Stevenson declared that America should be willing to give up its missile bases in Turkey *and* Italy *and* relinquish its naval base at Guantanamo in return for the withdrawal of the Russian missiles, a position widely regarded at the time as reminiscent of Munich in 1938.

After an exhaustive discussion, Robert Kennedy came up with the winning idea. He suggested that his brother ignore Khrushchev's second letter about trading the removal of the missiles in Turkey for the removal of the missiles in Cuba, and accept the proposal made in the first letter that the United States promise not to invade Cuba in return for the Soviets' withdrawing the missiles. President Kennedy agreed and sent Khrushchev a message on October 27 pledging not to invade Cuba if the missiles were withdrawn, but warning, in a virtual ultimatum, that if the missiles were not withdrawn on Sunday, October 28, he would conduct an air strike, and possibly an invasion, against Cuba on Monday the 29th or Tuesday the 30th.

Kennedy would not settle for the logical trade-off of the Turkish for the Cuban missiles, which would look too much like a compromise. Thus he was willing to risk thermonuclear war to obtain what amounted to virtual unconditional surrender from Khrushchev. It was indeed an extraordinarily dangerous, even reckless, position that John Kennedy took in sending his ultimatum to Khrushchev. As the British *Tribune* editorialized, "It may well be that

Kennedy is risking blowing the world to hell in order to sweep a few Democrats into office."

The *Tribune*'s remark may not have been far off base. The November elections were closing in. A mere compromise, such as the trade-off between the Turkish and Cuban missiles, was not quite heroic enough for Kennedy's taste. He needed to pull off a tremendous coup to help Democrats win the November elections. He needed to face Khrushchev down and make him surrender before the entire world.

Fortunately Khrushchev decided to risk humiliation and surrendered. On October 28 he announced the withdrawal of all Soviet missiles from Cuba. The crisis was over, and John F. Kennedy could tell his brother, "Well, I guess this is the week I earn my salary."

But was Khrushchev's surrender worth the risk of blowing up the world in a nuclear holocaust? Is *anything* worth taking such a risk?

Commenting on the crisis, Robert Kennedy told his brother: "I just don't think there was any choice. And not only that, if you hadn't acted, you would have been impeached."

"That's what I think," said JFK. "I would have been impeached."

The fact that the Kennedys were willing to go to nuclear war over the Cuban missiles was deeply disturbing to many, especially when nuclear war could have been so easily avoided by simply trading the removal of the American missiles in Turkey for the removal of the Russian missiles in Cuba (something the Kennedys were already prepared to do, although they would have had to clear it with NATO).

After the crisis was over, Robert Kennedy made this chilling comment to Arthur M. Schlesinger:

> We all agreed in the end that if the Russians were ready to go to nuclear war over Cuba they were ready to go to nuclear war, and that was that. So we might as well have the showdown then as six months later.

But, as it turned out, it was the Kennedys who were willing to go to nuclear war, not the Russians.

One must inevitably ask: "When, if ever, is nuclear war justified?"

And one must not hesitate in answering that the only circumstance when a leader is justified in risking a nuclear war is in the face of a mortal challenge to the very existence of a nation and a people. If the challenge is anything less than mortal, it is not worth risking a nuclear war.

One must admire President Kennedy for the magnificent way he handled himself during the crisis. Arthur M. Schlesinger delivered one of the most eloquent compliments when he wrote of "this combination of toughness and restraint, of will, nerve, and wisdom, so brilliantly controlled, so matchlessly calibrated, that dazzled the world." "It displayed," Schlesinger elaborated, "the ripening of an American leadership unsurpassed in the responsible management of power." And Harold Macmillan observed that "the way Bobby and his brother played this hand was absolutely masterly. . . . What they did that week convinced me that they were both great men." And of Bobby Kennedy, Robert McNamara said that in the midst of the greatest tension he had ever experienced he "came to know, admire, and love Robert F. Kennedy," who remained "calm and cool" throughout the crisis, combining "energy and courage, compassion and wisdom."

There was little doubt about it. From the standpoint of poise and courage and the deft use of great power in a time of overwhelming strain, the way the Kennedy brothers handled the Cuban missile crisis represented their finest hour.

And yet there is a disturbing side to the whole affair. There is the important question of follow-up, of pressing one's advantages. After the crisis was over, Kennedy failed to order the Navy to inspect the Russian ships carrying the missiles back to Russia to see if they were, in fact, carrying them. Aerial photographs were taken of the ships, but all they revealed were huge tarpaulins on the decks covering *something*. Whether they covered missiles or not could not be accurately determined. Then, in response to an administration probe to see whether Americans could inspect the missile sites in Cuba to determine whether the missiles had actually been removed, Castro refused to allow inspectors on Cuban soil.

So, in the end, the United States could never be quite sure that all the missiles had been, in fact, removed. Many could have simply been stored underground or hidden in one way or another.

The lack of vigorous Kennedy follow-up suggested that the Kennedys were satisfied with an *apparent* victory. John Kennedy had reached his personal objectives, which were to register a spectacular coup before the midterm elections and convey to the world the impression that he was a "winner."

Furthermore, after the crisis was over, Kennedy failed to stipulate what offensive weapons the Russians *could* send to Cuba and what Russian weapons Castro could deploy on Cuba. This led to the following Russian military aid to Cuba: In 1969 Soviet submarines, carrying nuclear weapons, docked in Cuba, and the United States did not ask them to get out; later the Russians began building a submarine base on Cuba, and the United States did not insist that the construction be halted; later still Cuba received from the Soviet Union twenty-five missile attack boats, twenty-one torpedo boats, and ten subchasers, enough ships to give the U.S. Navy a good tussle in the straits of Florida, and again the U.S. did nothing about it; then, in 1978, the Soviet Union sent a sizable number of MIG-23s, equipped with nuclear bomb delivery systems, to Cuba, and the U.S. did not ask the Soviets to remove them; and finally in 1979 it was discovered that there were some 5000 Soviet troops stationed on Cuba, a situation President Carter termed "intolerable" and then did nothing about.

Kennedy had been so lax in pressing his hard-won advantages that he set up no machinery to enforce his victory in the future. When Secretary of State Henry Kissinger, disturbed over the submarine base the Soviets were building on Cuba, hunted through the files looking for the written agreement he was sure President Kennedy had signed with Khrushchev, he found, to his utter amazement, there was none—which lends further credence to the belief that John F. Kennedy was willing to settle for an "apparent" victory.

Kennedy, however, was concerned with keeping up his own belligerencies against Cuba. Although he kept his promise to Khrushchev not to invade Cuba, and tried to discourage some exile groups from raiding the island, he did not wholly dismantle Operation Mongoose, and the attempts at sabotage and assassination in Cuba continued under the aegis of the CIA and the White House's Special Group. As proof of this we have the minutes of a meeting of the Special Group on June 19, 1963, at which McNamara, Harriman, McCone, and Bundy, among others, were present. At this meeting the CIA's Desmond FitzGerald, a close friend of Robert F. Kennedy, set forth a program of sabotage against Cuba aimed at electric power stations, petroleum refineries and storage facilities, railroad and highway transportation, and production and manufacturing facilities. The first operation was planned for mid-July. The raids were to be conducted from outside Cuba, using Cuban agents under CIA control. As for the Castro assassination plot, we shall soon see that it did not cease, but merely took on a different form. This would come to be known as the AM/LASH plot, and its chief promoter would be the same Desmond FitzGerald who set forth the sabotage program at the June 19 meeting of the Special Group. As Richard Helms testified at the Church committee hearings in 1975, the CIA continued its attempts to murder Fidel Castro right up to the afternoon of November 22, 1963, stating that the agency had "preexisting [presidential] authority" to do so.

There were many important consequences of the Cuban missile crisis. One was that Kennedy's long list of enemies now included the leader of the Soviet Union.

To evaluate Kennedy's policies in regard to the Soviet-Cuban relationship, we must ask what the status of that relationship is today. Had it deteriorated after the great showdown with Khrushchev, it could be confidently said that Kennedy's policy had paid off. Unfortunately, the exact opposite is true. Today the Soviet-Cuban rela-

Irish peasants in the nineteenth century, at the time of the great emigrations to America. (Library of Congress.)

The Kennedy homestead, Dunganstown, New Ross, as it looks today. Only the smaller building was standing when Patrick Kennedy left the farm for America in 1848. In Patrick's day the roof was thatched. (Sheehan Bros., New Ross.)

*A late-nineteenth-century Boston saloon, of the type
P. J. Kennedy owned and operated. (The Society for
the Preservation of New England Antiquities.)*

*P. J. Kennedy's house (center) on
Meridian Street, East Boston.
Joseph P. Kennedy was born here
in 1888. (Wide World Photos.)*

Rose Fitzgerald, age 15, with her father (at right), John F. "Honey Fitz" Fitzgerald, and her future father-in-law, P. J. Kennedy, during a vacation in 1905. (Wide World Photos.)

*Mr. and Mrs. Joseph P. Kennedy on their wedding day,
October 7, 1914. (United Press International Photo.)*

Rose Kennedy and three of her children, from left, Joseph Junior, Rosemary, and John. (Wide World Photos.)

Joseph P. Kennedy is congratulated by President Franklin D. Roosevelt after being sworn in as U.S. ambassador to the Court of St. James's by Justice Stanley Reed, February 18, 1938. (United Press International Photo.)

The Kennedy family at Antibes in 1939. Back row, from left: Kathleen, Joseph Junior, Rosemary, Mrs. Kennedy, Edward; middle row: John, Eunice, the ambassador, Patricia; front row: Robert and Jean. (Wide World Photos.)

Joseph P. Kennedy with sons Joseph Junior, left, and John at Harvard. (Wide World Photos.)

The Bouvier grandchildren at Lasata, East Hampton, 1934. From left: Edith Beale, carrying Lee Bouvier, Michel Bouvier, Phelan Beale, Jr., Bouvier Beale, Henry Scott, Jr., John Davis, Michelle Scott, and Jacqueline Bouvier. (Photo by Thomas F. Kelley. J. H. Davis Collection.)

John V. Bouvier III and his daughter Jacqueline at a Southampton horse show, 1934. (United Press International Photo.)

John V. Bouvier III, Miss Virginia Kernochan, and Mrs. Bouvier (far right) at a Tuxedo Park horse show, 1934. (United Press International Photo.)

Jacqueline Bouvier and her stepfather, Hugh D. Auchincloss, arrive at St. Mary's Church in Newport, Rhode Island, for her wedding to Senator John F. Kennedy, September 12, 1953. The bride's mother is to the left. (Wide World Photos.)

Senator John F. Kennedy returns to the Senate, accompanied by his wife, Jacqueline, after several months of convalescence in Palm Beach, 1955. (Wide World Photos.)

The three Kennedy brothers confer during a hearing of the Senate rackets committee, 1957. From left: Robert, committee counsel; Edward, on a visit to Washington; John, committee member. (Wide World Photos.)

James R. Hoffa, president of the Teamsters Union, points to a document held by Robert F. Kennedy, counsel of the Senate rackets committee, in the Senate hearing room, September 17, 1958. Walter J. Sheridan, a committee investigator, looks over Hoffa's shoulder. (Wide World Photos.)

Jacqueline Kennedy and her mother, Mrs. Hugh D. Auchincloss, at a November 2, 1960, Democratic Party fund-raiser at the Auchincloss Virginia estate, Merrywood. (Wide World Photos.)

The Kennedy family after the 1960 election. Standing, from left: Ethel Kennedy, Stephen Smith, Jean Smith, John F. Kennedy, Robert F. Kennedy, Patricia Lawford, Sargent Shriver, Joan Kennedy, Peter Lawford; seated: Eunice Shriver, Ambassador and Mrs. Joseph P. Kennedy, Jacqueline Kennedy, and Edward M. Kennedy. (United Press International Photo.)

President-elect John F. Kennedy and his wife, Jacqueline, thank supporters upon his winning the presidential election, November 9, 1960. (Photo by Henri Dauman. Pictorial Parade.)

President-elect John F. Kennedy announces the appointment of his brother Robert F. Kennedy as attorney general. (Wide World Photos.)

President John F. Kennedy delivers his inaugural address after taking the oath of office at the Capitol, January 20, 1961. (Wide World Photos.)

The new President and First Lady at the first of five inauguration balls held in Washington on January 20, 1961, this one at the Mayflower. (Wide World Photos.)

President and Mrs. Kennedy with 150 scientists, authors, statesmen, artists, and educators, after the dinner they gave on April 29, 1962, for Nobel Prize winners of the western hemisphere. The President is seated between Mrs. Ernest Hemingway, left, and Mrs. George C. Marshall. The First Lady is between Dr. Melvin Calvin and Dr. Robert Hofstadter. (Pictorial Parade.)

Jacqueline Kennedy rides with her children, Caroline and John Junior at the Kennedys' rented Virginia estate, Glen Ora. (Pictorial Parade.)

President John F. Kennedy and Attorney General Robert F. Kennedy with FBI Director J. Edgar Hoover at a White House meeting, February 23, 1961. (Wide World Photos.)

Singer Frank Sinatra and Senator John F. Kennedy at a fund-raising dinner in Los Angeles on the eve of the Democratic National Convention, July 10, 1960. (United Press International Photo.)

Judith Campbell in 1960, the year in which she first met John F. Kennedy and Sam Giancana. (Wide World Photos.)

Sam Giancana, boss of the Chicago underworld during the years of the Kennedy administration. (Wide World Photos.)

John Roselli, boss of the Mafia's rackets in Las Vegas and fellow conspirator with Sam Giancana and Santo Trafficante, Jr., in the CIA-Mafia Castro murder plots. (United Press International Photo.)

President Kennedy has tea with his Irish cousins, Mary Ryan and her daughter Josie, in the Kennedy homestead, Dunganstown, New Ross, June 27, 1963. (Lensmen, Dublin.)

President and Mrs. John F. Kennedy arrive at Love Field to begin their motorcade through Dallas, November 22, 1963. (Wide World Photos.)

President Kennedy is assassinated in Dallas, shortly after noon, November 22, 1963. The President is slumped in the back seat, while Mrs. Kennedy leans over him, then attempts to climb up on the back of the car. A secret serviceman has reached the bumper and is attempting to push Mrs. Kennedy back down into her seat. (Wide World Photos.)

Mrs. John F. Kennedy walks down the Capitol steps with Caroline and John Junior after the assassinated President's body was placed in the rotunda to lie in state, November 24, 1963. They are followed by Robert Kennedy, Mr. and Mrs. Peter Lawford, Mr. and Mrs. Stephen Smith, and President and Mrs. Lyndon Johnson. (Wide World Photos.)

Lee Harvey Oswald, President Kennedy's alleged assassin, in the Dallas police headquarters, seconds before being shot by Jack Ruby, November 24, 1963. (Wide World Photos.)

George de Mohrenschildt and his wife, Jeanne, with a photograph of President and Mrs. Kennedy arriving in Dallas the day of the President's assassination. This undated photo was found among de Mohrenschildt's possessions after his death. (Wide World Photos.)

Robert F. Kennedy and his wife, Ethel, celebrate his victory in the California primary, June 5, 1968, in the ballroom of the Ambassador Hotel. (Wide World Photos.)

Robert F. Kennedy lies wounded on the floor of the serving pantry of the Ambassador Hotel, moments after making his victory speech. (Wide World Photos.)

Mrs. Robert F. Kennedy and one of her sons, Robert F. Kennedy, Jr., at the funeral of her husband, St. Patrick's Cathedral, New York, June 7, 1968. (Pictorial Parade.)

Mrs. John F. Kennedy and her children, Caroline and John Junior, pay their respects to the body of Robert F. Kennedy lying in state in St. Patrick's Cathedral, New York, June 7, 1968. (Wide World Photos.)

"The boiler-room girls." Mary Jo Kopechne, extreme left, and other members of Senator Robert F. Kennedy's staff, at a meeting in the senator's office in 1967. A painting of Lt. Joseph P. Kennedy, Jr., hangs on the wall. (Wide World Photos.)

Mr. and Mrs. Aristotle S. Onassis leave the chapel in which they were married, October 20, 1968, on the island of Skorpios. With them are Caroline and John Junior. (Pictorial Parade.)

Santo Trafficante, Jr., boss of the Florida underworld, testifies before House Select Committee on Assassinations in Washington, September 28, 1978. (Wide World Photos.)

Carlos Marcello, boss of the Louisiana and Texas underworld testifies before House Select Committee on Assassinations, March 11, 1978. (United Press International Photo.)

Rose Kennedy at 84. (Pictorial Parade.)

Patriarch Joseph P. Kennedy celebrates his seventy-third birthday at Hyannis Port with seventeen of his grandchildren, September 1961. Front row, from left: Sydney Lawford, Robert F. Kennedy, Jr., Michael Kennedy, Maria Shriver, Courtney Kennedy, Mary Kennedy; middle row: Timothy Shriver, Victoria Lawford, Kara Kennedy, Caroline Kennedy, Robert Shriver, Kathleen Kennedy holding John F. Kennedy, Jr.; back row: Joseph P. Kennedy III, David Kennedy, the ambassador, Stephen Smith, Jr., and Christopher Lawford. (Wide World Photos.)

Joseph P. Kennedy III and his wife, Sheila, leave Boston's Brigham and Women's Hospital, October 10, 1980, with their newborn twins, Matthew Rauch Kennedy, left, and Joseph P. Kennedy IV. (Wide World Photos.)

Robert F. Kennedy, Jr., addresses a crowd of 18,000 at a "no nukes" rally in the Hollywood Bowl, June 15, 1981. (Wide World Photos.)

John F. Kennedy, Jr., and Caroline Kennedy in the Rose Garden of the White House, June 5, 1981, to attend the presentation by President Reagan of the Robert F. Kennedy medal for meritorious public service to Mrs. Robert F. Kennedy. (Wide World Photos.)

Senator Edward M. Kennedy campaigns in the New Hampshire primary for the Democratic nomination for President, February 1980. He is flanked by three secret servicemen and his niece Sydney Lawford. A New Hampshire glassblower is in the foreground. (James Hamilton.)

Senator Edward M. Kennedy celebrates his fifty-first birthday in Boston with his children, from left, Patrick, Kara, and Edward, Junior, February 1983. The second cake is to celebrate Kara's upcoming birthday. (Wide World Photos.)

tionship is thriving. And Cuba is stronger, militarily, than ever. So, in the last analysis, President Kennedy failed to obtain the only victory in Cuba worth risking a nuclear war over, the severing of the Soviet military connection with Cuba.

Finally, Kennedy's astonishing failure to press his hard-won advantages in Cuba did not go unobserved by his other enemies. As George F. Will pointed out in October 1982, on the occasion of the twentieth anniversary of the Cuban missile crisis, among those enemies who observed this failure to press advantages were the leaders of the Vietcong, who refused to be intimidated by the outcome of the Cuban missile crisis and, noting Kennedy's failure to follow it up, increased their pressure on the government of South Vietnam and its American military advisers.

45. Into the Quagmire

IN OCTOBER 1961, a little over five months after the Bay of Pigs disaster, John F. Kennedy decided to send two key members of his administration to southeast Asia to make a definitive estimate of the rapidly deteriorating situation in South Vietnam. On the basis of this report Kennedy would decide what action to take on the second major international problem he had inherited from the Eisenhower administration.

By this time the joint chiefs were pushing hard for a U.S. troop commitment in Vietnam, and the government of Premier Ngo Dinh Diem had begun to demand American combat troops for the first time.

John Kennedy could have sent almost any of his "brightest and best" over to Saigon. It is revealing, therefore, of Kennedy's basic attitude toward the problem that he sent not an advocate of a diplomatic solution, but two of his major hard-liners, or "hawks," both ardent counterinsurgency enthusiasts, Gen. Maxwell Taylor and Prof. Walt Whitman Rostow.

General Taylor, who was Kennedy's special military adviser and would one day be chairman of the joint chiefs, was the Kennedys' ideal general. He was handsome, urbane, athletic, and a strong advocate of building up America's guerrilla warfare capability. So taken with Maxwell

Taylor was Robert F. Kennedy that he named one of his sons Maxwell Taylor Kennedy.

Walt Whitman Rostow was another Kennedy adviser enthralled by counterinsurgency warfare. The former MIT professor, the hawk of hawks on Kennedy's White House staff, had already recommended that 25,000 SEATO troops be sent to Diem's aid in South Vietnam.

Before sending Taylor and Rostow off on their fact-finding mission, Kennedy told them: "There are limits to the number of defeats I can defend in one twelve-month period. I've had the Bay of Pigs and the pullout at Laos and I can't accept a third." Was this tantamount to telling them to recommend a stronger commitment?

And so, in sending these two men, and charging them as he did, Kennedy was virtually declaring war. Had he selected Stevenson, or Bowles, or Ball, he would have been making a peace-seeking gesture; in sending Taylor and Rostow he was asking for a report that would permit him to go to war.

Taylor and Rostow attended to their fact-finding in and around Saigon throughout October 1961, then issued their report to Kennedy in November. It called for a predictable initial U.S. troop commitment to South Vietnam of 8000 men, with the possibility of escalating to 200,000. It also called for a strong advisory and support mission, including helicopters, B-26s, and armored vehicles. And finally it called for certain reforms of the Diem government.

As Taylor put it, "Nothing would be more reassuring to the Diem government as [sic] sending in troops." Taylor declared that the risks of getting into a major war were "not impressive" and admitted that he had found Vietnam "not an unpleasant place" in which to operate. Summing up his recommendations, he declared, in regard to the sending of troops, "I do not believe that our program to save South Vietnam will survive without it." The troops, he thought, should be sent toward the last months of 1962 when Diem's own army was scheduled to reach a strength of 200,000.

The Taylor-Rostow report was barely out before Defense Secretary Robert McNamara and his deputy Roswell Gilpatric heartily endorsed it, agreeing to send up to 250,000 troops. Soon McGeorge Bundy also gave his stamp of approval, and other new frontiersmen signed on.

John F. Kennedy was now faced with one of the most momentous, and fateful, decisions of his life: whether to ignore the report's recommendations and continue with his present, extremely limited commitment, inherited from Eisenhower, or accept the Taylor-Rostow recommendations and substantially increase the commitment, to the point, almost, of going to war.

It was at this time that Kennedy had two encounters with one of his undersecretaries of state, George W. Ball, which could have led him to reject the report, but did not. George Ball, one of the saner minds in the Kennedy government, who always felt slightly out of place among the younger new frontiersmen, had expressed concern over Kennedy's sending Walt Rostow and Max Taylor to Vietnam because he felt Rostow was much "too fascinated with techniques of counterinsurgency," and he was aware of General Taylor's great interest in guerrilla warfare. Then, when Ball learned of the contents of their report, his worry turned to profound consternation. At a November 4, 1961, meeting in the White House, attended by Ball, McNamara, Rusk, and Gilpatric, among others, Ball, appalled at what he was hearing, declared, "We must not commit forces to South Vietnam or we would find ourselves in a protracted conflict far more serious than Korea." To which McNamara and Gilpatric replied, "But how else can the U.S. stop Vietnam from being taken over by the Vietcong?"

Ball's fateful second meeting with the President took place in the White House three days later. At this private meeting Ball told Kennedy that he strongly opposed the Taylor-Rostow recommendations. "To commit American forces to South Vietnam," he urged, "would be a tragic error. Once that process is started, there would be no end to it. Within five years we'll have three hundred thousand men in the paddies and jungles and never find them again. That was the French experience. Vietnam," Ball concluded, "is the worst possible terrain both from a physical and political point of view."

To Ball's utter astonishment Kennedy did not even want to argue the matter. He apparently had his mind already made up to accept the recommendations, for, responding to Ball's urgent plea with "an overtone of asperity," he said, "George, you're just crazier than hell. That just isn't going to happen."

Ball then left the White House in a mood of "dark futility," saying to himself, "We're heading hell-bent into a mess, and there's not a goddamn thing I can do about it. Either everybody else is crazy, or I am."

Throughout the remainder of November 1961, John F. Kennedy pondered what to do, receiving advice from all quarters. Chester Bowles was among those who recommended rejecting the Taylor-Rostow report. But Kennedy also refused to take Bowles's advice. Harris Wofford remarked in his book: "It took only man-eating sharks and crocodiles to get through to him." But, despite the fact that the doves could not get through to him, Kennedy must have agonized a good deal over the decision. He had always displayed some reluctance to become more deeply involved in what was happening in South Vietnam, and he had been so badly burned in the Bay of Pigs that he was not going to make a quick decision.

So there the Taylor-Rostow report lay on his desk, awaiting the President's decision. Now, with over twenty years of hindsight to illumine us, we know how momentously important the decision was. To decide in favor of implementing the report would set in motion a chain of events that would ultimately result in 57,939 Americans and over 1 million Vietnamese dead and the loss of South Vietnam to the communists.

As it turned out, Kennedy could not help himself. As a believer in the policy of containment and the so-called domino theory, and as a Kennedy, he could not withdraw from the fight in South Vietnam. He had to go in and win. And so, in December 1961, he made his decision to send a major military advisory and support team to Saigon and to order the Defense Department to prepare for the introduction of combat troops into South Vietnam. All this was to be done as secretly as possible, for, as with his Operation Mongoose, Kennedy did not want the American people to have any inkling of the extent of his commitment in Vietnam.

Soon fresh detachments of Special Forces Green Berets were reporting to Gen. Paul D. Harkins's military command in Saigon, and large numbers of U.S. Army vehicles and helicopters and B-26s began collecting at South Vietnamese military airfields and bases. The Americans' secret war against the Vietcong, and ultimately against Ho Chi Minh and Gen. Vo Nguyen Giap and the North Vietnamese army, had begun.

In retrospect, it is inconceivable that John F. Kennedy and his brother Robert and his band of the brightest and best could have had the arrogance to confront the victor over the French at Dien Bien Phu, believing there was any chance of winning in a conventional war. As the journalist David Halberstam, who, as reporter for the *New York Times* in Saigon, saw the deadly handwriting on the wall before most, later wrote, the Taylor-Rostow report was "arrogant and contemptuous of a foe who had a distinguished war record." And, by extension, Kennedy was arrogant and contemptuous to have approved it. But, as he confided to his advisers, Kennedy really believed that an American retreat in Asia would seriously upset the world balance of power.

As his brother Robert put it in the spring of 1962, in a speech in Hong Kong: "The solution of the war in South Vietnam lies in our winning it. We are going to win it, and we are going to stay here until we win."

It was not long after Kennedy's decision that Premier Diem's eccentric brother, Ngo Dinh Nhu, who had in the meantime been put in charge of South Vietnam's secret police, started, on his brother's orders, the Strategic Hamlet program, which provided for the "relocation" of peasants into fortified villages surrounded by barbed-wire fences and ditches filled with bamboo spikes. Along with this went such violations of the Geneva Convention as the spraying of poison from the air on crops and cattle and the dropping of napalm on villages suspected of harboring rebels, all of which was fully approved by the Pentagon. As it turned out, the Strategic Hamlet program had the effect of totally alienating the South Vietnamese peasants.

As might be expected, those members of Kennedy's administration who had strongly advocated intervention in South Vietnam now began to talk about how much good American aid was doing for the South Vietnamese war effort. In the spring of 1962, Robert McNamara, a man who knew very little about southeast Asia, a machinelike bureaucrat whose primary skills lay in industrial management and production, declared, "Every quantitative measurement we have shows we are winning this war." And Gen. Maxwell Taylor announced that he saw "a great national movement arising to destroy the Vietcong."

But in reality, despite the American aid, nothing much had changed. While the introduction of American helicopters into the war had an initial damaging effect on the Vietcong, the Cong soon adapted to it and changed their tactics so as to be less vulnerable to helicopter attack.

Likewise the Americans' attempt to "modernize" Vietnamese society, a society that had known the arts of civilization for thousands of years, got nowhere. The Nhu family and their followers carried on as before. An oriental family despotism stubbornly refused to become an American popular democracy. South Vietnamese peasants remained South Vietnamese peasants, stubbornly refusing to become American agribusinessmen.

In late 1962 and early 1963, it was clear to most close observers that the joint South Vietnamese–American war effort was not resulting in the defeat of the Vietcong. Nevertheless, President Kennedy, in his 1963 State of the Union address, declared that "the spearpoint of aggression has been blunted in South Vietnam." Robert McNamara in the spring of 1963 declared, "We have turned the corner in Vietnam." And Gen. Paul D. Harkins declared from Saigon, "The war will be won within a year."

There were others, however, who were less optimistic. Kennedy's new assistant secretary of state for the

Far East, Averell Harriman, was not at all sure we were winning the war, and he was virtually the only high U.S. government official who was not taken in by Diem and his devious relatives. Another who had not been deceived was the ambassador to India, John Kenneth Galbraith, who stated that American allegiance to Diem meant that the U.S. was "wedded to failure." But, of all the doubters, the members of the U.S. press in Saigon were the most clearsighted and outspoken. For they had almost all turned against Diem and his brother and Madame Nhu, regarding them as despotic, cruel, and out of touch with the people. As David Halberstam, who coined the epithet "quagmire" to characterize the Vietnam mess, put it in one of his dispatches: "The U.S. Embassy has turned into the adjunct of a dictatorship."

By the spring of 1963 the statistics had become grim indeed. Despite the Americans' use against the Vietcong of attack helicopters, defoliant sprays, napalm, and jet planes, the Vietcong were just as aggressive, powerful, and determined as ever, for they possessed the motivation the Americans could not buy. As for the 11,000 American soldiers sent so far to Vietnam, thirty-two had been killed in battle and eighty wounded. The United States was at war, had suffered casualties, and the American people were not yet fully aware of it.

A British cousin of mine, Col. Frank Brooke, who was on temporary duty at the Pentagon at the time, advising the U.S. Army on guerrilla warfare (he had fought in the Burmese jungles), told my mother and father in late 1963: "You Americans have no idea what you're doing in Indochina. You're getting into a big, nasty war down there and you don't even know it." Brooke also told the family that the Pentagon was "delighted" with the war because it gave them a perfect proving ground for new recruits and new weapons.

Part of the problem, so far as American awareness was concerned, was some of the statements high American officials were feeding the people. On April 22, 1963, Secretary of State Dean Rusk announced to the country that the Strategic Hamlet program had been "a success," morale in the countryside had begun to rise, and the Vietcong looked "less and less like winners."

Then, on the heels of this most unrealistic assessment, Premier Diem began cracking down on the Buddhists, many of whom had voiced opposition to his regime, and a whole new stage in the conflict began. When Diem forbade the Buddhist monks to display their flags on Buddha's 2587th birthday, the monks refused to obey. Diem's troops opened fire on them and the crowds around them, leaving many dead and wounded.

Soon Buddhist priests, or "bonzes," began soaking themselves with gasoline and igniting themselves in protest over Diem's anti-Buddhist policies. When American television viewers beheld these human bonfires in their living rooms, many began to sense for the first time that they were being deceived.

President Kennedy felt under pressure to install a new American regime in Saigon. Accordingly, he astonished all liberal Democrats by appointing the Republican Henry Cabot Lodge ambassador to South Vietnam, replacing Frederick E. Nolting, Jr. Lodge, as we know, had been defeated by Kennedy for the U.S. Senate, and, as Richard Nixon's running mate in 1960, had, in a sense, been defeated by Kennedy again in the presidential election of that year. Why did Kennedy appoint Lodge, of all people? Because if things ever *really* fell apart in Vietnam, he could share the blame with the Republicans.

Not long after the Massachusetts Republican reported for duty in Saigon, Diem made a massive assault on the Buddhist pagodas, arrested hundreds of Buddhist priests and monks, and seized many temples. This was nothing less than an all-out suppression of Buddhism in South Vietnam. It was a confusing situation. Here the United States was supporting Diem for his stand against communism, and Diem was taking an even stronger stand against a faction of his own people, who had nothing to do with communism. Apparently the Nhus took the Buddhists very seriously. When the ultra-Catholic Madame Nhu heard the news of the assault on the pagodas, she announced that it was the happiest day of her life.

The Nhu family's attack on the Buddhists took the Americans completely by surprise and clearly illustrated the despotic nature of Diem's regime. The ruthless suppression of the Buddhists was obviously an attempt to assure the supremacy of the Catholic minority of which the Nhus considered themselves the undisputed leaders.

The assault on the pagodas convinced American officials most concerned with affairs in South Vietnam that the United States was blindly committed to a narrow family depotism under whose leadership the war against the Vietcong could never be won. Accordingly, Henry Cabot Lodge began consulting secretly with the South Vietnamese generals to arrange for the overthrow of the Diem regime.

It was around this time, on July 17, 1963, that President Kennedy held a press conference during which he made what was to be his last public utterance on the Vietnam situation. In response to a reporter's questioning about his adminstration's commitment to South Vietnam, he said:

> We are not going to withdraw from that effort.
> In my opinion, for us to withdraw from that
> effort would mean a collapse not only of South
> Vietnam, but southeast Asia. So we are going
> to stay there.

Meanwhile things deteriorated in Saigon. The Diem government had succeeded in crushing the Buddhist dissidents, but, in so doing, in the words of George Ball, "The Nhus were destroying what little justification we had for being in Vietnam." On August 24 Washington sent Ambassador Lodge a cable stating that unless the Nhus were removed, the United States would find it impossible to continue its assistance to South Vietnam.

There followed visits to Saigon by Robert McNamara and Maxwell Taylor and a tremendous flurry of telegrams between Washington and Saigon. Before long, President Kennedy agreed to countenance a coup by the generals. As soon as the generals learned that Washington had withdrawn support of Diem, civil war broke out in Saigon. It was November 1, 1963. Troops loyal to the South Vietnamese generals took over key locations in the city. Diem and his brother managed to escape from the government palace to the suburb of Cholon, where they were quickly captured by insurgents who loaded them into an armored car and murdered them. The hated Nhu was stabbed many times, by many different knives, after his death. Somehow his wife, Madame Nhu, escaped, and later turned up in Paris after a brief stay in the United States, where she visited, among other cities, Dallas, Texas. Although the U.S. government was not directly involved in the murders, the fact that the United States had backed the coup led many to believe that Kennedy had countenanced the elimination of the Nhus.

Meanwhile, back in Washington, the news of the overthrow of the Diem regime hit hard. Arthur M. Schlesinger, Jr., saw President Kennedy immediately after he learned Diem and Nhu had been murdered. "He was somber and shaken," Schlesinger later wrote. "I had not seen him so depressed since the Bay of Pigs."

Needless to say, the coup in Saigon, fully condoned by President Kennedy, won him still another host of enemies. It wasn't long before Madame Nhu was publicly railing at Kennedy for having "betrayed" her husband's family and the people of South Vietnam.

John F. Kennedy now realized his Vietnam policy had, so far, been a failure. The leaders he had supported were now dead, the generals were in power, and the war against the Vietcong was going badly. When he, Kennedy, had taken office there had been only 600 U.S. military advisers in South Vietnam. Now, in November 1963, there were 16,263. Soon there would be 20,000, and the end of the commitment was still nowhere in sight.

But despite this sense of failure, Kennedy was still determined to persevere in South Vietnam. He was due to make a major foreign policy address at the Trade Mart in Dallas on November 22 in which he was going to reaffirm his Vietnam stand. In this address, which he did not live to present, he was planning to refer to America's "painful, risky, and costly effort in southeast Asia," declaring, "but we dare not weary of the task," and announcing, "We have increased our special counterinsurgency forces which are now engaged in South Vietnam by 600 percent." "Our mission in the world," he was going to say, "is to carry the message of truth and freedom to all the far corners of the earth. . . . We in this country are—by destiny rather than choice—the watchmen on the walls of world freedom."

Endless streams of ink have been spilled over the question of what John F. Kennedy would have done in South Vietnam had he not been killed twenty-two days after the assassination of Diem and his brother. It is a question which, of course, can never be fully answered, but, given what we know about Kennedy's personality, ambitions, and his last statements on South Vietnam, we can reasonably assume he would not have withdrawn from the war in Indochina.

Of course, Kennedy frequently expressed doubts over whether to persevere in Vietnam to his closest advisers. He apparently expressed them frequently enough to aide Kenneth O'Donnell to lead O'Donnell to write in his highly partisan book, *Johnny We Hardly Knew Ye,* that Kennedy would have withdrawn from Vietnam after the elections of 1964, but that he could not afford, politically, to get out until he had been reelected. It is said he expressed similar thoughts to Senators Mike Mansfield and Wayne Morse.

But, as Gore Vidal has pointed out, in Kennedy's second term he would be "holding the franchise for Bobby." He would be committed to safeguarding Bobby's chances of winning the presidency himself one day. For the sake of Bobby's political career, he could not afford to let the Kennedys appear weak in Vietnam. Furthermore, there is not one single written record among Kennedy's state papers, not so much as a memo, alluding to a projected U.S. withdrawal from South Vietnam.

John F. Kennedy had called a conference on Vietnam for Monday, November 25, over which President Lyndon Johnson eventually presided. Johnson held the conference on Sunday, November 24, and it was attended by all those Kennedy appointees who had helped lead Kennedy into the war: McNamara, Rusk, Bundy, McCone, Henry Cabot Lodge, and Maxwell Taylor. The question was should they persist in the war, or not? As it turned out, there was little debate. After the conference was over, Lyndon Johnson told press aide Pierre Salinger to announce to the press that he would "continue John Kennedy's policy." The war would go on.

Years later it was asserted in a Pentagon study of the war that it had been John F. Kennedy who had transformed the "limited risk gamble" of the Eisenhower administration to a "broad commitment to prevent the communist domination of South Vietnam."

John F. Kennedy was the first of the four American presidents involved with Vietnam to actually go to war in Indochina. His handpicked vice president continued the war, escalating it step by step, just as he had done. Most important, the cabinet officers and White House aides Kennedy had picked vigorously urged on the war under Lyndon Johnson. Not one of them ever thought they were not continuing John F. Kennedy's Vietnam policy in energetically pursuing the war.

But the most convincing evidence of all that John Kennedy would have pursued the war in South Vietnam had he lived was the fact that his brother Bobby continued to support the war for a full three years after his brother's death, believing he was furthering his dead brother's policy.

Years later, in his excellent book, *Why We Were in Vietnam*, Norman Podhoretz wrote, "He [Kennedy] steadily expanded the size of the U.S. Military Mission, sent combat support units, air combat and helicopter teams, still more military advisers, and 600 Special Forces Green Berets to train and lead South Vietnam in antiguerrilla tactics." For all intents and purposes, Podhoretz concluded, under John F. Kennedy "America went to war in Vietnam."

For Kennedy aide Harris Wofford, "Vietnam had become the fire in which the President was determined to prove he was made of steel."

In the last analysis, Kennedy was a victim of a way of thinking and behaving that was outmoded in a nuclear age. His administration, which started two secret wars, one in Cuba, the other in Vietnam, was basically confrontational, and therefore perilous indeed in an age when only the powers of compromise and conciliation can save the world from nuclear holocaust.

Yet, in the aftermath of the war, John F. Kennedy's extraordinary posthumous popularity made him all but invulnerable to blame over the Vietnam disaster. So popular was he, in fact, that Americans were more inclined to blame the President who ended the war, Kennedy's former rival, and the veterans who had fought in the war, rather than the President who had led them into it.

Although John F. Kennedy's name is nowhere inscribed on the ominous black granite Vietnam Veterans Memorial, there was once a symbol of his involvement in the Vietnam struggle in Washington, and it hung above his grave. After all the mourners had left the President's burial place at Arlington, guerrilla fighter Sgt. Maj. Frank Ruddy, who had been a member of a Special Forces honor guard during the burial ceremony, returned alone to his slain Commander in Chief, took off his green beret, and laid it on the pine boughs above his tomb.

46. "The Wonder of the World"

"Kennedy! Kennedy! Viva Kennedy!"
"Viva Kennedy! Viva Kennedy! Evviva Kennedy!"

NAPLES, July 2, 1963. A million and a half people line the avenues leading from NATO headquarters to the airport and give President John F. Kennedy the wildest, most exuberant welcome of his entire political career, a welcome even exceeding the mammoth crowds and mass hysteria of Berlin on June 26. Time and again the cheering Neapolitans break through the police barricades and engulf Kennedy's open limousine, where they are barely fended off by his Italian police escort. Women, young and old, cry and shriek. They hold out their arms as if to embrace, or supplicate, the handsome young American President. "Kennedy! Kennedy! Viva Kennedy! O mio Giovanni! Mio carissimo! Kennedy! Kennedy! Kennedy!"

John F. Kennedy, on his second major tour of Europe, had just delivered an address at NATO headquarters on the outskirts of Naples, and I had been invited to the ceremonies. There, in front of the offices of the commander in chief, Allied Forces Southern Europe, Kennedy had delivered a ringing speech in which he had summed up all he had been trying to tell Europe since his trip began:

The purpose of our military strength, the purpose of our partnership, is peace. Negotiations for an end to nuclear tests and attention to defense are all complementary parts of a single strategy of peace.

The United States welcomes the movement for the unification of western Europe and the greater strength it ensures. We did not assist in the revival of Europe to maintain its dependence on the United States; nor did we seek to bargain selectively with many and separate voices. We welcome a stronger partner. . . . The age of self-sufficient nationalism is over. The age of interdependence is here. . . . The Atlantic partnership is a growing reality.

As Kennedy spoke these words, under a glaring Neapolitan sun, before a predominantly American and Italian audience, with a sprinkling of British, French, Greeks and Turks, I was struck by how marvelous he looked. I had not seen him since the inauguration over two years before and expected him to show some signs of the burdens of his office. But, except for some puffiness about the jowls, caused, I later found out, by the massive doses of cortisone he was taking, he had hardly changed. Tanned, vibrant, slim, still youthful, with his reddish-brown hair barely flecked with gray, he was still Prince Charming, still the Golden Boy of the Western World. That unique combination of animal vitality, Irish charm, and veneer of wealth and Harvard was still intact. The magnetism was still there. Cuba, Berlin, Laos, Vietnam and the bloody racial disturbances in Alabama and Mississippi had not taken any visible toll.

It was a magnificent day. The excitement in Naples was palpable. The entire city was supercharged over Kennedy's visit. The Neapolitans are an exuberant people. On July 2, 1963, they were volcanic.

As the President's motorcade got underway for its eight-mile trip from NATO headquarters to the airport, a trip that would bring over a million Neapolitans to the motorcade route, I spoke to one wildly enthusiastic Neapolitan and asked him why he liked President Kennedy so much. The man, with his eyes popping out of his head, cried, *"Perché é lo 'Stupor Mundi!' Solo lui puó salvare l'umanitá!"* which, translated, means, "Because he is the 'Wonder of the World.' Only he can save humanity."

Then, as I digested this, he added, *"E la moglie é la Regina del Mondo!"* which means, "And his wife is the Queen of the World."

Lo Stupor Mundi. The expression stuck in my mind. It was one the Italian people had used for centuries to characterize great leaders. "The Wonder of the World." So that was the way the common people regarded John F. Kennedy. What exaggerated expectations Kennedy's charismatic personality evoked in people's hearts! "Only he can save humanity." How could any man live up to such hopes? And how could such a chasm have opened up between reality and expectation?

We now know that in the summer of 1963 John F. Kennedy was conducting two largely secret wars, but at the time no one but his closest advisers and those actually involved in his secret adventures knew it.

The fact was that by the summer of 1963, John F. Kennedy, the victor of the Cuban missile crisis, the handsome young President, had become a world figure, revered by millions upon millions of people, not only in his own country, but throughout the entire world. For Kennedy's greatest presidential asset was not his political or military judgment, or his powers of persuasion with Congress, or his vision, or his insight, or his wisdom; his outstanding asset was his incandescent personality, his extraordinary grace and charm. By exerting this charm he was able to influence large masses of people—and also the world's press. Kennedy cast a kind of hypnotic spell over both public and press; he had them in his thrall. In so doing he aroused impossible expectations, expectations no mortal could ever hope to fulfil.

John F. Kennedy's first step onto the world's stage had occurred in the late spring of 1961, when he and Jacqueline made their first trip to Europe as President and First Lady. One of our Bouvier cousins, a schoolmate of Jackie's, Michelle Crouse, had visited her in the White House shortly before this trip and found her in despair over it. The 31-year-old wife of the President had no idea how she was going to cope with Queen Elizabeth and Prince Philip, the de Gaulles, the Khrushchevs, and the rest. Then, to her relief, she succeeded in coping very well, becoming an instant hit with the European press and public and displaying remarkable poise for a woman her age, so much poise that Jack Kennedy was moved to make his now-famous quip: "I am the man who accompanied Jacqueline Kennedy to Paris and I have enjoyed it."

But John F. Kennedy made a tremendously favorable impression on the European public himself, despite the fact that he was suffering the entire time from a painful recurrence of his back problem and had to soak himself in a scalding hot tub after every public appearance.

As the Kennedys moved from Paris to Vienna to London, displaying their charms, the European press gushed praise. Jack and Jacqueline Kennedy felt comfortable in Europe, and it showed. Both had been students in Europe, and both had traveled widely in Europe during the most formative period of their lives. Their obvious delight in being in Europe again rubbed off on the crowds that greeted them. They returned to Washington confident their trip had been an enormous personal success. What they had achieved was nothing less than the seduction of Europe. The Kennedy charisma had found its first converts overseas.

When President Kennedy returned to Europe in the summer of 1963, for what was to be his last trip outside the United States, Jacqueline did not accompany him because she was pregnant (with Patrick Bouvier Kennedy) and she never liked to campaign, or take long trips, when she was pregnant, for fear of losing another baby. This time Kennedy's itinerary included West Germany, Berlin, Ireland, England, and Italy, and it was to put the seal on his image as a world leader and "Wonder of the World."

Kennedy's first stop was Cologne, where he went to

mass in the Cologne Cathedral with the Catholic West German chancellor, Konrad Adenauer. By the time mass was over and Adenauer and Kennedy had emerged, there were 400,000 people surrounding the cathedral, among whom were several thousand wildly cheering children holding little American flags.

He went on to even larger, more enthusiastic crowds in Bonn and Frankfurt, then the great climactic visit to West Berlin on June 26. Here Kennedy inspected the Berlin Wall, which, it will be recalled, had been put up as a way of resolving the differences between himself and Khrushchev over the status of West Berlin, and here he took a forty-mile tour of the city before the largest crowds he had ever seen—estimated at over a million and a half people—chanting "Kennedy! Kennedy! Kennedy!"

The tour of West Berlin climaxed in the square before the Berlin City Hall where Kennedy delivered the most celebrated speech of his career, a defiant challenge to communism. Using the rhetorical device of repetition, in response to a series of "If they [the communists] want to see what freedom means," "If they want to see what . . ." he cried out, in German, over and over:

> *Lass sie nach Berlin kommen!* Let them come to Berlin!

And then he uttered his great line, the line that drove the West Berliners to hysteria, and won him a lasting place in the hearts of all West Berliners:

> All free men, wherever they may live, are citizens of Berlin, and therefore, as a free man, I take pride in the words: *Ich bin ein Berliner!* I am a Berliner!

It was a thrilling, fighting speech that put Kennedy on the front page of every newspaper in the western world and sealed his position as leader of the west. Now there was no question who was the leader of the free world: it was not Harold Macmillan, or Konrad Adenauer, or Charles de Gaulle—it was John F. Kennedy.

Then it was on to Ireland, and more wildly cheering

crowds. Kennedy wanted very much to include Ireland in his European tour, not so much for political reasons, as for deeply personal, sentimental ones. He wanted to return to the land of his ancestors, to the village from which his great-grandfather had departed for the United States some 115 years before, and have a cup of tea with his cousins, who were still living on the same farm on which his great-grandfather had grown up. He wanted to go, even if, as McGeorge Bundy pointed out, there were "no political or diplomatic advantages to be gained by such a sensational excursion." What Bundy and some of the other brightest and best never seemed to see was that sometimes there were deep, personal reasons why the President should take a given course of action. As it turned out, Kennedy's return to the land of his ancestors, and the farm of his Irish cousins, was one of the most endearing episodes of his life.

President Kennedy arrived in Dublin on June 26 and promptly encountered another enormous crowd of enthusiastic, affectionate well-wishers who shouted "God bless you! God bless you!" as he made his way through the city. That night he stayed in the U.S. ambassador's residence in Phoenix Park, a splendid mansion surrounded by magnificently landscaped grounds that so impressed Kennedy he announced he wanted to become ambassador to Ireland once his two terms as president were up.

The next day he flew to New Ross, the small town on the river Barrow from which, it is believed, his great-grandfather Patrick sailed for the new world. In charge of the welcoming ceremonies was the mayor of New Ross, Andy Minihan, whom I met at New Ross in the fall of 1980.

Kennedy was scheduled to deliver an address from the riverside docks supposed to be the site of Patrick Kennedy's departure for the United States in 1848. The site was near a dredging dump and within sight of two New Ross landmarks, the Albatross Company, a fertilizer concern, and John V. Kelley's saloon, one of the town's favorite meeting places.

Before Kennedy's arrival, Andy Minihan, an imperious, bearded gentleman, had a run-in with the American ambassador, Matt McCloskey, a Philadelphia contractor who had been such a phenomenal fund-raiser for Kennedy's campaign that Kennedy had rewarded him with the ambassadorship to Ireland.

When McCloskey arrived at the riverside site of Kennedy's imminent speech and beheld an enormous heap of muck that had recently been dredged up nearby, he turned to Mayor Minihan, and in a gruff, presumptuous tone of voice said, "Whataya gonna do with this heap a muck? Get this heap a muck outa here."

Minihan, enraged by McCloskey's attitude, countered by telling the American ambassador: "You know what I'm goin' to do? I'm goin' to bring in 200 more loads of muck an' make 200 more heaps of muck so that when the President comes it will seem like he's talkin' from the bloody Alps here on this quay."

Later, after the President had arrived and the ceremonies were about to begin, McCloskey turned to Minihan and said, "Now I don't want any singing at the ceremony, understand?"

At that Minihan turned to Kennedy and said, "Mr. President, would you like to hear some songs?"

"I'd love to," replied Kennedy.

Minihan then signaled two choirs he had already stationed near the platform and the singers burst forth in Gaelic song.

McCloskey was also worried about security and asked Minihan why there did not seem to be many police in the vicinity of the platform. "They're all police out there," replied Minihan. What Minihan had done was to surround the podium with scores of plainclothesmen, all of whom knew each other and so would easily recognize a stranger in their midst.

Finally, after the arguing and the singing, John Kennedy got up and delighted his audience with the remark, "If my great-grandfather hadn't left New Ross I'd be working for the Albatross Company over there, or maybe here at John V. Kelley's."

After the ceremonies at New Ross, Kennedy and his

party, which included two of his sisters, Eunice and Jean, and aides O'Donnell and Powers, helicoptered to the Kennedy farm in Dunganstown, landing in a field behind the main house and barns.

The President was then greeted by his third cousin, Mary Ryan, a descendant of one of his great-grandfather's brothers, and her attractive daughters, Josie and Mary Anne, and welcomed into their house, a considerably larger building than the one great-grandfather Patrick had left 115 years before, which was now being used as sort of a shed.

There followed one of the most charming scenes of Kennedy's career. After posing with his Irish relatives for photographers in the Ryans' backyard, Kennedy and Mary Ryan and her two daughters went inside to sit in the little parlor, near a bright turf fire, and have some poached salmon and some hot scones and a cup of tea. The salmon was fresh from the nearby river Barrow, the tea was poured from a silver pot, and Mrs. Ryan had baked the scones herself.

For a while Mary Ryan, a delightful lady, and her two young daughters talked with the President about the farm, and they were amazed by how much he knew about it, even to the point of knowing they were about to hold an auction of some of the animals. Mrs. Ryan later told me that the President was completely natural and unpretentious and wholly at his ease.

It was a great moment in Kennedy family history. One hundred and fifteen years after Patrick Kennedy had left the house in Dunganstown and walked down the boreen to New Ross, there to begin his journey to America and the life of a cooper in East Boston, here was his great-grandson, John F. Kennedy, returning to the same house as President of the United States. Kennedy savored every minute of it, and as the visit drew to a close he raised his cup and said, "We want to drink a cup of tea to all the Kennedys who went and all those who stayed."

To conclude the visit Kennedy planted a juniper tree in Mary Ryan's front yard and after that he gave his cousin such a warm hug and a kiss that it astonished his sisters. They had never seen their normally cool brother display such affection.

From Dunganstown it was on to Wexford, then Cork, and finally back to Dublin where Kennedy delivered a speech before the combined houses of parliament, the Dail, in which he emphasized Ireland's literary achievements and her influence on American history. Judging from what I was told in Dublin in the fall of 1980, Ireland never got over John Kennedy's visit in the summer of 1963. The Irish took him to their hearts like a son, and his visit has since entered Irish folklore.

Upon returning to Washington, Kennedy received the welcome word that Khrushchev had endorsed his proposal for a limited nuclear test ban treaty. Coming on the heels of his triumphant tour of Europe, the news of Khrushchev's endorsement of one of Kennedy's most cherished projects raised Kennedy's prestige to its zenith. Throughout July 1963, all the major European magazines carried glowing photo-reportages of Kennedy's recent tour, and the world press was lavish in its praise of the American President.

And yet, as we now know, Kennedy's phenomenal grace and charm belied an administration whose style was hardly peace-loving. The discrepancy between image and reality was due principally to the press. If a journalist, such as Ben Bradlee of *Newsweek,* wrote flattering things about the President, he would be invited to White House parties where he would pick up fresh tidbits of information about the First Family. If he wrote unflattering things he would not be invited, and his source of information would be cut off. In its June 7, 1963, issue, *Time* magazine observed that Kennedy was "slavishly followed by the press" and was "more than slightly feared" by most journalists. And on June 24, 1963, I. F. Stone observed that "the atmosphere of Washington is like a reigning monarch's court," with sycophantic journalists falling all over themselves to flatter the monarch and his queen so they could pick up a juicy tidbit from the royal table. In this journalistic atmosphere Kennedy could get away with seeming like "the wonder of the world."

In the summer of 1963, with the triumphant tour of Europe and the limited nuclear test ban treaty resounding in the world's press, the carefully crafted Kennedy image was never more glowing. And, as a result, John F. Kennedy was more vulnerable than ever.

47. Jacqueline: On a Mission of Her Own

WHENEVER a member of the Bouvier family visited the White House during the Kennedy years, he or she would inevitably be struck by the enormous calm, and, in a sense, removal from reality, in which Jacqueline Kennedy apparently lived. A distinctly apolitical First Lady, far separated in her interests from great affairs of state and disliking politics, Jacqueline, by her own volition, and with the tacit approval of a husband who kept her at arm's length from his concerns, devoted herself chiefly to her own interests: riding in the Virginia hunt country, planning elaborate White House dinners and entertainments, buying and wearing haute couture clothes, bringing up two young children, going on long travels unaccompanied by her husband, and tracking down furniture and works of art to install in the White House. While hurricanes constantly whirled around her bedeviled husband, Jacqueline lived in the proverbial eye of the storm, trying to find a degree of happiness and achievement in a world of her own.

This was all very much in keeping with the way Jacqueline was brought up. Women in the Bouvier family were supposed to stay home, mind the children, and make a comfortable home for their husbands. A Bouvier wife was not supposed to discuss her husband's business, either with him or with anyone else. Careers for Bouvier women were always discouraged, even actively thwarted. Our Aunt Edith, who was to attain a measure of accidental celebrity in the seventies due to her unconventional way of life, possessed an extraordinary voice and an equally extraordinary theatrical presence and, quite possibly, could have enjoyed a successful theatrical career; but both her father and her husband dissuaded her and she became an eccentric recluse instead. It was an irony indeed that she finally got her opportunity to appear on the screen, in an underground film, *Gray Gardens,* in 1973, largely because of her niece's fame as an international superstar.

That Jacqueline Bouvier was brought up not to concern herself with such traditionally male pursuits as politics was probably, as it turned out, a blessing. For the great challenge of Jacqueline's married life was to maintain her own identity in the face of the Kennedys' unceasing demands that she adopt *their* interests and conform to *their* code. If Jacqueline had been a political animal like her husband she would not have accomplished half of what she eventually accomplished as First Lady.

As a couple, Jack Kennedy and Jacqueline Bouvier were distinguished more by their differences than by their similarities, and their marriage was racked by conflict. Their immediate predecessors in the White House, Harry and Bess Truman and Ike and Mamie Eisenhower, had both been cut out of the same cloth. Not so with the Kennedys. The character of the Kennedy administration, and the tone and style of the Kennedy White House, were more an expression of the differences between John and Jacqueline Kennedy than of the few traits and qualities they shared.

Put as simply as possible, whereas Harry and Bess Truman and Jimmy and Rosalynn Carter acted virtually as one person in the White House, John and Jacqueline Kennedy largely went their separate ways. John Kennedy had his own life as a political and sexual adventurer, and Jacqueline had hers as a mother, hostess, and finally, when she found herself, as a remarkably determined and talented restorer of the White House, a role that combined executive ability, artistic taste, and a strong sense of history. Because their lives and interests were so different, the John F. Kennedys stimulated one another. It was refreshing for President Kennedy, after a day of grappling, let us say, with the threat of Castro's Cuba, to meet with his wife and learn that she had just discovered in a government warehouse a china service that had been ordered by Abraham Lincoln. Likewise, it was stimulating for Jacqueline to help host a reception for a visiting head of state, because, being an apolitical person all her life, it was a new and different experience.

However, as might be expected, these differences also bred conflicts between the two. Certainly the President's sexual adventuring must have hurt and humiliated his proud, sensitive, and vain wife. We lack available witnesses to the scenes that probably took place in the White House family quarters, and Jacqueline has been very secretive with her relatives about her relationship with Jack; but it appears Jacqueline did not like what went on behind her back one bit, for she soon became one of the most absentee First Ladies in American history. Spending three or four days a week at Glen Ora, almost all summer in Hyannis Port, and a good deal of the winter in Palm Beach and taking a three-week trip to India and Pakistan, unaccompanied by her husband, and a three-week vacation in Italy, unaccompanied by her husband, and another long vacation in Greece, unaccompanied by her husband, Jacqueline left the President free to pursue his affairs at will.

Then there was the conflict over money. A tendency toward extravagance, stemming from her earliest years, carried over into Jacqueline's marriage and caused her to be reckless with John F. Kennedy's money. The only really major arguments between the President and the First Lady that were overheard and reported by their servants and secretaries were over money. Kennedy was frequently left aghast by how much money his wife spent. According to Jacqueline's personal secretary, Mary Barelli Gallagher, who kept the First Lady's accounts and submitted them to the President, Jacqueline's personal expenditures for 1961 were $105,446.14, and for 1962, a year in which she was supposed to "cut down," they were $121,461.61. This was more than the President's salary of $100,000 a year.

Since John F. Kennedy's income from his investments was in the neighborhood of $500,000 a year, perhaps more, he donated his entire salary as President to charity. But he never told Jackie this. Once, however, when Ben and Toni Bradlee were dining with the Kennedys in the White House, the President inadvertently let it slip out that he was donating his entire presidential salary to charity, whereupon Jacqueline, in a fit of surprise, cried, "Hey, how about donating some of it to me!"

Publicity was another bone of contention. John F. Kennedy consciously sought to create an idolatrous public, a public that would worship him and his family. Thus he would let no chance to publicize himself, Jackie, his children, and the rest of the Kennedys go by. To please her husband, Jackie would be compelled to submit to a seemingly endless series of intrusions into her private life. Nothing was sacred to Kennedy. Journalists were constantly fed tidbits of news about family life in the White House. Photographers were admitted everywhere, and they delighted the public with shots of Caroline skipping rope in the Oval Office.

It all made Jacqueline feel intensely claustrophobic. She hated to see all the people staring through the White House wrought-iron fence every time she went out for a stroll. "I'm sick to death of starring in everyone's home movies," she told White House chief usher J. B. West. Later West wrote, "If Mrs. Kennedy had her way the White House would be surrounded by high brick walls and a moat with crocodiles."

To my mother, on one of her visits to the White House, Jacqueline wistfully confessed she envied me living in Italy and said she "would go mad" if she could not get away from Washington soon.

To a friend she once exclaimed, "God, what targets we are in here!"

But to Kennedy, still smarting from his tiny margin of victory in the 1960 election, no amount of exposure was enough. It was always the more the better.

Eventually things came to a head between the John F. Kennedys over the President's forty-fifth birthday celebration in Madison Square Garden on May 29, 1962. The event was to be not only a massive birthday party, attended by 20,000 people, but also a fund-raiser for which several thousand of the guests were to pay $1000 apiece for the privilege of attending. The climax of the party was to be Marilyn Monroe (who later claimed she had had an affair with Kennedy) singing "Happy Birthday" to the President. This was just the sort of vulgar display that Jackie detested, and she refused to attend.

As it turned out, the party was a great success from Kennedy's standpoint. A great deal of money was taken in. Television viewers across the nation watched Jimmy Durante, Maria Callas, and Ella Fitzgerald perform for the President, and they went delirious when Marilyn Monroe in a skintight, sequined dress led the multitude in singing "Happy Birthday, dear President," hugging herself as she sang. After it was over Kennedy stood up and said, "I can now retire from politics after having had 'Happy Birthday' sung to me by such a sweet, wholesome girl as Marilyn Monroe." Jacqueline was not amused.

Yet despite conflicts over publicity, extramarital sex, and money, the John F. Kennedys were genuinely fond of one another. Jack Kennedy held great admiration and affection for Jackie, and not a little envy of her, and Jackie was, for the most part, an excellent wife and mother. The John F. Kennedys were very good friends and were very much married, in their own way.

Jacqueline's relationships with her blood relatives, the Lees and the Bouviers, were friendly but minimal. Jackie did not see very much of her mother even though Mrs. Auchincloss lived in Washington. When she did see her, Jackie usually appeared stiff and formal in her presence. Janet was given to criticizing her daughters, and Jackie simply could not tolerate criticism from her mother. Frequently she did not return her calls. The only other Lee relative Jackie saw was her sister, Lee Radziwill, who remained her closest friend and confidante. Whenever Lee visited the White House, Jackie would give her the royal treatment. And Lee accompanied her on all her major travels and vacations: to India and Pakistan, to Italy, and to Greece. Other members of the Lee family were shunned for fear they would give away the fact that they were Irish. As for nonrelative friends, Jackie had none besides her former prep school roommate, Nancy Tuckerman, whom she employed as one of her social secretaries in the White House. "Tucky," who never married, had always occupied a very special place in Jackie's affections. In her she could place ultimate trust. And Tucky's loyalty and devotion to Jackie were absolute.

Jacqueline's relations with her Bouvier aunts and cousins were somewhat complicated by all that had gone on during and after her parents' divorce, what had happened at her wedding in Newport, and her failure to appear at the reception the day of the inauguration.

Nevertheless, despite whatever feelings were left over from the past, various members of the family were invited to the White House on several occasions, and they invariably found Jackie warm and cordial, though a bit remote. When my mother and sister first visited Jackie in the White House she took them on a tour of the newly redecorated family quarters, and they were struck by her great delight in what she had accomplished. They were also struck by how spartan her regimen was. For lunch the First Lady had cold soup and a salad with no dressing. While the rich haute cuisine of chef René Verdon may have been impressive at lavish state dinners, it was not something weight-conscious Jacqueline could indulge in with great frequency. And finally they could not help being struck by how remote Jackie seemed to be from her husband's world and concerns. But most Bouviers agreed that Jackie really blossomed in the White House and that, despite her lamentations over lack of privacy, she came into her own as First Lady. Before Kennedy was elected President, Jackie had often struck her Bouvier relatives as being excessively worried and tense. Now, in the serene atmosphere of the White House, she seemed more natural and at ease.

One of the reasons for this, I believe, is that Jacqueline succeeded in finally imposing her own terms on her role as First Lady. She was able to create within the White House a world of her own making and engage in a mission that was entirely her own, and this gave her considerable satisfaction.

The world that Jacqueline Bouvier created in the Kennedy White House was the world of her extraordinary parties and entertainments and her restoration of the White House interior to its original glory after years of mistreatment and neglect.

First the parties and entertainments. John F. Kennedy met with seventy-four foreign leaders during his two and one-half years in office, twelve more than Franklin Roosevelt met in his twelve years in office. For sixty-six of these visits he and Jacqueline gave state receptions. Each of these was an exquisite creation, the product, almost exclusively, of Jacqueline's taste and imagination, with only a few touches provided by her assistants. Probably the most famous was her unique dinner party for the president of Pakistan at Mount Vernon, the first state dinner in history held outside the White House, at which the guests arrived after a sail down the Potomac in the presidential yachts, *Honey Fitz* and *Patrick J.* The other sixty-five have been endlessly described. What Jacqueline did was to bring a remarkable sense of appropriateness and a highly developed aesthetic sense to each affair. In addition to providing the very finest in food and drink and creating an atmosphere of gaiety and elegance, she was able to give each reception a character of its own in keeping with the statesman she was honoring. As British Prime Minister Harold Macmillan put it: "They certainly have acquired something we have lost, a casual sort of grandeur about their evenings, pretty women, music and beautiful clothes and champagne and all that." "All that" also included the exquisite haute cuisine of French chef René Verdon, with his wonderful salmon mousse, poulet à l'estragon, and casserole Marie-Blanche; Jackie's gorgeous flower arrangements; and after-dinner entertainments featuring such artists as Pablo Casals, Isaac Stern, and Eugene Istomin— not to mention Jackie herself in her bouffant hairdos and elegant Oleg Cassini evening gowns. These parties are, by now, a significant part of the cultural history of the United States, preserved in minute detail in an immense collection of photographs in the John F. Kennedy Library in Boston.

But it was not so much in her parties and entertainments that Jacqueline created a world of her own as in her project to transform the White House. No sooner were the Kennedys in the White House than both of them, and especially Jacqueline, were struck by how "depressing," "stark," "tasteless," and "unlived-in" the place looked. The old mansion was filled with accumulations of nondescript furniture and paintings that did not harmonize with the decor of the rooms that contained them, and there were no unifying themes to the individual rooms or to the mansion as a whole. Furthermore, the great house was so unlived-in that many of the windows did not open and most of the fireplaces did not draw. To Jacqueline's taste, the White House was simply a mess. To her dismay she found the upstairs family quarters decorated with what she called "early Statler"; it was so cheerless and undistinguished it wasn't even worthy of a second-class hotel. The upstairs Oval Sitting Room she complained was "like the Lubianka," alluding to the great Moscow prison. Certain bedroom curtains she termed "seasick green," and certain curtain fringes looked to her like "tired Christmas trees." The First Lady's sitting room was filled with "Mamie's ghastly pink." The ground floor hall looked like "a dentist office bomb shelter." The East Room looked like "a roller skating rink." And the East Wing garden was "atrocious."

And so before long, Jacqueline dreamed up the idea of restoring the White House to the way it was in the time of President Monroe (1817–1825), when it was wholly decorated in the then-fashionable French style. Her ultimate aim was to make the White House into a "national historic object" to be cared for as if it were a museum and, in so doing, to make it into "the most perfect house in America." This, of course, would be quite an enterprise, carrying heavy political overtones, and so when she broached it to her husband, Kennedy at first resisted. He was not at all sure how the idea would be received by the American public and wanted to consult with some of his closest political advisers about it. Clark Clifford confirmed Kennedy's worst fears by telling him, "The White House is a sacred cow to the American people and woe to any President who touches it." That was it, so far as Kennedy was concerned. Jackie would have to leave the White House alone.

There followed a furious argument, which Jackie finally won by sheer dint of will. Soon Jacqueline formed her White House Fine Arts Committee "to locate authentic furnishings reflecting the history of the presidency of the United States." As chief adviser to the committee she selected Henry Francis du Pont, the recognized supreme authority on the 1640–1840 period of American furniture and decorative objects. And in charge of restoring the decor to the French style of Monroe's presidency, she chose a renowned decorator from Paris, M. Stéphane Boudin. With a French chef loose in the kitchen and a French decorator loose in the rest of the White House, Jacqueline Bouvier Kennedy had embarked on the Frenchification of the Executive Mansion, just as President Monroe had done 144 years before.

In undertaking the restoration and redecoration of the White House Jacqueline was expressing a sense of history that was very much a Bouvier tradition. I remember undergoing as a young boy a profound experience of history with Grandfather Bouvier that all the Bouvier grandchildren underwent at one time or another. One Sunday in New York, Grandfather Bouvier, whom we called Grampy Jack, took me into his bedroom and pointed out the magnificent carved golden eagle that hung on the wall above his bed and said something like this: "You know where that golden eagle came from, my boy? It was a gift from Napoleon Bonaparte's brother to your great-great-grandfather. Now you know who Napoleon was, don't you?"

"Well," continued Grampy Jack, "your great-great-grandfather, Michel Bouvier, fought under Napoleon in the battle of Waterloo, and after the French were defeated, Michel Bouvier and Napoleon's brother Joseph fled to America and they both settled in Philadelphia and became friends. As a token of his friendship for your great-great-grandfather, Joseph Bonaparte gave him this golden eagle."

The effect of this kind of instruction on a boy who was studying European history in school was overwhelming.

Jacqueline Bouvier's experiences were similar. Grandfather Bouvier injected history into his grandchildren's blood and bones. Thus it was no frivolous whim when Jacqueline Bouvier Kennedy organized her plan to restore the White House.

Not long after Kennedy approved her plans, the White House and its warehouses in Fort Washington, Maryland, became an arena of high adventure for Jacqueline. The great search was on. Donning jeans and a pullover, she hunted through the White House's fifty-four rooms and sixteen bathrooms and plunged into the dusty White House basement, rummaging through its carpenters' shops and storage bins. And she became the first First Lady in history to go searching for hidden or forgotten treasures in the Fort Washington warehouses.

What treasures she came up with! In a closet off the dressing area of a downstairs White House men's room she found stained and chipped white marble busts of George Washington, Martin Van Buren, Christopher Columbus, John Bright, and Amerigo Vespucci. Sculpted in the Greek style in the early nineteenth century, they had been completely forgotten. In a ground-floor room that had been used as a broadcasting studio she discovered a massive piece of furniture entirely covered by green baize and loaded with broadcasting equipment. Underneath the baize she found a huge desk made from timbers taken from the *H.M.S. Resolute*. The desk had been presented to President Rutherford B. Hayes by Queen Victoria in 1878. In the White House basement she found a darkened, stained gold and silver flatware service that President Monroe had ordered from Paris in 1817. And in the Fort Washington warehouses she found services belonging to Presidents Polk and Harrison and discovered part of a fine china service decorated with the American eagle and banded with royal purple that Abraham Lincoln had ordered and that had been forgotten since his time.

Soon Jacqueline's White House Fine Arts Committee "to locate authentic furnishings reflecting the history of the presidency of the United States" was receiving priceless donations from all over the nation. Mr. and Mrs. Douglas Dillon gave a mahogany library table executed by the renowned Charles Honoré Lanvier, a French-born cabinetmaker who had worked in New York in the early 1800s. For the Blue Room George Wildenstein donated Jean Honoré Fragonard's *Apotheosis of Franklin.* Other gifts included furniture that had belonged to George Washington, Abraham Lincoln, James Madison, and Daniel Webster. Among the items loaned was a pier table that had belonged to Joseph Bonaparte at Point Breeze. And Mr. and Mrs. Henry T. MacNeill of Whitford, Pennsylvania, donated two maple chairs in Empire style made by Jacqueline's great-great-grandfather, Michel Bouvier, circa 1820.

Eventually, as her one-year $2-million restoration project was nearing completion, Jacqueline established the White House Historical Association and the position of White House curator, and produced an official *Historic Guide to the White House,* which she edited herself, the first one ever compiled.

Then, on February 16, 1962, Jacqueline Kennedy and CBS television's Charles Collingwood took an estimated 56 million television viewers on a tour of the recently restored Executive Mansion that inspired the admiration of millions, a strange manifestation of hostility from the novelist Norman Mailer, and a good deal of jealousy on the part of the President. Charles Collingwood told me that the President was genuinely piqued and could barely mask his annoyance at being so spectacularly upstaged by his wife.

However, these feelings did not prevent Kennedy from taking some credit for the whole enterprise. After the Congress passed a law making the White House restoration permanent, Kennedy made a public statement about it:

Through a wise provision of the Congress
in its last session, the White House, which had

become disfigured by incongruous additions and changes, has now been restored to what was planned by Washington.

The White House is the property of the nation and, so far as is compatible with living therein, it should be kept as it originally was for the same reasons that we keep Mt. Vernon as it originally was. . . . It is a good thing to preserve such buildings as historic monuments, which keep alive our sense of continuity with the nation's past.

Jacqueline had won a major victory in her ongoing battle with the President. With many of his own policies foundering, she had brought off the greatest achievement of her adult life, and she had done it in the face of his initial opposition.

Today, twenty years after the completion of her project, Jacqueline's White House restoration remains by and large intact. The upstairs family quarters have, of course, been redecorated by each new President and First Lady, the most extensive remodeling of which was accomplished by Nancy Reagan in 1981 and 1982. But the state rooms have remained exactly as Jacqueline restored them, and the guide she produced is still the official guide to the President's house.

What Jacqueline Bouvier Kennedy did for her country has never been fully appreciated because, unlike Eleanor Roosevelt and Bess Truman and Rosalynn Carter, her achievements were not in the more tangible realm of public affairs, but in the somewhat nebulous realm of style. For, in the last analysis, what Jacqueline gave the American people was precisely that which they so sorely lacked: she gave them beauty, elegance, grace, a high style, and a sense of the past.

Essentially what survives from the Kennedy administration is its style and its charm, and that style was in the largest part the achievement of the President's wife.

Since Jacqueline Kennedy, because of her extreme notoriety, is one of the most vulnerable women in the world, it is easy to criticize her. But to properly assess Jacqueline Kennedy's role as First Lady during her two and three-quarters years in the White House, we must assess the results of that stay. And here we cannot but offer praise. For during those years, while her husband recklessly hurtled toward destruction, she brought a beauty, an elegance, a dignity, and a grace to American life that had rarely, if ever, been achieved before and has not been equaled since. And in the restored White House she left an enduring legacy to the American people.

48. "The Enemy Within": Part II

*I'd like to be remembered as
the guy who broke the Mafia.*

Robert F. Kennedy

IN JUNE 1962 Joseph Valachi, serving time in the U.S.
penitentiary in Atlanta, and under a death sentence from
his former boss, Vito Genovese, also in the same prison,
asked to be put "in the hole," or solitary confinement,
telling prison officials he was "ready to talk." Agents from
the Bureau of Narcotics and the FBI were more than eager
to listen. Eventually he was transferred to the Westchester
County Jail where the interrogations continued. Finally,
on September 25, 1963, Valachi entered the national spotlight as chief witness at Senator John L. McClellan's Senate
hearings on the organization of La Cosa Nostra. Valachi
then became the first member of Cosa Nostra to break the
vow of *omertá* and testify in public.

Valachi revealed in minute detail the precise organizational structure of the Cosa Nostra, its code, its rules
and regulations, and its most important members, including those who sat on the national ruling body, the *commissione*. And he revealed the utter savagery of the Cosa
Nostra wars.

Valachi's testimony was, for Attorney General Robert F. Kennedy and the country at large, an astonishing

revelation. Although a national crime network had been suspected, its existence had never been confirmed until the discovery of the *commissione* meeting at Apalachin and the testimony of Joseph Valachi. As Ralph Salerno, a retired New York police official, put it: "The Valachi confessions are ranked next to Apalachin as the greatest single [intelligence] blow ever delivered to organized crime in the United States. This evaluation came from the lips of those most affected by it: members of the criminal network whose comments were overheard through bug and wiretap."

It is to the Kennedy brothers' credit that, unlike most Americans, they fully appreciated the extent of the menace of organized crime in America and did something about it. By the fall of 1963 Robert F. Kennedy could point with pride at the results of his war against the Mafia. Whereas in other areas, such as civil rights and space, the Kennedys had to be pushed into action through force of circumstances, with organized crime they were on the attack from the opening bell.

By the fall of 1963 Attorney General Kennedy had increased the number of attorneys in his Organized Crime and Racketeering Section from 17 to 63, had expanded his list of most-wanted crime bosses from 40 to 2000, and had got the IRS to assess $250 million more from various racketeers beyond the amounts they had paid when they filed their returns. Furthermore, by 1963 the number of indictments against organized crime members had risen to 615 from 121 in 1961, and the number of convictions had risen to 288 from 73.

But, as we know, Robert F. Kennedy did not limit his anticrime efforts solely to attacking the Cosa Nostra; he also went after labor leaders suspected of criminal activities, especially the boss of the Teamsters Union, James Riddle Hoffa. In the words of Prof. Monroe Freedman in an article he wrote for the *Georgetown Law Journal,* "When Kennedy became Attorney General satisfying this grudge [against Hoffa] became the public policy of the United States."

Hoffa's union, the International Brotherhood of Teamsters, had become, by the early sixties, the largest, richest, and most powerful labor union in the world, and its $200-million Teamsters Pension Fund had become "the biggest slush fund in history." In his book *The Enemy Within* Robert Kennedy wrote:

> The Teamsters Union is the most powerful institution in this country—aside from the United States Government itself. In many major metropolitan areas the Teamsters control all transportation . . . between birth and burial the Teamsters drive the trucks that clothe and feed us and provide the vital necessities of life. . . . Quite literally, your life—the life of every person in the United States—is in the hands of Hoffa and his Teamsters. . . . But though the great majority of Teamsters officials and Teamster members are honest, the Teamsters Union under Hoffa is often not run as a bona fide union. As Mr. Hoffa operates it, this is a conspiracy of evil.

Hoffa had indulged in practically every crime in the book in the course of running his vast union. He had indulged in bombing, shooting, and beating enemies and in blatant bribery and fraud.

What particularly horrified Kennedy about Hoffa was his connections with organized crime. For he had found out that Hoffa had created several phony locals and had put in charge of these "paper unions" officials who were connected with such notorious Cosa Nostra figures as Johnny Dioguardia (Johnny Dio) and Tony "Ducks" Corallo. It did not take Kennedy long to figure out that if the Cosa Nostra was in association with the Teamsters, it was in a position to paralyze the nation. All the Cosa Nostra would have to do would be to pressure Hoffa into calling a national Teamsters strike and the entire country would come to a standstill.

Accordingly, Robert Kennedy, in an unprecedented move, ordered an entire unit of the Justice Department devoted solely to pursuing Jimmy Hoffa and the Teamsters. Known as the "get Hoffa squad," its director was

Walter Sheridan, former FBI agent and staff member of the Senate rackets committee. Eventually Kennedy and Sheridan succeeded. On May 18, 1962, Hoffa was indicted under the Taft-Hartley Act in Nashville for receiving $1 million in illegal payments through a trucking company, the Test Fleet Corporation, which had been set up in his wife's name. The trial ended with a hung jury that was suspicious enough to prompt the judge to convene a grand jury to investigate charges of jury tampering. On May 9, 1963, the grand jury investigation resulted in indictments against Hoffa and the others for jury tampering. Then, on June 4, 1963, Hoffa was indicted in Chicago by the Justice Department for obtaining by fraud $20 million in loans from the Teamsters Central States Pension Fund, of which $1 million was diverted for Hoffa's own personal use. During the Chicago trial that followed, one of Hoffa's Teamsters officials, Ed Partin from Baton Rouge, turned on Hoffa and testified against him. He was then offered $1 million by Hoffa if he would retract his testimony with the proviso that if he refused the $1 million he would be killed.

By this time Partin had revealed to the FBI that Jimmy Hoffa had attempted to conspire with him to murder the attorney general. Since Partin was on friendly terms with certain members of Carlos Marcello's crime family in Louisiana, Hoffa had been sure that Partin could recruit someone capable of doing the job. Hoffa apparently favored using "a lone gunman equipped with a rifle with a telescopic sight" who would fire on Kennedy while he rode in an open convertible. When word of this plot was relayed to Robert Kennedy by the FBI, Kennedy ordered J. Edgar Hoover to authorize a lie detector examination of Partin, which eventually determined that Partin had been telling the truth. Subsequently the FBI uncovered more evidence of a Hoffa plot on Robert Kennedy's life. Finally the matter came to the attention of President Kennedy, who told several intimates, including Ben Bradlee, that he was very concerned about it.

Hoffa's jury tampering trial began January 20, 1964, and he was found guilty; on March 12 he was sentenced to twelve years in jail. Hoffa appealed the decision, but it was upheld by the Supreme Court in 1966. On August 17, 1964, Hoffa was convicted of fraudulent use of the Teamsters Pension Fund (literally looting it of $1 million) and was sentenced to five *more* years in jail. Hoffa finally went to prison in March 1967, after all his appeals had been exhausted. During this long process the Teamsters boss received support from everyone—from governors, mayors, judges, senators, congressmen, and police chiefs, but to no avail. In the end Bobby Kennedy had won.

Despite the controversy surrounding the appointment of the President-elect's brother as attorney general, by the fall of 1963 it was clear it was one of the best cabinet appointments Kennedy had made. For the first time in history organized crime had been identified for what it was, and enormous success in combating it had been attained by the Justice Department. Furthermore, the attorney general was on the verge of success in combating corruption in labor unions. These combined successes added up to what was unquestionably the Kennedy administration's foremost domestic achievement. Given another five years in office, the Kennedys could conceivably have exterminated the Cosa Nostra entirely, or at least have crippled it beyond repair.

Many have wondered what drove the Kennedys to be so adamant in their war against organized crime. It seemed as if they had a special grudge against the mob that went far beyond righteous indignation or sense of public duty. The truth was that the Kennedy family had been adversaries of organized crime ever since bootlegging days when Joe had both collaborated with, and been in rivalry with, the mob.

But how did the Kennedys keep the mob from damaging them by revealing what they knew about Joe Kennedy's bootlegging days? Evidently the ambassador kept the mob at arm's length by employing two strategies: one, by cultivating his friendship with Frank Sinatra, who, as we know, was supposed to be the Kennedys' means of communicating with the mob, and two, by accepting campaign "donations" from the mob in return for vague promises that the Kennedy government would leave the mob alone.

On December 9, 11, and 21, 1961, FBI listening devices picked up conversations between Sam Giancana, John Roselli, and other unidentified individuals that revealed what sort of deal Joseph P. Kennedy had made. The December 21st tape came to light during the 1978–1979 investigation by the House Committee on Assassinations of the murder of John F. Kennedy, and the other two were obtained from the FBI by Giancana's daughter, Antoinette, under the Freedom of Information Act.

The December 21st tape was revealing. After Roselli informed Giancana that Joe Kennedy had been in touch with Frank Sinatra, he observed that Sinatra "got it in his head that they [the Kennedys] are going to be faithful to him [and, by extension, to the mob]." To which Giancana replied, "In other words, then, the donation that was made . . ." "That's what I was talking about," interjected Roselli. Giancana then observed, "In other words, if I ever get a speeding ticket none of these fuckers would know me." "You told that right, buddy," said Roselli.

Evidently the mob vastly overrated the power of Frank Sinatra to intervene with the Kennedys in their behalf. During the House investigation of the JFK murder, the Committee on Assassinations discovered records in the FBI's Cosa Nostra file that showed how Carlos Marcello had hoped to prevent the U.S. immigration authorities from deporting him after the Kennedys came into power. According to a report by an FBI informant of a discussion between himself and Philadelphia underworld boss Angelo Bruno, Marcello had enlisted the aid of his friend and associate, Santo Trafficante, Jr., in pressing Frank Sinatra to use his friendship with the Kennedy family to persuade the immigration authorities not to deport him. To Marcello's bitter disappointment Sinatra was unable to do anything with the Kennedys, and Robert Kennedy was soon deporting him to Guatemala.

Thus the Kennedys had, from the mob's point of view, committed the cardinal sin against them. The mob had made its "donation" to the Kennedy presidential campaign through Frank Sinatra, and in return Joe Kennedy had apparently assured Sinatra his sons would not give the mob any speeding tickets. Then, once John and Robert Kennedy came into power, they turned around and went after the mob as no administration had ever done before. The mob also became convinced that the Kennedys used unfair and even illegal tactics against them. In retrospect, it appears that the more determined Robert Kennedy became to get Marcello, the more rash, naive, and ill-advised were the means he used. Because the Kennedys had accepted favors from the mob, this, in the mob's view, was a doublecross. According to the code of the Mafia the punishment for a doublecross is death.

It is worth noting, at this juncture, that at about the time Giancana, Roselli, Marcello, and other mob bosses had begun to realize that Frank Sinatra's connection to the Kennedys would do them no good and that the donation Giancana had made to the Kennedy presidential campaign through Joe Kennedy and Sinatra would do them no good either, Joe Kennedy suffered a massive stroke in Palm Beach. The stroke occurred only a few days after J. Edgar Hoover sent Robert Kennedy several memoranda (obtained by Antoinette Giancana) informing him of Giancana's contribution to his brother's campaign through his father and of Giancana's displeasure now that he wasn't getting his money's worth. If Robert Kennedy had telephoned this news to his father in Palm Beach in mid-December we can well understand how it could have contributed to the ambassador's stroke on December 18.

Electronic surveillance was a vital part of the Justice Department's drive against organized crime, and it resulted in the most comprehensive body of information on the mob ever collected. The buggings executed by the FBI not only revealed a great deal about the Cosa Nostra's activities, they also revealed a great deal about how the Cosa Nostra felt about the Kennedys.

These buggings were arguably illegal because they violated the Fourth Amendment. William Sullivan, then

Hoover's number three man at the FBI, told, in his memoirs, how Hoover got Robert Kennedy to tacitly approve them:

> Hoover set a trap for Bobby Kennedy when the attorney general, accompanied by Courtney Evans, was visiting our Chicago office. The special agent in charge asked Kennedy if he would like to listen to some "sensitive" tapes which his agents had collected during the course of a criminal investigation. Kennedy should have refused, should have asked to have transcripts sent through the usual channels. Instead, he sat down and listened to the tapes and by so doing compromised himself. After listening to the tapes for just a minute or two, Kennedy had to realize that they were the result of unauthorized taps. But he kept listening, which to Hoover implied tacit approval. Never a man to let an opportunity go by, Hoover insisted on and got sworn affidavits from every agent present stating that Kennedy had listened to the tapes and had not questioned their legality.

In time, thousands of hours of tapes on organized crime were collected by the FBI, many of which contained comments and threats by Cosa Nostra members against President Kennedy and his brother. For reasons that can only be surmised, FBI Director Hoover was very selective about what he told the attorney general was on the tapes he collected. While he revealed certain intelligence on the activities of certain Cosa Nostra families, he withheld from the attorney general most of the taped threats from Cosa Nostra members against him and the President.

Transcripts of these tapes finally surfaced in 1978 and 1979, during the hearings of the House Select Committee on Assassinations. They made chilling reading, for they revealed that the bitterness, frustration, and hatred of the mob for Robert Kennedy's anticrime policies were so intense that many members of the Cosa Nostra argued that the attorney general and his brother ought to be hit. Chief counsel of the House Committee on Assassinations, G. Robert Blakey, told me that when he took charge of the House's investigation he expected that what would turn up on organized crime would exonerate the mob from possible complicity in President Kennedy's assassination. Instead, the exact opposite proved to be the case. The tapes convinced him that if there had been a conspiracy to kill the President, the Mafia was probably behind it.

On February 9, 1962, Angelo Bruno, father of the Bruno family of Philadelphia, was overheard talking with one of his *caporegime,* Willie Weisburg:

> WEISBURG: See what Kennedy done. With Kennedy, a guy should take a knife, like one of them other guys, and stab and kill the fucker, I mean it. This is true. Honest to God. It's about time to go. But I tell you something. I hope I get a week's notice. I'll kill. Right in the . . . White House. Somebody's got to get rid of this fucker.

Angelo Bruno agreed with Weisburg, but advised him to be cautious, telling him that sometimes the man following the man eliminated turns out to be worse.

Three months later the FBI overheard Michelino Clemente, a *caporegime* in the Genovese family, express sentiments similar to Weisburg's: "Bob Kennedy won't stop today until he puts us all in jail all over the country. Until the commission meets and puts its foot down, things will be at a standstill." And at around the same time the FBI overheard this from an unidentified Cosa Nostra member:

> Since when is fucking a federal offense, and if it is I want the President indicted, because I know he was whacking all those broads. Sinatra brought them out. I'd like to hit Kennedy. I would gladly go to the penitentiary for the rest of my life, believe me.

By April 1963, the mob had realized someone was talking, and they believed it to be Joseph Valachi (whom they nicknamed Joe Cago), for the FBI overheard this exchange of remarks between Cosa Nostra member Angelo de Carlo and someone called Barney:

BARNEY: The thing they talk about today. Somebody must talk because they could never know these things. They know who's boss, underboss, the commission, the *caporegimes*. They talk like *amici nostra*. . . . And you can't do nothing about it.

DE CARLO: And oh, the other guy. In New York. What's his name? That was in the can with Vito?

BARNEY: Joe Cago.

DE CARLO: I hear he's talking like a bastard. . . . He must have known something about this thing?

BARNEY: He knows things from thirty-five years ago.

And on June 6, 1963, an FBI bugging device recorded Peter Magaddino, of the powerful Buffalo Cosa Nostra family, exclaiming, "The President should drop dead. . . . They should kill the whole family—the mother and the father too."

One major crime boss the FBI never succeeded in bugging was Carlos Marcello, who was reported to have issued death threats against both Kennedy brothers. Marcello enjoyed a unique status within the Cosa Nostra. As head of the New Orleans Mafia, which was the oldest in the United States, dating from the 1880s, the Louisiana boss enjoyed powers and privileges not accorded to any other Cosa Nostra leaders. As the head of "the first family" of the Mafia in America, Marcello alone enjoyed the privilege of being allowed to conduct syndicate operations without having to ask approval of the national *commissione*.

Marcello also enjoyed a peculiar relationship with the FBI. His case agent in New Orleans reported him to be a "legitimate businessman" and so, in the words of the

House assassinations committee report of 1979, "was less than enthusiastic about pressing an investigation of the Louisiana Mafia leader." This meant, among other things, that Marcello was never bugged. Some people believe Marcello's case agent, whose name was Regis Kennedy, had been turned. Regis Kennedy died in 1978, before the House Committee on Assassinations had an opportunity to interrogate him in any depth.

Another major Cosa Nostra boss the FBI experienced difficulty in penetrating electronically was CIA co-conspirator Santo Trafficante, Jr. Trafficante had a meeting in September 1962 at the Scott-Bryant Hotel in Miami with one José Alemán during which he intimated he knew John F. Kennedy would be assassinated. (Not long before this meeting Trafficante had met with Carlos Marcello at Churchill Farms.)

According to Alemán, who was a well-to-do Cuban exile with connections to Jimmy Hoffa and who doubled as an FBI informant, Trafficante said in reference to President Kennedy:

> Have you seen how his brother is hitting Hoffa, a man who is a worker, who is not a millionaire, a friend of the blue collars? He doesn't know that this kind of encounter is very delicate. . . . It is not right what they are doing to Hoffa. . . . Hoffa is a hard working man and does not deserve it. Mark my word, this man Kennedy is in trouble, and he will get what is coming to him.

Apparently Alemán disagreed with Trafficante, telling him that he thought Kennedy was doing a good job and, in his opinion, would probably be reelected, whereupon Trafficante said, very firmly, "You don't understand me. Kennedy's not going to make it to the election. He is going to be hit." As an informant for the FBI, Alemán promptly reported Trafficante's remarks to the Bureau, but, according to Alemán, the FBI chose to ignore him and never bothered to investigate Trafficante's assertions.

Furthermore, the FBI, in the person of its director,

also chose not to reveal the threatening recorded remarks of Sam Giancana, William Weisburg, Michelino Clemente, Peter Magaddino, and various other unidentified mobsters to either the attorney general or the President, or to the agency charged with protecting them, the Secret Service.

The Kennedy brothers' assault on the enemy within had led them to violate a fundamental tenet of the Cosa Nostra code: If you accept favors from the mob, you leave the mob alone. The Kennedys had accepted, or at least had not rejected, favors from the Cosa Nostra many times ever since the days of prohibition. But their mixture of pride, arrogance, and righteous indignation would not allow them to compromise with the mob. The Kennedys regarded the Cosa Nostra as a mortal enemy that had to be destroyed. They apparently never realized that the Cosa Nostra felt exactly the same way about them.

49. AM/LASH

IN RESPONSE TO Robert Kennedy's expressed disapproval of the plans to use gangsters to assassinate Fidel Castro, the CIA had to develop a different strategy. The new strategy was evolved principally by the CIA's Desmond FitzGerald, who had replaced the swashbuckling William K. Harvey as chief of Task Force W, that section of the CIA charged with covert operations in Cuba. When FitzGerald took over in January 1963, he renamed Task Force W the Special Affairs Staff, or SAS, and subsequently told Johnny Roselli to taper off his communications with his Cuban "assets." Roselli then broke off contact with his Cubans, but apparently never told them that the CIA's $150,000 offer for Castro's head had been withdrawn, an oversight that may well have resulted later in considerable confusion and disaffection among the Cuban conspirators. Upon retiring from his mission to kill Castro, Roselli did not request payment from the U.S. government, telling the CIA that, like a good "patriot," he had been motivated solely by "honor and dedication."

As was later revealed by the Senate Intelligence Committee's investigation of alleged assassination plots involving foreign leaders, Desmond FitzGerald then proceeded to come up with a number of curious schemes to kill Castro that all came to naught. One scheme called for the CIA's technical services division to devise a "rare exploding seashell," which would be placed conspicuously on the sea bottom in one of Castro's favorite skin-diving haunts. This scheme was eventually abandoned as seeming too much like something out of the CIA's dirty tricks department. Another of FitzGerald's ideas was to have James B. Donovan, the official who had been sent to Cuba to negotiate the release of the Bay of Pigs prisoners, give Castro a contaminated wet suit. The suit's breathing apparatus would be polluted with tuberculosis bacilli and the inside of the suit would be dusted with a fungus that would give Castro a chronic skin disease known as "madura foot." This plan was eventually rejected because if discovered, it would not be too difficult to determine who might have been behind it.

When these schemes were rejected, FitzGerald, apparently under considerable pressure from "above," then turned to a Cuban "asset" whom the CIA had been cultivating since 1961, when he had first been recruited by Santo Trafficante, Jr. His name was Rolando Cubela, a major in the Cuban army who knew Castro personally and saw him regularly, both in his office and at official functions. Cubela, and several of his closest friends, bitterly resented Castro's sellout to Russia and were convinced Castro had betrayed the revolution. By the fall of 1961 Cubela was anxious to find a way of overthrowing Castro, even if it involved assassination, which he preferred to call "elimination." Cubela already had experience in political assassination. In October 1956 he had shot and killed Blanco Rico, head of Premier Batista's department of military intelligence. The CIA regarded Cubela as a most valuable contact. When the agency began considering him as a possible serious conspirator in the effort to overthrow Castro, they assigned a case officer to him and gave him the code name AM/LASH.

For over a year the CIA's meetings with AM/LASH were inconclusive; then, with the advent of FitzGerald as head of Task Force W, soon to be renamed SAS, they began to get deadly serious. Meanwhile, on August 16, 1963, the *Chicago Sun-Times* carried an article reporting that the CIA and Sam Giancana were involved in some activity together, without specifying what the activity was. This startled CIA Director John McCone, who had never been told of the Giancana operation by his predecessor, Allen Dulles. Richard Helms then filled him in on the plot for the first time, telling him it involved assassination. It is not known whether McCone brought the matter to the attention of the Kennedy brothers at that time. By then, however, the Kennedy brothers were fully aware of the CIA-Mafia plots but apparently believed the plots had been abandoned by the CIA.

In early September 1963 Cubela met with a CIA agent in São Paulo, Brazil, and indicated he was now willing to try an "inside job" to "eliminate" Fidel Castro. This news was transmitted back to Washington on September 7. By coincidence, Castro was attending a reception at the Brazilian embassy in Havana that evening at which he told Daniel Harker of the Associated Press: "Kennedy is the Batista of our time, and the most opportunistic President of all time." He then went on to issue a warning against what he called "terrorist plans to eliminate Cuban leaders," declaring that he was "prepared to answer in kind." "United States leaders," Castro went on, "should think that if they assist in terrorist plans to eliminate Cuban leaders they themselves will not be safe."

This declaration caused not a little alarm back at CIA headquarters. Did Castro know about the CIA's plots against his life? Apparently Desmond FitzGerald thought not and continued to believe Cubela was "secure." Later in the fall Cubela requested from the CIA considerable military supplies, "a device with which to protect himself if the plots against Castro were discovered," and a meeting with Attorney General Robert F. Kennedy. FitzGerald assured him he would do his best.

Desmond FitzGerald was a personal acquaintance of Robert Kennedy. He and his second wife, Barbara, were among the most socially prominent and active couples in Washington during the years of the Kennedy administration. Thus not only did Robert Kennedy encounter Desmond FitzGerald at meetings of the Special Group, but he also saw him frequently at Washington receptions.

For some time Kennedy had been meeting with certain Cuban "assets" of the CIA in his continuing efforts to overthrow the Castro regime, so it would not have been very much out of the ordinary for him to meet with Cubela. Ultimately the CIA felt it unwise to expose the President's brother to a meeting with the man destined to be Castro's assassin just prior to that assassin's attempt on the Cuban dictator's life. Accordingly, Desmond FitzGerald agreed to meet with Cubela "as Robert Kennedy's personal representative," assuring Cubela he had the full support of Kennedy and the U.S. government behind him.

Although no written documents have survived indicating that FitzGerald really had the backing of Robert Kennedy in the AM/LASH operation, it is the opinion of some people close to both FitzGerald and Kennedy at the time that he did have that support. Thomas Hughes, then director of the State Department's Bureau of Intelligence and Research and now president of the Carnegie Endowment for International Peace, stated in an interview with me that he had not the slightest doubt that Robert Kennedy was aware of the AM/LASH plot and had given it his support. Since Kennedy and FitzGerald often met socially and at work, there was no need for formal authorization. The attorney general's approval could just as easily have been conveyed informally and be far less risky for all concerned. This opinion was confirmed by former CIA official, Samuel Halpern, who in 1963 had been executive assistant to the Task Force on Cuba and one of the four men directly involved in the AM/LASH operation. In an interview on November 18, 1983, Mr. Halpern told me that he was absolutely certain that "Des" FitzGerald "had full authorization from Attorney General Kennedy and President Kennedy to proceed with the AM/LASH plot against Castro," adding that he always felt that since they often met socially, Bobby Kennedy and "Des" FitzGerald conducted most of their business together at Washington cocktail parties and receptions, rather than in their respective offices.

Years later, Richard Helms testified under oath before the Senate Committee on Intelligence that he had "preexisting authority to deal with AM/LASH regarding a change in government [in Cuba] and that authority would have obviated the need to obtain Robert Kennedy's [explicit formal] approval." Helms testified:

> Given this Cuban of his standing and all the history of trying to find someone inside Cuba who might head a government and have a group to replace Castro . . . this was so central to the whole theme of everything we had been trying to do that I found it totally unnecessary to ask Robert Kennedy at that point [whether] we should go ahead with this. This is obviously what he had been pushing, pushing for us to try to do.

Helms was, of course, absolutely correct. After the Cuban missile crisis, the Kennedy brothers became more concerned than ever with getting rid of Castro and his regime. After all, Castro now emphatically deserved to be overthrown. He had sold out to the Soviets and had agreed to the installation of Soviet missiles aimed at the United States on Cuban soil. Although the morality of assassinating Castro prior to the Cuban missile crisis could be debated, now killing him could be considered in the national interest, virtually a patriotic act.

Following the Cuban missile crisis, the Kennedys' attitude toward Castro became somewhat ambiguous. On the one hand they continued to indulge their propensity for playing with fire by engaging in a number of provocative acts. On the other hand, the missile crisis seemed to have softened them somewhat, or at least slowed them down, for in the post–missile crisis period, the President for the first time began sending out feelers toward a possible rapprochement with Castro.

Discontinuing Operation Mongoose as basically ineffective and out of their control, the Kennedy brothers replaced it with the Special Group, or SG, of the National Security Council, on which they both, of course, sat. As various attacks on Soviet vessels off the Cuban coast by Cuban exile groups were occurring, the Special Group in

April 1963 discussed contingency plans in the event of Castro's death, leading one to assume that assassination of the Cuban leader was being contemplated. Then, according to the *Interim Report* of the Senate Committee on Intelligence, on June 19 President Kennedy ordered the Special Group to proceed with a top-secret sabotage program against Cuba. On October 3, 1963, the Special Group approved nine belligerent operations against Cuba. Again according to the *Interim Report,* on October 24, 1963, thirteen major sabotage operations, including the sabotage of an electric power plant, an oil refinery, and a sugar mill, were approved for the period November 1963 through January 1964.

We know that the SG discussed contingency plans in the event of Castro's death, but was that death ever officially decreed by the SG? Apparently not, if we are to judge from the testimony of the surviving members of the group. But that was principally because of the CIA's doctrine of "plausible denial," which asserted that an assassination attempt should always be planned and carried out in a way that would allow the person, or persons, who authorized it to plausibly deny participation in it.

Besides, the Kennedy administration had officially established an "executive action capability," or, non-euphemistically, a standby capability for political assassination, including the assassination of foreign heads of state. Once this "capability" had been established, there was no need for explicit orders to perform "executive action."

Although it is uncertain, it appears that Robert Kennedy was perhaps more anxious to get rid of Castro than his brother and that in the fall of 1963 the two brothers may have been working at cross-purposes, especially if Robert was actively promoting the AM/LASH plot—either that, or they were double-dealing. For at the same time, William Attwood, special adviser to the United States delegation to the United Nations, began holding a series of talks with the Cuban ambassador to the United Nations, Carlos Lechuga, to discuss opening negotiations on an accommodation between Castro and the United States. These discussions apparently had the blessing of President Kennedy and his national security advisor, McGeorge Bundy. Later, Attwood stated that he was told by Bundy that President Kennedy was in favor of "pushing towards an opening toward Cuba" to take Castro "out of the Soviet fold and perhaps wiping out the Bay of Pigs and maybe getting back to normal."

Meanwhile, the AM/LASH plot was nearing its critical phase. Although FitzGerald was strongly advised by his colleagues not to meet with AM/LASH directly, he went ahead and met him on October 29, 1963, in Paris, telling Cubela he was the personal representative of Robert F. Kennedy. At the meeting, attended also by Cubela's case officer, FitzGerald told Cubela he could be assured that the United States would fully support a coup d'état in Cuba engineered by Cubela. Cubela then requested a suitable assassination weapon, specifically a "high-powered rifle with telescopic sights that could be used to kill Castro from a distance." He also asked for high explosives.

Returning to Washington, FitzGerald told Cubela's case officer that AM/LASH should be told that the rifles, telescopic sights, and explosives would soon be provided. In addition to the rifles and other arms FitzGerald and the case officer decided to offer AM/LASH was another, more sophisticated weapon that had recently been developed by the CIA's technical services division. It was to be a special ballpoint poison pen rigged "with a hypodermic needle so fine that the victim would not notice its insertion." The pen would fire the tiny poisoned needle at the victim, and the victim would not feel a thing. Cubela's case officer, known to this day only as "2," had wanted "to devise some technical means of doing the job that would not automatically cause him [AM/LASH] to lose his life in the try." It was agreed that FitzGerald and the case officer would personally deliver the poison-pen device to AM/LASH in late November 1963.

Was it possible that the Kennedy brothers could have been discussing rapprochement with Castro and planning his assassination at the same time? Judging from what evidence we have, I believe it was well within their modus operandi. Based on the crucial testimony of one of the last surviving members of the AM/LASH operation, it thus appears that in late 1963, as the President was preparing for a political trip to Texas, the Kennedy brothers were simultaneously extending the olive branch to Castro with one hand and the poison pen with the other.

50. The Plans

ON SEPTEMBER 12, 1963, President and Mrs. John F. Kennedy celebrated their tenth wedding anniversary at Hammersmith Farm in Newport. As an anniversary gift the President presented his wife with the inventory of a New York art dealer, telling her she could have anything on the list, and the First Lady gave her husband a gold St. Christopher medal and a red leather and gold scrapbook with photographs of the newly landscaped White House Rose Garden. There was a small anniversary dinner, presided over by the Auchinclosses, during which toasts were made and gifts exchanged. Ben Bradlee, who was present with his wife, characterized the affair as "dicey," observing that "Jackie's stepfather is not exactly a swinger, and the toasts were pretty much in his image." After dinner the guests reminisced about that brilliant, windy September day ten years before, when, amid great family tension, John Kennedy and Jacqueline Bouvier had celebrated "The Wedding of the Year." How much had happened since then!

Although the summer of 1963 had been somewhat marred by the loss of Patrick Bouvier Kennedy in August, only two days after the infant was born, the John F. Kennedys had a good deal to be thankful for by September. Their marriage had survived many storms, sacrifices, crises, in-laws, disappointments, and Jack's infidelities and was still miraculously intact. They were both in excellent health—particularly the President—and had two healthy and attractive children.

John Kennedy at 46 and Jacqueline Kennedy at 34 were, that summer, the most celebrated couple in the world. Jacqueline was regaining her strength after the loss of her baby and was looking forward to a cruise in the Aegean she was going to take in October with the Greek shipowner, Aristotle Onassis, her sister Lee, and Lee's husband, Prince Stanislaus Radziwill. For icing on the tenth anniversary cake, the John F. Kennedy finances had never been more robust. *Time* magazine estimated that the President's personal fortune, which, as we know, had been entirely given to him by his father, had grown to around $10 million, making him the richest President in the history of the United States. The President was looking forward to being reelected in 1964 and getting most of his stalled legislative program passed during his second term. With four years of experience as the nation's first hostess and patroness of the arts behind her, Jacqueline was looking forward to more splendid accomplishments during her next four years in the White House. Yes, the Kennedy horizon in the summer of 1963 seemed to hold nothing but greater promise, glory, and magnificence.

But beneath the power and glamour of the Kennedys' world, there festered disappointments, hatreds, rivalries, and intrigues, some of which the President may have been aware of, others, not. For there were countless Americans who resented the Kennedys' beauty, wealth, and power, and countless others who were disenchanted with the country President Kennedy led. In addition to these malcontents there were certain elements in the country that detested the Kennedys so much they had already been overheard many times threatening their lives. In cities like Miami and New Orleans, where there were large concentrations of Cubans, and where the Mafia was deeply entrenched, I was told there was a general feeling in 1963 that either the Cuban exiles or the mob would eventually kill the President. The only question was who would get to him first.

Representative of those countless Americans who

were disenchanted with their country was a young political activist, leftist revolutionary, and admirer of Fidel Castro by the name of Lee Harvey Oswald. By an extraordinary twist of fate, a former friend of the First Lady's father and herself, and beau of her Aunt Michelle, had become the chief mentor and father figure to this young man.

George de Mohrenschildt, the White Russian émigré who had become so close to the Bouvier family during the years 1938 to 1940, had, fifteen years and three marriages later, wound up in Dallas as an oil and natural gas consultant. It was while he was in Dallas that he met and married his fourth wife, Jeanne Le Gron, also a White Russian. The de Mohrenschildts soon became leaders of Dallas's Russian colony, and it was somewhat in that capacity that they first visited, in September 1962, a young couple who had just returned from Russia, Lee and Marina Oswald. Before long the two couples became involved with one another in one of the most unlikely relationships imaginable. The distinguished White Russian émigré, whose family and property in Russia had been destroyed by the communist revolution, was clearly fascinated with the young American who had abandoned his country for Russia, married a Russian girl, then suffered such acute disillusionment in his adopted land that he returned to his native country again. And the "semi-educated hillbilly from Texas," of "very low category," as George de Mohrenschildt once described Oswald, was correspondingly interested in the Russian aristocrat whose family had suffered directly from the revolution he so much admired.

George de Mohrenschildt was an interesting and complex man. That Jacqueline Kennedy's father, mother, and twin aunts had been such good friends with the man who became, in turn, the best friend, and surrogate father, of her husband's alleged assassin seems to go beyond mere coincidence: one is tempted to speculate that there was some relationship, however tenuous, between these two disparate friendships and the tragic events of November 1963.

George de Mohrenschildt was born in 1911 in Minsk, where Oswald had gone to work during his expatriation in the 1950s. Before the Bolshevik revolution George's father had been an official of the Czar and had owned an estate of some 6000 acres. During the social hurricane unleashed by Lenin, the de Mohrenschildts lost everything and were compelled to flee Russia. George's older brother, Dimitri, went to the United States, where he earned degrees at Columbia and Yale, while George remained in Europe, taking degrees at Antwerp and Liège. Eventually Dimitri married an American girl by the name of Betty Hooker, who was a very good friend of the Bouvier family, particularly the twins, my mother and Aunt Michelle. In time Dimitri summoned brother George to America and introduced him to his wife's friends, the Bouviers. George immediately fell in love with Michelle, who had recently divorced her husband.

George de Mohrenschildt courted Michelle and the other Bouviers assiduously during the summer of 1938, becoming particularly close to Jack Bouvier and his daughters. He also took out the in-the-process-of-becoming-divorced Janet Bouvier occasionally, arousing the jealousy of her estranged husband, and kept up a friendship with her over the years.

De Mohrenschildt was, in many ways, an outrageous character. He loved to *épater le bourgeois,* to make provocative remarks in polite company that might conceivably puncture a few cherished prejudices or illusions. Although they were to remain good friends, Michelle ultimately realized she could never marry George and told him so. His shocking remarks, often enunciated before the entire family at Sunday luncheons, created too much ill will. Finally, George de Mohrenschildt gave up all hope of linking himself to the Bouviers. His exposure to the family, however, had been profound, and later, when the John F. Kennedys came into prominence, George de Mohrenschildt used to emphasize his great friendship with Mrs. Kennedy's family. Needing money badly, he eventually gravitated toward the burgeoning oil business, entering into partnership with his nephew by marriage, Eddie Hooker, another good friend of the Bouvier family who would function as sort of a link between the de Mohrenschildts and the Bouviers in the years to come. It was the oil business that took him to Texas and, in time, to Lee Harvey Oswald.

It has been estimated that the Russian nobleman and the Texan "hillbilly" met at least twenty times during the fall and winter of 1962 and 1963 and that the relationship that developed between them was fundamentally one of a father and son. Still, some observers, believing de Mohrenschildt to have been an intelligence agent of some sort, have suggested that his relationship to Oswald was one of CIA "handler," or "babysitter" or coconspirator, or possibly, debriefer. This possibility notwithstanding, the father-son relationship was evident to most of their mutual acquaintances. De Mohrenschildt had, in fact, lost a son who would have been about Oswald's age had he lived. And Oswald never knew his father; he had died of a heart attack two months before Oswald was born. Soon after they came to know each other, Lee Oswald began to look up to George de Mohrenschildt as to a father, an authority figure.

According to mutual friends in Dallas at the time, George de Mohrenschildt thought he had "discovered an original" in Oswald, a free spirit, a seeker, who acted firmly on his beliefs. In de Mohrenschildt's opinion, Lee Oswald was an "unbourgeois, uncalculating spirit who had dared go to Russia without giving a damn for the consequences." Yet he was, at the same time, fully cognizant of Lee's severe limitations, referring to him once as "a man of extremely poor background who read rather advanced books and did not even understand the words in them." Alas, Lee Harvey Oswald was the classic case of a little knowledge being a dangerous thing. He was a well-meaning seeker, but he really did not understand the large philosophical issues at stake in his search.

Nevertheless, for all the differences between them, George de Mohrenschildt and Lee Harvey Oswald formed a strong bond. A friend of both men in Dallas, one Samuel Ballen, observed "a mutuality, . . . an emotional complicity between Lee and George." And others observed that "Lee concentrated intensely on every word George said." One can easily understand how such abject attention could flatter the older man, who admitted to intimates that he lacked the emotional satisfaction of having a son look up to him. During their frequent meetings throughout the winter of 1962–1963, George de Mohrenschildt and Lee Harvey Oswald talked politics incessantly. According to an unfinished and unpublished manuscript of de Mohrenschildt's about his relationship with Oswald, found among the Russian émigré's possessions after his mysterious death in 1977, Lee was a great admirer of Fidel Castro and Che Guevara and told de Mohrenschildt that he thought "Cuba before Castro was a whorehouse for the American tourists," and a "headquarters of American racketeers." Although Lee admired President Kennedy, he told George that he regarded Kennedy's Cuban policy as "a disaster."

Another side to George de Mohrenschildt that stimulated the imagination of Lee Oswald was George's friendship with the First Lady of the United States and practically her entire family. According to his unpublished manuscript, George de Mohrenschildt talked often about Jacqueline Kennedy's family to Lee. The stories he told of the Bouviers undoubtedly stimulated Oswald's resentment against the rich (although in his manuscript de Mohrenschildt asserted, perhaps in self-defense, that he did not believe his stories about the Bouviers made Oswald resentful because Oswald regarded wealth and society as "big jokes"). What the stories did probably accomplish was to make President and Mrs. Kennedy much more immediate, vivid, and accessible to Oswald's imagination. Now, when someone would bring up the Kennedys in Oswald's presence, he could say that his very best friend, George de Mohrenschildt, knew them well and almost married into Jackie's family.

And George *had* become Lee's best friend by the spring of 1963. Oswald, the loner of loners, who despised his petit-bourgeois neighbors and who honestly believed he was destined to help establish a new world order, had no other male friends of any description. George de Mohrenschildt had become the central male influence in his life.

The friendship, however, also made Lee Oswald feel

inferior. Often he felt de Mohrenschildt was condescending to him. In the words of one of Oswald's biographers, Priscilla McMillan, "as the winter of 1963 began, the idea seems to have taken shape in Lee's mind that by a single, dramatic act whose political thrust George would approve, he might compel George's respect." Lee's wife, Marina, had gone on record to this effect, declaring that once when she and Lee and the de Mohrenschildts were driving through Dallas in George's big, gray convertible, George said something to Lee that elicited a pointed threat of violence from Lee.

In addition to talking politics with Lee, and belaboring his Kennedy-Bouvier connections, George de Mohrenschildt also tried to help smooth relations between Lee and his wife. These relations were poisonous, to put it mildly. The very bourgeois Marina, who wanted nothing more from life than a nice little house in the suburbs and enough money to take home a big brown bag of groceries from the supermarket each week, could not even begin to comprehend her hot-headed, messianic husband who imagined fate had singled him out for an extraordinary historical mission.

But in addition to that spiritual incompatibility, a more basic, sexual incompatibility complicated the conjugal life of Lee and Marina Oswald. Marina confided to friends that her husband was "not strong" sexually: he habitually came to climax too quickly. And Jeanne de Mohrenschildt testified that Marina often criticized her husband's sexual inadequacy in front of other people.

Once, Lee had had a long conversation with de Mohrenschildt about the ultraconservative John Birch Society and one of its members, retired Maj. Gen. Edwin A. Walker, who had led a group of antiblack demonstrators at the University of Mississippi at the time James Meredith was attempting to enroll and who was also militantly anti-Castro. De Mohrenschildt equated the John Birchers with the fascists, whom he hated, and habitually vented a good deal of spleen against Walker, who was constantly agitating for causes on the extreme right. It was not long after this discussion that Oswald acquired a revolver, and a rifle, with the alleged intention of assassinating General Walker.

The next events in the life of Lee Harvey Oswald are still the subject of much controversy; however, a reasonably accurate chronology can be pieced together.

Oswald, using the alias A. Hidell, ordered by mail a high-powered Mannlicher-Carcano rifle with telescopic sight with which allegedly to kill General Walker. On March 31, 1963, Oswald had himself photographed by his wife dressed entirely in black with a pistol at his side and holding a rifle and copies of two leftist publications, *The Militant* and *The Worker*. He apparently now regarded himself as a full-fledged Marxist revolutionary.

Early in April Oswald was fired from his job with a printing concern, Jaggers-Chiles-Stovall, where he had done photographic work with secret maps for the U.S. Army. His first full day out of work was April 8. On April 10 Oswald allegedly took a shot at General Walker through a window of the General's home and missed. The next day Oswald told his wife: "If someone had killed Hitler in time, many lives would have been saved."

The Oswalds were dreading a visit by the police, and when, two evenings after the shooting, they heard a commotion at their front door, they froze in fear. But they soon recognized the voice of George de Mohrenschildt. He was with his wife, Jeanne, and he burst into the house roaring in Russian, "Hey, Lee, how come you missed?"

After the de Mohrenschildts left, the Oswalds talked anxiously about George's remark, reassuring each other neither had told George about it. De Mohrenschildt had simply guessed. He had become so finely attuned to Lee's personality and ideas that when de Mohrenschildt heard about the shooting he immediately suspected Lee had pulled the trigger.

Then, in the middle of April, de Mohrenschildt announced he had found an interesting job in Haiti and would soon be leaving Dallas for good. The job was prospecting for oil and gas for Haiti's dictator, "Papa Doc" Duvalier, in return for luxurious living accommodations on a great estate and the right to operate a huge sisal plantation and take the entire profit from it. The de Mohrenschildts were to leave Dallas for Haiti on April 19.

The news came as a devastating shock to Lee Oswald. His newly found "father" and mentor cared for and respected him so little that he would abandon him at a moment's notice for a job in Haiti working for a *right-wing* dictator, precisely the type of political figure he abhorred.

Five days after the de Mohrenschildts departed from Dallas, Oswald left Dallas also, leaving his wife and daughter in the suburb of Irving with Marina's good friend, Ruth Paine. Lee went to New Orleans to stay with his uncle and aunt, Charles "Dutz" and Lillian Murret, who had helped bring him up after the early death of his father. Deciding to go live with the Murrets was quite probably a reaction to the recent loss of his "father," George de Mohrenschildt.

As it happened, Charles Murret was a bookmaker with connections to Carlos Marcello's crime family. One of "Dutz" Murret's closest associates had worked as a driver for Marcello, and Murret himself was in close association with several of Marcello's lieutenants. Because of Oswald's relationship to Murret it is entirely possible that the Marcello organization became aware of Oswald's existence in New Orleans in the summer of 1963, even to the extent of learning that he had made an attempt on General Walker's life some months before, and came to regard him as an ideal candidate for a "fall guy" in a plot to assassinate the President. Aside from Marcello's alleged death threat against President Kennedy in September 1962, an actual Marcello plot to kill the President may have been well advanced by the summer of 1963; a September 1963 FBI teletype reported that a discussion of such a plot had been overheard in March 1963.

At that time, Carlos Marcello was under federal indictment in New Orleans for having used a false Guatemalan birth certificate to obtain his illegal reentry into the United States. Marcello was scheduled to go on trial in New Orleans in late November, the same week in which President Kennedy was scheduled to visit Dallas.

The day after Oswald moved to New Orleans (April 24, 1963) it was announced in the Dallas *Times Herald* that President Kennedy would be visiting Dallas in November. The forthcoming presidential visit must have preyed on Oswald's mind during the months to follow, because on July 1 he went to the New Orleans Public Library and borrowed William Manchester's *Portrait of a President*. He subsequently took out another Kennedy book, the President's own *Profiles in Courage*.

We can only imagine what went through Oswald's mind as he read these two books. He had already learned a great deal about Jacqueline Kennedy's family background—from George de Mohrenschildt. Now he was learning practically everything that was available about the Kennedys themselves.

On August 9 Oswald was arrested on Canal Street for demonstrating for Castro and put in jail. A photograph has survived from this episode showing Oswald handing out "Fair Play for Cuba" pamphlets. Later he pleaded guilty to "disturbing the peace and creating a scene," paid a fine and was released on bail. It was his uncle "Dutz" Murret who paid the fine. Accompanying Murret to the courtroom proceedings was an associate of Marcello lieutenant Nofio Pecora. The associate arranged to put up Oswald's bail.

Meanwhile, on July 24, a group of ten Cuban exiles had arrived in New Orleans and had joined an exiles training camp north of the city. These exiles had been in touch with an anti-Castro conspirator known as "A," a lifelong friend of AM/LASH. It is not known whether Oswald was ever in touch with these exiles, though there is firm evidence that he attempted, unsuccessfully, to infiltrate an anti-Castro Cuban exiles group in New Orleans run by one Carlos Bringuier. If, however, Oswald had been in touch with these Cuban exiles, he might well have learned by mid-September of AM/LASH's association with the CIA, and his intention to kill Castro, just as he could well have learned by mid-August, from the article published in the *Chicago Sun-Times*, of the CIA's association with Giancana and what that probably involved. Given Oswald's apparently fanatical pro-Castro stance, knowledge of the AM/LASH operation, even though it was in an incipient stage at the time, might well have spurred Oswald to want to retaliate in behalf of his hero, the Cuban dictator.

It was during this time that Oswald apparently established a Fair Play for Cuba Committee office at 544 Camp Street from which he was to distribute his pro-Castro leaflets and a forty-page booklet entitled *The Crime against Cuba*, or, at the very least, he simply used 544 Camp Street as an address on the leaflets. Later it was learned that the same Camp Street address was shared by a curious assortment of groups: by the Cuban Revolutionary Council, the New Orleans umbrella organization of the anti-Castro exiles; by Guy Banister Associates, a detective agency run by a former FBI agent with strong links to Cuban exile organizations and American intelligence agencies; and also, quite probably, by organized crime, since one of Banister's agents was David Ferrie, a former Eastern airlines pilot who was working as a private investigator for Carlos Marcello. According to several witnesses Oswald was seen in the company of David Ferrie more than once that summer, not only in New Orleans, but also in Clinton, Louisiana.

One witness to these meetings later suggested that Ferrie might have lured Oswald into a plot to assassinate President Kennedy. Since Ferrie was close to Carlos Marcello, and Marcello probably knew about the Castro murder plots from his friend Santo Trafficante, Jr., it is conceivable that Ferrie could have told Oswald about the plots, hoping that would spur him to retaliate, on behalf of Castro, against Kennedy. But Oswald could likely have learned about the CIA-Mafia plots from still another source possibly connected to the tenants of 544 Camp Street. According to Guy Banister's personal secretary, Delphine Roberts, who was interviewed by Anthony Summers in 1978, none other than CIA-Mafia coconspirator John Roselli visited Banister's offices at 544 Camp Street during the same period in the summer of 1963 when Oswald visited them. Could Oswald, then, have learned about the Castro murder plots from one of the actual plotters?

On September 7 Oswald's idol, Fidel Castro, gave

an impromptu, three-hour interview to AP reporter Daniel Harker, during which he warned that U.S. leaders "aiding terrorist plans to eliminate Cuban leaders will themselves not be safe." Harker's article on the interview appeared in the *New Orleans Times-Picayune* on September 9 and therefore could have been read by Oswald.

Then, on September 13, the papers confirmed that President Kennedy would make a one-day visit to Texas on either November 21 or 22. Not long after the announcement, Oswald decided to go to Cuba, ostensibly to fight for Castro, exclaiming to his wife who had joined him in New Orleans, "I will become a revolutionary!" At the same time he would attempt to obtain a visa from the Soviet Embassy in Havana which would enable him eventually to return with his wife to Russia. Since Cuban consular facilities no longer existed in the U.S., he had to apply at the Cuban Embassy in Mexico City for a transit visa to visit Cuba.

On September 17 Oswald obtained a tourist visa to visit Mexico. Nine days later the Dallas press announced that President Kennedy would make a two-day visit to Texas on November 21 *and* 22. That same day Oswald departed by bus from Nuevo Laredo for Mexico City.

During the period September 27 to October 3 Oswald visited both the Soviet and Cuban embassies in Mexico City in an ostensible effort to obtain a transit visa for Cuba and to clear the way for an eventual return to the Soviet Union. On September 28 he allegedly saw an official by the name of Kostikov at the Soviet Embassy, who, it was later learned, was an intelligence officer of the KGB. He also allegedly saw a Cuban intelligence officer, Luisa Calderón, at the Cuban Embassy. In the end Oswald was unable to obtain his transit visa for Cuba and was compelled to return, in apparent disappointment, to Dallas.

On October 3 Lee Harvey Oswald returned to Dallas, where, on September 26, it had been confirmed in the papers that President Kennedy would visit on November 22. On October 4 Oswald applied for a job at a concern on Industrial Boulevard, one of the three possible presidential motorcade routes, and was turned down.

On October 7 Oswald took a room in Mrs. Bledsoe's rooming house. His wife Marina and their daughter were still living in a house belonging to Marina's friend, Ruth Paine, in the suburb of Irving. Mrs. Bledsoe evicted Oswald from her boardinghouse a few days later, and Lee went to Irving to visit his wife and daughter.

On October 14 Oswald took a room at 1026 North Beckley in the Oak Cliff section of Dallas, registering as O. H. Lee. Here he read copies of *The Worker* and *The Militant* containing extremely critical remarks about President Kennedy and his Cuba policy. One issue of *The Militant* hinted at the existence of certain assassination plots against Castro and the necessity of retaliating for them. Since Oswald registered at this new address using an alias, it appears the plan to murder the President had fully matured by this date. Further circumstantial evidence of this consists in the fact that he applied, unsuccessfully, for a job on Inwood Road, the probable return route of the presidential motorcade. As for his contacts with possible conspirators during this time, it is believed that they were made over a public telephone in a garage near his rooming house. A garage attendant later testified he had given Oswald change for several long-distance calls.

It was on October 15 that Oswald obtained, through the efforts of Ruth Paine, a job as an order filler in the Texas School Book Depository, a building covering *two* of the three possible presidential motorcade routes.

On November 1 Oswald rented a post office box in the names of the American Civil Liberties Union and the Fair Play for Cuba Committee. On the same day Marina Oswald was interviewed in Irving by FBI agent James Hosty, who asked for her husband's address, which she did not give him. Hosty interviewed her again on November 5. Oswald was much angered by this and left a note for Hosty at the FBI office threatening violence if the FBI did not desist from bothering his wife.

On November 9 Oswald sent a long letter to the Consular Division of the Soviet Embassy in Washington, which was intercepted by an FBI informant within the embassy. The letter brought the Soviet Consular Division up to date on his recent activities in Mexico, his wife's recent questioning by the FBI, and the birth of his daughter on October 20 and asked that he be informed of the arrival of his and his wife's entrance visas.

Also on November 9 a Miami police informer taped a conversation with an unidentified man who, claiming he was an organizer for a segregationist political party, told the informer "a plan to kill the President was in the works." "Kennedy would be shot," explained the informer, "with a high-powered rifle from an office building, and the gun would be disassembled, taken into the building, assembled, and then used for the murder. . . . They will pick up somebody within hours, just to throw the public off." This threat was immediately relayed to Miami police intelligence, which then vetoed the projected presidential motorcade in Miami on November 18. Instead, they decided to helicopter the President into the city. Inexplicably, the threat was never relayed to the Dallas police, who would approve a motorcade on the 22d, or to the Secret Service.

On November 18 President Kennedy delivered an inflammatory anti-Castro speech in Miami, which the CIA was to tell AM/LASH was meant to prove to him that Kennedy was prepared to countenance a coup and which could have been read in the local papers by Lee Harvey Oswald. The following day the President's motorcade route was published in the Dallas papers, and Oswald learned that Kennedy would pass right under the windows where he worked.

On November 19 President Kennedy was in the White House preparing for his trip to Texas on November 21. Between morning appointments he had a talk with his secretary, Evelyn Lincoln, during which they discussed Lyndon Johnson's protégé, Bobby Baker. Robert Kennedy was pursuing him with a vengeance for tax evasion and fraud. They also discussed the imminent trip to Texas and the question of who would be the President's running mate in the 1964 election.

When Mrs. Lincoln asked the President point-blank who that running mate would be, Kennedy, in Mrs. Lincoln's words, "looked straight ahead, and without hesitating, replied, 'At this time I am thinking about Governor Terry Sanford of North Carolina. But it will not be Lyndon.' "

Lyndon Johnson had been much angered by Robert Kennedy's pursuit of his former protégé, Mr. Baker, which pursuit Mr. Johnson believed was ultimately aimed at discrediting him as a vice-presidential candidate. Lyndon Johnson had not been seen in the White House since October when he left Washington for an extended stay in his native Texas. Mr. Johnson was scheduled to welcome the President and First Lady to Texas when they arrived in San Antonio on the first leg of their trip, the afternoon of November 21.

On the night of November 20, as President and Mrs. John F. Kennedy were preparing to go to bed in order to be well rested for their trip to Texas the following day, a 21-year-old prostitute and heroin addict known as Rose Cheramie was found in a road gutter near Eunice, Louisiana, by a state police officer. On the way to Louisiana State Hospital in Jackson to be treated for her injuries, Cheramie mumbled something to the police officer about her and some "Latins" going to Dallas to kill Kennedy, saying that "word was out in the underworld that Kennedy was going to be killed"; once in the hospital she told her attending physician that Kennedy was going to be killed in Dallas on November 22. Discounting her story as the ravings of a narcotics addict suffering from withdrawal symptoms, neither the police officer nor the physician took action on Miss Cheramie's prediction. Two days later, when the prediction came true, the state police called the hospital and ordered Rose Cheramie held for questioning.

On Thursday, November 21, after arriving in the Texas School Book Depository, Oswald allegedly asked a fellow worker, Wesley Frazier, for a ride to Irving to pick up some curtain rods. He then allegedly fashioned a bag made of brown paper and tape, and Wesley Frazier took him and the bag to Irving. That night, the night before the President's visit to Dallas, Oswald, according to his wife Marina, did several uncustomary things: he played with his daughter much longer than usual; he was angry and tense in bed with his wife, kicking her instead of making love to her; and he told Marina not to bother to get up to get his breakfast in the morning, the first time he had ever made such a request.

The following morning Oswald went into the garage and allegedly put his disassembled Mannlicher-Carcano rifle with telescopic sights into the paper bag he had brought from the Book Depository. When, after he returned to the house, Marina asked him what route President Kennedy was going to take through Dallas that day, he said he didn't know, which struck her as very odd since he had always shown such great interest in Kennedy's visit.

At 7:15 A.M. the morning of November 22 neighbor Linnie Mae Randle observed Lee Oswald coming from the Paines' garage carrying a brown package which he put in Wesley Frazier's car. She then called her brother Wesley and said Lee was waiting for his ride.

Before leaving for work Oswald told Marina to look in the bureau drawer after he left and she would find some money. As Wesley Frazier's car moved off, Marina looked in the drawer and found $170 in a wallet. She also noticed Lee's wedding ring in a cup. These constituted his entire known assets. By 8 A.M. Lee Harvey Oswald was at the Texas School Book Depository. By twelve noon he was observed by a fellow worker on the sixth floor of the Book Depository overlooking the area of Dealey Plaza where the President's motorcade would pass. The President was due in one-half hour. Also in Dealey Plaza that noon, it is now accepted by many, including a majority of the members of the 1979 House Committee on Assassinations, was at least one other armed individual waiting in ambush for the President.

Not long after the John F. Kennedys celebrated their tenth wedding anniversary, Jacqueline Kennedy embarked on a cruise of the Aegean on Aristotle Onassis's immense yacht, the *Christina*, accompanied by her sister, Lee, Lee's husband, Prince Radziwill, the Franklin D. Roosevelts, Jr., the designer Princess Irene Galitzine, and others.

While the First Lady was away on her travels, Robert

F. Kennedy was testifying in the United States Senate about organized crime in America, informing the senators about his campaign to rid the country of the Cosa Nostra, what had already been accomplished toward this end, and what still had to be done to rid America, once and for all, of this "horrible cancer," this "enemy within," which Kennedy believed threatened to destroy the very fabric of American society. And on October 7 the President signed the ratification of the limited nuclear test ban treaty. Ostensibly things were finally going reasonably well for the Kennedys. In early November the President delivered an optimistic report on national affairs to the Congress and held another of his dazzling nationally televised press conferences, his sixty-third since taking office.

But certain intrigues and crises were coming to a boil beneath the apparently optimistic surface. We will probably never know whether Sam Giancana and Johnny Roselli ever attempted to blackmail the President over his relationship with Judy Campbell or over their involvement with his government's plots to murder Fidel Castro. As for those Castro murder plots in which Giancana had figured so prominently, the then current plot, the AM/LASH operation, was nearing its critical phase. On November 18 President Kennedy had delivered that strongly worded anti-Castro speech in Miami which Desmond FitzGerald had informed AM/LASH was an official signal for the activation of the plan to kill the Cuban dictator. Then, on November 20, AM/LASH's CIA case officer phoned AM/LASH and told him that Desmond FitzGerald would be meeting with him on November 22 as AM/LASH had requested. It would be at this meeting that FitzGerald would give AM/LASH a device for killing Castro.

Then, in addition to the secret war against Cuba, there was the continuing war against organized crime and against corruption in organized labor, and all the animosities that *it* had stirred up. In the fall of 1963 some of the most vicious men in America were being pursued by the Kennedys. Sam Giancana was being hounded night and day by the FBI at Robert Kennedy's instigation. Carlos Marcello was under indictment by the Justice Department for conspiracy: his trial was due to come up in late November. Santo Trafficante, Jr., was, at Robert Kennedy's instigation, under investigation by the IRS. And Jimmy Hoffa, thanks to Robert Kennedy's relentless pursuit, was under indictment for both fraud and jury tampering. Three of these men had allegedly issued threats against the lives of either John Kennedy or Robert Kennedy.

But not only had organized crime vowed to destroy John Kennedy, elements within Kennedy's own government had vowed to destroy him. As the FBI's William Sullivan wrote in his memoirs, J. Edgar Hoover, detesting both Kennedy brothers and fearful of being fired, or retired, by the President, was assiduously "gathering damaging material" on both John Kennedy and Martin Luther King, Jr., "until he could unload it all and destroy them both."

And so, although the Kennedys were able to sail forth into the latter half of November 1963 still securely in possession of "the cloud capp'd towers, the gorgeous palaces, the great globe itself," they were nevertheless threatened on all sides by enemies of enormous power and resolve.

Was John F. Kennedy somehow aware that he had maneuvered himself into such a monstrous crossfire of hostility that his destruction was all but inevitable? With both pro-Castro Cubans and anti-Castro Cubans at his throat, with Castro smarting over Operation Mongoose and the CIA plots against his life, with many southern whites believing he was betraying them with his civil rights policy and many blacks believing he was betraying them by not doing enough for them, with the entire Cosa Nostra swearing vengeance against him and his brother, with Jimmy Hoffa vowing he would "get" him and his brother, with the embarrassed and out-of-favor Khrushchev out to avenge his humiliation over his defeat during the Cuban missile crisis, with J. Edgar Hoover bent on destroying him and his brother, with elements of the CIA believing he had betrayed them and with Dulles still in close touch with those elements, with the situation in Vietnam veering toward the murders of Diem and Ngo Dinh Nhu, and with

Sam Giancana, Carlos Marcello, John Roselli, and Santo Trafficante, Jr., in a position to blackmail him, did Kennedy have a premonition his days were numbered?

There is some indication that he did. At the conclusion of a speech to a group of representatives of several national organizations in June 1963, Kennedy had suddenly abandoned a recitation of all the problems besetting him and startled everyone by abruptly pulling a piece of paper out of a pocket and reading a speech of Blanche of Spain from Shakespeare's *King John:*

> *The Sun's o'ercast with blood; fair day, Adieu!*
> *Which is the side that I must go withal?*
> *I am with both: each army had a hand*
> *And in their rage, I having hold of both,*
> *They whirl asunder and dismember me.*

51. The Rendezvous

DURING THE WEEKS AND DAYS prior to the John F. Kennedys' visit to Texas, there were many who expressed strong reservations about the advisability of the Kennedys' making the trip. Adlai Stevenson told Arthur Schlesinger, Jr.: "I have serious doubts whether the President should go to Dallas." Senator J. William Fulbright told President Kennedy: "Dallas is a very dangerous place. *I* wouldn't go there. Don't you." At Robert Kennedy's birthday party on November 20, Ann Brinkley, wife of television commentator David Brinkley, told Kennedy aide Kenneth O'Donnell: "Keep the President away from Dallas."

There were many other admonitions about keeping the President away from Dallas, and many were passed on to Kennedy to no avail. As his former right-hand man Dave Powers emphasizes today, "Nobody had to force President Kennedy to go to Texas, least of all Lyndon Johnson: he could not have been held back from going."

That he could not have been held back from going had little to do with the Connally-Yarborough dispute that had so unsettled Democratic party politics in Texas; the real reason was that he needed to win Texas very badly if he was going to win reelection in 1964. His razor-thin 1960 triumph over Nixon had been due principally to winning

Texas and Illinois, but both states were won with tiny margins and not without dubious tactics.

His anxiety about Texas was especially intense in the light of all the anti-Kennedy feeling that had cropped up there since 1960, with so many of the big political bosses and a lot of the big oil money turning against him. Somehow he had to combat it. Kennedy believed in his and his wife's charm and charisma. He and Jackie were going down there, and they were going to charm those Texans into submission. With the November 1963 trip to Texas, the 1964 presidential campaign would begin.

By now Kennedy had realized what a valuable political asset Jacqueline was on a tour. Her extremely enthusiastic reception by the Europeans, especially the French, and her personal successes in Mexico and Miami, where she had addressed audiences in Spanish, had convinced him of this. The trip to Texas would be Jackie's first appearance on a presidential campaign tour. Kennedy wanted to make sure the Texans saw plenty of her. This meant maximum exposure to the public: wading into crowds and riding in long, open motorcades.

We now know, with the advantage of twenty years' hindsight, how numerous and powerful Kennedy's enemies were. And yet, despite this legion of enemies, Kennedy remained strangely incautious. This incaution raises the question of whether or not Kennedy was gripped by a death wish. Sometimes, when a person loses a sibling while still young, the survivor experiences intense guilt, and that sense of guilt can induce a subconscious yearning for death. Was John F. Kennedy overwhelmed with guilt over surviving his brother Joe and taking his place as the one destined for the presidency? It is impossible to say; however, there seems to be little doubt that John Kennedy was drawn toward taking risks that repeatedly brought him to the edge of the precipice. And what are we to make of the fact that his favorite poem was Alan Seeger's "I Have a Rendezvous with Death"?

So all the fateful, unwise decisions were made. There were reservations expressed about the great distance the motorcade would travel and the vulnerable route it would take (slowing down to a crawl of only ten miles per hour at the curve below the Texas School Book Depository). These were overruled: the route selected provided for maximum exposure for the President and First Lady, which was what the President wanted. There were discussions about whether to employ the bubble top on the presidential limousine. (Jacqueline liked to have it on because it kept the wind from mussing up her hair.) The bubble top was not bulletproof, but it would have made a gunman's aim more difficult and could have slightly deflected a bullet's trajectory. When it became known that the weather in Dallas would be good, Kennedy ordered the bubble top off. "I want all these Texas broads to see what a beautiful girl Jackie is," he is reported to have said. The President firmly vetoed a police motorcycle escort flanking either side of his limousine: it might prevent standees along the street from seeing him and Jackie, and so it was relegated some distance to the rear of the presidential car. Kennedy also firmly vetoed the presence of Secret Service bodyguards standing on the rear bumper of the presidential limousine for the same reason. Most people agree that if they had been there *they* would have received the bullets and not the President. As things were finally arranged, the Kennedys were to be easy targets.

At 1:30 P.M. (CST) the afternoon of Thursday, November 21, *Air Force One* touched down in San Antonio and the Kennedys were welcomed to Texas by Vice President Johnson. Along the route taken by the presidential motorcade a gratifying 125,000 people stood to get a look at the Kennedys. President Kennedy then dedicated the new Brooks Medical Center in San Antonio before a crowd of 6000 and returned with his party to *Air Force One*.

At 4:37 P.M. *Air Force One* touched down at Houston, and that evening Jacqueline Kennedy addressed a Hispanic group in carefully rehearsed Spanish, then attended, with her husband, a testimonial dinner for Congressman Albert Thomas, who had done so much for the space program. The Kennedys left for Dallas–Fort Worth shortly after eleven.

At 11:57 P.M. the Kennedys reached the Hotel Texas

in Fort Worth where they spent the night. During the night the *Dallas Morning News* was going to press with its full-page, black-bordered advertisement accusing the President of "the imprisonment, starvation, and persecution of thousands of Cubans" and of "selling food to Communist soldiers who were killing Americans in Vietnam." Marina Oswald was wondering why her husband was having such a troubled, fitful sleep.

At about 7:30 A.M. Lee Oswald got up and went into the garage to prepare his brown-paper package, and valet George Thomas woke President Kennedy to tell him it was raining. "That's too bad," Kennedy acknowledged.

At 8:53 A.M. President Kennedy addressed a crowd in a parking lot near the Hotel Texas under a light rain, shouting, in reference to the weather, "There are no faint hearts in Fort Worth!" Then, to calls of "Where's Jackie, where's Jackie?" he pointed to her hotel window and made his by now famous remark: "Mrs. Kennedy is organizing herself. It takes her a little longer, but, of course, she looks better than we do when she does it." Jacqueline heard the remarks over the PA system, glanced in the mirror, thought she looked tired, which she was, and said to her secretary, Mary Gallagher, "Oh, Mary, one day's campaigning can age a person thirty years." She was, however, grateful for the rain. That meant the bubble top would be on the car for the motorcade through Dallas.

But by the time the presidential motorcade was ready to move from the airport into Dallas, the weather had cleared up and the bubble top was ordered off. By 11:55 the President, wearing a blue-gray suit and gray-striped white shirt with blue tie, and the First Lady, in a pink suit and matching pillbox hat, were in the presidential limousine ready to roll into nearby Dallas. Dave Powers advised Jackie: "Be sure to look to your left, away from the President. Wave to the people on your side. If you both wave at the same voter, it's a waste."

The crowds along the route to the Trade Mart were discouragingly spotty at first, but soon turned out to be gratifyingly large and enthusiastic. Once the presidential motorcade got rolling, Jacqueline suffered considerably from the wind and the intense heat and glare, feeling comfortable only when going through shade or a tunnel. When, in a blinding glare, she put on her sunglasses, the President quickly ordered her to take them off, and she did. As the motorcade approached Dealey Plaza, Governor Connally's wife, Nellie, who was occupying one of the jump seats of the presidential limousine with her husband, turned around to Kennedy and said, "You sure can't say Dallas doesn't love you, Mr. President."

"No, you can't," said Kennedy with a grin.

52. Murder in Dallas: The Second Derailment

As THE MOTORCADE drove around a curve passing by the Texas School Book Depository, it slowed down. Entering Dealey Plaza, still moving more slowly than normal, Jacqueline noted, with relief, an underpass ahead, where she might receive a brief respite from the heat and glare.

At this point either Lee Harvey Oswald, or someone of still unknown identity using Oswald as a decoy, was taking aim at her husband's head from the sixth floor of the Texas School Book Depository. It is now widely believed that simultaneously, from behind a picket fence above a small grassy knoll overlooking Dealey Plaza to the right of the motorcade's advance, a second gunman was also taking aim at the President.

According to a police dictabelt recording of the sounds in Dealey Plaza at the time of the shootings, which was accepted as evidence by the 1979 House Assassinations Committee but which was later rejected by the National Science Foundation, at least four shots were fired, possibly more, three from the Book Depository, at least one from the grassy knoll. Precisely which shots struck the President and Governor Connally and where they struck them is still a matter of controversy. A fragment of a bullet, or of a curbstone hit by a bullet, also struck and wounded Dallas citizen James T. Tague who was standing near the triple underpass far from the line of sight between the Book Depository and the motorcade. One shot wounded Kennedy in the neck and back. The fatal shot wounded the right side of the President's head.

After this shot Jacqueline leaned toward her stricken husband and saw, in horror, pieces of his skull and bits of brain matter fly into the air. Recoiling at first, then appearing as if she were about to scramble out of the back of the car or reach for something, she screamed, "My God, what are they doing? My God, they've killed Jack, they've killed my husband . . . Jack, Jack!"

By now Governor Connally had collapsed from his wounds into his wife's lap, exclaiming, "My God, they are trying to kill us all!"

For the entire length of the trip to Dallas's Parkland Hospital the two wives held their unconscious husbands in their laps, believing both were dead.

The President's head wound was enormous. By the time the motorcade arrived at the hospital, Kennedy appeared dead to all who saw him, yet his vital signs had not yet stopped. Governor Connally, it was immediately ascertained, was badly wounded but still very much alive.

Meanwhile, Lee Harvey Oswald, after escaping from the Book Depository, shot and killed Police Officer J. D. Tippit in circumstances that remain mysterious to this day.

As the President lay dying in Parkland Hospital, with the doctors and nurses trying vainly to save him, three more events were taking place in three widely separated locations, one or more of which may have been connected to what had just happened in Dallas.

Cosa Nostra boss Carlos Marcello, on trial in New Orleans on criminal charges brought against him by Robert Kennedy, was acquitted of those charges shortly before the President's assassination (later he would be charged with jury bribery in the case). Assisting Marcello's lawyer in the courtroom was David Ferrie, the ex-pilot who had allegedly associated with Oswald in New Orleans and who would soon be arrested by the New Orleans district attorney on suspicion of having conspired with Oswald to kill the President.

Almost simultaneously, senior CIA official Desmond FitzGerald and AM/LASH case officer "2" were consigning a poison ballpoint pen with an ultrafine hypodermic needle to the Cuban AM/LASH conspirator Rolando Cubela, for possible use by Cubela against Fidel Castro. As they were consigning the weapon, they advised Cubela to use Blackleaf–40, a deadly poison that was commercially available, and they also told him they would soon be sending the explosives and high-powered rifle with telescopic sights he had requested. FitzGerald informed Cubela that he had helped write parts of John F. Kennedy's recent anti-Castro speech in Miami, notably Kennedy's characterization of the Castro government as "a small band of conspirators," which "once removed" would ensure U.S. support for "progressive goals" in Cuba, and that he had come to him with the poison pen as Robert F. Kennedy's "personal representative."

As for Robert Kennedy, he was holding a meeting of his anticrime staff with whom he was about to discuss the ongoing investigation of Sam Giancana, still a top priority in his effort to destroy the mob. It was during the lunch break of this meeting—1 P.M. (CST)—that John F. Kennedy was pronounced dead by Parkland's Dr. William Kemp Clark. An hour later Kennedy's body was forcibly and illegally removed from the hospital by his aides and the Secret Service, thus preventing an autopsy from being performed at Parkland. By 2:45, two hours and fifteen minutes after the shooting in Dealey Plaza, the President's body was on its way to Bethesda Naval Hospital aboard *Air Force One*.

In the course of a few seconds John F. Kennedy's life and administration had been destroyed. Suddenly the grace and the magic and the power were gone—the career that had taken several lifetimes to build had been shattered in less than a minute.

In an instant a family had lost a son and a nation had lost a leader upon whom both had placed boundless hopes. And an entire system of government had sustained a cynical attack. Those millions who had believed in the system and had voted for John F. Kennedy suddenly had their belief insulted and their votes annulled. This was not just a crime against a man, it was a crime against the faith and hope of a people.

President Kennedy once remarked that the two events in modern American history Americans most universally remember where they were when they first heard about them were Pearl Harbor and the death of Franklin D. Roosevelt. Now a third event would be added: Kennedy's own death at the hands of Lee Harvey Oswald and possible coconspirators.

The President's mother and father were in their house at Hyannis Port when they first heard the news. It was the habit of Rose and Joe Kennedy to take an afternoon nap in their respective rooms every day after lunch. Joe Kennedy, as we know, had suffered a massive stroke while playing golf in Palm Beach a little over a year after his son had been elected to the presidency. As a result of the stroke, his right side had been left partially paralyzed and he had lost the ability to speak. He was now under the care of his niece by marriage, Ann Gargan, and a trained nurse and therapist by the name of Rita Dallas.

At the time the President went to Dallas the talk in the Kennedy household at Hyannis was not so much of the President's trip to Texas, but of the upcoming Thanksgiving family reunion which was to fall on the first Thursday after the President returned from Dallas. Teddy and Joan were expected the next day. By Tuesday of the following week the other children and grandchildren would begin arriving. On Wednesday the President, Jacqueline, John Junior, and Caroline were to arrive on *Air Force One* at Otis Air Force Base and then helicopter to the lawn in front of the Kennedy house.

The Thanksgiving season was always a lovely season on the Cape. Preparations for the big Thanksgiving Day feast were already underway by November 22, when, shortly after 1:30 P.M., Joe Kennedy's personal maid Dora heard the terrible news of the shooting on the kitchen radio and ran into the hallway, near the stairwell, shrieking at the top of her lungs.

Rita Dallas and Ann Gargan were upstairs when they heard the commotion. Leaning over the banister, Rita Dallas heard Dora crying hysterically, "The President's been shot! The President's been shot!"

"Be quiet," Mrs. Dallas said, "what are you saying?" and she put her fingers to her lips and cast her eyes toward where Mr. and Mrs. Kennedy were sleeping.

Then Rose came out of her room in her bathrobe. "What's the matter with you two? . . . Please, can't you be quiet? I've never heard so much commotion. Now keep still. Do you want to disturb Mr. Kennedy?" Hearing the racket from Ann's room, she called to Ann to turn down her set. By this time Rita was in Ann's room reaching for the volume control. But before she could turn it down, Rose seemed to sense the import of the bulletins blaring forth, for she suddenly stiffened. Then Dora began crying again, hysterically clutching at Frank Saunders, the Kennedy chauffeur, and Ann came out of her room and leaned limply against the wall. "What *is* the matter?" Rose called. "Tell me, what's wrong?" There was a moment's hesitation, then Ann spoke: "Aunt Rose . . . Jack's been shot!" Freezing for a second, Rose pressed her fingers against her temples and said in a steady voice, "Don't worry, he'll be all right. . . . You'll see." And she went into her room and sat down on her bed. A few minutes later the phone rang. It was Bobby, calling her from his home in Virginia, to tell her what had happened.

Robert Kennedy was having lunch with Robert M. Morgenthau, the U.S. attorney for the Southern District of New York, when he learned the news of the shooting over the phone from J. Edgar Hoover. Later, after hearing his brother was dead, Bobby turned to his wife, Ethel, and said in a quiet, reflective voice: "He had the most wonderful life." At some point, he told his press aide, Edwin Guthman: "I thought they might get one of us, but Jack, after all he'd been through, never worried about it. . . . I thought it would be me." By "they" Robert Kennedy was apparently referring to the Cosa Nostra. Sometime later, when Pierre Salinger saw him, Kennedy struck Salinger as being the most shattered man he'd ever seen.

Meanwhile the news had reached Senator Edward M. Kennedy in the U.S. Senate, while he was signing some correspondence at the rostrum. It was a Senate page, Richard Reidel, who gave out the word: "The most horrible thing has happened! It's terrible, terrible!"

"What is it?" said Kennedy.

"Your brother, the President. He's been shot."

"How do you know?"

"It's on the ticker. Just came in on the ticker."

Ted Kennedy then quickly gathered up his papers and left. Without a moment's hesitation he knew exactly what he was going to do. He was going to fetch his wife Joan and his sister Eunice and together they would immediately fly up to Hyannis to be with their mother and father.

Now all five telephones in the house at Hyannis, each with its own number, began ringing incessantly, and the ambassador woke up, showing signs to his nurse that he felt vague presentiments that something was wrong. Ann Gargan, who felt officially in charge of him, went to him with the intention of telling him the news, but just before she could tell him, Rose came to her and told her to wait until "one of the boys" showed up.

After Bobby's call, Rose had paced her room for a while, then had gone out and walked up and down the cold, deserted beach, alone. When she returned to the house a call came through at 4:15 P.M. from *Air Force One*. It was the new President and First Lady. Rose accepted the Johnsons' condolences quietly. Shortly after the call, Teddy and Eunice and Joe Gargan appeared. They all put on heavy sweaters and set out for a walk on the beach. An icy November wind was sweeping in from the bay, and gulls were diving into the heavy surf for crabs and clams and minnows. As they walked along in silence, Rose astonished her nephew, Joe Gargan, by suddenly saying, "Joey, you should read more."

The dumbfounded young man could only say, "Yes, Aunt Rose."

"Read Marlborough, Fox, and Burke," Rose went on, "like Jack."

When they returned to the house, the great problem of the moment was to keep the news of Jack's murder from Father Joe. It was a rule in the Kennedy household not to divulge bad news in the afternoon or evening, if nothing could be done about it, but to wait until the following morning when one would be fresh and more able to bear a shock. Thus the family engaged in a long and emotionally draining charade until Joe finally went to bed for the night. Television and radio sets mysteriously went dead, animated discussions were held at dinner, just as in the old days, and high spirits were feigned.

Then, the next morning, after Rose came back from church, Ted and Eunice went into their father's room to tell Joe the news. The only other person present was the ambassador's nurse, Rita Dallas. Rose was too weak to face the ordeal and would not see her husband until dawn the next day.

Eunice leaned over her father's bed and took his hand, while Ted stood by with his hands folded behind his back. Eunice then took charge, as she always did in the Kennedy family, and, in a highly emotional and confused monologue managed to convey to her mute and semi-paralyzed father that something terrible had happened to his son Jack. As Joe's eyes began to show a cloud of fear, Teddy clarified the matter succinctly, saying, "Dad, Jack was shot." He then fell to his knees and held his hands to his face, and Eunice said, "He's dead, Daddy. He's dead."

It was the third time Joe had received news of the violent death of a child, and, even though the shock was devastating, he knew what to do. As his nurse, Rita Dallas, reported, he tried, despite his infirmities, to comfort Ted and Eunice. Then his doctor gave him a sedative and he went to sleep.

While the slain President's family was trying to cope with their sudden loss, the interrogation of Oswald in Dallas and the examination of the President's body in Bethesda proceeded clumsily. After his arrest (first, for the murder of Officer Tippit and then, some hours later, for the murder of President Kennedy), Lee Harvey Oswald was questioned for twelve hours by the Dallas police, the FBI, and the Secret Service, without legal counsel (Oswald is said to have repeated over and over again, "I am a patsy in this"), and an autopsy was performed on the President's body at Bethesda Naval Hospital just outside Washington.

The autopsy on President Kennedy was so botched it left a permanent legacy of doubt. The manner in which it was performed was deeply suspicious. The doctors at Parkland in Dallas had wanted to conduct the autopsy there, but the Secret Service had overruled them and had illegally removed the body from the hospital. Contrasting descriptions of the President's wounds soon emerged. The Dallas doctors claimed the wound in the President's throat, which they had further enlarged to perform a tracheotomy, was a wound of entry, but the Bethesda doctors, at first not detecting the wound at all because of the tracheotomy incision, eventually determined it to be a wound of exit. However, the Bethesda surgeons failed to track the wound through the neck and back and, in fact, were unable to manually probe the back wound to a depth of more than five inches.

Nor did the Bethesda doctors examine all the major organs and glands, as is usually the procedure in an autopsy. It is now widely believed that either Robert or Jacqueline Kennedy, who were following the progress of the autopsy by telephone from another room, told the surgeons through presidential physician Adm. George Burkley not to track the neck wound and not to conduct a complete autopsy, for fear that the doctors would discover the President's diseased adrenal glands. Because the President's neck was never opened up there is still doubt as to which wound was of entry and which was of exit. The question is important because the nature of the wounds reflected the direction from which the bullet, or bullets, were fired and the number of shooters involved.

Warren Commission archcritic Sylvia Meagher was particularly disturbed by the apparent acquiescence of the surgeons to the Kennedys' wish not to have the President's adrenals dissected. In *Accessories after the Fact,* she quoted the editors of *Current Medicine for Attorneys* who wrote, "The question is: was President Kennedy 'impaired for public life,' when he ran for public office—by reason of adrenal pathology? . . . Certainly the absence of findings in the autopsy on this point support that he was."

To further complicate the autopsy questions, FBI agents James Sibert and Francis O'Neill, who had been ordered to remain with the body and take notes on the autopsy, indicated in their final report that the bullet that caused the back wound did not transit, and thus the anterior neck wound could not have been one of exit. Furthermore, they stated that when the President's casket was opened up and the body removed and unwrapped, it was apparent that "surgery of the head area, namely in the top of the skull" had been performed. This observation has led several investigators to conclude that the President's body was surgically altered by someone before it arrived on the autopsy table at Bethesda in order to disguise the nature of the President's wounds. To even further complicate the autopsy issue, chief autopsy surgeon Cdr. James Humes burned his preliminary draft notes on the autopsy and then, on November 24, wrote a second draft, which was subsequently revised and submitted to Admiral Burkley in the White House and which has since disappeared altogether.

Thus no verbatim transcript was left by the police, FBI, or Secret Service of the questioning of the accused assassin, and no records were left by the chief autopsy surgeon of his original description of the President's wounds and the autopsy procedure at Bethesda.

After the autopsy and the embalming, the President's body was taken to the East Room of the White House, where it remained until Sunday, November 24. Sunday morning, preparations were begun to remove the body to the Capitol rotunda where it would lie in state.

Just as Jacqueline Kennedy was placing a letter to her dead husband in his coffin and the caisson bearing the coffin was about to leave the White House, one Jack Ruby, a Dallas striptease nightclub owner, with connections to the Marcello, Giancana, and Trafficante crime organizations and to Hoffa's Teamsters Union, made his way into the basement of the Dallas police headquarters, possibly with the cooperation of certain members of the Dallas police, at the precise moment Lee Harvey Oswald was about to be transferred from that headquarters to the county jail. Most of the police officers assigned to guard Oswald knew Ruby, for he used to cosign loans for them and give them free drinks and introductions to strippers at his clubs, passing out chits right at headquarters, and so they did not find his presence particularly out of the ordinary. Furthermore, he had been observed twice at Dallas police headquarters since Oswald's arrival and had also been seen at Parkland Hospital as the President lay dying. As Oswald was being led through the basement to the vehicle that was to take him to the county jail, Jack Ruby stepped out from behind Police Officer W. J. "Blackie" Harrison, with whom, it is suspected, he had been in touch by phone that morning, and silenced the President's murderer forever.

By now Ambassador Kennedy had recovered from the heavy sedation of the day before and was receiving visits from family members and friends. When news of the killing of Oswald reached the family, Mrs. Kennedy, in the words of Rita Dallas, "let out a weird, high cry of 'My God, my God.' " Then, "an eerie silence" fell upon the house and Ambassador Kennedy signaled for all visitors to leave his room. It was early afternoon and time for his nap. The muted, almost immobile invalid, who was unable to express his thoughts and feelings, must have felt terribly frustrated and drained. All he had worked so hard for all his life had been shattered. He was a closed, bottled-up, uncommunicative man anyway; now his loneliness was almost unbearable: he had to deal with enormous sorrows without being able to express his feelings to anybody but himself. A long and bitter agony stretched out before him. For the second time his grand design to hold the presidency for the house of Kennedy had been derailed.

53. A White House Wake

MONDAY, NOVEMBER 25, 1963. Washington: The funeral of President John F. Kennedy. At 11:30 A.M. the attention of virtually the entire world was focused, because of worldwide radio and television coverage via the new communications satellites, upon one event. It was an occurrence unmatched in the history of the human race.

By 11:45 I was standing outside St. Matthew's Cathedral with the other members of the Bouvier family, waiting for the funeral to begin. Soon the procession from the White House arrived on foot. There was the flag-draped caisson with the President's remains, and there was the mournful riderless horse, Black Jack, whose occasional random movements seemed to express the futility of it all. And there was Jacqueline, flanked by Robert and Edward Kennedy and followed by some thirty foreign heads of state, the Supreme Court, the cabinet, and many of her late husband's former assistants, presenting to the world an image of dignity and strength that did much to redeem her country's image and reputation at a moment when it was desperately needed.

As all the world now knows, Jacqueline had had to overcome formidable opposition to mount her funeral for her murdered husband. She had to overcome the opposition of the Catholic hierarchy to the choice of St. Matthew's Cathedral; the opposition of the Secret Service and others to her decision to march behind the caisson on foot from the White House to the cathedral; the opposition of the armed forces to having the Black Watch provide the music for the procession; the opposition of JFK aides Kenneth O'Donnell and David Powers to her and Robert Kennedy's choice of Arlington (over Boston) for the burial; the opposition of many to her having her husband's grave surmounted with an eternal flame.

Somehow all her decisions proved appropriate. As her mother had told my mother two days before the funeral, Jacqueline possessed "a truly remarkable sense of the fitness of things." Her special combination of style and steel had, in her behavior at the funeral, found its ultimate expression.

At the pontifical requiem mass I was sitting with my mother and father and sister in an assigned pew to the left of the center aisle, about fifteen rows from the front of the church. Since there were so many instantly recognizable world figures at the mass, it was often difficult to concentrate on the service. I was curious to see how Rose Kennedy was holding up. Huddled in the first pew, she appeared very withdrawn and alone. She had not felt well enough to march from the White House, and Mr. Kennedy had stayed behind in Hyannis on doctors' orders. Lyndon Johnson, towering over everybody but de Gaulle, looked very tired and worn and burdened. At one point in the service, Jacqueline, who was kneeling close to her husband's coffin, finally broke down and wept.

It was a long and occasionally inspiring ceremony. Toward the end, Cardinal Cushing provided a touching and welcome note. Suddenly abandoning the Latin and the text of the mass, he raised his long arms and cried:

> May the angels, dear Jack, lead you into Paradise. May the martyrs receive you at your coming. May the spirit of God embrace you, and mayest thou, with all those who made the supreme sacrifice of dying for others, receive eternal rest and peace. Amen.

A few minutes later, as the casket was being carried down the cathedral steps and the band was launching into "Hail to the Chief," little John Junior, who had that day just turned 3 years old, captivated everyone as he bid his father farewell with a salute.

After the services in St. Matthew's, those of us from the Bouvier family who had attended the funeral were unable to find our assigned official cars in the confusion outside the church and were forced to take taxis. The taxis, however, got caught in an immense traffic jam on the way to Arlington, and at a certain point we had to give up the idea of attending the burial and turn back. We therefore missed the muffled drums, the twenty-one gun salute, the fifty jet planes, the wing-dipping salute from *Air Force One*, the lighting of the eternal flame, and a final chance to pay our last respects to John F. Kennedy.

After the burial Jacqueline Kennedy returned to the White House to receive her family and some 200 representatives from 100 nations, including eight chiefs of state and ten heads of government. We had been told tea was to be served to family and friends in the upstairs sitting room and a reception for foreign diplomats was to be held downstairs in the State Dining Room. I made my way to the White House as soon as the burial was over.

What I beheld, upon my arrival there, was a gigantic wake: several parties were in the process of unfolding, including John Junior's birthday celebration, and the atmosphere in the executive mansion was electric with excitement. Heads of state, diplomats from every country in the world, Kennedys, Fitzgeralds, Bouviers, Auchinclosses, and friends were pouring in the main entrance. To all of us it seemed like yesterday that we had all gathered in the same place to celebrate the inauguration.

It is an Irish custom to hold a lively, boisterous party immediately after a burial of a relative or a friend, during which large amounts of alcohol are consumed and many funny stories are told. This practice is called "waking" and is supposed to help release the tension and allow a momentary escape from the overwhelming sense of horror and grief. Although in the White House that afternoon there was no one Irishman charged with organizing the President's wake, the mood of an Irish wake was somehow generated, especially upstairs in the family quarters where David Powers was holding forth. If the spirited mood in the White House after Kennedy's burial could be attributed to anyone in particular, it could be attributed to the man who had been John F. Kennedy's right arm for the past eighteen years, the man who people jokingly referred to as "John's other wife."

But there was another factor contributing to the animation in the White House that November afternoon. The past four days, witnessing first the murder of the President, then the murder of his assassin, had been so depressing and so bewildering that everyone was in a mood to forget temporarily what had happened and enjoy what turned out to be an unexpected reunion of family and friends. The nightmare was suspended. Friends and relatives were catching up on each other's lives. I spotted Janet Auchincloss, whom I had not seen since the inauguration. She was tearing here and there, trying to handle all the people who wanted to see Jackie, and *everyone* wanted to see Jackie. Janet looked so fresh and unworried that I was not in the least prompted to commiserate with her over the President's death. Instead I asked her how Jackie was holding up. "Oh, she's fine," she said, "she's in talking with de Gaulle, or maybe Prince Philip, now. She's used to this sort of thing."

Mac Bundy once wrote, "The end of the service at Arlington was like the fall of a curtain, or the snapping of taut strings." Perhaps this was why the White House felt so excited and alive. The curtain had fallen upon the President's death and had gone up again on Jackie's completely restored and redecorated White House to reveal a gathering of the high and mighty such as probably had never been seen before in the entire history of the executive mansion.

There was so much going on it made one's head spin. Downstairs Angier Biddle Duke, chief of protocol, was shepherding diplomats and heads of government from all over the world to a large buffet in the State Dining Room.

On their way, or after they had partaken of something from the buffet, they would be received by various members of the Kennedy family in the adjoining Red Room. At first the late President's sisters, Eunice, Patricia, and Jean, would do the honors. Later Jacqueline and Ted Kennedy would take over at the head of the receiving line.

While the big reception was getting underway downstairs, Jacqueline was receiving certain special heads of state upstairs in the oval study, where a high tea had been laid out. She had wanted a private word with only four favorite potentates: General de Gaulle, Prince Philip, President Eamon de Valera, and Emperor Haile Selassie.

While these meetings were beginning, two other parties were getting underway nearby in the family dining room and sitting room: tea, coffee, sandwiches, and drinks for family and friends presided over by Janet Auchincloss and Rose Kennedy, and a birthday party for John F. Kennedy, Jr.

I was shuttling back and forth between these upstairs events when I saw Jacqueline greet de Gaulle in the hall as he got out of the elevator. She welcomed him warmly, and together they went arm in arm into the oval study, where, I later learned, she made a brief attempt to patch up the enmity and tension that had developed of late between England, France, and the United States. She was functioning now on a wholly new level. No longer in the background, she was conducting relations among nations.

Once again I was struck by Jackie's extraordinary fortitude and poise. Jacqueline Bouvier Kennedy was, during this brief space of time, between 4 and 5 P.M. on Monday, November 25, 1963, the *real* President of the United States. Since Lyndon Johnson's reception for the heads of government at the State Department was not to begin until 5 P.M., the attention of the world was now focused wholly upon her. She *was* the United States of America to the foreign emissaries congregated in Washington. As I observed her, she seemed to be enjoying herself. It was a perfectly human reaction. She had always lived in Jack Kennedy's shadow, playing a supporting role to him; now she was number one, *she* was the king for a brief, one-hour reign. And she liked it, she liked it very much.

After she concluded her tête-à-têtes with her favorite world figures, Jacqueline had a few words with Mary Anne Ryan, the slain President's third cousin, who had come all the way from the family homestead in Dunganstown for the funeral; then she went downstairs to receive all the ambassadors and other heads of government in the Red Room.

When I arrived in the State Dining Room the reception was in full swing, with diplomats of every nation milling around and picking at the buffet. As I reached for a sandwich, I spotted Jean Monnet, with whom I had had a long conversation, principally about the Kennedys, on the plane to Washington. He seemed very excited.

"Have you ever seen anything like your cousin?" he asked.

"She was fantastic, wasn't she?" I replied.

"Extraordinary. Such strength I have rarely seen in all my years in public life. She was an example to the entire world. . . . Tell me, what is the talk about the assassination? What do the Kennedys think? Do they think there was a conspiracy?"

I told him I had not yet had a chance to talk with the Kennedys about it, but would, later, up in the family quarters, if it seemed appropriate.

"Well, I'll tell you," he said, "all the Europeans and Latin Americans are *absolutely convinced* it was a conspiracy, and almost all the Americans I've talked to think it was the work of a lone fanatic. Do you think this says anything about the American mentality or character?"

"I would say it denotes a streak of wishful thinking and self-deception on our part, which is very much in the American character."

"You want desperately to conserve your innocence, and protect your illusions, don't you?"

"Unfortunately, yes."

"Well, it will be interesting to see what Bobby Kennedy does. As attorney general, it will be his job to uncover the conspiracy. Do you think he will get along with President Johnson?"

"No. They have never gotten along. Lyndon Johnson always resented Bobby."

"There will be quite a power struggle, won't there?"

"It should be interesting to watch," I said.

We fell into line with all the dignitaries and others, and soon Jacqueline and Ted came into view. Jackie was standing between Kennedy and Angier Biddle Duke under a blazing bronze chandelier and against a bright red damask wall. Jackie was only 34 and Teddy 32. Youth had been in power and youth had been struck down. Now age would be in power—Johnson was almost twice Ted Kennedy's age.

As we approached Jacqueline, Monnet, knowing I was not in politics and was therefore less familiar than he with the cast of characters on the world political scene, started pointing out some of the people. There was the Queen of Greece. There was Anastas Mikoyan, deputy premier of the Soviet Union; there was Llevas Camargo, president of Colombia; there was Ludwig Erhard of West Germany. The entire globe, it seemed, was represented with the two Kennedys in the Red Room.

Finally I was only two diplomats away from Jacqueline and Ted. I was astonished at their vitality. After having gone through one of the most physically and emotionally draining days imaginable, here they both were: vibrant, dynamic, in control, receiving the sympathy of all the nations under the sun and giving of themselves unstintingly.

When I appeared before Jackie she registered surprise at seeing me in a line of only foreign diplomats. "Look, Ted, it's my *cousin!*" she cried. Then we embraced and I told her how proud I was of her and how heartsick I was over what had happened, and, in that low, breathless whisper of hers, she said, "Thanks, Jack," and I moved on, heading upstairs to join the party in the family sitting room.

Upstairs the wake had become a full-fledged party with wine and liquor flowing and laughter and high spirits prevailing. I quickly spotted Bobby Kennedy, Pat and Peter

Lawford, Lee and Stas Radziwill, Rose Kennedy, Janet Auchincloss, Dave Powers, little John Junior, Caroline, and many more familiar faces.

Robert Kennedy looked very tired and haggard. He had apparently taken the assassination of his brother harder than either Jackie or Ted. When I went up to him and offered my condolences, he was almost speechless and seemed completely drained. I noted he had not stood in the receiving line downstairs. I was tempted to ask him his opinion about the slaying, whether he thought it was the result of a conspiracy or not, but could not bring myself to do it, he looked so grief-stricken.

Today, in retrospect, I am convinced there was another reason why Robert Kennedy seemed so much more demoralized than the other Kennedys. Now that we know about the CIA-Mafia and AM/LASH plots to assassinate Castro, and how strongly Robert Kennedy had pushed for the elimination of Castro, we can imagine that he, Robert Kennedy, must have been enormously upset when he learned, almost immediately after the assassination, that Lee Oswald had been a Castro supporter and a member of the Fair Play for Cuba Committee. It is more probable than not, according to former AM/LASH operation officer, Samuel Halpern, that Robert Kennedy knew that on November 22 Desmond FitzGerald had been scheduled to meet with AM/LASH in Paris to assist him in effecting the violent overthrow of the Castro regime. Thus, in addition to grief, Robert Kennedy was probably also carrying a considerable burden of guilt.

In stark contrast to the attitude of Bobby Kennedy was the spirited, eternally clannish demeanor of his sisters. Eunice, Patricia, and Jean were, as usual, in a group by themselves. I remember the supercharged Eunice stabbing the air with her fist just as her brother Jack used to do.

A TV set had been turned on in the sitting room, and Peter Lawford was slumped in an armchair before it. What he, and a few others, were watching was a replay of the past three days' events: the presidential motorcade as it approached Dealey Plaza, Ruby shooting Oswald in the basement of the Dallas jail, the morning's funeral procession, stills of the assassinated President's gravesite at Arlington. Lawford, alone among those watching, seemed deeply moved by what he was seeing. From his sprawled slump in the armchair he kept shaking his head and throwing up his hands in gestures of futility.

The TV replay also gave *me* a sense of horror and futility. I wanted to express my sympathy to Rose Kennedy, but she was so surrounded by people, mostly relatives and former assistants to her slain son, that I could not see an appropriate opening. Meanwhile others moved about in a not-too-mournful state. Lee Radziwill, I thought, was acting a bit too carefree for the occasion. I speculated that Kennedy's death might have been, for her, something of a psychological relief. Her husband, Stas, normally a rather heavy, subdued personality, had also taken on a new dimension. Now he was the only husband of the Bouvier sisters left, and he need not defer anymore to the mighty Jack Kennedy. There was talk of his spending the night in the assassinated President's bedroom.

I was talking to Janet Auchincloss, who, just as she had done at the inauguration, had more or less taken command of the party, when we began to notice that everyone was drifting toward the family dining room. Janet said, "Oh, I guess it's time for the cake. Let's go see John blow out the candles."

We went into the dining room and found the 3-year-old boy marching around with a paper hat on his head and a toy rifle at right shoulder arms. He had seen marching all day and couldn't get it out of his system. From the sidelines his sister, Caroline, watched solemnly, saying hardly a word. Dave Powers was clapping his hands, trying to simulate a marching rhythm. Before long, young John Kennedy put away his gun and began opening up other presents. There was a circle of adoring onlookers around him, and they oohed and aahed each time he took a toy windup car or fire engine out of a box. "Happy Birthday, little John." "Long life, John!" A cake with three candles rested on the sideboard. When Jacqueline and Teddy came up from their handshaking in the Red Room it would be lighted and the birthday song would be sung. There could be no more fitting wake for the President, and everyone present was aware of it and waiting for the big moment.

As I was standing there with the others, an usher came up to Janet Auchincloss and told her it would be a while yet before Jacqueline would be able to get up to the birthday party; there were still so many diplomats to greet. I had to take the shuttle to New York that night to catch an early flight back to Rome the following morning and therefore could not wait all night for Jacqueline to come up. I had een her anyway. Deciding to leave, I spotted Rose Kennedy, now standing alone and somewhat apart from the festivities, and went over to her to offer my condolences.

She looked smaller and more inconspicuous than usual, as if her son's tragedy had somehow shrunken her. But she was poised and outwardly calm. Shaking her hand, I muttered some banality to her about how sorry I was for her and the family, and she surprised me by responding in a cool, utterly controlled voice:

"Oh, thank you, Mr. Davis, but don't worry. Everything will be all right. You'll see. Now it's Bobby's turn."

Part 4

POSTMORTEM

54. Aftermath and Cover-up

WHEN FIDEL CASTRO HEARD the news of the assassination of President Kennedy he was being interviewed by the French journalist Jean Daniel, who, coincidentally, had interviewed Kennedy only a few days before. According to Daniel, the Cuban dictator's immediate reaction to the news was to exclaim, *"Es una mala noticia,"* which he repeated three times, leading Daniel to believe that Castro was experiencing both shock and surprise. Then, some moments later, Castro turned to Daniel and asked, "What authority does Johnson exercise over the CIA?"

Castro's question was to raise other questions in the minds of those concerned with uncovering a possible plot to kill President Kennedy. Did it imply that Castro was fully aware that the CIA had been routinely plotting against him both with and without the authority of President Kennedy and was now wondering what the CIA would do under Johnson? Or did it imply that perhaps Castro suspected his own intelligence agency had acted without his authority in assassinating the American President, perhaps in retaliation for the CIA-Mafia and AM/LASH plots? Whatever the case, Cuba and Castro were high up on the United States government's list of suspects during the days immediately following the assassination.

No sooner was President Kennedy officially declared dead at 1 P.M. (CST) on Friday, November 22, than both the CIA and the FBI went into action to determine who was responsible for the murder. CIA Director John McCone immediately requested all agency material on Oswald, and shortly thereafter the Mexico station cabled CIA headquarters to inform them of Oswald's visit to Mexico City in late September and early October. That same evening FBI headquarters dispatched teletypes to all field offices, requesting that all FBI informants be contacted for information bearing on the assassination and further requesting that they attempt to "resolve all allegations pertaining to the assassination."

The following day, CIA headquarters cabled the AM/LASH case officer in Paris and told him to break off all contact with AM/LASH, because of the assassination of the President, and return immediately to headquarters in Washington.

That same day CIA Director McCone met with President Johnson and McGeorge Bundy and briefed them on what the Mexico station had reported on Oswald's visit to Mexico City in late September. We can well imagine the alarm Johnson and Bundy must have felt on learning that Oswald had visited both the Soviet and Cuban embassies before returning to Texas to kill Kennedy.

Later on in the day, President Johnson held his first cabinet meeting; Robert F. Kennedy arrived late. Some, including Johnson, believed the attorney general's lateness was intentional, a sign of disrespect. When Johnson mentioned Oswald's visit to the Cuban embassy in Mexico City, it must have been a terrible blow to the driving spirit behind the Kennedy vendetta against Castro, one more indication to Robert Kennedy that his and his brother's Cuban policy may have backfired in a way too horrible to imagine.

Later still, the FBI's legal attaché in Mexico City, known as the "legat," informed FBI headquarters in Washington that the U.S. ambassador to Mexico was convinced that Cubans were behind the assassination of President Kennedy and requested that "the CIA and the FBI do everything possible to establish or refute this Cuban connection." By then Mexican authorities had arrested Sylvia Duran, the Cuban embassy employee Oswald had had dealings with while he was in the Mexican capital. (She was subsequently released.) Undoubtedly news of the ambassador's opinion and Sylvia Duran's arrest was quickly transmitted to Robert Kennedy, who was already reeling from reports of Oswald's Cuban connections. Kennedy's reaction was to abdicate all responsibility concerning the investigation of his brother's murder and turn everything over to Deputy Attorney General Katzenbach and FBI Director Hoover. Hoover then sent out a cable to all FBI field offices rescinding an earlier order "to resolve all allegations pertaining to the assassination." By now the FBI did not want any more allegations investigated, much less resolved. It wanted the public to believe that Oswald was a "nut" who had acted alone.

The following day, Sunday, November 24, John McCone met with Johnson again and briefed him on what he knew about the CIA's covert operations against Cuba. It is not known whether the briefing included the AM/LASH operation, because McCone later denied having had knowledge of it at that time. McCone did know of the CIA-Mafia plots against Castro, but he apparently did not reveal them to the new President at this briefing. What he did reveal—the program of sabotage instituted first by Operation Mongoose, then followed up by the Special Group—must have made Johnson deeply suspicious that Cuba was behind the assassination.

Not long after this meeting, CIA headquarters received a cable from Mexico City stating that the U.S. ambassador to Mexico felt that the Soviets were too sophisticated to participate in a direct assassination of President Kennedy, but that the Cubans "would be stupid enough to have participated with Oswald." This news was soon communicated to Johnson and Robert Kennedy.

However, by now the Soviets were not above suspicion. Within twenty-four hours of Oswald's arrest, the FBI had discovered in its files the fact that Oswald had once defected to the Soviet Union and had declared himself to be a faithful Marxist. When this news spread, the Soviet Union went on nuclear alert and the United States followed suit, sending its force of nuclear bombers into the air. The stage was now set for World War III, and Johnson was compelled to telephone Khrushchev over the special "hot line" Kennedy had installed in the White House, to tell him that he was not going to launch a nuclear strike.

Later that same morning, the CIA's Mexican station dispatched a cable to headquarters in Washington containing the names of all known contacts of certain high-ranking Soviet personnel in Mexico City. Among the names listed in the cable was that of AM/LASH, Rolando Cubela, but since the CIA official who received the list was ignorant of the AM/LASH operation, he was unable to associate Cubela's name with it, and nothing was done about this potentially momentous information, which clearly implied Cubela might have been a double agent.

Meanwhile, AM/LASH's case officer had returned to Washington with SAS director Desmond FitzGerald and had made out a "contact report" on the November 22 meeting with AM/LASH, which he dated November 25 and in which, on instructions from FitzGerald, he omitted mention of having passed the poison pen to AM/LASH.

It was on that same day, Sunday, November 24, that Jack Ruby shot Lee Harvey Oswald in the Dallas jail. When word of this reached Robert Kennedy after a family mass for his brother in the White House, he must have realized immediately that the murder of Oswald had all the earmarks of a typical gangland slaying, and probably drew certain deeply disturbing conclusions. It now appeared that both Cuba and organized crime, Robert Kennedy's two major areas of concern as attorney general, may have been behind his brother's murder.

Meanwhile, not long after the killing of Oswald, Dallas FBI agent James Hosty, claiming he was acting on orders from a superior, J. Gordon Shanklin, destroyed a threatening note Lee Harvey Oswald had left him at his FBI office prior to the President's assassination. (Shanklin later denied any knowledge of the note.)

And in New Orleans on November 24, New Orleans District Attorney James Garrison, acting on a tip from Jack Martin, a private investigator, arrested David Ferrie, a Marcello associate and Oswald acquaintance, for possible complicity in the assassination and turned him over to the FBI for questioning. After determining that Ferrie was in a New Orleans courthouse with Carlos Marcello and his attorney, G. Wray Gill, at the time of the assassination, the FBI released Ferrie. FBI agent Regis Kennedy, the agent assigned to surveil Marcello, substantiated Ferrie's alibi. Needless to say, it seems deeply suspicious that the FBI released Ferrie so quickly after learning he was in a courthouse with the crime boss of Texas and Louisiana at the very time Marcello was being acquitted of charges brought against him by Robert Kennedy and Robert Kennedy's brother was being assassinated. Whose side was the FBI on?

Meanwhile, Lt. Francis Fruge, the police officer who had rescued injured prostitute and drug addict Rose Cheramie from a gutter near Eunice, Louisiana, the night of November 20 and had heard her prediction that President Kennedy would be killed in Dallas two days later, got in touch with the Louisiana State Hospital shortly after the assassination. He told the authorities there not to release Miss Cheramie until he had questioned her.

In 1978 the House Select Committee on Assassinations deposed both Rose Cheramie's physician, Dr. Victor Weiss, and Officer Fruge about Miss Cheramie's prediction. Weiss confirmed that Miss Cheramie had stated lucidly (while not under sedation), shortly after she had been admitted to the hospital on November 21, that "the word in the underworld" was that Kennedy would be assassinated and that the murder would occur in Dallas on November 22. Lieutenant Fruge testified that on the way to the hospital Miss Cheramie had told him that she had been driving from Florida to Dallas with two Latins. The three had stopped at the Silver Slipper lounge near Eunice for a drink and had got into an argument. She had been thrown out of the lounge by the manager. In attempting to hitchhike, she was struck by a passing car. When Fruge asked her what she was planning to do in Dallas, she replied she was going to pick up some money, pick up her baby, and kill Kennedy. (That she was supposed to pick up some money and her baby was subsequently verified.) Later, under questioning at the hospital, Cheramie told Fruge that the two Latins traveling with her from Miami had told her they were going to Dallas to kill the President. When Fruge notified the Chief of Homicide of the Dallas Police Department, Capt. Will Fritz, of Miss Cheramie's allegation, in Fruge's words, "Fritz answered he wasn't interested," allowing that he had already identified the assassin as Lee Harvey Oswald and had determined that Oswald had acted without confederates. Incredible as it seems, by this early date the lone-assassin hypothesis had become so accepted by the authorities that they had already closed their eyes to all other possible explanations of the crime. The investigation of Cheramie's allegation was then dropped and would not be revived again until New Orleans District Attorney Jim Garrison reopened the investigation of Kennedy's murder in 1967 and the House Select Committee on Assassinations began its hearings in 1976.

Meanwhile, a certain individual, later code-named "D" by the CIA, showed up at the U.S. Embassy in Mexico City and stated to embassy personnel that he had been in the Cuban consulate on September 28 and had seen Cubans pay Oswald a sum of money and talk about Oswald's assassinating someone (an allegation that was later disproved). Later that day the Mexico station dispatched a cable to CIA headquarters reminding headquarters of Castro's September 7, 1963, statement threatening U.S. leaders with retaliation if they continued to persist in plots against Cuban leaders.

On the morning of Tuesday, November 26, McCone met again with Lyndon Johnson and again they discussed the disturbing possibility that either Cuba or the Soviet Union might be behind the Kennedy assassination. At this meeting, Johnson informed McCone that he had given the FBI full authority to conduct the investigation of the assassination and directed McCone to make the CIA's resources available to assist the FBI's investigation. Not long after the meeting, the State Department received a telegram from the U.S. ambassador to Mexico, through CIA channels, giving his opinion that the Cubans were definitely behind the assassination.

By this time Robert Kennedy had apparently become persuaded that there had been a plot involving Cubans and organized crime to murder his brother, a plot that could conceivably have been in retaliation for his own policies, and this realization served to further depress him. G. Robert Blakey, who worked with Robert Kennedy in the Justice Department at the time, told me that Kennedy became "nonfunctional" to the point of ceasing to operate as attorney general. In the end he was compelled to delegate all power and authority to his deputy, Nicholas Katzenbach.

Katzenbach was in a difficult position. As the acting attorney general, it was up to him to take action on the assassination case. It was a time of high tension in Washington. Conspiracy allegations were pouring into the FBI and the CIA from all over the world. There were very real and well-founded suspicions that the governments of Cuba and the Soviet Union might have been involved in a plot to kill the President. Both the United States and the Soviet Union were on nuclear alert. Meanwhile, Hoover and the FBI were promoting the idea of Oswald as the lone assassin. Hoover had quickly realized that this theory would be far less embarrassing to the Bureau than if Oswald were a member of a conspiracy and the Bureau had failed to detect that conspiracy. Katzenbach did not know what we know today about Hoover and the FBI. Furthermore, he was unaware of the FBI's program of electronic surveillance of organized crime and of the threats against the Kennedys it had uncovered. He was also ignorant of the CIA-Mafia and AM/LASH plots. Anxious to defuse tensions, and with little reason to challenge Hoover's hasty conclusion that Oswald had acted alone, Katzenbach sent a memorandum on November 26 to presidential assistant Bill Moyers that defined the Justice Department's position on the case:

> It is important that all of the facts surrounding President Kennedy's assassination be made public in a way which will satisfy people in the United States and abroad that all the facts have

been told and that a statement to this effect be made now:

1. The public must be satisfied that Oswald was the assassin; that he did not have confederates who are still at large; and that the evidence was such that he would have been convicted at trial.
2. Speculation about Oswald's motivation ought to be cut off, and we should have some basis for rebutting thought that this was a Communist conspiracy or (as the Iron Curtain is saying) a right-wing conspiracy to blame it on the Commies.

The "lone gunman" explanation of the assassination of John F. Kennedy had begun, not as a conscious intention to obscure the facts or mislead the public, but as a sincere effort to defuse tensions and support Hoover's conclusions based on the FBI's three-day investigation of the case. It had also begun upon the default of Robert Kennedy, who, in Katzenbach's words, was simply "out of it," unable, emotionally, to pursue any line of investigation at all. As Katzenbach later stated to me, in reference to Robert Kennedy's apparent disinterest in the case: "Robert Kennedy never really wanted any investigation. I know he never read the FBI report, and I am quite sure he never read the Warren Report, even though I told him he should."

In the next few days there were more allegations of Cuban involvement in the assassination. On November 27 the FBI legat in Mexico City cabled FBI headquarters noting Castro's speech of September 7, threatening retaliation against United States leaders if they persisted in plots against Cuban leaders, and one CIA station cabled headquarters that AM/LASH had been so indiscreet in his conversations that word of his plot with the CIA might well have got back to the Cuban government. The following day, CIA cabled its Mexico station to "follow all leads," but warned the station chief in Mexico that the U.S. ambassador was pushing his case against Cuba too hard and his proposals could only lead to a "flap" with the Cubans.

By this time Lyndon Johnson appears to have wanted to avoid a flap with the Cubans at all cost. Deeply disturbed by the direction the CIA's and the FBI's investigations had been taking, Johnson became determined to set up his *own* investigation of John F. Kennedy's murder. Accordingly, after a conversation with J. Edgar Hoover the morning of November 29, Johnson ordered the formation of his own presidential commission to investigate the assassination, an unprecedented move since previous presidential assassinations had been investigated by independent judicial bodies.

Years later, in his memoirs, Johnson observed that most Americans had been prepared to believe that Lee Harvey Oswald was the lone assassin of President Kennedy until Jack Ruby silenced him in the Dallas jail. "With that single shot," wrote Johnson, "the outrage of a nation turned to skepticism and doubt. The atmosphere was poisonous and had to be cleared. I was aware of some of the implications that grew out of the skepticism and doubt. Russia was not immune to them. Neither was Cuba. Neither was Texas. Neither was the new President of the United States."

Thus, to clear the poison from the air, which, he admitted, contaminated even himself, President Johnson signed Executive Order No. 1130 on November 29, 1963, creating the President's Commission on the Assassination of President Kennedy, soon to be known as the Warren Commission after its chairman, the chief justice of the United States.

Meanwhile the FBI proceeded with *its* investigation, concluded hastily and under great pressure on December 9 with the issuance of a five-volume report indicating that Oswald was the lone assassin. On that day, Deputy Attorney General Nicholas Katzenbach, acting wholly on his own initiative, wrote each member of the Warren Commission recommending that the commission immediately issue a press release stating that the FBI report clearly showed there was no conspiracy, that Oswald was a loner.

Needless to say, most of these events between November 22 and December 9 were unknown to the press and the people and did not begin to surface until twelve years later, when the Senate began looking into the performance of the intelligence agencies in the investigation of the assassination of President Kennedy.

But whom did Robert Kennedy really think might have been behind the assassination of his brother? Judging from what evidence we have, he was deeply suspicious that there had been a conspiracy involving perhaps Jimmy Hoffa, or Cubans, or organized crime. Several days after the assassination he confided to President Johnson his suspicions about organized crime, and Johnson felt inclined to agree with him, adding that he was also deeply suspicious of Cuba.

And yet Robert Kennedy continued to disassociate himself publicly from the official investigation. In 1978 the House Select Committee on Assassinations discovered that while Robert Kennedy was remaining publicly silent and aloof from the FBI investigation, he and Kenneth O'Donnell worked behind the scenes with several close associates to investigate whether the Teamsters Union or certain members of organized crime were involved in his brother's assassination. Later, when the Warren Commission was formed, Kennedy unobtrusively arranged for the appointment of a Justice Department attorney, Charles Shaffer, to the Warren Commission so that Jimmy Hoffa's possible involvement would be closely watched. Unfortunately, however, the atmosphere of cover-up Kennedy himself had generated by refusing to concern himself with the official investigations prevented both his associates and the Warren Commission from uncovering the few leads indicating that Hoffa might have been involved.

As for Kennedy's other suspicions, about three weeks after the assassination, Arthur M. Schlesinger, Jr., confronted Robert Kennedy directly, asking what he thought about Oswald's role in the murder; Kennedy replied that there could be no serious doubt that Oswald was guilty, but there was still argument if he had done it himself or as part of a larger plot, whether organized by Castro or by the very gangsters he had been going after. Kennedy added that CIA Director John McCone had told him privately he was convinced there were two gunmen involved in the shooting.

But despite these suspicions, Robert Kennedy, as far as we know, did almost nothing about investigating the possible involvement of Castro, or Giancana, or Roselli, or Trafficante, or Marcello in his brother's murder, for he knew that if he probed these areas too deeply the CIA-Mafia plots against Castro and his slain brother's involvement with the girlfriend of two of the plotters might come to light. For the sake of the Kennedy image and his own political career he wanted to avoid that at all cost.

It would be a gross misstatement, then, to assert that Deputy Attorney General Nicholas Katzenbach and the members of the Warren Commission and the commission's staff and counsel consciously sought to cover up evidence pertaining to the assassination of John F. Kennedy. On the contrary, with one notable exception, the cover-up was perpetrated by those organizations and individuals whose responsibility it was to provide the Warren Commission with pertinent information. These were the CIA, the FBI, the Department of Defense, and Robert F. Kennedy, with the unwitting cooperation of the U.S. press, which by and large, failed to investigate what was unquestionably the most consequential crime in recent history.

The one notable exception was former CIA Director Allen W. Dulles, who was a member of the Warren Commission and who sat stone-faced through session after session, never revealing to the commission the most important information it could have received: the existence of CIA plots against Castro's life, which Dulles had authorized, and the Kennedys' possible involvement in those plots.

The question is raised: Why did Allen W. Dulles, Robert F. Kennedy, the CIA, the FBI, and the Department of Defense all withhold vital information from the Warren Commission so that it would be virtually impossible for the commission to uncover a plot, if one existed, to assassinate John F. Kennedy? The answer, I believe, is that these individuals and organizations feared that if they revealed certain information, they might suffer partial blame for the assassination or, as was the case with the FBI and the Pentagon, might be blamed for not having taken certain measures that could have prevented the assassination.

Thus, Allen W. Dulles did not reveal the existence of the CIA-Mafia plots to assassinate Castro to the commission he sat on because he feared that it might be discovered that John F. Kennedy's assassination was in retaliation for those plots, of which he, Dulles, had been the originator. (It was, of course, entirely conceivable that Oswald could have retaliated for those plots on his own initiative if he had learned of their existence.)

The same could be said for Robert F. Kennedy. He probably knew even more than Dulles. In addition to knowing about the CIA-Mafia plots, Robert Kennedy knew at least something about his brother's relationship with the girlfriend of two of the CIA-Mafia conspirators, and it is now reasonably certain that he also knew about the AM/LASH operation against Castro. Since he had been the principal force in the government both in the effort to overthrow Castro and in the war against organized crime, and since it became apparent to him soon after the assassination that both Cuba and organized crime could have been involved in the assassination, he knew that if it were discovered that Castro, or Cubans, and/or organized crime was behind his brother's murder that murder could be traced back to his own policies.

Further, if Desmond FitzGerald was indeed Robert Kennedy's personal representative when FitzGerald met AM/LASH on November 22 and passed him the poison pen, as former intelligence officers Thomas Hughes and Samuel Halpern told me he was, then he, Robert Kennedy, might well have borne a direct responsibility for his brother's murder, especially if it was true that Cubela was a Castro agent and the President's assassination had been in retaliation for the AM/LASH plot. (Unfortunately FitzGerald never lived to enlighten us on this subject—he died playing tennis with the French ambassador on July 23, 1967, long before the 1975 Senate Intelligence Committee hearings—and, of course, he was never called to testify before the Warren Commission.) In the end, then,

Robert Kennedy appeared much more comfortable with the idea that Oswald had acted alone.

Of all the individuals and agencies that prevented the Warren Commission from having the facts that it should have had, the most derelict was the CIA. In fact, several serious independent investigators have been forced to the conclusion that the CIA itself must have had a hand in the assassination.

To begin with, none of the top agency officials and case officers concerned with the CIA-Mafia and AM/LASH plots against Castro ever volunteered any information about those plots to the Warren Commission. Desmond Fitz-Gerald, in fact, withheld the existence of the AM/LASH plot from his own CIA colleague, Chief of Counterintelligence James J. Angleton, whose subordinate had been named CIA liaison with the Warren Commission.

Furthermore, when the commission requested the CIA to furnish it with its file on Oswald, the CIA delayed sending the file for four months and then sent an incomplete file. Years later, in 1975, when the Senate began investigating the CIA, it discovered that the agency had a much more substantial file on Oswald and had deliberately withheld it from the commission.

The same held true for the CIA's file on Jack Ruby. When the Warren Commission asked the agency for its file on Ruby, it was told, six months later—on September 15, 1964, just as the Warren Commission was about to announce its findings—that "an examination of Central Intelligence Agency files has produced no information on Jack Ruby or his activities." This was eventually found to be false, for thirteen years later CIA document 150–59 surfaced during the House Committee on Assassinations hearings, revealing that Ruby had probably visited none other than Santo Trafficante, Jr., in a Havana prison in 1959. Trafficante, as we know, had been contacted by John Roselli and the CIA to plot the murder of Fidel Castro.

Even the Department of Defense, division of Army Intelligence, had a hand in the cover-up. Army Intelligence had kept a file on Oswald and his alias, Hidell, but it was never brought to the attention of the Warren Commission and was shredded shortly before the 1975 hearings of the Senate Committee on Intelligence. Obviously it had contained enough significant material to show that Army Intelligence had been derelict in not bringing the file to the attention of the FBI or the Secret Service. If they had brought it to the attention of these agencies, Oswald's plan to kill Kennedy might have been thwarted.

As for the FBI, its performance in regard to the Warren Commission was nothing less than scandalous. It was Hoover who first urged that "the public must be satisfied that Oswald was the lone assassin." And it was Hoover who failed to have the Bureau investigate possible connections of the assassination to Cuba and organized crime, the two sources that promised most to reveal a possible conspiracy. It now appears that one of the reasons why Hoover directed his investigation away from Cuba and organized crime was because he knew that an arrest for complicity in the assassination of a major Mafia boss like Giancana, or Roselli, or Trafficante, or Marcello, might result in testimony at trial about the CIA-Mafia and AM/LASH plots, and both the FBI and the CIA did not want those top-secret operations revealed. Another reason why Hoover steered his investigation away from organized crime might have had something to do with the FBI's program of electronic surveillance, which Hoover may not have wanted to come to light, since it was arguably illegal.

From the very start, Hoover's relations with the Warren Commission were more those of an adversary than a partner. Not long after the commission came into being, Hoover began to investigate all the commission members and their staff and counsel so that any compromising information could be used as leverage in his dealings with them.

The FBI failed to reveal to the Warren Commission that two hours after Oswald was pronounced dead on November 24 FBI agent James P. Hosty, Jr., who had been conducting an investigation of Oswald in Dallas, flushed a threatening note he had received from Oswald down the toilet, allegedly on instructions from a superior, an event that vitiated the FBI's investigation from the start. The FBI failed to include a page from Oswald's address book listing Hosty's telephone number and auto license when it turned a copy of that address book over to the commission. It failed to reveal that Jack Ruby might have had dealings with CIA-Mafia conspirator Santo Trafficante, Jr. It failed to reveal that Hoover had disciplined seventeen FBI agents in connection with certain FBI deficiencies in the preassassination investigation of Oswald. It failed to investigate thoroughly Marcello associate David Ferrie when it questioned him, forty-eight hours after the murder, about his possible involvement in the assassination. When the FBI discovered that Oswald's uncle in New Orleans, Charles Murret, was found to have connections with organized crime, notably with the Marcello outfit, it failed to so inform the commission. It also failed to inform the commission of José Alemán's assertion that Santo Trafficante, Jr., had told him Kennedy was "going to be hit." And incredible as it seems, the FBI never told the commission about its vast electronic surveillance program, which had taped hundreds of conversations of major underworld figures during the Kennedy years, conversations revealing numerous threats against President Kennedy's life. Likewise, Hoover never told the commission about the FBI's mysterious failure to surveil electronically the two most important Mafia bosses in the south, Carlos Marcello and Santo Trafficante, Jr.

What was the reason for the FBI's withholding so much crucial information from the Warren Commission? Again it must have been fear of blame. If, for example, it was determined that the FBI had been derelict in its preassassination handling of the Oswald security case, failing to adequately assess Oswald as a possible threat to the President, the FBI would have had to accept part of the blame for the assassination. Likewise, if it was determined that organized crime had played a role in the assassination, either through Oswald or Ruby, or both, then the fact that the FBI had withheld many of the taped threats by organized crime figures against the President's life would mean the FBI would again have been vulnerable to blame for the assassination. In a similar vein, if it was determined that the Marcello organization was involved in the assassination, then the FBI's inadequate surveillance of Marcello would be called into question. Worse still, the possibility that the FBI agent who had been assigned to Marcello, Regis Kennedy, might have been on the Marcello payroll would have to be explored. It will be remembered that it was Regis Kennedy who had substantiated David Ferrie's alibi after he had been arrested for complicity in the assassination and who had subsequently released him, never bothering to investigate his possible involvement in the assassination any further.

But this is not to say that the Warren Commission itself was not derelict in its duty to leave no stone unturned in its investigation of the Kennedy and Oswald killings: It was not only derelict, but grossly inept.

The inept performance of Chief Justice Warren and certain members of his commission, such as Gerald Ford, was never more evident than in their treatment of Jack Ruby. It was obvious that if organized crime had recruited Ruby to silence Oswald and if the Dallas police had cooperated with the mob, as they had allegedly done in the past, by allowing Ruby to enter the police headquarters basement at precisely the moment when Oswald was about to be transferred to the county jail, Ruby was in mortal danger if he talked. Ruby and his lawyers were apparently suspicious that the Dallas police, acting in concert with the mob, were bugging him not only in the vicinity of his cell, but also in the room at the Dallas jail in which members of the Warren Commission questioned him. He therefore felt compelled to be very guarded in what he told his questioners, Chief Justice Warren, Representative Gerald Ford, and Commission Counsel J. Lee Rankin, because if his remarks were picked up by police electronic surveillance equipment and then transmitted to the mob he knew he would be silenced right there in jail.

Evidently Ruby was frightened to death of remaining in custody in Dallas. In testimony before Chief Justice Warren, Ruby said, "I want to tell you the truth, and I can't tell it here." "You understand my way of talking," he pleaded, "you have got to bring me to Washington," adding that his life was in danger in Dallas and his "whole family, was in jeopardy." To these pleas Warren turned a deaf ear, telling him simply that transferring him to Washington "could not be done."

Ruby then confronted Gerald Ford with the same plea. "Bring me to Washington," he begged Ford, "maybe certain people don't want to know the truth that may come out of me." Ford later remarked:

> We believe that we had fully probed from him all of the information that he had available. . . . The other members of the Commission agreed with the Chief Justice and myself that it was not necessary to bring Ruby from Dallas to Washington and to go through another interrogation of him in the nation's capital.

The truth of the matter seems to be that Chief Justice Warren did not *want* Ruby to talk any more than he did. Partial proof of this was the fact that Warren forbade the two attorneys who had been running the Warren Commision's investigation of Ruby for six months to question Ruby. They were Leon D. Hubert, Jr., and Burt W. Griffin, and they had committed the unpardonable sin of probing, in considerable detail, Ruby's activities in Cuba. That, in Warren's view, disqualified them from questioning Ruby, for, if they did, they might possibly uncover a conspiracy. Warren even reined in the otherwise unsuspecting Gerald Ford when *he* began questioning Ruby on his Cuban connections.

When Warren began winding down his inconclusive interrogation, Ruby seemed disappointed, telling the chief justice, "You can get more out of me. . . . Let's not break up too soon." Toward the end of Warren's examination of Ruby, the Dallas nightclub owner told the chief justice, "I have been used for a purpose," then reiterated his complaint that he could not reveal what that purpose was in the Dallas jail; he had to be transferred someplace where the mob could not get to him.

In the end, Ruby's protestations were to no avail. Giving up on Warren, he repeated them to others. To his psychiatrist he confessed, "I was framed into killing Oswald." To a reporter Ruby exclaimed, "If you knew the truth you would be amazed." In a lengthy television interview he declared:

> The only thing I can say—everything pertaining to what's happened has never come to the surface. The world will never know the true facts of what occurred—my motive, in other words. I am the only person in the background to know the truth pertaining to everything relating to my circumstances.

When the interviewer asked him if the truth would ever come out, Ruby replied:

> No. Because unfortunately these people, who have so much to gain and have such an ulterior motive to put me in the position I'm in, will never let the true facts come aboveboard to the world.

As it turned out, the Warren Commission failed to uncover the most important elements in the Ruby case. It failed to ascertain the significantly large extent of Ruby's connections to organized crime. It failed to investigate adequately Ruby's activities in Cuba, his gunrunning and dealings with American mobsters in Havana. It failed to develop what was ample evidence that Ruby had turned to the mob for money not long before the assassination, that prior to the assassination he had placed important phone calls to the Cosa Nostra's payoff man in Dallas, Paul Roland Jones, and to one of Jimmy Hoffa's henchmen, the six-foot five-inch, 370-pound Robert (Barney) Baker—not to mention his calls to Marcello lieutenant Nofio Pecora and reputed Giancana executioners Leonard Patrick and David Yaras. It failed to make anything of the fact that the financially strapped Ruby was seen shortly before the assassination by an officer in a Dallas bank with $7000 in cash, which he did not deposit into any account.

It failed to discover that shortly before the Kennedy assassination Ruby had bought a large safe to install in his club, the first time he had done this in his sixteen years as a Dallas nightclub operator. And it failed to discover how Ruby knew exactly *when* Oswald would be transferred to the Dallas County jail and *how* he would be transferred. (Seth Kantor, the foremost expert on Ruby, believes Ruby and certain members of the Dallas police force were in such close partnership that it may have been Ruby's appearance in the basement of police headquarters that was to be the signal to begin leading Oswald to the van that was to take him to the county jail.)

In the end, it was what the Warren Commission never learned, because of what the investigative agencies withheld, that prevented the commission from finding a conspiracy, if one existed. Marcello, Trafficante, and Hoffa, who knew each other, all had spoken to associates of assassinating one or both of the Kennedy brothers. Jack Ruby had solid connections to all three, and Oswald had solid connections to at least one, yet the Warren Commission never learned any of this.

There were many people to blame for this investigative debacle, but no one more to blame than the Kennedys themselves. By all rights, the Kennedys should have united in their determination to get to the bottom of John Kennedy's murder. Instead they did almost nothing, quietly acquiescing to Hoover's lone-gunman solution to the killing.

Apparently, in the end, few of those in power wanted to know who killed John F. Kennedy. Robert Kennedy was afraid to know. Chief Justice Earl Warren apparently only wanted to know that there was no conspiracy. And John F. Kennedy's successor, Lyndon B. Johnson, did not want to know if knowing was going to make problems. Johnson had clearly given himself away when he declared that "if certain rumors were not stopped they could lead the United States into a war which could cost forty million lives."

Of all the critics of the Warren Commission, the most eloquent was Sylvia Meagher, whose book *Accessories after the Fact* stands as a monument to what one brave and intelligent citizen can do in the face of massive deception, cowardice, and compromise:

> The Commission's failures manifest a contempt for the citizens whom this body pretended to serve—a contempt not only for their rights alone but for their intelligence. It must be said, without apology to the authors and advocates of the Warren Report that it resembles a tale told for fools, full of sophistry and deceit, signifying capitulation to compromise and the degradation of justice by its most eminent guardians.

The solution then was to offer a panacea to the American people. What this policy amounted to was a virtual surrender to the powers that might have been behind the assassination. To appreciate the consequences of this policy we need only examine what followed President Kennedy's assassination. First, a new administration came into power in the United States that would never have come into power had Kennedy lived, especially if it were true that Kennedy planned to eliminate Lyndon Johnson as his running mate in 1964. Second, the Russian-Cuban alliance became stronger than ever, the communist influence in Latin America became more pervasive, and once again Russia resumed arming Cuba to the teeth. Third, the Kennedy war against organized crime all but collapsed. When, following the assassination, a reporter asked Jimmy Hoffa about his troubles with the attorney general, Hoffa said, "Bobby Kennedy is just another lawyer now."

Hoffa was right. As Carlos Marcello had allegedly said to Edward Becker: The President was the dog, the attorney general was its tail. By chopping off the head, the dog would die, tail and all.

Beyond any doubt, organized crime in the United States benefited immensely from the assassination of John F. Kennedy. Slowly, inexorably, Robert Kennedy's anti-crime program fizzled out. In 1960 the Organized Crime and Racketeering Section attorneys spent 61 days in court,

660 days in the field, and 100 days before grand juries. In 1963, at the height of Kennedy's anticrime campaign, they spent 1081 days in court, 6177 days in the field and 1353 days before grand juries. By 1966, days in court had fallen to 606, days in the field to 3480, and days before grand juries to 373.

This partial collapse of the war on organized crime was even foreseen by the mob. On December 3, 1963, not quite two weeks after the assassination, an FBI listening device in Chicago's Armory lounge picked up a conversation between Sam Giancana and one of his lieutenants, Charles "Chuckie" English, which indicated that the Chicago mob knew only too well what would become of the FBI's crackdown on organized crime now that President Kennedy was dead. At a certain point in the conversation English said to Giancana:

> I will tell you something—in another two months from now the FBI will be like it was 5 years ago. They won't be around no more. They say the FBI will get it ["it" probably being the investigation of the President's assassination]. They're gonna start running down Fair Play for Cuba, Fair Play for Matzu. They call that more detrimental to the country than us guys.

And so it was that Robert Kennedy, in his grief and his guilt, was forced to admit to himself that in his and his brother's covert war against Cuba and open war against organized crime, both Cuba and organized crime had won. The fact that Kennedy gave up his war on organized crime and his pursuit of Castro after his brother's assassination seems to bear this out.

55. The Mysteries

IT TOOK A WHILE for the American people to begin to see through the deceptions practiced on them by those concerned with investigating the assassination of John F. Kennedy. Skepticism and doubt take time to develop, especially when people are in a state of shock. However, by the time the Warren Commission issued its final report on September 27, 1964, many people had already become deeply suspicious of the inquiry and were not disposed to accept its conclusion that Oswald had acted alone.

One of the reasons why most Americans had been so reluctant at first to accept the idea of a conspiracy was because they were so ignorant of the Kennedy administration's real, as distinguished from apparent, activities. They had been fed by the Kennedy publicity machine and an overobliging press such a relentless diet of adulatory prose about the Kennedys, and had been seduced so often by the President's dazzling press conferences and his and the First Lady's even more dazzling public appearances, that they had no idea there was anything seething beneath the glittering surface of the administration that would cause any group or combination of groups to conspire to kill the President. The reality, however, as we now know, was that the Kennedy brothers had been playing some very dangerous games, and almost no one, not even some of their closest aides and advisers, knew anything about them.

It was not until about a year after President Kennedy's death that people began to question seriously the investigation of the assassination. When the *Warren Report* finally came out, it was immediately denounced by a variety of critics. Soon books on the investigation began appearing that successfully challenged the methods, assumptions, and conclusions of the commission, and suggested valid reasons why some groups may have wanted to kill President Kennedy. The most convincing of these were Edward J. Epstein's *Inquest: The Warren Commission and the Establishment of Truth* and Sylvia Meagher's *Accessories after the Fact: The Warren Commission, the Authorities and the Report.* As a result of these books and others, there developed, by the mid-to-late sixties, a substantial body of public opinion disposed to believe that the Warren Commission's report was, at best, a tranquilizer and, at worst, a cover-up.

An investigation into the assassination conducted by New Orleans District Attorney Jim Garrison in 1967–1968, which resulted in actual arrests and indictments, did little to clarify all the questions that surrounded the crime. Garrison's accusations were, by and large, without foundation, and his principal suspect, New Orleans businessman Clay Shaw, was acquitted in 1969. Garrison did, however, uncover a plausible conspirator in David Ferrie, the Marcello associate whom witnesses had seen with Oswald on several occasions during the summer of 1963, and who, it will be remembered, had been briefly detained for questioning by the FBI forty-eight hours after the assassination. Ferrie, it was discovered, had made a mysterious trip to Texas and back the weekend of November 22–24, after having been present in a New Orleans courthouse with Carlos Marcello and his lawyer on the morning of November 22 when the Mafia chieftain was acquitted of charges brought against him by the Justice Department. One of the strange things Ferrie did before his weekend trip to Texas was to go to Oswald's former landlady in New Orleans and ask her whether she had come across his, Ferrie's, library card. (Marcello's lawyer, G. Wray Gill, had apparently told one of Ferrie's friends he had learned that the card had been found on Oswald shortly after his arrest. How Gill learned this was never determined.) It was also discovered that, the day before Ruby shot Oswald, Ruby had made a phone call to someone in Galveston; Ferrie had made a collect call to Carlos Marcello from Galveston. In 1967, eleven days after Garrison announced the imminent arrest of Ferrie for complicity in the Kennedy assassination, Ferrie died of an apparent brain hemorrhage, which Garrison characterized as a suicide because Ferrie had left two typed "suicide notes." Although Garrison made out a somewhat plausible circumstantial case to implicate Ferrie in a possible assassination conspiracy, he failed to make any mention of Ferrie's connection to the Marcello organization or of the possibility that Marcello himself could have been involved in the conspiracy. According to an FBI informant, in 1967 Garrison had accepted a $5000 gambling credit and free hotel accommodations from a Marcello operative who managed a Las Vegas casino. However, Garrison later denied any wrongdoing in connection with this alleged incident. Also in 1967, Garrison had a meeting in Las Vegas with Johnny Roselli, according to a report by the CIA Inspector General (cited in notes to the Assassinations Committee report).

During the course of Garrison's investigation the mysterious case of Rose Cheramie was revived, having remained relatively dormant for four years. (Miss Cheramie had died a violent death in September 1965, a month after volunteering her story to the FBI.) To reinvestigate the case, Garrison invited Lt. Francis Fruge of the Louisiana State Police to join his staff. Garrison and Fruge wanted to find out who the two men were who had been driving to Dallas with Miss Cheramie the evening of November 20 and who allegedly had told her they were going to Dallas to kill the President.

Accordingly, Fruge went to the Silver Slipper lounge, where Cheramie and her companions had stopped for a drink, and questioned the bar owner, Mac Manual, about Rose's companions. Fruge showed Manual a stack of photographs, some of which were of suspected assassination conspirators, others of which had been selected at random, asking him if he could identify any of them. The bar owner then chose photographs of two Cuban exiles, Sergio Arcacha Smith and a man called Osanto. Arcacha Smith was known to the district attorney's office as a former head of the New Orleans Cuban Revolutionary Front, a friend of David Ferrie, and a beneficiary of Carlos Marcello's financial contributions to the anti-Castro movement—an intriguing set of associations. After the collapse of the Garrison probe, which had been subjected to a merciless media attack, the investigation of Rose Cheramie and her Cuban friends was temporarily abandoned. The House Committee on Assassinations revived the case in 1978 and established beyond reasonable doubt that Rose Cheramie had indeed predicted the Kennedy assassination down to its date and place. However, when the committee deposed Sergio Arcacha Smith, the Cuban exiles' leader denied ever knowing Cheramie. It was clear to the committee that because Captain Fritz of the Dallas police had so quickly embraced the lone-assassin hypothesis, and had therefore refused to investigate Cheramie's allegations, any chance of establishing who her two companions might have been had long ago been lost. Thus the mystery of Rose Cheramie remains.

Although the Garrison inquiry was eventually discredited, and Garrison's chief suspect, New Orleans businessman Clay Shaw, was acquitted of conspiring to kill President Kennedy, the New Orleans District Attorney did turn up some testimony on the autopsy at Bethesda that future investigators of the assassination were to find disturbingly relevant. For it was during the Garrison probe that it was first publicly stated by one of the Army autopsy surgeons, Col. Pierre Finck, that "someone" of higher rank than the autopsy surgeons had prevented the tracking of the wound in the President's back and neck during the Bethesda autopsy. Later, during the investigation of the House Select Committee on Assassinations, FBI special agent Francis O'Neill testified that "Mrs. Kennedy had given permission for a partial autopsy and that Dr. Burkley, the President's physician, reiterated her remarks in the autopsy room." At the same time, special agent James

Sibert testified that he "had the impression the Kennedy family was somehow transmitting step-by-step clearances to the pathologists." Despite this testimony, the committee was unable to determine with certainty precisely why the President's wound through the back and neck was not tracked.

It is now widely believed that either Jacqueline Kennedy or Robert Kennedy told one of the high-ranking military officers in the autopsy room to prevent the dissection of the wound for reasons that are still unclear. Because of this, there has been controversy ever since over which puncture was of entry and which was of exit.

How did Robert Kennedy react to the Garrison investigation? As with the Warren Commission's investigation, he stayed clear of it, even though he must have been well aware of some of its potentially distressing implications. According to Arthur Schlesinger, when Robert Kennedy asked his Senate staff member Frank Mankiewicz whether he thought Garrison was onto something significant, and Mankiewicz started to tell him some of the things the New Orleans district attorney was turning up, Kennedy interrupted him, saying, "Well, I don't think I want to know."

In the end, Jim Garrison had seemed to be "onto something" but for some still inexplicable reason one of the potentially most important things he was onto—Ferrie's connection to the Marcello organization—was ignored. For example, in 1978 the House Committee on Assassinations discovered that only a few months after the Kennedy assassination the hitherto impecunious Ferrie had turned up as the owner of a Louisiana service station franchise, with none other than Carlos Marcello as backer. Garrison may have suspected that this was a payoff for Ferrie's possible role in the assassination because after his death he had confiscated business papers relating to Ferrie's ownership of the gas station. Still, he refrained from implicating Marcello in the assassination plot.

Eventually the Garrison probe ended ignominiously in a hail of media scorn, and the cause of the Warren Commission critics received a severe setback. It was not until the Senate Committee on Intelligence began uncovering the most shocking secrets of the Kennedy years in its 1975–1976 hearings that public opinion became so aroused against the *Warren Report* that it was only a matter of time before another investigation of President Kennedy's assassination was undertaken. In September of 1976, Congress established, staffed, and funded the House Select Committee on Assassinations, and a new investigation was begun.

In the meantime, several people who might have been involved in the assassination or who could have possibly given important testimony about it were murdered or committed suicide, thus lending further justification for a new effort to uncover a possible conspiracy.

Sam Giancana was the first to go. Staff members of the Senate Committee on Intelligence arrived in Chicago on July 19, 1975, to arrange for Giancana to appear before the committee in Washington five days later. He was to testify about his role in the Castro assassination plots. That same evening, around 10 P.M., Giancana was in the basement den of his Chicago home cooking sausage, escarole, and beans when the person he was with shot him seven times, first in the back of the head, then in the mouth and neck, a typical Mafia slaying of someone who had talked or might be planning to talk. The Chicago police suspected that Tony Accardo's gang was behind the murder, but Giancana's daughter, Antoinette, was sure her father had been killed by "the same people responsible for killing the Kennedys"—in her view, the CIA. As it turned out, the only solid clue in the case was the discovery that the gun used in the slaying came from Miami, which pointed toward Cubans, or possibly the Tampa-Havana gang of fellow conspirator, Santo Trafficante, Jr.

Jimmy Hoffa was next. Hoffa, a prime suspect in the Kennedy assassination, had received a grant of executive clemency from President Richard Nixon on December 23, 1971, on condition he not engage in labor union management of any kind. On July 30, 1975, eleven days after Giancana's murder, Hoffa went to an early afternoon appointment with, he thought, New Jersey Teamsters official

Anthony Provenzano and Detroit mobster Anthony Giacalone at the Red Fox restaurant outside Detroit. Hoffa
was never heard of again. Both Provenzano and Giacalone
failed to show up for the appointment and produced air-
tight alibis as to their whereabouts that afternoon. A U.S.
government informant associated with organized crime has
since declared that Hoffa was picked up at the restaurant
by someone he knew and trusted and was driven to a house
in the country, where he was murdered, stuffed in a fifty-
five-gallon oil drum, and transported by truck to a junkyard
where his body was crushed in a compactor for wrecked
cars destined to become scrap metal. Law enforcement
authorities believe that Hoffa was killed by the mob because he was trying to regain his power in the Teamsters
Union, despite the conditions imposed in Nixon's grant of
clemency. But in an interview on October 25, 1976, Hoffa's
attorney, William Bufalino, told author Dan Moldea he
believed the murder was related to Hoffa's possible early
participation in the CIA-Mafia plots against Castro. "Tell
the FBI to look into the CIA. And tell the CIA to look
into the FBI," Bufalino told Moldea. Whatever the case,
the crime was never solved. (As to Hoffa's participation
in the CIA-Mafia plots, Richard Helms told me he did not
believe it was true.)

Then came Johnny Roselli's turn. Roselli had already
begun to talk. In late January 1967, he had his lawyer get
in touch with *Washington Post* columnist Drew Pearson to
tell him he had important information to reveal about the
Kennedy assassination. The lawyer claimed that he represented someone who had been engaged by the CIA to
assassinate Fidel Castro, without revealing who that someone was, and that the Kennedy assassination had been in
retaliation for that plot.

After many delays, two FBI agents interviewed Roselli's lawyer, then drew up a "blind memorandum" reporting the interview, which was later summarized by the
Senate Committee on Intelligence as follows:

   1. The lawyer had information pertaining to
      the assassination, but it was necessary for

him in his capacity as an attorney to invoke the attorney-client privilege since the information in his possession was derived as a result of that relationship.

2. His clients, who were on the fringe of the underworld, were neither directly nor indirectly involved in the death of President Kennedy, but they faced possible prosecution in a crime not related to the assassinaton and through participation in such crime they learned of information pertaining to the President's assassination.

3. His clients were called upon by a governmental agency to assist in a project which was said to have the highest governmental approval. The project had as its purpose the assassination of Fidel Castro. Elaborate plans were made including the infiltration of the Cuban government and the placing of informants within key posts in Cuba.

4. The project almost reached fruition when Castro became aware of it; by pressuring captured subjects he was able to learn the full details of the plot against him and decided "if that was the way President Kennedy wanted it, he too could engage in the same tactics."

5. Castro thereafter employed teams of individuals who were dispatched to the United States for the purpose of assassinating President Kennedy. The lawyer stated that his clients obtained this information "from 'feedback' furnished by sources close to Castro," who had been initially placed there to carry out the original project.

6. His clients were aware of the identity of some of the individuals who came to the United States for this purpose, and he understood that two such individuals were now in the state of New Jersey.

7. One client, upon hearing the statement that Lee Harvey Oswald was the sole assassin of President Kennedy, "laughs with tears in his eyes and shakes his head in apparent disagreement."

8. The lawyer stated if he were free of the attorney-client privilege, the information that he would be able to supply would not directly identify the alleged conspirators to kill President Kennedy. However, because of the project to kill Fidel Castro, those participating in the project, whom he represents, developed through feedback information that would identify Fidel Castro's counterassassins in this country who could very well be considered suspects in such a conspiracy.

Meanwhile, Robert Kennedy had received word of Roselli's allegations and had his secretary phone J. Edgar Hoover to request a copy of CIA official Sheffield Edwards's memorandum of May 7, 1962, briefing Robert Kennedy on the Castro assassination plots. Apparently Kennedy wanted to see whether the wording of Edwards's memorandum could exonerate him from condoning the plots.

A few days later, on March 6 and 7, Drew Pearson's and Jack Anderson's columns published Roselli's allegations (without giving the name of the source) and the public became informed of the CIA-Mafia plots against Castro for the first time. Most people did not believe them, and Pearson was showered with criticism for having published such outrageous allegations.

Finally, the FBI's memorandum on Roselli's allegations was submitted to President Johnson on March 21. As soon as he read it, Johnson asked the CIA and the FBI for information on the CIA's plots to kill Castro, which he had apparently known little or nothing about. The following day an aghast Lyndon Johnson met with CIA director Richard Helms, who briefed him on the CIA-Mafia plots and, sketchily, on the AM/LASH operation, which, he told the President, had been condoned in principle by the Kennedy brothers. Johnson then ordered Helms to have the CIA's inspector general prepare a full report of all the CIA plots to murder Castro. This was done, and on May 23 Helms personally brought the report to Johnson and briefed him "orally on the contents."

It was after this meeting that a deeply shocked Lyndon Johnson became firmly convinced that President Kennedy had been murdered in retaliation for his government's plots to kill Fidel Castro. Later, Johnson told television newsman Howard K. Smith, "I'll tell you something that will rock you. Kennedy was trying to get Castro, but Castro got him first."

Strange as it may seem, however, nothing official was ever done about Roselli's revelations. After distributing the memorandum to the President and other high-ranking officials in the Johnson administration, the FBI decided not to investigate the allegations and calmly shelved the whole matter. J. Edgar Hoover was apparently still intent on protecting the Bureau's conclusion that Oswald had acted alone.

Nevertheless, Roselli had talked, and he was to talk again, to columnist Jack Anderson, and to certain U.S. senators when he appeared as a witness before the Senate Committee on Intelligence in 1975 and 1976. To Jack Anderson, Roselli confided that he believed Cubans once associated with Santo Trafficante, Jr., using Oswald as a decoy, had killed the President and that the fatal shot had been fired from close range, implying that it had come from the grassy knoll. To the Senate Committee on Intelligence he told in two hearings a good deal of what he knew about his and Giancana's and Trafficante's roles in the CIA-Mafia murder plots against Castro, and at a third top-secret hearing, held on April 23, 1976, in a suite at the Carroll Arms Hotel in Washington, he told representatives of the committee and Senator Richard Schweiker all he claimed he knew about the Kennedy assassination, indicating he believed Cubans associated with Castro and Trafficante were behind the crime.

Three months later and about ten days after a dinner in Miami with Santo Trafficante, Jr., Roselli disappeared without a trace. Then, one day in August 1976, some fishermen in Dumfoundling Bay, near Miami, found a fifty-five-gallon oil drum with a partially decomposed body inside it. The corpse, whose legs had been sawed off to accommodate it to the oil drum, was later identified as Johnny Roselli. He had apparently been cruising on a yacht with some friends and a stranger from Chicago when the man from Chicago strangled him, sawed off his legs, and crammed him into the oil drum with the help of accomplices on board. It was never found out who the murderer, or murderers, were, but a Mafia informant later told the investigators that he believed a Trafficante associate lured Roselli onto the yacht, and the House Committee on Assassinations, which investigated the crime, came to suspect that Trafficante had had a hand in the killing. On February 27, 1977, in a front-page article in the *New York Times*, Nicholas Gage wrote that "two men known to have had personal knowledge of the circumstances of the murder, provided solid information that Mr. Roselli was killed by members of the underworld as a direct result of his testimony before the Senate Committee." If Giancana was the first prospective witness before a Senate committee to be murdered, Roselli was the first actual witness to be killed for his testimony.

After Roselli it was George de Mohrenschildt. While the de Mohrenschildts were in Haiti they had received a postcard from Oswald, mailed from New Orleans, that contained just a conventional greeting. But when they returned to Dallas in 1967 they found that Oswald had left them a copy of the photograph Marina had taken of him dressed in black, pistol at his side, and holding a rifle. On the back was inscribed, "To my friend George from Lee Oswald 5/IV/63" and, in Russian, "Hunter of Fascists, ha-ha-ha!" The Russian words appeared to be in Marina Oswald's handwriting. Ten years later, on the very day a representative of the House Select Committee on Assassinations was going to question him about the assassination of the President, George de Mohrenschildt apparently committed suicide. He had just been interviewed extensively by a Dutch journalist, Willem Oltmans. Not long afterwards, de Mohrenschildt's nephew, Eddie Hooker, with whom he had been in business in Dallas, also committed suicide, leaving no explanatory note. In April 1977 Oltmans told the Associated Press and NBC that de Mohrenschildt had told him that he and Oswald had been hired by anti-Castro forces and Dallas oilmen to assassinate Kennedy and that he, de Mohrenschildt, had been "very, very much involved," an assertion that most investigators have concluded was without foundation.

After de Mohrenschildt's death a manuscript of a book George was writing about his relationship with Lee Harvey Oswald entitled *I Am a Patsy! I Am a Patsy!* was found among his possessions. Among other things, the manuscript asserted a belief in Oswald's innocence and told of a meeting the de Mohrenschildts had with the Auchinclosses at Merrywood in early 1964, at the time George was testifying before the Warren Commission. The unpublished manuscript is now part of the record of the House Select Committee's investigation of the assassination of John F. Kennedy.

"Janet, [de Mohrenschildt said] you were Jack Kennedy's mother-in-law, and I am a complete stranger. I would spend my own money and lots of my time to find out who were the real assassins or the conspirators. Don't you want any further investigation? You have infinite resources."

"Jack is dead and nothing will bring him back," replied she decisively.

"Since he was a very beloved President, I wouldn't let a stone unturned to make sure that the assassin is found and punished," implored Jeanne [Mrs. de Mohrenschildt]. "We both have grave doubts in Lee's guilt."

Later we discussed for a long time why a woman so close to President Kennedy, and likewise nor [sic] Robert Kennedy and the rest of the Kennedy family, would be so adamant on this subject. . . . Would it be possible, as much as it sounds like a sacrilege, that Lee was a "convenient" assassin to all the relatives and friends of the late President Kennedy? Convenient not in any derogatory sense but just because he was a *patsy*, a patsy not involved in any revenge arising out of JFK's biggest and costliest mistake—the Bay of Pigs.

Isn't it better to think, maybe subconsciously, that the assassin was a crazy, semiliterate, ex-Marine with an undesirable discharge, screwed-up, Marxist lunatic with a poverty-stricken childhood, unsuccessful in his pursuits both in USSR and in USA—and with a record of marriage verging on disastrous. It's better to hold this belief for them and for the rest of the country rather than to find out that the assassination was a devilishly clever act of revenge caused by the Bay of Pigs disaster. . . .

This would explain Lee's desperate scream: "I am a patsy!"

But we were still in the Auchincloss's luxurious mansion, about ready to leave. "Incidentally," said Mrs. Auchincloss coldly, "my daughter Jacqueline never wants to see you again because you were close to her husband's assassin."

"It's her privilege," I answered.

De Mohrenschildt concluded his narrative by protesting Lee Oswald's innocence, writing, "The Kennedy family did not want to pursue the matter of finding the real, unquestionable assassin, or a conspiracy. And they could have done it with their own immense, private resources. If somebody would kill my son or my brother, I certainly would want to be sure who did it. But possibly the personality of Lee Harvey Oswald suited perfectly the political purposes of the Kennedy family."

★   ★

What is the truth about this long tale of murder and suicide? Is there a truth we can know? Who killed President John F. Kennedy?

After two years of exhaustive, painstaking investigations led by G. Robert Blakey, the House Select Committee on Assassinations found that Lee Harvey Oswald had fired the shots that killed the President from the sixth floor of the Texas Book Depository, but that another gunman, believed to have been situated on the grassy knoll, also fired on the President, and missed. In the words of its final report, the committee determined that "on the basis of the evidence available to it John F. Kennedy was probably assassinated as a result of a conspiracy." However, the report concluded, "the committee was unable to identify the other gunman or the extent of the conspiracy." The decisive factor that led the committee to conclude that there had "probably" been a conspiracy was the testimony of acoustics experts, who, after analyzing a police dictabelt recording of the sounds in Dealey Plaza at the time of the assassination, testified that four shots had been fired, three from the Texas Book Depository and one from the grassy knoll.

The committee's determination that Oswald had indeed fired the shots that killed the President ruled out the widely held belief that Oswald had been a decoy, or a patsy, who had been framed by others to take the blame for the crime, a belief that the author still regards as extremely persuasive.

Among its secondary findings, the House committee concluded that neither the CIA, nor the FBI, nor the Secret Service, nor the government of Cuba, nor the government of the Soviet Union, nor any of the major Cuban exiles organizations, nor the Mafia *commissione* had been behind the assassination, but that these findings did not preclude the possibility that individual members of those organizations and institutions, acting on their own, could have been involved.

Of all the possible participants in a conspiracy to assassinate the President, the committee came to suspect that certain organized crime families, acting unilaterally, were the most likely to have been involved. The committee, in fact, delved into this possibility more intensively than any other and, in a most comprehensive investigation, succeeded in discovering many hitherto unknown associations between certain organized crime families and both Oswald and Ruby—especially Ruby, who, it was found, had been in contact with associates of the Giancana, Trafficante, and Marcello crime organizations during the months immediately preceding the assassination.

The committee noted, however, that conspiracy to commit murder is one of the most difficult crimes to prove, especially when, as is generally the case with Mafia executions, the originator of the plot is many persons removed from the individual who actually carries out the murder. Since, as of the date of the final report of the House Select Committee on Assassinations (March 29, 1979), no unimpeachable witnesses to a possible conspiracy had been found, the exact nature of the conspiracy, if one existed, was not discovered. With Oswald, Ruby, Ferrie, Cheramie, Hoffa, Giancana, Roselli, and de Mohrenschildt all dead and so many trails gone cold, it is now unlikely that the precise nature of the conspiracy, if one existed, will *ever* be discovered, much less proved.

Arthur M. Schlesinger, Jr., has aptly called the assassination of John F. Kennedy "a quagmire for historians." And so it is. Because of the gross deficiencies of the original investigations of the crime, Robert Kennedy's fear of uncovering facts that could damage his brother's reputation, Johnson's fear of discovering a conspiracy involving Cuba and the Soviet Union, the dishonesty of the FBI and the CIA, the cover-up of the CIA-Mafia plots by Allen Dulles and others, the inherent difficulties in proving conspiracy, and the fact that so many of the trails have turned cold and so many of the principals, and possible conspirators, have died, any historian trying to get to the truth of the Kennedy assassination is bound to sink into a quicksand of suspicions, contradictions, and enigmas.

However, we can at least safely say at this point that it is now certain that those responsible for conducting the original investigations of President Kennedy's assassination were not motivated by a sincere desire to get to the bottom of the crime, but by many other considerations, ranging from the desire to defuse tensions, both national and international (Katzenbach and Johnson), to the desire to avoid blame (Robert Kennedy, J. Edgar Hoover, Allen Dulles), to the desire to protect secrets and reputations (RFK, Dulles, the FBI, and the CIA). The House Select Committee on Assassinations did much to make up for prior obstructions to justice but was still not able to resolve doubt into certainty.

Nor have the most recent major books on the assassination been able to uncover all the unknowns, though they have made substantial progress in uncovering important facts overlooked by other investigators and have cleared up many former mysteries. Such serious, diligent, and able investigators as Sylvia Meagher, Edward Jay Epstein, Peter Dale Scott, Harold Weisberg, Seth Kantor, Anthony Summers, David Lifton, and G. Robert Blakey have braved Schlesinger's "quagmire" to make important contributions to our understanding of the crime.

Nevertheless, many mysteries remain. And they are likely to remain forever unless the Justice Department reopens the case and actual indictments are brought against suspected conspirators and witnesses are heard before a jury, something that does not seem likely to happen in the foreseeable future.

What are some of the major mysteries surrounding the Kennedy assassination that have never been entirely cleared up, by the Warren Commission, the House Select Committee, or the major private investigators of the assassination?

First, there is the mystery of Yuri Nosenko. On January 23, 1964, a KGB officer by the name of Yuri Nosenko informed a CIA agent in Geneva that he had important information to turn over to the CIA and desired to defect to the United States. Nosenko had a family in the Soviet Union and had enjoyed a successful career in the KGB, but he claimed he could no longer stand Soviet society. He had been the official supervisor of the KGB file on Lee

Harvey Oswald since Oswald's defection to the Soviet Union in 1959, and he could therefore inform the CIA of Oswald's relationship to Soviet intelligence.

As it turned out, Nosenko informed the CIA that "it was decided that Oswald was of no interest whatsoever, so the KGB recommended that he go home to the United States." As for Marina Oswald, Nosenko reported "she already had anti-Soviet characteristics. She was not too smart anyway and not an educated person. . . . The Soviets were glad to get rid of them both."

At the time this information was delivered to the CIA, the Warren Commission was just about to commence its hearings. It was immediately obvious to all concerned that Nosenko's testimony could account for Oswald's years in Russia and could conceivably exonerate the KGB and Chairman Khrushchev from any involvement in a plot to murder the American President.

Nosenko was eventually brought to Washington where the CIA's Richard Helms officially authorized Nosenko's defection to the United States, despite certain misgivings. Helms's misgivings were essentially those of the CIA's office of counterintelligence, which feared that Nosenko could well be a Soviet agent sent by the KGB to misinform the CIA and the Warren Commission about Oswald's activities in the Soviet Union. If this were true, the implications would be deeply disturbing. It would signify that the Soviet Union was trying to establish a "legend" for Oswald to cover up the fact that he was, in reality, an agent of the KGB.

After a good deal of discussion within the confines of CIA headquarters at Langley, it was decided that before allowing Nosenko to testify before the Warren Commission it would be wise to have him questioned by the CIA's chief of counterintelligence, James Jesus Angleton. Nosenko was then placed, illegally, in a CIA detention facility and subjected to relentless interrogation, including what is known in intelligence circles as "hostile interrogation," while in solitary confinement. In the end, James Jesus Angleton, a brilliant man who had once edited the poetry review *Furioso*, where he had worked with T. S. Eliot and

Ezra Pound, found so many holes in Nosenko's story that he came to the conclusion that he could not vouch for the defector's bona fides and that Nosenko could well be a Soviet agent sent over to misinform the CIA and the Warren Commission.

Unfortunately, this disturbing conclusion was reached too late to influence the Warren Commission. When the CIA informed Chief Justice Warren of Angleton's assessment of Nosenko, Warren, who was working against a deadline set by President Johnson, chose to disregard it and did not include the Nosenko affair in his final report.

Finally, in 1967, long after the *Warren Report* came out, Nosenko was officially declared by the CIA to be a Soviet disinformation agent. However, in 1976 this position was reversed, in what certain CIA officials called a "grotesque travesty," and Nosenko's bona fides were at last established. He was then given a job as a "consultant" to the CIA.

The Nosenko case still remains one of the great mysteries surrounding the Kennedy assassination. If Nosenko was a genuine defector and his information about the KGB's files on Oswald was true, then it could be assumed Oswald was not acting in behalf of the KGB when he assassinated President Kennedy. If, on the other hand, Nosenko was a Soviet disinformation agent sent to "defect" to the United States in order to misinform the Warren Commission, it meant that the Soviet government probably had something to hide. Since the 1976 report rehabilitating Nosenko was, and is still, so controversial, the mystery as to the nature of Nosenko's mission remains.

Another major mystery concerns what exactly Oswald did during his trip to Mexico City in late September and early October of 1963. One of the people he met with at the Soviet Embassy was Valery Kostikov, an official of the KGB attached to the infamous Thirteenth Division, the section concerned with political assassination and sabotage. Another person he met was Luisa Calderon, an employee of the Cuban Embassy in Mexico City, believed to be a member of the Cuban Directorate General of Intelligence, who, the CIA later claimed, was alleged to have expressed foreknowledge of the Kennedy assassination to her fellow embassy employees. Did Oswald visit the Cuban and Soviet embassies in Mexico City to obtain a transit visa for Cuba and to clear the way for eventual permission to return to the Soviet Union, or was he receiving instructions from the Soviets and the Cubans concerning his forthcoming mission to assassinate the President of the United States? And, if he was about to murder the American President, what was he doing trying to obtain visas to enter Cuba and the Soviet Union? Was he perhaps simply lining up his postassassination escape route? When allegedly halted by Officer Tippit after the assassination he appeared to be on his way to a Greyhound bus station from which he could catch a bus to the Mexican border. Once in Mexico, with a Cuban visa in hand, he could eventually find refuge in Cuba, and then perhaps take a plane from Havana to Moscow. In any case, the precise nature of Oswald's activities in Mexico City, prior to the assassination, is still a mystery.

The precise nature of Oswald's relationship to George de Mohrenschildt is also a mystery. Was de Mohrenschildt simply Oswald's friend, mentor, and surrogate father, or did he function in some intelligence capacity as well, perhaps as Oswald's "babysitter"? It is known that de Mohrenschildt had worked for French and Polish intelligence and that he was an acquaintance of J. Walton Moore, employed by the CIA's domestic contacts division in Dallas at the time de Mohrenschildt knew Oswald. He had even allegedly consulted Moore as to whether it was "safe" for him to recruit Oswald. (In 1977 Moore acknowledged he knew de Mohrenschildt, but denied he ever spoke with him about Oswald.) And there is some circumstantial evidence that he may have been a low-level agent of the CIA, though the CIA has denied it and the House Assassinations Committee has declared he was not. In any case, it is beyond dispute that de Mohrenschildt exercised considerable influence over Oswald. Did de Mohrenschildt really commit suicide? The evidence that he did is purely circumstantial. It will be remembered that his apparent suicide occurred on the very day a member of the House

Select Committee on Assassinations was going to question him about the Kennedy murder.

And what of Sam Giancana, Jimmy Hoffa, and Johnny Roselli? Were any involved in a conspiracy to blackmail or murder the President, and/or murder Lee Oswald? And why were Giancana, Hoffa, and Roselli murdered, and who murdered them? Were their murders connected, in any way, to the murder of the President? What passed between John F. Kennedy, Robert F. Kennedy, Sam Giancana, Jimmy Hoffa, and Johnny Roselli that we still do not know? It is worth mentioning, at this point, that the House assassinations committee chose not to explore the implications of the Kennedy-Campbell-Giancana-Roselli relationship and did not call either Judith Campbell or Frank Sinatra to testify to what they might have known. (Committee staff members did, however, review Miss Campbell's 1975 Senate testimony.) In the committee's own words, since President Kennedy "embodied aspects of the best characteristics of the American spirit," it chose to present the results of its investigation in a "dignified manner" in keeping "with the memory of a great leader." This attitude obviously precluded any delving into what might have been an unflattering side of Kennedy's life and administration.

And what of that other CIA plot to assassinate Castro, the AM/LASH operation? Was it, in any way, related to the Kennedy assassination? Several members of the Senate Committee on Intelligence came to believe that it possibly was related. However, the matter still remains a mystery. To this day no one is quite sure whether the AM/LASH operation did, in fact, backfire on its planners.

What is known is that Rolando Cubela was eventually arrested and sentenced to life imprisonment "for acts against the Cuban government." However, the government of Cuba has declared that it did not know who AM/LASH was until 1966, and when assassinations committee members interviewed Cubela in prison, Cubela told them that he did not believe Castro knew of the AM/LASH plot at the time of the Kennedy assassination. This was, in turn, challenged by the testimony of Joseph Langosch, the chief of counterintelligence of the CIA's special affairs staff in 1963. Langosch, whose section had been in charge of the AM/LASH operation, testified before the House assassinations committee that as of 1962 it was highly possible that Cuban intelligence was aware of AM/LASH, his seditious intentions, and his association with the CIA. If this was so, Cuban intelligence had a clear motive for killing President Kennedy. As of this writing, the issue has not been resolved. Despite the conclusion of several members of the Senate Committee on Intelligence, the House Committee on Assassinations in its final report of 1979 was unable to convincingly link the AM/LASH plot to a retaliatory plot against President Kennedy.

Other mysteries. Why wasn't Oswald questioned by the CIA on his return from the Soviet Union? Why did the White House order the interior of the presidential limousine destroyed before it could be examined by the Warren Commission? Why was the copy of the Zapruder film of the assassination that was examined by the Warren Commission cut and spliced by the FBI so that frames 208 to 212 and 334 to 434 were missing and a splice with frame reversals appeared at the frames where the commission believed Kennedy received his first bullet wound? And why did the commission ignore over twenty reliable witnesses who testified that they heard shots and/or saw puffs of smoke coming from the grassy knoll? (By the 1976–1979 investigation some sixty witnesses had testified to shots coming from the knoll.)

And where did the bullet come from that hit the curbstone near the triple underpass and wounded Dallas citizen James T. Tague? Neither the Warren Commission nor the House assassinations committee was able to resolve this mystery.

Another mystery concerns the possible alteration of the President's body between the time it was removed from Parkland Hospital and the time the autopsy was performed at Bethesda Naval Hospital. The crux of this mystery lies in the glaring discrepancy between descriptions of the President's wounds—between the descriptions submitted by the Parkland Hospital doctors and the FBI, both of which suggested more than one assassin had fired on the President, and that submitted by the doctors who performed the autopsy at Bethesda, which version was subsequently incorporated in the *Warren Report* without benefit of the autopsy surgeon's original notes (which were destroyed immediately after the autopsy) or the autopsy x-rays, photographs, and specimens, which were retained by the Kennedy family. The discrepancy was important because upon the descriptions hung the question of whether there was more than one assassin operating in Dealey Plaza on November 22. The FBI's description pointed toward two gunmen, the autopsy toward only one. After fifteen years of painstaking research on the subject, David S. Lifton, a computer engineer on the Apollo space program, produced in 1980 a book entitled *Best Evidence*, in which he contended, in a long and well-documented argument, that President Kennedy's body had been surgically altered between the time it left Parkland Hospital in Texas and the time the autopsy was performed at Bethesda Naval Hospital in Maryland, so that the nature of Kennedy's wounds observed at Bethesda would substantiate the contention they were caused by just one assassin. This conclusion led Lifton to believe that the plot to kill the President originated "in the highest levels of the United States government," and was "a covert operation." "I myself think," he wrote toward the end of this book, "that a sophisticated appraisal of the evidence must force one to the conclusion that there was a plot involving the executive branch of the government to remove Kennedy from office." Lifton ended his book with this chilling line: "Some time during Kennedy's thousand days, a secret veto was cast on his presidency and on his life."

David Lifton's suspicions suggest that future investigators into the assassination should not shrink from investigating the official investigators, particularly the FBI and the CIA, and should not rule out the possibility of a conspiracy reaching up to the highest levels of government. However, his hypothesis that the President's body had been surgically altered between Parkland and Bethesda has been convincingly disputed, if not demolished, by the panel of forensic pathologists engaged by the House Select Committee on Assassinations. The panel concluded that the contrasting descriptions of the President's wounds were due to simple human error. According to the panel, the Parkland doctors had missed the wound in the back because they never turned the President's body over to examine the back, and the Bethesda doctors missed the wound in the President's neck because the Parkland doctors had distorted the wound with a tracheotomy incision. Still, some doubts about the nature of the President's wounds and the conduct of the autopsy remain—most notably, why the Bethesda doctors did not dissect the neck-back wound—adding one more dimension to the morass Arthur Schlesinger insists awaits every historian of the Kennedy assassination.

As we wade into that morass, we must first ask the question: What individuals and groups stood to gain most from the assassination of President Kennedy? Of all Kennedy's enemies, the most likely to gain were the Cosa Nostra, the Cuban exiles, Fidel Castro and his loyalists, and certain disaffected elements of the CIA.

It is, however, somewhat unlikely that elements of the CIA or the Cuban exiles would have masterminded a plot to eliminate Kennedy, because what they stood to gain from Kennedy's destruction was marginal and uncertain: the remote possibility that Johnson's policies would be more advantageous to their interests. As for Castro and his loyalist Cubans, it does not appear likely that having Kennedy assassinated by Oswald—an ardent Castro supporter—could have served any interests other than revenge, since such an act could have provoked a U.S. attack on Cuba, the last thing Castro wanted.

But for the Cosa Nostra, the benefits to be derived from the death of President Kennedy would be enormous. The destruction of John F. Kennedy would neutralize his brother Robert and cripple his anticrime program. It was well known that Lyndon Johnson had little interest in fighting organized crime.

Thus when all the advantages from killing President

Kennedy are added up for each of his many enemies, there is no question which enemy stood the most to gain: It was "the enemy within." The Kennedys had crossed the line with this enemy time and again. They had accepted favors, collaborations, and donations, and yet they had gone after them with every weapon at their command.

After the assassination, the FBI continued its program of electronic surveillance of organized crime and was able to overhear the reactions of several notable Cosa Nostra bosses to the murder. Immediately after the President's death, Sam Giancana, who was in Chicago's Armory lounge with a member of his crime family, Charles "Chuckie" English, and was being secretly taped, was overheard observing, with evident satisfaction, "Bobby Kennedy will not have the power he once had."

On November 24, 1963, Stefano, Peter, and Antonio Magaddino of Buffalo were overheard speculating about Jack Ruby and Lee Oswald. Stefano Magaddino said, "It's a shame we've been embarrassed before the whole world by allowing the President to be killed in our own territory. You can be sure the police spies will be watching carefully to see what we think and say about this."

Then, on November 26, 1963, the FBI overheard a conversation about the assassination in Stefano Magaddino's funeral home in Niagara Falls. Frederico Randaccio, a Magaddino family underboss, suggested they all congratulate each other over Kennedy's murder, whereupon Magaddino said they should be more cautious because the FBI may be watching and recording them. Magaddino, who was then the chairman of the national Mafia *commissione*, observed that Robert Kennedy had caused his brother's death by "pressing too many issues." Three days later Magaddino was taped saying the murder of Oswald by Ruby was "arranged in order to cover up things."

On February 2, 1964, during a discussion between Philadelphia boss Angelo Bruno and some of his associates, an FBI listening device overheard someone say, "It's too bad his brother Bobby was not in that car too." Later, on August 13, the FBI overheard Russell Bufalino, a Pennsylvania mob leader, say, "The Kennedys are responsible for all my troubles. They killed the good one. They should have killed the other little guy."

The only two suspects we definitely know were involved in the tragic events in Dallas are Lee Harvey Oswald and Jack Ruby. Both men had contacts with organized crime, Oswald with the Marcello gang, Ruby with several other Cosa Nostra organizations, including the Giancana, Trafficante, and Marcello families, not to mention certain associates of Jimmy Hoffa, and both men had been very much involved with Cuba. Furthermore, both men were very well known to the intelligence agencies. Ruby had been an FBI informant, and the CIA had kept a file on him (which, as we know, it withheld from the Warren Commission). Both the FBI and the CIA had extensive files on Oswald, and many reputable investigators believe Oswald had been a low-level intelligence agent, or possibly an FBI informant in New Orleans, allegations that have never been proved and were declared to be without foundation by the House assassinations committee.

Thus in the respective backgrounds of these two known protagonists in the events of Dallas, there were at least two of the elements of the unholy alliance of the Cosa Nostra, the CIA, and the Cuban exiles. What more ideal "fall guy" for this alliance's murderous intentions could there have been than the ardently pro-Castro "nut," Lee Harvey Oswald?

Viewed in the perspective of the last twenty years, with all that we now know from three official assassination investigations, a major Senate investigation of the intelligence agencies, and the private investigations of writers like Sylvia Meagher, G. Robert Blakey, and Anthony Summers, it appears that there were possibly three separate and distinct conspiracies related to the Kennedy assassination. First, there was the possible conspiracy Oswald had entered into to murder the President, or the conspiracy of others to frame Oswald. Second, there was the possible conspiracy Ruby had entered into to murder Oswald. And third, there was the unorganized conspiracy or conspiracies various individuals and agencies of the U.S. government had entered into to obscure the circumstances surrounding the assassination, suppress important evidence, and withhold vital information from the Warren Commission, so that the plot to kill the President, if one had existed, would not be discovered.

Although the findings of the House Select Committee on Assassinations were essentially inconclusive, the committee members did develop deep suspicions that organized crime might have been involved in the Kennedy assassination. Of all the Cosa Nostra families that could have been involved, the committee came to believe that the vast Louisiana and Texas network of Carlos Marcello seemed the most likely candidate.

Certainly Marcello had a compelling motive to assassinate President Kennedy, and because he was head of the oldest Mafia family in the nation, he enjoyed the unique privilege among Mafia bosses of not having to consult the national *commissione* when making a major decision. Thus he could have conspired to assassinate the President without having obtained the blessing of the other Mafia bosses, an advantage that would contribute to the security of the operation. Furthermore, through his vast apparatus of corrupted law enforcement officials in Louisiana and Texas, including possibly New Orleans FBI agent Regis Kennedy and a member of the Dallas police who allegedly met with local Marcello associate Joseph Civello upon his return from the Apalachin conclave, Marcello also possessed the means to cover up the crime. In addition, through his close friendship with the anti-Castro conspirator, Santo Trafficante, Jr., Marcello could probably have been able to count on the CIA to aid in the cover-up. What more complete revenge could Carlos Marcello have obtained for Robert Kennedy's dumping him in Guatemala than having his brother killed on the same day he was acquitted of charges Robert Kennedy had brought against him? As they say in Sicily, "Revenge is a plate that is best served cold."

The House Select Committee on Assassinations found

evidence of many links between the Marcello organization and Lee Harvey Oswald and Jack Ruby that the Warren Commission had no knowledge of.

Granted associations do not prove guilt, nevertheless the number of associations the House assassinations committee discovered between the Marcello organization and Oswald and Ruby is impressive and seems to indicate that, if organized crime was in any way involved in the Kennedy assassination, the vast Marcello criminal network would have been the most likely Mafia family to have been involved.

Marcello and Trafficante, longtime friends, were called to testify before the House Select Committee on Assassinations in 1978, but both denied having participated in the assassination. In the months preceding Marcello's scheduled appearance before the committee, the FBI finally succeeded in bugging the Mafia chieftain in his New Orleans headquarters. Hoping to catch Marcello in a discussion of the Kennedy assassination with one of his henchmen, as his turn to testify before the committee drew near, the FBI picked up only one suspicious conversation. A few days before Marcello was due to depart for the hearing in Washington one of his lieutenants was overheard asking him how he planned to handle the assassinations committee. Marcello told him to shut up and step outdoors where they could talk. Marcello's demeanor at the eventual committee hearing also aroused suspicions, for when the name Robert Kennedy was mentioned the New Orleans Mafia don lost his cool and became visibly upset, complaining vociferously about how Kennedy had "kidnapped" him without warning. More composed, after he had been immunized, Trafficante admitted his role in the CIA-Mafia plots against Castro, but he denied José Alemán's allegation that he, Trafficante, had told Alemán that President Kennedy was "going to be hit." Trafficante and Marcello, as of November 1984, are still alive and their roles, if any, in the Kennedy and Oswald murders still remain a mystery. Recently Marcello, after a lifetime career of bribing judges and government officials on almost every level, was convicted of attempting to bribe Louisiana state government officials, a conviction that was upheld on appeal, and he is now in prison. Trafficante is seriously ill.

It is one of the still-unsolved mysteries associated with the Kennedy assassination that the FBI did not zero in on the Marcello organization immediately after the President's murder. The FBI had good reason to focus on the Marcello family. They knew the suspect they arrested forty-eight hours after the murder, David Ferrie, was connected to Marcello. The Secret Service had apparently found Ferrie's library card among Oswald's possessions after Oswald's arrest, along with documents indicating Oswald had recently lived in New Orleans. These had been turned over to the FBI. The most superficial investigation of Ruby would have quickly turned up his Marcello connections in both Dallas and New Orleans. But Hoover and the FBI suppressed every scrap of evidence and abandoned every lead that could possibly have led to the suspicion that the Marcello organization was involved in a conspiracy to assassinate the President, and/or the President's alleged assassin.

These suppressions can be summarized as follows. The FBI released Ferrie after the most superficial investigation imaginable. When, early in 1964, the FBI discovered Oswald's uncle's connections to the Marcello organization, it did not report them to the Warren Commission. The Dallas FBI office should have known about Jack Ruby's connections to organized crime in Dallas, including his connections to associates of Carlos Marcello, Joseph Civello, and Joseph Campisi, but it either ignored them or was told by headquarters to ignore them. An FBI report from Oakland, California, dated November 27, 1963, about Jack Ruby's activities in Dallas (a copy of which I received from former chief counsel of the House assassinations committee, G. Robert Blakey) stated that a reliable informant, who had lived in Dallas, had known Jack Ruby, and had worked for Joseph Civello, alleged that Ruby had been "a frequent visitor and associate of Civello." A copy of the report was sent to the Dallas FBI and must certainly have been read by that office, which should have known about the Ruby-Civello connection already.

To no avail. The Oakland FBI report eventually turned up among the Warren Commission exhibits with the part about Ruby's connection with Joseph Civello missing.

Although the FBI mounted an extraordinarily successful program of electronic surveillance of organized crime, we know it failed absolutely to penetrate Carlos Marcello. The FBI agent assigned to keep track of Marcello's activities, Regis Kennedy, reported that Marcello was "a legitimate businessman" who was not involved in organized crime. Later, when Edward Becker's allegations of Marcello's death threats against President Kennedy were brought to the attention of the FBI, the Bureau immediately sought to discredit Becker.

According to an FBI teletype, which I have seen and which has not been made public before this book, it appears that the FBI had even learned of a conspiracy allegation hinting of a possible involvement of the Marcello organization as early as six days after the assassination and did nothing about it. The teletype, marked "Urgent," had been sent by the Philadelphia FBI office to the Dallas and New Orleans offices on November 28, 1963. It reported on a conversation that had allegedly been overheard in March 1963, but about which the Philadelphia office had just learned. Three men—one reportedly a close associate of a Vincent Marcello and another a certain "professor" of unknown name—were talking of assassinating President Kennedy. As the three were looking at an advertisement in a detective-story magazine for a foreign-made rifle that sold for $12.98, Marcello's friend observed, "This would be a nice rifle to buy to get the President. . . ." He then went on to tell his friends that there was "a price on the President's head and on other members of the Kennedy family," adding that "somebody will get Kennedy when he comes South."

Ordinarily the Dallas and New Orleans FBI offices would have investigated the allegations in the Philadelphia office's report, but by November 28 the Oswald-as-lone-assassin hypothesis had been so firmly adopted by J. Edgar Hoover that he had rescinded an earlier order to his field agents to investigate all assassination allegations; and so no investigation was made. What makes the information intriguing twenty years later is that Vincent Marcello is one of Carlos Marcello's brothers and, according to New Orleans Metropolitan Crime Commission records, has been involved in a number of criminal enterprises. David Ferrie, who dabbled in hypnosis and chemistry, was nicknamed "the professor." Also, the foreign-made rifle Oswald bought in March, and with which he was alleged to have shot Kennedy, sold for $12.78 without telescopic sight. Oswald arrived in New Orleans two months after these remarks were reportedly made about the price on Kennedy's head and only a few days after it was announced that Kennedy would visit Dallas in November. Could Oswald have been recruited by the Marcello organization to participate in a plot to kill the President that was already in the works? The New Orleans FBI never made the slightest effort to find out.

So adamant was the FBI in suppressing all leads in the direction of a possible involvement of the Marcello organization in the Kennedy assassination, that one is inevitably led to the suspicion that the Bureau had something to hide in regard to Carlos Marcello. Was it that Hoover knew the FBI's surveillance of Carlos Marcello was deficient and did not want this deficiency known? Or was it that Lyndon Johnson told Hoover not to investigate a possible Marcello complicity because Marcello was so involved in the politics of Johnson's home state? Was it that Hoover was suspicious his agent in New Orleans, Regis Kennedy, had been corrupted by the Marcello organization and did not want this known either? Or, on a more sinister level, did Hoover know of a Marcello plot to kill the President and willfully do nothing about it? This explanation is not inconceivable because we now know that Hoover did not report threats by organized crime figures against the President's life, which FBI bugs had overheard, to either the Secret Service or to the attorney general.

Part of Hoover's effort to suppress all evidence leading to the possible involvement of the Marcello organization in the assassination was his apparent desire to convince the public that Jack Ruby was just a patriotic nightclub owner with no connection to organized crime, who had killed Oswald out of sympathy for the Kennedys. This hypothesis was later inadvertently demolished by Ruby himself. After his arrest, Ruby claimed he had killed Oswald so Mrs. Kennedy and Caroline would not have to testify at Oswald's trial and that his chief motive for shooting Oswald had been sorrow over the assassination and sympathy for the President's widow and children; however, a handwritten note from Ruby to his attorney, Joe Tonahill, discovered in 1967, revealed that this motive was but a legal ploy. The note told of some advice Ruby had received from his first lawyer, Tom Howard: "Joe, you should know this. Tom Howard told me to say that I shot Oswald so Caroline and Mrs. Kennedy wouldn't have to testify, o.k.?"

Judging from the range of associations with the Marcello crime family both Ruby and Oswald had, it is not inconceivable to suspect that the Marcello organization could have been behind both the conspiracy to kill the President and the conspiracy to kill the President's assassin, for the Marcello outfit had access not only to Oswald and Ruby, but also to the Dallas police and the Dallas jail.

The final conspiracy, the one to cloud or obscure certain circumstances surrounding the assassination, suppress important evidence, and withhold vital information from the Warren Commission so that a plot to kill the President, if one existed, would not be discovered, demonstrated what can happen when the demands of law clash with the demands of politics, personal ambition, and bureaucratic self-preservation.

As we know, those who had been directly involved in, or had been knowledgeable of, the plots to kill Castro—Dulles, Cabell, Bissell, McCone, Houston, Edwards, Helms, Harvey, FitzGerald, Hoover, and Robert Kennedy, among others—did not directly volunteer information about the plots to the commission. That they all saw fit to do this seems to indicate that what they were most fearful of was the possibility that the assassination of President Kennedy had been in retaliation for the Kennedy administration's

attempts to assassinate the president of Cuba. If this retaliation hypothesis was proved, the consequences for the
FBI and the CIA and for certain reputations, including
that of the slain President, would be devastating.

It would have also been devastating for certain reputations if J. Edgar Hoover had revealed to the Warren
Commission the taped threats against the President's and
Robert Kennedy's lives that FBI listening devices had recorded. First, the electronic surveillance was arguably illegal; second, Hoover had kept his boss, the attorney
general, ignorant of most of it; and third, the FBI had
taken no action in regard to the threats. No wonder Hoover
never turned the tapes over to the Warren Commission.
If he had, he would have completely destroyed his own
reputation and brought down Robert Kennedy's reputation with him.

J. Edgar Hoover apparently pushed so hard to mo-
nopolize the assassination inquiry and promote the idea
that Oswald was the lone assassin that he even aroused
the suspicions of certain members of the Warren Commission. On January 22, 1964, Allen Dulles, Hale Boggs,
and General Counsel J. Lee Rankin held a secret executive
session that does not appear in the final record but was
discovered later in a stenotypist's notes:

DULLES: Why would it be in their [FBI] interest to say he [Oswald] is clearly the only
guilty one? . . .

RANKIN: They would like to have us fold up
and quit.

BOGGS: This closes the case, you see. Don't
you see?

RANKIN: They found the man. There is nothing more to do. The commission supports
their conclusions, and we can go home and
that is the end of it.

BOGGS: I don't even like to see this being taken
down.

DULLES: Yes. I think this record ought to be
destroyed.

However, in assessing J. Edgar Hoover's role in pushing the lone-assassin hypothesis so hard, we must point out that his boss, Attorney General Robert Kennedy, did nothing to stop him from promoting that hypothesis. By all rights, Robert Kennedy, the arch crime-fighter, should have been deeply suspicious that either the Giancana, or the Marcello, or the Trafficante criminal organizations could have been behind his brother's murder, yet there is no record that he ever directed Hoover to investigate the possibility of their complicity. What was the reason for this astounding reluctance to pursue the most obvious possible conspirators, the gangsters he, Robert Kennedy, had vowed to destroy? Knowing what we now know, how would Hoover have responded to Robert Kennedy's urging him to investigate the possible complicity of a Giancana, or a Roselli, or a Trafficante, or a Marcello in his brother's murder? Hoover would have looked the young attorney general squarely in the eyes and asked him if he really wanted to open up all those cans of worms, if he really wanted the CIA-Mafia plots to become known. Then he might have asked the attorney general whether he would like his slain brother's relationship with Giancana's girlfriend to come to light. That could have been enough to dissuade Robert Kennedy from pushing for an investigation of the possible complicity in his brother's murder of Giancana, Roselli, Trafficante, or Marcello.

So, in the last analysis, what was being covered up after the Kennedy assassination was not so much the immediate circumstances surrounding that assassination, but the possibility that the CIA-Mafia and AM/LASH assassination plots against Castro and the President's involvement with the girlfriend of two of the Mafia plotters could have been related to the President's murder. According to G. Robert Blakey, CIA Director John McCone and Attorney General Robert Kennedy apparently met secretly to consider the advisability of bringing the CIA's attempts to murder Castro to the attention of the Warren Commission. Blakey believes, on the basis of evidence brought to his attention during the House Committee on Assassinations' investigation of the JFK murder, that both men probably agreed that for reasons of "national security" those plots should never be made public and should not be brought to the attention of the members of the commission and staff for fear they might leak.

When questioned by me on this matter on January 12, 1984, John McCone acknowledged having had many discussions with Robert Kennedy during the time of the Warren Commission's investigation. However, he asserted that he had no recollection of having discussed the Castro murder plots (which he did not refer to as such, but as "the matter to which [I] had referred") with Kennedy. Furthermore, he stated that he never had any intention of withholding information from the Warren Commission that he deemed pertinent to its investigation. Finally, he stated that he had no recollection of reaching an understanding with Robert Kennedy on withholding knowledge of the CIA-Mafia plots (which he again did not refer to as such, but as "the matter to which [I] had referred") from the commission.

This disclaimer notwithstanding, there remains the fact that in the voluminous Warren Commission investigation archive no records exist of John McCone, or Robert Kennedy, or anybody else, revealing the existence of the Castro murder plots to the commission.

Thus it can be said that the possible net results of the CIA's pact with the devil, which the Kennedy brothers ratified or tacitly condoned or failed to abrogate, were the moral discrediting of the CIA, the compromising of the Kennedy government and of the investigation of President Kennedy's assassination, and, quite possibly, the destruction of President Kennedy and his administration.

Many people had been fearful that President-elect Kennedy in appointing his brother to the position of chief law enforcement officer of the country would be placing himself and, in a certain sense, his administration, above the law. As attorney general, Robert Kennedy would be in a position to cover up any wrongdoing perpetrated by his brother. Little did those original skeptics imagine at the time the extent of what Robert Kennedy would one day be called upon to cover up: the plots to murder Castro, his brother's relationship with the girlfriend of two of the plotters, and how these could have borne on a plot to murder his brother, the President of the United States.

Seen in the perspective of the last twenty years, with all that has come to light during that period, the assassination of President Kennedy and the investigation of that assassination, coupled with the uncritical acceptance of that investigation by press and public, appear as a truly monumental failure of the administration of justice in the United States. The Kennedy assassination revealed, among many things, a staggering failure on the part of the law enforcement agencies and the criminal justice system. If the system did not work at the very highest level, how could it be expected to work at lower levels? If the FBI and the CIA could not be trusted, how could the Dallas police department or any other law enforcement agency be trusted? It also represented a most damaging blow to American prestige. A brutal act of violence had been committed against the American President, a man whose charm had captivated millions of people throughout the world. Then the President's apparent assassin was murdered within the confines of Dallas police headquarters, implying that the police were either corrupt or grossly negligent in letting the assassin's assassin in. And because the President's apparent assassin was silenced in the typical style of the Mafia, the world wondered about the extent of the Mafia's influence in the United States. That the ultimate authorship of that crime still remains a mystery, due principally to the willful withholding of vital information from the Warren Commission by the Justice Department, the Pentagon, and the CIA, only compounds the sense of demoralization. It is one thing to commit a horrible crime, it is another to let the guilty party get away with it.

It is the irony of all ironies that Robert F. Kennedy, the arch crime-fighter and enemy of the Cosa Nostra, was compelled to thwart the investigation of his own brother's murder even though there was a high probability that organized crime was involved. Robert Kennedy's sense of guilt must have been overwhelming. There was no way he could expiate that guilt. However, if he were to become

President, it was conceivable he could make up, at least in part, for what had happened to Jack, and might even be in a position to uncover and punish those who were responsible for his brother's assassination. "I now fully realize," he told an audience of students at San Fernando State College in California on June 3, 1968, "that only the powers of the Presidency will reveal the secrets of my brother's death." Three days later he himself was dead, the victim also of an assassin's bullet.

56. The Widow

JOHN F. KENNEDY was buried in Arlington on Monday, November 25. The following day the family debated whether to call off the Thanksgiving reunion, which was to fall on the following Thursday. In the end, they decided to go ahead with their original plans. As it turned out, the only member of the family who did not make it to Hyannis for the holiday was Bobby. Unable to face his mother and father, knowing what he now knew about Oswald and Ruby and the probable nature of the conspiracy behind his brother's murder, Bobby took his wife and children down to Hobe Sound, Florida, for the long weekend.

Jacqueline, however, decided to attend the reunion. Thanksgiving eve she suddenly arrived in Hyannis with no forewarning, and went straight to the Kennedy compound, bent on seeing Joe Kennedy. The ambassador's nurse, Rita Dallas, and Rose Kennedy did not want Jackie to disturb her father-in-law, but when Jacqueline arrived at the main house, carrying in her arms the flag that had draped her late husband's coffin, she expressed such a powerful determination to see him that no one had the courage to stand in her way.

Blocked by Rose Kennedy downstairs, she shouted, "I'm here to see Grandpa. No, no, I'm not upset. . . . Please, please, leave me alone. I'm fine. I just want to see Grandpa." And with that, she surged past Mrs. Kennedy, raced upstairs, and ran past Mrs. Dallas, crying, "Oh, Mrs. Dallas, I want to see Grandpa."

At first Mrs. Dallas tried to block her path, but then, realizing she could do nothing to stop her, she said, quietly, "He's waiting," and proceeded to lead her to the ambassador's room. Jacqueline handed the furled flag to Mrs. Dallas, telling her she wanted her to give it to Mr. Kennedy after she left.

"It was Jack's," she said.

Mrs. Dallas nodded and took the flag.

When Jacqueline finally gained access to the ambassador's room, she ran up to his bed, embraced him, and leaned her head against his shoulder. The aged patriarch, paralyzed and mute, tried to greet his daughter-in-law, but could only utter a little cry.

Jacqueline then drew back, and sitting on the bed, gave the ambassador a full and detailed account of everything that had happened since she and the President left Washington for Texas and returned for the funeral and the burial. She had wanted him to hear the full story from her before he read all the newspaper and magazine accounts. After she finished, the ambassador nodded, closed his eyes and fell back on his pillow.

Jacqueline then said goodnight and left, reminding Mrs. Dallas to give Mr. Kennedy the flag. As Jackie went downstairs, Mrs. Dallas reflected that she had never seen a woman who looked "so alone."

Later on that night, Mrs. Dallas awoke to a terrible commotion in the ambassador's room. The old man was groaning and retching. Mrs. Dallas found Mr. Kennedy in a state of wild panic, with his son's burial flag all crumpled up on his bed. Apparently Ann Gargan had taken it from where it had been put, and, not knowing what it was in the dark, had put it over the ambassador's bed like a blanket. It was getting chilly and she thought her uncle needed more cover. When Joe Kennedy awoke and saw his dead son's shroud over him, he came apart.

It was left to Ted Kennedy to try and pull the family together at Thanksgiving. Gamely he tried to get them all to laugh, and even succeeded now and then, much to the servants' disapproval. Immediately after lunch he organized a touch football game on the lawn during which sparks of the old Kennedy energy and drive were amply displayed. Eunice, especially, impressed everybody with her aggressive running game and high spirits. The ambassador's nurse and several of the servants found this boisterous behavior shocking less than a week after the President's murder. The next morning the governess of Ted Kennedy's children quit her job because, she said, Ted had thrown a loud party for his friends the night before and had stayed up until the early morning hours drinking and laughing. Explanations about Irish wakes were to no avail. She would not come back to work for the family. For the remainder of the weekend Teddy did his best to keep the family's spirits as high as he could.

Jacqueline, who had remained by herself with her children for most of the holiday weekend, was perhaps more deeply affected by the murder of John F. Kennedy than Ted. Not only had she lost a husband, she had suddenly lost her position as First Lady as well. Jacqueline Bouvier Kennedy had a terribly difficult adjustment to make. For a while she was utterly lost. She was a woman who had always drawn her identity from a man—a father or a spouse. For over ten years, she had defined herself in terms of her remarkable husband.

She was also no doubt consumed by guilt. All the times she could have been a help to Jack and wasn't. All the times he had pleaded with her to come on a campaign trip and she hadn't gone. "Oh, Mary, one day campaigning can age a woman thirty years," she had told her secretary, Mary Gallagher. Thank God she had at least gone with him on his last campaign. But she still felt guilty.

How to assuage the guilt? By not letting Jack down in death. By giving him a magnificent funeral. By placing an eternal flame over his grave. By glorifying his memory. And by placing under the Lincoln plaque in the Lincoln bedroom a plaque of her own: "In this room lived John Fitzgerald Kennedy with his wife, Jacqueline, during the two years, ten months, and two days he was President of

the United States—January 20, 1961–November 22, 1963."
(Mrs. Richard Nixon had the plaque removed soon after
she and her husband moved in.)

But there were other, far more spectacular ways of
glorifying the memory of her late husband. Not long after
the funeral, Jacqueline took the first step in the glorification process by persuading Lyndon Johnson to change
the name of Cape Canaveral to Cape Kennedy. Kennedy
had played a role in the space program, but by no stretch
of the imagination could he ever be conceived of as a space
pioneer, or even someone particularly interested in space
exploration. He had simply decided to go ahead with the
$30-billion Apollo project to put an American astronaut
on the moon by the end of the decade. As his own close
aide, Kenneth O'Donnell, admitted, it was a "snap weekend decision." Kennedy had made up his mind about it
one weekend "just like that." Surely there were many
dedicated space pioneers—such as Robert Goddard, Daniel and Harry Guggenheim, Wernher Von Braun, to name
only a few—who deserved a memorial much more than
someone who had merely signed an executive order allo-
cating a federal expenditure for a space project.

These considerations, however, meant nothing to
Jacqueline Kennedy, who was bent on glorifying her slain
husband at all cost. When Lyndon Johnson was informed
Jacqueline wanted to see him, not long after he had moved
into the White House, he feared the worst. But when she
simply asked him, in that childlike, whispery voice of hers,
to name Cape Canaveral after Jack, Johnson was so relieved that was all she wanted, he gushed: "Why sure,
Jackie, sure, we'll get it done right away." And so it was
done. (In 1973 Cape Kennedy was renamed Cape Canaveral.)

It was around this time that Jacqueline first expressed
to Theodore White, the ardently pro-Kennedy journalist
and historian, her conception of President Kennedy's reign
as resembling the mythical kingdom of Camelot, telling
White that as a boy Kennedy was often sick and used to
lie in bed and dream of performing valiant deeds like one
of King Arthur's knights, and that his favorite music, the

music he used to play before going to bed at night as President, was Lerner and Lowe's *Camelot*. And so the Camelot association with Kennedy and his administration was made, and Teddy White wrote about it in an article for *Life* magazine. Soon it was picked up by others in the media and it gained general acceptance. In time the Camelot metaphor would be used to epitomize the entire Kennedy presidency, as if that brief, turbulent era, so full of intrigue and vendetta, had been one thousand days of unmitigated beauty and light.

Not long after the birth of the Camelot myth, Mayor Robert Wagner of New York changed the name of Idlewild International Airport to John F. Kennedy International Airport. And then, not long after that, Congress changed the name of the planned natural cultural center in Washington to the John F. Kennedy Center for the Performing Arts, and appropriated $15.5 million in federal funds to match an equal amount to be raised privately for the new national monument.

Meanwhile, Jacqueline Kennedy vehemently pursued what had become her major personal contribution to the glorification, the John F. Kennedy Memorial Library in Boston. Here, in the city whose establishment the Kennedys felt had rejected them, she and her collaborators were to raise a monument to a Kennedy surpassing in grandeur that of any other son of Boston.

There was more to come. The U.S. Treasury minted a Kennedy half-dollar. Queen Elizabeth of England set aside three acres at Runnymede, where King John had signed the Magna Carta, as a Kennedy shrine. A huge John F. Kennedy Memorial Park was created in New Ross, in southern Ireland, near the Kennedy ancestral homestead in Dunganstown. Canada named one of its tallest peaks Mount Kennedy. Kennedy plazas, places, schools, boulevards, streets, and hospitals sprung up all over the globe. One could not escape the name Kennedy anywhere on the planet. In a very real sense, John F. Kennedy's murder had multiplied the Kennedys' power. With the name of Kennedy so universally glorified in stone, and bronze, and institutional lettering, it seemed certain that, sooner or later, a Kennedy would avail himself of the power of his name to regain the presidency.

Along with the glorification of John F. Kennedy, there went also his continued idealization and sentimentalization. If the press had gushed over John Kennedy before, now it became downright maudlin. The canonization had begun.

What are we to make of it all? The central fact leaps to mind that the glorification of John F. Kennedy was utterly unreasonable, but made some kind of emotional sense at the time. For the personality of John F. Kennedy, take him for "all in all," had struck some deep emotional chord in people, had fulfilled some widespread, and apparently fundamental, human need. In the last analysis, it seemed that what the American people wanted in a President was not so much wisdom and competence, but glamour, charisma, and the sense of hope and optimism Kennedy's incandescent personality projected. When all was said and done, they named all those landmarks and buildings after JFK not because of what he had done to deserve them, but because of what he had represented in the public imagination.

Unfortunately, what proceeded from all this was a monstrous distortion of the truth. A myth was created that could not possibly serve the interests of anybody but the Kennedy family. Jacqueline Kennedy's efforts at glorifying and mythologizing her late husband inadvertently did much to cloud what might have been behind her late husband's assassination.

The key elements in the myth-making process were the suppression of the truth about John F. Kennedy's past, the discouragement of any serious inquiry into the circumstances of his assassination, the lifelong inclination of Jacqueline Kennedy to construct and dwell in fairy tales, and the concerted attempt by the Kennedys and their court historians to manipulate history, including the suppression of books, such as William Manchester's *Death of a President*, they did not like.

All of these elements, however, would have been to no avail in building a Kennedy myth if the American people were not already emotionally disposed to accept one. In an America conditioned by the fabrications of Hollywood and Madison Avenue, the Camelot tale found fertile soil in which to grow.

Along with the sense of guilt, Jacqueline was also tormented by a sense of What Could Have Been Done to prevent the tragedy in Dallas. They should have heeded all the warnings and not gone to Texas. They should have spent more time at the Love Field airport shaking hands with the crowds: that would have delayed the motorcade considerably and the assassins might have lost nerve. She should have insisted on the bubble top. The driver of the presidential limousine should have speeded up after the first shot. There were so many things that could have been done, and weren't. However, reflecting on these once in the presence of her secretary, Mary Gallagher, Jacqueline showed she understood one facet of her late husband's character only too well. Turning to Mrs. Gallagher one day, after reciting a long litany of What Could Have Been Dones, she said, "Oh, well, I guess Jack would only have gotten more reckless as time went on anyway."

It is interesting to note that Jacqueline, despite her desire to glorify her husband's memory, seemed not to take any apparent interest in the official investigation of her husband's murder. Possibly this was because Robert Kennedy had encouraged her not to for the same reason he had adopted the policy of withholding vital information from the Warren Commission: He did not want certain things ever to come to light.

Jacqueline, in fact, in the immediate postassassination period, often appeared to her Bouvier relatives to be strangely withdrawn and inhibited in regard to the assassination. Certainly there was little in her attitude that bespoke wanting to get to the bottom of the crime and see justice done to those responsible for it.

What a contrast this was to Coretta King's attitude toward her husband's assassination four years later, as she helped in the investigation in every way she could, vigorously explored all possible conspiracies, and became instrumental in 1976 in persuading Congress to reopen the investigation of both Martin Luther King's and John F. Kennedy's murders.

However, there is little doubt about the sincerity and depth of Jacqueline's feelings about the loss of her husband. The remarks she contributed to a *Look* magazine memorial issue on the first anniversary of Kennedy's death eloquently expressed the way she felt:

> It is nearly a year since he has gone.
>
> On so many days—his birthday, an anniversary, watching his children run to the sea— I have thought, "But this day last year was his last to see that." He was so full of love and life on those days. He seems so vulnerable now, when you think that each one was a last time.
>
> Soon the final day will come around again— as inexorably as it did last year. But expected this time.
>
> It will find some of us different people than we were a year ago. Learning to accept what was unthinkable when he was alive changes you.
>
> I don't think there is any consolation. What was lost cannot be replaced . . .
>
> Now I think that I should have known that he was magic all along. I did know it—but I should have guessed it could not last. I should have known that it was asking too much to dream that I might have grown old with him and see our children grow up together.
>
> So now he is a legend when he would have preferred to be a man. . . .

The assassination left Jacqueline terribly vulnerable. She was vulnerable to the tabloids that exploited her, and she was vulnerable to those she had either snubbed, mistreated, or ignored. She no longer had the President of the United States to protect her. She no longer had her position as First Lady to protect her.

However, there were compensations. Jacqueline emerged from the assassination as a world celebrity. The entire globe had seen her leading the world's heads of state in the funeral procession. She had come out of this tragedy with virtually unlimited prestige.

The trouble was she didn't seem to know what to do with all the prestige she had. Since she had derived almost her total identity from a man, her husband, she had no real bedrock of selfhood to fall back on when he was gone, no selfhood that could successfully harness the immense prestige she had attained by force of circumstance. And so it seemed to many that she began to squander her prestige in aimless self-indulgences as she continued spending inordinate amounts of money on haute couture, frequented almost exclusively people of fashion, and jetted all over the world.

Then there was the problem of money. Kennedy had left Jacqueline well enough off, but not enormously well off, and all the money he had left her was tied up in a trust fund over which she had been given no control. Jackie's spending habits since childhood had been extravagant, and her living costs were now astronomical because she felt she had to keep up a standard of living appropriate to a former First Lady, *her* brand of First Lady. After the terms of Kennedy's will were made known to her, she wondered how she would ever make ends meet.

Fully cognizant of her extravagant ways, Kennedy had left his wife only $25,000 in cash. His major bequest was making her the beneficiary of a trust fund that would assure her an income of $200,000 a year, before taxes, not a vast income by any means, given her spending habits. It will be recalled that while she was in the White House Jacqueline spent over $100,000 a year on clothes alone.

There was also some money from the federal government, but not very much. From the government her husband had led she received only $43,229, representing civil service death benefits and salary owed the President for the period November 1–22, a widow's pension of $10,000 a year, and $50,000 a year in administrative expenses. So, in terms of actual cash she could lay her hands on, all she had was around $68,000.

Since she had long ago run through the $69,000 left

her by her father, she was left with very little money she could call her own. And she was given no control whatsoever over the trust fund that had been established for her. The trustees were all members of the Kennedy family and business staff, and part of the trust agreement stipulated that if she ever remarried, her trust fund would automatically revert to her children.

It was this feeling of being in relatively difficult straits that caused Jacqueline to be somewhat stingy with her employees, thereby creating resentments that would later find expression in critical books. The U.S. government had awarded Jacqueline $50,000 a year in expense money to maintain an office and a staff capable of handling the considerable official work left over from her husband's administration, including the assembling and organizing of his presidential papers. At first she balked at paying her secretary, Mary Gallagher, $12,000 a year out of her $50,000 allowance. Later she let Mary go. Mrs. Gallagher would tell the world about it in her book, *My Life with Jacqueline Kennedy*. Jacqueline also balked at paying her maid, Providencia Paredes—"Provi"—overtime, even though this faithful retainer had worked herself to the bone, usually late into the night, both before and after the President's murder.

Then, when President Kennedy's secretary, Evelyn Lincoln, was asked to leave, and she complained bitterly, Jackie told her, "Oh, Mrs. Lincoln, all this shouldn't be so hard for you, because you still have your husband. What do I have now? Just the Library." Before this episode, which Mrs. Gallagher related in her book, Jackie had asked Mrs. Lincoln why she needed such a big office, and Mrs. Lincoln had replied that she needed the space for all the President's things she was working on, the papers, the mementos, etc. To this Jackie replied, *"But these things are all mine!"*

Finally, there came the move to New York in the summer-fall of 1964, to the $200,000 apartment at 1040 Fifth Avenue. Much was made of this at the time, as if abandoning Washington was some kind of a mortal sin: the First Widow was supposed to be making daily visits to Arlington for the rest of her life. But for Jacqueline, living in New York was the most normal thing in the world. The Bouviers had been living in New York since 1869.

The move to New York brought a fresh rash of publicity. Once again Jacqueline was at the center of attention of an entire city, the city that had become, by the midsixties, the financial and cultural center of the western world.

But despite all the attention Jacqueline received she was nevertheless a lonely, unhappy woman. Every member of the Bouvier family who saw her during this period, including myself, was struck by her unhappiness and was deeply moved by her plight.

The first Bouvier, besides her sister, to visit her after the assassination was our oldest cousin, Michel Bouvier, who had grown up with Jackie as a brother, and was her godfather as well. (Jackie was, in turn, godmother to his son, John Vernou Bouvier IV, named after her father.) Unable to get to the funeral, Michel had paid a call on her at the Georgetown home she had moved into after moving out of the White House. There Jackie gave him a long, somewhat disjointed account of the assassination and the funeral that moved Michel deeply. He observed that the high-strung Jackie seemed unusually overwrought, so much so that he feared for the stability of her emotions and wondered whether her sanity would hold up under the terrible strain of the adjustment she was having to make. His heart went out to her, but he realized there was absolutely nothing he could do to assuage her grief or compensate for her loss. It was a feeling everyone in the Bouvier family would share.

My turn to see Jacqueline came in March 1966 upon the death of my father in New York. I was living in Italy at the time and flew from Rome to New York for the funeral. After the funeral Jackie came up to my mother's apartment to pay us her condolences. I had not seen her since I had gone to the White House after President Kennedy's burial to pay *her* my condolences.

When Jacqueline came in the front door I immediately noticed a startled expression in her eyes as she glanced here and there around the hall of my mother's apartment, as if on the lookout for a threat. Evidently my father's death had brought back childhood memories of her Uncle John, who had shared an office with her father on lower Broadway near the Stock Exchange, for she kept repeating "Uncle John" over and over, until we sat down on a couch in Mother's living room. There we reminisced for a while, and then she began staring into space and said, "Now they're all dead; they're all dead; they're all dead, all of them, all of them, all dead."

I nodded, and tried to change the subject by telling her how magnificent she had been at President Kennedy's funeral. She shrugged my compliment off in her customary unassuming way, and our conversation drifted back to our childhood days in East Hampton. I mentioned that I had been down in East Hampton the previous summer to take a look at Lasata, after not having seen it in ten years, and had found the old place much changed under its new owner, whereupon she remarked that she had been down there too, incognito, and the house had struck her this time as being "so small."

After talking a while about my father, Jackie got up to leave. As she was putting on her coat in the hall, glancing around with that startled, threatened look again, she appeared very vulnerable and alone, and, feeling suddenly protective, I decided to escort her down the elevator and through the apartment building lobby to her waiting limousine. Even walking through the lobby she looked guarded and tense. As she was to tell me several years later at the funeral of our Aunt Edith, "There are some things you never get over."

The consensus among the Bouviers, at least, seemed to be that Jackie should remarry. She was simply too exposed and unprotected on her own. But who could possibly deliver her? This was the unanswerable question. There seems to be an unwritten law of nature that a woman does not marry below her rank. Because Jackie had been married to the President of the United States, this narrowed the field of prospective husbands to zero. Jacqueline Bouvier Kennedy, the President's widow, had become the prisoner of her status, the victim of her fame.

57. The Legacies

ONE OF THE UNFORTUNATE CONSEQUENCES of the glorification of John F. Kennedy was its tendency to obscure Kennedy's true historical legacy. The glorification was essentially antihistorical, an exercise in fable building, in mythomania, whose only real beneficiaries were the Kennedys themselves.

"Don't let it be forgot, that once there was a spot, for one brief shining moment, that was known as Camelot," Jacqueline Kennedy had whispered to Teddy White, who then committed those whisperings to print in *Life* magazine not long after the assassination, thus giving birth to the Kennedy-Camelot legend.

Seduced by this Camelot image, most American journalists failed to evaluate, realistically, the Kennedy administration and investigate his murder, preferring a fable to reality. (Assassination investigators like Anthony Summers, an Englishman, observed that the American press failed to follow the most obvious leads in their investigations of the assassination. When Summers began his painstaking investigation in the late seventies he found, to his amazement, that many of the key people he interviewed had never been approached, much less interviewed, by the FBI, or by members of the Warren Commission staff, or by members of the American press.) It was, in fact, not until the findings of the Senate Select Committee on Intelligence and the House Select Committee on Assassinations were made public in the late seventies that the historical Kennedy, as distinguished from the mythical Kennedy, finally began to come into focus.

What, then, was the real Kennedy legacy, the legacy of historical truth?

First, let us consider the results of the Kennedy administration's foreign policy, of which the most consequential theaters of operation were Vietnam and Cuba. We have seen that President Kennedy's Vietnam policy, which was continued after his death by his handpicked successor, and secretaries of state and defense, not to mention his brother Robert, led to the longest and most disastrous war in the nation's history, resulting in over a million Vietnamese dead, 57,939 Americans dead or missing, and the loss of South Vietnam to the communists.

As for Kennedy's Cuban policy, and by that we mean all his administration's actions toward Cuba, from the Bay of Pigs through Operation Mongoose to the AM/LASH operation, that policy can only be judged in the light of what has happened in Cuba since Kennedy's death as another disaster. Seen in the light of 1984, even the Cuban missile crisis of 1962 appears to have been empty of favorable long-term results for the United States, for today Cuba is armed to the teeth by the Soviet Union. Furthermore, now that we know about the CIA-Mafia and AM/LASH plots, and Operation Mongoose, we can speculate, not unreasonably, that Kennedy's Cuban policy might well have cost him his life.

And yet, in stark contrast to these foreign policy disasters, there remains the magic of Kennedy's image as a world leader and inspirer of men and women everywhere. The world at large does not associate John F. Kennedy with the tragedy in Vietnam and the assorted belligerencies against Cuba and its leader; it still thinks of him as the knight in shining armor, the "Wonder of the World." This impression exerted a favorable influence on many areas of U.S. foreign policy while Kennedy was alive and continued to linger on in the world's consciousness after his death, with probably beneficial results for the United States. Kennedy's magic personality won many friends for America, both before and after his assassination, and this did much to counterbalance his blunders in Cuba and Vietnam.

In addition, there were some areas of foreign policy in which Kennedy registered a measure of success. One of the favorable consequences of the resolution of the Cuban missile crisis was the limited nuclear test ban treaty which put an end to nuclear testing in the atmosphere (but not underground). Then there was Kennedy's firm stand in West Berlin that may have prevented the Soviets from absorbing free Berlin into East Germany. And then, of course, there was the Peace Corps, which with a few exceptions won many friends for the United States and exposed many young Americans to their country's worldwide responsibilities at a most formative period in their lives.

As for Kennedy's domestic legacy, it was, at best, a mixed success. Although his space program did not spring from a passion for astronautics, it did culminate many years later (under his archrival Richard Nixon) in the successful Apollo 11 mission to the moon, and so we must give Kennedy credit for launching a $30-billion program that resulted in a great American technological triumph and set the stage for the future exploration of space.

We must also give Kennedy credit for his massive war against organized crime, although most of the credit for that program should go to his brother Robert. The Kennedy administration was the first in American history to fully recognize the extent of the Cosa Nostra's operations and the mortal threat they represented to American institutions, and to do something forceful about it. That, in the end, Kennedy's war against "the enemy within" may have cost him his life, and that his anticrime program fizzled out after his death, does not diminish his, and his brother's, achievement.

Then there was the matter of tax reform. Kennedy's proposed Tax Reform Bill of 1963, which became under Lyndon Johnson the Tax Reform Act of 1964, was a signal success in that it resulted in a period of sustained economic prosperity under his successor. Kennedy's revenue proposals were designed to please both liberals and conservatives in that they were crafted to stimulate both consumption and investment. Thus, his proposals called for no tax whatsoever on a family income of less than $4000 and a reduction of the tax rate on the highest income bracket from 91 to 77 percent. As it turned out, this mix made for significant economic recovery, but, since Kennedy spent so much money on military hardware (principally to fill the so-called missile gap), it also made for dangerously unbalanced federal budgets.

John Kennedy also displayed great courage in forcing the steel companies to rescind their price increases in April 1962. In remaining firm on this issue, he made his contribution toward restraining the inflationary wage-price spiral.

But it was in the area of civil rights that John F. Kennedy left his most enduring social legacy to the American people. For, combined with his own status as the first President of wholly Irish Catholic ancestry, his civil rights proposals, which became under Lyndon Johnson the Civil Rights Act of 1964, led to a virtual social revolution in the United States.

Before Kennedy, the United States of America was the almost exclusive domain of the male, white Anglo-Saxon Protestant. This class had dominated business, finance, government, education, and publishing since colonial times. After Kennedy, all this began to change. By the twentieth anniversary of his death something resembling a social revolution had taken place in America. Kennedy had helped cause this revolution. His civil rights proposals, eventually embodied in the Civil Rights Act of 1964, provided for an end to all government and private discrimination on the basis of race and made the Department of Justice into an enforcer of black rights throughout the nation. But it was Kennedy's status as the first non–Anglo-Saxon-Protestant President that really helped transform American society. Because he was who he was, Kennedy became a powerful social battering ram, knocking down the barriers to power and social acceptance for all peoples of America, not just the blacks, and in so doing helped transform American society.

As for that last bastion of society, the Social Register, we note with a smile that Teddy Kennedy is now happily ensconced within its orange and black covers. At last the Boston Irish are in society. Old Joe Kennedy would have been pleased.

What then was there about the Kennedy years that constituted the "one brief shining moment that was known as Camelot"? It had to do with the Kennedy personality and style, and particularly with the personality and style of Jacqueline Kennedy, who during her husband's 1000 days, succeeded in elevating the tone of the White House to a level it had never known before, and will probably never know again—which brings us to the legacy of style. To attempt to describe that style in words would only diminish its grace and brilliance. Fortunately for all of us, it is magnificently preserved in the John Fitzgerald Kennedy Library in Boston, dedicated in 1979. There one may view a film on John F. Kennedy's life showing Kennedy from youth to his forty-sixth year, with all his marvelous vitality, charm, and grace almost brimming over the screen. There one may watch his political campaigns on television screens scattered about the museum section and watch his scintillating press conferences on other television screens and understand how, in saying almost nothing of consequence, he could yet bedazzle millions of Americans with his quick wit, flashing smile, and easy, confident manner. There one can view huge collections of still photographs taken of Kennedy state ceremonies and dinners and be fairly blinded by the sheer grandeur and magnificence of it all. There one may trace, through photographs, Jacqueline Kennedy's restoration of the White House, comparing the way the various state rooms looked before her magic touch to the way they looked after she had transformed them. And there one may read John F. Kennedy's soaring eloquence inscribed in huge block letters on the walls:

> All this will not be finished in the first 100 days.
> Nor will it be finished in the first 1000 days,
> nor in the life of this Administration, nor even

perhaps in our lifetime on this planet. But let us begin.

If more politicians knew poetry, and more poets knew politics, I am convinced the world would be a better place in which to live.

The life of the arts, far from being an interruption, a distraction, in the life of a nation, is very close to the center of a nation's purpose— and is a test of the quality of a nation's civilization.

I look forward to an America which will not be afraid of grace and beauty . . . an America which will reward achievement in the arts as we reward achievement in business or statecraft.

This country cannot afford to be materially rich and spiritually poor.

Finally there is the legacy of John F. Kennedy's life, preserved in a detailed chronology, or time line, countless photographs from childhood to middle age, and collections of his personal possessions, including an exact replica of his White House office with his desk exactly as he had left it on November 21, 1963, to fly to Texas.

It was an extraordinary life, a life of overcoming, of fabulous luck, of rapid political success, only to be smashed by a sudden reversal of fate. This life was in itself a legacy to the American consciousness. A hundred years from now, when the events of 1963 in Cuba and Vietnam will be forgotten as the events of the Mexican War of 1848 are forgotten today, the brief life of John F. Kennedy will still cast its spell over the American mind. In the end, John F. Kennedy's principal legacy to the American people was his life.

Part 5

TOWARD RESTORATION:
The First Attempt, 1963-1968

"Doom was woven in your nerves."
Robert Lowell
Robert Kennedy 1925–1968

58. Blackmail, Ambition, and Guilt

IN THE WEEKS AND MONTHS following his brother's assassination, Robert Kennedy had to endure the hostility of Lyndon Johnson and J. Edgar Hoover along with the burdens of grief and guilt.

The tables had been turned. Johnson was now President and Hoover was now virtually director for life. Hoover was anxious to establish a closer relationship with Johnson, whom he had known for many years. No sooner had Johnson returned to Washington after the assassination than Hoover was meeting with him in the Oval Office. We do not have the minutes of that meeting, but we can gather from remarks made by Robert Kennedy to Arthur Schlesinger, Jr., that Hoover brought some dossiers with him that Johnson must have found very interesting.

Among those dossiers there was probably one on the recently slain President. Hoover, as we know, had been amassing a file on the Kennedys since the early 1930s, and, given his professed hatred of both John and Robert Kennedy, it is reasonably safe to assume he would have taken the first opportunity that presented itself to bring John Kennedy's dossier to the attention of the incoming President. According to Schlesinger (quoting Robert Kennedy), others contained information on certain members of the late President's staff who were now on Johnson's staff: McGeorge Bundy, Kenneth O'Donnell, Walt Rostow, Theodore Sorensen, and Pierre Salinger. Robert Kennedy later complained to Schlesinger that Hoover had brought those dossiers to Johnson "with the idea that President Kennedy had appointed a lot of rather questionable figures."

One of the purposes of the meeting was no doubt to discuss the FBI's investigation of the murder of John F. Kennedy. Most probably another purpose was to discuss the FBI's secret dossiers on Jack Kennedy and certain members of his staff. Harris Wofford, who had experienced the tensions of the Kennedy-Hoover-Johnson relationship firsthand as a White House aide, intimated as much in his memoir of the Kennedy administration, writing, "Within hours of Johnson's becoming President, J. Edgar Hoover established that direct access to the Oval Office that he had enjoyed with every President until Kennedy," and going on to state that "Robert Kennedy had to assume the FBI Director had disclosed to Johnson whatever damaging information he had on the Kennedys."

We have no record of what was discussed at the Johnson-Hoover meeting, but it is possible that Hoover disclosed to the new President a good deal of what he had on file about John F. Kennedy and his father and brother Robert. This possibly included John F. Kennedy's relationship with Judith Campbell, and her relationships with Sam Giancana and John Roselli; Sam Giancana's donation, through Joe Kennedy, to the 1960 presidential campaign; the $500,000 payment Robert Kennedy had allegedly made on his brother's behalf to the woman who had sued JFK for breach of promise during the 1960 campaign; something about the CIA-Mafia plots to assassinate Castro; and the successful assassination operation against Trujillo. The only indications we have that Hoover might have made these disclosures to President Johnson at this time come from certain statements attributed to Johnson during the postassassination period, most notably one quoted by Leo Janos of *Time*, who reported that in an interview with Johnson LBJ told him that just after he took office he learned that "we were running a damn Murder, Inc., in the Caribbean." Since it is known that the CIA did not brief Johnson on the CIA-Mafia plots until much later, he may have received his information about the operations against Castro and Trujillo from the director of the FBI.

With the information Hoover had given him, Johnson now had an important card to play in his continuing power struggle with Robert Kennedy. It was a card Johnson knew Robert Kennedy would never, under any circumstances, want played, face up, for all the world to see.

It was no secret that Lyndon Johnson bore little love for Robert Kennedy. In the years following the assassination Johnson occasionally gave vent to his feelings. Once he referred to Kennedy as "that little runt who acted like he was some kind of rightful heir to the throne." To White House aide Eric F. Goldman he confided, "That upstart's come too far and too fast. He skipped the grades where you learn the rules of life. He never liked me, and that's nothing to what I think of him."

As for Hoover, his treatment of Robert Kennedy after the assassination even exceeded in hostility that of Lyndon Johnson. According to Victor Navasky, in his book *Kennedy Justice,* "starting at 1:10 P.M. on November 22 they [the FBI] began pissing on the attorney general."

When Robert Kennedy finally returned to his office in the Justice Department and called Hoover on the direct line he had installed to the FBI director's office, Hoover refused to answer the call and told his secretary to put the phone in a cabinet and leave it there. When the attorney general went on trips outside Washington, the FBI no longer sent a car to pick him up at airports, hotels, and meetings. More importantly, beginning on November 26, the FBI director began communicating directly with the new President, rather than through the attorney general. Then, to add insult to insult, Hoover replaced Kennedy FBI favorite Courtney Evans (the man the Kennedys wanted to replace Hoover) with Cartha De Loach, a friend of Lyndon Johnson's right-hand man, Walter Jenkins.

As time passed, Johnson and Hoover drew closer and closer. Finally Johnson announced that he was exempting the FBI director from mandatory retirement at age 65. In a White House Rose Garden ceremony marking this event, Johnson stated, "The nation cannot afford to lose you. No other American, now, or in the past, has served the cause of Justice so faithfully and well."

It was in this atmosphere of hostility to Robert Kennedy that Lyndon Johnson called into being his presidential commission, chaired by Chief Justice Warren, to investigate the assassination of John F. Kennedy, and J. Edgar Hoover rushed to complete his own investigation of the assassination, the report on which he was to release prematurely, contrary to Chief Justice Warren's wishes.

Curiously, most of the American press and public passively accepted President Johnson's appointing the Warren Commission to investigate the assassination as a means of getting to the bottom of the crime, even though all members of the commission had close ties to the government and none of the previous presidential assassinations—Lincoln's, Garfield's, or McKinley's—had been investigated by a presidential commission. But many foreign writers and statesmen were not nearly so indulgent. In England Lord Bertrand Russell, with the prestige of a Nobel Prize behind him, formed the "Who Killed Kennedy Committee," which would count among its members such eminent Britons as the author Kingsley Martin, Sir Compton Mackenzie, and the historian Prof. Hugh Trevor-Roper of Oxford. These people soon proved to be highly suspicious of the Warren Commission and did not hesitate to voice their opposition to it.

Lord Russell demanded to know why all the members of the Warren Commission were so closely connected with the U.S. government and why, if Oswald was the lone assassin, the issue of national security was raised in defense of conducting the inquiry in the strictest secrecy. Finally Lord Russell felt compelled to issue a scathing indictment of the Warren Commission and its investigation. "There has never been," he thundered, "a more subversive, conspirational, unpatriotic or endangering course for the United States and the world than the attempt by the United States Government to hide the murder of its recent President."

That accusation could justifiably have been leveled at Robert Kennedy as well. According to House assassinations committee reports, Kennedy in the summer of 1964, while the Warren Commission was concluding its investigation, secretly ordered the FBI to investigate certain reputed underworld plots against Castro and, in late July, having learned that the AM/LASH plot had not yet been put to rest, still kept knowledge of these plots from the Warren Commission.

And so it was that in the matter of the investigation of John F. Kennedy's assassination, Lyndon Johnson and Robert Kennedy worked hand in hand. There were many reasons why Johnson and Kennedy wanted a hasty inquiry pointing to the guilt of a lone assassin without conspirators rather than a thorough investigation of John F. Kennedy's murder, but none were more pressing than the two men's political ambitions, specifically Johnson's intense desire to be elected President "in his own right" and Robert Kennedy's equally intense desire to be either Johnson's vice presidential running mate or a candidate for the U.S. Senate in the same general election.

As it turned out, Johnson succeeded in eliminating Kennedy as a contender for the vice presidential nomination through the ingenious device of issuing a blanket ruling that all members of his cabinet were disqualified from running for vice president in 1964, causing Kennedy, shortly thereafter, on August 22, to announce he would run for the U.S. Senate from New York.

In September, as the Johnson and Kennedy campaigns were gathering steam, the Warren Commission finally issued its report to the American people. The report conveniently made no mention of anything likely to have a negative impact on the two political campaigns.

And so, with the American public peacefully sedated by the *Warren Report,* which was published in September, Johnson went on to a landslide victory in November, with Robert F. Kennedy winning a seat from New York in the U.S. Senate by the large margin of 719,693 votes. Thus did the hasty, grossly deficient, and, in some instances, deliberately deceiving investigation of John F. Kennedy's assassination successfully advance the careers of America's two leading Democratic politicians, paving the way for a power struggle between them that would dominate Democratic party politics in the United States for the next three and a half years.

As a U.S. senator from New York, Kennedy possessed an ideal springboard for the realization of his ambition to become President of the United States. There, in the chamber that John F. Kennedy had used as a springboard for *his* presidential aspirations, Robert Kennedy could be the resurrected voice of his murdered brother.

From there, Robert Kennedy endeavored to promote the continuation of his dead brother's policies. Before his election he had vigorously called for the enactment of his brother's civil rights proposals and had been gratified by the passage of the Civil Rights Act of 1964. And he had also argued vigorously for the continued prosecution of the Vietnam war. Now he argued in behalf of other causes his brother had believed in, such as the effort to halt the spread of nuclear weapons.

However, not all the causes that had been dear to John Kennedy's heart were pursued by Robert Kennedy from the floor of the Senate. After the assassination, both Operation Mongoose and the war against organized crime gradually lost momentum, as did the CIA's assassination plots. In April 1964 President Johnson ordered a halt to all sabotage operations against Cuba. And in June 1965 the CIA, upon learning that the AM/LASH plot was insecure, discontinued it and stopped all assassination plots against Castro. Cuba and the Mafia were never major concerns of Johnson's, and it appears that Robert Kennedy lost heart for them when he came to suspect that his two secret wars might have boomeranged into his brother's murder.

Nevertheless, it was in the immediate postassassination period that Robert Kennedy finally "got" Jimmy Hoffa, on March 4, 1964, on a jury-tampering conviction, and on July 26 on misuse of union pension funds, although he was still unable to put the corrupt union chief behind bars. (Hoffa would finally go to jail on March 7, 1967.)

Pursuing his dead brother's policies from his position

in the Senate was one way Robert Kennedy could keep his brother's memory alive and, in so doing, bolster his *own* image, something he felt constantly obliged to do in his protracted struggle with Lyndon Johnson for preeminence in the Democratic party. Another way to accomplish the same goal was to find ways of continuously feeding "the Kennedy legend."

Capitalizing on the irrational mass guilt of the American people over John Kennedy's murder that had immersed him and the entire Kennedy family in a seemingly endless outpouring of exaggerated pity and compassion, Robert Kennedy began exploiting his brother's tragedy for his own advancement in whatever ways he could. Some of the ways Robert found of doing this were so dangerous that some observers felt he was trying not only to enhance his image but also to expiate his guilt.

One such exploit was the climbing of Mount Kennedy. In March 1966 the National Geographic Society decided to organize an expedition to scale the remote 13,900-foot peak and invited the two surviving Kennedy brothers to join. Ted Kennedy had recently broken his back in a plane crash and was unable to participate, but Robert Kennedy, even though he had something of a phobia about heights, accepted the challenge.

When Father Joe heard about the idea he vigorously opposed it. Understandably, he did not want his son to take any unnecessary risks. Bobby had never climbed anything higher than a hill before. Robert, however, was determined. He knew it would be arduous and risky, but he was going to do it, for Jack. Of course, he was also fully aware of the tremendous publicity the feat would generate.

And so, in the company of two veterans of a Mount Everest expedition, Kennedy helicoptered to a base camp at 8700 feet for the 5200-foot climb, over glaciers and deep crevasses, to the hitherto unclimbed summit. Roped between the two veterans, he made the dangerous climb in two days. Upon reaching the summit, he deposited some Kennedy memorabilia in the snow, made the sign of the cross, and spent a few minutes in meditation.

Of course, in the days following the climb photographs of Robert Kennedy on the summit of Mount Kennedy (one of the Everest veterans happened to be a good photographer) appeared in almost all the major newspapers and magazines of the world. Another chapter of the Kennedy legend had been composed.

The climbing of Mount Kennedy initiated a period during which Robert Kennedy took so many unnecessary physical risks that it appeared he was deliberately courting death. Kennedy historians, such as Arthur M. Schlesinger, Jr., dispute this interpretation because it suggests a desire to atone for the murder of John Kennedy. But I believe that Robert Kennedy knew deep in his heart that his relentless efforts to "get Castro" and destroy the Mafia had resulted in the destruction of his own brother, and this caused a suicidal sense of guilt to become lodged in his soul.

Robert Kennedy's grief and sense of guilt were frequently so overwhelming during the postassassination period that this very Catholic man was once moved to exclaim to a friend, "I don't know why God put us on earth. If I had my choice I would never have lived." So, in the grip of his guilt, Kennedy subconsciously courted the only fate that could rescue him from his despair and enable him to fully expiate his guilt. He courted it on the skiing slopes of Vermont and Idaho where he challenged the most dangerous runs. He courted it in the rapids of the Colorado River where he battled the fastest, most turbulent water. At one point on the Colorado he even jumped into the white water, something his guides observed they had never seen anyone do before.

Later, on a trip to Brazil, he tempted fate by wading into a piranha-infested lake. According to Ralph de Toledano's account of this incident, Kennedy remarked to his companions, "Piranhas have never been known to eat a United States senator." Later, when he returned home, Kennedy added a piranha to the collection of pets he kept at Hickory Hill.

Naturally, each one of these flirtations with death won Robert Kennedy headlines and resulted in more accretions to the Kennedy legend; so, in the end, they were not simply wasted attempts at atonement. On the one hand, we see his adventures as courting death, and on the other as furthering his career, the ultimate goal of which was the restoration of the Kennedys to maximum political power in the United States.

One major effort to bolster the Kennedy legend occurred in 1966 with the creation of the John Fitzgerald Kennedy School of Government and the Kennedy Institute of Politics at Harvard. The Kennedy family had agreed to give Harvard $3,500,000 on condition that its Graduate School of Public Administration be renamed the John Fitzgerald Kennedy School of Government, and the Kennedy Library Corporation agreed to donate $10 million to a Kennedy Institute of Politics within the JFK School of Government that would be controlled by an independent advisory committee of which one member had to be from the Kennedy family. Harvard accepted the Kennedy family's unprecedented conditions, and thus two new prestigious institutions bearing the Kennedy name were born. Now, in addition to the Harvard school and institute, the family name graced Cape Kennedy, the Kennedy Center for the Performing Arts, Kennedy Airport, and would soon adorn the John F. Kennedy Memorial Library in Boston.

It goes without saying that all the publicity attendant on Robert Kennedy's perilous adventures and continuous nourishment of the Kennedy legend galled Lyndon Johnson and his ally, J. Edgar Hoover, no end. Anxious to catch Robert Kennedy at *anything* that might compromise his reputation, Hoover even had his FBI agents shadow Kennedy at parties to see if they could catch him in a flirt, or with too many drinks under his belt. (According to William Sullivan they failed to get anything on him.)

But Hoover had another card to play to damage the Kennedy reputation. He asserted publicly that Robert Kennedy had approved of all FBI electronic surveillance while he was attorney general. In a letter to Representative H. R. Gross of Iowa of December 10, 1966, Hoover asserted that "all wiretapping and electronic eavesdropping carried out by the Federal Bureau of Investigation while Robert F. Kennedy was attorney general was done with the approval of Mr. Kennedy." We now know that Kennedy was aware that electronic surveillance was going on, and that he consented to the wiretapping of Martin Luther King, Jr. But at the time of Hoover's assertion Kennedy denied he knew anything about the electronic surveillance, "except in cases where national security was involved." Nevertheless, Hoover's revelations did make a dent in the Kennedy reputation.

If Hoover had ways of puncturing the growing Kennedy legend, what means did President Johnson have at his command to accomplish the same end? First, let it be said that Johnson knew full well what was going on. One of his aides, Louis Heren, expressed it succinctly:

> The entire postassassination series of events had been a calculated, contrived, emotional buildup, not for the sake of paying honest respect to, and showing genuine grief for, John F. Kennedy, but to enhance the image of the Kennedy family and the Kennedy name.

Johnson knew he could puncture this process of enhancing "the image of the Kennedy family and the Kennedy name" by leaking what he knew of Operation Mongoose, the CIA-Mafia plots against Castro, and the JFK-Campbell-Giancana affair. But he was afraid of being too overt in his hostility to the Kennedys, and so he confined himself to occasionally leaking little bits and pieces of what he knew, knowing that they would inevitably get back to Robert Kennedy.

Thus, alluding perhaps to the Trujillo assassination, or to the assassinations of Diem and his brother, or to the murder plots against Castro, he confided to Pierre Salinger that what had happened to John F. Kennedy "may have been divine retribution," and the remark was immediately reported to Robert Kennedy, who later told Arthur Schlesinger it "was the worst thing Johnson has said."

But, by and large, Johnson held his tongue, and the American public in the mid-sixties never learned of the darkest secrets of the Kennedy administration. While Johnson kept his secrets, and began sinking deeper and deeper into the Vietnam quagmire, Robert Kennedy, perceiving a growing opposition to Johnson's policies, began metamorphosing into a very different political bird than the predatory species he had been during his brother's administration. Gradually "Mr. Counterinsurgency," the man of the Green Berets, the implacable one who had been out "to get Castro," "to get Hoffa," "to get Marcello," "to get Giancana," and to win the war in Vietnam, began transforming into the great dissenter, the liberal dove. The process of metamorphosis was a most gradual one, and its various stages seemed to coincide with stages in the gradual deterioration of Lyndon Johnson's popularity.

In April 1965, while still advocating the continued prosecution of the Vietnam war, Robert Kennedy urged Lyndon Johnson to stop the bombing of North Vietnam. In January 1966 Robert Kennedy publicly expressed concern over the deterioration of life in the urban ghettos and announced he would advocate urban renewal. In February 1966 former hawk Robert Kennedy stunned the hawks of the Johnson administration by calling for a negotiated settlement in Vietnam that would include the participation of the Vietcong's political arm, the National Liberation Front.

By June 1966, the Vietnam war had given Robert F. Kennedy his proverbial golden opportunity, a chance to seize on an issue that would establish him as a national political figure in his own right. He would change course and begin challenging President Johnson's escalation of the war. However, though he became increasingly vocal in his opposition to escalation, he still could not bring himself to accept either surrender or unilateral withdrawal. Nor did he appear especially eager to antagonize Lyndon Johnson on the Vietnam war issue. Thus he refused to support Senator Fulbright's effort to rescind the Tonkin Gulf Resolution that had conferred wartime powers on Johnson without actually declaring war on North Vietnam.

Kennedy's address to the Senate on March 2, 1967, revealed a man who was becoming more and more appalled by the war, but still could not rid himself of the stance of a cold-war warrior committed to the policy of containment. "The fault for no peace," he told his fellow senators, "rests largely with our adversary. . . . If our enemy will not accept peace it cannot come." He then went on to enumerate the enormous costs in lives and money the war was exacting, but added, "Of course we are willing—we must be willing—to pay all these costs if the alternative is surrender or defeat." In conclusion he called for an "unconditional halt to the bombing of North Vietnam which could be resumed if negotiations failed."

In other words, although Kennedy would come to denounce the war he and his brother had played such a role in starting as "immoral," he, like a good Kennedy, could still not countenance the idea of unilateral withdrawal: That would contradict the Kennedy code.

However, there may have been another reason why Robert Kennedy could not bring himself to fully and unequivocally denounce Johnson's conduct of the war: his fear of Lyndon Johnson. "I am afraid that by speaking out I just will make Lyndon do the opposite, out of spite," Kennedy told a friend at this time; "he hates me so much that if I asked for snow he would make rain."

But was it only that? Or did his reluctance to speak out—that reluctance that so disappointed liberals like Jack Newfield—go deeper? Wasn't one of the chief reasons Robert Kennedy was so reluctant to speak out his fear of *Johnson's speaking out?* In his fear of pushing Johnson too far, Robert Kennedy became a virtual hostage to the Kennedy reputation. He could never let his criticism of either Hoover or Johnson push either man to the point of letting information out of their files. In such a fashion were the reckless indiscretions of John F. Kennedy responsible for inducing crippling compromises in his brother Robert's political positions. Robert Kennedy had had to go along with Hoover's wiretapping of Martin Luther King, Jr., for fear that if he did not Hoover would let certain things about the Kennedys out of his files. Likewise, Robert could not be too vehement in his criticism of Johnson's escalation of the Vietnam war for fear that if he was, Johnson would reveal things that would be irretrievably damaging to the Kennedy image. John F. Kennedy may, or may not, have been blackmailed for his indiscretions during his lifetime, but his brother, and the country, most certainly were blackmailed by them after his death.

59. Counterculture for Kennedy

By THE MID-SIXTIES Robert Kennedy's ambition to become President had developed into an all-consuming passion, an obsession that guided almost all his thoughts and actions. But to attain the presidency he had to build a constituency that would elect him. He could not rely wholly on the power of the Kennedy legend to propel him into the White House. He had to represent something special to a certain class of voters.

Since the mid-fifties a movement of generalized dissent had been gathering steam in the United States, and by the mid-sixties it embraced large numbers of Americans. One of the leaders of this movement was Allen Ginsberg, whose poem "Howl" won a large audience and helped incite a widespread revolt against most of the sacred gospels of American life. By the mid-sixties this movement had come to be known as the counterculture, after a word coined by the writer Theodore Roszak in his book *The Making of a Counterculture*.

By an extraordinary twist of fate, and through an apparently extraordinary metamorphosis of personality, Robert F. Kennedy, whose family had epitomized the culture, became, in the late sixties, one of the great heroes of the counterculture and certainly its leading political representative. It was a constituency composed of everything from blacks and Hispanics to "beatnik" poets to ultraliberal professors. The common bond of these disparate groups was a pervasive, shared discontent.

What had gone wrong with American society that it could produce such a huge army of malcontents as it produced in the sixties? And how did Robert Kennedy come to be the man so many of the malcontents looked to for salvation? It is a most complex subject about which libraries have been written. Certainly American society did not "go wrong" overnight. As Senator William Fulbright remarked after the assassination of John F. Kennedy: "Our national life has always been marked by a baleful and incongruous strand of intolerance and violence."

It had something to do with the quality of American life. Matthew Arnold had sensed something was missing from American civilization when he visited the United States in the late nineteenth century. After that visit he wrote, "The weakness of the United States lay at the heart of her success—the speed of change had made the quality of life in the U.S. very poor."

It also had something to do with unresolved racial issues. At a certain point in the mid-twentieth century, white upper- and middle-class Americans began abandoning the cities (and the blacks) for the suburbs, leaving the assorted poor behind to fester in the ghettos. American society, never very united or harmonious, became more disunited and more disharmonious.

By the mid-sixties the rebellious white children of the middle-class suburbs were joining forces with the rebellious children of the infernal ghettos in a common cause against what they called "the Establishment," or "the System," which they felt was responsible for their frustration and alienation.

Then, suddenly, there burst upon the scene all the professional rebels and rebel groups of the era: Jerry Rubin, Mark Rudd, Tom Hayden, Abbie Hoffman, Angela Davis, Timothy Leary, the psychedelics, Ken Kesey, Janis Joplin, the Beatles, the Hermann Hesse addicts, the denizens of Haight-Ashbury and the East Village, the rioters of Columbia in 1968, the Rolling Stones, the flower children, Bob Dylan, the Beatniks, the Hippies, the SDS, the Yippies, the Zen freaks, the Black Panthers, the Mailerian "hipsters," the I Ching people, and the dropout devotees of grass, hash, speed, and acid.

Joining them was a bewildering army of draft resisters, pacifists, prostitutes, academics, rock musicians, welfare mothers, artists, reservation Indians, frustrated suburban housewives, prison inmates, and assembly-line workers suffering from terminal boredom.

What were all these motley voices saying? They were saying that white American society was "slow death by conformity." They were also saying that American society was profoundly hypocritical. That the American gospel had promised certain inalienable civil rights to all, then had denied them to certain elements of society. That the American gospel had promised equality of opportunity to all and yet by the mid-twentieth century you had people like the Kennedy brothers being sent off into the competitive world with Ivy League educations and million-dollar trust funds, while millions of blacks and poor whites were being sent out into the same competitive world with no education or money.

They were also saying in Watts, and Harlem, and Detroit, and Chicago that the Kennedy-Johnson civil rights bill was not enough, that John F. Kennedy had promised them more, had given them expectations that had not yet been fulfilled.

And so, before long, there was under way in the land a widespread revolt against virtually all the orthodoxies of the American testament. A large segment of the population was conducting a spontaneous social and cultural revolution, a revolution on a scale never known in America before.

The youth of America was revolting against all the values that had driven the American, and Kennedy, engines for the past hundred years. It was revolting against striving to "get ahead," competing, making money, acquiring more and more power, more and more "respectability," higher and higher status. It was revolting against the competitive values and voting for the values of sharing, cooperation, and enjoyment. And, of course, it was high time such a revolt took place. For a simplistic value system based wholly on the muscular virtue of winning can only result in near-universal unhappiness and disappointment, since there will always be many more losers in a given society than winners.

In the last analysis, the counterculture was a massive revolt against the value system of the Kennedys, which had been the value system of "the culture" raised to the highest power. For the Kennedy family was, in a very real sense, one of Allen Ginsberg's "molochs" in "Howl": "moloch whose blood is running money." And yet, paradoxically, it was a Kennedy who came to be the principal political leader of the assorted rebels, dropouts, underdogs, and outcasts who composed the counterculture.

As Jules Witcover, who accompanied Kennedy on his political campaigns, put it: "Robert Kennedy since his election to the U.S. Senate from New York in November, 1964, had earned the role of political embodiment of the nation's dissatisfaction."

What had brought about this paradoxical situation, more than any other factor, was the steadily mushrooming nightmare of the Vietnam war. The Vietnam war, which, for so long, had been a Kennedy war, exacerbated all the discontent in the American soul and provided a single issue around which the discontented could coalesce.

Robert Kennedy had often despaired of ever finding a way to challenge successfully the enormous power of Lyndon Johnson. As it turned out, he finally found a way, opposing the escalation of the most unpopular war in American history. By going against his late brother's Vietnam policy, which Johnson had continued with an added degree of bellicosity, Robert Kennedy perceived that he could win over a large constituency. ("Dump Lyndon" they began chanting in the first months of 1968.) And it was entirely conceivable, Kennedy came to believe, that this constituency could carry him all the way to the White House.

This is not to say that Kennedy did not possess a basic sympathy for this constituency, that he embraced it only out of political expediency. Though its values clashed with his family's traditional code, Kennedy did come to identify, selectively, with the malcontents and the underdogs of this world. As the seventh-born child in a highly competitive family, Robert Kennedy had had to learn to fight to survive. Being smaller (only five feet nine inches and 150 pounds) than his brothers only aggravated his fundamental predicament. One of his biographers, Jack Newfield, described him as the "least poised, least articulate, least extroverted, and the most physical and passionate of the Kennedys."

He also became the most moralistic and self-righteous of the brothers, responding more fully than the others to his mother's Catholic indoctrination. In time, his moralistic streak gave him an arrogant, judgmental cast of mind that led him to gross oversimplifications when it came to deciding what was right and what was wrong.

Robert Kennedy was always an average student, and he failed to gain admittance to Harvard Law School—but he was a dogged worker who could put in long hours on a tough task. Shy, insecure, and inarticulate throughout his adolescence and early manhood, he found in the woman he married, Ethel Skakel, an emotional support that brought out his personality and never failed him. If ever there was "a marriage made in heaven," the Kennedy-Skakel marriage was it. The two were so alike that one friend was prompted to remark that when Bobby was talking with Ethel it was like he was talking with himself.

Robert Kennedy identified with the underdog; however, sympathy for the underdog, and for people who suffered in general, was not a quality he displayed very often in his early years, but one which he developed as he grew older and experienced suffering himself. Gradually, as he came to experience pain and loss, Robert Kennedy moved away from the Kennedy ethos of confrontation and winning toward adopting some of the gentler ideals of the counterculture. More than likely it was the grief and guilt he felt over his brother's murder that eventually caused him to feel pity and compassion for the other unfortunates of this world.

Thus we find Robert Kennedy in 1967 and 1968 becoming more and more outspoken in his opposition to Johnson's escalations of the Vietnam war and primarily through this public stance, gradually attracting a larger and larger constituency who felt as he did.

By the election year of 1968, when Kennedy began to wear his hair long and shaggy, and declared, "If I was not born a Kennedy I would be a juvenile delinquent or a revolutionary," he had in his camp most of the counterculture, a sizable constituency and certainly a most vocal one. If it could somehow be wedded to a significantly large segment of the "square" white middle class, the coalition could possibly sweep him all the way into the White House.

And so, as the time of the 1968 primaries approached, Robert Kennedy, still somewhat hesitant about declaring his candidacy, pursued his dual policy of wooing his motley new constituency while systematically feeding the family legend, which latter policy he felt might lure to his side that much-needed chunk of the square white middle class.

60. The Desperate Quest

BY JANUARY 1968 ROBERT KENNEDY had despaired of successfully challenging the power of Lyndon Johnson, despite the President's waning popularity; he announced to the nation that under no circumstances would he be a candidate for the presidency in 1968. His professed rationale for not running was to avoid splitting the Democratic party, for a schism in the ranks would obviously play right into the Republicans' hands.

However, at the time he announced his withdrawal from the race Kennedy also wistfully told the reporters: "There's affluence, yet a feeling of unhappiness in the country. If someone touched the heart of that . . ." The truth was that Robert Kennedy wanted very much to touch "the heart of that" and run, but, being an astute politician with a superb sense of political timing, he realized that the circumstances were not yet quite favorable enough for him to throw his hat in the ring.

Then, suddenly, in February the circumstances began to change dramatically. The Vietcong launched their Tet offensive on February 1, the American Embassy in Saigon was attacked, Gen. William Westmoreland pleaded for more troops, and the joint chiefs recommended hurling another 200,000 Americans into the Vietnam quagmire. Taking advantage of the new burst of anti-Vietnam feeling the Tet offensive had occasioned, Kennedy lashed out at

Lyndon Johnson's Vietnam policy in his strongest statement on the war to date. Not long thereafter, a frustrated Johnson, at the limits of his patience, replaced his secretary of defense, Robert McNamara, with that good old Washington trusty, Clark Clifford.

Meanwhile, the New Hampshire primary was approaching, and all the political antennae in the nation quivered in anticipation of who would win the Democratic contest between Eugene McCarthy and Lyndon Johnson. When the results of the primary were proclaimed on March 12, Robert Kennedy, the noncandidate, was stunned to learn that McCarthy had walked off with twenty out of the state's twenty-four delegates to the national convention, polling 42.2 percent of the state Democratic vote and slightly over half the total vote after all the Republican write-ins had been tabulated. So Lyndon Johnson *could* be beaten!

As it turned out, the results of the New Hampshire primary changed everything for Robert Kennedy. Four days after McCarthy's victory, Kennedy reversed his previous stand and announced that he too was a candidate for the presidency of the United States, making the announcement in the same Senate Caucus Room in which his late brother had announced his candidacy for the presidency eight years before. Contrary to what most people believe, both Joseph Kennedy, Sr., and Ted Kennedy were against Bobby's running, and Jacqueline Kennedy tried to get Arthur Schlesinger to stop him because she was sure someone would kill him if he did.

There followed one of the most hastily put together political campaigns in American history. As Kennedy aide William vanden Heuvel put it, "A nationwide political apparatus had to be created overnight." Many observers thought it was all sheer madness, and, in many ways, it was.

Meanwhile Lyndon Johnson began to have second thoughts about his *own* candidacy. The insoluble Vietnam war had destroyed his popularity, crippled his effectiveness, and soured his mood. Several of his closest aides felt he had begun to lose his taste for the job. Things came to a head on March 31. On that day, when a Gallup poll showed Johnson's popularity had sunk to an all-time low, and Martin Luther King, Jr., preached a sermon against the Vietnam war in the National Cathedral, Lyndon Johnson startled Robert Kennedy and the world by announcing he would not run for reelection.

For Robert Kennedy the President's withdrawal was an impossible dream come true. Now he would not have to confront the mighty Lyndon Johnson, a battle that had promised much nastiness, and, quite possibly, the leaking of unsavory revelations about his slain brother, something Robert had to avoid at all cost if he was going to continue to exploit the Kennedy legend successfully. Now he would have to confront only McCarthy and Hubert Humphrey. Against *them* he thought he had a chance.

On April 3, Robert Kennedy and Lyndon Johnson met for the last time, and Kennedy exacted a limited degree of cooperation from the President about not unduly disturbing the political waters. Granted they were enemies, but, after all, they were also both loyal Democrats. Although there is no record of their conversation, it is reasonable to assume, judging from what followed, that something of a deal was made. Kennedy could, of course, criticize Johnson during the campaign, within limits, within very certain, restricted limits. In return Johnson would keep the lid on what he knew.

The following day, as Kennedy was beginning his campaign in Indiana, Martin Luther King, Jr., was murdered in Memphis, an event that shook Kennedy badly and caused riots to break out in over a hundred American cities, resulting in the deaths of thirty-seven people.

On learning the terrible news as his campaign jet was landing in Indianapolis, Kennedy went straight to the city's ghetto and spoke to a crowd of some six hundred blacks on a street corner:

> We must make an effort, as Martin Luther King did, to understand with compassion and love. . . . I had a member of my family killed, but he was killed by a white man. But we have to make an effort in the United States, we have

to make an effort to understand. What we need is not violence, but love and wisdom, and compassion towards one another, and a feeling of justice towards those who still suffer within our country, whether they be white or black.

He then went on to quote from Aeschylus: "In our sleep, pain which cannot forget falls drop by drop upon the heart until, in our own despair, against our will comes wisdom through the awful grace of God."

As it turned out, the riots following Dr. King's murder worked mostly to Kennedy's political disadvantage, since they made the white middle class so uneasy they began to look with suspicion on that "nigger lover" Robert Kennedy. However, Kennedy did not let that daunt him, and, fueled by his outrage over Martin Luther King's murder, he threw himself into the campaign with even more gusto than before.

What a boil of emotions powered Robert Kennedy's quest for the presidency in 1968! The other candidates' motivations were relatively simple, a mixture of personal ambition and desire to do something for the country. But Robert Kennedy's motivation was infinitely more complex. Robert Kennedy wanted to be President to make up for his brother's death: to complete his brother's truncated presidency, and to atone for his brother's murder, which he felt he was indirectly responsible for.

It was an emotional campaign, and a dangerous one. Everybody was aware that, after he announced, Kennedy immediately became the most vulnerable target in the country. For besides his sworn enemies (Hoffa was smoldering in prison; Giancana was in exile in Cuernavaca waiting for the right moment to return; deportation proceedings against Marcello continued), there were bound to be scores of assorted maniacs and fanatics waiting out there to eliminate another Kennedy—not to mention all those who would be disposed to kill him for political reasons. Robert Kennedy was fully aware of this himself, and yet he recklessly plunged into crowds with inadequate protection and repeatedly exposed himself to potential danger in literally hundreds of situations. Some called this behavior courage; others saw in it a subconscious desire to join his dead brother.

Once, in Lansing, Michigan, the local police advised one of Kennedy's bodyguards, Bill Barry, that a man with a rifle had been spotted entering the building directly opposite Kennedy's hotel. Barry then told Kennedy aide Fred Dutton about it, and Dutton went to Kennedy's room to draw the shades on his windows. When Kennedy noticed what he was doing he stopped Dutton, saying, "I don't want that! Don't ever do that. I'm not going to start ducking, or running." Later that day he told Dutton, "You know if I'm ever elected President, I'm never going to ride in one of those goddamn bubble top cars."

And so here is Robert Kennedy arriving at the Kansas City airport where 2500 people, mostly young women, are waiting to greet him. As Kennedy steps off the plane several hundred women burst through the police barricades, race to the plane, shrieking, "Bobby! Bobby! Bobby!" pin Kennedy against the plane, and begin pulling at his clothes and his hair before being yanked away by the police. And here is Robert Kennedy, his hair longer than he has ever worn it before, speaking before 14,500 students at Kansas University in Lawrence, the largest gathering in the university's history. Many of the students are holding aloft large placards reading I LOVE BOBBY, KISS ME, BOBBY, BOBBY IS GROOVY, BOBBY IS SEXY, SOCK IT TO 'EM BOBBY.

It was a wild and desperate campaign, an "orgy of emotion," as one writer put it, and one remains in awe of how Robert Kennedy stood up to it. For Robert Kennedy was basically a very shy, somewhat awkward man, who never really felt at ease with people unless he was with members of his own family. Meeting new people, shaking hands, and speaking in public did not come easily to him. Many observers noted that his hands always trembled while he spoke. And yet here he was, going against his basic nature, trying as hard as he could to be the outgoing politician, rather than the back-room manager, which was probably his true political vocation.

Robert Kennedy got into all sorts of subjects that

are not ordinarily the province of politicians. He got into philosophy, psychology, and religion. He made the happiness/unhappiness of Americans and the state of the American soul into political issues. "We are in a time of unprecedented turbulence, of danger, and questioning," he cried on March 18. "It has its roots in the question of national soul." "There is a contest on," he would cry, "not for the rule of America, but for the heart of America." Most politicians did not talk in those terms.

He also indulged in the politics of high expectations, as his brother before him had done, promising everything to everybody. Unlike the Republicans, whose traditional constituency is the white Anglo-Saxon Protestant bloc, the democrats, as the party of all the "others," are compelled to play ethnic politics to the hilt, and Kennedy proved a master at the game. To the young he promised an end to the Vietnam war (though he still remained against surrender or a unilateral withdrawal) and an administration of beauty and light. To the blacks he promised jobs, the elimination of the ghettos, and an end to all racial discrimination. To the Mexican-American farm workers, the Chicanos, he promised higher wages and better living conditions. To the malcontent and disaffected everywhere he promised a "rebirth of the national soul." To all who suffered he promised an end to their sufferings. "Starvation in Mississippi is unacceptable!" he would cry. "Suicides on Indian reservations are unacceptable!" he would cry again. It was a dangerous game, for it is one thing to promise, and another to deliver; often great expectations are followed by even greater disappointments, and dealing with a disappointed electorate is, of course, the politician's ultimate nightmare.

Did Robert Kennedy stand a chance in his desperate quest for the presidency? Kennedy knew that to win the nomination he had to attract large segments of white labor and the white middle class. But he had lost a lot of labor votes through his persecution of Jimmy Hoffa and almost the entire white south because of his championing of civil rights for blacks.

There was one important group of white middle-class

voters, however, which Kennedy believed he could attract to his side, and that was the Jews. Sixty percent of all the Jews in the country live in two states, California and New York, and these, of course, are the two states that send the largest delegations to the national convention. The equation was simple. To win the nomination he had to win New York and California. To win New York and California he had to win the Jewish vote. To win the Jewish vote he had to take a strong pro-Israel stand.

Robert Kennedy had a long record of sympathy for Israel and the Jews. In April 1948, the last month of the British mandate in Palestine, he went to Palestine to write some articles on the Jewish-Arab struggle for the now defunct *Boston Post*, a paper that was indebted to his father.

The struggle between the Palestinian Arabs and the Jews was intensifying in anticipation of the imminent expiration of the British mandate. Soon thousands of Palestinian Arabs would be forced out of their country by the new Jewish state of Israel. In this violent struggle, the lines were neatly drawn.

Being a Kennedy, and therefore an advocate of the virtues of toughness, hard work, competitiveness, and ambition, Kennedy soon took the side of the Jews against that of the Palestinian Arabs. The Jews seemed to possess the qualities he admired most. In his articles for the *Boston Post* he wrote that the Jews were "a young, tough, determined" people, "and will fight as such." "If a Jewish state is formed," he wrote, "it will be the only stabilizing factor remaining in the near and middle East." Of course the exact opposite proved to be true.

Just as he praised the Jews in his articles for the *Post,* Kennedy had nothing good to say for the Arabs. "The Jews," he wrote, in an especially simplistic passage, have "an undying spirit that the Arabs, Iraqi, Syrians, Lebanese, Saudi Arabians, Egyptians, and those from Trans-Jordan can never have."

When Kennedy visited Jersualem in 1948, not long before the expiration of the British mandate, a Palestinian Arab family by the name of Sirhan, one of whose members was destined to put an end to Kennedy's desperate quest for the presidency, was living in a hillside community just outside the city's walls. After Kennedy left Palestine, and the mandate expired, all hell broke loose in the country, with the Arabs and Jews fighting it out for whatever territory each could capture. In the violent struggle the Sirhans lost a son, and their house was captured by the Jews, causing the family to flee to a refugee shelter within Jerusalem's walls. Twenty years later Sirhan Sirhan, who had been four years old at the time his family lost their home, recalled those days of violence at his trial in Los Angeles for the murder of Robert F. Kennedy.

Robert Kennedy, as we know, was a black-and-white thinker, with a pronounced strain of the moralist in his makeup. After his 1948 experience in Palestine he became a black-and-white thinker on the Jewish-Arab question. The Jews were good; the Arabs were bad. It was an attitude characteristic of most Americans' thinking on the subject at the time. Thus Kennedy proved incapable of seeing any justification in the Palestinian Arabs' cause. When the Jews began expelling the Palestinian Arabs from the new state of Israel (300,000 were forced out after April 1, 1948, and many more later) and the refugee camps in Syria and Jordan began filling up to overflowing, Robert Kennedy, the supposed champion of the underdog, took no pity on them. Later, when the UN General Assembly voted not to have Jordanian Jerusalem incorporated into the new state of Israel, Kennedy protested the vote.

Two and a half million Jews lived in New York state at the time Robert Kennedy ran for senator from New York in 1964. Assiduously he cultivated the Jewish vote in that whirlwind "hit and run" campaign, doing things few non-Jewish candidates had ever done before. Having himself photographed eating a knish was pretty innocent. But donning the yarmulke, the traditional Jewish skullcap, for speeches in synagogues and having himself photographed wearing it was a bit much. No non-Jewish politician running for the Senate had ever done that before.

Naturally, in all his speeches before Jewish audiences Kennedy reminded his listeners of John F. Kennedy's support for Israel, recalling that during his late brother's administration JFK had advocated sending Hawk missiles to the Jewish state. Joseph Kennedy had had a reputation for being an anti-Semite, and, of course, as ambassador to Great Britain, he had advised Roosevelt not to go to war against Hitler. But Robert Kennedy, with his pro-Israel sympathies, succeeded in overcoming that reputation. He won the New York Jewish vote and that probably won him his election to the Senate. As a token of thanks to the Jews of New York, the Kennedy family gave $1,450,000 to Yeshiva University after the election.

But Robert Kennedy, in his courting of the Jewish vote, went several steps further. He openly criticized the Arabs. In June 1967, speaking at a meeting of Jewish labor union leaders, he made a remark that reverberated throughout the Arab world like a cannon volley. Clearing his throat in a mock cough, he made a sour face and said, "I've just drunk a cup of bitter Arab coffee and have not had time to wash my mouth." The remark elicited a big laugh from his audience, and feelings of shock and outrage throughout the entire Arab world, where it was interpreted as an insult to the Arab people and to Arab hospitality.

As it turned out, Kennedy's "bitter Arab coffee" remark was to dog him throughout the remaining days of his life—he would eat knishes, the Arabs would say, and attend bar mitzvahs, and wear the yarmulke, but he would not drink Arab coffee. The line was even quoted in his obituaries in Arab newspapers after his death at the hands of a young Palestinian Arab.

But Robert Kennedy, like most Americans, was not at all concerned with the Arabs during the 1968 campaign. By the time his campaign was in high gear, half a million Palestinian Arabs had been driven from their homeland by the Israeli state, or had left voluntarily, and were living in miserable refugee camps in Lebanon, Jordan, and Syria. Kennedy's brother, Edward, had been chairman of the Special Senate Subcommittee on Refugees and Escapees, and in that role had made an inspection of the Palestinian refugee camps in Jordan and Lebanon in 1966, which resulted in his calling for the repatriation and compensation of those refugees. Even so, Robert Kennedy refused to acknowledge the plight of the Palestinian Arabs. It was essentially because of this limitation that his quest for the presidency was eventually thwarted.

One wonders if Kennedy would have been able to see the Arab side if there were as many Arabs in the American electorate as Jews. As it was, the Arab-Americans were a tiny minority in the United States in 1968. Estimates vary, but most experts agree there were no more than 400,000 to 500,000 of them living in the United States at the time. Among these were 2000 Palestinian Arab refugee families that had been allowed to immigrate to the United States by a special decree of President Eisenhower. And among these was the Sirhan family of Jerusalem. Leaving Beirut by ship in 1956, the Sirhans had arrived in New York, via Naples, in 1957 and then had taken a train for Los Angeles where their American sponsors lived. Eventually the family settled in Pasadena. Sirhan Sirhan was thirteen years old at the time.

Much has been theorized about Robert Kennedy's profound metamorphosis of personality after the assassination of his brother. Yet Kennedy's attitude toward the Arabs, and the Palestinian Arabs in particular, completely belies that hypothesis. The Palestinian Arabs were among the most oppressed, downtrodden peoples of the world in 1968, and Robert Kennedy took no note of their plight. Was it that he did not want anything to interfere with his capturing the Jewish vote?

Sometimes it is more enlightening to discover what a politician *omits* from campaign rhetoric than what he or she keeps repeating. A study of Robert Kennedy's 1968 campaign speeches reveals some truly extraordinary omissions. We know that as attorney general, and de facto "assistant President" of the United States, Kennedy's major concerns had been fighting organized crime and trying to sabotage Castro's Cuba. Civil rights for blacks came third. And we know that Kennedy believed that quite possibly Cubans and the Cosa Nostra were involved in the plot to assassinate his brother. Yet, in the campaign of 1968, Kennedy barely uttered a word about Cuba and organized crime; the blacks, the poor, and the counterculture got all his attention.

The fateful campaign ground on to its tragic conclusion. In May, Kennedy won in Indiana and Nebraska. Indiana was a particularly satisfying victory because it was determined that the white working-class vote had come out for him rather than for McCarthy. Asked why, Kennedy quipped, "I think part of it is that Gene comes across lace curtain Irish to these people. They can tell I'm pure shanty Irish."

Then, later on in May, Kennedy lost in Oregon. Kennedy's utterances about a disturbed America that had lost its way did not seem to strike a sympathetic chord in the healthy-minded Oregonians, who did not feel particularly disturbed and did not feel they had lost their way. And his anti-Vietnam war pronouncements seemed but an echo of Gene McCarthy's statements on the same issue. Also there were not many blacks and Mexican-Americans in Oregon. McCarthy emphasized this and took advantage of the fact to compliment the Oregonians by calling them the elite electorate, one not suited to Robert Kennedy, who, he said, "appealed mainly to the uneducated." The strategy worked, and the flattered Oregonians came out for Gene McCarthy.

However, one elite, educated group Kennedy did court in Oregon was the Jews. While campaigning in Portland Kennedy made one of the most impassioned pro-Israel declarations of his career. In a speech he gave in the Temple Neveh Shalom on May 26, he took a stronger position on Israel than any other U.S. presidential candidate had ever taken.

> The U.S. must defend Israel against aggression from whatever source. Our obligations to Israel, unlike our obligations towards other countries, are clear and imperative. Israel is the very opposite of Vietnam. Israel's government is democratic, effective, free of corruption, its people united in its support.

Kennedy followed these remarks with what might have been a fatal statement: "The United States should, without delay, sell Israel the fifty Phantom jets she has so long been promised."

The next day, May 27, a picture of Robert Kennedy appeared in a Pasadena paper, *The Independent,* to which the Sirhan family subscribed. Underneath the photo the caption read: "BOBBY SAYS SHALOM—Sen. Robert F. Kennedy, wearing a traditional Jewish 'yarmulke,' addressed the Neveh Shalom congregation in Portland on his campaign tour of Oregon. He told the congregation the U.S. must support Israel against outside aggression."

The sight of this photograph appears to have profoundly unnerved the Palestinian Arab refugee, Sirhan Sirhan, whose people had been victims of Israeli bombings, and he reaffirmed what he had already scribbled in a notebook on May 18, possibly in reaction to another instance of pro-Israeli activity by Kennedy: "Robert F. Kennedy must be assassinated before June 5, 1968."

61. The Fifty Phantoms

ON TO CALIFORNIA. The crucial state. The state that could make or break him. At stake were 174 delegates. He had to make a comeback after the defeat in Oregon. If he lost in California, it was all over.

Robert Kennedy knew there were two keys to winning California: the Mexican-Americans and the Jews. The Mexican-Americans he already had in his pocket. His passionate and much-publicized support of Cesar Chavez and the Mexican farm workers had assured that. But the Jews were still considered uncommitted. And the Jews were vitally important because a higher percentage of them voted in primary elections than any other so-called ethnic group. The largest concentrations of Mexican-Americans and Jews in California were located in Los Angeles and its environs, and so it was in the Los Angeles area that Kennedy had to make his major campaign effort.

By an incredible convergence of fate, the odds against which were beyond calculation, Kennedy's life would intersect disastrously in Los Angeles with the life of a young Palestinian Arab refugee. Sirhan Sirhan, at the time of Kennedy's visit to Los Angeles, was an unemployed worker who had dropped out of Pasadena City College, which he had scorned as a "diploma factory," and had worked, off and on, exercising horses at a thoroughbred racehorse breeding ranch in Corona, east of Pasadena, and also at the Santa Anita racetrack. The breeding ranch, called the Granja Vista Del Rio, belonged, in part, to the Cuban actor-singer Desi Arnaz, former husband of actress Lucille Ball. Arnaz was a fervent opponent of Fidel Castro and a leader of Cuban exiles in his area.

Sirhan's immediate superior at the ranch was one Frank Donnarauma, whose real name was Henry Ramistella. Ramistella, it was later discovered, had a record of narcotics violations in New York and Florida and, it was suspected, may have been connected with organized crime. The young Sirhan had apparently become very friendly with Donnarauma/Ramistella and left this cryptic reference to him in his notebook: "happiness hppiness Dona Donaruma Donaruma Frank Donaruma pl please ple please pay to 5 please pay to the order of Sirhan Sirhan the amount of 5. . . . " Sirhan had first met Donnarauma/Ramistella at the Santa Anita racetrack where Sirhan had been employed as a "hotwalker," or walker of horses after training. It was, in fact, Donnarauma who got Sirhan his job at the Corona ranch.

Sirhan Sirhan was a thoughtful, articulate young man of 24, passionately committed to the Arab cause. An admirer of John F. Kennedy because he had opened serious dialogues with such great Arab leaders as Nasser of Egypt, Sirhan had been originally well disposed toward Robert F. Kennedy because Kennedy had styled himself the champion of the underdog, and Sirhan considered himself, and his fellow Palestinian Arabs, the underdogs of underdogs.

But then, in late May 1968, while Kennedy was campaigning in Oregon, Sirhan saw a film on television called "The Story of Robert Kennedy," which caused him to change his mind completely about his hero. The half-hour film had been made by Jewish film producer John Frankenheimer and had obviously been targeted for a Jewish audience. At one point early in the film, the narrator informed his listeners that young Robert Kennedy had been in Israel as a correspondent in 1948 at the time Israel was born. "He wrote his dispatches, and came to a decision," the narrator goes on, at which point, an Israeli flag is seen fluttering in the wind, "and then," the narrator says, in dramatic tones, "Bobby Kennedy decided his future lay in the affairs of men and nations."

Sirhan Sirhan was watching the film in Pasadena, and when he saw this episode something in him snapped. Later, at his trial for the murder of Robert Kennedy, he testified:

> The film presented Kennedy as being for the underdog and also being for the disadvantaged and for the scum of society, that he wanted to help the poorest people and the most prejudiced and the weakest and at that moment, sir, they showed on the television where Robert Kennedy was in Israel helping to, so I thought, helping to celebrate the Israelis, sir, there, and the establishment of the state of Israel, and the way that he spoke, well, it just bugged me, sir, it burned me up and up until that time I had loved Robert Kennedy, I cared for him very much, and I hoped that he would win the Presidency, but when I saw, heard, he was supporting Israel, sir, not in 1968, but he was supporting it from all the way from its inception in 1948, sir. And he was doing a lot of things behind my back that I didn't know about and, until that time when I watched him on television, it burned me up, sir. And that is most likely, sir, the time I had written this [Robert F. Kennedy must die].

Although the Frankenheimer documentary did not air until May 20, Sirhan claimed it had prompted his famous May 18 diary entry:

> My determination to eliminate R.F.K. is becoming more the more of an unshakable obsession. . . . R.F.K. must die—RFK must be killed, Robert F. Kennedy must be assassinated. . . . Robert F. Kennedy must be assassinated before June 5, '68. Robert F. Kennedy must be assassinated I have never heard please

> pay to the order of of of of of of of of of of of
> this or that 8 00 00 0 0 HL
> Please pay to the order of

Then, on May 26, while Kennedy was winding up his campaign in Oregon, Sirhan read an article by David Lawrence in the *Pasadena Independent* that further enraged him. The gist of the article, entitled "Paradoxical Bob," was that while Kennedy was advocating disengagement from the war in Vietnam, condemning the war as cruel and wasteful and a "national tragedy," he was at the same time advocating the arming of Israel and pledging full and total U.S. military support to the Jewish state. The paradox was obvious. Kennedy, the "peace candidate," was only selectively a peace candidate. While he was a dove on Vietnam, he was a hawk on Israel. The article enraged Sirhan. Again he felt betrayed by Kennedy.

It was on the next day, May 27, that Sirhan beheld in the *Pasadena Independent* the photo of Robert Kennedy wearing the yarmulke in the Portland synagogue and declaring that the U.S. should send fifty Phantom bombers to Israel.

Later, when Sirhan was arrested for murdering Kennedy, a copy of David Lawrence's article in the May 26 *Pasadena Independent* was found in his pocket. Later still, at his trial, Sirhan testified that Robert Kennedy's willingness to send fifty Phantom bombers to Israel "solidified" in his mind his determination to kill Kennedy.

Meanwhile, Kennedy had come to Los Angeles to wind up his California campaign. His motorcade sailed through the Los Angeles suburbs of Watts and Venice. Kennedy made a quick trip to San Diego and back. Wearing the yarmulke again, he spoke at the Temple Isaiah in Beverly Hills on June 1, where he again advocated sending fifty Phantom bombers to Israel, and the speech was carried over station KFWB and was heard by Mrs. Sirhan, who duly reported it to her son.

Then, on June 2, Sirhan drove from Pasadena to downtown Los Angeles where he attended a Robert Kennedy open house at the Ambassador Hotel. Apparently

Kennedy impressed Sirhan favorably at this event because later, during his trial, he stated, "When I saw him that day, he looked like a saint to me."

But when he was asked at the trial whether anything had happened between June 2 and 4 that had changed his mind, he replied, "I don't know sir, because his willingness, his commitment to send those fifty Phantom jet bombers to Israel was still solidified in my mind. . . ."

The next day, June 3, Sirhan visited the ranch in Corona where he had once worked for Frank Donnarauma/Henry Ramistella. We still do not know what transpired during this visit. At his trial Sirhan both asserted and denied he had gone to the ranch that day. But he did admit that he practiced with a pistol on a firing range near Corona the day he revisited the ranch.

On June 4, the day of the voting, Robert Kennedy, with his wife and children, went to swim at the beach in Malibu with friends. Later he had an early supper with film producer John Frankenheimer and film director Roman Polanski and his wife, Sharon Tate.

While Kennedy and his family were at the beach in Malibu, Sirhan was out at the San Gabriel Gun Club in Fish Canyon doing some more pistol practice. Remaining at the gun club from 11:30 A.M. to 5:30 P.M., Sirhan fired some 700 to 800 rounds. By six, Sirhan was eating a hamburger with a friend at Bob's Big Boy restaurant on Colorado Boulevard in Pasadena.

A little after seven, John Frankenheimer deposited Robert Kennedy and his family at the Ambassador Hotel where Kennedy's election headquarters had been established. Two hours later Sirhan parked his De Soto nearby and entered the hotel himself.

62. Murder in Los Angeles: The Third Derailment

WHEN SIRHAN SIRHAN ARRIVED at the Ambassador Hotel around nine he went first to the campaign party of Republican senatorial candidate Max Rafferty in the hotel's Venetian Room. Sirhan had known Rafferty's daughter, Kathleen, in high school, and it was primarily to see her that he had decided to go to her father's party.

Sirhan was an inconspicuous figure at the event. The short, slim, dark-skinned Palestinian with bushy hair was dressed in blue jeans, a white shirt, and a loose blue sweater, and apparently did nothing at the party but drink two Tom Collinses and make a few objectionable remarks.

According to the testimony of two individuals, a Mexican and a Puerto Rican, who claimed they ran into Sirhan in a hallway outside the Venetian Room after he had apparently been ejected from the Rafferty party, Sirhan left the party muttering curses about "the rich Rafferty people who step all over the poor." To that the Mexican observed, "But Kennedy will help the poor," and Sirhan angrily retorted, "Kennedy! He should never be President. You think he really wants to help the poor? Kennedy helps himself. He's just using the poor. Can't you see that?"

After this exchange, Sirhan wandered into the Kennedy party in the main ballroom, known as the Embassy Room, where he promptly drank two more Tom Collinses while he watched the election returns, along with Kennedy's campaign workers, coming in over the teletype. Apparently security was so lax that Sirhan experienced no difficulty whatsoever in gaining access to the Kennedy party.

Meanwhile, Robert Kennedy was watching the election returns with his family, friends, and aides upstairs in the hotel's Royal Suite. On the brink of collapse from what had been the most strenuous effort of his life, Kennedy looked very tired. A mood of nervous uncertainty pervaded his entourage. The California returns were coming in slowly because of a computer breakdown, and the outcome was still anybody's guess.

At about 11 P.M., Sirhan, according to his testimony at his trial, decided to return home and went back to his car; once there, he realized he was too drunk to drive. So instead of driving home he took his Iver Johnson 22-caliber pistol from the back seat, "so the Jews wouldn't get it" (there was supposed to be a Jewish parade in the area that evening to commemorate the first anniversary of the Six-Day War), tucked his pistol into the top of his pants, and returned to the Kennedy party. (This story is widely regarded with skepticism as having been concocted to avoid a charge of premeditated murder.)

From this point on, according to Sirhan's own testimony again, Sirhan's mind went blank and he remembered nothing that followed. However, later under hypnosis, he recalled going back to the Kennedy party in the main ballroom, drinking two cups of coffee to sober up, and then going into the Colonial Room, where the press had gathered to watch the election returns coming in over the teletype.

At approximately 11:40 a shout of joy went up in the Royal Suite as it was announced on television that Robert Kennedy had won a double victory. In South Dakota he had defeated Hubert Humphrey by 50 to 30 percent, and in California he had triumphed over Eugene McCarthy by 46 to 42 percent.

Kennedy then went down to the ballroom to thank his campaign workers and deliver his victory speech. Without any security protection to speak of he took the service elevator to the kitchen pantry, which was full of kitchen workers, and from there proceeded through a crowded corridor to the podium in the ballroom. Later a Los Angeles fireman, stationed in the corridor, testified that he had noticed a swarthy, bushy-haired young man carrying what appeared to be a rolled-up poster in the corridor as Kennedy came through. By the time Kennedy reached the podium the young man had gone into the pantry area with his package, and, standing among ten or twelve kitchen workers near the steam tables, began waiting for Kennedy to come through again. It was generally known by this time that, after his victory speech, Kennedy was going to go to the adjacent Colonial Room to meet the press. The short cut to the Colonial Room was through the pantry area.

It must be emphasized, at this point, that Kennedy's security guard was virtually nonexistent. All he had to protect him were an Ace Agency guard and two athletes, decathlon champion Rafer Johnson and football tackle Rosie Grier. These last two were brawny and agile enough, but neither was expert in security. This lack of adequate protection in Los Angeles was typical of the campaign throughout the rest of the country. Later the Los Angeles Police Department declared that it had offered Kennedy a twelve-man "hot squad" to provide security during his Los Angeles visit and he had refused it. (Kennedy's aides said they knew nothing of the offer.) By all rights, the pantry area should have been cleared before each of Kennedy's sorties through it, but no one on Kennedy's staff had had the sense to even suggest it, never mind make sure it was done. And Kennedy himself was apparently oblivious to the possible dangers of a hotel pantry full of unchecked busboys, waiters, and dishwashers.

When Kennedy arrived at the podium, a huge cheer went up from his supporters. When it subsided, he launched into his victory speech. Its burden was contained in one paragraph:

> What I think is quite clear is that we can work together in the last analysis, and that what has been going on within the United States over a period of the last three years—the divisions,

the violence, the disenchantment with our society; the divisions, whether it's between blacks and whites, between the poor and the more affluent, or between age groups or on the war in Vietnam—is that we can start to work together. We are a great country, an unselfish country and a compassionate country. I intend to make that a basis for running.

While Kennedy was delivering his victory speech, Sirhan Sirhan climbed up on a tray stacker in the pantry area and, holding the rolled-up, posterlike object close to his stomach, went into a crouch. A security guard would have become instantly suspicious of this crouching figure, who did not appear to be a hotel employee, but there was no guard anywhere near the pantry at the time. Soon a pretty young girl in a polka-dot dress, whom Sirhan had apparently met earlier, joined him on the tray stacker, and the two were observed in animated conversation.

Before long, Kennedy ended his victory speech by making the V sign and shouting, "On to Chicago! Let's win there!" As the crowd roared, there was some discussion at the podium about how Kennedy was going to get to the Colonial Room to meet the press. Kennedy apparently wanted to go through the pantry again, but some of his aides thought he could just as well get there through the ballroom. The discussion was resolved by the hotel's assistant maître d', Karl Uecker, who took the candidate by the arm and guided him into the corridor leading to the pantry area. Kennedy's security personnel, wife and aides followed.

Entering the crowded serving pantry, with Ace security guard Thane Cesar and amateur bodyguards Johnson and Grier trailing him, Kennedy began shaking hands with the busboys and kitchen helpers. It was at this moment that someone noticed Sirhan and the girl in the polka-dot dress smile at each other, after which Sirhan suddenly tore the wrapping paper away from his pistol, jumped down from the tray stacker, and holding the weapon over the heads of the people surrounding Kennedy, began firing at Kennedy's head from close range.

One witness said Ace security guard Thane Cesar then fired several shots, presumably at Sirhan, that hit Kennedy. Later this account was discredited by the police and the witness was not called to testify at Sirhan's trial. Still, certain investigators allege that more than one gun was fired, and FBI reports of the scene suggest there were nine to fifteen shots. Sirhan's gun held only eight rounds.

Upon being hit, Kennedy wheeled around and grabbed Thane Cesar by the throat, pulling off the guard's clip-on necktie and falling to the floor with him. Later photos revealed Thane Cesar's clip-on tie on the floor close to Kennedy's bleeding head.

As Kennedy fell back, Sirhan continued to fire, even after he was subdued by Karl Uecker, getting off eight rounds in all and wounding five other people. Finally Rafer Johnson and Rosie Grier caught up with the struggling pair, and a furious fight ensued. Sirhan battled his captors fiercely, and none was able to break his grip on his gun. In the end, it took eight people to subdue Sirhan and force him to release his grip on his revolver. As he was being subdued Sirhan was heard to cry out, "I can explain . . . let me explain . . . I did it for my country . . . I love my country."

About thirty seconds later, three people in the Embassy Room, Sandy Serrano and a Mr. and Mrs. Bernstein, saw a girl in a white polka-dot dress rush by them on her way to an emergency exit shouting, "We shot him! We shot him!"

By that time pandemonium had broken out in the Embassy Room, where the mood of jubilation over Kennedy's victory had turned to horror and hysteria. As word of what happened spread, people began shrieking and crying and some collapsed on the ballroom floor.

Twenty-six hours later Robert F. Kennedy, 43, died at the Good Samaritan Hospital in Los Angeles. The fate he had so recklessly tempted over the past four and a half years had finally taken him at a time when it meant the most, at a moment of triumph, of victory. Kennedy's desperate quest for the presidency had ended. He had set out to redeem the tragedy of his brother's murder and ended in further compounding the tragedy, in doubling its horror.

As for Sirhan Sirhan, he was taken into custody by the Los Angeles police who arraigned him at 7:40 A.M. on June 5, charging him with six counts of assault with intent to murder. Soon it was learned that the David Lawrence article critical of Kennedy's politics, "Paradoxical Bob," had been found in his pocket, and two notebooks had been discovered by the police in his Pasadena home. In one Sirhan had apparently written, "Robert F. Kennedy must be assassinated before June 5th, '68," which, the Los Angeles press observed, was the first anniversary of the Six-Day War between Israel and her neighboring Arab states.

Later, during his trial, Sirhan was asked, under hypnosis, to relive his shooting of Kennedy, and all the 24-year-old Palestinian refugee could do was cry out: "You can't send the bombers! You can't send the bombers! You can't send the bombers!"

When, during the trial, Sirhan was asked why he had been so upset with Kennedy's policy in regard to Israel and the Arabs, he replied:

> Well, sir, when you move—when you move a whole country, sir, a whole people, bodily from their own homes, their own land, from their businesses, sir, outside their country, and introduce an alien people, sir, into Palestine— the Jews and the Zionists—that is completely wrong, sir, and it is unjust and the Palestinian Arabs didn't do a thing, sir, to justify the way they were treated by the West. It affected me, sir, very deeply. I didn't like it. Where is the justice involved, sir? Where is the love, sir, for fighting for the underdog? Israel is no underdog in the Middle East, sir. It's those refugees that are underdogs. And because they have no way of fighting back, sir, the Jews, sir, the Zionists,

just keep beating away at them. That burned
the hell out of me.

In view of the nature of these thoughts, Sirhan's
lawyers, in their effort to save him from the gas chamber,
probably might have given more emphasis to political considerations in establishing their psychiatric defense, but
they concentrated almost entirely on the "doctrine of di-
minished responsibility" because of psychological impair-
ment. As it turned out, this one-sided defense did not
work, for Sirhan demonstrated to the jury that he was
eminently sane. The jury found him guilty of premeditated
murder in the first degree and recommended the death
sentence. Largely as a result of Senator Edward Kennedy's
plea for leniency, his sentence was eventually commuted
to life imprisonment with the possibility of parole in 1984.
Sirhan's first petition for parole was denied in 1983.

Partly because Sirhan's lawyers chose a wholly psychiatric defense, the political significance of Sirhan's act
was almost completely lost. For if we rule out the possibility of a Mafia conspiracy, the murder of Robert Kennedy
clearly appeared to be a political crime and not simply the
act of "a lone crazed gunman" with no reasoned motivation.

63. The Explanation

IF AN OFFICIAL effort to hide and obscure truth followed the murder of John F. Kennedy, an unofficial obfuscation, or distortion of truth, followed the murder of Robert F. Kennedy. That unofficial distortion was first perpetrated, with few exceptions, by the world's press and later by most of the biographers of Robert F. Kennedy.

For, as it turned out, an overwhelming majority of the world's journalists, historians, and biographers writing of Robert F. Kennedy's life and death either deliberately ignored or neglected to explore the political implications of his murder, preferring to paint it as an act of madness, as the work of a "crazed lunatic," and a symptom of a "sick society."

James Reston of *The New York Times* dismissed Sirhan's motive as "a wholly irrational act" with no political overtones and went on to write of "lawlessness threatening modern public order everywhere."

The *Boston Globe,* in an editorial, proclaimed, "So now it develops that Sirhan Bechara Sirhan was a mad man, truly mad . . . 'I did it for my country. I love my country.' Sirhan is said to have cried out as he watched Sen. Kennedy fall. And thus he proved his madness, for this deluded young Jordanian from Jerusalem, a victim of the senseless conflict in the Middle East, is in truth a man without a country to love anymore."

And so it went. All over the world the press, as in one unified chorus, proclaimed Sirhan a "madman," the assassination a "senseless killing," and the United States of America a "sick," "violent" society. The plight of the Palestinian Arab refugees was hardly mentioned.

There were, however, two important exceptions to this chorus: *Le Monde* and *The Economist*.

On June 7 *Le Monde* editorialized:

> Whether the murderer of Robert Kennedy acted of his own volition, or whether he was the unwitting instrument of a dark conspiracy, the criminal act of a Palestinian nationalist on June 5, the anniversary of the Six Day War, has a symbolic importance. A year after the victory of the troops of General Dayan, twenty years after the creation of the State of Israel, never has despair and hatred been so intense among a people that believes that it has been robbed of its homeland. Sirhan Sirhan is precisely one of the hundreds of thousands of Palestinians who have had to leave their homes, some to find shelter in a neighboring Arab country, others to settle in a foreign land. The resolutely pro-Israeli declarations of Robert Kennedy in the course of his electoral campaign, his appeals for an increase in the supply of American arms to the government of Mr. Eshkol, could have exasperated this young, twenty-four-year-old man who, like so many of his compatriots, dreams only of revenge and "liberation."

Echoing *Le Monde, The Economist* of London on June 8 declared, "The man charged with killing Senator Kennedy is a Palestine Arab. When are we all going to tackle the root of the refugee problem?"

But these two instances were voices crying in the wilderness. For the overwhelming majority of the world's newspapers, including the Arab press, which was clearly disturbed over an Arab killing a Kennedy, saw the Kennedy murder as a "senseless killing" by a "lone madman."

Even more serious than the world press's unwillingness to face the truth of why Robert Kennedy was killed was the reluctance of Kennedy's biographers to face the issue.

Arthur M. Schlesinger, Jr., Jack Newfield, Jules Witcover, William vanden Heuvel, and Milton Gwirtzman all failed to consider the political motive for Sirhan's act. Robert Kaiser, in his *R.F.K. Must Die!* flatly rejected it. Was it because these biographers, all (but Kaiser) being friends of Robert Kennedy, were too close to their subject to be objective about it? Or was it because the non-Arab world had stubbornly insisted on looking upon the Arab-Israeli conflict in a wholly one-sided way: that is, the Israeli cause was all good and the Arab cause all bad? Or was it because the Palestinians themselves had made their cause so unpopular through their violent terrorist retaliations that few non-Arabs would be willing to sympathize with their plight?

Whatever the case, there seems to have been a national blind spot in the American consciousness in regard to the struggle between the Israelis and the Palestinian Arabs. That blind spot blotted the Palestinian Arabs out of the American field of vision entirely. The American public, and especially the American press, could see clearly only the cause of the Israelis. What was, of course, desperately needed was not a pro-Arab vision, or a pro-Israel vision, but a *balanced* view of the struggle, one that could understand and sympathize with both sides.

The only differing account of the RFK assassination I know of was written by a Burmese journalist and diplomat, Godfrey H. Jansen, whose *Why Robert Kennedy Was Killed: The Story of Two Victims,* was published in 1970 by The Third Press. Mr. Jansen's book is a carefully reasoned analysis of Sirhan Sirhan's background, personality, and motivation and is the only account of the tragedy I know of that delves into Robert Kennedy's courting of the Jewish vote in 1968 in any significant detail.

Might there also have been a conspiracy to murder Robert Kennedy in which Sirhan Sirhan was only a pawn? Sirhan Sirhan was a very sensitive, impressionable, and suggestible young man, who fell under hypnosis easily;

several students of his crime have theorized that he killed Kennedy as a result of hypnotic suggestion.

But who was the programmer? William W. Turner, a former FBI special agent, and John G. Christian, a former broadcast newsman for ABC, in their book *The Assassination of Robert F. Kennedy,* published by Random House in 1976, relate the testimony of two call girls who "serviced" a noted hypnotist by the name of William Joseph Bryan, Jr., who, in turn, told them, before his death, he had hypnotized Sirhan Sirhan. Bryan also told the two girls he was involved with the CIA and was privy to certain "top-secret projects." The call girls' questionable assertions have never been thoroughly investigated.

Turner and Christian also introduced a "second gunman" theory in their book, naming Ace security guard, Thane Cesar, as their prime second-gunman suspect, an hypothesis which has yet to be authoritatively upheld, since the witnesses involved were not called to testify at the trial. And they wondered, not without reason, about the identity of the girl in the polka-dot dress who had been seen with Sirhan on the tray stacker just before Sirhan fired at Kennedy. In the end, however, Turner and Christian were unable to put forth a convincing case for conspiracy.

Nevertheless, there remain some unsettling aspects to the Robert Kennedy murder that suggest a conspiracy could have existed. We have mentioned Sirhan's association with Frank Donnarauma of the Santa Anita racetrack and the Corona horse ranch. It took the FBI ten months to find out who Donnarauma was, that his real name was Henry Ramistella and that he had a criminal record. Could the Cosa Nostra, through Ramistella, have recruited Sirhan to murder Kennedy? Sirhan would have been an ideal candidate for the job because, like Oswald, he was already motivated for political reasons of his own.

Sirhan wrote in his notebook after his "Robert F. Kennedy must be assassinated" entries: "please pay to the order of of of of of of of of of of of this or that 8 000 000 HL," suggesting a payment for the assassination might have been offered. And we are reasonably certain that Sirhan visited Corona two days before the assassination.

However, although the Mafia certainly did not want Robert Kennedy to be President, one wonders why they would have attempted to kill him so early in the campaign. Being prudent men of business, wouldn't they have waited until after Kennedy's nomination and not have made a move until it began to appear certain that Kennedy was going to win over his Republican opponent? Perhaps not. Perhaps it would have been smarter to eliminate him early, when the crime would receive less attention (and investigation).

According to Turner and Christian, an FBI report that was released ten years after the RFK murder gave evidence that the Mafia was at least contemplating the assassination of Robert Kennedy. The report mentioned an informant who claimed that a wealthy southern California rancher, who hated Robert Kennedy because of his support of Cesar Chavez, had pledged $2000 toward a $500,000 to $750,000 Mafia contract to kill Senator Kennedy "in the event it appeared he could receive the Democratic nomination for President."

Why wasn't Sirhan's possible link to organized crime fully investigated at the time of the assassination? Because, for one thing, the CIA-Mafia-Cuban exiles alliance was not yet public knowledge and was still not associated in the public mind with John F. Kennedy's assassination. In fact, the only people who knew about this alliance, outside the FBI, the CIA, and a few Kennedy intimates, were the Mafia plotters and Lyndon Johnson, Allen Dulles, and Robert Kennedy, and they had all covered up what they knew. Also, the FBI conducted the principal investigation of the crime, and if it had kept the CIA-Mafia plots from the Warren Commission, it was certainly not going to air them in their investigation of Robert Kennedy's murder. That would have clearly shown they had withheld vital information from the commission.

This brings us to the FBI, which, at the time of RFK's assassination, was still under the direction of Robert Kennedy's archenemy, J. Edgar Hoover. According to William Sullivan's memoirs, when Robert Kennedy's name came up at a top-level FBI meeting in the spring of 1968, Clyde

Tolson, then the number two man at the Bureau, who was presiding at the meeting, said, "I hope someone shoots and kills that son-of-a-bitch," indicating, quite clearly, that the Bureau's attitude toward Kennedy had not changed at all since Kennedy's days as attorney general.

Sullivan went on to state that there were "many holes in the [Sirhan] case." "We never could account for Sirhan's presence in the kitchen of the Ambassador Hotel," he wrote. "Did he know Kennedy would be walking through?" "There are so many unknowns," he went on, "in the end we were never sure." However, the FBI did conclude that Sirhan Sirhan had acted alone.

My own belief is that, based on the current status of the evidence, the Robert F. Kennedy assassination remains an unsolved crime. The possibility that Sirhan could have been framed, or programmed hypnotically to fire at Kennedy—from the Senator's right, while another gunman administered the fatal shot from Kennedy's rear, is feasible, given what we now know about the crime. However, even if Sirhan Sirhan did not act alone, his participation in the crime, given his anti-Israel prejudices, could still be regarded as just one more violent episode arising from the struggle between the Israelis and the Palestinian Arabs. For if there was a plot, the conspirators surely exploited Sirhan's prejudices to lure him into it.

64. The Family

ROBERT KENNEDY'S DEATH had an even greater impact on the Joseph P. Kennedy household than John's death had. The ambassador and Mrs. Kennedy had maintained a certain stoicism over the assassination of John F. Kennedy, but when Bobby was killed, they, and all the members of the household, broke down completely. In a sense, Bobby's tragedy became an occasion for the family to grieve openly for Jack as well.

For the Robert F. Kennedy household the murder was nothing less than a devastation. Bobby and his wife had been very close, and Robert had enjoyed a strong and loving relationship with his ten children. The impact of Robert Kennedy's murder on some of his sons seems to have been especially cruel. While his daughters and younger sons appear to have survived the tragedy with minimal injury, his three oldest sons—Joe, Bobby Junior, and David—seem to have suffered psychological damage, for all three were destined to get into serious trouble as they grew older.

News of the shooting of Robert Kennedy reached Hickory Hill, Kennedy's home in Virginia, at dawn, June 5, when his 14-year-old son, Robert Kennedy, Jr., went down to the front door to pick up the morning paper. When he read the headline that his father had been shot in Los Angeles he couldn't think or move. After he recovered his senses, he took the paper inside and burned it in the family fireplace. Then he phoned his mother and his brothers Joe and David in Los Angeles.

News of the shooting reached the Joseph P. Kennedy house in Hyannis in the very early morning, long after Joe and Rose had gone to bed. One of Bobby's sisters had phoned the news from Los Angeles to Anne Gargan around 4 A.M. Hyannis time, telling her not to inform Mr. and Mrs. Kennedy until they woke up. Thus for several hours a terrified Anne Gargan had to keep the news bottled up inside her.

When dawn came and the early-rising Kennedy household began to stir, Anne was about to break the news to Rose Kennedy when Mrs. Kennedy suddenly burst out of her room crying, "It's Bobby! It's Bobby!" She had turned on her television as soon as she had wakened to find out how Bobby had done in the California primary and had immediately received the news he had been shot.

After the initial shock wore off, Mrs. Kennedy pulled herself together and decided to go to mass. All her life the Catholic religion had been her greatest consolation. Her faith in God was absolute. "God does not give us burdens we cannot bear" had always been a central canon of her faith. When Rose Kennedy arrived at the church the reporters and photographers were already there, just as they had been when she had gone to mass after her son John's murder. And they were no less importunate and obtrusive this time as they exploded flashbulbs in her face and asked her how she had felt when she had heard the news about Bobby.

Returning from mass, Rose went immediately to her husband's room to tell him what had happened in Los Angeles. According to Rita Dallas and Frank Saunders, who were the only witnesses to record what went on in the house at Hyannis that sad morning, this was the first time Rose had been alone with her husband in years. For a long time there had been virtually no communication between them.

Joe Kennedy, by June 1968, was almost 80; he could not walk, or speak, and his hearing was rapidly failing him.

Trapped inside himself, he received the news of his son's murder without being able to express his feelings openly. After his wife left his bedside, the ambassador signaled for Rita Dallas to turn on his television set.

When Rose Kennedy left her husband's room Rita Dallas noticed she was crying. It was the first time Mrs. Dallas had ever seen the normally stoic Mrs. Kennedy break down. With tears in her eyes, and looking utterly distraught, Rose then went to her room and turned on her television.

Soon all the radios and television sets in the house were blaring, and everyone in the household was weeping. Bobby was not yet dead, but the medical bulletins had already indicated he was dying. Joe Kennedy sat up in bed all morning, watching the coverage of his son's agony, with the tears streaming down his face. Throughout the entire morning everyone in the Kennedy household stared at television sets, weeping for Bobby. It was a great letting go, a purge. By the time Bobby finally died, twenty-six hours after he had been shot, the household in Hyannis had already spent their tears.

Meanwhile Lyndon Johnson had sent a presidential jet to Los Angeles to bring Robert Kennedy's body, and those members of the Kennedy family who were in Los Angeles, back to New York. It had been decided that Robert Kennedy's body would be brought directly to St. Patrick's Cathedral, where it would lie in state until the funeral two days later. Among those accompanying the body would be Jacqueline Kennedy, who had flown to Los Angeles immediately after hearing the news of the shooting and had remained at Bobby's bedside in the Good Samaritan Hospital as he lay dying.

When Rose Kennedy finally recovered her composure, she decided she would go directly to St. Patrick's, in her own words, to "wait for Bobby." And so, the evening of June 6, she sat alone in the vast, empty cathedral waiting for her son. After the casket arrived from Los Angeles, she was joined in her vigil by Jacqueline, Ethel, and Edward Kennedy.

The funeral service on June 8 was attended by some

2000 people, including many representatives of Robert Kennedy's special constituency. The blacks and Hispanics had gathered early in front of St. Patrick's so as not to miss the chance of paying their last respects to the one national leader they believed in.

The high requiem mass in St. Patrick's was far more elaborate and moving than John F. Kennedy's funeral had been, due partly to its much more grandiose setting. Its most emotional moment came when Edward Kennedy delivered a short, unscheduled eulogy. Standing next to the casket, the last surviving son of Joe and Rose Kennedy said, in the most eloquent address of his life:

> He gave us strength in time of trouble, wisdom in time of uncertainty, and sharing in time of happiness. . . . He loved life completely and he lived it intensely.
>
> My brother need not be idealized, or enlarged in death beyond what he was in life, but to be remembered simply as a good and decent man, who saw wrong and tried to right it, saw suffering and tried to heal it, saw war and tried to stop it.

There followed some remarks by Archbishop Cooke, a movement from Gustav Mahler's Fifth Symphony led by Leonard Bernstein, and Andy Williams's rendition of "The Battle Hymn of the Republic." Then, to Handel's Hallelujah Chorus, Ted Kennedy and young Joe Kennedy led the procession out of the cathedral.

Next came the funeral train to Washington. So that people along the 226-mile route could see Robert Kennedy's casket as the train passed, it was set upon chairs at window level. The idea was to give Robert Kennedy's supporters a chance to pay him their last respects. As it turned out, it was an irresponsible idea that only served to compound the tragedy of Robert Kennedy's death. Many bystanders along the route jumped down onto the tracks to touch the funeral car, some with disastrous consequences. Just past Elizabeth, New Jersey, two people who had jumped down on the tracks were killed by a train coming from the opposite direction, and six others were seriously injured. Then, at Trenton, an 18-year-old youth climbed up on a boxcar for a better view of the Kennedy train and was almost electrocuted by a high-tension wire. Badly burned, he was taken to the hospital in critical condition, but fortunately did not die.

The final act in Robert Kennedy's eighty-five-day campaign for the Democratic nomination was played out at Arlington National Cemetery twenty feet from the grave of John F. Kennedy, who had been killed four years, six months, and thirteen days before. There, by the gravesite, was Ethel Kennedy with her ten children, and expecting an eleventh, looking terribly drained, but strong and staunch to the end. And there was Jacqueline Kennedy, and her two children, reliving the agony of 1963.

One individual who hated Bobby was still nurturing his hatred, even with Bobby dead, and that was J. Edgar Hoover. According to William Sullivan, Hoover deliberately held up the news of the June 7 capture of Martin Luther King, Jr.'s, assassin, James Earl Ray, so he could interrupt TV coverage of Bobby's burial on June 8 with the news of the capture.

When the remaining children of Joe and Rose Kennedy returned to Hyannis from Washington to see their father after the burial, Rita Dallas was amazed by what she called "their recuperative powers." Bursting into their father's room, Joe's daughters cried out: "Daddy, Teddy was magnificent, absolutely magnificent!" And referring to Bobby's son, young Joe, they exclaimed, "Daddy, he's got it! You should have seen him!" Then, alluding to Joe's greeting all 1000 mourners on the train to Washington, they enthused, "Nobody put him up to it, Daddy, he did it on his own!"

Later, in a more somber mood, Jacqueline Kennedy arrived at the house, went up to Joe's room, and sat alone with him for a while, trying to give the mute and paralyzed patriarch what comfort she could. But now there was no comfort left for Joe Kennedy. It had been Bobby who had held the Kennedy family together after Jack's assassination. It had been Bobby who had become Joseph P. Kennedy's reason for living. Although he had been reluctant to give Bobby's candidacy his blessing, he had finally decided he would, and would spend up to $20 million to get Bobby elected. Before leaving for California, Bobby had told his father, "I'm going to win this one for you, Dad." What then happened was more than any father should ever have to bear—a third son was lost in the prime of life.

Part 6

IMAGE IN DISTRESS, 1968-1979

65. The Remarriage

IT DID NOT TAKE LONG after the murder of Robert Kennedy for the press to begin referring to the late senator in much the same terms, and tones, it had been using to portray his slain brother John during the past four and a half years. Thus, in the days immediately following his burial in Arlington, Robert Kennedy underwent yet a third metamorphosis of personality, changing, in the press's view, to a "martyred hero," "a martyr to freedom," and "a knight fallen in battle." The second Kennedy glorification had begun.

Granted, the glorification of Robert Kennedy was not nearly as intense and exaggerated as that of John F. Kennedy. Still, it was sufficiently hysterical and widespread to cause the name Kennedy to be bestowed on several more landmarks and institutions and to inspire a fresh new rash of adulatory Kennedy books.

As the tumultuous Democratic convention of August 1968 approached, the journalistic apotheosis of the slain Kennedy brothers intensified to such an extent that the 36-year-old surviving Kennedy brother, Edward, could probably have ridden the public mood and captured the Democratic nomination himself had he chosen to fight for it, which, as it turned out, he was not prepared to do.

And if the American people had felt irrational mass guilt over the murder of John F. Kennedy, now, after the murder of Robert F. Kennedy, they were thrown into a veritable frenzy of self-laceration. A widespread feeling began to arise among the people that they now *owed* the presidency to the Kennedys. Consequently it soon became a matter of virtual certainty that young Edward Kennedy would be handed the presidency one day, as a kind of grant from the people, most likely in 1972 or 1976.

However, in order to win the presidency back, the Kennedys had to keep aloft the inflated image. They could not reveal themselves to be mere human beings with human frailties, who occasionally got into accidents or made unseemly marriages. The presidency would be granted to the last of the Kennedy brothers only if he and his family did not destroy the illusions about themselves they had so pointedly built up.

But with both John F. Kennedy and Robert F. Kennedy gone, a lot of restraints had been removed from the Kennedy field of action. Both Jacqueline Kennedy and Edward Kennedy had had to hold themselves in check for the sake of Bobby's political ambitions. Now they no longer had to behave quite so virtuously. They could finally let themselves go.

Ironically, the first Kennedy to let go, and in so doing cause a puncture in the family image, was the Kennedy who had done so much to inflate the image, who, in fact, had been the main force behind the glorification of John F. Kennedy, and that was the late President's widow, Jacqueline.

On October 18, 1968, barely four months after the assassination in Los Angeles, Jacqueline Kennedy made an announcement that so deflated the Kennedy image it has never been quite the same since. She announced that she was going to marry the divorced Greek shipowner and multimillionaire, Aristotle Onassis, a man twenty-nine years older than she, with an unsavory reputation, who was so unlike the late John F. Kennedy in looks and manners and values, that her marriage to him suddenly raised disturbing questions about the nature of her marriage to her first husband. Had that union also been just for money and power?

*   *

On the few occasions in the mid-sixties that I had a chance to talk with Jacqueline Kennedy, I was always struck by the aura of loneliness, vulnerability, and insecurity that seemed to envelop her. Then she became Mrs. Aristotle Onassis and changed dramatically, becoming much more cheerful, outgoing, and sure of herself. Noting the tremendous difference, I came to the conclusion that, for a while at least, the marriage to Onassis had been good for her, and hence made some sense.

But to the world at large it made no sense at all. Rather, it was widely regarded as some sort of incredible disaster. A worldwide negative reaction to the marriage of Jacqueline Kennedy and Aristotle Onassis resulted. The American public had conceived of Jackie as the loving wife of an American hero, as a radiant, queenly First Lady of unimpeachable virtue, and then as a grieving widow devoted to her slain husband's memory and ideals. They had thought of her as a sacred American legend, as a living saint.

When this paragon of American womanhood virtually eloped with a disreputable old man who seemed to have no ideals whatsoever beyond piling up enormous sums of money and collecting yachtfuls of celebrities, people were stunned.

"Jackie—How Can You?" headlined a London tabloid. "The Reaction Here Is Shock and Dismay," headlined *The New York Times.* "America Has Lost a Saint," headlined the West German *Bild-Zeitung,* adding in a subtitle, "All the World Is Indignant." "John Kennedy Dies Today for a Second Time," headlined Rome's *Il Messagero.*

In France news of the marriage broke as a national tragedy. *Le Monde* opined that Onassis represented "the antithesis of President Kennedy's dream of a less cruel world," and went on to observe that "Mr. Onassis is concerned more with dominating this world than reforming it." "Is it this appetite for power, with all that it reveals of a quasi-animal energy that charmed the widow of John Kennedy?" *Le Monde* asked. In conclusion, the French paper observed that "the second Mrs. Onassis will cause to be forgotten the radiant Snow White who contributed so much to the popularity of her husband."

Even the Vatican's ultraconservative *L'Osservatore della Domenica,* normally reticent, leveled a broadside at the former First Lady, declaring that, as a result of her remarriage, Jacqueline was in "a state of spiritual degradation" and was now "a public sinner," an assertion that showed how hysterically unfair the reaction to the remarriage could be.

Along with this journalistic castigation of the marriage went a near-universal condemnation of Onassis. Italy's *L'Espresso* was particularly severe on the Greek shipowner, describing him as "this grizzled satrap, with his liver-colored skin, thick hair, fleshy nose, the wide horsey grin, who buys an island and then has it removed from the maps to prevent the landing of castaways."

But not everybody was shocked by the Kennedy-Onassis marriage. Those who knew Jackie best saw nothing especially unusual about it. Most members of the Bouvier family, for example, were surprised by the marriage, but hardly shocked. Those of us who had grown up with Jackie felt that Onassis was precisely the type of man we thought she would marry. She had always liked older men, much older men, even as a teenager. And we all knew that her mother and father had relentlessly coached her to marry a very rich man. Furthermore, Onassis was, in many ways, a man very much like Jackie's father, whom she had adored. Like Black Jack Bouvier, Onassis was a very masculine, protective type who loved to indulge women. Both men were totally materialistic. Both were very "worldly." And both had a way of making a woman feel very appreciated and secure. Security was what Jackie needed after Bobby's murder.

Jack Bouvier, had he lived to see the marriage, would have no doubt been delighted with Onassis. Over and over again he had drummed it into Jackie's ears that she should marry a very rich man. Jackie's mother used to urge her to do the same thing. In marrying Onassis Jackie was doing exactly what she had been brought up to do—which brings up the question of money. In marrying Onassis, Jackie was finally able to break her financial dependence on the Kennedys and indulge her extravagant tastes at whim. To Jackie's Bouvier relatives this was reason enough for her to wed Onassis.

There was also another good reason for Jackie to marry Aristotle Onassis: escape. Jackie had been very close to Robert Kennedy. He had been her confidant, her adviser, and her most devoted male friend. When he was murdered she was shattered. Some say she became incoherent. The whole Kennedy adventure had ended in horror. Her husband had been murdered. And now her brother-in-law had also been murdered. In the weeks following Bobby Kennedy's assassination Jackie was seized with a desperate desire to escape the Kennedy nightmare. What more sublime escape could there be than a shimmering island in the Aegean sea and one of the most luxurious yachts in the world? For Jacqueline, after what she had gone through, the beauty and serenity of Skorpios and the luxury of the *Christina* were heaven-sent.

Finally, she could also realize her childhood "dream of glory." With a 68-year-old shipping emperor by her side she could finally be "la fille naturelle de Charlemagne," with Camelot replaced by a new fairyland on an enchanted Greek island.

Nevertheless, despite Jacqueline's quite valid personal reasons for marrying Aristotle Onassis, the marriage was, in a larger perspective, a mistake. For Jacqueline had become a world figure whose conduct was watched and copied everywhere. This was a considerable responsibility. By all rights, Jackie should have weighed the possible public reaction to marrying a man like Onassis, but she did not. In fact, she resented the limitations on her freedom being a public figure imposed.

I remember being shocked, when I returned to Italy in 1972 to write a book on Venice, by my European friends' reactions to Jackie's marriage. I was, in fact, much more shocked by these reactions than I had been shocked by the news of her remarriage. Everywhere I went—Paris, Rome, Naples, Venice—I was compelled to defend Jackie's marriage. "She threw it all away, didn't she?" was a typical remark. "We all thought she would marry someone like André Malraux," a Polish writer friend told me, "and here she goes off with a gangster."

It was astonishing how many European friends of mine had totally misread Jackie. Malraux was the *last* type of man Jackie would marry. Marry a man of no independent means, who lived off royalties from books and the modest salary of a French government official? That wasn't Jackie's cup of tea at all. But what about her supposed intellectualism and devotion to the arts? Wouldn't that have brought her closer to a Malraux than to an Onassis, many inquired? Jacqueline was never particularly interested in the world of ideas. And her interest in the arts was never more than superficial. Although she was endowed with a sense of history, she was never concerned with history as a search for truth. For Jackie history was a kind of aesthetic antiquarianism. It was being concerned that a James Monroe pier table be rescued from the White House storage bins and placed in the Red Room where it belonged. The idea that Jackie would marry a man of ideas was preposterous. Jacqueline needed to be married to a man of material power. It had been power that had attracted her to Kennedy, and it was power that attracted her to Onassis. Jacqueline had always derived her sense of identity from association with a powerful man. When she was young she was Daddy's best girl. Then she was a senator's wife, and then the President's wife. For Jackie being someone's wife was very important. Now she was Mrs. Aristotle Onassis, the wife of one of the richest men in the world. This status gave her a tremendous satisfaction. You see, she seemed to be telling the world, you thought I had lost everything; but look at me now, married to one of the richest men on earth!

Still her reputation suffered grievously from the marriage, especially in Europe where Onassis was emphatically not liked. It wasn't long before the former Mrs. John F. Kennedy, widow of the late President of the United States, was reduced to being called "Jackie O." As if to give her a monument appropriate to her new status, a new disco off the Via Veneto in Rome was named "Jackie O."

Then there was the problem of her much-coveted privacy. One of the reasons she had married Onassis was that he was in a position to guarantee her privacy with his yacht and island. As it turned out, Onassis's fortune, yacht, and island failed to bring her the privacy she craved. As the marriage wore on she drew more attention and harassment than ever and became the unwitting star of a seemingly never-ending media circus. The *paparazzi* became merciless in their exploitation of her. It wasn't long before fourteen photos of Jackie sunbathing nude on Skorpios appeared in an Italian magazine.

Unflattering books became another unpleasant consequence of the Onassis marriage. Before Jacqueline married Onassis, she had received nothing but praise from biographers, historians, and memoirists. After the marriage she began receiving abuse from them.

Jackie's marriage to Onassis also put her in the annoying position of no longer being able to criticize people (such as writers) convincingly for exploiting the Kennedy tragedies, for, in a sense she had, in marrying Onassis, profited from them herself. It is safe to say that if she had not been the widow of the assassinated President, Onassis, the celebrity collector, desirous of enlarging his fame, would not have married her and shared his vast wealth with her.

If Jacqueline's reputation suffered from her marriage to Onassis, the Kennedy reputation suffered from it also, by extension. The Kennedys, both blood and honorary, did not, in fact, like the idea of the marriage at all. Realizing full well that it would damage the image they had labored so mightily to inflate, the Kennedys had first tried to talk her out of her marriage plans. Ted Kennedy was understandably wary of the effect the marriage might have on public opinion. However, Jackie held firm and succeeded in getting him to give her his reluctant public blessing. Rose Kennedy also gave her a reluctant public blessing, conceding that the marriage made some sense in that it should finally give Jackie the financial independence she so desired. But the "honorary Kennedys" were less hypocritical about the whole affair. Dave Powers, for example, told me in Boston that he never could understand why she married the shipping magnate, allowing that it certainly did not do John Kennedy's memory any good.

The marriage, according to what Jacqueline told certain Bouvier relatives, worked until the death of Onassis's son, Alexander, from an air accident, in January 1973. After that tragic event the marriage turned sour. A dispirited Onassis began regretting he had not married a younger woman who could have given him another son. He reputedly told Jackie, who could no longer have children, that she was "bad luck."

Onassis had his good points but he was also a cruel and vulgar man. He had married Jackie for prestige and had proudly displayed her in public as he would an old master or a jewel. He enjoyed making Jackie jealous and went out of his way to be photographed in public with old flames like Maria Callas, knowing Jackie would see the pictures in the papers. And it was said that he took a perverse delight in taking guests on whale hunts where they would watch the whales being harpooned and taken aboard the ships of his whaling fleet, a pastime that certainly did not endear him to his sensitive, animal-loving wife. It was, all things considered, a tense menage. Onassis's children did not care for their new stepmother, and John F. Kennedy, Jr., it has been reported, came to regard his stepfather as "a joke." As might be expected, Jacqueline's extravagance bothered Onassis not a little, as it had bothered her father and John F. Kennedy. It was widely rumored that she spent some $1.5 million of Onassis's money in the first year of her marriage alone.

Jacqueline had naturally expected to inherit an enormous fortune from Onassis some day, but after the death of son Alexander that hope was extinguished. As soon as he began to recover from the shock of his loss, Onassis drew up a new will, creating the Alexander Onassis Foundation and bequeathing a substantial share of his fortune to it. He also added to daughter Christina's share. The foundation was designed to promote "nursing, education, literary works, religious and scientific research, and journalistic and religious endeavors" and effectively put an end to Jacqueline's dream of one day possessing great wealth. During the last two years of Onassis's life, he and Jacqueline became more and more estranged; in 1974 the aging shipping magnate began contemplating divorce, calling his wife, according to biographer Lee Guthrie, "coldhearted and shallow." To columnist Jack Anderson he complained of Jackie's extravagance and the complaint found its way into Anderson's column. As Onassis's health began to fail and his mood grew darker and darker, Jacqueline found herself being gradually excluded from his life. On March 15, 1975, he died in Paris with only his daughter Christina at his side.

After the funeral Jacqueline issued a statement to the press that probably contained a kernel of truth:

> Aristotle Onassis rescued me at a moment when my life was engulfed with shadows. He meant a lot to me. He brought me into a world where one could find both happiness and love. We lived through many beautiful experiences together which cannot be forgotten, and for which I will be eternally grateful.

The estate of Aristotle Onassis was estimated to be worth close to a billion dollars, less debts, which were considerable, and taxes. According to Greek law, Jacqueline's legal share of a billion-dollar estate would have been something in the neighborhood of $125 million. However, Onassis had arranged things so that she would get far, far less, even going to the extent of persuading the Greek parliament to change some of the inheritance laws to protect his fortune. In the end, as all the world knows, executrix Christina settled $20 million of her father's estate on Jacqueline. Thus, since she had had to renounce her Kennedy trust upon marrying Onassis, Jackie ended up with not a great deal more money than she would have had had she not married Onassis. By the mid-seventies the Kennedy trust, worth $10 million in 1963, would have probably grown to be worth at least $20 million, or the same amount Onassis had left her.

And so it was that Jacqueline's marriage to Aristotle Onassis failed to enrich her significantly beyond her condition under the Kennedy trust, yet it damaged both her reputation and the Kennedy image. It was, in fact, the first major blow to the Kennedy image that, in the summer of 1968, had seemed absolutely unassailable. But this was no great calamity. As certain members of the Bouvier family observed at the time, Jackie had done more than her duty by the Kennedys; she had done quite enough for them. Where would they have been, *who* would they have been, without her?

Although criticism of Jacqueline for her marriage to Onassis has persisted, I believe it is basically unfair. That Jacqueline kept her sanity through two assassinations and was able to begin a new life was an achievement that far outweighed her apparent failure to protect the vanity of an inflated image.

66. Chappaquiddick: The Fourth Derailment

As THE SUMMER OF 1969 APPROACHED, with its promise of the United States landing a man on the moon, Edward M. Kennedy's star shone in the political heavens with a special brilliance. Earlier in the year he had been elected assistant majority leader of the Senate, or Democratic party whip, by cleverly outmaneuvering Louisiana's Senator Russell Long, a veteran of twenty-two years. This coup had given him the distinction of being the youngest whip in the entire history of the U.S. Senate. It meant that, among other things, Kennedy, at only 37, was but one step away from being the leader of his party in Congress. Neither of his two older brothers had even come close to reaching such eminence in their senatorial careers.

Upon attaining his new prestigious role, Senator Kennedy was suddenly emboldened to speak out on many issues of some importance, and, in so doing, he attracted a new measure of national attention. Moving up from his back-row seat, where for years he had been relatively silent, to a front-row seat only one removed from the majority leader's chair, he lashed out at President Nixon's handling of the Vietnam war, criticized Nixon's ABM missile program, and assailed the President's apparent lack of concern for the poor and for civil rights.

By the summer of 1969 Kennedy was clearly the man of the hour in the Democratic party, destined, without question, to be his party's candidate for the presidency in 1972. What was more, as a potential added bonus to his prestige, the Kennedy image was on the verge of receiving a new burst of light. Although Jacqueline Kennedy's marriage to Aristotle Onassis in the fall of 1968 had somewhat bedimmed its former radiance, an event was to take place in July 1969 that promised to help restore the image to its former brilliance, and that was the Apollo XI moon landing, scheduled for July 21. As the long-awaited space event approached, Kennedy lost no time in reminding the world that it had been his brother John F. Kennedy who had launched Project Apollo eight years before. And so, in July 1969, the Kennedy image continued to shine in the American political firmament as a star of the first magnitude. There was nothing visible on the horizon that seemed capable of seriously dimming its light.

However, as fate would have it, a calamity occurred two days before the expected moon landing that so clouded the Kennedy image it would never shine with quite the same luster again. For, on the night of July 18–19, Senator Edward Kennedy drove his car off a narrow bridge on a Cape Cod island, killing his passenger, a 28-year-old unmarried woman; then, as if that were not bad enough, he left the scene of the accident without reporting what had happened to the police.

On the surface, the accident appeared to have been a most unlikely tragedy to have happened to the handsome young senator who seemed to have everything going for him. But, in reality, there were certain things in Kennedy's character and background that persuaded otherwise. These things disclosed an immature, erratic, self-destructive streak in Kennedy's personality, and several disquieting episodes in his past clearly indicated that driving a woman to her death and then not reporting the accident for ten hours was something well within his capacity to do.

As the last and most indulged child of Rose and Joe Kennedy, young Teddy was spoiled practically from birth. With his father and older brothers frequently absent, he had been brought up by four women, his mother and three sisters. As he himself has put it: "It was like having a whole army of mothers around me." And, of course, the army spoiled him to death. Mother Rose confirmed this indulgence in her memoirs, when she wrote of the last child she knew she would have: "He was my baby and I tried to keep him my baby." Furthermore, with his three older brothers all giving promise of accomplishing the great things demanded of them by their ambitious parents, there was much less pressure on young Teddy to achieve. As a much-indulged child and adolescent, Teddy had every reason to believe that life would be handed to him on a silver platter—and it was. His first significant job, undertaken long after his graduation from the University of Virginia Law School and arranged through his family's political contacts, was as assistant district attorney for Suffolk County in Massachusetts, a position in which he did not distinguish himself in the slightest. Then, not long after his thirtieth birthday, he "won" a seat in the U.S. Senate, the seat that had been vacated by brother Jack and had been "kept warm" for Teddy by an old friend of the family, Ben Smith, who had taken Jack's seat on the understanding he would one day relinquish it to Teddy. Joe Kennedy had once explained it all to Jack and Bobby, both of whom had been a bit put out at their younger brother's being given a seat in the Senate at the absolute minimum required age: "You boys have what you want now, and everybody else helped you work to get it. Now it's Ted's turn. Whatever he wants, I'm going to see he gets it."

Thus, young Teddy grew up, a chubby, rosy-cheeked, good-natured youngster, and later a strapping (over six feet and 210 pounds) young man, indulged in all his desires and assured by all that his way in life would be made smooth. The result was a very slow-maturing personality that acknowledged few restraints and was exceedingly impatient when thwarted.

It was not surprising therefore that such a personality would soon get into trouble. Trouble came for Teddy during his sophomore year at Harvard. A good football player, he had wanted to make the varsity team. But he was failing Spanish, and at Harvard one could not fail a foreign language requirement and hope to make a team. Frustrated,

Teddy took the easy way out and paid a friend to take the exam for him. Both were caught, and Teddy was expelled from the university, an embarrassment that his family was able to cover up for the next ten years.

When in 1953, after a two-year hitch as an enlisted man in the Army (during which he was unable to rise above the rank of private), Teddy reentered Harvard, something else happened that cast some doubt on his character. During a rugby match against the New York Rugby Club he lost control of himself three times, getting into three separate fistfights with opponents, and was expelled from the game. The umpire has since testified that he had never known a player before who, after repeatedly being warned, had gotten into three violent fights in one game.

After failing to gain admission to Harvard Law School, Teddy entered the University of Virginia Law School in Charlottesville. During his law-school years Teddy was arrested no fewer than four times for extremely reckless driving. Among his offenses were running through red lights at night at ninety miles per hour in suburban Charlottesville, driving at night with his headlights off at ninety miles per hour, also in a suburban area, and hiding from a policeman.

Upon graduating from Virginia Law, Kennedy bounced around, taking a number of odd jobs, including working for his brother's presidential campaign. Of the eleven states assigned to him in that campaign, most of which were in the traditionally Republican west, brother Jack lost eight. However, this apparently did not bother Teddy very much because, after all, Jack won the election. Since he was benefiting from the million-dollar trust fund established for him by his father when he was only a young child, and was about to come into another substantial trust, Teddy did not *have* to work for a living. He was, therefore, able to do what he pleased a good deal of the time. This, of course, gave him plenty of time to get into trouble. One such episode occurred during a yachting cruise. According to Kennedy biographer Joe McCarthy, Kennedy was on a cruise from Cape Cod to Maine one summer with Bobby, Ethel, Jean, friend David Hackett, and Red Fay and his wife, Anita, when, one afternoon near Northeast Harbor, as Teddy was rowing ashore to buy supplies, he was taunted by a yachtsman aboard another yacht. After a sharp exchange, the physically powerful Teddy boarded the yacht and threw the yachtsman overboard. Then, when other members of the crew appeared on deck, he threw them overboard too, without knowing whether they could swim or not. Fortunately none of the yachtsmen brought charges.

In 1964, during his campaign for the Democratic nomination for his second Senate term, Kennedy was severely injured in a private plane crash, principally because he was the only passenger on board who had not buckled his seat belt. As a result of the crash he suffered six spinal fractures, two broken ribs, and was listed in critical condition. He remained in the hospital six months.

Teddy Kennedy's next episode of recklessness came the winter after Bobby's murder. He and Joan had rented a house in Palm Beach, not far from his father's house on North Ocean Drive. One night the family chauffeur Frank Saunders was awakened by a loud pounding on his door. It was the senator. According to Saunders's account in his book *Torn Lace Curtain,* he got out of bed, opened the door, and beheld Teddy breathing heavily and smelling of alcohol. What was wrong? "Car's stuck," said Teddy, "the fucking thing's stuck down the road. . . . I missed the turn. Take care of it," he told Saunders, "and do it so nobody will spot the car." Then, after telling Saunders where the car was, the senator took off.

Saunders found the car about two-tenths of a mile from the Joseph P. Kennedy house. The senator had missed a sharp turn to the left and had gone over a curb and into a mass of bushes just short of a cement wall. Saunders called the wrecker and took care of everything, including giving the wreckers a good tip so they would keep their mouths shut. According to Saunders, when he saw the senator the next time Kennedy didn't say a word about the accident. In Saunders's words, "Ted's accident was another lesson for me in how ungrateful the Kennedys could be toward the people who worked for them. They *expected* you to do everything for them, no matter how dirty the work. If only they'd show some appreciation every so often . . . yet getting any kind of thanks from them was about as likely as getting a pay raise."

Teddy Kennedy also took some rather reckless chances with women. Though he had married the pretty, blonde, Catholic Joan Bennett while in law school, he, like his brother Jack, had never taken the vow of fidelity very seriously, and reports repeatedly linked him in extramarital relationships, any one of which, if true, could have backfired on him with serious consequences for his career. According to Judith Campbell's memoirs, during his brother's campaign for the presidency Teddy had made an unsuccessful play for her at about the same time Jack was first introduced to her. According to an investigation conducted by the *New York Post,* during the two years prior to the Chappaquiddick mishap he had carried on an affair with a certain Countess Llana Campbell, an attractive blonde European whom he brought up to rented cottages on Martha's Vineyard on several occasions for long weekend parties. At the time of his accident at Chappaquiddick he was reportedly involved with a stunning young Austrian woman by the name of Helga Wagner who was living in Key Biscayne, Florida.

Then, recently, there had been the drinking problem. After the death of Robert Kennedy, which he had taken very hard, Teddy had begun drinking quite heavily. In April 1969 he had traveled to Alaska to investigate poverty among the Eskimos, one of brother Bobby's pet causes. During the trip he worried aides and journalists considerably with his incessant drinking. Carrying a little silver hip flask with him, he was constantly taking nips throughout the trip, and in the evenings he spent long hours in Alaska's saloons. Once, when he was slightly drunk, he told his entourage: "They're going to shoot my ass off the way they shot Bobby's." According to biographer Burton Hersh, on the plane home from Fairbanks he got so drunk that he kept walking up and down the aisle roaring "Eskimow Pow-er, Es-ki-mow Pow-er" over and over again, while spilling his drinks on the other passengers.

Thus, by the summer of 1969, though ostensibly on

top of the world, with the presidency a definite possibility in 1972, Edward Kennedy was, in reality, a troubled, still-immature, accident-prone young man with a shaky marriage and a past that he would just as soon see forgotten.

Teddy had two sides to his personality. There was his noble, eloquent side, the side he displayed so convincingly in his funeral eulogy for his brother Robert, when he said,

> Like my three brothers before me, I pick up a fallen standard. Sustained by the memory of our priceless years together, I shall try to carry forward that special commitment to justice, to excellence, to courage that distinguished their lives.

And then there was what can only be called his underside, the spoiled, overindulged, lastborn son, the cheater at Harvard, the young man bent on finding an easy way out, the reckless driver, the philanderer, the heavy drinker, the accident-prone taker of unnecessary chances. It was this underside that took over the night of July 18–19, 1969.

If the assassination of John F. Kennedy is "a quagmire for historians," then the Chappaquiddick affair is in many ways almost as deep and treacherous a bog. The facts are, by now, fairly well known. Senator Kennedy was in Edgartown, Martha's Vineyard, for a sailing regatta he had been competing in ever since he was a child. After the race, in which he had come in ninth, he went to a party in an isolated cottage on nearby Chappaquiddick Island, a party which had been arranged, with his knowledge, by his cousin Joe Gargan and his lawyer-friend Paul Markham. Six former campaign workers of Robert Kennedy's, all unmarried females, had been invited, along with three other men, two of whom were married. The party had been organized ostensibly to pay back six of Bobby Kennedy's most devoted assistants. However, since it was held in an isolated cottage on a somewhat desolate island (and not, for example, in a restaurant or hotel in Edgartown), and the six women attending were all unmarried and in their twenties and the six men attending were all but one married and all but one in their thirties and were without their wives, it is easy to presume the party may have had other purposes, if only in the minds of the organizers.

Sometime after 11:30 P.M., quite probably after midnight, after a good deal of eating and drinking, Edward Kennedy left the party with one of the women, slim, blonde, 28-year-old Mary Jo Kopechne, who left both her purse and hotel keys in the cottage as she headed for Kennedy's car.

Kennedy and Miss Kopechne then drove away from the cottage together in the senator's Oldsmobile, ostensibly, according to Kennedy, to take Mary Jo back to her hotel in Edgartown. Soon Kennedy turned down a bumpy, dirt-and-sand road which led over a narrow bridge, with no guardrail, spanning a small pond. The car, traveling at considerable speed, careened off the bridge and landed upside down in seven to ten feet of water. Somehow Kennedy was able to struggle free of the car and swim to the surface, while Miss Kopechne was unable to get out.

From here on, the controversy begins. According to Kennedy's testimony, he repeatedly dove into the "murky current" in an effort to rescue Miss Kopechne but failed in the attempts. (According to a 1980 *Reader's Digest* investigation this is a questionable contention.)

Then Kennedy proceeded to do some very strange things. He walked a mile and a half back to the cottage where the party had been going on, without stopping to call for help at two lighted buildings along the way—the Malm house, near the scene of the accident, and the Chappaquiddick firehouse, where he could have stopped and pulled an alarm that would have awakened the whole island and brought volunteer firemen to the rescue within fifteen minutes.

Arriving back at the cottage, Kennedy spotted one of the men, Raymond La Rosa, by the entrance and called softly, "Ray, get me Joe." Then he slipped into the back seat of a Valiant parked outside the house. When Gargan appeared at the car Kennedy asked him to get Paul Markham. The three men talked inside the car and, according to their later testimony, then returned to the scene of the accident and tried, in vain, to rescue Miss Kopechne from the car. After a while they gave up. Lights were still on in both the firehouse and the Malm house, and still Kennedy and his friends did not call for help.

Things were very murky from here on. According to Senator Kennedy's testimony at the official inquest, he told Gargan and Markham to return to the cottage and not tell anyone what had happened, while he would return to Edgartown and report the accident to the police. Although the ferry had shut down for the night, the ferryman could have been telephoned and, for a fee, would have been obligated by his contract to ferry the senator across the 500-foot channel to Edgartown. But again according to his testimony, Kennedy chose not to summon the ferry, but to swim the channel instead, fully clothed.

Eventually he reached his room at the Shiretown Inn. Although no one saw the senator dripping wet from the swim, the official inquest revealed that he was spotted by one of the owners of the Shiretown Inn, Russell E. Peachey, who testified that at 2:25 A.M. he noticed Kennedy standing at the foot of the stairs on the deck just outside the office, or lobby, wearing a jacket and slacks.

"May I help you in any way?" asked Peachey.

According to Peachey's testimony, Kennedy at first replied, "No," then said he had been awakened by a noise coming from a party next door and had gone to look for his watch and couldn't find it. He asked Peachey for the time.

Glancing through the office window, Peachey noticed that the time on the office clock was 2:25 A.M. and so informed the senator. Kennedy then thanked him, turned and went upstairs to his room, without commenting any further on the alleged noise from the party next door.

By 7:30 A.M. Kennedy was up and about, looking neat and clean in dry yachting clothes, as if he were about to race again shortly. Soon he was talking unconcernedly with Ross Richards, winner of the previous day's regatta, and before long Stanley Moore and Mrs. Richards joined them. To those who observed Kennedy during these moments he looked fresh, alert, and relaxed.

Kennedy was chatting away with the Richardses and Mr. Moore on the deck of the Shiretown Inn when, all of a sudden, Joe Gargan and Paul Markham appeared, looking, according to Mr. Richards's testimony at the inquest, "ruffled" and "damp." Kennedy, Gargan, and Markham then immediately headed for Kennedy's room, with Gargan first retrieving the senator's key from the front desk. Once in the room, according to Markham's inquest testimony, Markham and Gargan simultaneously asked the senator what had "happened," and Kennedy replied, to his friends' astonishment, that he had not reported the accident. Then, again according to Markham's inquest testimony, Gargan and Markham advised Kennedy to notify legislative aide David Burke, attorney Burke Marshall, and "the family" of the accident by phone immediately. (It was not clear whether "family" referred to the Kennedys or the Kopechnes.)

At 8:30 A.M. Kennedy emerged from his room, went to the front desk, bought the New York and Boston papers, and borrowed a dime from the desk clerk for a phone call. After he made the call, Kennedy, Gargan, and Markham then went down to the ferry and took the ferry to Chappaquiddick Island, ostensibly to make a telephone call from the pay phone at the Chappaquiddick landing which they considered more "private" than the pay phone at the Inn. The person they were most anxious to reach was Burke Marshall, former assistant attorney general in the Kennedy administration and "defuser of blockbusters" for the Kennedy family, as Kennedy biographer Burton Hersh characterized him. However, no one at the ferry landing noticed Kennedy, Gargan, or Markham making a call.

While the three men milled around the landing, as if they were waiting for somebody, the ferry went back to Edgartown and returned to Chappaquiddick with the wrecker from Jon Ahlbum's service station. According to the Reader's Digest's 1980 investigation of the accident, as the wrecker was coming off the ferry, one of the workers called toward Kennedy, Gargan, and Markham: "Hey, did you hear about the accident?" Markham replied calmly, "Yes, we just heard about it."

So the car had been discovered! There was nothing Kennedy could do now but report the accident. The police had probably already identified the owner of the Oldsmobile from the license plates. Without making any more calls (if he ever made any), Kennedy took the ferry back to Edgartown and headed for police headquarters.

The submerged, overturned car had been discovered by fishermen, and Police Chief Dominick J. Arena and scuba diver John N. Farrar had been summoned to the scene. Farrar found the pale, rigid body of Mary Jo Kopechne in the rear of the car, clutching the bottom of the rear seat with both hands, her head thrust up and back as if in quest of a pocket of air. He promptly removed the body. After her body was brought to the surface, it was briefly examined by Chief Arena, who determined that Mary Jo had on a blouse, bra, and slacks, but no panties. He also determined that the purse found in the car did not belong to Mary Jo but to Rosemary Keough.

Soon Police Chief Arena identified Senator Kennedy as the owner of the car and phoned police headquarters in Edgartown in an effort to locate the senator. He was told the senator was already there to report the accident. Arena then spoke briefly with Kennedy and agreed to meet with him at headquarters and take his statement.

The statement Kennedy then gave turned out to be the first of three blows in the assassination of his own character.

On July 18, 1969, at approximately 11:15 P.M. in Chappaquiddick, Martha's Vineyard, Mass., I was driving my car on Main Street on my way to get the ferry back to Edgartown. I was unfamiliar with the road and turned right onto Dike Road instead of bearing hard left on Main Street. After proceeding for approximately one-half mile on Dike Road, I descended a hill and came upon a narrow bridge. The car went off the side of the bridge. There was one passenger with me, one Miss Mary

————,* a former secretary of my brother, Senator Robert Kennedy. The car turned over and sank into the water and landed with the roof resting on the bottom. I attempted to open the door and the window of the car but have no recollection of how I got out of the car. I came to the surface and then repeatedly dove down to the car in an attempt to see if the passenger was still in the car. I was unsuccessful in the attempt. I was exhausted and in a state of shock. I recall walking back to where my friends were eating. There was a car parked in front of the cottage, and I climbed into the back seat. I then asked for someone to bring me back to Edgartown. I remember walking around for a period of time and then going back to my hotel room. When I fully realized what had happened this morning, I immediately contacted the police.

When Supervisor George W. Kennedy of the Massachusetts Registry of Motor Vehicles read the statement he allowed that he was not satisfied with it and asked the senator if he would elaborate on it.

"I have no comment," Kennedy said.

Gargan and Markham then assured the supervisor that the senator would answer some questions later, but, as it developed, he never did. Chief Arena then allowed Kennedy to leave without interrogating him. He did not interrogate Gargan or Markham either, for there had been nothing in Kennedy's brief statement indicating that Gargan and Markham had been involved in the episode in any way. Before leaving police headquarters, Kennedy told Arena he wished to speak with his lawyer, Burke Marshall, before making any more statements, and Markham then pleaded with the chief to withhold the senator's first statement from the press until Kennedy had conferred with Marshall.

*The original statement did not contain the complete name of Miss Kopechne because Kennedy was uncertain of its spelling.

As soon as Kennedy, Gargan, and Markham left police headquarters, the press descended en masse on the hapless Chief Arena, demanding to know why Kennedy had not called for help to save Miss Kopechne, why he had not reported the accident sooner, etc. The chief told them he would answer their questions later, after he received more information from the senator.

As it turned out, Kennedy, after finally reaching Burke Marshall, through a most circuitous route, and conferring with him at length over the phone, never did return to police headquarters to elaborate on his original statement. Instead he left the island and went straight to the family compound in Hyannis Port.

Meanwhile, everyone who had been at the cookout on Chappaquiddick the night before was being taken away from the island by Kennedy aides; Chief Arena, who had been kept ignorant of the cookout attendees by Kennedy, never had a chance to question any of them.

Mary Jo's body was also taken away by a Kennedy aide, Dun Gifford, who had arrived on Martha's Vineyard in a chartered plane early in the day (in response to an urgent call from Kennedy administrative assistant David Burke) with the apparent mission of expeditiously returning the body to the Kopechne family in Pennsylvania, and hence out of the jurisdiction of the state of Massachusetts. By early afternoon the embalming of the body had been completed, and Mr. Gifford had obtained associate medical examiner Donald R. Mills's signature on a death certificate ascertaining death by drowning with no evidence of "foul play." According to Dr. Mills's testimony at the inquest he did not recommend an autopsy; however, he admitted he had not conferred with District Attorney Edmund Dinis, who was officially in charge of the case, on the matter. By noon the following day (Sunday), after delays caused by bad weather and problems with the chartered aircraft, Dun Gifford was on his way to Pennsylvania with Mary Jo's body. As it turned out, District Attorney Edmund Dinis, who had assumed charge of the case, had wanted an autopsy very urgently, but Gifford, with the indulgence of Chief Arena, removed the body from the island in his chartered plane before Mr. Dinis set in motion the necessary procedures. (However, Gifford later claimed he had waited until the last minute.)

Before the body left Martha's Vineyard, however, associate medical examiner Mills and mortician Eugene Frieh had had a chance to go over it. Like Chief Arena, they noted that Mary Jo was wearing a blouse, bra, and slacks, but no panties. Although they found no bruises on the body, they found what appeared at first to be blood stains on the back of Mary Jo's blouse but which were later determined by chemical analysis to be grass stains. No such stains were found on either her bra or her slacks. Mortician Frieh also noticed that there was surprisingly little water in the body and concluded that Mary Jo could have probably died of suffocation in an air void, despite Dr. Mills's official conclusion that the cause of death was drowning.

Senator Kennedy attended the funeral of Mary Jo Kopechne in Plymouth, Pennsylvania, on July 22, 1969, the day after the Apollo moon landing, wearing a very conspicuous white neck brace which he was not observed wearing again. He was accompanied by his wife, Joan, and sister-in-law Ethel Kennedy. During the funeral service in St. Vincent's Catholic Church, Mary Jo's mother, sitting across the aisle from the Kennedys, wept uncontrollably, as did the other "boiler-room girls" who had attended the fateful cookout on Chappaquiddick. It was a highly charged moment. Mary Jo had been a slender, pretty woman with fair skin and sandy blonde hair; she had a reputation for loyalty, intelligence, and the ability to do hard work under pressure. She had been particularly devoted to the late Robert Kennedy, for whom she had worked late hours uncomplainingly.

After the burial, during which Mrs. Kopechne broke down again, the Kennedys flew back to Hyannis in a private DC-3 belonging to Ethel Kennedy and her children. Later it was learned that the Kennedys had offered to pay for Miss Kopechne's funeral, but her proud parents had refused the offer and paid for the funeral with a bank loan and the money they had saved for their daughter's wedding. (Much later attorney Joseph Flannagan, representing the Kopechne family, announced the Kopechnes had received $140,923 in settlement from the Kennedys through Senator Kennedy's insurer. Whether any more money was ever given the Kopechnes is not known, but sometime after the insurance settlement, the press reported that Mr. and Mrs. Joseph Kopechne, a couple of modest means, had bought a second home in the Poconos.)

Upon returning to the Kennedy compound, Senator Kennedy and his aides, on what should have been a day of celebration because of the moon landing, convened a grand council to decide what to do next. Soon there would be a trial, and Kennedy would have to enter a plea. The senator would also have to explain his actions publicly on television to his constituents, the people of Massachusetts, and his possible future constituents, the people of the United States.

The "honorary Kennedys" responded to the call in a most heartening way. They were all potential high-office holders in a prospective Edward Kennedy administration, and they had been quick to realize that there never would be any high offices to hold unless this Chappaquiddick mess was settled. Among those attending the council were former Secretary of Defense Robert McNamara, former Special Assistant to the President Theodore Sorensen, speechwriter Richard Goodwin, Representative John Culver, Representative John Tunney, former Assistant Attorney General Burke Marshall, Kennedy speechwriter Milton Gwirtzman, and Kennedy brother-in-law, campaign manager, and manager of the Kennedy business enterprises, Stephen Smith. Consulted by telephone were former Special Assistant to the President and Harvard historian Arthur M. Schlesinger, Jr., and Harvard professor and former ambassador to India, John Kenneth Galbraith. It fell to certain of these distinguished gentlemen to draft a second Kennedy statement on the accident, since Kennedy's first statement had not held up to public scrutiny and was taking a daily beating from the press.

Meanwhile, Kennedy's lawyers were bargaining with the Dukes County special prosecutor in Edgartown, who happened to be an acquaintance of the senator's, Walter

E. Steele. (They had once been colleagues in the Suffolk County district attorney's office.) In time they came up with a deal, and Senator Kennedy, in a brief court appearance, pleaded guilty to a misdemeanor charge of leaving the scene of an accident. The judge, with the concurrence of the prosecution, then imposed the minimum sentence: two months in jail, suspended, and revocation of the defendant's driver's license for one year. After the sentence was read, Kennedy was noticed to heave a visible sigh of relief.

Upon returning to Hyannis from the trial, Kennedy was presented with a draft of a second statement prepared for him by his advisers. He was to read it to the people of Massachusetts, and the nation, on television that night. For seventeen minutes, Edward Kennedy assassinated his own character a second time by delivering a rambling, banal, self-pitying statement on television that differed substantially from the first statement he had submitted to Chief Arena. (For example, he never told Chief Arena about Gargan and Markham, but on TV he mentioned their attempt to rescue Mary Jo.) He alluded to "the Kennedy curse" and to assorted great statesmen from Massachusetts history, and wondered out loud whether he should stay in politics. The statement, in the words of biographer Burton Hersh, "turned the stomachs of alert people all over the country."

Several members of the grand council agreed. Richard Goodwin observed that "almost anything he could have done would have been better than what did happen. He did the worst thing he could have, he Nixonized the situation." Theodore Sorensen was of the same opinion and, according to Burton Hersh, quietly took out several passages from his book *The Kennedy Legacy* which had alluded to Edward Kennedy's bright political future.

Such public uproar followed Kennedy's statement that District Attorney Edmund Dinis felt compelled to petition Judge James A. Boyle to hold an official inquest into the death of Miss Kopechne to determine whether any criminal charges should be brought against Senator Kennedy.

The inquest was held January 5–8, 1970, in secret, at Kennedy's request, and, again at Kennedy's request, the Supreme Court of Massachusetts issued a ruling that the transcript could not be released to the press until nine months after the inquest.

When the transcript was finally released, its 700-odd pages revealed that Senator Kennedy had assassinated his own character a third time. Kennedy testified at the inquest that, after obtaining his car keys, he had left the cottage on Chappaquiddick at 11:15 P.M. to drop Mary Jo Kopechne off at her hotel in Edgartown. Instead of continuing on the paved macadam road, he had mistakenly turned right and gone down a dirt road, which turned out to be Dike Road that led over Dike Bridge. He had not realized his error until his car went off the bridge. After unsuccessfully trying to rescue Mary Jo from the car, he had gone back to the cottage to get Joe Gargan and Paul Markham, and together they had tried to rescue Mary Jo and had failed. Kennedy had then swum the 500-foot channel back to Edgartown and had returned to the Shiretown Inn. At 2:25 he had put on dry clothes and had gone downstairs to ask the innkeeper what time it was.

"Why didn't you report the accident until ten hours later?" District Attorney Dinis asked.

To this Kennedy replied,

> I tossed and turned in the room unable to gain the strength within me, the moral strength, to call Mrs. Kopechne.
>
> I somehow believed that when the sun came up and it was a new morning that what had happened the night before would not have happened and did not happen . . . it was a nightmare. I was not even sure it happened.

District Attorney Edmund Dinis had asked a Pennsylvania judge to authorize an autopsy and the request had been denied, principally because of strenuous objection by Mr. and Mrs. Joseph Kopechne, who had been advised by Richard Cardinal Cushing to forbid exhumation of Mary Jo as "their Christian duty to prevent the desecration of their daughter's body." Dinis thus had to indicate at the inquest that there was a "gaping hole" in the case. And so the court of inquiry never learned whether or not Miss Kopechne was pregnant or whether she had had sexual intercourse the day of her death. Nor did they ever learn for sure whether Miss Kopechne died as a result of drowning or of suffocation.

There were many other gaping holes in the proceedings, as we shall see, especially in regard to the records of Senator Kennedy's telephone calls the morning of July 19. But these gaping holes were never satisfactorily filled. Kennedy stood by his statement, as he still does today. In the end, Judge Boyle found that Kennedy had been reckless and was "probably guilty of criminal conduct," but he did not suggest that the senator be indicted for any crimes. Many journalists dubbed the inquest a "noquest." So unsatisfied was the public with the inquest that Dukes County grand jury foreman Leslie Leland, one of the honest, dedicated law enforcement officials concerned with the case, succeeded in convening a grand jury to return an indictment against Senator Kennedy. However, because of the Supreme Court ruling, the grand jury was not allowed to read the transcript of the secret inquest, nor was it allowed to question any of the inquest witnesses. Without the findings of the inquest, or the testimony of the witnesses, the grand jury literally had nothing to go on and was therefore compelled to disband in frustration without returning an indictment. The presiding judge, Wilfred J. Pacquet, a 67-year-old Democratic party stalwart, who had rigidly enforced the no-transcript rule, had done his duty toward the party that had sustained him all his life. He had even gone so far as to have a Catholic priest present during the grand jury proceedings, who, before the deliberations, had prayed that the jury would exercise "justice and charity" toward the defendant.

Had Kennedy been a man of lesser importance he could have been tried for criminal manslaughter and possibly sent to prison. For the doubts remain. First of all, few could accept Kennedy's claim that he was taking Mary Jo back to Edgartown that night because she wasn't feeling well. Kennedy had not told anyone but his chauffeur that he was leaving the party, and Kennedy only told him because he had the keys to Kennedy's car. Furthermore, Kennedy, with his history of reckless driving, rarely drove by himself, leaving that chore up to his chauffeur. The day of the tragedy his chauffeur had driven him to the party and had also driven him down Dike Road to the beach and back. If Mary Jo had really been ill and had wanted to return to her hotel, the logical person to drive her there would have been the chauffeur. Also, although Kennedy was the host of the cookout, he had not said goodnight to any of his guests, and neither had Miss Kopechne when he and Miss Kopechne left. Nor had Miss Kopechne told any of the other guests at the party she was ill and wanted to return to the hotel. She had also failed to ask her roommate for the key to her hotel room, and she had left her purse behind in the cottage. That Kennedy had been heading for the ferry seems preposterous. The difference between the paved road to the ferry and the narrow, bumpy, "washboard" road to the beach, which leads off at a right angle to the paved road, is so pronounced that a reasonably sober driver would sense it immediately. In his final report of the inquest Judge Boyle stated, "I infer a reasonable and probable explanation of the totality of the above facts is that Kennedy and Kopechne did *not* intend to return to Edgartown at that time; that Kennedy did not intend to drive to the ferry slip, and his turn onto Dike Road was intentional."

Senator Kennedy was the first driver to go off Dike Bridge in forty years. Most drivers slow down to a crawl when they approach Dike Bridge. In 1980 an exhaustive investigation by *Reader's Digest* determined, in a scientific test, that Kennedy's speed, as he approached the bridge, had probably been about 34 miles per hour. At the inquest Judge Boyle declared that even 20 miles per hour on Dike Road was "reckless."

Secondly, virtually no one has been willing to accept Senator Kennedy's contention that he left the party with Mary Jo at 11:15. At the inquest Deputy Sheriff Christopher S. Look, Jr., testified that he had seen Senator

Kennedy's car at the intersection of School Road and Cemetery Road at approximately 12:45. On patrol at the time, Sheriff Look had noted there were two passengers in the car, that some object, perhaps a purse, was sitting on the rear window shelf, and that the license plate number "began with L and had two sevens, one at the beginning and one at the end." (Senator Kennedy's license plate number was L78-207.) Look testified in a sworn statement:

> The car passed directly in front of me, about 35 feet away from my car, my headlights were on this car, and right across and then it stopped. It continued around the corner and stopped and I noticed the headlights were backing up, and I said to myself, well, they probably want some information; so I stopped my car and got out and started to walk back to them on Cemetery Road. I got about 25 or 30 feet when the car was backing up and backed toward the ferry landing on the macadamized road, then it drove down Dike Road.

Look testified that the next morning, when the wrecker hauled Kennedy's car out of Poucha Pond, "As soon as they started to pull it out and it became visible, I walked over and told Officer Brougier, gee, that is the same car I saw last night."

Kennedy no doubt felt compelled to state that he had left the party early because the ferry to Edgartown stopped running at midnight. Having been spotted by Sheriff Look at 12:45 meant that he probably had left the party with Mary Jo after the ferry had shut down for the night. Since shortly after Look's sighting, Kennedy had gone off Dike Bridge, the time of the accident was probably around 12:50 or 12:55.

Other doubts. Kennedy testified that there were very strong currents running in Poucha Pond that had prevented him from getting Miss Kopechne out of the car. But according to the *Reader's Digest*'s scrupulous scientific investigation of the tidal currents in Poucha Pond, conducted in 1979, the current was "not so strong as to constitute an insurmountable obstacle." Furthermore, Kennedy testified that Gargan and Markham had made an attempt to rescue Miss Kopechne and that Gargan had been severely bruised in the attempt. However, when Gargan and Markham returned to the cottage none of the girls had noticed anything extraordinary about them and the following morning no one had noticed any bruises on either Mr. Gargan or Mr. Markham. They were not wet and no cuts or scratches or black and blue marks were spotted on either of them. These facts led the *Digest* to the opinion that no genuine attempts had been made to rescue Mary Jo, especially if the accident had happened after 12:45. For Kennedy had been seen at the Shiretown Inn dry and neatly clothed at 2:25. Between the time of the accident (12:50?) and the time Kennedy was spotted at the Inn, there simply had not been sufficient time to have mounted much of a rescue effort to save Mary Jo. For after the accident Kennedy had had to walk back to the cottage to fetch Gargan and Markham and then somehow return to Edgartown, go to his room, change, and appear by the front desk and be recognized at 2:25.

This brings up the subject of the famous "swim" (with all his clothes on) across the 500-foot channel between the Chappaquiddick and Edgartown ferry slips, a feat one wag called "Leander swimming the Hellespont." No one testified to having seen Kennedy walk dripping wet from the Edgartown ferry slip to the Shiretown Inn, nor had he been observed entering the Inn dripping wet. However, a certain Mr. Ballou from Rhode Island testified that he had seen three men crossing the Edgartown Channel in a small boat around 2 A.M. And Gargan and Markham had told the girls at the cottage that they were looking for a boat. Later a young boy testified that he had discovered the following morning that his rowboat had been used during the night and had been tied up in another place. Why would Kennedy have claimed to have swum the channel? Perhaps because he was supposed to have been "in shock," rather than methodically searching for a boat with which to escape the scene of the accident. Also he was supposed to have told Markham and Gargan "You take care of the girls; I'll take care of [reporting] the accident" as he plunged into the water. But if Markham and Gargan had aided him in his escape from the scene of the accident they would have been implicated in that escape. What could have been the purpose of taking a boat? To allow the senator to be recognized at the Shiretown Inn dry as a bone at 2:25. It is known as establishing an alibi.

But the most nagging doubt of all concerns the related questions of why Kennedy hadn't called for help immediately and why he had waited ten hours to report the accident. As we have noted, the Malm house near Dike Bridge had a lighted window as Kennedy passed it on his way back to the cottage, and the lighted, open Chappaquiddick firehouse with its alarm switch accessible twenty-four hours a day stood only a stone's throw from the cottage. Kennedy in 1974 told the *Boston Globe* that he had been "in shock" at the time and had kept telling himself, "I just can't do it. I just can't do it." In the morning he had still hoped to find the accident nothing but a bad dream, and he "willed Mary Jo alive."

But again this seems a doubtful contention. One plausible explanation for the apparent contradictions is that Kennedy, from the very beginning, was desperately trying to find a way out. The way out might have been his cousin, Joe Gargan. As in the past, the idea was to let someone else take the blame: cousin Joe could have been the likely choice. This was, in fact, the hypothesis the *Boston Globe* put forth in October 1974, after an exhaustive two-month investigation of the case.

Both Kennedy and Gargan have denied that Gargan was asked to take the blame. Nevertheless, Joe Gargan had in the past stood ready to "cover" for his illustrious cousin, Senator Kennedy. It had been he who had, in fact, rented the Chappaquiddick cottage for four days and nights in his own name, telling the owner that it was going to be used only by himself and his wife and children. The owner thus had no idea that Kennedy and the "boiler-room girls" would be visiting the cottage. No one, in fact, least of all Kennedy's parents and his wife, had known the senator would be there except for those invited to the cookout.

What might have happened was that Kennedy had thought to have Gargan take the blame soon after the accident, or Gargan could have volunteered to take the blame. The first thing for Kennedy to do was to establish an alibi. Hence his appearance, dry, hair combed, neatly dressed, at 2:25 A.M., on the deck outside the Inn's lobby. And hence his not reporting the accident for ten hours. If it was not *his* accident, why report it?

When would such a plan have broken down? Probably when it was learned that the accident had been discovered. The motive for returning to Chappaquiddick in the morning may not have been to make that "private" telephone call (any number of "private" phones in Edgartown could have been used), but to return to the scene of the accident to see whether or not the accident had been discovered, whether the car was still there, and whether Mary Jo was dead or alive. After all, the swift tidal currents could conceivably have swept the vehicle further out into Poucha Pond where it could have disappeared from sight. Or the reverse current could have swept it out into Cape Poge Bay where it could have disappeared entirely.

Then there is the mysterious matter of all the telephone calls. On March 12, 1980, *The New York Times* revealed that "records of Senator Edward M. Kennedy's telephone calls in the hours after the accident at Chappaquiddick were withheld by the telephone company from an inquest into the death of Mary Jo Kopechne without the knowledge of the assistant district attorney who asked for them."

For some time there had been rumors of some sixteen or seventeen calls made by the senator during the night and early morning of July 18–19. On August 13 the conservative *Manchester Union Leader* of New Hampshire published an article by Arthur C. Egan, Jr., stating that Senator Kennedy had made seventeen calls in the early hours of July 19, immediately after the accident. Mr. Egan said he had obtained the records from one James T. Gilmartin, a lawyer from the Bronx. Mr. Gilmartin confirmed to the *Times* that he had obtained the telephone records from a friend who worked for the New England Telephone company in Boston.

Another individual who claimed he had seen the telephone records was Anthony T. Ulasewicz, a former New York City police detective who had been sent to Chappaquiddick by President Nixon's White House staff immediately after the accident to investigate the case. Ulasewicz has maintained that several calls had been made in the middle of the night.

The issue is important because Kennedy claimed he had been so disoriented, and so "in shock," after the accident that he had been unable to call the police, or the fire department, or anybody else, to rescue Miss Kopechne that night. If it was true that he had been able to make seventeen calls to friends and associates during the night, it would discredit that claim.

At the time of the official inquest New England Telephone records showing Senator Kennedy's telephone calls on July 18–19 were subpoenaed and the company's general accounting supervisor, A. Robert Molloy, brought four lists of those calls to the inquest. For some reason still not clear, only one list of sixteen calls was presented into evidence. All the calls had been made after 10:57 A.M. on July 19, or *after* the senator had reported the accident. The other three lists were not introduced.

The attorney representing the company, a Mr. Parrott, did however tell District Attorney Dinis, in a private colloquy during the inquest, there were no calls charged to Senator Kennedy's credit card before 7:52 A.M. So there *had been* calls made before 10:57, after all. On inquiring of Mr. Parrott what had happened to the three lists of calls not introduced as evidence, the *Times* was told that those lists no longer existed.

What about the call at 7:52 A.M.? At the inquest Kennedy said it was a call to find out how he could get in touch with his brother-in-law, Stephen Smith. Asked by *The New York Times* on March 12, 1980, whom precisely had he called at 7:52 A.M. on July 19, Senator Kennedy responded, "A Mrs. Wagner. She had his [Stephen Smith's] address, but she didn't have his number."

Who was Mrs. Wagner? Soon the whole world learned who Mrs. Wagner was, as the press went to work on her and her beautiful face began to appear on the front page of the *New York Post* and other papers. Helga Wagner was an attractive blonde divorcée, originally from Austria, who was living in Key Biscayne, Florida, and who had known Senator Kennedy for some time. Her most recent companion had been Charles, Prince of Wales. Well known in international society, Mrs. Wagner had become a talented jewelry designer and is now designing jewelry in New York. In addition to Senator Kennedy, she also knew his brother-in-law, Stephen Smith; however, it is doubted whether Kennedy's call to her at 7:52 on July 19 was solely to get his brother-in-law's telephone number.

So before Kennedy had phoned the police, or the fire department, or his wife, or the Kopechnes, or his parents, he had phoned Helga Wagner in Florida. Senator Kennedy also claimed he had made a call to administrative assistant David Burke at about nine from the Chappaquiddick ferry slip, but the ferry operator testified at the inquest that he had not seen anyone in the Kennedy party use the phone, and, as we know, as soon as the Kennedy party had learned the accident at Dike Bridge had been discovered they had immediately taken the ferry back to Edgartown.

In 1980 Senator Kennedy told *The New York Times* that he had phoned David Burke at about nine from the ferry slip to get Burke Marshall's telephone number. It was Marshall whom Kennedy had been most anxious to reach. The *Times* then got in touch with Mr. Burke, at that time an official with ABC News, and he confirmed that he had received a call from Kennedy early in the morning. The call had awakened him, and he had immediately attempted to phone Burke Marshall, as the senator had requested. Mr. Marshall, then general counsel of IBM, had not been at home and his wife, Violet Marshall, had taken the call. Upon being questioned by the *Times,* Mrs.

Marshall stated that she had received a call from David Burke shortly after she had awakened in the morning, sometime between 6 and 9 A.M. If Mrs. Marshall was correct, this indicated that Senator Kennedy may have called David Burke sometime *before* the time he testified to.

What other calls had Kennedy made before reporting the accident?

W. A. Rock, a Cape Cod pilot, told the *Times* that he had been called at 9 A.M. by Kennedy's legislative assistant, Dun Gifford, the aide entrusted with removing Miss Kopechne's body to Pennsylvania. Mr. Rock stated that Mr. Gifford had asked to be flown to Martha's Vineyard immediately. They had then left Nantucket for Edgartown around 9:30 A.M., dipping over the bridge at Chappaquiddick on the way. Mr. Rock told the *Times* he and Mr. Gifford could see Kennedy's car "still submerged in the water" as they flew over Dike Bridge.

Upon being questioned about this by the *Times,* Mr. Gifford said that he had been called by Mr. Burke at his home in Nantucket that morning and could not dispute Mr. Rock's recollection of a 9 A.M. call. If Mr. Rock was correct it indicates, of course, that Mr. Burke had phoned Mr. Gifford some time before Kennedy had called Mr. Burke. When asked by the *Times* about this discrepancy, Mr. Gifford abruptly changed his mind and said he must have called Mr. Rock *after* 9 A.M. He had then phoned Senator Kennedy's attorneys and had asked Mr. Rock to get in touch with them too. Things were beginning to fall apart.

From these revelations, which did not come to light until 1980, it appeared that Senator Kennedy had, in fact, made several calls before he had reported the accident and during the time he had supposedly been "in shock." Why were the three lists of telephone calls, upon which these early calls may have been registered, never introduced as evidence at the inquest? And why were these lists eventually destroyed?

Senator Kennedy's counsel at the inquest was Mr. Edward P. Hanify, a partner in the Boston law firm of

Ropes and Gray. When I interviewed him later, Mr. Hanify stated that only one list of telephone calls was introduced as evidence because only one list of calls was asked for by District Attorney Dinis. Mr. Hanify also stated that he had no knowledge whatsoever concerning the destruction of the other three lists of calls.

But what about the known calls, the sixteen made after Kennedy reported the accident that *were* presented as evidence during the inquest? To whom had these calls been made? Apparently they had all been made to Kennedy family members and aides and associates, as would be expected. Only one call, the first on the list, made at 10:57 A.M., remains mysterious. This call, billed to Kennedy's credit card, had lasted 23 minutes and 24 seconds; it had been made from Vineyard Haven to the home of Jacqueline Kennedy Onassis at Hyannis. Since Kennedy himself was at police headquarters with Markham at the time the call was made, it is thought that the call was made by the senator's cousin, Joe Gargan, using the senator's credit card number. What was mysterious about the call was the fact that Mrs. Onassis and her children were away at the time, and there was apparently no one else staying at the house. It is therefore believed that someone had been told to go to the Onassis house to receive an important call. Mr. Gargan had then traveled to neighboring Vineyard Haven to make the call when he could have easily made it from Edgartown. Who was Gargan calling and why? Mr. Gargan refused to be interviewed by *The New York Times* on this matter.

Could Mary Jo Kopechne have been saved? Another big question. Scuba diver John Farrar had been called at his Turf and Tackle shop at 8:45 A.M. on July 19 to investigate the sunken car near Dike Bridge. By 8:55 he had extricated Mary Jo's body from the car. At the inquest Farrar testified that if he had been called the night of the accident he could have reached Mary Jo in fifteen or twenty minutes. Both he and mechanic John Ahlbum also testified there were still air pockets in the car and the trunk was full of air when the car was hauled out of the water. Asked if Mary Jo could have been saved, Farrar testified that if

Kennedy had pulled the firehouse alarm and he, in his capacity as captain of the scuba, search, and rescue division of the Edgartown Volunteer Fire Department, had been alerted, he would have had Mary Jo out of the car alive in twenty-five minutes.

Still more doubts. What about Senator Kennedy's sworn statement at the inquest in 1970 that he had never been on Chappaquiddick until July 18 and was therefore totally unfamiliar with the roads? (This, of course, was to explain why he made the "accidental" ninety-degree turn onto bumpy Dike Road from the macadamized Main Street leading to the ferry landing.)

In January 1980 the *New York Post* interviewed several residents of Martha's Vineyard to find out whether the senator's statement was true. From their testimony it appeared that Kennedy had been on Chappaquiddick several times before July 18, 1969. Among those who told the *New York Post* that they were certain the senator had been on the island before were John Edwards, the ferry operator, Dodie Silva, the realtor who had helped arrange the rental of the cottage where the cookout was held, Harold B. Kelley, Jr., manager of the Chappaquiddick Beach Club, and Russell Stearns, a Boston investment banker and Chappaquiddick summer resident. (In addition to these refutations of his contention that he was unfamiliar with Chappaquiddick Island, the senator's contention was also authoritatively demolished by *The New York Times,* the *Washington Star,* and the *Reader's Digest.*)

But Kennedy need not have visited the island before July 18 to have become familiar with its roads; he had driven over the macadam road leading from the ferry to the cottage twice the afternoon of the accident and had also driven down Dike Road twice that same afternoon on the way to the beach for a swim and then returning from the beach to the cottage.

For now, one can only speculate on what *really* happened the night of July 18–19, 1969, on Chappaquiddick. Perhaps one day in the not-too-distant future something approximating the full truth will be known, for I have been informed that former District Attorney Edmund Dinis is now prepared to "tell all" and will probably do so in a forthcoming book. Certainly some convincing account is badly needed. For what emerged from the incomplete, inconclusive legal proceedings against Kennedy was a pattern of deliberate indulgence toward the senator. Clearly the Kennedy attorneys were able to manipulate the Massachusetts criminal justice system to meet their client's needs. Toward the end of all the legal proceedings, it became obvious that in Massachusetts there was one law for the people and another for the Kennedys.

And yet at the time of President Ford's pardon of former President Nixon, Senator Kennedy had the nerve to issue a statement criticizing the pardon, asking, "Do we operate under a system of equal justice under law? Or is there one system for the average citizen and another for the high and mighty?"

There is, of course, one system for the average citizen, and another for the high and mighty, and Kennedy had taken full advantage of that system. This, combined with all the apparent untruths Kennedy had told about the events of July 18–19, 1969, soon led to widespread public outrage over the senator's conduct and the way he had been able to get off scot-free.

Why was there such an intense public outburst over the Chappaquiddick affair? After all, scandals of this nature happen every day. The truth was that the American people had been fed so many myths about the Kennedys, and had built up such vast illusions about them, that when they were confronted with the reality of Chappaquiddick their disillusionment was so great as to provoke not merely a sense of disgust, or annoyance, or disappointment, but an outburst of genuine rage.

The appalling reality of Chappaquiddick was that a Kennedy, who seemed destined for the presidency, was evidently willing to place his political ambitions above the life of a young woman, a young woman who had dedicated a good part of her life to serving the political ambitions of his late brother Robert. The appalling reality was that the instinct of this Kennedy was not to save a life he had endangered, but to save his own political skin.

But that wasn't all. It was one thing to commit this crime, but it was quite another to get away with it. What truly angered the American people was Kennedy's attempt to escape from the accident politically unharmed and the obvious cooperation of certain authorities in helping him make that escape.

In the end, it didn't work. Because he had been so obviously untruthful to both the authorities and the American people over what had happened on Martha's Vineyard on July 18–19, Senator Kennedy did not escape the accident politically unharmed. In fact, the Chappaquiddick affair effectively ruined his chances of becoming President of the United States, as the outcome of the primary fight against President Carter in 1980 was to show.

In November 1979, before that fight began, Senator Kennedy was interviewed by CBS correspondent Roger Mudd. When Mudd brought up Chappaquiddick, Kennedy seemed to fall apart all over again. In answer to Mudd's question, "Do you think, Senator, that anybody really will ever fully believe your explanation of the Chappaquiddick . . . ?" Kennedy replied:

> Oh, there's . . . the problem is . . . from that night . . . I found the . . . the . . . the . . . the . . . the . . . conduct and behavior almost a sort of . . . beyond belief myself.
>
> That's why it's been . . . but I think that that's, that's the way it was.
>
> That's, that's that happens to be the way it was.
>
> Now . . . I find it as I've stated, that . . . I've found that the conduct, that . . . that evening, in, in, in, in the . . . as a result of the impact, of the accident, and the . . . and the the sense of loss, the sense of hope, and the, and the sense of tragedy and the whole set of circumstances, that . . . the, the behavior was inexplicable.
>
> So I find that those, those . . . those types

of questions as they apply to that . . . they're
questions in my own . . . soul, as well.

But that happens to be the way it was.

That, unfortunately for Edward M. Kennedy, was
the way it was. Could Kennedy have saved himself politically if he had behaved honestly and courageously that
night on Chappaquiddick? Suppose, as soon as the accident
had happened, he had phoned the police from the Malm
house near Dike Bridge, then gone to the firehouse to
sound the alarm, then gone to the cottage and got all the
men and women at the party to come to Dike Bridge, and,
as the result of everybody's efforts, Mary Jo's life had been
saved?

It, of course, would have immediately come to light
that he, Kennedy, a married man and a U.S. senator,
accompanied by a young, attractive, unmarried woman,
had been driving down a lonely, isolated road toward an
empty beach at an hour of the night after the last ferry
had returned to Edgartown. This alone would have damned
him among a certain segment of American society. But
whatever damage this might have done him, it would have
been more than compensated for by his having demonstrated to the world that in a moment of crisis he had been
able to act coolly and decisively to save a young woman
whose life he had endangered. Especially if the rescue
effort had been successful, Kennedy might have emerged
from the affair a hero, with his political career relatively
unimpaired.

The accident at Chappaquiddick, and the public reaction
to it, was a devastating blow to the Kennedy family. Joseph
Kennedy's nurse, Rita Dallas, has described the family's
reactions at the compound.

After the tragedy became known, calls went out to
the entire family, and, before long, the various members
began arriving from around the globe to do what they could
for Teddy. Jean and Stephen Smith arrived from Europe.
Patricia showed up "hollow-eyed and nervous." Eunice

arrived from Paris, and in Mrs. Dallas's words, "came storming into the house, her face set, her eyes smarting. 'Where's Teddy,' she snapped, 'where's my brother?'" Jacqueline Onassis arrived from Greece and turned her house over to the grand council.

When Teddy told his father about the accident, the old man, almost totally paralyzed and going blind and deaf, nodded weakly and closed his eyes. It was the final blow to his ambitions for his sons and he knew it.

Rose Kennedy was so disturbed by the affair that she would not speak to anybody in the house about it and would only speak with Teddy about it outdoors, near the flagpole, so no one could hear what they said.

As for Teddy himself, he was utterly distraught. In Mrs. Dallas's words he looked "drawn, downcast, intimidated." During the convening of the family, the lawyers, the brain trust, he "walked around in a stupor, more alone than I had ever seen him," Mrs. Dallas observed.

Chappaquiddick was a terrible personal tragedy for Ted Kennedy, and one cannot help but feel deep compassion for him. For Ted Kennedy is a very likeable person, and basically a very decent human being. People never fail to be struck by his fundamental niceness. There is almost no malice in him, and certainly the last thing he ever wanted to do was harm Mary Jo Kopechne. However, by acting the way he did during and after the Chappaquiddick affair, Teddy Kennedy destroyed an image that the Kennedys had paid a vast fortune and spent many years to create, and he certainly may have disqualified himself for the presidency. Not only did the Kennedy image never recover from the Chappaquiddick disaster, but, according to Rita Dallas, Joe Kennedy's spirit never recovered either. From the moment Ted Kennedy told his father about the accident, the mute and paralyzed old man appeared to lose the last sparks of fire remaining to him, and the man of limitless ambition lost the ambition to live.

67. Death of a Patriarch

ON DECEMBER 19, 1961, not quite one year after his son John's accession to the presidency, Joseph P. Kennedy suffered a massive stroke while playing golf in Palm Beach that left him permanently disabled. During the next seven years and eleven months the ambassador lived through a long and bitter agony that saw two of his sons murdered, one fall into disgrace, and his own powers deteriorate steadily to his death on November 18, 1969.

After the murder of John F. Kennedy, the ambassador had fastened all his hopes on his middle son, Robert. As his nurse, Rita Dallas, has observed, Bobby became the focus of his life, and watching the progress of his middle son's political career became his primary reason for living. Then, after Bobby was murdered, the old man became absorbed in his lastborn son, Teddy. Rita Dallas has testified that it was only when Teddy was around that the old man managed to smile and take some measure of enjoyment from his crippled life. Teddy would come to his father's bedroom and read him the newspapers. He would tuck him into bed at night and remain in the darkened room until his father fell asleep. "The relationship that grew between these two men," wrote Mrs. Dallas, "was powerful in its gentleness, strong in its understanding, and unique in its love."

In time Teddy became the only consolation left to

his father, who failed to respond to anyone in the family but him. Then came the disgrace over Chappaquiddick, and even Teddy failed to console him anymore. After Teddy's disastrous telecast confession, the compound emptied of relatives, in-laws, and advisers, and a deathly quiet fell over the house in Hyannis. Observers noted the ambassador seemed to go rapidly downhill. As the summer wore on, the old patriarch lost his appetite and his nurse realized he had given up. After Chappaquiddick, Mrs. Dallas would have to place ice cubes in the ambassador's mouth to open his ever-tightening throat. Before long it became evident that the old man was also going blind. With his one good hand he would rub his constantly tearing eyes until they were blood-red; then he would let his hand fall, and he would stare blankly into space. As breathing became more difficult, he was given oxygen from time to time. By autumn he could barely hear or see, and he experienced great difficulty in breathing and swallowing. Occasionally he suffered periods of cardiac arrest. For short lengths of time his heart would actually stop beating; then it would miraculously recover and the beats would resume. By November, he could no longer utter a sound. Then, one gray day he showed no signs of recognizing Teddy when his son came into his room, and the family knew it was the beginning of the end. The call went out for a gathering of the clan. Joseph P. Kennedy's deathwatch had begun.

By November 15 almost everyone was on hand. Jacqueline Onassis arrived from Greece. Eunice and her husband, Sargent Shriver, the ambassador to France, arrived from Paris. The next day Teddy was horrified to note that his father failed to respond to his voice. Then, on the 17th, the aged ambassador fell into a coma. It was then that Ethel Kennedy arrived from McLean, Virginia, ill with a fever, and had to be put to bed. During the night Jacqueline and Teddy stayed up all night in the ambassador's room, as the old man sank deeper and deeper into a coma. By mid-morning of November 18 word went out through the compound that the ambassador was dying. Soon his entire family was at his bedside. The last to arrive was

Rose, who was brought in on the arm of her son, Teddy.
When they were all assembled, Jacqueline Onassis took a
rosary from the ambassador's dresser, returned to the bedside, and gave the rosary to Mrs. Dallas, who then gave
it to Mrs. Kennedy. Rose Kennedy touched the rosary's
cross to her husband's lips and placed the beads in his
hand. As the ambassador died, his wife and children and
in-laws recited the Our Father. Death came at 11:05 A.M.
Joseph P. Kennedy was 81 years old.

The white-vestment funeral mass was held at St.
Francis Xavier Church in Hyannis, and the ambassador
was buried in the Kennedy family plot in Brookline. Cardinal Cushing officiated at the mass and delivered a long
eulogy of the deceased, beginning with the grandiose statement, "Brethren, we have become a spectacle to the whole
world, to angels as well as men." Nine years before, he
had delivered the long, monotonal invocation at the inauguration of John F. Kennedy. The intervening years may
be considered the Kennedy era in the history of the United
States. For, even though Joseph P. Kennedy's dynastic
plans had been thwarted by calamities, his family had dominated the American consciousness during the sixties as
few, if any, families in the nation's history had done.

They had also provided a valuable moral lesson. The
tragic careers of the four Kennedy brothers showed how
terrible the consequences of a family code rooted in the
values of exaggerated competitiveness and will to power
could be. For the values Joseph P. Kennedy had instilled
in his sons resulted, ultimately, not in victory, but in destruction. The ancient Greeks had a word to describe the
trait that destroyed the Kennedy brothers—*hubris,* which
to the Greeks meant "excessive pride and arrogance that
offends the gods." The Germans have a word that de-
scribes the process of destruction—*Totsiegen,* which means
"winning oneself to death."

There are no memorials in metal and masonry to Joseph
P. Kennedy, as there are to his sons Joseph Junior, John,
and Robert, but in Room 1850 of 125 Park Avenue in New

York City there is a suite of offices bearing his name that can be considered a fitting monument to the patriarch of the Kennedys.

As one approaches the door to this Kennedy sanctum sanctorum, one encounters a single sign on the wall, reading, "Joseph P. Kennedy Enterprises." This entity does not technically exist as a business organization. Rather it is an umbrella name that embraces the Park Agency, Inc., which is the family holding company, and the Joseph P. Kennedy Jr. Foundation.

Upon entering the suite, which the Kennedy enterprises occupied in early 1983 after having been located for many years in the Pan Am Building, one is greeted by a large, airy room with shell-white walls and a light-blue carpet. To one side there is a large island counter behind which sits the receptionist. Doors to the various offices lead from the room at intervals. At the far end of the room, on a pedestal, stands a bust of Joseph P. Kennedy. Before long it will be joined by a bust of John F. Kennedy. Although the walls are still bare, they will soon be adorned with a blowup of Chicago's colossal Merchandise Mart, the Kennedy family's principal business asset.

Overseeing this enterprise is Kennedy stalwart, Brooklyn-born Stephen E. Smith, husband of Jean Kennedy and chief executive of the Park Agency, Inc. He, in turn, is assisted by a staff of some eight accountants, two of whom are usually former agents of the Internal Revenue Service, and a bevy of secretaries.

The Kennedy enterprises that are managed in Room 1850 of 125 Park Avenue represent money accumulated by Joseph P. Kennedy during the years 1920 to 1969 and consist of a set of trust funds the patriarch established for his wife and children, several charitable foundations, and a string of businesses that feed those trusts and foundations. The aggregate value of these enterprises, which, taken together, constitute "the Kennedy fortune," has never been revealed, but it is thought to amount to something in the neighborhood of $350 million, perhaps a bit more, perhaps a bit less.

The amassing and managing of this fortune was Joseph P. Kennedy's principal achievement in a lifetime of many and diverse achievements. It was, of course, upon this broad financial base that the political careers of his sons were launched and sustained. And since the ambassador was not only a superb money-maker, but also a money manager *sans pareil,* the Kennedy fortune was never dissipated through unwise investments or poor tax planning. For if there was one thing this father of a president labored to avoid at all cost, it was the tax bite of the federal government of the United States.

When the inventory of Joseph P. Kennedy's estate was entered into the records of Palm Beach County Court on November 4, 1970, everybody but the Kennedy family and their closest advisers was astonished to learn how small it was. All the ambassador left for distribution to his heirs was some Florida real estate worth $345,000; real estate in Aransas County, Texas, worth $116,000; Albany's Standard Building; unspecified equity in a ranch in Corpus Christi, Texas; the family's Palm Beach home, appraised at $250,000; a one-eighth interest in Chicago's Merchandise Mart, worth around $12,500,000; miscellaneous non-producing oil and mineral properties in Alabama, Florida, Illinois, Kansas, Mississippi, Texas, and Oklahoma valued at $100,000; $36,000 in cash, clothing worth $100, accounts receivable amounting to $83,000, three pairs of cuff links, and one Movado pocket watch.

By the terms of Joseph P. Kennedy's will, which had been drawn up on December 30, 1955, Kennedy's sisters, Loretta Connelly and Margaret Burke, received bequests of $25,000 each and Rose Kennedy received $500,000 and Albany's Standard Building. All the rest and residue of the estate, after taxes and costs, went to the Joseph P. Kennedy Jr. Foundation. Estate taxes amounted to a trifling $134,330.44.

Joseph P. Kennedy had planned well. Since his overriding concern in managing his fortune had been to minimize estate taxes, he had given away most of his money during his lifetime, leaving but a few scraps here and there to be distributed after his death. Kennedy had given the bulk of his fortune to his wife and children and grandchildren, in the form of four trusts established in 1926, 1936, 1949, and 1959. By 1960 the value of these trusts was such that Rose Kennedy and her seven surviving children were each worth something in the neighborhood of $10 million, which meant that each received an income of around $400,000 to $500,000 a year. In addition, since two of the Kennedy children, Joseph Junior and Kathleen, had died, the surviving children also benefited from income generated by their deceased siblings' trusts.

Today, in 1983, it is believed that each of the trust funds established for Rose Kennedy and her children is worth anywhere from $15 to $20 million, from which each beneficiary derives an income of from $500,000 to $1 million a year. Naturally these substantial incomes go only to Rose Kennedy, Senator Edward Kennedy, Patricia Kennedy Lawford, Eunice Kennedy Shriver, Jean Kennedy Smith, and the permanently institutionalized Rosemary Kennedy. Since John F. Kennedy and Robert F. Kennedy are dead, their trusts have passed on to their children. John F. Kennedy, Jr., and Caroline Kennedy receive income from Kennedy trusts worth from $7 to $10 million each, in addition to the substantial trusts established for them by Aristotle Onassis; and the children of Robert F. Kennedy receive income off trusts worth about $1 million each. Thus, in the upcoming generation, there are already considerable disparities of wealth.

The remainder of the Kennedy fortune, that part which is not held in trust for family members, is tied up in several charitable foundations and memorials and is believed to have an aggregate value of some $75 million. These include the Joseph P. Kennedy, Jr. Foundation, devoted mostly to helping retarded children and contributing to the Catholic Archdiocese of Boston; the John Fitzgerald Kennedy Memorial Library in Boston; and Robert F. Kennedy Memorial; the Park Foundation (which regularly makes gifts to schools the Kennedy grandchildren attend); and the Special Olympics, Inc., which sponsors athletic events for retarded young people.

Feeding the Kennedy trusts, foundations, and memorials are the various Kennedy-owned businesses that are either held or managed by the Park Agency.

The largest of these, by far, is the Merchandise Mart, a twenty-four-story structure in Chicago with 1000 tenants, which is currently worth about $200 million and which generates an annual income of about $25 million in rentals. Next door is the new Kennedy-owned Apparel Center, a huge fashion and clothing emporium that produces a rental income of around $10 million a year. Other Kennedy businesses include the Corpus Christi–based Mokeen Oil Corporation, and the Kenoil Corporation, worth around $20 million, with oil-producing properties in Texas, Louisiana, Mississippi, and California. These are the principal money makers. Other Kennedy-controlled businesses include the Park Agency's considerable real estate holdings; the Sutton Producing Corporation, a small oil company based in San Antonio; and the Forest Oil Corporation of Bradford, Pennsylvania, which is wholly owned by Senator Edward Kennedy. Finally, rounding out the Kennedy holdings is a substantial portfolio of stocks and bonds containing such standard blue chips as Exxon, IBM, and Eastman Kodak.

For the most part, the heirs to this vast cornucopia of riches take little interest in the businesses that produce their wealth. They leave the management of those concerns to the accountants who keep family business so secret that none of the heirs knows how much he or she or the others is worth. When President Kennedy once asked former Kennedy business manager Thomas Walsh whether Teddy was richer than he, Walsh refused to tell.

However, though the heirs take little interest in the management of the Kennedy businesses and are largely kept in ignorance of their own and each other's finances, they all enjoy having their bills and taxes paid by the Park Agency, which acts as a combination Big Daddy and Mother Hen to the family. There is even an employee of the agency whose special task it is to cater to the financial needs of the Kennedy grandchildren. Before Onassis, the agency bought and sold horses for Jacqueline Kennedy. Regularly the agency buys and sells cars and houses for the heirs. It also pays many of the Kennedy grandchildren's school and college tuitions. Since most Kennedys, especially the children of Joseph P. Kennedy, seem to dislike handling money directly, the Park Agency very conveniently pays most of their bills. Buy a new fur coat? Send the bill to the Park Agency. Take a long trip? Send the air fare and hotel bills to the agency. Annoyed with having to pay domestic and secretarial help? Let the agency pay them. Kennedy heirs are also spared the messy business of preparing and filing income tax returns. It is all done by the agency. How John, Robert, and Edward Kennedy, who, as politicians, have been entrusted with spending the people's money, ever learned anything about money under this dispensation is indeed a wonder. For the most part, the Kennedy heirs live in a financial fairyland. Theirs is the ultimate American Dream. To be a Kennedy means to be taken care of financially from birth.

Si monumentum requiris circumspice—"If you seek his monument, look around"—goes the classic epitaph. In the last analysis, Joseph P. Kennedy's monument is his fortune and the heirs to that fortune: his wife, five surviving children, twenty-eight surviving grandchildren, and the foundation he established in memory of his firstborn son. Looking around, that monument is as conspicuous as ever.

68. Revelations, Revelations...

ON JANUARY 21, 1971, Senator Edward M. Kennedy was ousted as Democratic party whip; his fellow senators elected West Virginia's Robert C. Byrd to the post of assistant majority leader of the Senate by a vote of 31 to 24.

The defeat came as a shock to the young senator and clearly reflected the influence Chappaquiddick was to have on his image and career. It also presaged, in a sense, what would happen to his family's image during the nineteen-seventies. For, if the sixties had been a decade of triumph and disaster for the Kennedys, the seventies would witness a steady erosion of the family's image as, one by one, certain disturbing allegations out of the family's immediate past would come to light.

If the accident at Chappaquiddick had not occurred, and Joseph P. Kennedy had not died, Edward Kennedy would have most likely been the Democratic party's candidate for the presidency in 1972. But, as things turned out, Kennedy's reputation had been so damaged by Chappaquiddick and his family responsibilities had been so enlarged by his father's death that running for the presidency in 1972 was absolutely out of the question. Citing increased family responsibilities as his reason, Kennedy announced that he would not be a candidate for the presidency, or the vice presidency, in 1972 and would not accept a draft at the convention if one were offered.

733

The Democratic convention then chose Senator George McGovern for the presidency and Kennedy's brother-in-law, Sargent Shriver, for the vice presidency after their original choice, Senator Thomas Eagleton, withdrew because of past health problems. So, as it happened, there would be a "Kennedy" running in the presidential election after all. Dutifully the Kennedy clan came out to cheer on dear old Uncle Sarge. But Uncle Sarge and George McGovern turned out to be no match for long-standing Kennedy rival Richard Nixon and were severely trounced in one of the most lopsided presidential elections in the nation's history. Thus, for a second time in the new decade a Kennedy sustained an important political defeat. This was something new.

But in terms of their effect on the family image, Edward Kennedy's defeat as party whip and Sargent Shriver's defeat as his party's vice presidential candidate were almost inconsequential compared to what began to slowly come to light about certain aspects of the lives and activities of John and Robert Kennedy. For it was during the mid-seventies that word of John and Robert Kennedy's respective relationships with Marilyn Monroe surfaced, and, most damaging of all, John Kennedy's mysterious relationship with the former Judy Campbell became known.

It was Norman Mailer who first brought Robert Kennedy's relationship with Marilyn Monroe to the attention of the world. Miss Monroe had apparently deluded herself into believing that Robert Kennedy would divorce his wife, Ethel, to marry her, thus putting her in the position of possibly becoming First Lady of the United States one day. According to Mailer, this preposterous notion became "absolutely indispensable to her need for a fantasy in which she could begin to believe." As everybody now knows, Robert Kennedy was in California the weekend of August 4, 1962, when the 36-year-old actress apparently killed herself through an overdose of sleeping pills, some say because of dejection over unrequited love for Robert Kennedy, others because of more sinister reasons. Whether Robert Kennedy, the most puritanical of the Kennedy men, ever had sexual relations with Miss Monroe is a matter of controversy. Many believe not. William Sullivan wrote in his memoirs that J. Edgar Hoover had tried to "get something on" Bobby Kennedy and Miss Monroe and had failed.

Then, in 1974, columnist Earl Wilson came out with a book asserting that John F. Kennedy had had an affair with Marilyn Monroe. Wilson claimed that he had conducted an exhaustive three-year investigation of the President's relationship with the actress, had withheld the story for years, and then had finally decided to tell it "to set the record straight" in the light of Norman Mailer's book, which concentrated on Miss Monroe's relationship with Robert Kennedy, omitting her affair with the President.

According to Wilson, Miss Monroe had been thoroughly infatuated with John F. Kennedy, whom she liked to refer to as "The Prez," believing that her "sexual pyrotechnics" with him eased Kennedy's chronic backache, a novel theory since such pyrotechnics usually have the opposite effect. She had apparently been trying to arrange another rendezvous with President Kennedy through a mutual friend, New York textile manufacturer Henry Rosenfeld, when she died the night of August 4. Still according to Wilson, Miss Monroe had been planning to go to Washington, using Mr. Rosenfeld as a cover, to attend a performance of the new play, *The President,* and have a date with the President after the show.

Wilson's revelations about the presidential affair with Marilyn Monroe, which, of course, have never been indisputably substantiated because both the principals are dead, were not especially damaging to the Kennedy image—in the minds of many they made the President into sort of a sexual hero—but unfortunately they gave rise to dozens of stories of Kennedy amours. Suddenly women who claimed they had gone to bed with the President began popping up everywhere, giving Kennedy a posthumous reputation as a philanderer.

One of the most persistent rumors of John F. Kennedy's marital infidelities concerned his alleged affair with the extraordinarily beautiful, Vassar-educated Mary Pinchot Meyer, sister of Toni Bradlee, Ben Bradlee's wife, and ex-wife of high-ranking CIA official Cord Meyer, Jr., and, according to her friend, Timothy Leary, a reputed dabbler in LSD and pot. Kennedy had made no secret of his attraction to Mary Meyer, inviting her to the White House dozens of times, both before and after his breakup with Judith Campbell.

About a year after Kennedy's assassination, at the height of Robert F. Kennedy's campaign for the Senate, Mary Meyer was murdered under very mysterious circumstances. She had been taking her daily walk on a towpath along the Potomac when someone came up to her and shot her twice in the head. Immediately after the murder, which has never been solved, ugly rumors began circulating in Washington about who may have been responsible for the killing.

In February 1976, James Truitt, a former assistant to Philip Graham, publisher of the *Washington Post,* claimed in interviews with the Associated Press and the *Washington Post* that the President's affair with Mary Meyer had lasted from January 1962 to November 1963 and that the two had been together at least thirty times. Truitt also claimed that Mary Meyer had kept a diary in which her affair with the President was given considerable space. Still according to Truitt, Mary's sister, Toni Bradlee, found Mary's diary after the murder and turned it over to James Jesus Angleton, chief of CIA counterintelligence and a close friend of Mary Meyer's. Angleton allegedly destroyed the diary. After the *Washington Post* published Truitt's revelations, Kenneth O'Donnell acknowledged that Mary Meyer had made many visits to the White House but denied there had been a love affair between her and the President. Toni Bradlee stated to the Associated Press that she had known nothing about her sister's relationship with Kennedy while Mary was alive. And James Jesus Angleton, when questioned by the *Washington Post,* refused to say whether Mary Meyer had kept a diary or not. Mary's murder has never been solved.

Meanwhile, the Chappaquiddick affair refused to blow away. On September 23, 1974, Senator Edward Kennedy announced his withdrawal from the 1976 presidential race, again citing his considerable family responsibilities as his reason. The senator also knew, but of course did not acknowledge, that the *Boston Globe* had been conducting an exhaustive investigation of the Chappaquiddick accident and was about to make some disturbing revelations. These finally came out in a series of articles in October 1974, about a month after Kennedy's announcement of withdrawal.

As it turned out, the *Globe*'s two-month investigation disclosed more than 100 discrepancies between Senator Kennedy's testimony and the testimony of others involved in the case, and advanced the novel idea that the senator's cousin, Joseph Gargan, may have been going to take the blame for the accident but that it was decided at the last minute that the senator's alibi wouldn't wash and so Kennedy had finally been compelled to report the accident as his own, ten hours after it had happened. The *Globe* claimed it had acquired its information from "a highly knowledgeable source" and that its conclusions were based "on more than speculation and testimonial inconsistencies." Although Kennedy denied plotting to have his cousin take the blame for the accident, he did tell the *Globe* that his actions were "irrational and indefensible and inexcusable and inexplicable." Both Markham and Gargan refused to be interviewed on the matter. Later Gargan denied he had ever been asked to take the blame.

It was at about the time the *Boston Globe* was dredging up the Chappaquiddick mess again that another skeleton was let out of the Kennedy closet—Joan Kennedy's alcoholism. On September 12, 1974, it was reported that Joan had entered a drying-out clinic. Then on November 6 it was reported that she had been fined $200 and her driver's license had been suspended for drunken driving on October 9.

Joan Kennedy had begun drinking heavily after Chappaquiddick. She had been pregnant at the time and suffered her third miscarriage not long after the accident. Whether or not the shock of Chappaquiddick had anything to do with the miscarriage has never been determined. All that became known was that after the miscarriage Joan began drinking more heavily than ever, and it wasn't long before she became a confirmed alcoholic.

The accident at Chappaquiddick, the Kennedy brothers' affairs with Marilyn Monroe and others, Joan's alcoholism, and certain unsavory revelations about Jacqueline Onassis's husband, who died in Paris on March 15, 1975, combined in the mid-seventies to seriously undermine the once seemingly impregnable Kennedy image. Then, in December 1975, word of President Kennedy's relationship with a certain "friend" began to leak out of the hearings of the Senate Select Committee on Intelligence; that revelation was destined to give the Kennedy image a most severe battering.

What had happened was that as the Senate committee proceeded with its various investigations into the past activities of the CIA and the FBI, it stumbled across the darkest secrets of the Kennedy administration: the CIA-Mafia and AM/LASH plots to murder Castro, and Operation Mongoose. It was during the course of uncovering those secrets that the committee learned that President Kennedy had a friend whose name was Judith Campbell who was also associated with two of the gangsters the CIA had hired to kill Castro. The senators were stunned. They had been looking for the culprit in the master's barn and had apparently found the master there.

This startling discovery immediately led the committee to infer that the President had been using Miss Campbell as a conduit to the CIA-Mafia plotters; in September 1975 it subpoenaed her to give secret testimony to determine whether this had been the case.

Judith Campbell, who had married golf pro Dan Exner several months earlier, claimed later in a book that her "first awareness of the Senate Committee's existence was on June 19, 1975, when Sam was murdered in the basement kitchen of his Oak Park home." The murder, as we know, occurred just before Sam Giancana was to meet someone from the committee to arrange for his appearance at the hearings. Ever since the Giancana murder, Judy herself had lived in mortal dread of being subpoenaed to appear before the committee.

She finally did appear before them in secret session to answer questions about her relationships with President John F. Kennedy, Sam Giancana, and John Roselli. Before the committee hearing began, she had a meeting with her assigned attorney, Henry A. Hubschman, who was associated with Sargent Shriver's law firm. According to Mrs. Exner's memoirs, Hubschman immediately asked her if she had any records or diaries covering the years of her relationship with JFK, and she replied that she had a suitcase full of records and diaries. Hubschman then asked her if there was anything relating to CIA assassination plots in her records and diaries and she replied, "Absolutely not." Still according to Mrs. Exner, Hubschman then advised her not to volunteer any information to the committee, but to simply answer yes or no to all questions.

During her testimony before the Senate committee, Judy Campbell Exner told her questioners, Chief Counsel F. A. O. Schwarz, Jr., Minority Counsel Curtis R. Smother, and six other staffers, that during the most intense period of her relationship with the President—April 29, 1961 to March 22, 1962—she had met with the President in the White House many times, and that each meeting had been a purely "social occasion." She also replied "yes" when asked if she had also met frequently with Giancana and Roselli. When she was asked if she knew about the CIA-Mafia plots, she responded simply "no." By and large, the committee accepted her testimony, which was immediately sealed and will not be made public until 2025.

In the end, the Select Committee on Intelligence chose not to pursue its investigation of the relationships between Judy Campbell, John F. Kennedy, Sam Giancana, and John Roselli in any great depth, possibly out of fear of what it might have turned up. Toward the end of the committee's hearings, Chairman Senator Frank Church, who had been a friend of John F. Kennedy, issued a brief statement on the matter: "We have no evidence she was a conduit of any kind." It was almost as if the committee had not *wanted* to know what her role might have been in the life of President Kennedy.

Out of respect for the reputation of the late President, and the realities of Democratic party politics, the committee at first did not even reveal the identity, or gender, of the President's friend in its *Interim Report.** But four days before the committee issued its report, word leaked out that the friend was Judith Campbell Exner, and the *Washington Post* published the news on November 16, 1975, burying it in the back pages.

The committee's avoidance of the Kennedy-Campbell-Giancana-Roselli relationship did not go unnoticed, and several journalists, notably William Safire of *The New York Times*, were quick to brand the Church committee's inquiry a "cover-up." Noting that Kennedy family attorney Burke Marshall had told Senator Church he would serve as a consultant to the committee in recruiting suitable lawyers and had, in fact, recruited Chief Counsel F. A. O. Schwarz, Jr., Safire demanded to know why "the Frank Church cover-up committee has decided not to question Frank Sinatra on his role in making possible the first penetration of the White House by organized crime," and (alluding to the recent Giancana murder) why the committee did not ask the FBI "to investigate the first murder of a prospective Senate witness."

In a major essay in *The New York Times* Safire claimed that Senators Church and Tower were "duty bound" to ask Frank Sinatra when he had introduced Sam Giancana

---

*The actual wording of the committee's *Interim Report* is as follows: "Evidence before the committee indicates that a close friend of President Kennedy had frequent contact with the President from the end of 1960 through mid-1962. FBI reports and testimony indicate that the President's friend was also a close friend of John Roselli and Sam Giancana and saw them often during the same period. . . . White House telephone logs show 70 instances of phone contact between the White House and the President's friend whose testimony confirms frequent phone contact with the President himself." Later the *Report* stated in a footnote in parenthesis "(Sinatra is not the President's friend discussed in the preceding subsection)".

to Judith Campbell and when he had introduced Miss Campbell to the President. Safire also insisted that the senators were "duty bound" to ask Sinatra if, through his friendship with Giancana, he knew anything about the CIA-Mafia plots. Needless to say, the Church committee ignored Mr. Safire's protestations.

For Judith Campbell Exner the revelation that she had been the President's friend and also the friend of the recently slain Sam Giancana put her in a dangerous position. She had to find a way of reassuring the mob that she had not given away any Cosa Nostra secrets during her Senate testimony and would not give away any secrets in the future. Eventually her attorney advised her to call a press conference, which she did on December 17, 1975, in San Diego. The press conference, her attorney assured her, was virtually her only chance for survival.

Judith Exner, then 41, appeared at her press conference wearing huge dark glasses and looking very nervous and ill at ease. Once the reporters had assembled, she proceeded to issue a series of denials. No, she had not been used by President Kennedy as a conduit to Sam Giancana and John Roselli as part of a CIA-sponsored plot to murder Fidel Castro. No, she had not discussed her relationship with Giancana and Roselli with the President. No, she had not known that the CIA had hired Giancana and Roselli to murder the Cuban dictator. No, Castro's name had never been mentioned during the numerous calls she had made to the President in March and April 1961, when the Bay of Pigs invasion of Cuba was being planned and executed. Her relationship to President Kennedy had been purely personal and had nothing to do with political machinations of any kind. Asked whether she had known Robert F. Kennedy, she replied, "No comment." (Later a government source claimed she had attended a couple of parties in Washington at which Robert Kennedy had been present.) Asked if she had known that Giancana and Roselli were in the Mafia, she replied that she "didn't really know" they were, but then conceded she "probably knew they were members of the underworld."

Through her testimony and press conference, Judith

apparently succeeded in convincing both the senators and the mob that she had not engaged in conspiratorial machinations injurious either to the United States or to the Mafia. Yet the doubts remain. Whatever the case, we shall probably never know the ultimate truth about the intricate relationships between John F. Kennedy, Robert F. Kennedy, Sam Giancana, John Roselli, and Judith Campbell Exner, because four of the principals have been murdered and one is not talking anymore.

Judith Campbell Exner, however, did write a book in collaboration with Ovid Demaris about her relationships with Kennedy, Giancana, and Roselli, in which she substantially reiterates what she had said at the Senate committee hearings. Entitled *My Story,* the book came out in 1977 and inflicted a heavy blow to the image of John F. Kennedy. In it she implied that she and Jack Kennedy, among others, had been regularly treated by Dr. Max Jacobson with injections of amphetamines, that the JFK-Jackie marriage was "not in good shape," that Jackie thought to divorce Jack Kennedy but couldn't for obvious political reasons, and that Jack was determined to establish a Kennedy presidential dynasty stretching right down to the "grandkids," with himself as "patriarch."

At one point in her book Judy summarizes quite aptly the fix the Kennedy brothers and the U.S. government had got themselves into by hiring gangsters to kill Castro: "The CIA was protecting Sam and Johnny. The FBI [read Robert Kennedy] was trying to get them, and then the White House was scared to death they might get them." These remarks seem to indicate that, despite her protestations to the contrary, Judy had known what had been going on all along.

Toward the end of her book Judith summarizes her contact with men of crime and men of politics with these philosophical remarks: "No one really knows why Sam was murdered, or Jack, for that matter, and now Johnny. Life in the underworld of crime and the netherworld of politics is cheap. From what I have observed, it is impossible to tell the good men from the bad."

My own beliefs about the nature and significance of

the Kennedy-Campbell-Giancana triangle, and its possible relationship to the Castro assassination plots and even possibly to the Kennedy assassination, are based essentially on information from three sources: one, Ovid Demaris's revelation to me in October 1983 that Judy Campbell had told him that Kennedy knew she was seeing Giancana during the same period that he, Kennedy, was seeing her; two, the established fact, documented by the Senate Committee on Intelligence, that the FBI knew as early as October 18, 1960, that Giancana was involved in some plot to kill Castro; and three, the FBI electronic surveillance tapes of December 9, 11, and 21, 1961, revealing that Giancana had made a "donation" to the JFK presidential campaign through Frank Sinatra and Joseph P. Kennedy to obtain Kennedy indulgence toward himself and the mob.

On the basis of these I believe that President Kennedy was aware his girlfriend was seeing Sam Giancana, that he knew who Giancana was, and also knew that Giancana was involved in some kind of plot to kill Castro. I also believe that it was entirely possible that Kennedy might have been monitoring Giancana's progress through his contact with Judy, even though she might not have been aware of it at the time. I do not, however, believe that Kennedy learned that Giancana had been hired by the CIA to kill Castro until the spring of 1962, when his brother was given a full briefing on the CIA-Mafia plots by the agency. Until then, I believe Kennedy was under the impression that Giancana was plotting against Castro only on behalf of the mob, which, as we know, had its own plans to kill the Cuban leader entirely independent of those of the CIA.

I further believe that it is entirely possible that Joseph P. Kennedy did not tell his sons that Giancana had made a donation to the presidential campaign through him, so that John and Robert Kennedy probably did not learn about the donation until mid-December, 1961, just before their father suffered his stroke.

How could all of this have been related to the Kennedy assassination? Since Joseph P. Kennedy had compromised himself and his sons by accepting a donation from the boss of the Chicago underworld, and the Kennedy administration had been compromised by its involvement in the CIA-Mafia plots, and President Kennedy had been compromised by his relationship with the girlfriend of one of the Mafia plotters, the underworld could have felt reasonably sure they could get away with assassinating the President. They knew that neither Ambassador Kennedy, nor Attorney General Kennedy, nor the FBI, nor the CIA would press for an investigation that might turn up the moral compromises each had made and the secrets each had been protecting during John F. Kennedy's thousand days in the White House.

At about the time Judith Exner's book appeared, still another unflattering episode in the romantic life of John F. Kennedy was revealed by William Safire in the *Times*. Under the Freedom of Information Act, Safire had petitioned the FBI for J. Edgar Hoover's file on John F. Kennedy, and among the documents he received was a memorandum on the Kennedy-Campbell-Giancana affair and a report that Robert Kennedy had paid a $500,000 settlement to a woman in early 1961 who claimed she had been engaged to John F. Kennedy in 1951 and had sued Kennedy for breach of promise. According to the FBI documents Safire received, Robert Kennedy had not denied paying the settlement for his brother and so Hoover believed the episode was true.

Then, on the heels of this revelation, the diary of a former French ambassador to the United States and friend of the Kennedys, Herve Alphand, was published. It revealed that Alphand believed John F. Kennedy had been terribly vulnerable to blackmail and/or attack from his enemies because of "his amorous behavior."

Such were the storms of doubt and suspicion raised about the Kennedy assassination by the Senate Committee on Intelligence that certain members of Congress, notably Senator Richard Schweiker of Pennsylvania and Representatives Henry B. Gonzalez of Texas and Thomas N. Downing of Virginia, began pressing for a fresh new investigation of the assassination. A crucial impetus for proceeding with this undertaking was the murder of John Roselli just before he was scheduled to testify again before the Senate Intelligence Committee. Finally, in September 1976, almost thirteen years after Kennedy's murder, the House Select Committee on Assassinations was formed "to investigate the circumstances surrounding the deaths of John F. Kennedy and Martin Luther King, Jr. . . ." This committee conducted exhaustive researches and heard testimony throughout 1977 and 1978 until it went out of existence in January 1979. Its final report was published on March 29, 1979.

As we know, the House Select Committee's findings were basically inconclusive in that the committee determined that there probably had been a conspiracy to assassinate President Kennedy, but "was unable to identify the other gunman or the extent of the conspiracy."

The committee did, however, lay some of the blame for the success of the assassination on John F. Kennedy himself. For the committee's final report stated,

> Not only did Kennedy enjoy traveling, but he almost recklessly resisted the protective measures the Secret Service urged him to adopt. He would not allow blaring sirens, and only once—in Chicago in November 1963—did he permit his limousine to be flanked by motorcycle police officers. Furthermore, he told the special agent in charge of the White House detail that he did not want agents to ride on the rear of his car.

(The presence of such agents probably would have prevented his assassination in Dallas.)

The committee also laid some of the blame for the original inadequate investigation of the assassination on Robert F. Kennedy, stating, in its final report, that "the Department of Justice failed to exercise initiative in supervising and directing the investigation by the Federal Bureau of Investigation in the assassination." However, the committee chose not to speculate on why the normally vindictive, crime-busting attorney general had failed to vigorously investigate his brother's murder.

Since the final report of the assassinations committee was so inconclusive, it was unable to resolve beyond a reasonable doubt certain central mysteries: one, whether John F. Kennedy was aware of the CIA-Mafia operation against Castro and had given it his support, or whether he was not aware of it and had therefore been duped by the CIA; two, whether he was aware of his friend Judith Campbell's relationship with two of the Mafia plotters, or whether he was not, and had therefore been set up by the mob; three, whether Kennedy's assassination had been in retaliation for the operation against Castro, or in retaliation for the war against the mob, or both. Finally, the committee was unable to satisfactorily explain why Hoover's FBI manipulated so much evidence, failed to pursue so many promising leads, and, in general, consistently sought to subvert and obscure the truth in its investigation of the assassination. In its final report on the investigation of the murder of Martin Luther King, Jr., the committee concluded that the FBI's activities "encouraged an attack on Dr. King" and characterized the conduct of the FBI, in regard to Dr. King, as "morally reprehensible, illegal, felonious, and unconstitutional." Could the same have been said about the conduct of Hoover's FBI in regard to Dr. King's supporter, President John F. Kennedy?

What has become of the House assassinations committee findings? They were forwarded to the Justice Department for review, without results as of this writing. No proceedings have yet been brought in any court. So far the only reaction to the report to come from the FBI has been a December 12, 1980, declaration denying the validity of the acoustical evidence accepted by the committee that points to the existence of a second gunman in the assassination. Two years later, the National Science Foundation also denied the validity of the acoustical evidence. In June 1985 the Justice Department is scheduled to make its review of the assassinations committee's findings public.

Meanwhile both private and public investigators continue to produce books on the assassination that stress the probable involvement of organized crime. The two most convincing are by G. Robert Blakey, whose *The Plot to*

Kill the President was based on his work as chief counsel of the House Select Committee on Assassinations, and Anthony Summers, whose excellent *Conspiracy*, published in 1980, attracted widespread attention. Blakey, a national authority on organized crime and currently a professor of law at Notre Dame, is unshakably convinced that the Cosa Nostra had a hand in the assassination and that a trial must eventually be held. Blakey contends,

> Between historical truth and judicial truth, there's a difference. We cannot continue to live the lie that this case was solved in 1963 and 1964. It wasn't. It is still open and unsolved. Charges, trial, and judgment are what we must strive for in the fullest sense. For the sanity of the society we live in, we must do it. It may well be that we will never be able to determine the judicial truth, to discover who was really responsible for the assassination of John Fitzgerald Kennedy in Dallas on November 22, 1963. But the important thing is that we never, never stop trying.

A major part of the problem of why no action on the assassinations committee's findings has been taken so far lies in the continuing apparent reluctance of key members of the Kennedy family, notably Senator Edward Kennedy, to press the Justice Department on the matter. On August 1, 1966, Edward Kennedy issued the incredible statement that he had not read the Warren Commission's report but was nevertheless convinced that Lee Harvey Oswald alone had assassinated his brother, a position from which he has never publicly deviated, even though he was fully apprised of the House assassinations committee's findings of possible conspiracy in 1979. In February 1975, as the Senate Committee on Intelligence was beginning its inquiry, which promised to address itself also to the Kennedy assassination, Eunice Kennedy Shriver, speaking by her own admission in behalf of the entire Kennedy family, stated publicly that the Kennedys were satisfied with the Warren Commission's findings and saw no need for another investigation. Then, when the House Committee on Assassinations began its investigations of the murders of John F. Kennedy and Martin Luther King, Jr., the Kennedy family refrained from directly involving themselves in the investigation, designating family attorney Burke Marshall as their representative in any dealings they might be compelled to have with the committee, whereas members of the King family volunteered to help in any way they could. (Mrs. King had even pressed for the investigation.)

Even the "honorary Kennedys" have so far displayed a reluctance to concern themselves with the investigations of the JFK assassination, least of all undertake investigations of the crime themselves. Such a hitherto determined investigator as Walter Sheridan, former head of Bobby Kennedy's "get Hoffa squad," and such staunch Kennedy loyalists as Sorensen, Goodwin, O'Donnell, Powers, and Schlesinger, who would be expected to have left no stone unturned in an effort to discover, and punish, the President's assassins, appear to have consistently displayed a strange passivity in regard to the case. What might be the reason for this perplexing attitude?

I believe the reason is the fear that by delving into the crime too deeply it may be discovered that the assassination of John F. Kennedy represented a personal failure, or a failure of his administration, that Kennedy's own reckless policies and intrigues, or those of his brother Robert, or those of his advisers might have brought on his destruction. And if this were irrefutably determined, it would both desanctify John F. Kennedy's image and damage the historical reputation of his administration.

Given all the new cracks in the Kennedy image, the question inevitably arose as the decade drew to a close: Would the American people ever be disposed to elect a Kennedy to the presidency again? By the fall of 1979 the question began to loom larger and larger as it became widely, and authoritatively, rumored that Edward Kennedy's time had come, that, after having refused to run in 1968, 1972, and 1976, he would, in 1980, make an attempt to restore the Kennedys to the White House by running for the presidency of the United States.

Part 7

TOWARD RESTORATION:
The Second Attempt, 1979-1982

69. Kennedy '80 - Part I: The Debacle

IT HAD TAKEN EDWARD KENNEDY some time to make up his mind to run for president. Back in April 1978 he had told a *New York Times* reporter, "Why should I be talking about running for President? There's a Democrat in the White House. There's no moral crisis in the country. What's the reason? For power? For what?"

As it turned out, the President himself unwittingly supplied the reason. For some time President Carter's popularity had been collapsing throughout the country as the American people began to perceive an aimless drift to his policies, both domestic and foreign, and a general lack of presidential timber in his somewhat naive and feckless personality. As this erosion became more and more evident, Kennedy sensed a power vacuum opening up, and only Governor Jerry Brown of California seemed prepared to fill it. To have Brown step in and possibly steal the nomination from Carter in 1980 was an intolerable idea to the Kennedys. Furthermore, Kennedy was becoming more and more disillusioned with Carter from an ideological standpoint. The more he examined the President's policies and pronouncements, the more it seemed that Carter was going against nearly everything that he, Senator Edward Kennedy, stood for, and nearly everything the Democratic party had traditionally stood for as well.

When a popularity poll conducted in California showed

that 59 percent of those polled were for Kennedy, 17 percent for Brown, and 15 percent for Carter, and a Gallup poll showed Kennedy winning by a margin of 2 to 1, it looked as if Kennedy could have the nomination for the asking. With his mother and sisters now behind his decision to run, his chance seemed to have finally come. It was a situation, on a grander scale, analogous to having that congressional seat magically become available for young John Kennedy upon James Michael Curley's renunciation of it in 1945.

Then too, the press, sensing a bonanza of news stories, responded enthusiastically to the idea of a Kennedy candidacy and constantly urged him on. In New York the *Post* practically begged him to come forward and save the country.

And so Edward Kennedy came forth. Yet no sooner was his hat finally in the ring than his foot was in his mouth. When Roger Mudd asked him in a television interview on November 4 why he wanted to be president, Kennedy left his viewers gasping with disbelief as he responded,

> Well, I'm—were I to—to make the—announcement . . . is because I have a great belief in this country, that it is—has more natural resources than any nation in the world . . . the greatest technology of any country in the world . . . the greatest political system in the world . . . and the energies and the resourcefulness of this nation, I think, should be focused on these problems in a way that brings a sense of restoration in this country by its people to . . . and I would basically feel that—that it's imperative for this country to either move forward, that it can't stand still, or otherwise it moves back.

As it turned out, the Mudd interview was only the first of a seemingly endless succession of debacles. Within a relatively short space of time the Ted Kennedy candidacy became something of a national joke. Everything seemed to go wrong at once. The press that had lured him into the fight turned against him and began dredging up his cheating at Harvard, his running traffic lights in Virginia, his rumored links with Helga Wagner and other women, his wife's alcoholism, and, of course, Chappaquiddick.

Exasperated by Carter's indecisive handling of the Iranian crisis, Kennedy recalled how courageously his brother had handled the Cuban missile crisis. But when he castigated the Shah, calling him a "crook" and his regime "one of the most violent in the history of mankind," although he may have been echoing the sentiments of many, the timing of his remarks could not have been more wrong. At that moment the United States was in a mortal struggle with the Khomeini regime, and it certainly did not help for Senator Kennedy to begin attacking Khomeini's former adversary, whom we had been supporting for the past decade. After he made this untimely utterance, it seemed as if everyone in the country suddenly turned against Ted Kennedy. The *New York Post,* which had so encouraged his candidacy, headlined on its front page: TEDDY THE TOAST OF TEHERAN. And George Bush, echoing the thoughts of many, publicly declared that Kennedy's remarks raised "serious questions about his judgment of foreign policy."

It wasn't long before Kennedy's candidacy became somewhat preposterous, if it had not been somewhat preposterous from the very beginning. To challenge an incumbent President of one's own party was potentially destructive of both incumbent and party. It violated one of the basic rules of party politics: the party first, the party above personal ambition. Even Robert Kennedy had refrained from such an arrogant maneuver. The Kennedys, it appeared, were only nominally Democrats. In reality they were a party unto themselves. In any other major western democracy something similar to a Ted Kennedy candidacy would have been virtually unthinkable. The Europeans, by and large, had long ago firmly rejected the idea of family political dynasties.

If it was presumptuous for the Kennedys to run Teddy against Carter, it was also a gross miscalculation, the result of a collective self-deception. For the Kennedys threw themselves into the presidential campaign of 1980 thinking it was still 1960. The whole clan came out thinking it would be like old times. But now, in 1980, many of the rules and conditions of the game had changed; most of all, the candidate had changed. Furthermore, by virtue of the events of 1969 and the unsavory revelations of the seventies, the Kennedy image had also changed.

The rules and conditions of the game had changed. The rules governing finances were different. No longer could the Kennedys pour their own millions into a political campaign. To be eligible for the new federal matching funds the Kennedys had to raise money from donations. And it was against the law now for any one individual to contribute more than $1000 to any one candidate. Thus a Rose Kennedy could not blithely write out a check for $500,000 for Teddy's campaign. The best she could do would be to hold a party at her house in Hyannis and invite six hundred guests at $25 a head. That would net $15,000. Granted Teddy had the old *Caroline* to toot around the country in, but now its costs had to be supported by contributions and fees if they were to be partially defrayed by federal matching funds.

There was another new set of conditions: The Democratic party's "outreach" rules had introduced affirmative action into the primary elections. Now the various minorities in each state were to be represented in each state's delegation in accordance with fixed quotas. For example, in New York it did not make any difference how the people actually voted in the primary; 19 percent of the delegates at the convention *had* to be black, 7.2 percent *had* to be Hispanics, 50 percent *had* to be women.

The new rules were sexist, racist, confusing, and undemocratic. Theoretically, in a Democratic primary election the voters should be free to elect an entire delegation of Hispanic women, or Wasp men, if they so choose. But this was a different America from 1960. During the intervening years the American people had become fragmented into a welter of different ethnic, racial, and sexual groups. One was no longer just an American. One was a Wasp, or a Jew, or a black, or an Hispanic, or an Italian, or a woman, or a handicapped person, or a youth, or a senior citizen, or a gay, and each group had to be represented and courted. Furthermore, each of the thirty-six states holding primaries had its own specific outreach rules regarding ethnic, racial, and sexual proportioning. No longer could a Jack Kennedy just march into a state primary and mop up a majority of the delegates simply on the basis of his charm. Now the ethnic, racial, and sexual ratio of a particular delegation was preordained. Now the Democratic candidates had to devise entirely new strategies to capture the primaries.

But the fact that the rules and conditions had changed over the past twenty years need not have affected the flexible, pragmatic Kennedys unduly—except possibly in the area of finances. They could adapt to them, and did. What they could not adapt to successfully was the candidate. Here was the major difference between 1960 and 1980, the difference between John F. Kennedy and Edward M. Kennedy.

Ted Kennedy himself admitted there was "an enormous sense of expectancy" about his candidacy. This was both an advantage and a disadvantage. If Ted Kennedy had turned out to be as adroit and graceful and articulate a candidate as brother John, it would have been an enormous advantage. But, alas, Teddy was no Jack Kennedy. Jack Kennedy himself had even said as much long ago when he once allowed publicly that "Teddy shouldn't ever want to be president."

Ted Kennedy is much more formal and reserved than his brothers were, and, during the campaign, he often looked painfully ill at ease, as if he had rather not be doing all this, but, for some reason not entirely clear to himself, he had to. Where was the relaxed grace of Jack Kennedy? Where was that gutsy, sleeves-rolled-up, necktie-loosened, reaching out to the people of Robert Kennedy? Strange as it seemed, emanating from a Kennedy, there was a kind of tiredness, a kind of staleness, to the last of the Kennedy brothers. Watching him at a public appearance one wanted to go up and help him get through it, the whole thing seemed so painful to him, such an unpleasant ordeal.

Then there was the problem of language, of speaking

on his feet. Sometimes, especially when he did not have a prepared text, Kennedy was inarticulate to the point of incoherence—which is not to mention the curious Cape Cod accent and all the circumlocutions and malapropisms:

"I want a chahnce to ahnswer the Shar's claim."

"We should expedite the synfuels program through the process of expediting."

"We must face the problems we are facing as we have always faced the problems we have faced."

"Roll up your sleeves and your mothers and fathers."

Then, whenever he began to feel he was losing his audience, he inevitably resorted to the kind of wooden bellowing that went out of style with the disappearance of the likes of Honey Fitz and James Michael Curley.

What a contrast to John Kennedy's carefully crafted rhetoric! John Kennedy, who had totally rejected the old-fashioned bellowing of his grandfathers' generation. John Kennedy, who was familiar with the oratory of Burke and Pitt and Webster and was capable of writing clear, meticulous, eloquent prose and delivering it with both grace and passion.

Now, with his younger brother, the Kennedy utterances seemed cramped, bloodless, contrived, labored, unnatural. It was a labored, unnatural feeling that characterized, so disadvantageously, that first Kennedy '80 event, the formal declaration of candidacy in Faneuil Hall, Boston, November 7, 1979. One by one the Kennedys were introduced on stage, as in a circus sideshow, a curious procedure for a declaration of high political candidacy. In came Jacqueline Onassis, looking wooden and stiff. Then Rose walked on, smiling her lopsided smile, and waving tentatively at the audience, which was composed almost entirely of her relatives and their hangers-on. Then came the candidate, not striding forward with the brisk, purposeful, grace of his brother John, but walking hesitantly. And then his wife Joan, overly made up, overperoxided, and looking utterly bored. She stood there stiffly, several feet away from her husband, a vacant stare in her eyes. She, like Jacqueline Onassis, had the appearance of a prop some invisible stagehand had guided into place. There followed the children, the handsome, 18-year-old Teddy Junior, the perky 20-year-old Kara, and freckled-faced little Patrick, 12. Now the sideshow was complete. They all stood there as if to say, "Well here we are folks, the Kennedy freaks." Then, on cue, Uncle Teddy launched into his stiff, unmoving declaration of candidacy and, before long, the little carnival was over.

A little over two weeks later, around the time of Thanksgiving weekend, I attended a reception for Rose Kennedy in Palm Beach given by that indefatigable Palm Beach hostess, Brownie McClean. At this early stage in Kennedy's campaign, even before the Iowa precinct caucuses, I found the Kennedys supremely confident. Rose Kennedy announced, "I'm very happy about everything. I've always been behind my sons when they wanted to do something. And I believe Ted will make a good president." Whereupon she began handing out "Kennedy '80" buttons. Her daughter Pat Lawford and Pat's daughters Victoria and Robin echoed her sentiments, telling everybody they were sure Teddy would win. It was clear to me that Rose and Pat really believed what they were saying—they had deluded themselves into thinking that nothing had changed.

In the weird, often illogical landscape of the American primary elections of 1980, the Democratic precinct caucuses of Iowa, held on January 21, 1980, were the first of four little elections to choose the state's fifty delegates to the national Democratic convention. The fourth and last of these elections would not come until mid-June, but Kennedy had to do well in this first little essay to make his already sagging candidacy believable, that is, worthy of being financed by campaign contributions.

Not only Ted Kennedy's candidacy, but the entire Kennedy legend was now on the line—nationally—for the first time since Bobby's candidacy of 1968. For this exercise the Kennedys were prepared to pull out all the stops. Half the family would come out to trudge through the Iowa snow talking to hog farmers, Jaycees, and housebound farm wives. On hand would be Joan and Teddy Junior, and Kara and Patrick and Joseph P. Kennedy III, the indefatigable Eunice, and even the everlasting Rose.

It was a time of national humiliation over the captivity of the American hostages in Iran, deep concern over the Soviet invasion of Afghanistan, and deeper concern over the 16 percent inflation rate, almost the highest in American history, and ever-soaring interest rates, these last two terrors threatening to utterly destroy the high standard of living Americans had come to take for granted as a virtual birthright.

But instead of attacking these problems, Kennedy seemed more intent on parading his fragmented family around. After Chappaquiddick and Joan's troubles, and all the "womanizing" talk, he obviously felt compelled to project the image of the family man above all—as if this had anything to do with being qualified to cope with the vast and dangerous problems of the presidency.

Day after day, in Indianola, in Marengo, in Amana, in Knoxville, in Oskaloosa, in Springfield, in Council Bluffs, in Des Moines, he paraded his estranged wife and bewildered children from farm, to gym, to union hall, to seed company, to courthouse, to drugstore, to community center, to radio station, occasionally joined by another member of the family, Eunice, or his 89-year-old mother, a traveling sideshow of Kennedys, to demonstrate to everyone that he was *indeed* a family man. Not a mistress or a chorus girl was in sight.

The audiences were there mostly out of curiosity. It is not every day that one got to see real live Kennedys. But they were, by no means, overwhelmed. Ginger Foti, a restaurant hostess who came to the Jasper County courthouse to hear Kennedy, told a reporter: "We're not so quick to believe what's on the surface. There's still something underneath there that's not right."

Meanwhile the family sideshow went into its various routines. Joan and the kids acted as ushers and greeters in a Kennedy union hall appearance. Joe Kennedy II set up a storefront campaign headquarters in Des Moines and was stared at as if he were the living reincarnation of his Grandfather Joe, Uncle Jack, and Father Bobby. Eunice Kennedy astonished farmers and reporters by chasing squawking chickens around a barnyard. Rose Kennedy tried to bring tears to Iowa eyes by saying, in a speech, "I know you helped my sons when they aspired to the great position of president of the United States, so I am delighted you are going to help my youngest son—my last child."

It was indeed a strange spectacle, this Kennedy sideshow. In what other great democracy in the western world would a candidate for the highest political office lug his wife and children and nephew and sister and aged mother around with him as he campaigned? No, only in America does a politician feel so compelled to project a "family image" that he must always appear in public with a bevy of close relatives.

But the Kennedy family sideshow didn't work in Iowa. This overemphasis on the presence of the wife and kids was somehow grotesque beside the ambulance, and the doctor, and the nurse, and the welter of secret servicemen with their submachine guns that accompanied the Kennedys wherever they went. If Ted Kennedy was widely acknowledged to be "a moving target," was it advisable that he move about with an innocent wife and three young children constantly by his side?

Nor did the words work. The Iowans heard nothing but generalities:

> I think people would have asked why it is that American hostages are held, that American embassies are burned, that there are Cuban troops in Africa and Soviet troops in Afghanistan. I can remember when our allies and our adversaries respected the United States. . . .
>
> There are no problems—energy problems, health-care problems—that we cannot deal with. After all, this is America, and we have faced up to such problems before. . . .
>
> So I come here because I believe that as

difficult as the problems that we face, overseas and here at home, that we can be effective in dealing with them. . . .

And what does Mobil Oil do with the profits they received from decontrol? They go out and buy Montgomery Ward department store. . . . Now how much oil do you think they are going to find drilling in the aisles of Montgomery Ward department store? . . .

(Mobil Oil bought Montgomery Ward in 1976, before oil was decontrolled. And it is worth noting that Kennedy's major sources of income are from oil and department stores.)

I refuse to accept that there is a malaaaaaise [he draws the word out] in the spirit of the American people. I have not found it to be so. . . . And I believe very sincerely that we in this country have the natural resources in abundance, have the greatest political system that has ever been described by mankind, or womankind. . . .

And we can make our country once again the all-American country we know it can be. . . .

And then there were all the old New Deal ideas Kennedy pulled out of his hat. He was going to beef up social security benefits. He was going to make sure the poor and needy and unemployed got "their full benefits." He was going to plug with all his might for national health insurance. These ancient ideas hung around in the air like, to use a phrase from Nietzsche, so many "rancid hams." Who was going to *pay* for all the beefed up social security benefits, the welfare and unemployment, the national health insurance? The Iowans, strapped with high taxes, high interest rates, and high prices? They didn't want to hear about essentially unproductive giveaway programs. They knew who would have to pay for all the free lunches.

In the end nothing worked. The rancid old New Deal ideas didn't work. The vague generalities didn't work. The

Kennedy family sideshow didn't work. After spending almost $3 million on his campaign, Kennedy lost Iowa to Carter by the overwhelming vote of 59 to 31 percent.

It was nothing less than a debacle, and the Kennedy campaign was in a shambles for lack of funds. The all-important New Hampshire primary was only a month away, and contributions to the campaign were already drying up. Now the press, which had gradually withdrawn its initial support for Kennedy, suddenly intensified its criticism of the candidate. As one cancellation of speaking engagements after another reached his office (with consequent drying up of funds), Ted Kennedy had to cope with a flood tide of anti-Kennedy articles dealing with everything from running red lights in Charlottesville to failing to report a fatal accident on Martha's Vineyard.

Then came the Georgetown speech in late January and a sudden reprieve, a new lease on life. Ted Kennedy is not very able as an ad-lib speaker, or in a question-and-answer situation, but with a prepared text which he has memorized and rehearsed he can often be very effective. The Kennedy forces were taking no chances with the Georgetown appearance. At the insistence of his advisers Kennedy memorized his speech and rehearsed it in the hall at Georgetown University in which he was scheduled to deliver it. Then the Kennedy people rounded up some 200 supporters to provide periodic wild clapping and cheering during the speech (much to the annoyance of the president of Georgetown, who claimed Kennedy forces kept his students from attending). And finally the Kennedy people made sure the event enjoyed maximum media coverage.

As it turned out, Ted Kennedy's Georgetown speech was an unqualified success. It was delivered with great force and apparent conviction to a standing ovation. Gone were the hesitations and the vague generalities. In a speech reiterating everything Roosevelt's New Deal and Harry Truman's Fair Deal had ever stood for, Kennedy certified himself as the only genuinely liberal candidate in the field. Asserting that President Carter's program had grossly neglected the young, the aged, the sick, the minorities, the poor, the underprivileged, and women, Kennedy defined his constituency as essentially that of his brother Bobby: all those who have been "left out of the American dream." As one Kennedy staffer attending the speech put it: "We knew we were liberals finally."

Being liberal, however, did not help very much in Georgia. The Kennedy forces knew they were going to lose, and they did, badly. A small Kennedy sideshow, headed by Jean Kennedy Smith, was sent there and was largely ignored, both by the press and the public.

Then came the New Hampshire primary in February, the first big one. Kennedy absolutely had to do well in New Hampshire, in order to do as well as he wished in his own bordering state of Massachusetts whose primary fell immediately after. If he did not make a decent showing in New England he was finished.

Jimmy Carter, however, was not standing idle. Since January he had been slushing New Hampshire with federal money. First he announced a $34-million grant to the state for a four-lane highway from Manchester to Portsmouth. Then, as the primary approached, he allocated $100,000 to the state's ski resorts and announced that the federal government would finance a commuter railroad from Concord to Boston.

To counteract this largesse from the American taxpayer, Kennedy rolled out the Kennedy family sideshow, apparently still convinced that the "family man" image was the principal quality the voters were looking for in a presidential candidate. It was a lugubrious sight, this Kennedy '80 caravan through cold, snowbound New Hampshire. Reporters called their assignment "the death watch," and the candidate "the moving target."

Picture the line of cars and buses carrying Kennedy, his staff, his relatives, the over 100 reporters and media people (whose cases were searched regularly for bombs), the double detail of secret servicemen (each with a wire coming out of his ear and a tiny flesh-colored microphone out of his cuff, and carrying a gray Samsonite briefcase holding an UZI submachine gun), the candidate's car followed immediately by an ambulance containing a doctor, a nurse, and two paramedics. Picture this train of mostly black and gray vehicles winding its way through the desolate, snowy hills of New Hampshire under a gray, overcast sky, this horde of busbound media people with their tele-cameras and klieg lights ready to go into action should anything *happen*. If there should be another Dallas, or Los Angeles, the networks wanted the American people to see it—*live*. Picture this small rolling armed camp and portable emergency room accompanying the third Kennedy brother to campaign for the presidency. This was the new image of the once-invincible Kennedys.

When the votes were tallied, it was Carter with 47.1 percent of the delegates and Kennedy with 37.3 percent, a disaster to the Kennedy forces. This was New England, not Georgia. What had happened? A Kennedy state, a state that had given John F. Kennedy a nine-to-one margin of victory in the 1960 primary, had just rejected his youngest brother by a margin of 10 percent.

As if this were not disaster enough, no sooner were the New Hampshire votes tabulated than the February 1980 *Reader's Digest* came out with a major feature on the Chappaquiddick incident, headlined CHAPPAQUIDDICK: SHOCKING NEW FACTS against a photo of Dike Bridge at night. It was followed immediately by another February publication, an entire magazine devoted to the scandal, entitled *Death at Chappaquiddick* and based on the Tedrow brothers' authoritative book of the same title. The *Reader's Digest* has the largest circulation of any magazine in the world. It was, as we know, the magazine that had launched Jack Kennedy's career in 1945 with the publication of John Hersey's "Survival," the inflated account of the exploits of the PT-109 in the Solomons. Having helped build one Kennedy career, it was now helping to destroy another. It was a sign of the times. This was not 1945 or 1960 when the Kennedy star was ascendant. This was 1980 when it was most decidedly on the wane.

Thus in February 1980 there were two major rehashes of the Chappaquiddick affair on the newsstands of America. The scandal would not die, and its resuscitation was very damaging to the candidacy of Senator Edward M. Kennedy.

Throughout March things proceeded from bad to worse. In his public appearances Kennedy went from blunder to blunder. Observers kept saying over and over again that he was a far cry from his brothers. By now he was not only running against Jimmy Carter, he was running against his brothers' reputation and image. Every time he made a public appearance he had to risk unfavorable comparison to them.

More primary disasters. In the Florida primary on March 11 Kennedy was annihilated, with Carter taking seventy-six delegates to Kennedy's twenty-three. The Kennedy people blamed the staggering defeat on Carter's slushing the state with federal funds and on the President's commandeering of all the air-conditioned buses in the state to take voters to the polls, but these were mere excuses. It remained a crushing defeat.

By now Ronald Reagan was scoring victory after victory over his rivals in the primaries, winning the Florida contest with 58 percent of the vote to George Bush's 30 and John Anderson's 8. Although he was over twenty years older than Ted Kennedy, Reagan somehow appeared more youthful, more loose and supple and quick, and his ideas seemed fresher and more exciting. Observers began noting that Reagan acted the way one would have expected John Kennedy to have acted at a similar age, and John Kennedy would have been 63 in 1980, only six years Reagan's junior. The favorable comparison of John Kennedy with Ronald Reagan only accentuated the unfavorable comparison of Ted Kennedy with his older brother and led to further deterioration of his image.

Then, after the Florida disaster, came the defeat in Illinois, the state that had given John Kennedy the 1960 presidential election. Early in this primary, Mayor Jane Byrne of Chicago had made a grudging endorsement of Carter. But when Kennedy telegraphed her, "Remember I've loved you, and Chicago, longer," Byrne reversed herself and went with Kennedy. To no avail. It was a rout. Carter captured an overwhelming 165 delegates to Kennedy's pitiful 14.

Now the debacle of Ted Kennedy's candidacy for the

presidency of the United States was complete. A vague sense of disappointment had plagued his campaign from the beginning. Expectations had been too high. But nobody could possibly have ever lived up to the vastly inflated Kennedy legend. Now disappointment had turned to disarray and despair.

Quietly, the Kennedy grandchildren gathered at Trader Vic's in the Plaza Hotel in New York and discussed ways of extricating their Uncle Teddy from the race with the least embarrassment possible. Even the normally unpolitical Jacqueline Onassis sensed something had to be done to save the Kennedy reputation and convened a gathering of top-level Kennedy aides and various old-guard honorary Kennedys in her apartment in New York to find a way to get Ted out of the campaign before he destroyed his and his family's reputation. Uncle Teddy had been running against the images of Jack and Bobby and had lost. With a *Daily News* poll of New York voters awarding sixty-one delegates to Carter and only thirty-four to Kennedy and talk at Kennedy's New York headquarters of the offices "being vacant soon," it appeared that Ted Kennedy's campaign for the presidency of the United States had come to an ignominious end. Who, what could save the last of the Kennedy brothers now?

70. Kennedy '80 - Part II:
"Rehearsal '84"

As MARCH 25, the day of the New York primary, approached, nearly everyone close to Edward Kennedy was advising him to withdraw from the race. New York was the Kennedys' "other home state." He could not afford the embarrassment of losing as big in New York as the Harris poll had predicted. Jacqueline Onassis, who, of course, lived in New York, was moved to advise Teddy to withdraw rather than risk that embarrassment. Many of the Kennedy grandchildren urged him to get out before the enormity of his possible defeat crushed him, and perhaps them, politically, forever.

Furthermore, after the terrible defeats in Iowa, New Hampshire, Florida, and Illinois, contributions to the Kennedy campaign had almost entirely dried up, leaving the campaign exposed to staggering debts. And under the new election financing laws the Kennedys were forbidden to make up the deficit themselves. First to feel the crunch would be all the campaign workers, from top to bottom, who would have their stipends and budgets slashed to nothing. Finally, to pay off the huge debt, the Kennedy family would have to become virtually a business unto itself, a constantly traveling troupe, performing at an endless series of fund-raising events.

I attended one of those events not long before the New York primary. This fund-raiser was hosted in a Manhattan art gallery by Patricia Kennedy Lawford and two of Robert F. Kennedy's daughters, Kerry and Courtney, and its main purpose was to sell large, poster-sized lithographs of Ted Kennedy by Andy Warhol for $1500 apiece. It soon became obvious to me that the lithos weren't selling, and, upon inquiring of Kerry and Courtney how things were going, I found my suspicions confirmed. The girls appeared quite desperate. Soon I learned there was desperation in just about every Kennedy campaign headquarters in the country.

Then, just as all looked utterly dark, something happened that seemed to promise a sudden reprieve. President Carter's ambassador to the UN, Donald F. McHenry, voted in favor of a resolution which condemned Israel's aggressive settlements policy in occupied territories and denied Israel's sovereignty over the holy city of Jerusalem. Immediately the American Jewish community exploded, raining a hail of invective down on President Carter and his UN ambassador. Carter quickly disavowed the vote, blaming the whole incident on a "communications failure." It was yet another example of the Carter bungling that Americans had become so fed up with. But to America's Jews it went far beyond bungling. For them it was a deadly serious matter. Carter's ambassador at the UN had voted on the side of the Arabs about such sacred matters as the status of Jerusalem! The largest concentration of Jews in America was in the state of New York. They had been a major factor in Bobby's winning the 1964 senatorial race. If Ted Kennedy could capitalize on their outrage at Carter perhaps he could win in New York after all.

To further aggravate Carter's position, and therefore enhance Kennedy's, both the rate of inflation and interest rates went up again, while the stock market plummeted to 765 on the Dow-Jones average, its lowest level in years.

Ted Kennedy consulted with his aides and decided to come out swinging. He was in the race to stay. Promptly, he attacked Carter on all fronts: inflation, the economy, the hostage crisis, and the question of Israel's right to settle her conquered territories and assert sovereignty over Jerusalem. All of a sudden, he and his campaign workers began to sense strong new support for his campaign in New York. There was a big Jewish anti-Carter vote out there, and maybe he could capture it.

When it became apparent that Ted Kennedy was not giving up, Anthony Lewis, in an article in the *New York Times,* lauded Kennedy's "guts" and courage for not quitting, and the Kennedy people took heart from this approbation. *Finally,* a good word from the press.

Before long the Kennedy camp in New York was undergoing a rejuvenation of sorts, and various Kennedy family sideshows began hitting the road again. Among the grandchildren some proved more effective campaigners than others. According to Kennedy staffers and delegates I spoke with, the most able were Willie Smith, Maria and Bobby Shriver, Bobby Kennedy, Jr., Kathleen Kennedy, and Joseph P. Kennedy III. Joe III's wife, Sheila Rauch Kennedy, was considered the best of all. Among the older Kennedys, Jacqueline Onassis proved quite effective in some of the "ethnic" neighborhoods, Puerto Rican Harlem and the large Greek enclave in Astoria, Queens. All Jackie Onassis had to do at the big meeting at the Astoria Manor was smile, and the Greek-Americans gathered there went wild. By the time Ted Kennedy showed up the crowd had been prepared. Of course he told them exactly what they wanted to hear, that one of his three birthday wishes was for Turkish troops to withdraw from Cyprus. On cue, Miss Cyprus 1979 then gave him a birthday bouquet "on behalf of all the 200,000 refugees in Cyprus." A great cheer went up.

But it was the Jews that Kennedy concentrated on the most in New York, knowing full well that the Jews usually voted in greater numbers in the primaries than any other ethnic group in the country. Over and over again he criticized the Carter administration's opposition to Israel's right to settle her conquered territories. He stuck to issues and refrained from exploiting the Kennedy legend.

The strategy paid off. To the joy of the Kennedy camp, Ted Kennedy took the New York primary 58.9 percent to 41.1 percent for Carter, capturing 164 delegates to 118 for Carter. When the vote was analyzed, it turned out

that Kennedy had won the Jewish vote 4 to 1. The Jewish
vote also helped in Connecticut, for the same day as the
New York contest Kennedy won the Connecticut primary
46.9 percent to 41.5, taking 29 delegates to Carter's 25.

Now there was jubilation at Kennedy headquarters.
At last they had the big win they so sorely needed. With
a double victory under Kennedy's belt, the campaign would
now take on new life. But no sooner had Kennedy's campaign found a new momentum than it was blunted again
by severe losses in Virginia, Kansas, and Wisconsin. The
Wisconsin defeat was a serious setback because Wisconsin
was a traditionally liberal state and Kennedy had by now
identified himself with all the liberal causes. Carter, however, had wisely remained "in the Rose Garden," concerning himself chiefly with foreign affairs, and most of all
with the Iranian crisis, rather than trying to best Kennedy
on domestic issues. Just before the primary was held, he
announced the imminence of a dramatic breakthrough in
the crisis, one which would soon lead to the release of the
hostages. Immediately, the patriotic Wisconsinites rallied
around their President and gave him a plurality over Kennedy. Then, no sooner were the votes history, than it became evident that the "breakthrough" would not materialize.
Kennedy had been had.

On to Michigan, where the dogged Kennedy tried to
blame the Japanese invasion of the U.S. automobile market on Carter. Concentrating his attention on factory workers, blacks, ethnics, women, and the unemployed, he eked
out a narrow victory over Carter 71 to 70. Kennedy's victory in Michigan had undoubtedly received an unexpected
boost from yet another Carter administration bungle, the
abortive military mission to rescue the hostages, which saw
three American helicopters fail, eight would-be rescuers
die, and Secretary of State Cyrus Vance resign. As if this
were not enough, it was then revealed that Fidel Castro
had unloaded his jails on Miami, with Carter's approval,
flooding the city with a fresh batch of criminals, derelicts,
and the insane.

The Pennsylvania primary came next (April 22), and
there a heartened Kennedy took off his gloves and con-

ducted a barefisted attack on the President that revealed
a whole new candidate. Gone were the hesitations, the
unsureness, the awkwardnesses of the previous months.
He blasted Carter over inflation, high interest rates, and
neglect of the poor, the elderly, youth, women, and blacks;
he hit hard at Carter's weak "surprised" response to the
Soviet invasion of Afghanistan and hammered away again
at the continued captivity of the hostages in Iran. Again
the result was a squeaker. With Mayor Bill Green of Philadelphia giving Kennedy a boost by throwing his full support to him, Kennedy took the state by the infinitesimal
margin of 93 to 92.

The victory in so large and important a state as Pennsylvania encouraged the Kennedy forces to fight on to what
had come to be called "super Tuesday," June 3, when no
fewer than eight key states were to hold primaries. By now
it was clear to the Kennedy people that they would probably lose the fight for the nomination but that by continuing
to challenge Carter they could assure his defeat in the
general election in November and in so doing pave the
way for a possible Kennedy candidacy in 1984. Kennedy
against Reagan would, of course, be the ultimate ideological contest, the archliberal against the archconservative.

During the weeks leading up to super Tuesday, the
expression "rehearsal for 1984" began to find currency in
the Kennedy camp. If Kennedy '80 failed, the campaign
would not be a total loss—it could be thought of as a dress
rehearsal for the next presidential campaign. Later, at a
campaign breakfast at "21" which I attended and at which
almost the entire Kennedy family was present, I found that
the expression "rehearsal for '84" had become sort of a
rallying cry for both the Kennedy family and Senator Kennedy's supporters.

The super Tuesday primaries included three "big-
gies," as the Kennedy people liked to call them: California,
New Jersey, and Ohio. These states, then, became the
focus of Kennedy's most determined campaigning. Meanwhile, however, Kennedy absorbed new defeats in Texas,
Indiana, North Carolina, Tennessee, Maryland, and Ne-

braska. By the time June 3 rolled around Carter had 1207 delegates and Kennedy 667, with 1666 needed to win.

On June 3, to the Kennedy camp's glee, their man won California by 45 percent to 38 and New Jersey by 56 percent to 37. But Carter took Ohio 51 percent to 44 and two other states. By Wednesday June 4, Carter had won the nomination on paper, having captured 1971 delegates to Kennedy's 1221. Kennedy's only hope now was to make a last-ditch effort to overturn the Democratic party rule that bound the delegates to the candidates to whom they were pledged. If Kennedy could somehow engineer an open convention, he might be able to persuade enough delegates committed to Carter to change their allegiance and come over to his side. Unexpected "stampedes" had occurred on convention floors before.

After super Tuesday the Kennedy campaign became concerned chiefly with a rules fight, the drafting of the Democratic platform, and a desperate attempt to raise money to pay off the campaign's staggering debts. Thus the Kennedy staffers went to work on the problem of over-turning the rules and writing ultraliberal planks to be pre-sented to the platform committee, and the Kennedy family hit the fund-raising circuit with a vengeance. All manner of Kennedy sideshows were organized, including lunch-eons in the Hamptons and "Rose Parades" in Massachu-setts to honor the candidate's mother on her ninetieth birthday.

I attended a luncheon given by investment banker Robert Towbin and his wife Irene in East Hampton. The party fell on June 19, a little over two weeks after the primaries of super Tuesday that had sealed Kennedy's de-feat, and the candidate appeared somewhat deflated. When I spoke with him about the campaign he told me it had been "rough," but "worth it," adding that he was confident he would win the rules fight. His big problem at the mo-ment was money. After the luncheon he had to attend two more fund-raisers.

At a certain point early in the campaign the Ken-nedys had realized that the public curiosity about them was so pronounced that all they had to do was appear at some event and people would pay to come and see them. The biggest draws in the family were Rose, Ted, Joan, and Jackie. But people would also pay to see the lesser lights: Ethel, Patricia, Jean, Eunice, and all the grand-children.

What greater Kennedy family event to exploit than Rose Kennedy's ninetieth birthday on June 21, 1980? The Kennedy family pulled out all the stops. Hundreds paid to attend the big party in the house at Hyannis Port. And thousands more paid for the privilege of marching in the various "Rose Parades." For $2 you could fall in line be-hind Rose's open car in Boston and trek a mile and a half with her to the cheers of the assembled multitudes. "Rose Parades" were not only held in Boston, but also in Spring-field, Worcester, Lowell, and Taunton. In each of these localities thousands of $2 marchers trudged behind the indomitable Rose. By the time Rose had become ninety years and one day a tidy sum had been gathered to help defray her son's colossal campaign debt.

It was an ironic situation. The Kennedys were wealthier than ever, and yet they were reduced to literally selling themselves to raise money to pay off Teddy's debts. By 1980 the Kennedy family fortune, comprising all the trust funds and the assets of the Joseph P. Kennedy Jr. Foun-dation, was estimated to amount to something in the neigh-borhood of $350 million. Edward Kennedy's personal fortune, entirely given to him by his father, amounted to slightly less than $20 million. In 1979 Kennedy had de-clared an annual taxable income of $501,197, upon which he had paid a total of $161,197 in taxes, and yet Kennedy was compelled to spend most of his time raising money.

Fortunately for Kennedy, people would pay more to see Rose and Joan and Jackie perform than they would to see Miz Lillian, Rosalynn, Amy, and Billy, the same Billy who it was later reported was doing $220,000 worth of business with the terrorist government of Colonel Kha-dafi's Libya.

And so down to the wire. The Democratic National Convention was to open on Monday, August 11. The Kennedy campaign continued unto the eleventh hour, with a big fund-raiser the night of August 10 at the Shubert theater; it was billed as "Broadway for Kennedy." Kennedy supporters were invited to pay $100 apiece to see such artists as Lauren Bacall, Betty Comden, Cy Coleman, Jule Styne, and Leonard Bernstein perform, and then hear Kennedy, who would be accompanied by his wife, make a rousing preconvention speech.

I attended this event and found myself sitting in the midst of the Robert Kennedy family, Ethel and about eight of her children. From what I was able to observe, the entire Kennedy family was present in the theater save for Rose, Jackie, Caroline, and JFK Junior. Teddy Kennedy, Jr., was sitting directly in front of me, and he certainly was an extraordinarily handsome young man.

After many speeches and songs by the entertainers, out came Ted Kennedy and his wife Joan. For a man who had been through such an ordeal he looked surprisingly rested and relaxed. He beamed with vitality and good spirits. Kennedy began the last speech of his campaign saying that he spoke not for his own candidacy, but for his commitment "to democratic principles" and for his "commitment to the common man and the common woman." The Democratic party was "the longest-lasting party on this planet," and it always had "a deep commitment toward the common man and the common woman."

Lacing into Ronald Reagan, he called Reagan's economic program "food stamps for the rich" and his stand against the ERA irresponsible. "There were founding *mothers*, as well as founding fathers!" he bellowed. As for health care, Reagan had no program at all. "The health of a family," Kennedy asserted, "should not depend on the wealth of a family."

That said, to rousing cheers, he thanked all his supporters and told them he would make a "real fight for an open convention" the next day, a fight he had absolutely no chance of winning.

It was a mad scene as we all exited from the theater. An enormous crowd had assembled in front of the Shubert, along with an intimidating array of policemen, photographers, and television cameramen. Having sat among them all evening, I was in the middle of the phalanx of Kennedys as I reached the sidewalk. Suddenly there was an explosion of flashbulbs, and it seemed as if a hundred cameras zoomed in on us. Then came the shouts from the crowd pressing against police barrier sawhorses: "Hey, there's Ethel, there's Ethel! Hi, Ethel, hi!" "Look it's Bobby Kennedy Jr." "Hey, there's Joan. Joan! Joan!" "Where's Jackie?" "Jackie! Jackie! Jackie!" "Teddy. Teddy. Teddy." It was pandemonium. I looked at the wild-eyed crowd pressing against the barricades. The flashbulbs and klieg lights were blinding. I wondered how I would ever get through the crowd, once I got past the barricades. Then, I noticed some of the Kennedy grandchildren were waving at the crowd. "Look, there's Teddy Junior. It's him. It's him. I know it's him!" For the Kennedys that night the old high was back. They could not have asked for more attention. When I finally got through the melee and into a taxi, I couldn't help reflecting that despite Ted Kennedy's overwhelming defeat the Kennedys still represented something magic to the American people. They remained, like the great stars of the film world, demigods and demigoddesses. What effect, I wondered, would this have on the younger generation, on Bobby Junior and Teddy Junior and Joe II? With no effort on their part, they had already achieved "star" status. One thing was certain. The Kennedys were never to be underestimated. Even in ignominy. Even in defeat. On to 1984.

71. "Tho' Much Is Taken, Much Abides..."

As EXPECTED, SENATOR EDWARD M. KEN-
NEDY lost the rules fight at Madison Square Garden during the afternoon and early evening of August 11. A frantic,
last-minute attempt to get some of the Carter people on
the rules committee to switch over to the Kennedy side
had resulted in only a handful of converts. The 158-mem-
ber committee voted by a margin of roughly two to one
to uphold the White House–sponsored rule that every delegate must vote for the candidate to whom he or she was
first committed or risk being deprived of credentials and
replaced by a presumably more loyal alternate.

Since there were around 1900 delegates pledged to
President Carter, that meant the President already had
some 300 more votes than he needed to be nominated on
the first roll call of the convention. Once the rules committee voted to uphold the Carter rule, it was all over for
Ted Kennedy. He had lost the nomination. Later that
evening, from his suite in the Waldorf-Astoria, he formally
withdrew from the race. President Carter would run on
Wednesday unopposed.

For Ted Kennedy, losing the Democratic nomination
was, in a very real sense, a preordained defeat. He should
never have been expected to live up to the excessive demands Joe and Rose Kennedy had imposed on their sons.
Perhaps John F. Kennedy was able to live up to them, but

it was utter madness to expect the same of his two younger brothers.

And so the Democratic National Convention of August 1980 rejected the candidacy of the lastborn child of Joe and Rose Kennedy. But, as it turned out, the convention was far from through with Senator Edward M. Kennedy. On the following evening, Tuesday, August 12, Kennedy was scheduled to address the entire convention at 8 P.M. It was to be the major speech of the convention before Carter's acceptance speech. For Kennedy, personally, it would be a chance to turn a defeat into a victory.

All weekend before the convention opened, Kennedy and his speechwriters and advisers worked on the address. The speech had been originally drafted by Kennedy aides Robert Shrum and Carey Parker. Kennedy then added elements of his own. Finally it was further bolstered, and polished, by those two veterans of Kennedy campaigns, Arthur M. Schlesinger and Ted Sorensen. Sorensen's hand in the final document was unmistakable. The speech turned out to have a generous dash of the high rhetoric of John F. Kennedy's better speeches, and occasionally reminded one of JFK's ringing inaugural address. Ted Kennedy rehearsed the speech twice on the teleprompter in his suite at the Waldorf and once on the teleprompter in Madison Square Garden. He even tried out elements of it in a talk before the California delegates' caucus over the weekend and at the breakfast in his honor at "21" Monday morning.

On Tuesday evening the entire Kennedy family was assembled in a large box over one of the entrances to the convention floor. They had gathered in the same box the previous evening for the rules battle. All during that evening, while the rules battle was fought and lost, an unceasing barrage of exploding flashbulbs fired on the Kennedys as delegates and others pulled up under their box to snap pictures. Now with Ted Kennedy about to speak, the barrage intensified. It seemed that every delegate to the convention, whether a Kennedy or a Carter supporter, wanted to bring home a picture of the Kennedy family assembled to hear their standard-bearer address the convention, and the nation.

It was a grand occasion and Ted Kennedy rose to it magnificently. As he strode toward the podium and prepared to deliver his speech, he seemed to grow larger than life, and his whole being took on a kind of glow. For the first time since the campaign began he manifested a presidential aura. Now more than a century of Kennedy political life rose up in Ted Kennedy. The early struggles of his family in East Boston were with him—those days when the Kennedys were a despised, poverty-stricken minority, like the groups Kennedy was now championing. The first American Kennedy, the unfortunate Patrick, was there with his great-grandson on this night of August 12, 1980. And grandfathers Honey Fitz and P. J. were there with him, too. The ambitions and resentments and pride of his father were with him. And the struggles and death of Jack. And the struggles and death of Bobby. And the ambitions and sorrows of his mother. His own struggles and his own tragedies were with him, including all the disappointments, failures, and successes of his recent campaign. His deep belief in the social and economic ideals of the New Deal was with him. As Kennedy strode into the glare of the television lights and launched into his speech, all these memories, experiences, forces, and ideas coalesced within him and gave his words an enormous strength and sense of conviction.

The speech was the quintessential liberal utterance, the liberal litany raised to the one-hundredth power. Kennedy called upon the Democratic party to renew its commitment to "economic justice" and a "fair and lasting prosperity." He urged his party to espouse the cause of the common people. He criticized the Republicans for fighting and blocking "the forward surge of average men and women in their pursuit of happiness." He ripped into Ronald Reagan on the Republican candidate's stand on unemployment insurance, the environment, and his interpretation of the New Deal. He called for the reindustrialization of America, real tax reform, and national health insurance. He spoke of the "hard hours" of his campaign when he "sailed against the wind." Finally he said,

> And someday, long after this convention, long after the signs come down, and the crowds stop cheering, and the bands stop playing, may it be said of our campaign that we kept the faith. May it be said of our party in 1980 that we found our faith again.
>
> May it be said of us, both in dark passages and in bright days, in the words of Tennyson that my brothers quoted and loved and that have special meaning for me now:
>
> I am a part of all that I have met . . .
> Tho' much is taken, much abides . . .
> That which we are, we are—
> One equal temper of heroic heart . . .
> Strong in will
> To strive, to seek, to find and not to yield.
>
> For me, a few hours ago, this campaign came to an end. For all those whose cares have been our concern, the work goes on, the cause endures, the hope still lives and the dream shall never die.

As Ted Kennedy pronounced these last words, the Democratic convention at Madison Square Garden erupted in a sustained demonstration that lasted, with no letup, for a full half hour. It was pandemonium. Vainly Tip O'Neill attempted to gavel the house to order to call for votes from the delegates on certain platform resolutions that were in contention. His voice and gavel were overwhelmed by the avalanche of cheers and applause. Take Kennedy's ideas or leave them: The address had an undeniable power. Gone were the hesitations; he had been every bit as eloquent as his brother Jack. Whatever weaknesses were contained in the speech, Kennedy's delivery negated them. What he said he said magnificently, and with overwhelming force and conviction. And though his own defeat at the hands of Jimmy Carter had been monumental, utterly destroying the myth of Kennedy political invincibility, Ted

Kennedy had found in the depths of his being the courage and power to give this hurricane of a speech. In so doing, he transformed a crushing political defeat into a personal victory of the spirit.

After his defeat for the nomination, Edward Kennedy went on to campaign halfheartedly for Jimmy Carter, exacting, as his price for supporting the President (according to a book by Hamilton Jordan), that the Carter forces help pay off some of his enormous campaign debt, which they agreed to do, with considerable reluctance.

As it turned out, Kennedy campaigned more against Ronald Reagan than for Jimmy Carter, and in so doing made his not-inconsiderable contribution to Reagan's victory.

Kennedy was then compelled to witness the most extraordinary mastery of Congress displayed by any President since Franklin D. Roosevelt, as Ronald Reagan managed to get almost his entire legislative program passed during his first year in office.

The contrast between Reagan's first hundred days and John F. Kennedy's first hundred was, of course, nothing less than overwhelming. Ted Kennedy could not help realizing, with a certain chagrin, that by the end of Reagan's first 100 days an entire economic program had been launched, for better or for worse, while by the end of his late brother's first 100, nothing had happened but the debacle in the Bay of Pigs.

As President Reagan's second year in office was coming to a close, the time came for his potential challengers in 1984 to step forward and announce their candidacies for the Democratic nomination.

Edward Kennedy seemed a definite possibility, but on December 1, 1982, he surprised most everyone by announcing his withdrawal from the race. Family considerations were given as his reason for not running. It was true that his three children, fearful of assassination, did not want him to run, and, as an additional discouragement, he was in the process of getting a divorce.

However, there was also the chance that an imminent re-airing of the Chappaquiddick mess might have influenced Kennedy's decision. For by the time of his withdrawal announcement, it had become known that former District Attorney Edmund Dinis, who had prosecuted Kennedy, was now willing to tell all, and author Leo Damore was working on a book about the Chappaquiddick case that promised to reveal wholly new information about the accident and the investigation.

Furthermore, from a purely political standpoint, Kennedy had to realize that the time for his candidacy was just not right. In the off-year election of November 1982 the Democrats, including Kennedy, had not done as well as they had expected (Kennedy's own margin of victory was less than in 1976), making it seem highly unlikely that a Democrat could successfully challenge Reagan in 1984, especially if the President's economic program had by that time produced a genuine recovery. If Kennedy were to be beaten by Reagan in 1984, his chances of ever becoming president would be negligible. But then why feel compelled to run for president at all? Running for president had been a role that had always been thrust on Edward Kennedy by circumstances; it had never been one he adopted out of pure, unfettered choice. Besides, Ted Kennedy is a man who likes to enjoy himself, and from what I observed of him during the 1980 contest, he did not strike me as someone who really enjoys political campaigning, especially presidential campaigning.

There remained the remote possibility that Edward Kennedy might change his mind at the last minute about running in 1984, as his brother Robert did in 1968. A pattern, however, seems to have become firmly established in Edward Kennedy's political life: he seems perennially a presidential possibility, never a president.

Yet, in spite of everything it would be a mistake to underestimate Edward Kennedy, or the other Kennedys. The Kennedys have suffered the foulest indignities. They have known both ignominy and defeat. But they have borne their misfortunes with dignity and grace; and Edward Kennedy has shown he has been able to recover from disasters that would have surely defeated a lesser man. As the last-born child of Joe and Rose Kennedy proved the night of August 12, 1980, "Tho' much is taken, much abides. . . ."

Epilogue 1984

IN JULY 1984, television viewers across the United States witnessed a spectacular political debut. The setting was the 1984 Democratic National Convention, and the debut was made by 26-year-old Edward M. Kennedy, Jr., eldest son of the senior senator from Massachusetts. Senator Kennedy had remained true to his promise not to run for the 1984 Democratic nomination, but he had seen to it that the American people would hear a new Kennedy voice at the convention.

Handsome, poised, charming, with his curly blond hair glistening in the spotlights and his prominent features and winning smile reminding his audience of his famous uncles, young Teddy Kennedy confidently delivered an address that was forceful, eloquent, and perfectly paced. From time to time the television cameras turned from the son to the father, who was seated on the convention floor beaming with pride. By the time the address was over, it was clear to many that this was a young Kennedy with promise.

Teddy's sterling performance at the convention came at a time when the reputation of the younger generation of Kennedys had been severely damaged. Earlier in the year, Teddy's cousin Robert F. Kennedy, Jr., had been convicted of felony possession of heroin and Bobby's younger brother David had died at 28 of an overdose of cocaine and Demerol. The family, shocked by these disasters, which had seemed to portend a gruesome future for the grand-children of Rose and Joe, hoped Teddy's achievement at the convention would help to restore the younger Kennedys' battered reputation.

As 1984 drew to a close, however, the investigation of David Kennedy's death attracted more attention from the press than any other event associated with the family that year—more than Rose Kennedy's crippling stroke in the spring, and more than Senator Kennedy's vigorous last-minute campaigning in behalf of the Democratic presidential nominees, Walter Mondale and Geraldine Ferraro. Once again it was not an achievement but a disaster that focused massive public attention on the Kennedys. Once again, a Kennedy had died young. But in contrast to the four untimely deaths in the preceding generation, all of which were redeemed by heroic overtones, David Kennedy's death was squalid and demeaning.

The involvement with drugs of two of Robert F. Kennedy's oldest sons first became public knowledge in September 1979, when David Kennedy, then 23, was beaten and robbed in a Harlem hotel alleged to be a drug supermarket, or "shooting gallery" as the press described it. A subsequent police investigation, which did not result in any charges but findings of which were leaked to the press, revealed that young David had gone to the East 116th Street hotel often to "score" heroin and other drugs. On his way through the hotel's dingy lobby, David would pass a bulletproof cashier's cage decorated with a faded photograph of his uncle John F. Kennedy. The pushers there knew David as "White James" and "Sweetwater." A few weeks after his mugging, David was hospitalized for bacterial endocarditis, a heart disease often caused by heroin abuse.

Four years later, in September 1983, Bobby Kennedy, Jr., was arrested in Rapid City, South Dakota, where he had gone to visit a friend. He was charged with possession of heroin, a felony punishable by two years in jail and a $2,000 fine. The following March, Bobby was convicted, given a suspended sentence, and put on two-year probation. Local police had found the heroin in young Kennedy's bag after he had collapsed on the plane, apparently from drug withdrawal. In no time the entire world learned that the son and namesake of the former attorney general of the United States was involved in drugs.

Though this was startling news to the world, the drug problems of some members of the younger generation were well known to the Kennedy family and their closest friends. For some time it had been the despair of Senator Ted Kennedy and Robert F. Kennedy's widow, Ethel, and also of Eunice Kennedy Shriver and Patricia Kennedy Lawford, for Eunice's son Bobby and Patricia's son Christopher had occasionally joined Bobby and David Kennedy in their adventures with drugs. It had been a constant source of concern for Ted Kennedy during his 1980 campaign for the Democratic nomination.

The troubles of Ethel Kennedy and her sons derived directly from the murder of Robert F. Kennedy in 1968, an event that devastated his immediate family. Robert's 12-year-old son David had urged him not to run for the 1968 Democratic nomination, because of the misery it might bring his family if he too was assassinated. Robert did not heed his son's admonition, and later David witnessed the horror of his father's murder on television from his room in Los Angeles' Ambassador Hotel.

The assassination scarred the sensitive David permanently and led him to reject the Kennedy ethos of winning at all cost. As the months passed, David became more and more rebellious, and within two years of his father's death he was into drugs.

According to sources close to the family, Ethel Kennedy, consumed with grief after her husband's murder, seemed slowly to fall apart, letting her household lapse into chaos and her older children run wild. Devoting most of her time and energies to her seven younger children, especially the infant, Rory, who was born after Robert's death, Ethel had little left for her three oldest sons, Joe, Bobby, and David, though they needed their mother more than ever. In time the three hyperactive, rambunctious teenagers became too much for her to handle. She grew impatient with their questions about their father's life and death, especially with those concerning the assassination, and eventually refused to answer them. Furious arguments would break out, sometimes culminating in Ethel's throwing the offending boy out of the house. After Bobby was arrested in Hyannis Port one summer for possession of marijuana, she hurled him into the bushes, screaming, "You've dragged your family's name through mud." Young Bobby then ran away from home, ending up on the West Coast with so little money (he had no control of his trust fund) that he resorted to panhandling on the Berkeley campus and hopping freights. Soon he gravitated toward drugs to ease his pain.

Bobby's younger brother David had, in the meantime, been badly hurt in a jeep crash caused by the negligent driving of his oldest brother, Joe. The accident, which left a female passenger semiparalyzed below the waist for life, seriously injured David's back. The painkillers administered to him in the hospital led to his addiction to such prescription drugs as Demerol, Percodan, and Mellaril, and ultimately to his later dependence on heroin and cocaine.

Besides grief over their father's death, the lack of a steady male influence in their lives, and their mother's inability to discipline their energies and cope with their problems, Bobby and David also suffered from the burden of the Kennedy name. In 1962 a dynastically minded John F. Kennedy had given his eight-year-old nephew David a photo of the boy posing before the White House, inscribing it, "A future President inspects his property." It was not easy for a boy like David, who was very sensitive and not especially gifted, to grow up thinking such an exalted destiny might be expected of him. One can imagine how he felt when he passed the photograph of JFK in the hotel where he scored his drugs. Pressured to meet the exaggerated expectations of their elders, David and his brother Bobby grew up feeling guilty and unworthy, as their own identities diverged from the patterns cut out for them to follow.

The guilt and feelings of unworthiness led Bobby straight to heroin. He now lives with his wife, Emily, in Katonah, New York, near the drug rehabilitation clinic he must attend until April 1986. Unfortunately, Bobby's ear-

lier achievements—which included writing a respected biography of a southern integrationist judge, Frank Johnson—
have been obscured by the worldwide headlines about his
arrest. In the summer of 1984, however, his reputation was
somewhat redeemed by the birth of his son, Robert F.
Kennedy III.

While Bobby was making progress toward conquering his drug problem, his brother David went from bad to
worse. In and out of several drug rehabilitation programs
over the years, he eventually proved beyond help. His
struggle finally ended in Palm Beach's Brazilian Court Hotel
the morning of April 25, 1984.

The Kennedy clan had gathered in Palm Beach that
April because it was feared that the matriarch Rose would
soon die as a result of her recent stroke. This might be the
last chance for her children and grandchildren to say goodbye to her.

Not long after he arrived on the scene, David began
drinking large amounts of vodka and snorting cocaine while
taking Demerol, a painkiller, and Mellaril, a sedative. According to sources close to the family, the young man was
very upset over some unflattering stories about him in a
national magazine. The stories intensified his guilt and
sense of unworthiness at having let the Kennedy name
down and prompted him to go out on all-night binges of
drinking and doing cocaine. One of these proved to be his
last. After a wild night during which he may have drunk
as many as ten vodkas on the rocks and done at least two
grams of cocaine, in addition to taking his usual dose of
Demerol and Mellaril, he collapsed in his hotel suite early
in the morning of April 25. Hotel employees found him
sprawled dead on the floor between the two beds, the
telephone off the hook, at 11:32 A.M.

By November 1984, the investigation of David Kennedy's death being conducted by the Florida state attorney
of Palm Beach County had become most complex, giving
rise to yet another set of Kennedy mysteries. Although the
state medical examiner's report was made public in October,
over a thousand pages of testimony, including the toxologist's
report, are still being kept secret as of this writing.

Complicating the case are the depositions, released in October, of the two hotel employees, concierge Douglas Moschiano and staffer Betty Barnett, who found David dead. Following a phone call from David's mother, who was worried because she had not been able to reach her son by phone, Moschiano and Barnett had gone to David's two-room suite to see if he was all right. Preliminary reports of the scene indicated that no drugs were found in David's suite and that no one had visited his room since he died. A few days later the police reported that 1.3 grams of high-quality cocaine had been found among David's effects, but that no other evidence of drugs had been found in the suite. In mid-October, however, after the state of Florida had charged two former bellhops, David Dorr and Peter Marchant, with selling cocaine to David, police investigators testified at a pretrial hearing that they had found traces of drugs in the bathroom toilet when they first inspected David's suite. Then, concierge Moschiano testified that David's 27-year-old cousin Caroline Kennedy had come to the hotel the morning of David's death, accompanied by another woman, possibly her cousin Sydney Lawford. An hour before Moschiano discovered the body, he saw Caroline heading toward David's suite, having been unable to reach him on the house phone.

Defense lawyer Michael Salnick suggested in a supplementary discovery motion submitted by written brief that Caroline and Sydney might have entered the room (using the room key that was left on the ledge above David's door) and found their cousin dead; noticing all the drugs on the bed table, either Caroline or Sydney may have picked them up and thrown them into the toilet. Then, according to the defense attorneys' hypothetical reconstruction of what might have happened, instead of reporting the death to the police, either Caroline or Sydney may have notified their Aunt Ethel of the tragedy. Ethel, in turn, instructed the hotel to find out what had happened to her son. If the defense could establish all of this, they could claim that Caroline and Sydney were guilty of not reporting the death to the police and of tampering with evidence. Later, in another discovery motion, the defense suggested that the Demerol David used in conjunction with the cocaine might have been stolen from Rose Kennedy's bedroom, either by David or by one of his cousins, and that it was the interaction of the Demerol and cocaine that killed David, not the cocaine alone. At a pretrial hearing, counsel for the defense raised the possibility that Caroline, Sydney, or another Kennedy cousin might have stolen the fatal drug from their grandmother to give to David, then unsuccessfully tried to flush it down the toilet upon finding him dead.

On October 17, however, Caroline publicly denied that she ever entered David's hotel room (a denial she reiterated in a sworn statement released January 14 by Palm Beach County State Attorney David Bludworth).

At this the defense attorneys, in another discovery motion, demanded that the fingerprints lifted from David's room by the police be compared with those of Caroline Kennedy, Sydney Lawford, Douglas Kennedy (one of David's younger brothers), and other Kennedys who may have visited David's room that morning. The prosecution initially refused to release the pertinent documents, but meanwhile the *Palm Beach Daily News* and the *Palm Beach Post* had filed a civil suit against the Palm Beach County state attorney to force him to make public the full investigative record of the case. The two newspapers won their suit in early November and awaited release of the record, especially the fingerprint evidence.

The prosecution, however, insisted on holding a separate hearing for the release of each of the more than 1,000 documents associated with the case, thus slowing the disclosure process to a crawl. Finally, on November 14, as pressure mounted, Palm Beach police chief Joseph Terlizzese released to the defense a statement on the fingerprints which, in accordance with the Florida Public Records Law, was immediately made public. Referring to concierge Moschiano's testimony that he had seen Caroline Kennedy and her companion heading in the direction of David Kennedy's room the morning of David's death, Chief Terlizzese declared: "We concluded that they had made an attempt to visit him, but we never found any evidence they were in the room." Terlizzese then went on to state that fingerprints found in David's suite did not belong to Caroline or Sydney, though he added that all of the fingerprints found had not been identified and refused to say whose fingerprints had so far been identified.

As the case stands in mid-December 1984, pretrial hearings will continue for another two and a half months, and the trial of the two alleged drug pushers will commence in West Palm Beach on March 4, 1985. Among the potential witnesses the defense has listed are Sydney Lawford, Douglas Kennedy, and Caroline Kennedy. At first the defense attorneys were disposed to plea bargain, but then, as they began to sense they might be able to get their clients off, they appeared to be pushing for an acquittal. The latter possibility was placed in doubt, however, when assistant state attorney Pablo Perhacs, the active prosecutor in the case, announced on December 12th that David Kennedy had written a $120 check to defendant Peter Marchant two days before he died and that Kennedy's signature on the check had been authenticated by a crime laboratory analyst. Meanwhile, the Kennedy family remains apprehensive over the prospect of Caroline, Sydney, and Douglas being grilled by the defense in a courtroom, and the publicity that might erupt from a trial.

As might be expected, Kennedy damage-control squads are making a concerted effort to minimize the damage David Kennedy's death is inflicting on the family image. In November some seven family lawyers reportedly appeared before a federal judge in Miami in an effort to prevent the defense in Palm Beach from viewing the photographs taken of the death scene on April 25. Observers in Palm Beach, notably Chuck Holmes and Tony Wharton of the *Palm Beach Post* and John Purnell of *USA Today*, are of the opinion that a close relationship has developed between the Kennedy family and the prosecution.

Caroline Kennedy's involvement in the David Kennedy investigation is ironic, for of the twenty-eight surviving grandchildren of Joe and Rose she is one of the most exemplary. A Harvard graduate and enthusiast of the arts, she is (as of December 1984) the hard-working manager and coordinating producer of the Office of Film and Television of New York's Metropolitan Museum of Art and the dedicated vice-president of the John F. Kennedy Library Foundation in Boston. On November 23, 1983, at a memorial mass marking the twentieth anniversary of John F. Kennedy's assassination, she delivered a moving eulogy of her father. Caroline Bouvier Kennedy was, to use her mother's family motto, "*sans peur et sans reproche.*"

Jacqueline Kennedy Onassis has brought up her children exceptionally well. Her handsome son, John, has led, like his sister, a relatively unblemished career during his first 24 years. After graduating from Brown, John knocked around for a while, working on a Cape Cod fishing boat and doing a stint with a Peace Corps–type program in India. Under pressure from his mother and Uncle Teddy, he buckled down to a nine-to-five job in October 1984, as assistant to New York City's commissioner of business development—following the traditional Kennedy path of public service. Why wasn't John as severely affected by his father's assassination as were Robert Kennedy's older sons by their father's murder? Because he does not even remember his father; he turned three the day of JFK's funeral. Also, since Jacqueline had only two children to worry about, in contrast to Ethel's eleven, neither John nor Caroline felt neglected in their youth.

While the probe into the circumstances surrounding David Kennedy's death was widely reported in the press throughout the fall of 1984, various investigators behind the scenes were still busy trying to unravel the murders of John and Robert Kennedy. Compared to these ongoing investigations, the David Kennedy investigation is trivial, for upon the outcome of the assassinations investigations depends the resolution of the most crucial issues of the Kennedy saga. These issues can be reduced to four momentous questions: (1) to what extent were the Kennedys themselves indirectly responsible for the disasters that befell them?; (2) was the JFK assassination related in any way to the Kennedy administration's obsession with "getting rid of Fidel Castro" (bearing in mind that there were at least eight attempts on Castro's life during the Kennedy administration, including one that was in progress the very day Kennedy was killed)?; (3) did organized crime plot and carry out the murder of one or both of the Kennedy brothers?; and (4) if it did, why did the United States government's two major investigative agencies, the FBI and the CIA, let the Mob get away with the two crimes?

Since the hardcover publication of this book in July 1984, I have become more convinced than ever that organized crime had a hand in the JFK assassination, and I am beginning to believe that the Mob may have also been behind the RFK murder. Among the developments that have influenced my thinking was my interview in October 1984 of a distinguished newspaper publisher who knew CIA-Mafia anti-Castro conspirator John Roselli for twenty years and spoke with him about the JFK assassination shortly before Roselli's murder. According to this source, who has requested anonymity, Roselli knew how and why President Kennedy was killed: in retaliation for Bobby Kennedy's crackdown on the Mafia. The conspirators, who were members of organized crime with connections to Castro's Cuba, had recruited the pro-Castro Oswald as a scapegoat, luring him into the plot by informing him of the secret CIA-Mafia murder plots against Castro. While Oswald certainly fired on the President, another gunman— a professional killer hired by the conspirators—fired also, from close range. Oswald was supposed to have been identified as the lone assassin immediately after the crime and killed as he was making his escape. When this plan failed, Jack Ruby, a figure connected to several major crime families, including the Giancana, Marcello, and Trafficante organizations, and also to Jimmy Hoffa's Teamsters, was quickly recruited by the conspirators to silence Oswald. Why did the FBI and the CIA fail to identify the conspiracy? Because they realized that if they did, the secret assassination plots against Castro would have become known. For reasons of "national security" (and probably also of national honor), the FBI and the CIA decided this should never happen.

It is worth noting that, despite all that has come to light over the past nine years about the Kennedy brothers' knowledge of, and possible involvement in, the CIA's plots to assassinate Fidel Castro during the Kennedy administration, the glorification of John and Robert Kennedy continues unabated, often to the sacrifice of historical truth.

During the 1984 presidential election campaign, it was revealed that the Reagan administration's CIA had given a handbook for guerrilla warfare to the Nicaraguan "contras" that advocated such terrorist tactics as "hiring professional criminals to bring about uprisings and shootings that will create martyrs" and "neutralizing selected and planned targets such as court judges and security officials." When former Attorney General (under Lyndon Johnson) Ramsey Clarke was interviewed about this on a call-in radio show, a caller asked him whether President Kennedy had ever been knowledgeable of the CIA Castro assassination plots during his administration. Clarke replied, "No, President Kennedy did not know anything about them and had nothing to do with them." When I once stated on a radio talk show that there was conclusive evidence that the Kennedy brothers were aware of at least two or three of the CIA-Mafia plots and certainly were behind the CIA-AM/LASH plot, a storm of outraged callers blasted me for defaming the late President's memory. Later on in the program, when I stated that one of the CIA's AM/LASH plotters had told me on the record that the plot "to get rid of Castro" had had the full authorization of President Kennedy and his brother, irate callers told me that either the CIA officer or I was lying. And how dare I insinuate that President Kennedy might have been assassinated in retaliation for his own administration's efforts to assassinate Castro?

The principal investigators of the Robert F. Kennedy murder case at this writing are Gregory Stone, former special assistant to Representative Allard K. Lowenstein, and Dr. Robert F. Joling, a former president of the American Academy of Forensic Sciences, who came to dispute the official findings in the case. Lowenstein was killed by a former associate as he was pushing for the re-investigation of the RFK assassination; he and Dr. Joling were collaborating on a book about the assassination. The Low-enstein estate and Dr. Joling have since authorized Gregory Stone to revise and complete the manuscript.

According to Stone, who is now involved in legal efforts to reopen the investigation, the current status of the evidence suggests that "reasonable grounds for doubt exist that Sirhan Sirhan acted alone in the assassination of Robert F. Kennedy" and that "the balance of available evidence establishes a rebuttable assumption that at least two guns were fired in the Ambassador Hotel pantry the night of the shooting." Crucial to Stone's belief is the evidence contained in some 4000 previously classified FBI documents on the case obtained by various independent assassination investigators—principally by Bernard Fensterwald, Jr., a Washington, D.C., attorney—as the result of Freedom of Information Act petitions. These documents clearly indicate that more than eight shots were fired in the Ambassador Hotel pantry the night of June 5, 1968. Also, according to Stone, Los Angeles coroner Thomas Noguchi's autopsy report establishes that the fatal shot was fired into the back of Kennedy's head from no more than two or three inches away. This finding would rule out the possibility that Sirhan fired the fatal shot, for he was three or four feet to Kennedy's right when he commenced firing.

Stone conjectures that Sirhan had been set up as a fall guy, perhaps through hypnotic suggestion, and that the security guard who followed the senator into the pantry, only a step behind him, may have fired the fatal shot. William Turner and Jonn Christian speculated in their book on the RFK assassination that Sirhan's role in the murder conspiracy was to attract attention away from "the killer-gunman immediately behind Kennedy who administered the fatal shot." In his 1983 book *Contract on America*, David Scheim suggests the possibility of Mafia involvement, citing a 1975 Boston University symposium during which a Chicago crime investigator, Alex Bottus, alleged that the security guard, Thane Cesar, had been affiliated with reputed California Mafia boss John Alessio. When the police questioned Cesar in the course of the RFK assassination investigation, he denied firing his gun at the time of the shooting. However the police did not impound Cesar's gun after questioning him.

Dr. Thomas Noguchi offers his interpretation of the crime in his 1983 book, *Coroner*:

> Forensic evidence suggested that the shooting occurred in a different way. An instant after Kennedy entered the pantry, a gun appeared three inches from the back of his head, fired, then disappeared. Kennedy threw up his right arm and started to turn. Other shots were fired [from Sirhan's position]. . . .
>
> That . . . forensic re-creation of the scene could mean only one of two things: (1) either Sirhan lunged toward Kennedy and fired, a move unseen by anyone, and then as Kennedy spun, lunged *back* to fire from further away, a second move also invisible to all, or (2) a second gunman triggered the first shots up close, ducked away, and then Sirhan fired the other bullets from three feet away as Kennedy turned.

Noguchi speculates in his book that there might indeed have been a second gunman in the pantry and that "Sirhan, consumed with hatred for Kennedy, had agreed to jump into the middle of the room and start firing wildly to divert attention from the real killer." To support the speculation, Noguchi cited the statement of Karl Uecker, the assistant maître d' who led Senator Kennedy into the pantry and was standing between Kennedy and Sirhan when the shooting broke out. "I told the authorities that Sirhan never got close enough for a point blank shot. Never," Uecker told the former chief medical examiner. Noguchi concludes that "until more is positively known of what happened that night the existence of a second gunman remains a possibility. Thus I have never said that Sirhan Sirhan killed Robert Kennedy."

If the violently anti-Israel Sirhan had been hired to divert attention from the real killer, at a time when Kennedy was assiduously courting the Jewish vote, who might have put such an ingenious plot together? Stone has a host of suspects but will not speculate on them until more hard evidence is assembled. Kennedy's principal enemies at the time included Jimmy Hoffa, who had already conspired to kill Kennedy in 1963 and who was now in jail because of him; certain Mafia bosses, including Marcello, Giancana, and Trafficante, whom Kennedy had tried to destroy; certain elements of the CIA who had never forgiven him and his brother for the Bay of Pigs disaster and the firing of Dulles and Cabell; and FBI director J. Edgar Hoover, who was destined to be retired once and for all should Kennedy be elected President.

To these should be added whoever might have been behind John Kennedy's assassination. The chilling contents of the FBI teletype alleging the existence of a March 1963 New Orleans plot to kill JFK, possibly involving the Marcello family, may be pertinent also to the Robert Kennedy murder. One of the alleged conspirators mentioned in the document had stated that there was "a price on the President's head and on other members of the Kennedy family." Were the same conspirators who were behind the JFK assassination also involved in the murder of his brother? Researchers have found some possible connections, including one member of organized crime who was both in Dealey Plaza on November 22, 1963, and near the Ambassador Hotel the night of June 5, 1968, but have so far been unable to link the two crimes.

Although Gregory Stone, with Dr. Joling's support, continues to work on his book about the RFK assassination, and Dr. Noguchi has urged that the crime be reinvestigated, there are as yet no official plans to reopen the case. The Department of Justice apparently has no interest in probing the murder of its former attorney general any further, and neither Sirhan nor the Kennedy family wishes there to be another investigation—Sirhan because he still wishes to appear a martyr in the eyes of the Arab world, and the Kennedys for reasons that have never been made clear.

The Justice Department is, however, continuing its investigation of the John F. Kennedy assassination case, specifically the findings and supporting volumes of hearings and exhibits of the House Select Committee on Assassinations' 1976–1979 re-investigation of the murder. The department was to have announced the results of its review of the case in 1983, but after repeated delays, for which no reasons have been made public, it now estimates that the results will be published in June 1985.

Among the evidence the department has been reviewing are: the Dallas police dictabelt recording of the sounds at the assassination site, which led the House committee to conclude that four shots had been fired at the President—three from the Book Depository and one from the grassy knoll; a film of the assassination scene by an amateur photographer, Charles L. Bronson (originally dismissed by the FBI when turned over to them on November 25, 1963, then not rediscovered until 1978), that purports to show two figures in the window from which Oswald allegedly fired on the President; and all the new evidence of organized crime associations shared by Oswald and Ruby that the House Assassinations Committee discovered during its investigation in the late seventies.

After making public its review of the House committee's findings, the Justice Department will either reopen the case or shelve it. Most authorities on the subject who regard the case as still unsolved believe that the Justice Department will probably do the latter. If it does, then we may never arrive at the judicial truth of the assassination, and it will be left to private investigators to try to reach the historical truth. One such effort was initiated by the *Reader's Digest* three years ago but is temporarily stalled because of a recent shake-up of the *Digest's* editorial board. Another is the ongoing unofficial investigation being conducted by former chief counsel of the House assassinations committee, G. Robert Blakey, who has said, "I am now firmly of the opinion that the Mob did it. It is an historical fact."

Many doubts and mysteries continue to thwart the resolution of both cases, and the question of questions remains unanswered: Was organized crime able to eliminate the Kennedy brothers and get away with it? If the Justice Department and the American people choose not to face this question,

the cause of justice and personal liberty in America will
receive a severe setback. To honor the courage and vision
of the slain Kennedy brothers, especially their brave attack
on organized crime, truth and justice in the Kennedy assassination cases should be pursued as long as significant doubts
and unsolved mysteries remain.

Do the Kennedys have a future of leadership in the
United States, or are the failings of David Kennedy and
Robert F. Kennedy, Jr., indicative of a general decline in
the family's capacity for the self-discipline and resolve needed
to maintain a position of leadership in American society?

I do not believe these two instances of failure portend
anything for the Kennedy family as a whole. The self-
destructive impulses of Bobby and David Kennedy, though
present to a lesser degree in a few of their cousins, do not
characterize the entire younger generation. Several of the
young Kennedys have already demonstrated exceptional
promise and ability. RFK's oldest daughter, Kathleen, for
example, has become a leader in social service work in the
southwest. Maria Shriver is a talented television reporter
who often displays flashes of the charm and charisma of
her famous uncles. Her brother Bobby, a brilliant student
at Yale who wrote his undergraduate thesis on his grandfather Joe, has become a successful California attorney
with ambitions to enter national politics. Steve Smith, Jr.,
is a bright, energetic young man who graduated from Harvard and Columbia Law and is eager to get into politics.
Helping his father manage several major campaigns, including Ted Kennedy's 1980 campaign, young Steve has
already gained an extraordinary political education. Joe
Kennedy III successfully launched a low-cost fuel oil business in Boston, and in 1976 effectively managed his Uncle
Teddy's campaign for re-election to the Senate. He is the
father of twins named Matthew Rauch Kennedy and Joseph P. Kennedy IV, born in October 1980. Edward M.
Kennedy, Jr., showed courage, strength, and determination in overcoming a cancerous bone tumor that cost him
one of his legs, and at the 1984 Democratic convention
proved himself equal, if not superior, to his father and

uncles as an orator. There is little doubt that one of these young Kennedys will someday attain high political office. It is only a question of who and when.

No, the squalid end of David Kennedy is by no means indicative of a general decline of the Kennedys. Nietszche once wrote that "the strength of an organism may be judged from how much disease it can stand." This aphorism can be applied to families, institutions, nations, even entire civilizations. In the last two generations, the Kennedy family has survived one case of hopeless mental retardation, two young deaths from air accidents, two brutal murders witnessed by the entire world, a tragic auto accident, two crippling strokes, and now another young death, this time from an overdose of drugs. Yet the family has withstood all this and remained strong.

To insinuate, as some writers have, that the Kennedys are finished because one out of twenty-nine grandchildren died of a drug overdose, and two or three others have taken drugs, is tantamount to saying that the current high incidence of drug addiction and alcoholism in America, the increased suicide rate among the young, and the prevalence of other social ills in 1984 mean that American society is in an irreversible decline. The Kennedy family and American society are strong enough to withstand much more than what has assailed them so far.

"Though much is taken . . . much abides." The line from Tennyson that Edward Kennedy quoted in his great victory-in-defeat speech at the 1980 Democratic convention applies just as much to the family disaster of 1984 as to the calamities of 1944, 1948, 1963, 1968, 1969, and 1980. We remain aware of the pride and arrogance that accompanied the Kennedys' rise to power, the *hubris* for which the gods demanded, and received, their due. Still, despite everything, the last lines of Tennyson's poem continue to define the family's spirit, not only today but probably for many years to come:

> *"That which we are, we are—*
> *One equal temper of heroic heart . . .*
> *Strong in will*
> *To strive, to seek, to find and not to yield."*

Bibliography and Sources

THE FOLLOWING constitutes only the source material for this book and is not to be considered a comprehensive bibliography on the Kennedys.

Owing to the John F. Kennedy Library's policy of keeping much of its most important resources closed to the public, there is a regrettable lack of primary sources on the Kennedys available to researchers and writers. In fact, this book represents about as far as an author can go, given the present availability of primary sources.

A veil of secrecy has enshrouded the lives of several Kennedys and the presidential administration of John F. Kennedy. It was not until the Senate's 1975–1976 investigation of the intelligence agencies that some of the secrets of the Kennedy administration, and of the life of President Kennedy, began coming to light.

The researcher or writer bent on discovering new information about the Kennedy family or the John F. Kennedy administration is advised to consult pages 818–822 of this bibliography to discover how much material the John F. Kennedy Library is still withholding from the public. In general, material closed to the public falls into three categories: papers classified for purposes of national security; papers relating to an individual's strictly personal affairs; and papers that "might be used in some way to injure or harass any person." The library staff will review all closed documents on request to determine whether the reasons for closing no longer exist and the documents concerned can be reopened.

Further contributing to the atmosphere of secrecy is the welter of important material about the life and death of John F. Kennedy and his administration from three major investigations, listed herein, that cannot by law be released to the public until the twenty-first century. These are much of the Warren Commission testimony and exhibits, not due to be released until 2014, testimony taken by the Senate Select Committee to Study Governmental Operations with respect to Intelligence Activities, not due to be released until 2025; and much of the testimony and evidence taken by the House Select Committee on Assassinations, not due to be released until 2029. Furthermore, some 200 documents associated with the Warren Commission's inquiry were classified by President Johnson unreleasable until 2039.

The Kennedy Family: Biographies, General, and Related Works

Adler, Bill. *The Kennedy Children: Triumphs and Tragedies.* New York: Franklin Watts, 1980.

American Heritage Editors. *RFK: His Life and Death.* New York: Dell, 1968.

Beschloss, Richard R. *Kennedy and Roosevelt.* New York: Norton, 1980.

Blair, Joan, and Clay Blair, Jr. *The Search for JFK.* New York: Berkley, 1976.

Bradlee, Benjamin C. *Conversations with Kennedy.* New York: Norton, 1975.

Brown, Gene, editor. *The Kennedys, A New York Times Profile,* with introduction by Harrison E. Salisbury. New York: Arno Press, 1980.

Burns, James MacGregor. *John Kennedy: A Political Profile.* New York: Harcourt Brace Jovanovich, 1960.

Cameron, Gail. *Rose: A Biography of Rose Fitzgerald Kennedy.* New York: Putnam, 1971.

Clinch, Nancy Gager. *Kennedy Wives, Kennedy Women*. New York: Dell, 1976.

———. *The Kennedy Neurosis*. New York: Grosset & Dunlap, 1973.

Cutler, John Henry. *Honey Fitz: Three Steps to The White House: The Life and Times of John F. (Honey Fitz) Fitzgerald*. New York: Bobbs-Merrill, 1962.

Dallas, Rita, and Jeanira Ratcliffe. *The Kennedy Case*. New York: Putnam, 1973.

Davis, John H. *The Bouviers*. New York: Farrar, Straus & Giroux, 1969.

De Toledano, Ralph. *RFK: The Man Who Would Be President*. New York: Putnam, 1967.

Dinneen, Joseph. *The Kennedy Family*. Boston: Little, Brown, 1959.

Donovan, Robert J. *PT-109: John F. Kennedy in World War II*. New York: McGraw-Hill, 1961.

Exner, Judith, with Ovid Demaris. *My Story*. New York: Grove Press, 1977.

Fay, Paul B., Jr. *The Pleasure of His Company*. New York: Harper & Row, 1966.

Halberstam, David. *The Unfinished Odyssey of Robert Kennedy*. New York: Bantam, 1969.

Hersh, Burton. *The Education of Edward M. Kennedy*. New York: Dell, 1980.

Gallagher, Mary Barelli. *My Life with Jacqueline Kennedy*. New York: McKay, 1969.

Guthrie, Lee. *Jackie, the Price of the Pedestal*. New York: Drake, 1978.

Kelley, Kitty. *Jackie Oh!* Secaucus, N.J.: Lyle Stuart, 1978.

Kennedy, Rose Fitzgerald. *Times to Remember*. New York: Doubleday, 1974.

Koskoff, David E. *Joseph P. Kennedy: A Life and Times*. Englewood Cliffs, N.J.: Prentice-Hall, 1974.

Krock, Arthur. *Memoirs: Sixty Years on the Firing Line*. New York: Funk & Wagnalls, 1968.

Lasky, Victor. *JFK: The Man and the Myth*. New York: Macmillan, 1966.

———. *RFK: The Myth and the Man*. New York: Trident Press, 1968.

Lerner, Max. *Ted and the Kennedy Legend: A Study in Character and Destiny.* New York: St. Martin's, 1980.

Lincoln, Evelyn. *My Twelve Years with John F. Kennedy.* New York: McKay, 1965.

_____. *Kennedy and Johnson.* New York: Holt, Rinehart and Winston, 1968.

McCarthy, Joe. *The Remarkable Kennedys.* New York: Popular Library, 1960.

Newfield, Jack. *Robert Kennedy: A Memoir.* New York: Atheneum, 1971.

O'Donnell, Kenneth P., and David F. Powers. *Johnny We Hardly Knew Ye: Memoirs of John Fitzgerald Kennedy.* Boston: Little, Brown, 1972.

Olsen, Jack. *Aphrodite: Desperate Mission.* New York: Putnam, 1970.

Parmet, Herbert. *Jack: The Struggles of John F. Kennedy.* New York: Dial, 1980.

_____. *JFK: The Presidency of John F. Kennedy.* New York: Dial, 1983.

Rainie, Harrison, and John Quinn. *Growing Up Kennedy.* New York: Putnam, 1983.

Salinger, Pierre. *With Kennedy.* New York: Doubleday, 1966.

Saunders, Frank. *Torn Lace Curtain.* New York: Holt, Rinehart and Winston, 1982.

Schlesinger, Arthur M., Jr. *A Thousand Days: John F. Kennedy in the White House.* New York: Houghton Mifflin, 1965.

_____. *Robert F. Kennedy and His Times.* New York: Houghton Mifflin, 1978.

Searls, Hank. *The Lost Prince: Young Joe, the Forgotten Kennedy.* New York: New American Library, 1969.

Shannon, William. *The Heir Apparent: Robert Kennedy and the Struggle for Power.* New York: Macmillan, 1981.

Sidey, Hugh. *John F. Kennedy, President.* New York: Atheneum, 1964.

Sorenson, Theodore C. *Kennedy.* New York: Harper & Row, 1965.

Stein, Jean, edited by George Plimpton. *American Journey: The Times of Robert Kennedy.* New York: Harcourt Brace Jovanovich, 1970.

Swanson, Gloria. *Swanson on Swanson*. New York: Random House, 1980.

Thayer, Mary Van Rensselaer. *Jacqueline Bouvier Kennedy*. Garden City, N.Y.: Doubleday, 1961.

Thompson, Nelson. *The Dark Side of Camelot*. Chicago: Playboy Press, 1976.

vanden Heuvel, William, and Milton Gwirtzman. *On His Own: Robert F. Kennedy, 1964–1968*. Garden City, N.Y.: Doubleday, 1970.

Whalen, Richard J. *The Founding Father: The Story of Joseph P. Kennedy*. New York: New American Library, 1964.

White, Theodore H. *The Making of the President, 1960*. New York: Atheneum, 1961.

———. *The Making of the President, 1964*. New York: Atheneum, 1965.

———. *The Making of the President, 1968*. New York: Atheneum, 1969.

———. *America in Search of Itself: The Making of the President, 1956–1980*. New York: Harper & Row, 1982.

Wicker, Tom. *Kennedy without Tears*. New York: Morrow, 1964.

Wills, Garry. *The Kennedy Imprisonment: A Meditation on Power*. Boston: Little, Brown, 1981.

Witcover, Jules. *85 Days: The Last Campaign of Robert Kennedy*. New York: Putnam, 1969.

Wofford, Harris. *Of Kennedys and Kings: Making Sense of the Sixties*. New York: Farrar, Straus & Giroux, 1980.

The John F. Kennedy Presidential Administration

Abel, Elie. *The Missile Crisis*. Philadelphia: Lippincott, 1966.

Ball, George W. *The Past Has Another Pattern: Memoirs*. New York: Norton, 1982.

Bishop, Jim. *A Day in the Life of President Kennedy*. New York: Random House, 1964.

Clinch, Nancy Gager. *The Kennedy Neurosis*. New York: Grosset & Dunlap, 1973.

Fairlie, Henry. *The Kennedy Promise: The Politics of Expectation*. Garden City, N.Y.: Doubleday, 1973.

Galbraith, John Kenneth. *A Life in Our Times*. New York: Ballantine, 1981.

Halberstam, David. *The Best and the Brightest*. New York: Harper & Row, 1969.

Lincoln, Anne H. *The Kennedy White House Parties*. New York: Viking, 1969.

Lincoln, Evelyn. *Kennedy and Johnson*. New York: Holt, Rinehart and Winston, 1968.

Manchester, William. *Portrait of a President: John F. Kennedy in Profile*. Boston: Little, Brown, 1963.

Moldea, Dan E. *The Hoffa Wars: Teamsters, Rebels, Politicians and the Mob*. New York: Paddington, 1978.

Navasky, Victor S. *Kennedy Justice*. New York: Atheneum, 1977.

Parmet, Herbert. *JFK: The Presidency of John F. Kennedy*. New York: Dial, 1983.

Podhoretz, Norman. *Why We Were in Vietnam*. New York: Simon and Schuster, 1982.

Powers, Thomas. *The Man Who Kept the Secrets: Richard Helms and the CIA*. New York: Knopf, 1979.

Rostow, Walt W. *The Diffusion of Power*. New York: Macmillan, 1972.

Schlesinger, Arthur M., Jr. *A Thousand Days: John F. Kennedy in the White House*. New York: Houghton Mifflin, 1965.

Sheridan, Walter. *The Fall and Rise of Jimmy Hoffa*. New York: Saturday Review Press, 1972.

Sullivan, William C. *The Bureau: My Thirty Years in Hoover's FBI*. New York: Norton, 1979.

Thayer, Mary Van Renssalaer. *Jacqueline Kennedy: The White House Years*. Boston: Little, Brown, 1967.

United States Senate. *Interim Report of the Select Committee to Study Government Operations with Respect to Intelligence Activities: Alleged Assassination Plots Involving Foreign Leaders*. U.S. Government Printing Office, November 20, 1975.

West, J. B. *Upstairs at the White House: My Life with the First Ladies*. New York: Coward-McCann, 1973.

Wolff, Perry. *A Tour of the White House with Mrs. John F. Kennedy*. New York: Doubleday, 1962.

Wyden, Peter. *Bay of Pigs, the Untold Story.* New York: Simon and Schuster, 1979.

The Assassinations of John F. Kennedy and Robert F. Kennedy

a. The Assassination of John F. Kennedy

Anson, Robert Sam. *They've Killed the President: The Search For the Murderers of John F. Kennedy.* New York: Bantam, 1975.

Ashman, Charles. *The CIA-Mafia Link.* New York: Manor Books, 1975.

Belli, Melvin M. *Dallas Justice: The Real Story of Jack Ruby and His Trial.* New York: McKay, 1964.

Bishop, Jim. *The Day Kennedy Was Shot.* New York: Funk & Wagnalls, 1968.

Blakey, G. Robert, and Richard N. Billings. *The Plot to Kill the President.* New York: New York Times Books, 1981.

Brashler, William. *The Don: The Life and Death of Sam Giancana.* New York: Harper & Row, 1977.

Canfield, Michael, and Alan Weberman. *Coup d'Etat in America: The CIA and the Assassination of John F. Kennedy.* New York: Third Press, 1975.

Committee to Investigate Assassinations. *American Political Assassinations: A Bibliography of Works Published 1963–1970.* Washington, D.C., 1973.

Cornell Institute on Organized Crime. *Organized Crime: A Bibliography.* Ithaca, N.Y.: Cornell University Press, 1977.

Demaris, Ovid. *Captive City.* New York: New American Library, 1968.

Eddowes, Michael. *The Oswald File.* New York: Potter, 1977.

Epstein, Edward J. *Inquest: The Warren Commission and the Establishment of Truth.* New York: Viking, 1966.

————. *Legend: The Secret World of Lee Harvey Oswald.* New York: Reader's Digest Press, 1978.

Fensterwald, Bernard J. *Coincidence or Conspiracy?* New York: Kensington, 1977.

Garrison, Jim. *A Heritage of Stone.* New York: Putnam, 1970.

Guth, DeLloyd J., and David R. Wrone. *The Assassination of John F. Kennedy: A Comprehensive Historical and Legal Bibliography, 1963–1979.* Westport, Conn.: Greenwood, 1980.

Kantor, Seth. *Who Was Jack Ruby?* New York: Everest House, 1978.

Lane, Mark. *Rush to Judgment.* New York: Holt, Rinehart and Winston, 1966.

Library of Congress. *The Assassination of John F. Kennedy: An Alphabetical Bibliography.* Washington, D.C.: Library of Congress, Congressional Research Service, 1979.

Lifton, David. *Best Evidence. Disguise and Deception in the Assassination of John F. Kennedy.* New York: Macmillan, 1980.

Maas, Peter. *The Valachi Papers.* New York: Putnam, 1968.

Manchester, William. *The Death of a President.* New York: Harper & Row, 1967.

McMillan, Priscilla Johnson. *Marina and Lee.* New York: Harper & Row, 1977.

Meagher, Sylvia. *Accessories after the Fact.* New York: Vintage, 1976.

——— and Gary Owens. *Master Index to the JFK Assassination Investigations.* Metuchen, N.J.: Scarecrow, 1980.

Morrow, Robert D. *Betrayal: A Reconstruction of Certain Clandestine Events from the Bay of Pigs to the Assassination of John F. Kennedy.* Chicago: Henry Regnery, 1976.

Powers, Thomas. *The Man Who Kept the Secrets: Richard Helms and the CIA.* New York: Knopf, 1979.

The President's Commission on the Assassination of President Kennedy. (The Warren Commission) *Hearings and Exhibits.* Vols. I–XXXVI. U.S. Government Printing Office, September 1964.

Ramparts Magazine. *In the Shadow of Dallas. Ramparts,* June 1967.

Reid, Ed. *The Grim Reapers, The anatomy of organized crime in America.* Chicago: Henry Regnery Co., 1969.

Russell, Brian, and Charles E. Sellier, Jr. *Conspiracy to Kill a President.* New York: Bantam, 1982.

Scott, Peter Dale, Paul Hoch, and Russell Stetler. *The Assassinations, Dallas and Beyond—A Guide to Cover-ups and Investigations.* Berkeley: Westworks, 1977.

Summers, Anthony. *Conspiracy.* New York: McGraw-Hill, 1980.

Thompson, Josiah. *Six Seconds in Dallas: A Microstudy of the Kennedy Assassination.* New York: Bernard Geiss, 1968.

Thompson, Nelson. *The Dark Side of Camelot.* Chicago: Playboy Press, 1976.

United States House of Representatives. *Report of the Select Committee on Assassinations. Ninety-Fifth Congress—Second Session. Findings and Recommendations.* Accompanied by 12 volumes of Hearings and Evidence. U.S. Government Printing Office, March 29, 1979.

United States Senate. *Interim Report of the Select Committee to Study Governmental Operations with Respect to Intelligence Activities. Alleged Assassination Plots Involving Foreign Leaders.* U.S. Government Printing Office, November 20, 1975.

United States Senate. *Final Report of the Select Committee to Study Governmental Operations with Respect to Intelligence Activities. Book V. The Investigation of the Assassination of John F. Kennedy: Performance of the Intelligence Agencies.* U.S. Government Printing Office, April 23, 1976.

The Warren Report, New York: Associated Press, 1964.

Weisberg, Harold. *Whitewash,* Vols. I & II. New York: Dell, 1966. *Whitewash,* Vols. III & IV. Self-published, 1967.

b. The Assassination of Robert F. Kennedy

Blakey, G. Robert, and Richard N. Billings. *The Plot to Kill the President.* New York: New York Times Books, 1981.

Jansen, Godfrey. *Why Robert Kennedy Was Killed: The Story of Two Victims.* New York: Third Press, 1970.

Kaiser, Robert Blair. *R.F.K. Must Die! A History of the Robert Kennedy Assassination and Its Aftermath.* New York: Dutton, 1970.

Noguchi, Thomas I., and Joseph DiMona. *Coroner.* New York: Simon and Schuster, 1983.

Stone, Gregory. *Robert F. Kennedy Assassination: Current Status of Evidence.* Unpublished monograph, 1984.
Turner, William W., and Jonn G. Christian. *The Assassination of Robert F. Kennedy: A Searching Look at the Conspiracy and Cover-Up 1968–1978.* New York: Random House, 1978.
Witcover, Jules. *85 Days: The Last Campaign of Robert Kennedy.* New York: Putnam, 1969.

Organized Crime and Assassination Plots Involving Foreign Leaders

Sources for chapters dealing with organized crime and the CIA-Mafia and AM/LASH plots against Castro and their possible bearing on the assassination of President Kennedy and the investigation of the assassination.

1. Report of the Select Committee on Assassinations, U.S. House of Representatives, 95th Congress, Findings and Recommendations.

2. Hearings and Evidence, Select Committee on Assassinations, U.S. House of Representatives: Investigation of the Assassination of President John F. Kennedy:

VOLUME I	Hearings, September 6, 7, 8, 1978
VOLUME II	Hearings, September 11, 12, 13, 14, 15, 1978
VOLUME III	Hearings, September 18, 19, 20, 21, 1978
VOLUME IV	Hearings, September 22, 25, 26, 1978
VOLUME V	Hearings, September 27, 28, 29, December 29, 1978
VOLUME VI	Photographic Evidence
VOLUME VII	Medical, Autopsy, and Ballistics Evidence
VOLUME VIII	Acoustics, Polygraph, Handwriting, and Fingerprints
VOLUME IX	Organized Crime, including FBI electronic surveillance transcripts, staff report on Carlos Marcello, and possible

3. Alleged Assassination Plots Involving Foreign Leaders. Interim Report of the Select Committee to Study Governmental Operations with Respect to Intelligence Activities. United States Senate, together with Additional, Supplemental, and Separate Views.

Includes assassination plots against Patrice Lumumba, Congo; Fidel Castro, Cuba; Rafael Trujillo, Dominican Republic; and the November 1963 coup against Ngo Dinh Diem, South Vietnam; the question of authorization of the plots, findings and conclusions; and additional supplemental and separate views of Senators Hart, Morgan, Baker, Goldwater, and Mathias.

4. The Investigation of the Assassination of President John F. Kennedy: Performance of the Intelligence Agencies. Book V of Final Report of the Select Committee to Study Governmental Operations with respect to Intelligence Activities, United States Senate.

a. Cuba and the Intelligence Agencies
b. The United States Government Response to the Assassination: November 22, 1963 to January 1, 1984
  • The CIA Response
  • The FBI Response
c. The Intelligence Agencies and the Warren Commission. January to September 1964
  • Relationship between the FBI and the Warren Commission
  • Relationship between the CIA and the Warren Commission
  • Unpursued Leads and Knowledge of Plots to Assassinate Castro
d. Developments after the Warren Commission
  • 1965: Termination of AM/LASH Operation
  • 1967: Allegation of Cuban Involvement in the Assassination
e. The FBI and the Oswald Security Case. The FBI and the Destruction of the Oswald Note

5. FBI documents obtained under the Freedom of Information Act. Includes allegations of Marcello complicity in Kennedy assassination plot and involvement of Jack Ruby with Marcello associates in Dallas.

The Chappaquiddick Case

LEGAL PROCEEDINGS TRANSCRIPTS

In re: Kopechne
Petition for Exhumation and Autopsy
No. 1114 of 1969
   Clerk of Courts Office
   Luzerne County Court House
   N. River Street
   Wilkes-Barre, Pa. 18711
Inquest into the Death of Mary Jo Kopechne
Docket No. 15220 1970
   Joseph E. Sollitto, Jr.

Clerk of Courts
County of Dukes County
Edgartown, Mass. 02539

BOOKS

Olsen, Jack. *The Bridge at Chappaquiddick.* Boston: Little, Brown, 1964, and Ace Books, 1970.

Rust, Zad. *Teddy Bare.* Western Islands, 1971.

Sherrill, Robert. *The Last Kennedy.* New York: Dial, 1976.

Tedrow, Richard L., and Thomas L. Tedrow. *Death at Chappaquiddick.* Ottawa, Ill.: Green Hill, 1976.

Willis, Larryann. *Chappaquiddick Decision.* Portland, Ore.: Better Books, 1980.

ARTICLES

"Kennedy: The Unanswered Questions." *Life,* August 8, 1969.

"Chappaquiddick Mystery." *National Review,* November 18, 1969.

"Chappaquiddick Suspicions Renewed." *Time,* May 11, 1970.

"Judge's Harsh Verdict on Teddy Kennedy." *Newsweek,* May 11, 1970.

"Official Report on the Kennedy Case; with Excerpts from Testimony by E. M. Kennedy." *U.S. News and World Report,* May 11, 1970.

Kopechne, Mrs. Joseph, as told to Suzanne James. "The Truth about Mary Jo." *McCall's,* September 1970.

"Chappaquiddick after the Bridge." *Esquire,* February 1972.

Sherrill, R. "Chappaquiddick + 5." *New York Times Magazine,* July 14, 1974.

"Chappaquiddick Story." *Newsweek,* October 7, 1974.

"Chappaquiddick Investigation." *Boston Globe,* October 26, 27, 28, 29, 30, and 31, 1974.

Franke, David. "The Chappaquiddick Mystery: 40 Questions for Teddy Kennedy." *Human Events,* November 2, 1974.

"Back to Chappaquiddick." *Time,* November 11, 1974.

"Chappaquiddick: Kennedy Faces Lingering Doubts." *Oakland Tribune,* July 15, 1979.

Barron, John. "Chappaquiddick—the Still Unanswered Questions." *Reader's Digest,* February 1980.

Thomas, Jo. "Gaps Found in Chappaquiddick Phone Data." *New York Times,* March 12, 1980.

Books by Members of the Kennedy Family

Kennedy, Edward M. *Decisions for a Decade.* 1968. Reprint. New York: Doubleday, 1977.

Kennedy, Edward M., editor. *The Fruitful Bough. Reminiscences of Joseph P. Kennedy.* Privately printed.

Kennedy, John F. *Why England Slept.* Honors thesis in Government, Harvard University, 1940. New York: Funk & Wagnalls, 1940, 1961.

_____. *As We Remember Joe.* Privately printed, 1945.

_____. *Profiles in Courage.* New York: Harper & Row, 1965.

_____. *Public Papers of the President 1961, 1962, 1963.* 3 vols. U.S. Government Printing Office, 1962, 1963, 1964.

_____. *A Nation of Immigrants.* New York: Harper & Row, 1964.

Kennedy, Joseph P. *I'm for Roosevelt.* New York: Reynal and Hitchcock, 1936.

Kennedy, Robert F. *The Enemy Within.* New York: Harper & Row, 1960.

_____. *Thirteen Days: A Memoir of the Cuban Missile Crisis.* New York: Norton, 1969.

_____. *To Seek a New World.* Garden City, N.Y.: Doubleday, 1967.

Kennedy, Robert F., Jr. *Judge Frank M. Johnson, Jr., a Biography.* New York: Putnam, 1978.

Kennedy, Rose Fitzgerald. *Times to Remember.* New York: Doubleday, 1974.

General Works on Irish and American Life, History and Politics, and Miscellaneous Works

Adams, William Forbes. *Ireland and the Irish Emigrant to the New World.* New Haven: Yale University Press, 1932.

Allen, Frederick Lewis. *Only Yesterday.* New York: Harper, 1931.

Beard, Charles A., and Mary R. Beard. *The Rise of American Civilization.* New York: Macmillan, 1927.

Bonanno, Joseph. *A Man of Honor: The Autobiography of Joseph Bonanno.* New York: Simon and Schuster, 1983.

Boston 200 Corp. *East Boston.* Neighborhood History Series. Boston: Boston 200 Corp., 1976.

Bouvier, Jacqueline, and Lee Bouvier. *One Special Summer.* New York: Delacorte, 1974.

Bouvier, John Vernou, Jr. *Our Forbears.* Privately printed, 1931, 1942, 1944, 1947.

Bouvier, Kathleen. *To Jack with Love. Black Jack Bouvier: A Remembrance.* New York: Kensington, 1979.

Byrne, Stephen. *Irish Emigration to the United States.* New York: Arno Press and The New York Times, 1969.

Churchill, Winston S. *Blood, Sweat and Tears.* New York: Putnam, 1941.

————. *The Unrelenting Struggle.* New York: Little, Brown, 1942.

Coyne, Franklin E. *The Development of the Cooperage Industry in the United States 1620–1940.*

Danaher, Kevin. *Ireland's Vernacular Architecture, Cultural Relations Committee of Ireland.* Cork: Mercier, 1975.

Hale, Edward E. *Letters on Irish Emigration.* Freeport, N.Y.: Books for Libraries, 1972.

Handlin, Oscar. *Boston's Immigrants.* Cambridge, Mass.: Harvard University Press, 1979.

————. *The Uprooted. The Epic Story of the Great Migrations That Made the American People.* Boston: Atlantic Monthly–Little, Brown, 1951.

Giancana, Antoinette, and Thomas C. Renner. *Mafia Princess: Growing Up in Sam Giancana's Family.* New York: Morrow, 1984.

Green, James R., and Hugh Carter Donahue. *Boston's Workers, a Labor History.* Boston: Boston Public Library, 1977.

Hodgson, Godfrey. *America in Our Time.* Garden City, N.Y.: Doubleday, 1976.

Johnson, Lyndon Baines. *The Vantage Point. Perspectives on the Presidency 1963–1969.* New York: Holt, Rinehart and Winston, 1971.

Lash, Joseph P. *Roosevelt and Churchill 1939–1941.* New York: Norton, 1976.

Lemass, Sean F. *A Memory of John Fitzgerald Kennedy's Visit to Ireland, June 21–29, 1963.* Dublin: Wood Printing, 1964.

Nevins, Allan, and Henry Steele Commager. *The Pocket History of the United States.* New York: Pocket Books, 1956.

Neustadt, Richard E. *Presidential Power: The Politics of Leadership.* New York: Wiley, 1960.

New Ross Tourist Association. *Guide to Historic New Ross and Neighborhood.* New Ross, June 1978.

O'Brien, George. *Economic History of Ireland in the Eighteenth Century.* 1918. Reprint. Philadelphia: Porcupine, 1976.

Peters, Joan. *From Time Immemorial: The Origins of the Arab-Jewish Conflict over Palestine.* New York: Harper & Row, 1984.

Reedy, George E. *The Twilight of the Presidency.* New York: New American Library, 1970.

Schrier, Arnold. *Ireland and the American Emigration 1850–1900.* Minneapolis: University of Minnesota Press, 1958.

Thompson, Jacqueline. *The Very Rich Book—America's Supermillionaires and Their Money—Where They Got It, How They Spend It.* New York: Morrow, 1980.

Trench, W. Stuart. *Realities of Irish Life.* New York: John W. Lovell, 1868.

Wallace, Martin. *A Short History of Ireland.* Devon: Newton & Charles, Newton Abbot, 1973.

White House Historical Association. *The White House: An Historic Guide.* Washington, D.C., 1962.

White, Theodore H. *In Search of History: A Personal Adventure.* New York: Harper & Row, 1978.

_____. *America in Search of Itself: The Making of the President, 1956–1980.* New York: Harper & Row, 1982.

Woodham-Smith, Cecil. *The Great Hunger: Ireland 1845–1849.* New York: Harper & Row, 1963.

Miscellaneous Sources and Collections

A. BIBLIOGRAPHIES

Crown, James Tracey. *The Kennedy Literature: A Bibliographical Essay on John F. Kennedy*. New York: New York University Press, 1968.
Sable, Martin Howard. *A Bio-Bibliography of the Kennedy Family*. Metuchen, N.J.: Scarecrow, 1969.

B. WARREN COMMISSION PAPERS

Documents and evidence, including some testimony and some exhibits, but not all, pertaining to the Warren Commission's investigation of the assassination of John F. Kennedy. United States National Archives Records Group 272, Washington, D.C.

C. BOUVIER FAMILY PAPERS 1820–1983 in possession of John H. Davis and Maude Bouvier Davis.
Includes letters, birth, marriage, and death certificates, wills, diaries, divorce papers, financial records of the Bouviers since 1820.

D. SPECIAL COLLECTIONS

Significant material relating to the Kennedys may be found in the following library collections:
Franklin D. Roosevelt Library, Hyde Park, N.Y. (Extensive correspondence between President Roosevelt and Joseph P. Kennedy.)
Princeton University Library, Princeton, N.J. The papers of Arthur Krock (extensive correspondence between Arthur Krock and various members of the Kennedy family).
Princeton University Library, Princeton, N.J. The Seeley G. Mudd Manuscript Library. The Bernard M. Baruch papers (correspondence with and about Joseph P. Kennedy). The papers of Allen W. Dulles (some papers relating to the Kennedy administration).
The Lyndon Baines Johnson Library, Austin, Texas. (Correspondence, memoranda, etc., between Lyndon B. Johnson and John F. Kennedy.)
Library of Congress: The Stewart and Joseph Alsop pa-

pers. The James Landis papers. The Harold Ickes papers.
(Many references to the Kennedys in all three collections.)
Southeastern Louisiana University Library. Kennedy assassination section. Sims Memorial Library. Large collection of JFK assassination documents open to the public.
University of Wisconsin, Stevens Point Library JFK assassination collection. Learning Resources Center. Extensive collection of JFK assassination documents.

Magazine and Newspaper Articles

NOTE: *Thousands of newspaper and magazine articles have been written about the Kennedys. The following is a list of those that were particularly important sources for this book.*

Anderson, Jack. "Late Mobster's View of JFK Killing." *Washington Post,* October 23, 1978.

Brody, Jane. "Doctor Analyzes Kennedy Ailment." *New York Times,* July 11, 1967.

Cantwell, Robert. "Mr. Kennedy, the Chairman." *Fortune,* September 1937.

Coogan, Tim Pat. "It's Kennedy County Now!" *Irish Digest,* September 1973.

Crewdson, John M. "Mrs. Exner Plans a Book on Kennedy Friendship." *New York Times,* January 15, 1976.

"Day of the Dearos." Unsigned article on Honey Fitz in JFK Library.

De Deddt, Ralph F. "The First Chairman of the Securities Exchange Commission." *American Journal of Economics and Sociology.* Undated.

Gage, Nicholas. "Rosselli Called a Victim of Mafia Because of His Senate Testimony." *New York Times,* February 25, 1977.

Green, Abel. "Joe Kennedy's Film Career." *Variety,* November 26, 1969.

Jensen, Michael C. "Managing the Kennedy Millions." *New York Times,* June 12, 1977.

Klemesrud, Judy. "The Reaction Here Is Shock and Dismay." *New York Times,* October 19, 1968.

Laski, Harold J. "British Democracy and Mr. Kennedy." *Harper's,* April 1941.

Life. "The 'Little Man' is Bigger Than Ever: Louisiana Still Jumps for Mobster Marcello." An investigative report. April 10, 1970.

New York Post. "Chappaquiddick: Ted Has Been There Before." January 21, 1980.

New York Times. "Former French Ambassador Herve Alphand, in His Published Diary, Notes JFK Vulnerable for His Amorous Behavior." October 6, 1977.

―――. "Kennedys Are Satisfied on Murder Findings" (according to Eunice Kennedy Shriver). February 23, 1975.

―――. "Kennedy Friend Denies Plot Role." December 18, 1975.

―――. "Mrs. Onassis Said to Get 20 Million in a Pact with Christina Onassis." September 20, 1977.

People. "Two Worlds of a Kennedy" (about RFK Jr.). October 3, 1983.

―――. "David A. Kennedy, 1955–1984." May 14, 1984.

―――. "Ethel Kennedy, Behind a Brave Front, Fought to Maintain a Dynasty and a Home." May 14, 1984.

Rawls, Wendell. "F.B.I. Files Disclose Letter on Kennedy." *New York Times,* December 15, 1977.

Safire, William. "Murder Most Foul" (about murder of Sam Giancana). *New York Times,* December 22, 1975.

―――. "Put Your Dreams Away. The Sinatra Connections." *New York Times,* January 5, 1976.

―――. "All in the Family." *New York Times,* January 23, 1976 and January 29, 1976.

―――. "Frank and Jack and Sam and Judy." *New York Times,* June 13, 1977.

―――. "J. Edgar's Private Files." *New York Times,* December 15, 1977.

Time. "Profitless Paramount." July 27, 1936.

Vidal, Gore. "The Holy Family." *Esquire,* 1967.

Walton, Richard J. "Tough Guys in the Years of Kennedy's Presidency." *New York Times,* June 8, 1975.

Whalen, Richard J. "How Joe Kennedy Made His Millions." *Fortune,* January 1963.

Interviews and Conversations

From 1940 to 1983 the author has either formally interviewed or held informal conversations with the following people used as sources for this book:

Janet Auchincloss, Letitia Baldrige, George W. Ball, Bouvier Beale, Edith Bouvier Beale, Prof. G. Robert Blakey, John V. Bouvier, Jr., John V. Bouvier III, Kathleen Bouvier, Michel Bouvier, Colonel Frank Brooke, Charles Collingwood, Michelle Bouvier Crouse, John E. Davis, Maude Bouvier Davis, Ovid Demaris, George de Mohrenschildt, John Ficke, Thomas S. Gates, Eric F. Goldman, Patrick Grennan, Samuel Halpern, Richard Helms, Thomas Hughes, Nicholas Katzenbach, Edward M. Kennedy, Joan Kennedy, John F. Kennedy, Joseph P. Kennedy, Rose Fitzgerald Kennedy, J. Patrick Lannan, James T. Lee, David Lifton, Charles "Lucky" Luciano, Sylvia Meagher, Andrew Minihan, Jean Monnet, Philip Ober, Jacqueline Kennedy Onassis, David E. Powers, Michelle Bouvier Putnam, Harrington Putnam, Cornelius Ryan, Mary Ryan, Mary Anne Ryan, Gloria Swanson, Harris Wofford. Other persons interviewed, or spoken with off the record, have asked that their names not be revealed.

Author's Files on the Bouvier and Kennedy Families

1. The Bouvier Family—1758–1984

   In addition to the above-cited Bouvier family papers, the author has, for this book, drawn upon his files of Bouvier genealogical documents, notes, records of interviews, and impressions already used as a source material for his 1969 book, *The Bouviers*. These include impressions of various members of the Bouvier family the author knew and various Bouvier family gatherings the author attended.

2. The Kennedy Family—1953–1984

   The author has collected material on the Kennedy family ever since Jacqueline Bouvier's marriage to John F. Kennedy in 1953. This includes, in addition to thousands of newspaper and magazine articles, accounts of the Kennedy-Bouvier courtship and wedding, impressions of the various Kennedy inaugural events the author attended January 19 and 20, 1961, impressions of the various events associated with the funeral, burial, and wake of President Kennedy the author attended on November 25, 1963, and various encounters with members of the Kennedy family and entourage during Robert F. Kennedy's campaign for the Democratic nomination in 1968 and Edward M. Kennedy's campaign for the Democratic nomination in 1980. The author also visited the Kennedys' Irish relations in Dunganstown, county Wexford, in October–November 1980.

The Campaign of Senator Edward M. Kennedy for the Democratic Nomination for President in 1980

Sources for Part 7, dealing with Senator Edward Kennedy's campaign for the Democratic presidential nomination in 1980 were as follows:

1. Interviews with Rick Stearns, number four man in hierarchy of Kennedy's campaign managers. Interviews conducted by author's chief researcher, Timothy James, in Washington campaign headquarters, on June 25 and 26.
2. History of Kennedy's campaign. At the author's request, Mr. James wrote a complete history of the campaign, which he followed day by day. The monograph is the basis for chapters 69 and 70.
3. The 1980 Democratic Convention. Mr. James, a delegate to the convention from New York, provided the author with a full account of the proceedings of the convention.
4. The author attended a number of campaign events, which are described in the text, at which he had opportunities to talk with Senator Kennedy and various members of his staff.

Note: Books and articles dealing with the campaign are listed in the bibliography.

Resources in the John Fitzgerald Kennedy Library, Boston

LIBRARY CATALOGUES AND PAMPHLETS AVAILABLE ON REQUEST

The Kennedy Collection: A Subject Guide, a 299-page book catalogue.
Historical Materials in the John F. Kennedy Library.
Guide to the Use of Historical Materials in the John F. Kennedy Library.
The John F. Kennedy Audiovisual Collection.
John F. Kennedy: A Reading List.
The John F. Kennedy Library and History Program and the Use of Oral History Interviews.

THE KENNEDY AND FITZGERALD GENEALOGICAL ARCHIVE

Extensive collection of papers, documents, and letters relating to the ancestors of President Kennedy, including birth, marriage, and death certificates, wills, former addresses, and personal chronologies.

THE PAPERS OF PRESIDENT JOHN F. KENNEDY

The following categories of JFK papers are available to the public at the JFK Library. Note some files are closed.
1. Personal Papers
   Biographical materials, Harvard records, correspondence, 1943–1952, manuscripts, notes
2. Prepresidential Papers, 1947–1960
   House of Representatives files, 1947–1952
   Campaign files, 1946 campaign, 1952 campaign, 1958 campaign
   Senate files, 1953–1960
   1960 campaign files
   Transition files
3. Presidential Papers, 1961–1963
   President's office files (excluding recordings)
   National Security files (major portions closed)
   White House central files
   White House social files (closed)
   Miscellaneous presidential files
   White House Staff files (many closed)

President Kennedy's outgoing correspondence (closed)
Presidential recordings (closed)

PAPERS OF THE POSTASSASSINATION PERIOD—1963–1964

COLLECTIONS OF PERSONAL AND ORGANIZATIONAL PAPERS

Includes 1200 linear feet of Robert F. Kennedy papers, 1937–
1968; John Kenneth Galbraith papers, 1930–1963; Arthur M.
Schlesinger papers, 1948–1965; Theodore Sorensen papers,
1953–1964; Theodore H. White papers, including draft manuscripts of *The Making of the President 1960, 1964, 1968.*

RECORDS OF GOVERNMENT AGENCIES

ORAL HISTORY INTERVIEWS

Includes interviews of Leonard Bernstein, Chester Bowles,
Arleigh Burke, Chiang Kai-Shek, Cardinal Cushing, William
J. Fulbright, Grace de Monaco, Averell Harriman, Arthur
Krock, Henry Luce, Robert S. McNamara, James Reston,
Dean Rusk, and Wernher von Braun.

PAPERS, TAPES, AND ORAL INTERVIEWS CLOSED TO THE PUBLIC

While many papers and recordings of members of the Kennedy
family, both personal and official, are available to the public
in the John Fitzgerald Kennedy Library, many important ones
are closed. Likewise, while many papers and recordings of
Kennedy aides, friends, cabinet members, ambassadors, and
White House staffers are available to the public, many
important ones are closed. So that scholars and writers will
not make useless trips to the library, the following is a selection of what remains closed to the public as of January 1,
1983:

1. Three hundred twenty-five secretly taped conversations
   held in the White House between President Kennedy and
   various officials, friends, and relatives, January 20, 1961
   to November 19, 1963. President Kennedy also taped
   hundreds of telephone conversations from July 1962 through
   November 1963. The recording system was removed from
   the Oval Office the day of his assassination.

   In February 1982, the *Washington Post* obtained a twenty-
   nine-page log of the 325 tapes. According to the log, among

those individuals secretly taped by the President were the following:

Jacqueline Kennedy
Robert F. Kennedy
Robert Wagner, mayor of New York
Henry Kissinger, special counsel on foreign affairs
Dean Rusk, secretary of state
McGeorge Bundy, national security advisor
John McCone, CIA director
Lyndon Johnson, vice president
Adlai Stevenson, ambassador to UN
Barry Goldwater, senator from Arizona
Hubert Humphrey, senator from Minnesota
Dwight D. Eisenhower, former President
Gen. Douglas MacArthur, retired general
John McCormack, Speaker of the House
William Fulbright, senator from Arkansas
Mike Mansfield, Senate majority leader
George Meany, head of the CIO
Henry Jackson, senator from Washington
Ross Barnett, governor of Mississippi
Pat Brown, governor of California
Edward M. Kennedy
Archibald Cox, later special Watergate prosecutor

In the twenty-nine-page log of the tapes several entries of conversations are entirely canceled out, with no explanations. As of July 1, 1983, nearly twenty years after Kennedy's death, only 5 percent of these tapes has been made public. The JFK Library contends that 75 percent of the recorded material involves national security. Also closed:

2. John F. Kennedy financial records.
3. Chronological file. Outgoing correspondence of President Kennedy.
4. White House social files and other records of Mrs. John F. Kennedy and the White House social staff.
5. White House telephone memoranda and toll tickets.
6. Janet Travell, physician to the President. Kennedy medical records.
7. Paul B. Fay, Jr. Personal correspondence between Fay and President Kennedy.

8. Richard Goodwin, assistant special counsel to the President. Memoranda, reports, and correspondence from the White House and State Department.
9. Edward M. Kennedy. Papers 1962–1975.
10. Joseph P. Kennedy. Ambassadorial business and family papers (including all financial records) 1920–1969.
11. Rose F. Kennedy. Family papers, including research with background material for writing of autobiography *Times to Remember.*
12. Frank Mankiewicz, press secretary to Robert F. Kennedy. Correspondence, memoranda, etc.
13. Jacqueline Kennedy Onassis. Correspondence and assorted materials.
14. David Powers, special assistant to the White House and political aide of President Kennedy. Correspondence, memoranda, etc.
15. Walter Sheridan, author and head of Justice Department's "get Hoffa" squad under Robert F. Kennedy. Background materials for writing of *The Fall and Rise of Jimmy Hoffa.*
16. Stephen Smith, brother-in-law of President Kennedy and chief executive of Joseph P. Kennedy Enterprises. Files of political activities in preparation for presidential campaigns of John, Robert, and Edward Kennedy.
17. William vanden Heuvel, aide to Robert Kennedy. Papers, correspondence, campaign materials, 1963–1968.
18. U.S. Secret Service. White House appointment slips.
19. Oral history interviews:
    a. Lemoyne K. Billings, friend of JFK, 63 pp.
    b. McGeorge Bundy, special assistant to the President for national security affairs, 1961–1966, 7 pp. (portions closed).
    c. Lord Harlech, friend of JFK, 26 pp.
    d. Robert F. Kennedy, attorney general of the U.S., 1026 pp. (portions closed).
    e. Dean Rusk, secretary of state, 1961–1969, 401 pp.
    f. Terry Sanford, governor of North Carolina, 55 pp.
    g. George Smathers, senator from Florida and friend of JFK, 68 pp. (portions closed).
    h. Theodore Sorensen, special counsel to the President, 238 pp. (portions closed).

Appendix I

A KENNEDY FAMILY CHRONOLOGY, 1823–1984*

1823	Patrick Kennedy, born to Patrick and Mary Johanna Kennedy, in Dunganstown, Ireland.
1845	Potato famine strikes Ireland.
1848	Patrick Kennedy, cooper, emigrates to the United States.
1849	Patrick Kennedy, cooper, marries Bridget Murphy in Boston.
1854	Michael Hannon, laborer, marries Mary Ann Fitzgerald in Boston.
1857	Thomas Fitzgerald, peddler, marries Rose Cox in Boston.
1858	Son, Patrick J., born to Patrick and Bridget Kennedy in East Boston.
	Patrick Kennedy dies.
1863	John F. Fitzgerald born in North End.
1881	Patrick J. Kennedy works as lager beer retailer in East Boston.
1882	Patrick J. Kennedy buys saloon on Haymarket Square.

*The primary source for this chronology is a time line on the Kennedy family in the John Fitzgerald Kennedy Library in Boston. The author has made changes and additions where appropriate and has brought the chronology up to date.

1884	Kennedy and Quigley, liquors, opens at 2 Elbow Street and 81 Border Street, East Boston.
1885	Patrick J. Kennedy wins first of five terms as state representative for East Boston.
1887	P. J. Kennedy marries Mary Hickey.
1888	Joseph Patrick Kennedy born in East Boston to P. J. Kennedy and Mary Hickey.
	Bridget Kennedy dies.
1889	John F. Fitzgerald, customs clerk, weds Mary Josephine Hannon.
1890	Rose Fitzgerald born in North End to John F. Fitzgerald and Mary Hannon.
1891	John F. Fitzgerald elected to common council from Ward 6.
1892	P. J. Kennedy and John F. Fitzgerald elected to state senate.
1894	John F. Fitzgerald elected to first of three terms in U.S. Congress.
1895	P. J. Kennedy helps form Columbia Trust Company.
1900	P. J. Kennedy appointed election commissioner.
1901	John F. Fitzgerald purchases *The Republic*, a Boston Catholic weekly.
1902	P. J. Kennedy appointed wire commissioner.
1905	John F. Fitzgerald elected mayor of Boston.
1907	Mayor Fitzgerald defeated in reelection attempt.
1910	John F. Fitzgerald elected again as mayor.
1914	Joseph P. Kennedy and Rose Fitzgerald married.
1915 July	Joseph P. Kennedy, Jr., born in Hull, Massachusetts.
1917 May	John F. Kennedy born in Brookline.
1918	Joseph P. Kennedy serves as assistant general manager of Fore River shipyards.
Sept.	Rosemary Kennedy born in Brookline.
1919 Jan.	Joseph P. Kennedy joins brokerage firm of Hayden, Stone and Co.
1920 Feb.	Kathleen Kennedy born in Brookline.
1924 May	Patricia Kennedy born in Brookline.
1925 Nov.	Robert F. Kennedy born in Brookline.
1926 Jan.	Joseph P. Kennedy buys into films; produces seventy-six films in two years.

1928 Feb.	Jean Kennedy born in Boston.
1928 Sept.	Kennedy family moves to New York.
1929 Jan.	Kennedys purchase summer home in Hyannis Port.
May	P. J. Kennedy dies.
1932 Feb.	Edward M. Kennedy born in Boston.
June	Joseph P. Kennedy works for FDR's nomination at Democratic convention.
1933 Sept.	Joseph P. Kennedy becomes U.S. distributor for Scotch whiskey and British gin.
1934 July	Joseph P. Kennedy appointed chairman of new Securities and Exchange Commission.
1937 Mar.	Joseph P. Kennedy appointed chairman of Maritime Commission.
1938 Mar.	Joseph P. Kennedy takes post as U.S. ambassador to Court of St. James's's.
May	Rosemary, Kathleen, and Mrs. Kennedy presented at Court of St. James's's.
1940 June	John F. Kennedy graduates *cum laude* from Harvard.
July	*Why England Slept* published.
Nov.	Ambassador Kennedy submits resignation to Roosevelt.
1941 Jan.	Joseph P. Kennedy opposes lend-lease.
Sept.	John F. Kennedy joins the Navy.
1943 June	Kathleen Kennedy returns to England to work with Red Cross.
Aug.	PT-109 rammed by Japanese destroyer in South Pacific.
1944 May	Kathleen Kennedy and Lord Hartington married.
Aug.	Lt. Joseph P. Kennedy, Jr., killed on mission in England.
Sept.	Lord Hartington killed in action in France.
1945 June	Joseph P. Kennedy, Jr., awarded Navy Cross posthumously.
July	Joseph P. Kennedy buys Chicago's Merchandise Mart.
1946 Feb.	Robert F. Kennedy reports for duty on *USS Joseph P. Kennedy, Jr.*
Apr.	JFK announces for Congress.
June	JFK wins primary with 42 percent of vote.

Aug.	Joseph P. Kennedy Jr. Foundation is established.
Nov.	JFK elected to House of Representatives.
1947 Feb.	Eunice Kennedy heads juvenile delinquency project at Department of Justice.
Apr.	JFK opposes Taft-Hartley labor bill.
July	Joseph P. Kennedy named to Hoover Commission on Organization of Executive Branch.
Oct.	Joseph P. Kennedy disagrees with JFK; calls Truman Doctrine dangerous public policy.
1948 Feb.	JFK cosponsors National Veterans Housing Conference.
May	Kathleen Kennedy Hartington killed in air crash in France.
June	Leading Massachusetts Democrats urge JFK to run for governor.
Nov.	JFK reelected to House unopposed.
1949 Jan.	JFK condemns U.S. policymakers for "loss" of China.
Oct.	JFK introduces bills for low-rent public housing and aid to public and private schools.
1950 Jan.	JFK receives honorary degree from Notre Dame.
June	Robert F. Kennedy marries Ethel Skakel.
Oct.	John F. Fitzgerald dies at 87.
1951 Feb.	JFK visits Europe to study U.S. role in NATO's defense.
Aug.	JFK proposes cutting aid to Africa and Near East; cites waste and inefficiency.
Nov.	JFK, Robert F. Kennedy, and Patricia Kennedy travel around world.
1952 Apr.	JFK announces he will run for U.S. Senate.
June	Robert F. Kennedy becomes JFK's campaign manager.
Aug.	JFK promises in campaign to "do more" for Massachusetts.
Oct.	Rose Kennedy greets 50,000 women at receptions during her son's campaign.
Nov.	JFK elected senator, defeating Henry Cabot Lodge, Jr., by narrow margin.
1953 Mar.	JFK proposes UN-sponsored plebiscite for Trieste.
May	Eunice Kennedy married to R. Sargent Shriver.

	In major Senate speeches, JFK proposes economic program for New England.
July	Robert F. Kennedy resigns after six months as attorney for Senator Joseph McCarthy's subcommittee.
Sept.	JFK, Jacqueline Bouvier married in Newport, Rhode Island.
1954 Jan.	JFK backs bill for St. Lawrence Seaway over heavy opposition in Massachusetts.
Apr.	Patricia Kennedy married to Peter Lawford.
	Robert F. Kennedy is Democratic counsel in Army-McCarthy Senate hearings.
	JFK urges France offer independence to Indochina.
Oct.	JFK undergoes complex back surgery; nearly loses his life.
1955 Feb.	JFK undergoes second back operation; writes *Profiles in Courage* during convalescence.
May	JFK urges increase in immigration quotas.
Aug.	Robert F. Kennedy travels extensively in Soviet Union with Justice William O. Douglas.
1956 Mar.	JFK opposes radical changes in electoral college system.
	JFK endorses Adlai Stevenson for Democratic presidential nomination.
May	Jean Kennedy married to Stephen E. Smith.
June	JFK receives honorary degree from Harvard.
	JFK pushes for reform in military academy appointments.
Aug.	JFK narrowly loses bid for Democratic vice presidential nomination.
1957 Jan.	JFK appointed to Senate Foreign Relations Committee.
	Robert F. Kennedy appointed counsel to labor racketeering investigation.
May	JFK wins Pulitzer Prize for *Profiles in Courage*.
June	JFK elected to Harvard Board of Overseers.
July	JFK calls on France to free Algeria.
Nov.	Caroline Kennedy is born.
1958 May	JFK's proposal to extend unemployment benefits defeated in Senate.

Aug. Robert F. Kennedy battles Teamsters' Jimmy Hoffa in televised labor rackets hearings.

JFK claims Soviet missile gains shifting world balance of power.

Nov. JFK reelected to Senate by record 874,608 votes.

Edward M. Kennedy married to Joan Bennett.

1959 Jan. JFK leads fight to end loyalty oath requirements for students.

Feb. JFK opposes federal aid to parochial schools.

Apr. First major strategy meeting for 1960 presidential campaign; Robert F. Kennedy designated JFK's campaign manager.

Sept. Congress passes labor-management reform bill; JFK is Senate manager.

Oct. JFK's *A Nation of Immigrants* published.

1960 Jan. JFK announces candidacy for President.

Apr. JFK beats Humphrey in Wisconsin primary.

May JFK defeats Humphrey in West Virginia primary.

July Nixon and Lodge win GOP nominations.

JFK nominated at Democratic convention.

JFK picks LBJ as running mate.

Sept. JFK faces Catholic issue in Houston.

JFK debates Nixon.

Nov. JFK wins presidential election.

John F. Kennedy, Jr., is born.

Dec. President-elect Kennedy appoints Robert F. Kennedy as attorney general.

1961 Jan. JFK inaugurated.

JFK signs order increasing surplus food to jobless Americans.

First live telecast of a presidential news conference.

Mar. Peace Corps established; R. Sargent Shriver named director.

JFK announces Alliance for Progress.

JFK warns cease-fire must precede negotiations for a neutral Laos.

Apr. RFK deports Carlos Marcello to Guatemala.

Attorney General Robert F. Kennedy proposes antiracketeering legislation, launches war on organized crime.

Bay of Pigs invasion fails; JFK accepts the blame.

JFK increases U.S. military mission in Vietnam.

May   Gallup Poll: 83 percent of Americans approve of JFK's performance as President.

RFK sends 400 U.S. marshals to protect Freedom Riders in Montgomery.

JFK urges national goal of landing American on moon before 1970.

July   JFK urges new physical fitness programs in schools.

JFK calls up reserves in response to Berlin crisis.

Aug.   JFK signs Cape Cod National Seashore bill.

Sept.   ICC approves RFK petition banning interstate bus segregation.

First federal program established to combat juvenile delinquency.

JFK challenges Soviets to "peace race."

Nov.   Pablo Casals performs in special White House concert.

Food for Peace director, George McGovern, expedites grain to starving in Africa.

Operation Mongoose, a covert war against Cuba, is launched.

Dec.   At Football Hall of Fame banquet, JFK warns U.S. is becoming "a nation of spectators."

Joseph P. Kennedy, Sr., suffers a stroke.

JFK establishes Commission on the Status of Women.

1962 Jan.   JFK reports 1961 rise in prices held to less than 1 percent.

Feb.   Jacqueline Kennedy hosts first televised tour of White House.

RFK acts as U.S. emissary in Indonesian-Dutch territorial dispute.

Mar.   JFK announces resumption of nuclear testing in absence of treaty.

First presidential consumer protection message sent to Congress.

Apr.   Steel companies forced to rescind price increases.

Forty-nine Nobel Prize winners entertained at White House dinner.

May   Secretary of Interior Stewart Udall presides over White House conference on conservation.

RFK indicts Jimmy Hoffa under Taft-Hartley Act.

June   JFK proposes $2.5 billion business tax cut to stimulate economy.

July   JFK urges freer trade with a united western Europe.

Rose Kennedy serves as hostess during visit of president of Ecuador.

JFK signs welfare amendments providing new services to families.

Aug.   JFK meets with representatives of American Indian nations.

Meeting of Special Group Augmented; stepped-up Mongoose activity is decided upon and "liquidation" of Castro is discussed.

JFK signs Communication Satellite Act.

Sept.   RFK leads fight to enroll first black at University of Mississippi.

Oct.   Aerial photos show Soviet missiles in Cuba.

JFK orders naval blockade of Cuba.

U.S. prepares for possible military action in Cuba.

U.S.S.R. agrees to remove missiles from Cuba.

Nov.   JFK bars discrimination in federal housing.

Operation Mongoose ends and Special Group Augmented takes over covert operations against Cuba.

Dec.   JFK and British Prime Minister Macmillan discuss Skybolt missile project cancellation.

RFK concludes negotiations to release Bay of Pigs prisoners.

1963 Jan.   Edward M. Kennedy takes office as junior senator from Massachusetts.

JFK proposes major tax cut to strengthen all segments of economy.

Feb.   JFK delivers congressional message on mental illness and mental retardation.

JFK proposes job program for youth and domestic "peace corps."

Mar.   JFK urges states to pass Twenty-fourth Amendment barring poll tax.

Apr.   JFK delivers address at Boston College centennial ceremonies.

May   JFK meets with Canadian Prime Minister Pearson at Cape Cod.

RFK initiates discussions on voluntary desegregation of public facilities in the south.

RFK indicts Jimmy Hoffa for fraud.

June   At American University JFK proposes "strategy of peace" to end cold war.

JFK sends comprehensive civil rights bill to Congress.

JFK tours Ireland; visits relatives.

July   JFK has audience with Pope Paul VI.

JFK proposes eliminating immigration quota system.

Aug.   Patrick Bouvier Kennedy born; dies two days later.

JFK signs bill averting nationwide railroad strike.

"Hot line" between Kremlin and White House goes into operation.

Sept.   RFK testifies before Senate committee on organized crime.

Oct.   JFK signs ratification of nuclear test ban treaty.

JFK approves sale of 5 million tons of wheat to U.S.S.R.

JFK signs first major act to combat mental illness and mental retardation.

JFK dedicates Robert Frost Library at Amherst College.

Nov.   Vietnam Premier Diem and his brother are assassinated following a coup encouraged by JFK.

JFK holds sixty-fourth news conference since taking office 1028 days before.

JFK delivers an anti-Castro speech in Miami.

President and Mrs. Kennedy arrive in Texas for political tour.

JFK assassinated in Dallas. Lee Harvey Oswald, the suspected assassin, is killed by Jack Ruby.

1964 Jan.   RFK in Asia; negotiates cease-fire between Indonesia and Malaysia.

Apr.   RFK testifies for antipoverty bill.

May   RFK urges support of civil rights bill in Georgia speech.

June   Edward M. Kennedy suffers broken back in small-plane crash during Senate campaign.

Enthusiastic crowds greet RFK in West Berlin and Warsaw.

Aug.   RFK announces candidacy for New York Senate seat.

Sept.   Stephen E. Smith named RFK campaign manager.

Warren Commission issues report on JFK assassination, declaring Oswald was assassin, acting alone.

Nov.   RFK elected to U.S. Senate by 719,693 votes.

1965 Jan.   RFK and Edward M. Kennedy first brothers to serve in Senate together since Dwight and Theodore Foster in 1803.

Mar.   RFK climbs Mount Kennedy in Yukon.

Apr.   RFK urges LBJ to suspend bombing of North Vietnam.

June   In first major Senate speech RFK asks for halt in spread of nuclear weapons.

Nov.   RFK visits Latin America.

1966 Jan.   RFK proposes program to stimulate employment and community development in urban ghettos.

Mar.   RFK criticizes delay of legal assistance programs for New York City poor.

June   RFK tours Africa, condemns apartheid.

RFK successfully leads reform forces in New York surrogate court election.

Aug.   RFK charges Vietnam war decreases urban aid.

Oct.   RFK campaigns for Democratic candidates throughout the nation.

Dec.   RFK announces community development project in Brooklyn's Bedford-Stuyvesant.

1967 Feb.   RFK proposes new Communist China policy.

Mar.   RFK attacks Vietnam war escalation.

Apr.   RFK inspects hunger conditions in Mississippi delta.

May   RFK calls for renewed commitment to principles of Alliance for Progress.

July   RFK visits East Harlem after riot.

Sept.	RFK offers bill to curb cigarette ads on radio and TV.
Dec.	RFK holds hearings on Indian education needs.
1968 Jan.	RFK disclaims presidential candidacy.
Feb.	RFK assails Vietnam war; condemns bombing and deception.
Mar.	RFK attends mass marking the end of Chavez twenty-day fast.
	RFK announces candidacy for President.
	RFK carries campaign to south and west.
May	RFK wins Indiana and District of Columbia primaries.
	RFK wins in Nebraska.
	McCarthy beats Kennedy in Oregon.
June	RFK wins in California and South Dakota.
	RFK assassinated in Los Angeles. Sirhan Sirhan is charged with the murder.
Oct.	Jacqueline Kennedy marries Aristotle S. Onassis on Skorpios, Greece.
1969 July	Edward M. Kennedy has auto accident on Chappaquiddick Island; Mary J. Kopechne killed.
Nov.	Joseph P. Kennedy dies.
1970 Nov.	Edward M. Kennedy reelected to U.S. Senate.
1971 Jan.	Senator Edward M. Kennedy loses post as assistant Senate majority leader.
1973	Cape Kennedy renamed Cape Canaveral.
1975	Senate Select Committee on Intelligence discovers CIA-Mafia and AM/LASH plots against Castro during JFK administration.
1976 Sept.	House Select Committee on Assassinations is formed to reopen the investigation of the assassination of John F. Kennedy.
Nov.	Edward M. Kennedy reelected to U.S. Senate.
1977 May	Senator Edward M. Kennedy attacks President Carter on health reforms.
1979 Mar.	House Select Committee on Assassinations issues its final report on the assassination of John F. Kennedy, concluding that Kennedy was "probably killed as a result of a conspiracy."

Apr.   Senator Edward M. Kennedy attacks President Carter on deregulation of oil and gas.

Oct.   Dedication of John Fitzgerald Kennedy Library in Boston.

Nov.   Senator Edward M. Kennedy announces candidacy for presidency.

1980 Aug.   Senator Edward M. Kennedy is defeated for the Democratic party nomination by President Carter.

Oct.   Mr. and Mrs. Joseph P. Kennedy III announce birth of twins, Matthew Rauch Kennedy and Joseph P. Kennedy IV.

1981 Jan.   Senator Edward M. Kennedy loses chairmanship of Senate Judiciary Committee.

Senator and Mrs. Edward M. Kennedy announce plans to divorce.

1982 Dec.   Senator Edward M. Kennedy withdraws from 1984 presidential election.

1983 Nov.   Memorial service held in Washington to commemorate twentieth anniversary of death of John F. Kennedy. Edward M. Kennedy and Caroline Kennedy deliver eulogies.

1984 Apr.   David A. Kennedy, third oldest son of Robert and Ethel Kennedy, dies in Palm Beach.

July   Edward M. Kennedy, Jr., addresses Democratic National Convention in San Francisco.

Sept.   Mr. and Mrs. Robert F. Kennedy, Jr., announce birth of a son, Robert F. Kennedy III.

Appendix II

CHRONOLOGY:
THE UNITED STATES, JOHN F. KENNEDY,
ROBERT F. KENNEDY,
ORGANIZED CRIME, AND CUBA, 1959–1979*

1959

January 1	Fidel Castro takes over Cuban government. Batista and his personal aides leave Cuba.
December 11	CIA Director Allen Dulles approves "thorough consideration be given to the elimination of Castro."

*The primary sources for this chronology are the chronologies in two reports of the United States Senate Select Committee to Study Governmental Operations with Respect to Intelligence Activities: the *Interim Report on Alleged Assassination Plots Involving Foreign Leaders* and Book V of the final report, *The Investigation of the Assassination of President John F. Kennedy: Performance of the Intelligence Agencies*. The author has made changes and additions where appropriate and has brought the chronology up to date.

1960

Early February
John F. Kennedy is introduced to Judith Campbell by Frank Sinatra in Las Vegas and allegedly begins a relationship with her.

Late March
Judith Campbell allegedly begins a relationship with Sam Giancana, boss of the Chicago underworld.

March–December
John F. Kennedy carries on an affair with Judith Campbell. Miss Campbell is also seeing Sam Giancana on a regular basis.

August
CIA Deputy Director of Plans Richard Bissell and CIA Chief of Security Sheffield Edwards have discussion concerning use of underworld figures in assassinating Castro. Certain figures in organized crime are already involved in a plot to kill Castro.

Late September
Bissell and Edwards brief Dulles and CIA Deputy Director Charles Cabell about operations against Castro.

Initial meeting is held between John Roselli, a Las Vegas underworld figure, Robert Maheu, a private investigator, and CIA support chief for the purpose of planning assassination of Castro. Roselli then asks Giancana to participate in the plot. Giancana agrees and approaches Santo Trafficante, Jr., boss of the Florida underworld, who agrees to recruit a Cuban "asset" to carry out the murder.

A subsequent meeting takes place in Florida and includes Roselli's coconspirators, Sam Giancana and Santo Trafficante, Jr., boss of the Florida underworld.

October 18
Hoover sends memo to CIA about Giancana's involvement in Castro assassination plot. Apparently FBI does not yet know CIA is behind the plot.

November
John F. Kennedy is elected President of the United States.

| Late November | Dulles briefs President-elect Kennedy on plans for Cuban exiles and CIA to invade Cuba and probably alludes to plot to assassinate Castro (according to Bissell) in circumlocutious terms, without telling him Giancana, Roselli, and Trafficante are involved. |

| Throughout 1959, 1960 | Jack Ruby, Dallas nightclub operator, is active in gunrunning activities in Cuba, in close association with organized crime. On one of his trips to Havana he reportedly visits Trafficante in a Cuban prison. |

1961

| January 20 | President Kennedy succeeds President Eisenhower. |

| February–April | President Kennedy is receiving an average of two telephone calls a week from Judith Campbell, who is also seeing CIA-Mafia conspirator Sam Giancana. |

| March 31 | CIA approves sending carbines to Dominican dissidents to help in plot to assassinate President Trujillo. |

| March, April | Final plans are drawn up for CIA–Cuban exiles invasion of Cuba. They receive President Kennedy's approval. |

Early April	Roselli passes poison pills with which to kill Castro to a Cuban associate of Trafficante in Miami. Sam Giancana is also in Miami with Santo Trafficante, Jr. Assassination attempt is, in Bissell's words, "an auxiliary operation" of the Bay of Pigs invasion.
	Judith Campbell sees Sam Giancana and John Roselli.
	Cuban fails in attempt to poison Castro.

April 4	Attorney General Robert Kennedy deports New Orleans underworld boss Carlos Marcello to Guatemala. Marcello, a friend of Trafficante, had been active in anti-Castro movement.
April 15–17	Bay of Pigs invasion fails. President Kennedy accepts blame.
April 18–20	President Kennedy meets with Cuban exile leaders, including Cuban hired by the underworld to kill Castro.
Late April, early May	President Kennedy and Judith Campbell allegedly meet for first time since Kennedy became President. Miss Campbell continues seeing Sam Giancana. She now also sees Roselli, whom she met again with Giancana in early April after not having seen him for several years. According to Miss Campbell, President Kennedy was aware of her relationship with Sam Giancana.
May 22	Hoover sends memorandum to Attorney General Robert Kennedy noting CIA had used Giancana in "clandestine efforts" against Castro.
May 30	President Trujillo is assassinated in Dominican Republic by dissidents armed by the CIA.
May to December	Judith Campbell allegedly visits President Kennedy in White House at least twenty times. She continues seeing Giancana and Roselli.
October 5	National Security Action Memorandum 100 directs assessment of potential courses of action "if Castro were removed from the Cuban scene."
November	Operation Mongoose, a covert war against Cuba, is launched. Robert Kennedy is named "supreme commander." CIA's JM/WAVE station in Miami becomes second largest CIA station in the world.

November 9	President Kennedy tells Tad Szulc that he is under pressure from advisors to order Castro's assassination, but does not name advisors.
November 29	Kennedy fires Allen Dulles, who is succeeded as director of the CIA by John McCone. Deputy Director of the CIA Gen. Charles Cabell is also dismissed.
December 9, 11, 21	FBI electronic surveillance overhears evidence of Giancana "donation" to Kennedy presidential campaign through Frank Sinatra and Joseph P. Kennedy. J. Edgar Hoover informs Attorney General Robert F. Kennedy.

1962

January	President Kennedy orders "massive Mongoose activity" against Cuba.
February 19	Richard Helms succeeds Bissell as CIA deputy director of plans.
February 27	J. Edgar Hoover informs Attorney General Robert F. Kennedy that Judith Campbell has been phoning the White House, adding that Miss Campbell is a friend of Sam Giancana and John Roselli.
March 22	J. Edgar Hoover has lunch with President Kennedy at the White House and informs him of Judith Campbell's connections with Sam Giancana and John Roselli. After the luncheon Kennedy places his last telephone call to Miss Campbell from the White House.
April	CIA's William Harvey establishes contact with John Roselli and reactivates plan to assassinate Castro.
Late April	Harvey passes poison pills to Roselli in Miami (the second attempt).

May 7   CIA's Houston and Edwards brief Attorney General Kennedy on pre–Bay of Pigs underworld assassination plots. Kennedy does not object to plots, only to the use in those plots of Mafia figures he is currently investigating. CIA does not tell Kennedy that the underworld assassination plots will continue.

May 10   Attorney General Kennedy tells J. Edgar Hoover that the CIA has used underworld figures in an effort to assassinate Castro. Kennedy realizes they are the same criminals Judith Campbell has been seeing.

Late June   John F. Kennedy breaks off relationship with Judith Campbell. She still continues to see Giancana and Roselli.

July, August   William Harvey decides to stop using Sam Giancana in plan to kill Castro. He retains Roselli, however.

August 10   Meeting of Special Group Augmented is held at which "liquidation" of Castro is discussed. SGA recommends increased Mongoose activity.

September   Roselli informs Harvey the poison pills are still with "asset" in Cuba.

Carlos Marcello allegedly threatens the life of President Kennedy. Santo Trafficante allegedly tells Jose Aleman Kennedy "is going to be hit."

September 29   Teamster official Edward G. Partin informs Justice Department that Jimmy Hoffa is planning to murder Robert Kennedy.

October 4   Robert Kennedy advises Special Group Augmented that President Kennedy wants more priority given to operations against Castro regime.

October 22–28   Cuban missile crisis. JFK orders naval blockade of Cuba. U.S.S.R. agrees to remove missiles from Cuba.

November	Operation Mongoose ends.
December	Special Group takes over covert operations against Cuba.
	Robert Kennedy steps up investigation of Giancana. The FBI harasses Judith Campbell.

1963

Early 1963	William Harvey tells underworld figures the CIA is no longer interested in using them to assassinate Castro. AM/LASH plot against Castro is revived, using Castro government official Rolando Cubela, an associate of the Cuban "asset" who had been recruited by Santo Trafficante, Jr., for first CIA-Mafia attempt against Castro.
March 18	Attack on a Soviet vessel off the northern coast of Cuba by members of Alpha 66, assisted by members of the Second National Front of Escambray, reportedly occurs.
March 26	Attack on a Soviet vessel by members of Commandos L-66, another anti-Castro group, reportedly occurs.
April	Special Group discusses the contingency of Castro's death.
April 25	It is announced in papers that President Kennedy will visit Dallas in November.
May–September	Lee Harvey Oswald moves to New Orleans; becomes involved with Fair Play for Cuba Committee. He contacts anti-Castro Cubans as well, attempting to infiltrate their ranks and meets with David Ferrie, an associate of Carlos Marcello, who reportedly participated in Bay of Pigs invasion and is militantly anti-Kennedy.

Mid 1963   Series of meetings among major leaders of the anti-Castro movement.

June 19   Special Group decides to step up covert operations against Cuba.

July 24   Ten Cuban exiles arrive in New Orleans from Miami and join training camp north of New Orleans. This training camp is directed by the same individuals who were previously involved in procuring dynamite for the exiles' anti-Castro activities. "A," a lifelong friend of AM/LASH, had helped procure the dynamite. Lee Harvey Oswald is in New Orleans and may have learned of Castro assassination plot at this time.

Late July   Carlos Bringuier is requested to assist exiles at the training camp in returning to Miami. Oswald attempts to penetrate Bringuier's group.

July 31   The FBI seizes more than a ton of dynamite, twenty bomb casings, napalm material, and other devices at a Cuban exile's home in the New Orleans area. Articles appear in the *New Orleans Times-Picayune* on August 1, 2, and 4, 1963.

August 16   *Chicago Sun-Times* carries an article that reports CIA had dealings with the underworld figure Sam Giancana. Helms then informs McCone of the CIA operation against Castro involving Giancana, and tells him it involved assassination.

August   Oswald distributes pro-Castro leaflets in New Orleans and makes two broadcasts in behalf of the Castro regime. He is arrested and jailed for disturbing the peace. An associate of a Marcello lieutenant pays his bail.

         According to FBI report, a Latin American military officer attends a Cuban exile group meeting and talks of assassination.

Early September

Talks between the Cuban delegate to the United Nations, Carlos Lechuga, and a U.S. delegate, William Attwood, are proposed by the Cubans.

September 7

CIA case officers, after their first meeting with AM/LASH since prior to the October 1962 missile crisis, cable headquarters that AM/LASH is interested in attempting an "inside job" against Castro and is awaiting a U.S. plan of action. This news could have leaked to Cuban exiles groups in New Orleans and found its way to Oswald.

Castro gives an impromptu, three-hour interview with AP reporter Daniel Harker. He warns that U.S. leaders aiding terrorist plans to eliminate Cuban leaders will themselves not be safe. Oswald could have read Harker's article in the *New Orleans Times-Picayune* on September 9.

Mid-September

Oswald is seen in Clinton, Louisiana, in company of David Ferrie and Guy Banister, a private investigator and former FBI agent.

September 12

Cuban Coordinating Committee meets to conduct a broad review of the U.S. government's Cuban contingency plans. They agree there is a strong likelihood that Castro will retaliate in some way against the rash of covert activity in Cuba; however, an attack on U.S. officials within the United States is considered unlikely.

Late September

Oswald is in Mexico City and visits both the Cuban and Soviet embassies. A confidential intelligence source later asserts that Oswald had talked of killing President Kennedy at the Cuban Embassy.

September 27

The coordinator of Cuban affairs circulates a memorandum listing assignments

	for contingency plans relating to possible retaliatory actions by the Castro regime. No responsibility is assigned for attacks on U.S. officials within the United States.
October 6	FBI headquarters learns of Oswald contacts in Mexico City.
October 10	The FBI is told by an informant that the CIA is meeting with AM/LASH. Oswald could have received this news from David Ferrie or Guy Banister by phone.
October 14	Oswald rents room in Oak Cliff section of Dallas, registering with an alias, O. H. Lee. Receives copies of *The Worker* and *The Militant* containing extremely critical articles about President Kennedy and his Cuban policy. On October 15 Oswald obtains job in Texas School Book Depository. It is believed that a conspiracy to assassinate President Kennedy could have matured by this date.
October 24	Jean Daniel, the French reporter, conducts a brief interview with President Kennedy before setting off on an assignment in Cuba. President Kennedy expresses his feeling that Castro has betrayed the revolution.
October 29	Desmond FitzGerald, a senior CIA officer, meets AM/LASH. FitzGerald tells AM/LASH that a coup against Castro would receive U.S. support. FitzGerald is introduced to AM/LASH as a "personal representative of Attorney General Kennedy." FitzGerald and Kennedy, are in fact, friends.
October–November	Jack Ruby places telephone calls to associates of Jimmy Hoffa, Carlos Marcello, and Sam Giancana.
November 1	Diem is assassinated following a coup encouraged by President Kennedy.

Case officer is told by FitzGerald that AM/LASH may be informed that the rifles, telescopic sights, and explosives will be provided.

November 18

President Kennedy makes a public appearance in Tampa and delivers a speech on Cuban policy in Miami that FitzGerald hopes will convince AM/LASH the U.S. government is behind his desire to overthrow Castro.

November 19

Castro contacts Daniel and spends six hours talking to him about U.S.–Cuban relations.

President Kennedy's motorcade route in Dallas is published in Dallas newspapers. Oswald learns motorcade will pass beneath window where he works.

November 20

CIA officer telephones AM/LASH and tells him there will be a meeting on November 22. AM/LASH is told that it is the meeting he has requested.

Rose Cheramie, a Louisiana prostitute, tells Louisiana State Police Officer Francis Fruge and Louisiana State Hospital physician Dr. Bowers that two Latins would kill President Kennedy in Dallas on November 22.

November 21

Jack Ruby sees Joe Campisi, a friend of Carlos Marcello, and has dinner in Campisi's restaurant.

November 22

President Kennedy is assassinated.

FitzGerald meets with AM/LASH. He refers to President Kennedy's speech of November 18 in Miami and indicates that he helped write the speech. He tells AM/LASH the explosives and rifles with telescopic sights will be provided. FitzGerald and the case officer also offer AM/LASH the poison-pen device, but AM/LASH is dissatisfied with it.

Oswald slays Dallas police officer J. D. Tippit and is arrested.

Lyndon Johnson is sworn in as President.

Daniel spends the day with Castro and later reports his reaction to news of the assassination.

David Ferrie, present with Carlos Marcello in a New Orleans courtroom at the time of the murder, makes a mysterious trip to Texas and phones Marcello collect from Galveston.

McCone requests all agency material on Oswald.

Mexico station cables CIA headquarters at 5:30 P.M. to inform them of Oswald's October visit to Mexico City and visits to Cuban and Soviet embassies.

FBI headquarters dispatches a teletype at 9:40 P.M. to all field offices requesting contact of all informants for information bearing on the assassination.

FBI headquarters dispatches a teletype at 11 P.M. to all field offices requesting they resolve all allegations pertaining to the assassination.

November 23   Oswald is charged with the murder of John F. Kennedy.

Director McCone meets with President Johnson and McGeorge Bundy and briefs them on information CIA headquarters has received from Mexico station. By now it is known that Oswald is a member of the Fair Play for Cuba Committee and is an avowed Marxist who once defected to the Soviet Union.

CIA headquarters cables the AM/LASH case officer and orders him to break contact with AM/LASH because of the President's assassination and to return to headquarters. AM/LASH plot against Castro temporarily abandoned.

CIA personnel prepare a memorandum suggesting that Oswald's contacts in

Mexico City with Soviet personnel might have sinister implications. This information is transmitted to CIA's liaison with FBI by telephone at 10:30 A.M.

Desk officer is put in charge of CIA investigation of the assassination.

CIA headquarters telephones the Mexico station to call off the planned arrest of Sylvia Duran, the Cuban Embassy official who had dealt with Oswald, but learns the arrest cannot be called off. Thomas Karamessines, Richard Helms's deputy, sends a cable to Mexico station saying, the arrest "could jeopardize U.S. freedom of action on the whole question of Cuban responsibility."

Legat informs FBI headquarters that the U.S. ambassador to Mexico is concerned that Cubans are behind Oswald's assassination of President Kennedy. The ambassador requests both the CIA and FBI do everything possible to establish or refute this Cuban connection.

FBI headquarters dispatches a teletype to all field offices rescinding the early teletype of November 22 requesting contact of all informants for information bearing on the assassination and the resolution of all allegations pertaining to the assassination.

November 24   Mexico station dispatches a cable to headquarters with the names of all known contacts of certain Soviet personnel in Mexico City. Among the names in the cable is that of AM/LASH, Rolando Cubela.

At 10 A.M., Director McCone meets with the President and briefs him about CIA's operational plans against Cuba.

Cablegram is sent from Mexico to CIA headquarters stating that the U.S. ambassador to Mexico feels that the Soviets are too sophisticated to participate in a direct assassination of President Kennedy, but the Cubans would be stupid enough to have participated with Oswald.

Oswald is murdered at 12:21 P.M. EST. Jack Ruby is arrested. Later it was learned that Ruby had been involved in gunrunning operations in Cuba and had probably met Santo Trafficante, Jr., in Havana. It is also learned that Ruby was close to Dallas Marcello associates Joseph Civello and Joseph Campisi.

Marcello associate and anti-Castro militant David Ferrie, upon returning to New Orleans from Texas, is arrested and held for questioning by the FBI on suspicion he had conspired to assassinate President Kennedy. Later the FBI releases him.

November 25   The case officer prepares a "contact report" on the November 22 meeting with AM/LASH. On FitzGerald's orders, no mention is made of the poison pen being offered to AM/LASH. Contact report is postdated November 25.

At noon, "D" shows up at the U.S. Embassy in Mexico City. He tells embassy personnel that he was in the Cuban Consulate on September 18 and saw Cubans pay Oswald a sum of money and talk about Oswald's assassinating someone.

At 12 P.M., Mexico station dispatches a cable to CIA headquarters reminding headquarters of Castro's September 7, 1963, statement threatening U.S. leaders.

A senior U.S. Embassy official in Mexico City tells a senior Mexican government official known facts about Oswald's visit to Mexico City and raises questions of Cuban involvement. Later the CIA receives an allegation that Luisa Calderon, an intelligence officer at the Cuban Embassy who had dealings with Oswald, had expressed foreknowledge of the Kennedy assassination to her coworkers.

Rose Cheramie's foreknowledge of the assassination is communicated to Dallas police by Louisiana state police, and her testimony is ignored. By now the Dallas police are convinced Oswald was the lone assassin and will not investigate other allegations.

November 26

McCone again meets with President Johnson. The President tells him the FBI has responsibility for the investigation of the President's death and directs him to make CIA resources available to assist the FBI's investigation.

The American ambassador in Mexico sends a cable to the State Department through CIA channels. He gives his opinion that the Cubans are involved in the assassination.

CIA headquarters cables CIA stations in Europe and Canada for all information on the assassination issue, noting they should carefully examine material obtained from a specified resource.

Deputy Attorney General Katzenbach writes Presidential Assistant Bill Moyers, stating "that the facts should be made public in such a way as to satisfy the people of the U.S. and abroad, that the facts have been told and a statement to this effect be made now. . . . The public should be satisfied that Oswald was the assassin and speculation about his motive ought to be cut off." Katzenbach is acting on his own initiative. Robert Kennedy has delegated all authority to him in matters pertaining to the assassination. J. Edgar Hoover has by now adopted the "lone assassin" hypothesis and begins to ignore, and suppress, all evidence pointing to someone other than Oswald as the President's assassin.

November 27

Legat cables FBI headquarters and notes a press release referring to Castro's speech of September 7, 1963.

One CIA station cables information received from the specified resources that AM/LASH had been indiscreet in his conversations.

FBI sends a supervisor to Mexico City to coordinate the investigation and to pursue it vigorously until the desired results are obtained.

An FBI report quotes an informant alleging Jack Ruby's association with Dallas Mafia Boss Joseph Civello, a lieutenant of Carlos Marcello. The allegation is ignored by the FBI.

November 28   CIA headquarters cables a reminder to the Mexico station to "follow all leads" and to continue to investigate the possibility of Cuban or Soviet involvement.

CIA headquarters warns the station chief in Mexico that the ambassador is pushing the case too hard and his proposals could lead to a "flap" with the Cubans.

An FBI teletype quotes an informant alleging that an associate of Carlos Marcello's brother Vincent was overheard discussing a plot to murder President Kennedy. The allegation is not investigated by the FBI.

November 29   President Johnson announces formation of the Warren Commission after discussing other possibilities with Director Hoover.

November 30   Director McCone meets with President Johnson at 11 A.M. and they discuss the Cuba question. "D" is mentioned.

December 1   McCone meets with both Bundy and President Johnson. McCone's memorandum indicates they discussed "D's" story of Oswald's receiving a sum of money at the Cuban Embassy.

December 2   At 10 A.M., McCone meets with the President and Bundy.

McCone's calendar reveals that at 3 A.M. he attended a meeting at the CIA with the subject being Cuba.

December 4

CIA receives a report from one of its Cuban agents that he thought he had met Oswald in Cuba, Mexico City, or the United States. This agent believes that the Cuban government employs assassins and had carried out at least one assassination in Mexico.

FBI memorandum from Sullivan to Belmont indicates there is no evidence that Oswald's assassination of the President was inspired or directed by (pro-Castro) organizations or by any foreign country.

December 6

Warren Commission holds its first meeting, as the FBI and CIA are completing their own investigations.

December 8

CIA headquarters cables its Miami station, ordering a halt to an operation to supply weapons to AM/LASH, pending a high-level policy review.

December 9

A memorandum to Director McCone discusses U.S. operations against Cuba, but does not mention the AM/LASH operation or any other specific operation.

FBI's five-volume report on the assassination is completed. It concludes that Lee Oswald was the lone assassin, acting without confederates.

Acting on his own initiative, Deputy Attorney General Katzenbach writes the Warren Commission and recommends that the commission immediately state that the FBI report clearly shows Oswald was a loner.

December 10

Hoover receives report on the investigative deficiencies in the handling of the preassassination Oswald case and takes disciplinary action against seventeen Bureau officials.

Director McCone meets with CIA staff and the subject of the meeting is Cuba.

December 12   CIA Mexico station reports the FBI is pushing to wind up the Mexican aspects of the case.

Late December   CIA desk officer completes a brief report on his investigation, which is submitted to the President.

The CIA decides to have the counterintelligence division continue the investigation.

1964

January 23   A subordinate to the chief of counterintelligence is designated the "point of record" for all matters relating to the assassination and the Warren Commission. This official is ignorant of the AM/LASH plot.

January 24   FBI liaison is told by CIA official that there are no active plots against Castro.

January 28   Warren Commission Counsel Lee Rankin meets with Hoover and they discuss the allegation that Oswald was an FBI informant.

March   Desmond FitzGerald, now western hemisphere division chief, tells CIA agents in Buenos Aires: "If Jack Kennedy had lived I can assure you we would have gotten rid of Castro by last Christmas."

Rankin requests that the FBI furnish the commission with information on certain pro-Castro and anti-Castro organizations.

Allen Dulles, Robert F. Kennedy, Richard Helms, Desmond FitzGerald, William Harvey, J. Edgar Hoover, and other CIA and FBI officials do not disclose CIA-Mafia and AM/LASH plots to the Warren Commission. Hoover also does not disclose electronic surveillance of organized crime to the commission.

March 26	The President's commission requests the FBI respond to fifty-two questions.
April 7	President Johnson orders a halt to all sabotage operations against Cuba.
May 14	Both Hoover and Helms testify the JFK assassination case will always be open.
May 20	Rankin requests additional information on certain pro-Castro and anti-Castro organizations.
June 11	Warren Commission receives a summary of the pro-Castro and anti-Castro organizations from the field offices but not from FBI headquarters. Hoover's letter informs the commission that the CIA and Department of the Army "may have pertinent information concerning these organizations."
July	The FBI learns some details of the CIA's AM/LASH operation from one of the FBI's informants.
September 25	Bureau receives a copy of the Warren Commission's report. Shortly thereafter the report is made public. The report concludes that Oswald killed President Kennedy without conspirators.
Late 1964	AM/LASH becomes more insistent that the assassination of Cuban leadership is a necessity. He is told that the U.S. government cannot become involved in the "first step." He is put in contact with B-1, and the CIA through B-1 is kept informed of the plotting.
November	Lyndon Johnson is elected President and Robert Kennedy is elected senator from New York.

1965

May	"A," a Cuban associate of Rolando Cubela, contacts the Immigration and Naturalization Service with information about

the AM/LASH operation. He is turned over to the FBI for handling. The FBI informs the CIA about "A."

June

Both agencies interrogate "A" and establish that he knew who was involved in the AM/LASH operation, including the CIA.

June 23

CIA headquarters cables its stations stating the entire AM/LASH group is insecure and further contact constitutes a menace to CIA operations. AM/LASH operation is discontinued.

July 2

FBI writes that the details of the meeting with "A" and the CIA were sent to the White House, the attorney general, and the director of Central Intelligence.

1967

Early January

New Orleans District Attorney Jim Garrison launches an investigation of the assassination of John F. Kennedy, suspecting a plot involving the CIA and Cuban exiles. He names David Ferrie and others among suspects. Ferrie dies during the investigation.

Late January

Drew Pearson meets with Chief Justice Warren and informs Warren that a lawyer was told by an underworld contact that Castro planned Kennedy's assassination. The contact was John Roselli.

January 31

James J. Rowley, head of the Secret Service, meets with Warren; Rowley is informed of the lawyer's story.

February 13

FBI is informed by James J. Rowley that Chief Justice Warren has recently been informed of U.S. attempts to assassinate Castro in 1962 and 1963, that Castro has decided to utilize the same procedure, and that Warren wants these allegations looked into.

February 15	Hoover informs Rowley that the Bureau "is not conducting any investigation" but would accept volunteered information.
March 4	Robert Kennedy's secretary calls Hoover and requests a copy of Edwards's memo of May 7, 1962, at which time Robert Kennedy was briefed on assassination plots.
March 7	Drew Pearson's column on assassination is published.
March 17	Presidential Assistant Marvin Watson advises White House FBI liaison Cartha De Loach that President Johnson has instructed the FBI to interview the lawyer concerning any knowledge he has of the assassination of Kennedy. Watson says request "stemmed from a communication the FBI had sent the White House some weeks ago."
March 20	The lawyer interviewed by the Washington field office will not identify his source of the information that Castro plotted to kill Kennedy. Agents interviewing the lawyer are instructed to make it clear the FBI was "not interfering with any current investigation in New Orleans."
March 22	The FBI forwards results of the interview with the lawyer to the White House. The information indicates that the lawyer's sources were allegedly used by the CIA in attempts against Castro. The White House also receives information from CIA relating to CIA's use of Roselli, Maheu, and Giancana in a plot against Castro. Material also includes information that Robert Kennedy advised on May 9, 1962, that CIA should never take such steps without first checking with the Department of Justice. Helms meets the President at the White House in early evening.

March 23	Helms assigns the inspector general the task of reporting on CIA assassination attempts against Castro.
April 4	Watson calls De Loach and advises that the President is convinced there was a plot in connection with Kennedy's assassination.
April 24	Inspector general's report is delivered to Helms in installments.
May 22	Helms returns copy of report to the inspector general after showing it to President Johnson. Johnson confides to intimates he is convinced President Kennedy was assassinated in retaliation for plotting the murder of Castro.
May 23	All notes and other derived source material of the inspector general's report are destroyed.
Some time after June	President Johnson tells television newsman Howard K. Smith, "I'll tell you something that will rock you. Kennedy was trying to get Castro, but Castro got to him first." Later, Johnson tells Leo Janos of *Time* magazine that just after he took office he discovered that "we were running a damn Murder, Inc., in the Caribbean."
July 23	Desmond FitzGerald, author of AM/LASH plot, dies of a heart attack.

1968

June 5	Robert F. Kennedy is assassinated in Los Angeles.

1969

Russian submarines, carrying nuclear weapons, dock in Cuba. Later a Russian submarine base is constructed on Cuba, and the Soviet Union delivers twenty-five missile attack boats, twenty-one torpedo boats, and ten subchasers to Cuba.

1975

June–October | Senate Committee on Intelligence discovers CIA-Mafia and AM/LASH plots against Castro; Operation Mongoose; John F. Kennedy's relationship with Judith Campbell and Miss Campbell's relationship with CIA-Mafia plotters Sam Giancana and John Roselli.

June | Sam Giancana is murdered in Chicago just before he is to testify before Senate Committee on Intelligence about CIA-Mafia plots against Castro.

November 16 | The *Washington Post* leaks the identity of the President's friend, Judith Campbell Exner, four days before the Senate Committee on Intelligence releases its report.

November 20 | Senate Committee on Intelligence releases its *Interim Report,* which reveals that circumstantial evidence was developed indicating that John and Robert Kennedy were aware of the CIA's plans to kill Castro and had either given their explicit or tacit approval of the plans or had issued orders comprehensive enough to be considered official authorization.

December 17 | Judith Campbell Exner holds press conference in San Diego at which she denies having role in CIA-Mafia plots against Castro.

1976

August | John Roselli is murdered near Miami after testifying before the Senate Committee on Intelligence on the CIA-Mafia plots against Castro and the assassination of John F. Kennedy.

September | Several members of the Senate Committee on Intelligence become convinced

President Kennedy was assassinated in retaliation for the CIA-Mafia plots against Castro. House Select Committee on Assassinations is formed to reopen the investigation of the assassination of President John F. Kennedy. G. Robert Blakey is appointed chief counsel.

1977

June

Judith Campbell Exner publishes memoirs in which she recalls her relationships with John F. Kennedy, Sam Giancana, and John Roselli and protests her ignorance of the CIA-Mafia plots against Castro at the time she knew Kennedy, Giancana, and Roselli.

1978

April 2

Soviet Union delivers MIG-23s, equipped with nuclear bomb delivery systems, to Cuba.

Members of the House Committee on Assassinations question Fidel Castro in Havana about his possible complicity in the assassination of John F. Kennedy. Castro denies any role.

September–
December

House Select Committee on Assassinations holds public hearings during which CIA-Mafia plots against Castro are discussed. Richard Helms and Santo Trafficante testify to their roles in the plots. Carlos Marcello is questioned about his possible role in the JFK assassination. Marcello denies any role.

1979

March 29

In its final report, the House Select Committee on Assassinations finds "on the basis of the evidence available to it, that President John F. Kennedy was probably assassinated as a result of a conspiracy."

Although the committee finds that both Carlos Marcello and Santo Trafficante, Jr., had "the motive, means, and opportunity to have President Kennedy assassinated," it was unable to establish direct evidence of their complicity.

The committee further finds that "the Cuban government was not involved in the assassination of John F. Kennedy" and that "anti-Castro Cuban groups, as groups, were not involved in the assassination of President Kennedy, but that the available evidence does not preclude the possibility that individual members may have been involved."

ACKNOWLEDGMENTS

WHEN I BEGAN this book I did not have a clear idea where it would lead. In fact, it was not until I had written about half the book that I began to realize only too clearly where it would lead. It was at this point that the book became, for me, emotionally difficult to write. I am therefore doubly grateful to all those people who put up with me during the writing and gave me their encouragement and support. Without them my ordeal would have been even more difficult than it was. My principal debt of gratitude goes to Nancy Davis, whose consistent encouragement and help from beginning to end helped me to push forward. My thanks go also to my agent, Marianne Strong, who, among her many contributions, introduced me to several key sources for the book, and my editors at McGraw-Hill, Gladys Justin Carr, editor-in-chief and chairman of the editorial board, who commissioned the book for publication, and Gail Greene, editor, who displayed a genius for concision and succeeded in whittling down what was at first an immense manuscript to something that could fit between the covers of a book. The copy editors, David Damstra and Ursula Smith, and assistant editor Lisa Grotheer also made significant contributions toward improving the manuscript. Particular thanks go to Harris Wofford, former special assistant on civil rights to President John F. Kennedy and later deputy director of the Peace Corps, for his thorough review of the entire manuscript and his many perceptive suggestions toward improving it. I am also most grateful to Prof. G. Robert Blakey of Notre Dame, former Justice Department attorney under Robert F. Kennedy and chief counsel to the House Select Committee on Assassinations, for his many insights into the JFK assassination and what may have been behind it, which he discussed with me in at least a dozen lengthy telephone interviews, and to Sylvia Meagher and Gary Owens, whose painstakingly complete *Master Index to the J.F.K. Assassination Investigations* was an indispensable tool in researching the John F. Kennedy assassination. In addition I would like to thank all those who granted me interviews—especially such busy men as former CIA Director Richard Helms, former Attorney General Nicholas Katzenbach, and former Undersecretary of State George W. Ball—and all those authors who gave me permission to quote from their books, particularly David E. Koskoff, Richard Whalen, Paul B. Fay, Jr., Jeanira Ratcliffe, and Rose Fitzgerald Kennedy. In addition, several last-minute contributors of vital information for this book deserve special thanks. They are Ovid Demaris, coauthor of Judith Campbell's memoirs, who provided important information on Miss Campbell's relationships with John F. Kennedy and Sam Giancana as this book was nearing completion, and Antoinette Giancana and Laurie Lister, editor at William Morrow who allowed me to consult the galleys of Miss Giancana's book, *Mafia Princess*. My thanks go also to Raymond Leone, Craig Fuller, and Garry Smith of Chemical Bank, my mother, Maude Bouvier Davis, my aunt, Michelle Bouvier Putnam, my researchers, Petunia Camero Newman, Kevin Connor, Wendy Davis, Claude d'Estree, Sarah Hospodar, Timothy James, Peter Weiss, and Deborah Greene of the John F. Kennedy Library, my former professor at Princeton, Eric F. Goldman, who recommended two of my researchers, and certain friends who made special contributions to the book, namely Adam Brody, Mercedes Darrow, and the late Phil Ober. I am also greatly indebted to all those who helped type the manuscript, particularly Mike Kaplan at Typing Etcetera, Maureen Simmons of SOHO Typing, and Nancy Davis. And I wish to record a debt of thanks to my quick, efficient, and economical photocopiers, William S. Marbit and Henry B. Trattner of Reader's. Special thanks go also to Milton and Gloria Gunzburg in whose villa in Puerto Vallarta, Casa Las Estacas, and under whose hospitality the present form and structure of this book was first conceived and its initial outline written, and to Andrew Minihan, former mayor of New Ross, Ireland, who guided me through the land of the Kennedys' ancestors. For the illustrations, I am grateful for the help given me by Wendy Davis, who served as picture editor for the book, Bill Fitzgerald of Wide World, Pete Sansone of UPI, and Allan Goodridge of the John F. Kennedy Library.

It was Paul Valery who said that books are never completed, only abandoned. That wisdom certainly holds true for this book. There are so many unsolved mysteries associated with the Kennedy saga that an author foolish enough to attempt to unravel them must inevitably suffer from a sense of incompleteness after he or she has finally abandoned the task.

Among the sources listed in the bibliography that were essential for this book are fifteen U.S. Government Printing Office publications without which the book, as it came to stand, could not have been written. They are the *Final Report* (and twelve supporting volumes of Hearings and Evidence) *of the House Select Committee on Assassinations;* the U.S. Senate's *Interim Report of the Select Committee to Study Governmental Operations with Respect to Intelligence Activities; Alleged Assassination Plots Involving Foreign Leaders;* and the *Final Report of the Select Committee to Study Governmental Operations with Respect to the Intelligence Activities,* Book V, *The Investigation of the Assassination of John F. Kennedy: Performance of the Intelligence Agencies.* To the anonymous authors of these publications, my deepest thanks.

Since this book is an attempt at an overview of Kennedy family history, spanning a period of 135 years, I have had to consult many books on the Kennedys by authors who have gone before me. It would have been an impossible task to have researched the entire history myself, in the space of three years, while engaged in the arduous task of actually writing the book. Those books and their authors are listed in the bibliography, and I am exceedingly grateful to all of them.

J. H. D.
New York, February 10, 1984

Index

865

875

884